T0262677

Applications of Cryptography and Network Security

Applications of Cryptography and Network Security

Edited by **Stephen Mason**

New Jersey

Published by Clanrye International,
55 Van Reypen Street,
Jersey City, NJ 07306, USA
www.clanryeinternational.com

Applications of Cryptography and Network Security
Edited by Stephen Mason

International Standard Book Number: 978-1-63240-065-9 (Hardback)

Printed in the United States of America.

Contents

Preface

Cryptography is the essential and efficient ingredient to the recipe of security solutions. With the arrival of new age communication systems and high speed networks in the future, cryptography will have a key role to play. This book talks about the crucial security challenges that the computing world is facing today and also discusses several techniques to fight against such attacks. The chapters in this book discuss various facets of cryptography and their applications. It will cater to the needs of researchers, engineers, graduates and PhD students working in this field. It will also be beneficial to teachers at universities and colleges as a reference.

This book unites the global concepts and researches in an organized manner for a comprehensive understanding of the subject. It is a ripe text for all researchers, students, scientists or anyone else who is interested in acquiring a better knowledge of this dynamic field.

I extend my sincere thanks to the contributors for such eloquent research chapters. Finally, I thank my family for being a source of support and help.

Editor

Part 1

Security and Privacy in Computing and Communication Networks

1

Secure and Privacy-Preserving Authentication Protocols for Wireless Mesh Networks

Jaydip Sen
Innovation Lab, Tata Consultancy Services Ltd.
India

1. Introduction

Wireless mesh networks (WMNs) have emerged as a promising concept to meet the challenges in next-generation wireless networks such as providing flexible, adaptive, and reconfigurable architecture while offering cost-effective solutions to service providers (Akyildiz et al., 2005). WMNs are multi-hop networks consisting of *mesh routers* (MRs), which form wireless mesh backbones and *mesh clients* (MCs). The mesh routers provide a rich radio mesh connectivity which significantly reduces the up-front deployment cost of the network. Mesh routers are typically stationary and do not have power constraints. However, the clients are mobile and energy-constrained. Some mesh routers are designated as gateway routers which are connected to the Internet through a wired backbone. A gateway router provides access to conventional clients and interconnects ad hoc, sensor, cellular, and other networks to the Internet. The gateway routers are also referred to as the *Internet gateways* (IGWs). A mesh network can provide multi-hop communication paths between wireless clients, thereby serving as a community network, or can provide multi-hop paths between the client and the gateway router, thereby providing broadband Internet access to the clients.

As WMNs become an increasingly popular replacement technology for last-mile connectivity to the home networking, community and neighborhood networking, it is imperative to design efficient and secure communication protocols for these networks. However, several vulnerabilities exist in the current protocols of WMNs. These security loopholes can be exploited by potential attackers to launch attack on WMNs. Absence of a central point of administration makes securing WMNs even more challenging. Security is, therefore, an issue which is of prime importance in WMNs (Sen, 2011). Since in a WMN, traffic from the end users is relayed via multiple wireless mesh routers, preserving privacy of the user data is also a critical requirement (Wu et al., 2006a). Some of the existing security and privacy protection protocols for WMNs are based on the trust and reputation of the network entities (Sen, 2010a; Sen, 2010b). However, many of these schemes are primarily designed for *mobile ad hoc networks* (MANETs) (Sen, 2006; Sen, 2010c), and hence these protocols do not perform well in large-scale hybrid WMN environments.

The broadcast nature of transmission and the dependency on the intermediate nodes for multi-hop communications lead to several security vulnerabilities in WMNs. The attacks can be external as well as internal in nature. External attacks are launched by intruders who are not authorized users of the network. For example, an intruding node may eavesdrop on the packets and replay those packets at a later point of time to gain access to the network resources. On the other hand, the internal attacks are launched by the nodes that are part of the WMN. On example of such attack is an intermediate node dropping packets which it was supposed to forward. To prevent external attacks in vulnerable networks such as WMNs, strong authentication and access control mechanisms should be in place for practical deployment and use of WMNs. A secure authentication should enable two communicating entities (either a pair of MC and MR or a pair of MCs) to validate the authenticity of each other and generate the shared common session keys which can be used in cryptographic algorithms for enforcing message confidentiality and integrity. As in other wireless networks, a weak authentication scheme can easily be compromised due to several reasons such as distributed network architecture, the broadcast nature of the wireless medium, and dynamic network topology (Akyildiz et al., 2005). Moreover, the behavior of an MC or MR can be easily monitored or traced in a WMN by adversaries due to the use of wireless channel, multi-hop connection through third parties, and converged traffic pattern traversing through the IGW nodes. Under such scenario, it is imperative to hide an active node that connects to an IGW by making it anonymous. Since on the Internet side traditional anonymous routing approaches are not implemented, or may be compromised by strong attackers such protections are extremely critical (X. Wu & Li, 2006).

This chapter presents a comprehensive discussion on the current authentication and privacy protection schemes for WMN. In addition, it proposes a novel security protocol for node authentication and message confidentiality and an anonymization scheme for privacy protection of users in WMNs.

The rest of this chapter is organized as follows. Section 2 discusses the issues related to access control and authentication in WMNs. Various security vulnerabilities in the authentication and access control mechanisms for WMNs are first presented and then a list of requirements (i.e. properties) of a secure authentication scheme in an open and large-scale, hybrid WMN are discussed. Section 3 highlights the importance of the protection user privacy in WMNs. Section 4 presents a state of the art survey on the current authentication and privacy protection schemes for WMNs. Each of the schemes is discussed with respect to its applicability, performance efficiency and shortcomings. Section 5 presents the details of a hierarchical architecture of a WMN and the assumptions made for the design of a secure and anonymous authentication protocol for WMNs. Section 6 describes the proposed key management scheme for secure authentication. Section 7 discusses the proposed privacy protection algorithm which ensures user anonymity. Section 8 presents some performance results of the proposed scheme. Section 9 concludes the chapter while highlighting some future direction of research in the field of secure authentication in WMNs.

2. Access control and authentication in WMNs

Authentication and authorization is the first step towards prevention of fraudulent accesses by unauthorized users in a network. Authentication ensures that an MC and the corresponding MR can mutually validate their credentials with each other before the MC is allowed to access the network services. In this section, we first present various attacks in WMNs that can be launched on the authentication services and then enumerate the requirements for authentication under various scenarios.

2.1 Security vulnerabilities in authentication schemes

Several vulnerabilities exist in different protocols for WMNs. These vulnerabilities can be suitably exploited by potential attackers to degrade the network performance (Sen, 2011). The nodes in a WMN depend on the cooperation of other nodes in the network for their successful operations. Consequently, the *medium access control* (MAC) layer and the network layer protocols for these networks usually assume that the participating nodes are honest and well-behaving with no malicious or dishonest intentions. In practice, however, some nodes in a WMN may behave in a selfish manner or may be compromised by malicious users. The assumed trust (which in reality may not exist) and the lack of accountability due to the absence of a central point of administration make the MAC and the network layer protocols vulnerable to various types of attacks. In this sub-section, we present a comprehensive discussion on various types of attacks on the existing authentication schemes of WMNs. A detailed list various attacks on the different layers of WMN communication protocol stack can be found in (Sen, 2011; Yi et al., 2010).

There are several types of attacks that are related to authentication in WMNs. These attacks are: (i) unauthorized access, (ii) replay attack, (iii) spoofing attack, (iv) denial of service attack (DoS), (v) intentional collision of frames, (vi) pre-computation and partial matching attack, and (vi) compromised or forged MRs. These attacks are discussed in detail below.

Unauthorized access: in this attack, an unauthorized user gets access to the network services by masquerading a legitimate user.

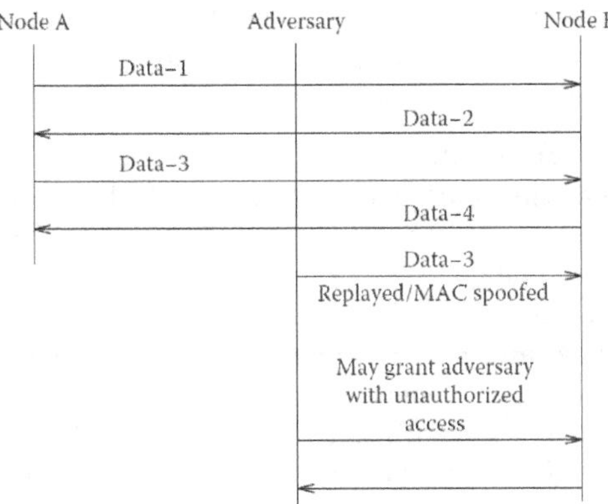

Fig. 1. Illustration of MAC spoofing and replay attacks [Source: (Sen, 2011)]

Replay attack: the replay attack is a type of *man-in-the-middle* attack (Mishra & Arbaugh, 2002) that can be launched by external as well as internal nodes. An external malicious node can eavesdrop on the broadcast communication between two nodes (*A* and *B*) in the network as shown in Fig. 1. It can then transmit legitimate messages at a later point of time to gain access to the network resources. Generally, the authentication information is replayed where the attacker deceives a node (node *B* in Fig. 1) to believe that the attacker is a legitimate node (node *A* in Fig. 1). On a similar note, an internal malicious node, which is an intermediate hop between two communicating nodes, can keep a copy of all relayed data. It can then retransmit this data at a later point in time to gain unauthorized access to the network resources.

Spoof attack: spoofing is the act of forging a legitimate MAC or IP address. IP spoofing is quite common in multi-hop communications in WMNs. In IP spoofing attack, an adversary inserts a false source address (or the address of a legitimate node) from the packets forwarded by it. Using such a spoofed address, the malicious attacker can intercept a termination request and hijack a session. In MAC address spoofing, the attacker modifies the MAC address in transmitted frames from a legitimate node. MAC address spoofing enables the attacker to evade *intrusion detection systems* (IDSs) that may be in place.

DoS attack: in this attack, a malicious attacker sends a flood of packets to an MR thereby making a buffer overflow in the router. Another well-known security flaw can be exploited by an attacker. In this attack, a malicious attacker can send false termination messages on behalf of a legitimate MC thereby preventing a legitimate user from accessing network services.

Intentional collision of frames: a collision occurs when two nodes attempt to transmit on the same frequency simultaneously (Wood & Stankovic, 2002). When frames collide, they are discarded and need to be retransmitted. An adversary may strategically cause collisions in specific packets such as acknowledgment (ACK) control messages. A possible result of such collision is the costly exponential back-off. The adversary may simply violate the communication protocol and continuously transmit messages in an attempt to generate collisions. Repeated collisions can also be used by an attacker to cause resource exhaustion. For example, a naïve MAC layer implementation may continuously attempt to retransmit the corrupted packets. Unless these retransmissions are detected early, the energy levels of the nodes would be exhausted quickly. An attacker may cause unfairness by intermittently using the MAC layer attacks. In this case, the adversary causes degradation of real-time applications running on other nodes by intermittently disrupting their frame transmissions.

Pre-computation and partial matching attack: unlike the attacks mentioned above, where the MAC protocol vulnerabilities are exploited, these attacks exploit the vulnerabilities in the security mechanisms that are employed to secure the MAC layer of the network. Pre-computation and partial matching attacks exploit the cryptographic primitives that are used at the MAC layer to secure the communication. In a pre-computation attack, or *time memory trade-off* (TMTO) attack, the attacker computes a large amount of information (e.g., key, plaintext, and the corresponding ciphertext) and stores that information before launching the attack. When the actual transmission starts, the attacker uses the pre-computed information to speed up the cryptanalysis process. TMTO attacks are highly effective against a large number of cryptographic solutions. On the other hand, in a partial matching attack, the attacker has access to some (ciphertext, plaintext) pairs, which in turn decreases the encryption key strength, and improves the chances of success of the brute force mechanisms. Partial matching attacks exploit the weak implementations of encryption algorithms. For example, the IEEE 802.11i standard for MAC layer security in wireless networks is prone to the session hijacking attack and the *man-in-the-middle* attack that exploits the vulnerabilities in IEEE802.1X. DoS attacks are possible on the four-way handshake procedure in IEEE802.11i.

Compromised or Forged MR: an attacker may be able to compromise one or more MRs in a network by physical tampering or logical break-in. The adversary may also introduce rogue MRs to launch various types of attacks. The fake or compromised MRs may be used to attack the wireless link thereby implementing attacks such as: passive eavesdropping, jamming, replay and false message injection, traffic analysis etc. The attacker may also advertise itself as a genuine MR by forging duplicate beacons procured by eavesdropping on genuine MRs in the network. When an MC receives these beacon messages, it assumes that it is within the radio coverage of a genuine MR, and initiates a registration procedure. The false MR now can extract the secret credentials of the MC and can launch spoof attack on the network. This attack is possible in protocols which require an MC to be authenticated by and MR but not the vice versa (He et al., 2011).

2.2 Requirements for authentication in WMNs

On the basis of whether a central authentication server is available, there are two types of implementations of access control enforcements in WMNs: (i) centralized access control and (ii) distributed access control. For both these approaches, the access control policies should be implemented at the border of the mesh network. In the distributed access control, the access points could act as the distributed authentication servers. The authentication could also be performed in three different places:

- A remote central authentication center
- Local entities such as IGWs or MRs that play the role of an authentication server
- Local MRs

The main benefit of central authentication server is the ease of management and maintenance. However, this approach suffers from the drawback of having a single point of failure. Due to higher *round trip time* (RTT) and authentication delay, a centralized authentication scheme in a multi-hop WMN is not desirable. Instead, authentication protocols are implemented in local nodes such as IGW or MRs. For ensuring higher level of availability of the network services, the authentication power is delegated to a group of MRs in order to avoid single point of failure.

The objective of an authentication system is to guarantee that only the legitimate users have access to the network services. Any pair of network entities in a WMN (e.g., IGW, MR, and MC) may need to mutually authenticate if required. An MR and MC should be able to mutually authenticate each other to prevent unauthorized network access and other attacks. The MCs and MRs should be able to establish a shared pair-wise session key to encrypt messages. The protocol should have robust key generation, distribution and revocation procedures.

Several requirements have been identified in (Buttyan et al., 2010) for authentication mechanisms between MC and MRs in a WMN. These requirements are summarized below:

- *Authentication should be fast enough to support user mobility.* In order to maintain the *quality of service* (QoS) of user applications on mobile MCs, the authentication process should be fast. Also, the re-authentication delays should be within the acceptable limit of handoff delay.
- *MCs and MRs should be able to authenticate themselves mutually.* During the authentication process, the MR authenticates the MC, but the MR also should prove its authenticity to the MC.
- *Authentication process should be resistant to DoS attacks.* Since a successful attack against the central authentication server will lead to a complete compromise of the security system in the network, the authentication process should be robust.

- *Authentication protocols should be compatible with standards.* In a multi-operator environment, it is mandatory that the authentication protocols are standardized so that an MC of one vendor should be able to authenticate with the MR of a different network operator.
- *Authentication protocols should be scalable.* Since the mesh networks have large number of MCs, MRs and IGWs, the authentication protocol should be scalable and must not degrade in performance as the network size increases.

The mutual authentication protocols for MCs and MRs must use several keys for encrypting the credentials. The connection key management should satisfy the following requirements.

- *The connection keys should not reveal long term keys.* The connection keys that the MRs obtain during the authentication of the MCs should not reveal any long-term authentication keys. This requirement must hold because in the multi-operator environment, the MCs may associate to MRs operated by foreign operators.
- *The connection keys should be independent of each other.* As the neighboring MRs may not fully trust each other in a multi-operator environment, the authentication and key generation mechanism have to prevent an MR from deriving connection keys that are used at another MR.
- *The connection keys must be fresh in each session.* It must be ensured that the connection key derived during the authentication protocol for both participants (MC and MR) is fresh.

3. User privacy requirement in WMNs

Privacy provision is an important issue to be considered for WMN deployment. However, privacy is difficult to achieve even if messages are protected, as there are no security solutions or mechanisms which can guarantee that data is not revealed by the authorized parties themselves (Moustafa, 2007). Thus, it is important that complementary solutions are in place. Moreover, communication privacy cannot not be assured with message encryption since the attackers can still observe who is communicating with whom as well as the frequency and duration of the communication sessions. This makes personal information susceptible to disclosure and subsequent misuse even when encryption mechanisms are in place. Furthermore, users in WMNs can be easily monitored or traced with regard to their presence and location, which causes the exposure of their personal life. Unauthorized parties can get access to the location information about the MC's positions by observing their communications and traffic patterns. Consequently, there is a need to ensure location privacy in WMNs as well.

To control the usage of personal information and the disclosure of personal data, different types of information hiding mechanisms like anonymity, data masking etc should be implemented in WMN applications. The following approaches can be useful in information hiding, depending on what is needed to be protected:

- *Anonymity*: this is concerned with hiding the identity of the sender or receiver of the message or both of them. In fact, hiding the identity of both the sender and the receiver of the message can assure communication privacy. Thus, attackers monitoring the messages being communicated could not know who is communicating with whom, thus no personal information is disclosed.

- *Confidentiality*: it is concerned with hiding the transferred messages by using suitable data encryption algorithms. Instead of hiding the identity of the sender and the receiver of a message, the message itself is hidden in this approach.
- *Use of pseudonyms*: this is concerned with replacing the identity of the sender and the receiver of the message by pseudonyms which function as identifiers. The pseudonyms can be used as a reference to the communicating parties without infringing on their privacy, which helps to ensure that the users in the WMNs cannot be traced or identified by malicious adversaries. However, it is important to ensure that there exist no indirect ways by which the adversaries can link the pseudonyms with their corresponding real world entities.

Privacy has been a major concern of Internet users (Clarke, 1999). It is also been a particularly critical issue in context of WMN-based Internet access, where users' traffic is forwarded via multiple MRs. In a community mesh network, this implies that the traffic of a residence can be observed by the MRs residing at its neighbors premises. Therefore, privacy in WMNs has two different dimensions: (i) data confidentiality (or privacy) and traffic confidentiality. These issues are briefly described below:

- *Data confidentiality*: it is obvious that data content reveals user privacy on what is being communicated. Data confidentiality aims to protect the data content and prevent eavesdropping by intermediate MRs. Message encryption is a conventional approach for data confidentiality.
- *Traffic confidentiality*: traffic information such as with whom, when and how frequently the users are communicating, and the pattern of traffic also reveal critical privacy-sensitive information. The broadcast nature of wireless communication makes acquiring such information easy. In a WMN, attackers can conduct traffic analysis as MRs by simply listening to the channels to identify the "ups and downs" of the target's traffic. While data confidentiality can be achieved via message encryption, it is much harder to preserve traffic confidentiality (T. Wu et al., 2006).

4. Secure authentication and privacy protection schemes in WMNs

Since security and privacy are two extremely important issues in any communication network, researchers have worked on these two areas extensively. However, as compared to MANETs and *wireless sensor networks* (WSNs) (Sen, 2009; Sen & Subramanyam, 2007), WMNs have received very little attention in this regard. In this section, we first present a brief discussion on some of the existing propositions for secure authentication and user privacy protection in WMNs. Later on, some of the mechanisms are discussed in detail in the following sub-sections.

In (Mishra & Arbaugh, 2002), a standard mechanism has been proposed for client authentication and access control to guarantee a high-level of flexibility and transparency to all users in a wireless network. The users can access the mesh network without requiring any change in their devices and softwares. However, client mobility can pose severe problems to the security architecture, especially when real-time traffic is transmitted. To cope with this problem, *proactive key distribution* has been proposed in (Kassab et al., 2005; Prasad & Wang, 2005).

Providing security in the backbone network for WMNs is another important challenge. Mesh networks typically employ resource constrained mobile clients, which are difficult to protect against removal, tampering, or replication. If the device can be remotely managed, a distant hacking into the device would work perfectly (Ben Salem & Hubaux, 2006). Accordingly, several research works have been done to investigate the use of cryptographic techniques to achieve secure communication in WMNs. In (Cheikhrouhou et al., 2006), a security architecture has been proposed that is suitable for multi-hop WMNs employing PANA (Protocol for carrying Authentication for Network Access) (Parthasarathy, 2006). In the scheme, the wireless clients are authenticated on production of the cryptographic credentials necessary to create an encrypted tunnel with the remote access router to which they are associated. Even though such framework protects the confidentiality of the information exchanged, it cannot prevent adversaries to perform active attacks against the network itself. For instance, a malicious adversary can replicate, modify and forge the topology information exchanged among mesh devices, in order to launch a denial of service attack. Moreover, PANA necessitates the existence of IP addresses in all the mesh nodes, which is poses a serious constraint on deployment of this protocol.

Authenticating transmitted data packets is an approach for preventing unauthorized nodes to access the resources of a WMN. A *light-weight hop-by-hop access protocol* (LHAP) has been proposed for authenticating mobile clients in wireless dynamic environments, preventing resource consumption attacks (Zhu et al., 2006). LHAP implements light-weight hop-by-hop authentication, where intermediate nodes authenticate all the packets they receive before forwarding them. LHAP employs a packet authentication technique based on the use of one-way hash chains. Moreover, LHAP uses TESLA (Perrig et al., 2001) protocol to reduce the number of public key operations for bootstrapping and maintaining trust between nodes.

In (Prasad et al., 2004), a lightweight *authentication, authorization and accounting* (AAA) infrastructure is proposed for providing continuous, on-demand, end-to-end security in heterogeneous networks including WMNs. The notion of a security manager is used through employing an AAA broker. The broker acts as a settlement agent, providing security and a central point of contact for many service providers.

The issue of user privacy in WMNs has also attracted the attention of the research community. In (T. Wu et al., 2006), a light-weight privacy preserving solution is presented to achieve well-maintained balance between network performance and traffic privacy preservation. At the center of the solution is of information-theoretic metric called *traffic entropy*, which quantifies the amount of information required to describe the traffic pattern and to characterize the performance of traffic privacy preservation. The authors have also presented a penalty-based shortest path routing algorithm that maximally preserves traffic privacy by minimizing the mutual information of traffic entropy observed at each individual relaying node while controlling the possible degradation of network within an acceptable region. Extensive simulation study proves the soundness of the solution and its resilience to cases when two malicious observers collude. However, one of the major problems of the solution is that the algorithm is evaluated in a single-radio, single channel WMN. Performance of the algorithm in multiple radios, multiple channels scenario will be a really questionable issue. Moreover, the solution has a scalability problem. In (X. Wu & Li, 2006), a mechanism is proposed with the objective of hiding an active node that connects to a gateway router, where the active mesh node has to be anonymous. A novel communication protocol is designed to protect the node's privacy using both cryptography and redundancy. This protocol uses the concept of *onion routing* (Reed et al., 1998). A mobile user who requires anonymous communication sends a request to an *onion router* (OR). The OR acts as a proxy to the mobile user and constructs an onion route consisting of other ORs using the public keys of the routers. The onion is constructed such that the inner most part is the message for the intended destination, and the message is wrapped by being encrypted using the public keys of the ORs in the route. The mechanism protects the routing information from insider and outsider attack. However, it has a high computation and communication overhead.

In the following sub-sections, some of the well-known authentication and privacy preservation schemes for WMNs are discussed briefly. For each of the schemes, its salient features and potential shortcomings are highlighted.

4.1 Local authentication based on public key certificates

In the localized authentication, a *trusted third party* (TTP) serves as the trusted *certificate authority* (CA) that issues certificates. In (Buttyan & Dora, 2009), a localized authentication scheme is proposed in which authentication is performed locally between the MCs and the MRs in a hybrid large-scale WMN operated by a number of operators. Each operator maintains its own CA. Each CA is responsible for issuing certificates to its customers. Each CA maintains its own *certificate revocation list* (CRL). The CAs also issue cross-certificates among each other for enabling entities (MCs or MRs) subscribing to different operators to perform certificate-based authentications and key exchanges. To minimize authentication delay, the *provably secure key transport protocol* (Blake-Wilson & Menezes, 1998) proposed by Blake-Wilson-Menezes (BWM) has been used.

For authentication in multiple domains in a metropolitan area network, a localized authentication scheme has been proposed in (Lin et al., 2008). In this scheme, an *embedded two-factor authentication* mechanism is utilized to verify the authenticity of a roaming MC. The authenticity verification does not need any intervention of the home *Internet service provider* (ISP) of the MC. The two-factor authentication mechanism includes two methods of authentication: password and smart card. To minimize the *ping-pong effect*, the session key is cached in the current network domain. Whenever the MC requests a handoff into a neighboring MR which has a valid shared session key with the MC, a user-authenticated key agreement protocol with secret key cryptography is performed. Thus an expensive full authentication based on an asymmetric key encryption is avoided. The protocol execution is fast since it involves encryption using only the symmetric key and keyed *hash message authentication codes* (HMACs).

The localized authentication schemes are based on the assumption that the MRs are trusted and fully protected by robust certificates. In practice, MRs are low cost devices and without extra protection, these devices can easily be compromised. In the event an MR gets compromised, the local authentication schemes will fail. To defend against compromised MRs, a scheme based on local voting strategy (Zhu et al., 2008) is adopted which work on the principle of *threshold digital signature* mechanism (Cao et al., 2006).

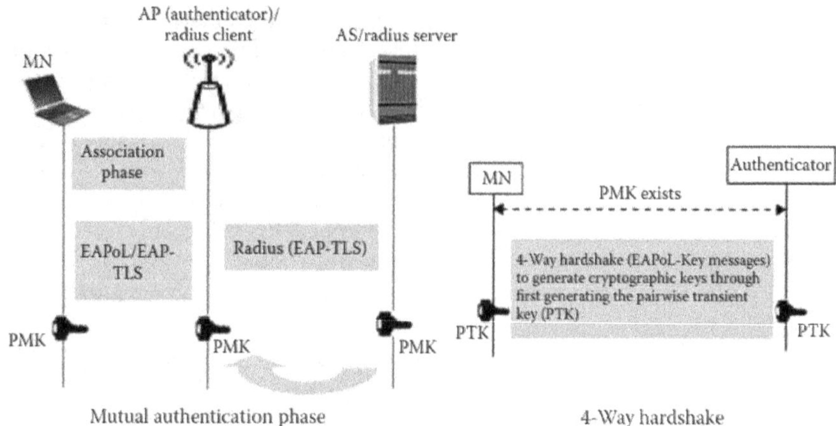

Fig. 2. Schematic diagram of IEEE 802.11i authentication protocol [Source: (Moustafa, 2007)]

4.2 Authentication model based on 802.11i protocol

In most commercial deployments of wireless local area networks (WLANs), IEEE 802.11i (IEEE 802.11i, 2004) is the most common approach for assuring authentication at the layer 2. However, the IEEE 802.11i authentication does not fully address the problem of WLAN vulnerability (Moustafa, 2007). In IEEE 802.11i authentication, as described in Fig. 2, the MC and the *authentication server* (AS) apply the 802.1X (IEEE 802.1X, 2001) authentication model carrying out some negotiation to agree on *pair-wise master key* (PMK) by using some upper layer authentication schemes or using a pre-shared secret. This key is generated by both the MC and the AS, assuring the mutual authentication between them. The *access point* (AP) then receives a PMK copy from the AS, authenticating the MC and authorizing its communication. Afterwards, a four-way handshake starts between the AP and the MC to generate encryption keys from the generated PMK. Encryption keys can assure confidential transfer between the MC and the AP. If the MC roams to a new AP, it will perform another full 802.1X authentication with the AS to derive a new PMK. For performance enhancement, the PMK of the MC is cached by the MC and the AP to be used for later re-association without another full authentication. The features of 802.11i exhibit a potential vulnerability because a compromised AP can still authenticate itself to an MC and gain control over the connection. Furthermore, IEEE 802.11i authentication does not provide a solution for multi-hop communication. Consequently new mechanisms are needed for authentication and secure layer 2 links setup in WMNs (Moustafa, 2007).

Wireless dual authentication protocol (WDAP) (Zheng et al., 2005) is proposed for 802.11 WLAN and can be extended to WMNs. WDAP provides authentication for both MCs and APs and overcomes the shortcomings of other authentication protocols. The name "dual" implies the fact that the AS authenticates both the MC and the AP. As in the four-way handshake in IEEE 802.11i, this protocol also generates a session key for maintaining confidentiality of the messages communicated between the MC and the AP after a successful authentication. WDAP provides authentication during the initial connection state. For roaming, it has three sub-protocols: an authentication protocol, a de-authentication protocol, and a roaming authentication protocol.

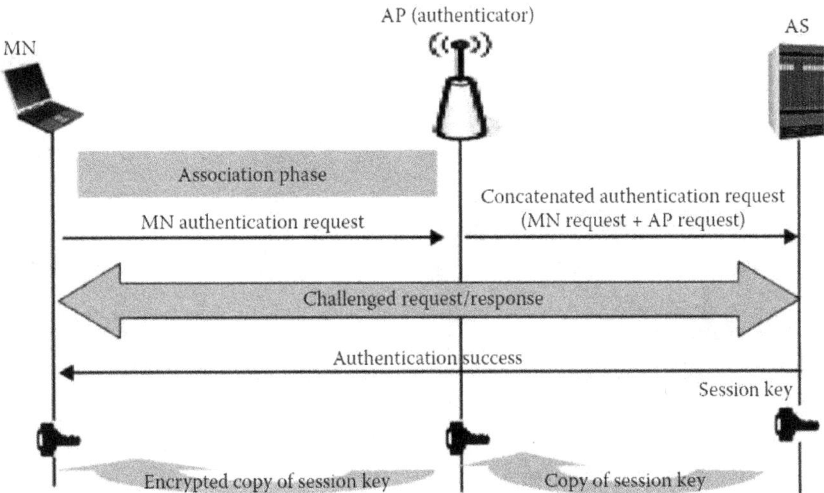

Fig. 3. Schematic diagram of the authentication process in WDAP [Source: (Moustafa, 2007)]

Fig. 3 illustrates the WDAP authentication process. In the authentication protocol, the AP receives the authentication request from the MC. It then creates an authentication request for itself and concatenates this request to the received request from the MC. The concatenated request is then sent to the AS. Since both the mobile station and the AP do not trust each other until the AS authenticates both of them, WDAP is a dual authentication protocol. If the authentication is successful, AS generates a session key and sends the key to the AP. The AP then sends this key to the MC encrypting it with the shared key with MC. This key is thus shared between the AP and the MC for their secure communication and secure de-authentication when the session is finished. When an MC finishes a session with an AP, secure de-authentication takes place to prevent the connection from being exploited by an adversary. Use of WDAP in WMN environments ensures mutual authentication of both MCs and MRs. Also, WDAP can be used to ensure authentication between the MRs through authentication requests concatenation. In case of multi-hop communication in WMNs, each pair of nodes can mutually authenticate through the session key generated by the AS. However, a solution is needed in case of open mesh networks scenarios, where the AS may not be present in reality. Another problem arises in case of roaming authentication. WDAP is not ideally suited for use in roaming authentication since it works only for roaming into new APs, and does not consider the case of *back roaming* in which an MC may need to re-connect with another MC or an AP with whom it was authenticated earlier. As a result, the WDAP session key revocation mechanisms has some shortcomings that makes it unsuitable for deployment in real-world WMNs.

An approach that adapts IEEE 802.11i to the multi-hop communication has been presented in (Moustafa et al., 2006a). An extended forwarding capability in 802.11i is proposed without compromising on its security features to setup authenticated links in layer 2 to achieve secure wireless access as well as confidential data transfer in ad hoc multi-hop environments. The general objective of this approach is to support secure and seamless access to the Internet by the MCs situated near public WLAN hotspots, even when these nodes may move beyond the coverage area of the WLAN. To accomplish the *authentication, authorization and accounting* (AAA) process for an MC within the WLAN communication range, classical 802.11i authentication and message exchange take place.

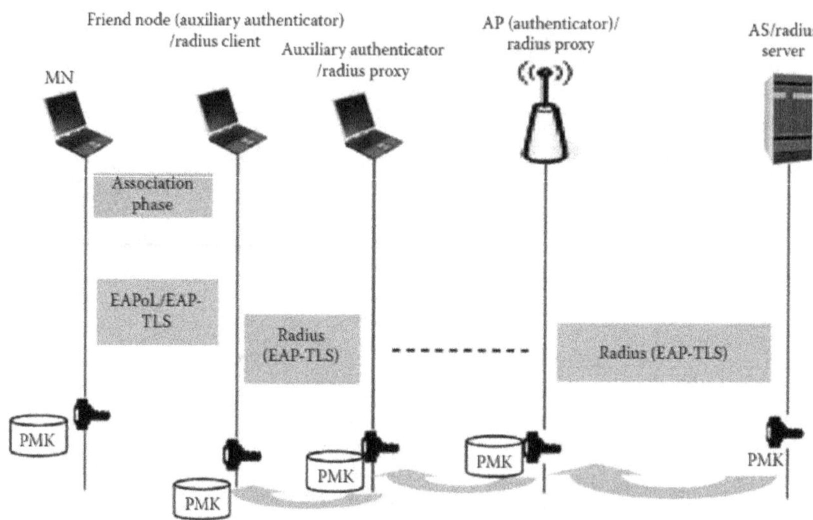

Fig. 4. Schematic diagram of adapted 802.11i with EAP-TLS for multi-hop communication [Source: (Moustafa, 2007)]

As shown in Fig. 4, for accomplishing the AAA process for MCs that are beyond the WLAN communication range but belong to the ad hoc clusters, 802.11i is extended to support forwarding capabilities. In this case, the notion of *friend nodes* is introduced to allow each MC to initiate the authentication process through a selected node in its proximity. The friend node plays the role of an auxiliary authenticator that forwards the authentication request of the MC to the actual authenticator (i.e., the AP). If the friend node is not within the communication range of the AP, it invokes other friend nodes in a recursive manner until the AP is reached. The concept of proxy RADIUS (Rigney et al., 2000) is used for ensuring forwarding compatibility and secure message exchange over multi-hops. Proxy chaining (Aboba & Vollbrecht, 1999) takes place if the friend node is not directly connected to an AP. To achieve higher level of security on each authenticated link between the communicating nodes, 802.11i encryption is used by invoking the four-way handshake between each MC and its authenticator (AP or friend node). This approach is useful in open mesh network scenarios, since it allows *authentication by delegation* among the mesh nodes. In addition, since the authentication keys are stored in the immediate nodes, the re-authentication process is optimized in case of roaming of the MCs. However, an adaptation is needed that allows establishment of multiple simultaneous connections to the authenticators - APs and the friend nodes – in a dense mesh topology. Also, a solution is needed to support fast and secure roaming across multiple *wireless mesh routers* (WMRs). A possible solution is through sharing session keys of authenticated clients among the WMRs (Moustafa, 2007).

4.3 Data packet authentication

An approach to prevent unauthorized node getting access to the network services in WMNs is to authenticate the transmitted data packets. Following this approach, a *light-weight hop-by-hop access protocol* (LHAP) (Zhu et al., 2003; Zhu et al., 2006) has been proposed for authenticating MCs for preventing resource consumption attacks in WMNs. LHAP implements light-weight hop-by-hop authentication, where intermediate nodes authenticate all the packets they receive before forwarding them further in the network. In this protocol, an MC first performs some light-weight authentication operations to bootstrap a trust relationship with its neighbors. It then invokes a light-weight protocol for subsequent traffic authentication and data encryption. LHAP is ideally suited for ad hoc networks, where it resides between the data link layer and the network layer and can be seamlessly integrated with secure routing protocols to provide high-level of security in a communication network.

LHAP employs a packet authentication technique based on the use of *one-way hash chains* (Lamport, 1981). Moreover, it uses TESLA (Perrig et al., 2001) protocol to reduce the number of public key operations for bootstrapping and maintaining trust among the nodes. For every traffic packet received from the network layer, LHAP adds its own header, which includes the node ID, a packet type field indicating a traffic packet, and an authentication tag. The packet is then passed to the data link layer and control packets are generated for establishing and maintaining trust relationships with the neighbor nodes. For a received packet, LHAP verifies its authenticity based on the authentication tag in the packet header. If the packet is valid, LHAP removes the LHAP header and passes the packet to the network layer; otherwise, it discards the packet. LHAP control packets are passed to the network layer with the goal to allow LHAP execution without affecting the operation of the other layers.

LHAP is very suitable for WMN applications. For secure roaming, LHAP can be useful in distributing session keys among MCs employing a special type of packet designated for this purpose. However, the focus of this protocol is on preventing resource consumption attack on the network. However, LHAP cannot prevent insider attacks and hence complementary mechanisms are needed for this purpose (Moustafa, 2007).

4.4 Proactive authentication and pre-authentication schemes

In (Pack & Choi, 2004), a fast handoff scheme based on prediction of mobility pattern has been proposed. In this scheme, an MC on entering in the coverage area of an access point performs authentication procedures for multiple MRs (or APs). When an MC sends an authentication request, the AAA server authenticates the all the relevant APs (or MRs) and sends multiple session keys to the MC. A prediction method known as *frequent handoff region* (FHR) selection is utilized to reduce the handoff delay further. FHR selection algorithm takes into account user mobility pattern, service classes etc. to make a selection of frequent MRs suitable for handoff. To increase the accuracy of the user mobility prediction, a proactive key distribution approach has been proposed in (Mishra et al., 2004). A new data structure - neighbor graphs - is used to determine the candidate MR sets for the MC to associate with.

A reliable re-authentication scheme has been proposed in (Aura & Roe, 2005), in which an MR issues a credential for the MC it is currently serving. The credential can be used later (by the next MR) to certify the authenticity of the MC.

A fast authentication and key exchange mechanism to support seamless handoff has been proposed in (Soltwisch et al., 2004). The mechanism uses the *context transfer protocol* (CTP) (Loughney et al., 2005) to forward session key from the previous router to the new access router.

4.5 Extensible authentication protocols

IEEE 802.1X has been applied to resolve some of the security problems in the 802.11 standard, where the MC and the AS authenticate each other by applying an upper layer authentication protocol like *extensible authentication protocol encapsulating transport layer security* (EAP-TLS) protocol (Aboba & Simon, 1999). Although EAP-TLS offers mutual authentication, it introduces high latency in WMNs because each terminal acts as an authenticator for its neighbor to reach the AS. This can lead to longer paths to the AS. Furthermore, in case of high mobility of terminals, re-authentication due to frequent handoffs can make be detrimental to real-time applications. Consequently, variants of EAP have been proposed by researchers to adapt 802.1X authentication model to multi-hop communications in WMNs. Some of these mechanisms are briefly discussed below.

EAP with token-based re-authentication: a fast and secure hand-off protocol is presented in (Fantacci et al., 2006), which allows mutual authentication and access control thereby preventing insider attacks during the re-authentication process. To achieve this, old authentication keys are revoked. Thus, a node should ask for the keys from its neighbors or from the AS when its needs the keys. The mechanism involves a token-based re-authentication scheme based on a two-way handshake between the node that performs the handshake and the AS. The AS is involved in every hand-off to have a centralized entity for monitoring the network. An authentication token, in the form of keying material is provided by the authenticator of the network to the AS to obtain the PMK key. The authenticator can be an AP or a host in the WMN. Initially, the MC performs a full EAP-TLS authentication, generating a PMK key that is then shared between the MC and its authenticator. Whenever the MC performs hand-off to another authenticator, the new authenticator should receive the PMK key to avoid a full re-authentication. The new authenticator issues a request to the AS for the PMK and adds a token to the request. The token is a cryptographic material to prove that the authenticator is in contact with the MC which owns the requested PMK. The token was earlier generated by the MC while performing the hand-off and was transmitted to the new authenticator. The AS verifies the token, and issues the PMK to the new authenticator. This protocol is secure and involves centralized key management. However, the need to involve the AS in each re-authentication is not suitable for scenarios where MCs have random and frequent mobility (Moustafa, 2007). A distributed token verification will be more suitable for open and multi-hop WMN environments.

EAP-TLS over PANA: a security architecture suitable for multi-hop mesh network is presented in (Cheikhrouhou et al., 2006) that employs EAP-TLS over *protocol for carrying authentication and network access* (PANA) (Parthasarathy, 2006). It proposes an authentication solution for WMNs adapting IEE 802.1X so that MCs can be authenticated by MRs. The authentication between MCs and MRs requires MCs to be directly connected to the MRs. Since PANA enables MCs to authenticate to the access network using IP protocol, it is used in this mechanism to overcome the problem of association between MCs and MRs that can be attached through more than one intermediate node. When a new MC joins the network, it first gets an IP address (pre-PANA address) from a local DHCP server. Then, the PANA protocol is initiated so that the mobile node discovers the *PANA access* (PAA) router to authenticate itself. After successful authentication, the MC initiates the *Internet key exchange* (IKE) protocol with the MR for establishing a security association. Finally, IPSec tunnel ensures data protection over the radio link and a data access control by the MR. During the authentication and authorization phases, PANA uses EAP message exchange between the MC and the PAA, where PAA relays EAP messages to the AS using EAP over RADIUS. EAP-TLS message is used in this approach. The protocol is suited for heterogeneous WMNs since it is independent of the technology of the wireless media. However, PANA requires use of IP addresses in the mesh nodes. This puts a restriction in its use since all elements of a WMN may not use IP as the addressing standard.

EAP-TLS using proxy chaining: the combinations of (Moustafa et al., 2006a; Moustafa et al., 2006b) propose adaptive EAP solutions for authentication and access control in the multi-hop wireless environment. In (Moustafa et al., 2006a), an adapted EAP-TLS approach is used to allow authentication of mobile nodes. A delegation process is used among mobile nodes by use of auxiliary authenticators in a recursive manner until the AS is reached. To allow extended forwarding and exchange of EAP-TLS authentication messages, proxy RADIUS is involved using proxy chaining among the intermediate nodes between the MCs requesting the authentication and the AS. This approach permits the storage of authentication keys of the MCs in the auxiliary authenticators. This speeds up the re-authentication process and enhances the performance of the adaptive EAP-TLS mechanism. This solution is applicable for WMNs, especially in multi-hop communications. However, to support secure roaming across different *wireless mesh routers* (WMRs), communication is required between the old and the new WMRs. This can be done by using central elements or switches that link the WMRs and allow storing of information in a central location and distribution of information among the WMRs.

EAP-enhanced pre-authentication: an EAP-enhanced pre-authentication scheme for mobile WMN (IEEE 802.e) in the link layer has been proposed in (Hur et al., 2008). In this scheme, the PKMv2 (public key management version 2) has been slightly modified based on the key hierarchy in a way that the communication key can be established between the MC and the target MR before hand-off in a proactive way. The modification allows the master session key generated by the authentication server to bind the MR identification (i.e., base station identification) and the MAC address of the MC. In the pre-authentication phase, the authentication server generates and delivers the unique public session keys for the neighbor MRs of the MC. The neighboring MRs are the access points that the MC potentially moves to. These MRs can use the public session key to derive an authorization key of the corresponding MC. In the same way, the MC can derive the public session key and the authorization key for its neighbor MRs, with the MR identification. Once the handoff is complete, the MC only needs to perform a three-way handshake and update the encryption key since the MC and MR already possess the authentication key. Thus a re-authentication with the authentication server is avoided and the associated delay is reduced.

Distributed authentication: a distributed authentication for minimizing the authentication delay has been proposed in (Lee et al., 2008), in which multiple trusted nodes are distributed over a WMN to act on the behalf of an authentication server. This makes management of the network easy, and it also incurs less storage overhead in the MRs. However, the performance of the scheme will degrade when multiple MCs send out their authentication requests, since the number of trusted nodes acting as the authentication server is limited compared to the number of access routers. In (He et al., 2010), a distributed *authenticated key establishment scheme* (AKES) has been proposed based on *hierarchical multi-variable symmetric functions* (HMSF). In this scheme, MCs and MRs can mutually authenticate each other and establish pair-wise communication keys without the need of interaction with any central authentication server. The authors have extended the polynomial-based key generation concept (Blundo et al., 1993) to the asymmetric function for mutual authentication among the MCs and MRs. Based on the symmetric polynomial and an asymmetric function, an efficient and hierarchical key establishment scheme is designed This substantially reduces the communication overhead and authentication delay.

Secure authentication: an improved security protocol for WMNs has been proposed in (Lukas & Fackroth, 2009). The protocol is named "WMNSec", which is based on the four-way handshake mechanism in 802.11i. In WMNSec, a dedicated station - *mesh key distributor* (MKD) - generates one single dynamically generated key for the whole network. This key is called the *global key* (GK). The GK is distributed from the MKD to the authenticated stations (MRs) using the four-way handshake from 802.11i. A newly joined MR would become another authenticator after it is authenticated and become the authenticated part of the WMN. Thus, the iterative authentication forms a spanning tree rooted as the MKD and spanning the whole network. To provide a high level of security, each key has a limited validity period. Periodic re-keying ensures that the keys used in all stations are up-to-date.

4.6 Authentication using identity-based cryptography

Identity-based cryptography (IBC) is a public key cryptography in which public key of a user is derived from some publicly available unique identity information about the user, e.g. SSN, email address etc. Although the concept of IBC was first introduced by Shamir (Shamir, 1984), a fully functional IBC scheme was not established till Boneh and Franklin applied Weil pairing to construct a bilinear map (Boneh & Franklin, 2001). Using IBC, an attack-resilient security architecture called "ARSA" for WMNs has been proposed in (Zhang & Fang, 2006). The relationship among three entities in this scheme, e.g., brokers, users and network operators are made analogous to that among a bank, a credit card holder, and a merchant. The broker acts as a TTP that distributes secure pass to each authenticated user. Each secure pass has the ID of the user enveloped in it and the WMN operator grants access to all the users those possess secure passes. The users are not bound to any specific operator, and can get ubiquitous network access by a universal pass issued by a *third-party broker*. ARSA also provides an efficient mutual *authentication and key agreement* (AKA) between a user and a serving WMN domain or between users served by the same WMN domain.

4.7 Privacy protection schemes in WMNs

Traffic privacy preservation is an important issue in WMNs. In a community mesh network, the traffic of mobile users can be observed by the MRs residing at its neighbors, which could reveal sensitive personal information. A mesh network privacy-preserving architecture is presented in (T. Wu et al., 2006). The mechanism aims to achieve traffic confidentiality based on the concept of *traffic pattern* concealment by controlling the routing process using multi-paths. The traffic from the source (i.e., IGW) to the destination (i.e., MR) is split into multiple paths. Hence, each relaying nodes along the path from the source to the destination can observe only a portion of the entire traffic. The traffic is split in a random manner (both spatially and temporally) so that an intermediate node can have little knowledge to figure out the overall traffic pattern. In this way the traffic confidentially is achieved. The mechanism defines an information-theoretic metric, and then proposes a penalty-based routing algorithm to allow traffic pattern hiding by exploiting multiple available paths between a pair of nodes. Source routing strategy is adopted so that a node can easily know the topology of its neighborhood. The protocol can also ensure communication privacy in WMNs, where each destination node is able to consistently limit the proportion of mutual information it shares with the observing node. However, the traffic splitting can increase delay in communication and hence this mechanism may not be suitable for real-time applications in WMNs.

A novel privacy and security scheme named PEACE (Privacy Enhanced yet Accountable seCurity framEwork) for WMNs has been proposed in (Ren et al., 2010). The scheme achieves explicit mutual authentication and key establishment between users (i.e. MCs) and MRs and between the users themselves (i.e., between the MCs). It also enables unilateral anonymous authentication between users and the MRs and bilateral anonymous authentication between a pair of users. Moreover, it enables user accountability by regulating user behaviors and protects WMNs from being abused and attacked. Network communications can be audited in cases of disputes and frauds. The high level architecture of PEACE trust model consists of four kinds of network entities: the network operator, user group managers, user groups and a *trusted third party* (TTP). Before accessing the WMN services, each user has to enroll in at least one user group whose manager, thus, knows the essential and non-essential attributes of the user. The users do not directly register with the network operator; instead, each group manager subscribes to the network operator on behalf of its group members. Upon registration from a group manager, the network operator allocates a set of group secret keys to this user group. The network operator divides each group secret key into two parts - one part is sent to the requesting group manager and the other part to the TTP. To access network services, each user request one part of the group secret key from his group manager and the other part from the TTP to recover a complete group secret key. The user also needs to return signed acknowledgments to both the group manager and the TTP. PEACE uses a variation of the short group signature scheme proposed in (Boneh & Shacham, 2004) to ensure sophisticated user privacy. The scheme is resistant to bogus data injection attacks, data phishing attacks and DoS attacks (Ren et al., 2010).

A security architecture named "SAT" has been proposed in (Sun et al., 2008; Sun et al., 2011). The system consists of ticket-based protocols, which resolves the conflicting security requirements of unconditional anonymity for honest users and traceability of misbehaving users in a WMN. By utilizing the tickets, self-generated pseudonyms, and the hierarchical identity-based cryptography, the architecture has been demonstrated to achieve the desired security objectives and the performance efficiency. The system uses a blind signature technique from the payment systems. (Brands, 1993; Wei et al., 2006; Figueiredo et al., 2005; Chaum, 1982), and hence it achieves the anonymity by delinking user identities from their activities. The pseudonym technique also renders user location information unexposed. The pseudonym generation mechanism does not rely on a central authority, e.g. the *broker* in (Zhang & Fang, 2006), the *domain authority* in (Ateniese et al., 1999), the *transportation authority* or the *manufacturer* in (Raya & Hubaux, 2007), and the *trusted authority* in (Zhang et al., 2006), who can derive the user's identity from his pseudonyms and illegally trace on an honest user. However, the system is not intended for achieving routing anonymity. *Hierarchical identity-based cryptography* (HIBC) for inter-domain authentication is adopted to avoid domain parameter certification in order to ensure anonymous access control.

5. The hierarchical architecture of a WMN

In this section, we first present a standard architecture of a typical WMN for which we propose a security and privacy protocol. The architecture is a very generic one that represents majority of the real-world deployment scenarios for WMNs. The architecture of a hierarchical WMN consists of three layers as shown in Fig. 5. At the top layers are the *Internet gateways* (IGWs) that are connected to the wired Internet. They form the backbone infrastructure for providing Internet connectivity to the elements in the second level. The entities at the second level are called wireless *mesh routers* (MRs) that eliminate the need for wired infrastructure at every MR and forward their traffic in a multi-hop fashion towards the IGW. At the lowest level are the *mesh clients* (MCs) which are the wireless devices of the users. Internet connectivity and peer-to-peer communications inside the mesh are two important applications for a WMN. Therefore design of an efficient and low-overhead communication protocol which ensure security and privacy of the users is a critical requirement which poses significant research challenges.

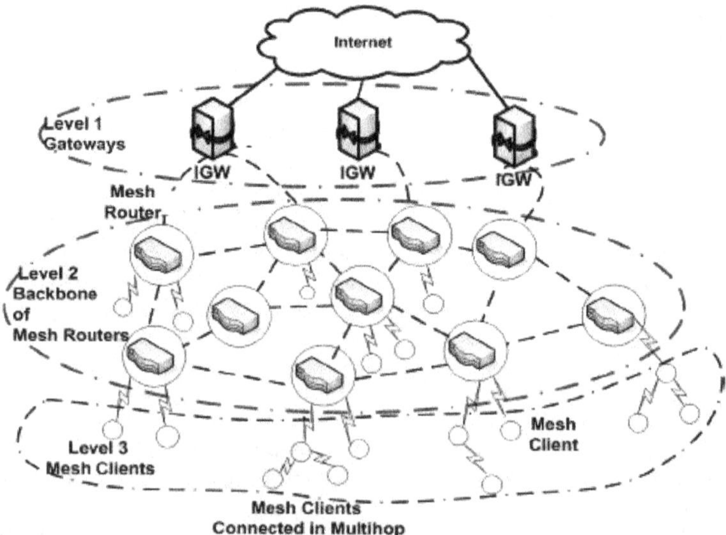

Fig. 5. A three-tier architecture of a wireless mesh network (WMN)

For designing the proposed protocol and to specify the WMN deployment scenario, the following assumptions are made.

1. Each MR which is authorized to join the wireless backbone (through the IGWs), has two certificates to prove its identity. One certificate is used during the authentication phase that occurs when a new node joins the network. EAP-TLS (Aboba et al., 2004) for 802.1X authentication is used for this purpose since it is the strongest authentication method provided by EAP (Aboba et al., 2004), whereas the second certificate is used for the authentication with the *authentication server* (AS).
2. The certificates used for authentication with the RADIUS server and the AS are signed by the same *certificate authority* (CA). Only recognized MRs are authorized to join the backbone.
3. Synchronization of all MRs is achieved by use of the *network time protocol* (NTP) protocol (Mills, 1992).

The proposed security protocol serves the dual purpose of providing security in the access network (i.e., between the MCs and the MRs) and the backbone network (i.e., between the MRs and the IGWs). These are described the following sub-sections.

5.1 Access network security

The access mechanism to the WMN is assumed to be the same as that of a *local area network* (LAN), where mobile devices authenticate themselves and connect to an *access point* (AP). This allows the users to the access the services of the WMN exploiting the authentication and authorization mechanisms without installing any additional software. It is evident that such security solution provides protection to the wireless links between the MCs and the MRs. A separate security infrastructure is needed for the links in the backbone networks. This is discussed in Section 5.2.

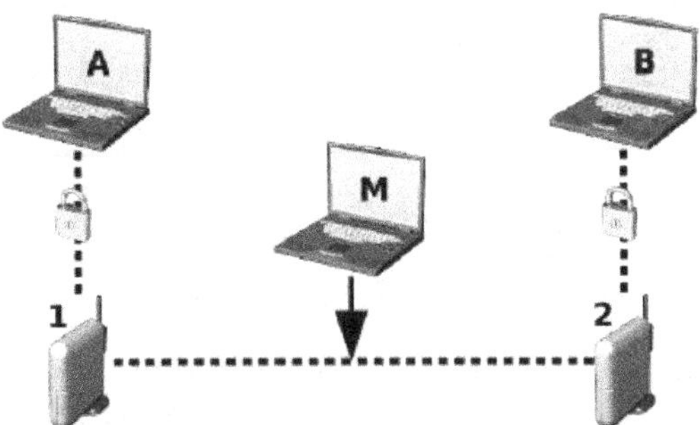

Fig. 6. Secure information exchange among the MCs *A* and *B* through the MRs 1 and 2

Fig. 6 illustrates a scenario where users *A* and *B* are communicating in a secure way to MRs 1 and 2 respectively. If the wireless links are not protected, an intruder *M* will be able to eavesdrop on and possibly manipulate the information being exchanged over the network. This situation is prevented in the proposed security scheme which encrypts all the traffic transmitted on the wireless link using a stream cipher in the data link layer of the protocol stack.

5.2 Backbone network security

For providing security for the traffic in the backbone network, a two-step approach is adopted. When a new MR joins the network, it first presents itself as an MC and completes the association formalities. It subsequently upgrades its association by successfully authenticating to the AS. In order to make such authentication process efficient in a high mobility scenario, the key management and distribution processes have been designed in a way so as to minimize the effect of the authentication overhead on the network performance. The overview of the protocol is discussed as follows.

Fig. 7 shows the three phases of the authentication process that a MR (say *N*) undergoes. When *N* wants to join the network, it scans all the radio channels to detect any MR that is already connected to the wireless backbone. Once such an MR (say *A*) is detected, *N* requests *A* for access to network services including authentication and key distribution. After connecting to *A*, *N* can perform the tasks prescribed in the IEEE 802.11i protocol to complete a mutual authentication with the network and establish a security association with the entity to which it is physically connected. This completes the Phase I of the authentication process. Essentially, during this phase, a new MR performs all the steps that an MC has to perform to establish a secure channel with an MR for authentication and secure communication over the WMN.

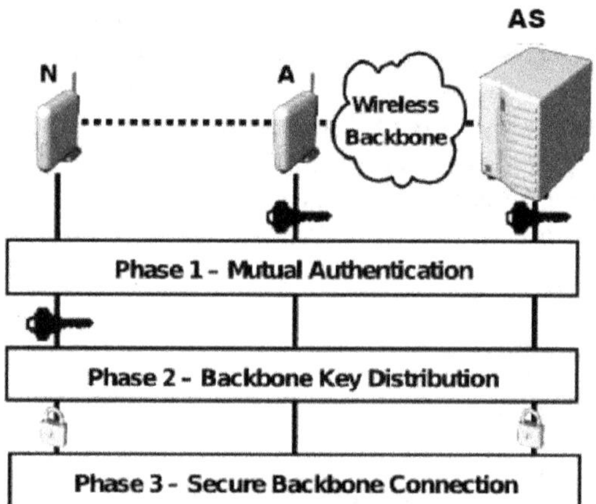

Fig. 7. Steps performed by a new MR (*N*) using backbone encrypted traffic to join the WMN

During Phase II of the authentication process, the MRs use the *transport layer security* (TLS) protocol. Only authorized MRs that have the requisite credentials can authenticate to the AS and obtain the cryptographic credentials needed to derive the key sequence used to protect the wireless backbone. In the proposed protocol, an end-to-end secure channel between the AS and the MR is established at the end of a successful authentication through which the cryptographic credentials can be exchanged in a secure way.

To eliminate any possibility of the same key being used over a long time, a server-initiated protocol is proposed for secure key management. The protocol is presented in Section 6. As mentioned earlier in this section, all the MRs are assumed to be synchronized with a central server using the NTP protocol.

Fig. 8 shows a collection of four MRs connected with each other by five wireless links. The MR *A* is connected with the AS by a wired link. At the time of network bootstrapping, only node *A* can connect to the network as an MR, since it is the only node that can successfully authenticate to the AS. Nodes *B* and *C* which are neighbors of *A* then detect a wireless network to which can connect and perform the authentication process following the IEEE 802.11i protocol. At this point of time, nodes *B* and *C* are successfully authenticated as MCs. After their authentication as MCs, nodes *B* and *C* are allowed to authenticate to the AS and request the information used by *A* to produce the currently used cryptographic key for communication in the network. After having derived such key, both *B* and *C* will be able to communicate with each other, as well as with node *A*, using the ad hoc mode of communication in the WMN. At this stage, *B* and *C* both have full MR functionalities. They will be able to turn on their access interface for providing node *D* a connection to the AS for joining the network.

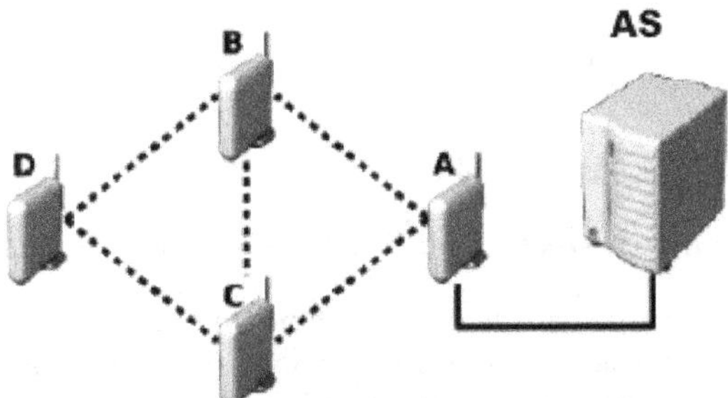

Fig. 8. Autonomous configuration of the MRs in the proposed security scheme

6. The key distribution protocol

In this section, the details of the proposed key distribution and management protocol are presented. The protocol is essentially a server-initiated protocol (Martignon et al., 2008) and provides the clients (MRs and MCs) flexibility and autonomy during the key generation.

In the proposed key management protocol delivers the keys to all the MRs from the AS in a reactive manner. The keys are used subsequently by the MRs for a specific time interval in their message communications to ensure integrity and confidentiality of the messages. After the expiry of the time interval for validity of the keys, the existing keys are revoked and new keys are generated by the AS. Fig. 9 depicts the message exchanges between the MRs and the AS during the execution of the protocol.

A newly joined MR, after its successful mutual authentication with a central server, sends its first request for key list (and its time of generation) currently being used by other existing MRs in the wireless backbone. Let us denote the *key list timestamp* as TS_{KL}. Let us define a *session* as the maximum time interval for validity of the key list currently being used by each node MR and MC). We also define the duration of a session as the product of the *cardinality of the key list* (i.e., the number of the keys in the key list) and the longest time interval of validity of a key (the parameter *timeout* in Fig. 9).

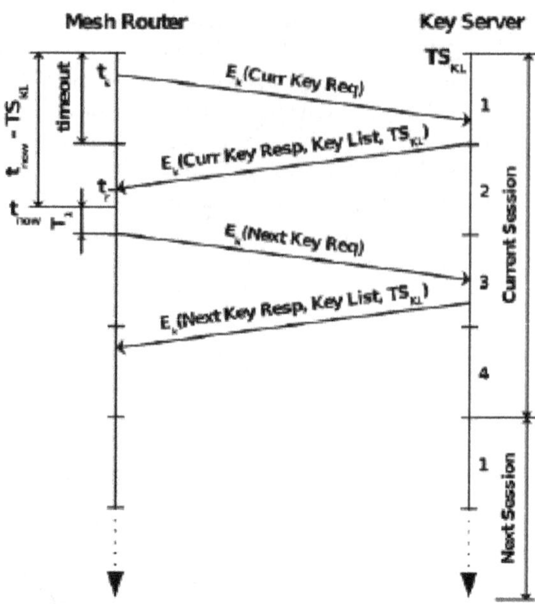

Fig. 9. Message exchanges between an MR and the AS in the key management protocol

The validity of a key list is computed from the time instance when the list is generated (i.e., TS_{KL}) by the AS. An MR, based on the time instance at which it joins the backbone (t_{now} in Fig. 9), can find out the key (from the current list) being used by its peers (key_{idx}) and the interval of validity of the key (T_i) using (1) and (2) as follows:

$$key_{idx} = \left\lfloor \frac{t_{now} - TS_{KL}}{timeout} \right\rfloor + 1 \qquad (1)$$

$$T_i = key_{idx} * timeout - (t_{now} - TS_{KL}) \qquad (2)$$

In the proposed protocol, each WMN node requests the AS for the *key list* that will be used in the next session before the expiry of the current session. This is feature is essential for nodes which are located multiple hops away from the AS, since, responses from the AS take longer time to reach these nodes. The responses may also get delayed due to fading or congestion in the wireless links. If the nodes send their requests for key list to the AS just before expiry of the current session, then due to limited time in hand, only the nodes which have good quality links with the AS will receive the key list. Hence, the nodes which will fail to receive responses for the server will not be able to communicate in the next session due to non-availability of the current key list. This will lead to an undesirable situation of network partitioning.

The *key index* value that triggers the request from the nodes to the server can be set equal to the difference between the *cardinality of the list* and a *correction factor*. The correction factor can be estimated based on parameters like the network load, the distance of the node from the AS and the time required for the previous response.

In the proposed protocol, the correction factor is estimated based on the time to receive the response from the AS using (3), where t_s is the time instance when the first key request was sent, t_r is the time instance when the key response was received from the AS, and *timeout* is the validity period of the key. Therefore, if a node fails to receive a response (i.e., the key list) from the AS during timeout, and takes a time t_{last}, it must send the next request to the AS before setting the last key.

$$c = \left\lceil \frac{t_{last} - timeout}{timeout} \right\rceil \text{ if } t_{last} \geq timeout \tag{3}$$

$$= 0 \text{ if } t_{last} < timeout$$

$$t_{last} = t_r - t_s$$

The first request of the key list sent by the new node to the AS is forwarded by the peer to which it is connected as an MC through the wireless access network. However, the subsequent requests are sent directly over the wireless backbone.

7. The privacy and anonymity protocol

As mentioned in Section 1, to ensure privacy of the users, the proposed security protocol is complemented with a privacy protocol so as to ensure user anonymity and privacy. The same *authentication server* (AS) used in the security protocol is used for managing the key distribution for preserving the privacy. To enable user authentication and anonymity, a novel protocol has been designed extending the *ring signature authentication* scheme in (Cao et al., 2004). It is assumed that a symmetric encryption algorithm E exists such that for any key k, the function E_k is a permutation over b-bit strings. We also assume the existence of a family of *keyed combining functions* $C_{k,v}(y_1, y_2, \ldots, y_n)$, and a publicly defined *collision-resistant* hash function $H(.)$ that maps arbitrary inputs to strings of constant length which are used as keys for $C_{k,v}(y_1, y_2, \ldots, y_n)$ (Rivest et al., 2001). Every keyed combining function $C_{k,v}(y_1, y_2, \ldots, y_n)$ takes as input the key k, an initialization b-bit value v, and arbitrary values $y_1, y_2, \ldots, y_n$. A user U_i who wants to generate a session key with the authentication server, uses a ring of n logged-on-users and performs the following steps.

Step 1. U_i chooses the following parameters: (i) a large prime p_i such that it is hard to compute discrete logarithms in $GF(p_i)$, (ii) another large prime q_i such that $q_i \mid p_i - 1$, and (iii) a generator g_i in $GF(p_i)$ with order q_i.

Step 2. U_i chooses $x_{A_i} \in Z_{q_i}$ as his private key, and computes the public key $y_{A_i} = g_i^{x_{Ai}} \bmod p_i$.

Step 3. U_i defines a trap-door function $f_i(\alpha, \beta) = \alpha . y_{Ai}^{\alpha \bmod q_i} . g_i^{\beta} \bmod p_i$. Its inverse function $f_i^{-1}(y)$ is defined as $f_i^{-1}(y) = (\alpha, \beta)$, where α and β are computed as follows (K is a random integer in Z_{qi} .

$$\alpha = y_{Ai}.g_i^{-K.(g_i^K \bmod p_i) \bmod q_i} \bmod p_i \qquad (4)$$

$$\alpha^* = \alpha \bmod q_i \qquad (5)$$

$$\beta = K.(g_i^K \bmod p_i) - x_{Ai}.\alpha^* \bmod q_i \qquad (6)$$

U_i makes p_i, q_i, g_i and y_{A_i} public, and keeps x_{A_i} as secret.

The *authentication server* (*AS*) chooses: (i) a large prime p such that it is hard to compute discrete logarithms in $GF(p)$, (ii) another large prime q such that $q \mid p - 1$, (iii) a generator g in $GF(p)$ with order q, (iv) a random integer x_B from Z_q as its private key. *AS* computes its public key $y_B = g^{x_B} \bmod p$ and publishes (y_B, p, q, g).

Anonymous authenticated key exchange: The key-exchange is initiated by the user U_i and involves three rounds to compute a secret session key between U_i and *AS*. The operations in these three rounds are as follows:

Round 1: When U_i wants to generate a session key on the behalf of n ring users $U_1, U_2, \ldots U_n$, where $1 \le i \le n$, U_i does the following:

i. (i) U_i chooses two random integers x_1, $x_A \in Z_q^*$ and computes the following: $R = g^{x_1} \bmod p$, $Q = y_B^{x_1} \bmod p \bmod q$, $X = g^{x_a} \bmod p$ and $l = H(X, Q, V, y_B, I)$.

ii. (ii) U_i Chooses a pair of values (α_t, β_t) for every other ring member U_t $(1 \le t \le n, t \ne k)$ in a pseudorandom way, and computes $y_t = f_t(\alpha_t, \beta_t) \bmod p_t$.

iii. (iii) U_i randomly chooses a b-bit initialization value v, and finds the value of y_i from the equation $C_{k,v}(y_1, y_2, \ldots\ldots y_n) = v$.

iv. (iv) U_i computes $(\alpha_i, \beta_i) = f_i^{-1}(y_i)$ by using the trap-door information of f_i. First, it chooses a random integer $K \in Z_{q_i}$, computes α_i using (6), and keeps K secret. It then computes α_i^* using (5) and finally computes β_i using (6).

v. (v) $(U_1, U_2, ., U_n, v, V, R, (\alpha_1, \beta_1), (\alpha_2, \beta_2), ., (\alpha_n, \beta_n))$ is the ring signature σ on X.

Finally, U_i sends σ and I to the server *AS*.

Round 2: *AS* does the following to recover and verify X from the signature σ.

i. *AS* computes $Q = R^{x_B} \bmod p \bmod q$, recovers X using $X = V.g^Q \bmod p$ and hashes X, Q, V and y_b to recover l, where $l = H(X, Q, V, y_B, I)$.

ii. *AS* computes $y_t = f_i(\alpha_t, \beta_t) \bmod p_i$, for t = 1,2,.....n.

iii. *AS* checks whether $C_{k,v}(y_1, y_2, \ldots\ldots y_n) = v$. If it is true, *AS* accepts X as valid; otherwise, *AS* rejects X. If X is valid, *AS* chooses a random integer x_b from Z_q^*, and computes the following: $Y = g^{x_b} \bmod p$ $K_s = X^{x_b} \bmod p$ and $h = H(K_s, X, Y, I')$. *AS* sends $\{h, Y, I'\}$ to U_i.

Round 3: U_i verifies whether $K_S^{'}$ is from the server AS. For this purpose, U_i computes $K_S^{'} = Y^{x_a} \bmod p$, hashes K, X, Y to get $h^{'}$ using $h^{'} = H(K_s^{'}, X, Y, I^{'})$. If $h^{'} = h$, U_i accepts K_s as the session key.

Security analysis: The key exchange scheme satisfies the following requirements.

User anonymity: For a given signature X, the server can only be convinced that the ring signature is actually produced by at least one of the possible users. If the actual user does not reveal the seed K, the server cannot determine the identity of the user. The strength of the anonymity depends on the security of the pseudorandom number generator. It is not possible to determine the identity of the actual user in a ring of size n with a probability greater than $1/n$. Since the values of k and v are fixed in a ring signature, there are $(2^b)^{n-1}$ number of $(x_1, x_2, ... x_n)$ that satisfy the equation $C_{k,v}(y_1, y_2, ... y_n) = v$, and the probability of generation of each $(x_1, x_2, ... x_n)$ is the same. Therefore, the signature can't leak the identity information of the user.

Mutual authentication: In the proposed scheme, not only the server verifies the users, but the users can also verify the server. Because of the hardness of inverting the hash function *f(.)*, it is computationally infeasible for the attacker to determine (α_i, β_i), and hence it is infeasible for him to forge a signature. If the attacker wants to masquerade as the *AS*, he needs to compute $h = H(K_s, X, Y)$. He requires x_B in order to compute X. However, x_B is the private key of *AS* to which the attacker has no access.

Forward secrecy: The forward secrecy of a scheme refers to its ability to defend leaking of its keys of previous sessions when an attacker is able to catch hold of the key of a particular session. The forward secrecy of a scheme enables it to prevent *replay attacks*. In the proposed scheme, since x_a and x_b are both selected randomly, the session key of each period has not relation to the other periods. Therefore, if the session key generated in the period *j* is leaked, the attacker cannot get any information of the session keys generated before the period *j*. The proposed protocol is, therefore, resistant to replay attack.

8. Performance evaluation

The proposed security and privacy protocols have been implemented in the Qualnet network simulator, version 4.5 (Network Simulator, Qualnet). The simulated network consists of 50 nodes randomly distributed in the simulation area forming a dense WMN. The WMN topology is shown in Fig. 10, in which 5 are MRs and remaining 45 are MCs. Each MR has 9 MCs associated with it. To evaluate the performance of the security protocol, first the network is set as a full-mesh topology, where each MR (and also MC) is directly connected to two of its neighbors. In such as scenario, the throughput of a TCP connection established over a wireless link is measured with the security protocol activated in the nodes. The obtained results are then compared with the throughput obtained on the same wireless link protected by a static key to encrypt the traffic.

After having 10 simulation runs, the average throughput of a wireless link between a pair of MRs was found to be equal to 30.6 MBPS, when the link is protected by a static key. However, the average throughput for the same link was 28.4 MBPS when the link was protected by the proposed security protocol. The results confirm that the protocol does not cause any significant overhead on the performance of the wireless link, since the throughput in a link on average decreased by only 7%.

The impact of the security protocol for key generation and revocation on packet drop rate in real-time applications is also studied in the simulation. For this purpose, a VoIP application is invoked between two MRs which generated UDP traffic in the wireless link. The packet drop rates in wireless link when the link is protected with the proposed security protocol and when the link is protected with a static key. The transmission rate was set to 1 MBPS. The average packet drop rate in 10 simulation runs was found to be only 4%. The results clearly demonstrate that the proposed security scheme has no adverse impact on packet drop rate even if several key switching (regeneration and revocation) operations are carried out.

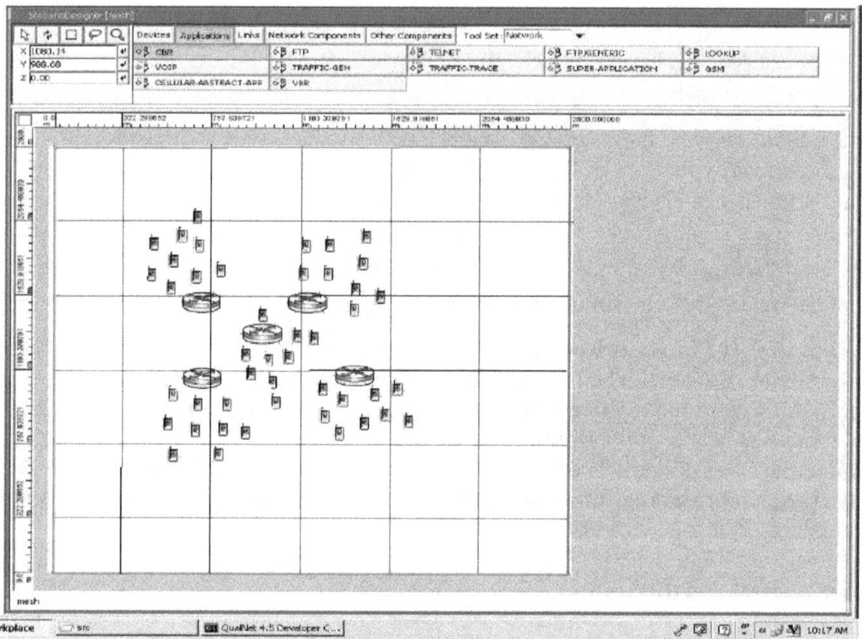

Fig. 10. The simulated network topology in Qualnet Simulator

The performance of the privacy protocol is also analyzed in terms of its storage, communication overhead. Both storage and communication overhead were found to increase linearly with the number of nodes in the network. In fact, it has been analytically shown that overhead due to cryptographic operation on each message is: $60n + 60$ bytes, where n represents the number of public key pairs used to generate the ring signature (Xiong et al., 2010). It is clear that the privacy protocol has a low overhead.

9. Conclusion and future work

WMNs have become an important focus area of research in recent years owing to their great promise in realizing numerous next-generation wireless services. Driven by the demand for rich and high-speed content access, recent research has focused on developing high performance communication protocols, while security and privacy issues have received relatively little attention. However, given the wireless and multi-hop nature of communication, WMNs are subject to a wide range of security and privacy threats. This chapter has provided a comprehensive discussion on the current authentication, access control and user privacy protection schemes for WMNs. It has also presented a novel security and key management protocol that can be utilized for secure authentication in WMNs. The proposed security protocol ensures security in both the access and the backbone networks. A user privacy protection algorithm has also been presented that enables anonymous authentication of the users. Simulation results have shown the effectiveness of the protocol. Future research issues include the study of a distributed and collaborative system where the authentication service is provided by a dynamically selected set of MRs. The integration with the current centralized scheme would increase the robustness of the proposed protocol, maintaining a low overhead since MRs would use the distributed service only when the central server is not available. Authentication on the backbone network in a hybrid and open WMN is still an unsolved problem. In addition, authentication between MRs and IGWs from different operators in a hybrid WMN environment is another challenge. Authentication and key distribution in a mobile WMN such as mobile WiMAX or LTE networks is another open problem. High mobility users make the challenge even more difficult. Owing to very limited coverage IEEE 802.11-based MRs (e.g., 100 meters), the high-mobility users (e.g. a user on a fast moving car) will migrate from the coverage area of an MR to that of another. It is not acceptable for the user to authenticate and negotiate the key with each MR. Novel solutions possibly using group keys are needed for this purpose. The requirements of user anonymity and privacy of users should be integrated to most of the applications in WMNs.

10. References

Aboba, B.; Bluk, L.; Vollbrecht, J.; Carlson, J. & Levkowetz, H. (2004). *Extensible Authentication Protocol (EAP).* RFC 3748, June 2004.

Aboba, B. & Simon, D. (1999). *PPP EAP TLS Authentication Protocol.* RFC 2716, 1999.

Aboba, B. & Vollbrecht, J. (1999). *Proxy Chaining and Policy Implementation in Roaming, RFC 2607,* October 1999.

Akyildiz, I. F.; Wang, X. & Wang, W. (2005). Wireless Mesh Networks: A Survey. *Computer Networks,* Vol 47, No 4, pp. 445–487, March 2005.

Ateniese, G.; Herzberg, A.; Krawczyk, H. & Tsudik, G. (1999). Untraceable Mobility or How to Travel Incognito. *Computer Networks,* Vol 31, No 8, pp. 871–884, April 1999.

Aura, T. & Roe, M. (2005). Reducing Reauthentication Delay in Wireless Networks. *Proceedings of the 1st IEEE International Conference on Security and Privacy for Emerging Areas in Communications Networks (SecureComm'05),* pp. 139-148, Athens, Greece, September 2005.

Ben Salem, N. & Hubaux, J.-P. (2006). Securing Wireless Mesh Networks. *IEEE Wireless Communication,* Vol 13, No 2, pp. 50-55, April 2006.

Blake-Wilson, S. & Menezes, A. (1998). Entity Authentication and Authenticated Key Transport Protocols Employing Asymmetric Techniques. *Proceedings of the 5th International Workshop on Security Protocols, Lecture Notes in Computer Science,* Vol

1361, pp. 137–158, Christianson et al. (eds.), Springer-Verlag, Heidelberg, Germany, 1998.

Blundo, C.; Santis, A. D.; Herzberg. A.; Kutten, S.; Vaccaor, U. & Yung, M. (1993). Perfectly-Secure Key Distribution for Dynamic Conferences. *Proceedings of the 12th Annual International Cryptology Conference on Advances in Cryptology (CRYPTO'92). Lecture Notes in Computer Science*, Brickell (ed.), Vol 740, pp. 471-486, 1993.

Boneh, D. & Franklin, M. (2001). Identity-Based Encryption from the Weil Pairing. *Proceedings of the Annual International Cryptology Conference (CRYPTO'01). Lecture Notes in Computer Science*, Vol 2139, pp. 213–229, Springer-Verlag, Berlin, Germany, August 2001.

Boneh, D. & Shacham, H. (2004). Group Signatures with Verifier-Local Revocation. *Proceedings of the 11th ACM Conference on Computer and Communication Security (CCS)*, pp. 168-177, Washington DC, USA, October 2004.

Brands, S. (1993). Untraceable Off-Line Cash in Wallets with Observers. *Proceedings of the Annual International Cryptology Conference (CRYPTO'93). Lecture Notes in Computer Science* Vol 773, pp. 302–318, August 1993.

Buttyan, L. & Dora, L. (2009). An Authentication Scheme for QoS-Aware Multi-Operator Maintained Wireless Mesh Networks. *Proceedings of the 1st IEEE WoWMoM Workshop on Hot Topics in Mesh Networking (HotMESH '09)*, Kos, Greece, June 2009.

Buttyan, L.; Dora, L; Martinelli, F. & Petrochhi, M. (2010). Fast Certificate-based Authentication Scheme in Multi-Operator Maintained Wireless Mesh Networks. *Journal of Computer Communications*, Vol 33, Issue 8, May 2010.

Cao, T.; Lin, D. & Xue, R. (2004). Improved Ring Authenticated Encryption Scheme. *Proceedings of 10th Joint International Computer Conference (JICC), International Academic Publishers World Publishing Corporation*, pp. 341-346, 2004.

Cao, Z; Zhu, H. & Lu, R. (2006). Provably Secure Robust Threshold Partial Blind Signature. *Science in China Series F: Information Sciences*, Vol 49, No 5, pp. 604–615, October 2006.

Chaum, D. (1982). Blind Signatures for Untraceable Payments. *Proceedings of the Annual International Cryptology Conference (CRYPTO'82). Advances in Cryptology*, pp. 199–203, Plenum Press, New York, USA, August 1983.

Cheikhrouhou, O.; Maknavicius, M. & Chaouchi, H. (2006). Security Architecture in a Multi-Hop Mesh Network. *Proceedings of the 5th Conference on Security Architecture Research (SAR 2006)*, Seignosse-Landes, France, June 2006.

Clarke, R. (1999). Internet Privacy Concerns Confirm the Case for Intervention. *Communications of the ACM*, Vol 42, No 2, pp. 60–67, February 1999.

Fantacci, R.; Maccari, L.; Pecorella, T. & Frosali, F. (2006). A Secure and Performant Token-Based Authentication for Infrastructure and Mesh 802.1X Networks. *Proceedings of the 25th IEEE International Conference on Computer Communications (INFOCOM'06)*, Poster Paper, Barcelona, Spain, April 2006.

Figueiredo, D.; Shapiro, J. & Towsley, D. (2005). Incentives to Promote Availability in Peer-to-Peer Anonymity Systems. *Proceedings of the 13th IEEE International Conference on Network Protocols (ICNP'05)*, pp. 110–121, November 2005.

He, B.; Xie, B.; Zhao, D. & Reddy, R. (2011). Secure Access Control and Authentication in Wireless Mesh Networks. *Security of Self-Organizing Networks: MANET, WSN, WMN, WANET*, Al-Sakib Khan Pathan (ed.), CRC Pres, USA, 2011.

He, B.; Joshi, S.; Agrawal, D. P. & Sun, D. (2010). An Efficient Authenticated Key Establishment Scheme for Wireless Mesh Networks. *Proceedings of IEEE Global Telecommunications Conference (GLOBECOM'10)*, pp. 1-5, Miami, Florida, USA, December 2010.

Hur, J.; Shim, H.; Kim, P.; Yoon, H. & Song, N.-O. (2008). Security Consideration for Handover Schemes in Mobile WiMAX Networks. *Proceedings of IEEE Wireless Communications and Networking Conference (WCNC '08)*, Las Vegas, NV, March, 2008.

IEEE Standard 802.11i (2004). *Medium Access Control Security Enhancements*, 2004.

IEEE Standard 802.1X (2001). *Local and Metropolitan Area Networks Port-Based Network Access Control*, 2001.

Kassab, M.; Belghith, A.; Bonnin, J.-M. & Sassi, S. (2005). Fast Pre-Authentication Based on Proactive Key Distribution for 802.11 Infrastructure Networks. *Proceedings of the 1st ACM Workshop on Wireless Multimedia Networking and Performance Modeling (WMuNeP 2005)*, pp. 46–53, Montreal, Canada, October 2005.

Lamport, L. (1981). Password Authentication with Insecure Communication. *Communications of the ACM*, Vol. 24, No. 11, pp. 770-772, November 1981.

Lee, I.; Lee, J.; Arbaugh, W. & Kim, D. (2008). Dynamic Distributed Authentication Scheme for Wireless LAN-Based Mesh Networks. *Proceedings of International Conference on Information, Networking, Towards Ubiquitous Networking and Services (ICOIN '07)*, Estril, Portugal, January, 2007. *Lecture Notes in Computer Science*, Vazao et al. (eds.), Vol. 5200, pp. 649–658, Springer-Verlag, Heidelberg, Germany, 2008.

Lin, X.; Ling, X.; Zhu, H.; Ho, P.-H. & Shen, X. (2008). A Novel Localised Authentication Scheme in IEEE 802.11 Based Wireless Mesh Networks. *International Journal of Security and Networks*, Vol. 3, No. 2, pp. 122–132, 2008.

Loughney, L.; Nakhjiri, M.; Perkins, C. & Koodli, R. (2005). *Context Transfer Protocol (CXTP)*. IETF RFC 4067, July 2005.

Lukas, G. & Fackroth, C. (2009). WMNSec: Security for Wireless Mesh Networks. *Proceedings of the International Conference on Wireless Communications and Mobile Computing: Connecting the World Wirelessly (IWCMC'09)*, pp. 90–95, Leipzig, Germany, June, 2009, ACM Press, New York, USA.

Martignon, F.; Paris, S. & Capone, A. (2008). MobiSEC: A Novel Security Architecture for Wireless Mesh Networks. *Proceedings of the 4th ACM Symposium on QoS and Security for Wireless and Mobile Networks (Q2SWinet'08)*, pp. 35-42, Vancouver, Canada, October 2008.

Mills, D.L. (1992). *Network Time Protocol*, RFC 1305, March 1992.

Mishra, A. & Arbaugh, W. A. (2002). *An Initial Security Analysis of the IEEE 802.1X Standard. Computer Science Department Technical Report CS-TR-4328*, University of Maryland, USA, February 2002.

Mishra, A.; Shin, M.H.; Petroni, N. I.; Clancy, J. T. & Arbauch, W. A. (2004). Proactive Key Distribution Using Neighbor Graphs. *IEEE Wireless Communications*, Vol. 11, No. 1, pp. 26–36, February 2004.

Moustafa, H. (2007). Providing Authentication, Trust, and Privacy in Wireless Mesh Networks, pp. 261-295. *Security in Wireless Mesh Networks*. Zhang et al. (eds.), CRC Press, USA, 2007.

Moustafa, H.; Bourdon, G. & Gourhant, Y. (2006a). Authentication, Authorization and Accounting (AAA) in Hybrid Ad Hoc Hotspot's Environments. *Proceedings of the 4th ACM International Workshop on Wireless Mobile Applications and Services on WLAN Hotspots (WMASH'06)*, pp. 37-46, Los Angeles, California, USA, September 2006.

Moustafa, H.; Bourdon, G. & Gourhant, Y. (2006b). Providing Authentication and Access Control in Vehicular Network Environment. *Proceedings of the 21st IFIP TC- 11 International Information Security Conference (IFIP-SEC'06)*, pp. 62-73, Karlstad, Sweden, May 2006.

Network Simulator QUALNET. URL: http://www.scalable-networks.com.

Pack, S. & Choi, Y. (2004). Fast Handoff Scheme Based on Mobility Prediction in Public Wireless LAN Systems. *IEEE Communications*, Vol. 151, No. 5, pp. 489–495, October 2004.

Parthasarathy, M. (2006). *Protocol for Carrying Authentication and Network Access (PANA) Threat Analysis and Security Requirements.* RFC 4016, March 2005.

Perrig, A.; Canetti, R.; Song, D. & Tygar, J. (2001). Efficient and Secure Source Authentication for Multicast. *Proceedings of the Network and Distributed System Security Symposium (NDSS 2001)*, pp. 35-46, San Diego, California, USA, February 2001.

Prasad, N. R.; Alam, M. & Ruggieri, M. (2004). Light-Weight AAA Infrastructure for Mobility Support across Heterogeneous Networks. *Wireless Personal Communications*, Vol 29, No 3–4, pp. 205–219, June 2004.

Prasad, A. R. & Wang, H. (2005). Roaming Key Based Fast Handover in WLANs. *Proceedings of IEEE Wireless Communications and Networking Conference (WCNC 2003)*, Vol 3, pp. 1570–1576, New Orleans, Louisiana, USA, March 2005.

Raya, M. & Hubaux, J.-P. (2007). Securing Vehicular Ad Hoc Networks. *Journal of Computer Security, Special Issue on Security of Ad Hoc and Sensor Networks*, Vol 15, No 1, pp. 39–68, January 2007.

Reed, M.; Syverson, P. & Goldschlag, D. D. (1998). Anonymous Connections and Onion Routing. *IEEE Journal on Selected Areas in Communications*, Vol 16, No 4, pp. 482-494, May 1998.

Ren, K.; Yu, S.; Lou, W. & Zhang, Y. (2010). PEACE: A Novel Privacy-Enhanced Yet Accountable Security Framework for Metropolitan Wireless Mesh Networks. *IEEE Transactions on Parallel and Distributed Systems*, Vol 21, No 2, pp. 203–215, February 2010.

Rigney, C.; Willens, S.; Rubins, A. & Simpson, W. (2000). *Remote Authentication Dial in User Service (RADIUS), RFC 2865*, June 2000.

Rivest, R.; Shamir, A. & Tauman, Y. (2001). How to Leak a Secret. *Proceedings of the 7th International Conference on the Theory and Applications of Cryptology and Information Security: Advances in Security (ASIACRPT'01). Lecture Notes in Computer Science*, Vol 2248, pp. 552-565, Boyd, C. (ed.), Springer, Heidelberg, December 2001.

Sen, J.; Chowdhury, P. R. & Sengupta, I. (2006). *Proceedings of the International Symposium on Ad Hoc and Ubiquitous Computing (ISAHUC'06)*, pp. 62-67, Surathkal, Mangalore, India, December, 2006.

Sen, J. & Subramanyam, H. (2007). An Efficient Certificate Authority for Ad Hoc Networks. *Proceedings of the 4th International Conference on Distributed Computing and Internet Technology (ICDCIT'07)*, Bangalore, India, December 2007. *Lecture Notes in Computer Science*, Janowski & Mohanty (eds.), Vol 4882, pp. 97-109, 2007.

Sen, J. (2009). A Survey on Wireless Sensor Network Security. *International Journal of Communication Networks and Information Security (IJCNIS)*, Vol 1, No2, pp. 59-82, August 2009.

Sen, J. (2010a). A Distributed Trust and Reputation Framework for Mobile Ad Hoc Networks. *Recent Trends in Network Security and its Applications*, Meghanathan et al. (eds.), pp. 528–537, *Communications in Computer and Information Science (CCIS)*, Springer- Verlag, Heidelberg, Germany, July 2010.

Sen, J. (2010b). Reputation- and Trust-Based Systems for Wireless Self-Organizing Networks, pp. 91-122. *Security of Self-Organizing Networks: MANET, WSN, WMN, VANET*, A-S. K. Pathan (ed.), Aurbach Publications, CRC Press, USA, December 2010.

Sen, J. (2010c). A Robust and Efficient Node Authentication Protocol for Mobile Ad Hoc Networks. *Proceedings of the 2nd International Conference on Computational Intelligence, Modelling and Simulation (CIMSiM'10)*, pp. 476-481, Bali, Indonesia, September 2010.

Sen, J. (2011). Secure Routing in Wireless Mesh Networks, pp. 237-280. *Wireless Mesh Networks*, Nobuo Funabiki (ed.), InTech, Croatia, January 2011.

Shamir, A. (1984). Identity-Based Cryptosystems and Signature Schemes. *Proceedings of the International Cryptology Conference (CRYPTO'84). Lecture Notes in Computer Science*, Vol. 196, pp. 47–53, Springer-Verlag, Berlin, Germany, August 1984.

Soltwisch, R.; Fu, X.; Hogrefe, D. & Narayanan, S. (2004). A Method for Authentication and Key Exchange for Seamless Inter-Domain Handovers. *Proceedings of the 12th IEEE International Conference on Networks (ICON '04)*, pp. 463–469, Singapore, November 2004.

Sun, J.; Zhang, C. & Fang, Y. (2008). A Security Architecture Achieving Anonymity and Traceability in Wireless Mesh Networks. *Proceedings of the 27th IEEE International Conference on Computer Communications (IEEE INFOCOM'08)*, pp. 1687–1695, April 2008.

Sun, J.; Zhang, C. ; Zhang, Y. & Fang, Y. (2011). SAT: A Security Architecture Achieving Anonymity and Traceability in Wireless Mesh Networks. *IEEE Transactions on Dependable and Secure Computing*, Vol 8, No 2, pp. 295–307, March 2011.

Wei, K.; Chen, Y. R.; Smith, A. J. & Vo, B. (2006). WhoPay: A Scalable and Anonymous Payment system for Peer-to-Peer Environments. *Proceedings of the 26th IEEE International Conference on Distributed Computing Systems (ICDCS'06)*, July 2006.

Wood, A. D. & Stankovic, J. A. (2002). Denial of Service in Sensor Networks. *IEEE Computer*, Vol 35, No. 10, pp. 54–62, October 2002.

Wu, T.; Xue, Y. & Cui, Y. (2006). Preserving Traffic Privacy in Wireless Mesh Networks. *Proceedings of the International Symposium on a World of Wireless, Mobile and Multimedia Networks (WoWMoM'06), pp.* 459-461, Buffalo-Niagara Falls, NY, USA, June 2006.

Wu, X. & Li, N. (2006). Achieving Privacy in Mesh Networks. *Proceedings of the 4th ACM Workshop on Security of Ad Hoc and Sensor Networks (SASN)*, pp. 13-22, October 2006.

Xiong, H.; Beznosov, K.; Qin, Z. & Ripeanu, M. (2010). Efficient and Spontaneous Privacy-Preserving Protocol for Secure Vehicular Communication. *Proceedings of IEEE International Conference on Communications (ICC'10)*, pp. 1-6, Cape Town, South Africa, May 2010.

Yi, P.; Wu, Y.; Zou, F. & Liu, N. (2010). A Survey on Security in Wireless Mesh Networks. *IETE Technical Review*, Vol 27, No 1, pp. 6-14.

Zhang, Y. & Fang, Y. (2006). ARSA: An Attack-Resilient Security Architecture for Multihop Wireless Mesh Networks. *IEEE Journal of Selected Areas in Communication*, Vol. 24, No. 10, pp. 1916–1928, October 2006.

Zhang, Y.; Liu, W.; Lou, W. & Fang, Y. (2006). MASK: Anonymous On-demand Routing in Mobile Ad Hoc Networks. *IEEE Transactions on Wireless Communications*, Vol. 5. No. 9, pp. 2376–2385, September 2006.

Zheng, X.; Chen, C.; Huang, C.-T.; Matthews, M. & Santhapuri, N. (2005). A Dual Authentication Protocol for IEEE 802.11 Wireless LANs. *Proceedings of the 2nd IEEE International Symposium on Wireless Communication Systems*, pp. 565–569, September 2005.

Zhu, S.; Xu, S.; Setia, S. & Jajodia, S. (2003). LHAP: A Lightweight Hop-by-Hop Authentication protocol for Ad-hoc Networks. *Proceedings of the 23rd IEEE International Conference on Distributed Computing Systems Workshops (ICDCSW'03)*, pp. 749–755, May 2003.

Zhu, S.; Xu, S.; Setia S. & Jajodia, S. (2006). LHAP: A Lightweight Network Access Control Protocol for Ad Hoc Networks. *Ad Hoc Networks*, Vol 4, No 5, pp. 567-585, September 2006.

Zhu, H.; Lin, X.; Lu, R.; Ho, P.-H. & Shen, X. (2008). SLAB: A Secure Localized Authentication and Billing Scheme for Wireless Mesh Networks. *IEEE Transactions on Wireless Communications*, Vol 7, No. 10, pp. 3858–3868, October 2008.

2

Anonymous Authentication Protocols for Vehicular Ad Hoc Networks: An Overview

Hu Xiong, Zhi Guan, Jianbin Hu and Zhong Chen
Key Laboratory of Network and Software Security Assurance of the Ministry of Education, Institute of Software, School of Electronics Engineering and Computer Science, Peking University
P. R. China

1. Introduction

According to car crash statistics, over six million motor vehicle crashes occur on U.S. highways each year. More than 42,000 people are killed in these accidents which injure three million others, and cost more than $230 billion each year. Astonishingly, five people die every hour in these crashes in the United States which is about one death every 12 minutes IVI (2001). In order to alleviate the threats of these crashes and improve the driving experience, car manufactures and the telecommunication industry have made great efforts to equip each vehicle with wireless devices that allow vehicles to communicate with each other as well as with the roadside infrastructure located in critical points of the road, such as intersections or construction sites. Misener (2005); VII (2011). Technologies built on 802.11p and IEEE 1609 standards, 5.9 GHz Dedicated Short Range Communications (DSRC) protocols [1] DSRC (1999), are proposed to support these advanced vehicle safety applications such as secure and effective vehicle-to-vehicle (V2V) (also known as Inter-Vehicle Communica- tion (IVC)) and vehicle-to-infrastructure (V2I) communications, which are also known as Vehicle Safety Communications (VSC) technologies. As shown in Fig. 1, the wireless communication devices installed on vehicles, also known as onboard units (OBUs), and the roadside units (RSUs), form a self-organized Vehicular Ad Hoc Network (VANET) Lin (2008); Sun (2007). Furthermore, the RSUs are connected to the backbone network via the high speed network connections. In this way, VANETs inherently provide a way to collect traffic and road information from vehicles, and to deliver road services including warnings and traffic information to users in the vehicles. Thus, an increasing interest has been raised recently on the VANETs-based applications Bishop (2000), aiming to improve driving safety and traffic management by the method of providing drivers and passengers with Internet access.

Due to the open broadcasting of wireless communications and the high-speed mobility of the vehicles, extensive research efforts have been launched by academic institutions and industrial research labs several years ago to investigate key issues in VANETs, especially

[1] The United States Federal Communications Commission (FCC) has allocated in the USA 75MHz of spectrum in the 5.9GHz band for DSRC and the European Telecommunications Standards Institute (ETSI) has allocated in the Europe 30 MHz of spectrum in the 5.9GHz band for Intelligent Transportation Systems in October 1999 and August 2008, respectively

security and privacy preservation for mobile vehicles Calandriello *et al.* (2007); Chen *et al.* (2011); Daza *et al.* (2009); Hubaux *et al.* (2004); Kamat *et al.* (2006); Kounga *et al.* (2009); Li *et al.* (2008); Lin *et al.* (2007; 2008a;b); Lu *et al.* (2008; 2009; 2010); Mak *et al.* (2005); Plößl & Federrath (2008); Raya & Hubaux (2005; 2007); Sun *et al.* (2007; 2010a;b); Wasef *et al.* (2010); Wang *et al.* (2008); Wu *et al.* (2010); Xu *et al.* (2007); Xi *et al.* (2007; 2008); Xiong *et al.* (2010a;b); Zhang *et al.* (2008a;b). Obviously, any malicious behaviors of user, such as injecting beacons with false information, modifying and replaying the previously disseminated messages, could be fatal to the other users. Thus, identifying the message issuer is mandatory to reduce the risk of such attacks. Meanwhile, in order to protect the user-related private information, such as the driver's name, the license plate, speed, position, and travelling routes along with their relationship, authentication in VANETs should be privacy-preserving.

It is natural to observe that achieving privacy and liability simultaneously is conflicting goal. On one aspect, a well-meaning OBU is willing to offer as much local information as possible to RSUs and other OBUs to create a safer driving environment so long as its locations cannot be tracked. And on the other, a misbehaving OBU may abuse the privacy protection mechanism to avoid legal responsibility when it involved in a dispute involving safety messages [2]attempts. Therefore, the *conditional privacy-preserving authentication* should be fulfilled in VANETs where a trusted authority can reveal the real identity of targeted OBU in case of a traffic event dispute, even though the OBU itself is not traceable by the public.

This chapter surveys the literature on privacy issues in VANETs from different perspectives, and thus provides researchers with a better understanding of this primitive. This chapter does not propose or advocate any specific anonymous authentication mechanisms. Even though some sections might point out vulnerabilities in certain classes of authentication protocols, our purpose is not to criticize, but to draw attention to these problems so that they might be solved.

The remainder of this chapter is organized as follows. Section 2 presents attack model, security requirements and related VANETs network architecture. All previous privacy-preserving protocols for VANETs are classified in Section 3, together with the basic cryptographic primitives. An example of Ring-signature based anonymous authentication protocol based on bilinear pairing are given in Section 4. Section 5 discusses how to use the taxonomies. Section 6 concludes the paper by stating some possible future research directions.

2. Motivation

2.1 Attack model

According to Lin (2008); Lin *et al.* (2007); Raya & Hubaux (2005; 2007); Sun *et al.* (2007), several possible security attacks in VANETs have been defined and listed as follows:

- Fake information attack: The adversary may diffuse bogus messages to affect the behavior of others. For instance, in order to divert traffic from a given road, one may send a fake traffic jam message to the others.
- Message replay attack: The adversary replays the valid messages sent by a legitimate user some time before in order to disturb the traffic.

[2] A safety message reports on the state of the sender vehicle, e.g., its location, speed, heading, etc.

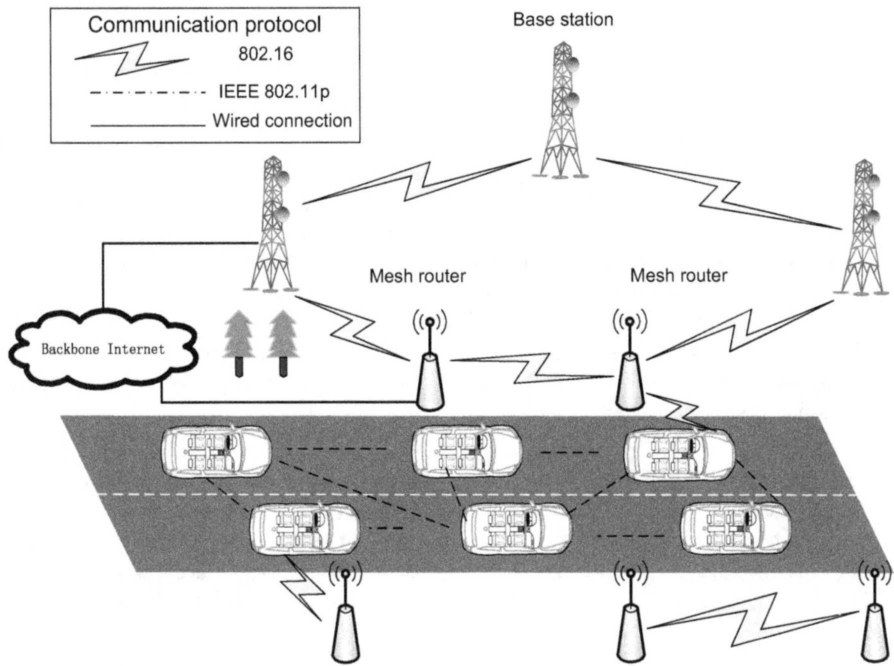

Fig. 1. Vehicular Ad Hoc Networks

- Message modification attack: A message is altered during or after transmission. The adversary may wish to change the source or content of the message in terms of the position and/or time information that had been sent and saved in its device notably in the case of an accident.
- Impersonation attack: The adversary may pretend to be another vehicle or even an RSU by using false identities to fool the others.
- RSU preemption/replication attack: An RSU may be compromised such that the adversary can relocate the compromised RSU to launch any malicious attack, such as broadcasting fake traffic information. Moreover, the adversary may illegally interrupt and manipulate traffic lights which is controlled by the corrupted RSU to get a better traffic condition
- Denial of service (DoS) attack: The adversary injects irrelevant jamming and aggressive dummy messages to take up the channels and consume the computational resources of the other nodes, such as RF interference or jamming or layer 2 packet flooding.
- Movement tracking: Since wireless communication is on an openly shared medium, an adversary can easily eavesdrop on any traffic. After the adversary intercepts a significant amount of messages in a certain region, the adversary may trace a vehicle in terms of its physical position and moving patterns simply through information analysis. Assuming that the attacker does not make use of cameras, physical pursuit, or onboard tracking devices to reveal the identity of his target; otherwise, the tracking problem becomes simpler but also more expensive and limited to few specific targets.

2.2 Security requirements

To countermeasure and mitigate the potential threats in the aforementioned attack models, a security system for safety messaging in a VANET should satisfy the following requirements.

1. *Efficient anonymous authentication of safety messages*: The security system should provide an *efficient* and *anonymous* message authentication mechanism. First of all, all accepted messages should be delivered unaltered, and the origin of the messages should be authenticated to guard against impersonation attacks. Meanwhile, from the point of vehicle owners, it may not be acceptable to leak personal information, including identity and location, to unauthorized observers while authenticating messages. Therefore, providing a secure yet anonymous message authentication is critical to the applicability of VANETs. Furthermore, considering the limited storage and computation resource of OBUs, the authentication scheme should have low overheads for safety message verification and storage.
2. *Efficient tracking of the source of a disputed safety message*: An important and challenging issue in these conditions is enabling a trusted third party (such as police officers) to retrieve a vehicle's real identity from its pseudo identity. If this feature is not provided, anonymous authentication can only prevent an outside attack, but cannot deal with an inside one. Furthermore, the system should not only provide safety message traceability to prevent inside attacks, but also have reasonable overheads for the revealing the identity of a message sender.
3. *Threshold authentication* Chen *et al.* (2011); Daza *et al.* (2009); Kounga *et al.* (2009); Wu *et al.* (2010): A message is viewed as trustworthy only after it has been endorsed by at least n vehicles, where n is a threshold. The threshold mechanism is a *priori* countermeasure that improves the confidence of other vehicles in a message. In addition, the threshold in the proposed scheme should be adaptive, that is to say, the sender can dynamically change the threshold according to the traffic context and scenarios.
4. *Confidentiality* Kamat *et al.* (2006); Li *et al.* (2008); Plößl & Federrath (2008); Wang *et al.* (2008) Some research teams pointed out that the privacy of the communication content should be protected against unauthorized observers. While confidentiality of communicating message can be negligible in most cases, it is e.g. crucial for services subject to costs. Besides application data administrative messages like routing protocol information or messages containing cryptographic material, the cryptographic information held by participants or centralized instances should also be protected against unauthorized access.

2.3 Network model

Similar to previous work Calandriello *et al.* (2007); Chen *et al.* (2011); Daza *et al.* (2009); Hubaux *et al.* (2004); Kamat *et al.* (2006); Kounga *et al.* (2009); Li *et al.* (2008); Lin *et al.* (2007; 2008a;b); Lu *et al.* (2008; 2009; 2010); Mak *et al.* (2005); Plößl & Federrath (2008); Raya & Hubaux (2005; 2007); Sun *et al.* (2007; 2010a;b); Wasef *et al.* (2010); Wang *et al.* (2008); Wu *et al.* (2010); Xu *et al.* (2007); Xi *et al.* (2007; 2008); Xiong *et al.* (2010a;b); Zhang *et al.* (2008a;b), the security system should include at least three types of entities: the top Trusted authority (TA), the immobile RSUs at the roadside, and the moving vehicles equipped with on-board units (OBUs).

- OBU: A vehicle can not join the VANETs unless it registers its own public system parameters and corresponding private key to the TA. The secret information such as private keys to be used generates the need for a tamper-proof device in each vehicle. According to existing works, only the authorized parties can access to this tamper-proof device. OBUs are mobile and moving most of the time. When the OBUs are on the road, they regularly broadcast routine safety messages, such as position, current time, direction, speed, traffic conditions, traffic events. The information system on each vehicle aggregates and diffuses these messages to enable drivers form a better awareness of their environment (Fig. 2). The assumed communication protocol between neighboring OBUs (IVC) or between an OBU and a RSU (V2I) is 5.9 GHz Dedicated Short Range Communication (DSRC) DSRC (1999) IEEE 802.11p.

- RSU: The RSUs, which are subordinated by the TA, form a wireless multi-hop mesh network (mesh mode in WiMax) aiming to extend the wireless coverage and increase the network robustness and throughput. Some of these RSUs are connected to the backbone networks with wired connections or to the WiMax base stations with wireless connections. Vehicles and passengers can gain access to the Internet for a short moment when passing through any of the RSUs by communicating with it. Thus, the RSUs should be able to perform fast handoff in order to support basic Internet services such as e-mail and TCP applications. We remark that the handoff process should be predictive when the moving pattern and speed of the vehicle are given. In addition, the RSUs should work as gateways which also support the 802.11p protocol and can transform the safety messages broadcasted by the vehicles into IP packets. With the support from RSUs, the workload of the vehicles is reduced. Otherwise, the vehicles need to send multiple copies of safety messages in different formats: one to the other vehicles with 802.11p, and one to the base stations with 802.16e. Different from the vehicles, we assume that RSUs have neither computation and energy constraints nor buffer size constraints.
- TA: The TA is in charge of the registration of all RSUs and OBUs each vehicle is equipped with. The TA can reveal the real identity of a safety message sender by incorporating with its subordinate RSUs. To the end, the TA requires ample computation and storage capability, and the TA cannot be compromised and is fully trusted by all parties in the system.

The network dynamics are characterized by quasi-permanent mobility, high speed, and (in most cases) short connection times between neighboring vehicles or between a vehicle and a roadside infrastructure network access point.

3. Taxonomy of privacy-preserving authentication protocol for VANETs

3.1 RSU-based approach

Zhang *et al.*Zhang *et al.* (2008a;b) presented a novel RSU-aided message authentication scheme (RSUB), in which the RSUs are responsible for validating the authenticity of messages sent from vehicles and for sending the results back to peer vehicles. Compared to the solutions without support from RSUs, this kind of schemes enables lower computation and communication overheads for each vehicle. Independently, Lu *et al.* Lu *et al.* (2008) introduced another anonymous authentication protocol for VANETs based on generating on-the-fly short-lived anonymous keys for the communication between vehicles and RSUs. These keys enable fast anonymous authentication and conditional privacy. All of these schemes employ RSUs to assist vehicles in authenticating messages. To keep a centralized certificate issuer from

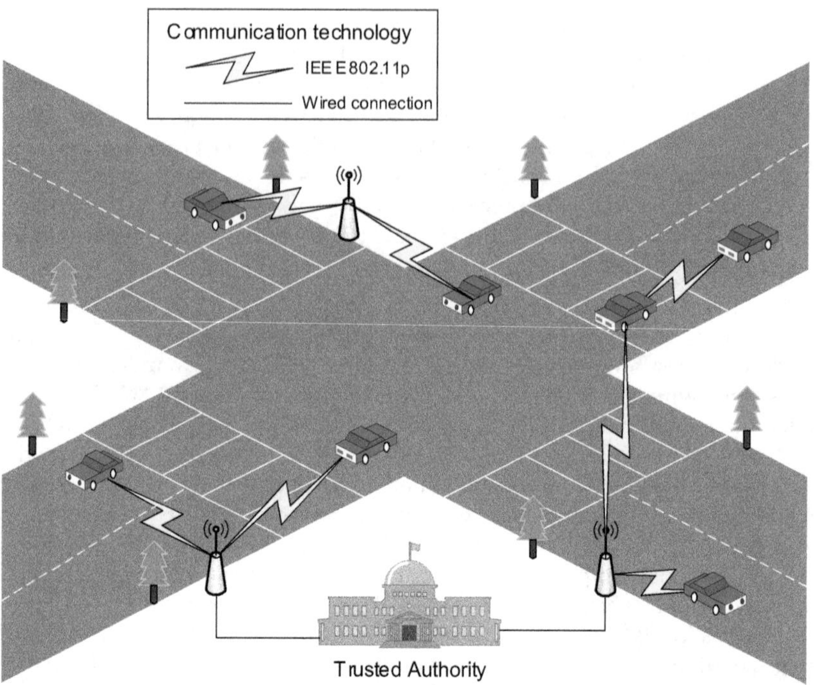

Fig. 2. VANETs Architecture

being a bottleneck, an RSU is allowed to issue certificates for the vehicles. However, it brings a privacy risk when an RSU is compromised by the adversaries. Once the service records of an RSU are leaked, it is easy for the adversary to link the pseudonymous certificates that a vehicle has obtained from the compromised RSU. In particular, when the number of compromised RSUs increases, it possibly provides a solution for the adversaries to revert the mobile trace of the target vehicles. However, relying on the roadside infrastructure for safety message authentication is a precarious solution: while these messages enable critical assisted driving features the roadside infrastructure will likely offer only partial coverage (for example during the deployment stage, for economic considerations, or simply due to physical damage).

3.2 Group-oriented signature-based approach

3.2.1 Group signature-based scheme

In Chaum & Hevst (1991), Chaum and Heyst proposed a new type of signature scheme for a group of entities, called group signatures. Such a scheme allows a group member to sign a message on the group's behalf such that everybody can verify the signature but no one can find out which group member provided it. However, there is a trusted third party, called the group manager, who can reveal the identity of the originator of a signature in the case of later dispute. This act is referred to as "opening" a signature or also as revocation of a signer's anonymity. The group manager can either be a single entity or a number of coalitions of several entities (e.g., group members). Dozens of group signature schemes Boneh *et al.*

(2004); Boneh & Shacham (2004); Chaum & Hevst (1991); Nakanishi & Funabiki (2005) have been proposed since 1991 due to its attractive features.

Lin *et al.* Lin *et al.* (2007; 2008a); Sun *et al.* (2007) proposed the group signature based (GSB) protocol, based on the efficient group signature Boneh *et al.* (2004). With GSB, each vehicle stores only a private key and a group public key. Messages are signed using the group signature scheme without revealing any identity information to the public. Thus privacy is preserved while the trusted authority is able to expose the identity of a sender. However, the time for safety message verification grows linearly with the number of revoked vehicles in the revocation list in the entire network. Hence, each vehicle has to spend additional time on safety message verification. Furthermore, when the number of revoked vehicles in the revocation list is larger than some threshold, the protocol requires every remaining vehicle to calculate a new private key and group public key based on the exhaustive list of revoked vehicles whenever a vehicle is revoked. Lin *et al.* Lin *et al.* (2007; 2008a); Sun *et al.* (2007) do not explore solutions to effectively updated the system parameters for the participating to vehicles in a timely, reliable and scalable fashion. This issue is not explored and represents an important obstacle to the success of this scheme.

3.2.2 Ring signature-based scheme

Ring signature scheme, introduced by Rivest, Shamir and Tauman Rivest *et al.* (2001), offers two main properties: anonymity and spontaneity. In practice, anonymity in a ring signature means 1-out-of-n signer verifiability, which enables the signer to keep anonymous in these "rings" of diverse signers. Spontaneity is a property which makes the distinction between ring signatures and group signatures Boneh *et al.* (2004); Chaum & Hevst (1991). Different from group signatures which allow the anonymity of a real signer in a group can be revoked by a group manager, the ring signature only gives the group manager the absolute power to control the formation of the group, and does not allow anyone to revoke the signer anonymity, while allowing the real signer to form a ring arbitrarily without being controlled by any other party. Since Rivest *el al.*'s scheme, many ring signature schemes have been proposed Abe *et al.* (2002); Bresson *et al.* (2002); Dodis *et al.* (2004); Wong *et al.* (2003); Xiong *et al.* (2009; 2011). In 2007, Liu *et al.* Liu *et al.* (2007) have introduced a new variant for the ring signature, called revocable ring signature. This scheme allows a real signer to form a ring arbitrarily while allowing a set of authorities to revoke the anonymity of the real signer. In other words, the real signer will be responsible for what has signed as the anonymity is revocable by authorities while the real signer still has full freedom on ring formation.

To address the scalability concern in Lin *et al.* (2007), Xiong *et al.* Xiong *et al.* (2010a) proposed a spontaneous protocol based on the revocable ring signature Liu *et al.* (2007), which allows the vehicle to generate the message without requiring online assistance from the RSUs or the other vehicles. In this solution, the remaining vehicles are not required to update their system parameters regardless of the number of revoked vehicles. However, this protocol suffers larger communication overhead than that of other protocols because the length of ring signature depends on the size of the ring. Furthermore, Xi *et al.* Xi *et al.* (2007; 2008) also introduced a random key-set-based authentication protocol to preserve the vehicle's privacy based on ring signature. However, this solution only provides unconditional anonymity without an effective and efficient mechanism to reveal message sender's identities when necessary.

3.2.3 *k*-TAA-based scheme

In a *k*-times anonymous authentication (*k*-TAA) system Teranisi *et al.* (2004), participants are a group manager (GM), a number of application providers (AP) and a group of users. The GM registers users into the group and each AP independently announces the number of times a user can access his application. A registered user can then be anonymously authenticated by APs within their allowed numbers of times (*k* times) and without the need to contact the GM. Dishonest users can be traced by anyone while no one, even the GM or APs, can identify honest users or link two authentication executions performed by the same user. Finally no one, even the GM, is able to successfully impersonate an honest user to an AP. In *dynamic* *k*-TAA Nguyen & Safavi-Naini (2005), APs have more control over granting and revoking access to their services and so have the required control on their clients.

Sun *et al.* Sun & Fang (2009); Sun *et al.* (2010c) proposed a new misbehavior defense technique leveraging the idea of dynamic revocation, to provide a means of limiting the impact of misbehavior by adjusting it to an acceptable level during the vulnerable period existing in the automatic revocation technique based on *dynamic* *k*-TAA. However, the downside of Sun *et al.*'s scheme is obviously the lack of capability to trace misbehaving users.

3.3 Pseudonyms-based approach

3.3.1 Basic scheme

Raya *et al.*Raya & Hubaux (2005; 2007) introduced the large number of anonymous key based (LAB) protocol. Their key idea is to install on each OBU a large number of private keys and their corresponding anonymous certificates. To sign each launched message, a vehicle randomly selects one of its anonymous certificates and uses its corresponding private key. The other vehicles use the public key of the sender enclosed with the anonymous certificate to authenticate the source of the message. These anonymous certificates are generated by employing the pseudo-identity of the vehicles, instead of taking any real identity information of the drivers. Each certificate has a short life time to meet the drivers'privacy requirement. Although LAB protocol can effectively meet the conditional privacy requirement, it is inefficient and may become a scalability bottleneck. The reason is that a sufficient numbers of certificates must be issued to each vehicle to maintain anonymity over a significant period of time. (Raya *et al.*Raya & Hubaux (2005; 2007) suggest using *large pseudo* certificates for each vehicle). As a result, the certificate database to be searched by the TRC in order to match a compromised certificate to its owner's identity is huge. In addition, the protocols of Raya & Hubaux (2007) are extended for providing confidentiality in specific scenarios of VANET implementations in Wang *et al.* (2008).

3.3.2 TESLA-based scheme

TESLA is an efficient and message-loss tolerant protocol for broadcast authentication with low communication and computation overhead Perrig *et al.* (2002a). It is widely used in areas of sensor networks Perrig *et al.* (2002b). It uses one-way hash chain where the chain elements are the secret keys to compute message authentication code (MAC). With TESLA, a sender sends data packets at a predefined schedule, which has been known in advance to the receivers as well as the commitment to a hash chain as a key commitment. Each hash chain element as a MAC key corresponds to a certain time interval. For each packet, the sender attaches a

MAC tag to it. This MAC tag is derived using the next corresponding MAC key in the hash chain based on negotiated key disclosure delay schedule between the sender and the receiver. Obviously, upon receiving the packet, the receiver canąŕt verify the authenticity of the packet yet. After key disclosure delay, the sender discloses MAC key, and then the receiver is able to authenticate the message after verifying the released MAC key is indeed the corresponding element of the chain. One requirement for TESLA scheme is the loose synchronization among the nodes. The disadvantage is the delayed message authentication.

Lin *et al.* Lin *et al.* (2008b) developed the 'time-efficient and secure vehicular communication' scheme (TSVC) based on the Timed Efficient Stream Loss-tolerant Authentication (TESLA) standard (RFC 4082) Perrig *et al.* (2002a). With TSVC, a vehicle first broadcasts a commitment of hash chain to its neighbors and then uses the elements of the hash chain to generate a message authentication code (MAC) with which other neighbors can authenticate this vehicles' following messages. Because of the fast speed of MAC verification, the computation overhead of TSVC is reduced significantly. However, TSVC also requires a huge set of anonymous public/private key pairs as well as their corresponding public key certificates to be preloaded in each vehicle. Furthermore, TSVC may not be robust when the traffic becomes extremely dynamic as a vehicle should broadcast its key chain commitment much more frequently.

3.3.3 Proxy re-signature-based scheme

Proxy re-signature schemes, introduced by Blaze, Bleumer, and Strauss Blaze *et al.* (1998), and formalized later by Ateniese and Hohenberger Ateniese & Hohenberger (2005), allow a semi-trusted proxy to transform a delegateeąŕs signature into a delegatorąŕs signature on the same message by using some additional information. Proxy re-signature can be used to implement anonymizable signatures in which outgoing messages are first signed by specific users. Before releasing them to the outside world, a proxy translates signatures into ones that verify under a system's public key so as to conceal the original issuer's identity and the internal structure of the organization. Recently, Libert et al. Libert & Vergnaud (2008) have introduced the first *multi-hop unidirectional* proxy re-signature scheme wherein the proxy can only translate signatures in one direction and messages can be resigned a polynomial number of times.

The size of the certificate revocation list (CRL) and the checking cost are two important performance metrics for the revocation mechanism in VANETs. Unfortunately, the pseudonymous authentication schemes are prone to generating a huge CRL, whereas the checking cost in the group-signature-based schemes is unacceptable for the vehicles with limited computation power. Since the CRL is usually transmitted by vehicle-to-vehicle communication, the quick increase of the CRL in the pseudonymous authentication schemes brings large communication cost. Moreover, the larger the CRL size, the longer the transmission delay to all vehicles, and during this period, the misbehaving vehicles can compromise VANETs continually. Sun et al. Sun *et al.* (2010a;b) proposed an efficient authentication protocol which supports RSU-aided distribution certificate service that allows a vehicle to update its certificate set from an RSU on the road based on the proxy re-signature Libert & Vergnaud (2008). In their scheme, the vehicle only needs to request the re-signature keys from an RSU and re-sign numbers of the certificates issued by the TA to be the same as those issued by the RSU itself, and thus significantly reduces the revocation cost and the certificate updating overhead. However, their scheme also rely on the RSUs which only cover partial high-way or city roads during the deployment stage.

3.3.4 Confidentiality-oriented scheme

The need for confidentiality in specific scenarios of VANET implementations has also been discussed in recent works Kamat *et al.* (2006); Li *et al.* (2008); Plößl & Federrath (2008); Wang *et al.* (2008). Specifically in Wang *et al.* (2008), the protocols of Raya & Hubaux (2007) are extended: session keys for pairs of vehicles are established by using the Diffie-Hellman key agreement protocol while group session keys are established using the key transfer approach. These keys are used for both message authentication and confidentiality Wang *et al.* (2008). A lightweight authenticated key establishment scheme with privacy preservation and confidentiality to secure the communications in VANET is proposed by Li *et al.* Li *et al.* (2008). Meantime, two security frameworks for VANETs to provide authentication, confidentiality, non-repudiation and message integrity have also been proposed by Plößl & Federrath (2008) and Kamat *et al.* (2006) independently. Nevertheless, all of these works Kamat *et al.* (2006); Li *et al.* (2008); Plößl & Federrath (2008); Wang *et al.* (2008) suffer from the same criticism in LAB, in other words, each OBU has to take a large storage space to store a huge number of anonymous key pairs.

3.4 *Priori*-based approach

By taking strict punitive action, a *posteriori* countermeasures can exclude some rational attackers, but they are ineffective against irrational attackers such as terrorists. Even for rational attackers, damage has already occurred when punitive action is taken. To reduce the damage to a bare minimum, the *priori* countermeasures have been proposed to prevent the generation of fake messages. In this approach, a message is not considered valid unless it has been endorsed by a number of vehicles above a certain threshold.

3.4.1 Basic scheme

Most recently, Kounga *et al.* Kounga *et al.* (2009) proposed a solution that permits vehicles to verify the reliability of information received from anonymous origins. In this solution, each vehicle can generate the public/private key pairs by itself. However, the assumption in this solution is very restricted in that additional hardware is needed on the OBU. However, Chen and Ng Chen & Ng (2010) showd that the Kounga *et al.*'s scheme does not achieve the goals of authenticity of a message, privacy of drivers and vehicles, reliability of distributed information, and revocation of illegitimate vehicles.

After that, a proposal is also presented following the *priori* protection paradigm based on threshold signature by Daza *et al.* Daza *et al.* (2009). Nevertheless, to obtain the anonymity, this protocol assumes that the OBU installed on the vehicle can be removable and multi OBUs could alternatively be used with the same vehicle (like several cards can be used within a cell phone in the same time). Thus, this assumption may enable malicious adversary to mount the so-called Sybil attack: vehicles using different anonymous key pairs from corresponding OBUs can sign multiple messages to pretend that these messages were sent by different vehicles. Since multi OBUs can be installed on the same vehicle, no one can find out whether all of these signatures come from the same vehicle or not.

	Anonymous authentication	Traceability	Confidentiality	GSBS	RSUS	*Priori* -based	PBS
Zhang *et al.* (2008a;b)	✓	✓			✓		
Lu *et al.* (2008)	✓	✓			✓		
Lin *et al.* (2007; 2008a)	✓	✓		✓			
Sun *et al.* (2007)	✓	✓		✓			
Xiong *et al.* (2010a)	✓	✓		✓			
Xi *et al.* (2007; 2008)	✓			✓			
Sun & Fang (2009)	✓			✓			
Sun *et al.* (2010c)	✓			✓			
Raya & Hubaux (2005; 2007)	✓	✓					✓
Lin *et al.* (2008b)	✓	✓					✓
Sun *et al.* (2010a;b)	✓	✓		✓			✓
Li *et al.* (2008)	✓	✓	✓				✓
Plößl & Federrath (2008)	✓	✓	✓				✓
Kamat *et al.* (2006)	✓	✓	✓				✓
Wang *et al.* (2008)	✓	✓	✓				✓
Kounga *et al.* (2009)[3]						✓	
Daza *et al.* (2009)	✓	✓				✓	
Wu *et al.* (2010)	✓	✓		✓		✓	

GSBS: Group-oriented signature based scheme; RSUS: RSU based scheme; PBS: Pseudonyms-based scheme

Table 1. Summary of related protocols

3.4.2 Group signature-based scheme

A linkable group signature Nakanishi *et al.* (1999) is a variant of group signatures. In a linkable group signature, it is easy to distinguish the group signatures produced by the same signer, even though the signer is anonymous. Linkable group signatures can thwart the Sybil attack but are not compatible with vehicle privacy due to the linkability of signer identities, i.e., the various message endorsements signed by a certain vehicle can be linked. Wu *et al.* Wu *et al.* (2010) proposed a novel protocol based on linkable group signature, which is equipped with both *priori* and *posteriori* countermeasures. However, they face the same adverse conditions in GSB protocol in which the verification time grows linearly with the number of revoked vehicles and every remaining vehicle need to update its private key and group public key when the number of revoked vehicles is larger than some threshold.

4. An example of ring-signature based anonymous authentication protocols

In order to be self-contained, we give an example of Ring-signature based authentication protocol along with the notion of bilinear pairing Xiong *et al.* (2010a) as follows.

4.1 Bilinear pairing

Note that the publication of an identity based encryption scheme Boneh & Franklin (2001) built on bilinear pairings has triggered a real upsurge in the popularity of pairings among cryptographers. Following Boneh and Franklin, a lot of cryptosystems based on pairings have been proposed which would be hard to construct using more conventional cryptographic primitives. At this moment, pairing-based cryptography is a highly active field of research, with several hundreds of publications.

Let $\mathbb{G}_1$ denote an additive group of prime order q and $\mathbb{G}_2$ be a multiplicative group of the same order. Let P be a generator of $\mathbb{G}_1$, and $\hat{e}$ be a bilinear map such that $\hat{e} : \mathbb{G}_1 \times \mathbb{G}_1 \rightarrow \mathbb{G}_2$ with the following properties:

1. Bilinearity: For all $P, Q \in \mathbb{G}_1$, and $a, b \in \mathbb{Z}_q$, $\hat{e}(aP, bQ) = \hat{e}(P, Q)^{ab}$.
2. Non-degeneracy: $\hat{e}(P, P) \neq 1_{\mathbb{G}_2}$
3. Computability: It is efficient to compute $\hat{e}(P, Q)$ for all $P, Q \in \mathbb{G}_1$

4.2 Ring-signature based

4.2.1 System initialization

Firstly, as described in section 2.3, we assume each vehicle is equipped with a tamper-proof device, which is secure against any compromise attempt in any circumstance. With the tamper-proof device on vehicles, an adversary cannot extract any data stored in the device including key material, data, and codes. We assume that there is a trusted Transportation Regulation Center (TRC) which is in charge of checking the vehicle's identity, and generating and pre-distributing the private keys of the vehicles. Prior to the network deployment, the TRC sets up the system parameters for each OBU as follows:

- Let $\mathbb{G}_1, \mathbb{G}_2$ be two cyclic groups of same order q. Let $\hat{e} : \mathbb{G}_1 \times \mathbb{G}_1 \rightarrow \mathbb{G}_2$ be a bilinear map.
- The TRC first randomly chooses $x_{TRC} \in_R \mathbb{Z}_q$ as its private key, and computes $y_{TRC} = x_{TRC}P$ as its public key. The TRC also chooses a secure cryptographic hash function $\mathcal{H} : \{0,1\}^* \rightarrow \mathbb{Z}_q$.
- Each vehicle V_i with real identity RID_i generates its public/private key pair as follows:
  - The vehicle V_i first chooses $x_i \in_R \mathbb{Z}_q$ as its private key, and computes $y_i = x_iP$ as its public key.
  - V_i randomly selects an integer $t_i \in_R \mathbb{Z}_q$ to determine the verification information of y_i: $a_i = \mathcal{H}(t_iP \parallel RID_i)$ and $b_i = (t_i + x_i \cdot a_i)$. Then V_i sends $\{y_i, RID_i, a_i, b_i\}$ to TRC.
  - After receiving $\{y_i, RID_i, a_i, b_i\}$, TRC checks whether the following equation holds:

  $$a_i \stackrel{?}{=} \mathcal{H}((b_iP - a_iy_i) \parallel RID_i)$$

  If it holds, then $\{y_i, RID_i\}$ is identified as the valid public key and identity. Otherwise, it will be rejected. In the end, the TRC stores the (y_i, RID_i) in its records.
- Each vehicle is preloaded with the public parameters $\{\mathbb{G}_1, \mathbb{G}_2, q, y_{TRC}, \mathcal{H}\}$. In addition, the tamper-proof device of each vehicle is preloaded with its private/public key pairs (x_i, y_i) and corresponding anonymous certificates (these certificates are generated by taking the vehicle's pseudo-identity ID_i). Finally, the vehicle will preload the revocation list (RL) from the TRC.

4.2.2 OBU safety message generation

Vehicle V_π signs the message M before sending it out. Suppose $S = \{y_1, \cdots, y_n\}$ is the set of public keys collected by vehicle V_π and it defines the ring of unrevoked public keys. Note that the public key set S, collected and stored temporarily by V_π, is dynamic. We assume that all public keys y_i, $1 \leq i \leq n$ and their corresponding private keys x_i's are generated by TRC, and π $(1 \leq \pi \leq n)$ is the index of the actual message sender. In other words, as V_π travels through the road network, the set of public keys collected by it keeps changing over time. Otherwise, a unique set of public keys used by a vehicle may enable the adversary to infer its traveling trajectory. The signature generation algorithm $Sig(S, x_\pi, y_{TRC}, M)$ is carried out as follows.

1. Randomly select $r \in_R \mathbb{Z}_q$ and compute $R = rP$.
2. For y_{TRC}, compute $E_{TRC} = \hat{e}(y_\pi, y_{TRC})^r$.
3. Generate a non-interactive proof $SPK(1)$ as follows: $SPK\{\alpha : \{E_{TRC} = \hat{e}(R, y_{TRC})^\alpha\} \bigwedge \{\bigvee_{i \in [1,n]} y_i = \alpha P\}\}(M)$. The signature σ of M with respect to S and y_{TRC} is (R, E_{TRC}) and the transcript of $SPK(1)$.

For clear presentation, we divide $SPK(1)$ into two components:

$$SPK\{\alpha : E_{TRC} = \hat{e}(R, y_{TRC})^\alpha\}(M), \tag{1a}$$

$$SPK\{\alpha : \bigvee_{i \in [1,n]} y_i = \alpha P\}(M). \tag{1b}$$

To generate a transcript of $SPK(1a)$, given E_{TRC}, R, y_{TRC}, the actual message sender indexed by π proves the knowledge of x_π such that $E_{TRC} = \hat{e}(R, y_{TRC})^{x_\pi}$ by releasing (s, c) as the transcript such that

$$c = \mathcal{H}(y_{TRC} \parallel R \parallel E_{TRC} \parallel \hat{e}(R, y_{TRC})^s E_{TRC}^c \parallel M)$$

This can be done by randomly picking $l \in_R \mathbb{Z}_q$ and computing

$$c = \mathcal{H}(y_{TRC} \parallel R \parallel E_{TRC} \parallel \hat{e}(R, y_{TRC})^l \parallel M)$$

and then setting $s = l - cx_\pi \bmod q$.

To generate the transcript of $SPK(1b)$, given S, the actual message sender indexed by π, for some $1 \leq \pi \leq n$, proves the knowledge of x_π out of n discrete logarithms x_i, where $y_i = x_i P$, for $1 \leq i \leq n$, without revealing the value of π. This can be done by releasing $(s_1, \cdots, s_n, c_1, \cdots, c_n)$ as the transcript such that $c_0 = \sum_{i=1}^n c_i \bmod q$ and

$$c_0 = \mathcal{H}(S \parallel s_1 P + c_1 y_1 \parallel \cdots \parallel s_n P + c_n y_n \parallel M).$$

To generate this transcript, the actual message sender first picks randomly $l \in_R \mathbb{Z}_q$ and $s_i, c_i \in_R \mathbb{Z}_q$ for $1 \leq i \leq n, i \neq \pi$, then computes
$c_0 = \mathcal{H}(S \parallel s_1 P + c_1 y_1 \parallel \cdots \parallel s_{\pi-1} P + c_{\pi-1} y_{\pi-1} \parallel lP \parallel s_{\pi+1} P + c_{\pi+1} y_{\pi+1} \parallel \cdots \parallel s_n P + c_n y_n \parallel M)$

Payload	Timestamp	Signature	Public Key Sets
100 bytes	4 bytes	40n+60 bytes	20n bytes

Table 2. Message Format for OBU

and finds c_π such that $c_0 = c_1 + \cdots + c_n \bmod q$. Finally the actual message sender sets $s_\pi = l - c_\pi x_\pi \bmod q$.

Now we combine the constructions of $SPK(1a)$ and $SPK(1b)$ together. First, the actual message sender randomly picks $l_1, l_2 \in_R \mathbb{Z}_q$ and $s_i, c_i \in_R \mathbb{Z}_q$ for $1 \le i \le n$, $i \ne \pi$, then computes

$$c = \mathcal{H}(S \parallel y_{TRC} \parallel R \parallel E_{TRC} \parallel \hat{e}(R, y_{TRC})^{l_1} \parallel s_1P + c_1y_1 \parallel \cdots \parallel s_{\pi-1}P + c_{\pi-1}y_{\pi-1} \parallel l_2P \parallel s_{\pi+1}P + c_{\pi+1}y_{\pi+1} \parallel \cdots \parallel s_nP + c_ny_n \parallel M).$$

After that, the actual message sender sets $s = l_1 - cx_\pi \bmod q$, finds c_π such that $c = c_1 + \cdots + c_n \bmod q$, and sets $s_\pi = l_2 - c_\pi x_\pi \bmod q$. The transcript of $SPK(1)$ is therefore $(s, s_1, \cdots, s_n, c_1,$
$\cdots, c_n)$.

According to DoT (2006), the payload of a safety message is 100 bytes. The first two fields are signed by the vehicle, by which the "signature" field can be derived. A timestamp is used to prevent the message replay attack. The last field is the public key sets, which records the public key pairs employed by the OBU. The format of messages in our protocol is defined in Table 2.

4.2.3 Message verification

Once a message is received, the receiving vehicle first checks if the $RL \bigcap S \stackrel{?}{=} \emptyset$. If so, the receiver performs signature verification by verifying of $SPK(1)$ as follows:

$$\sum_{i=1}^{n} c_i \stackrel{?}{=} \mathcal{H}(S \parallel y_{TRC} \parallel R \parallel E_{TRC} \parallel \hat{e}(R, y_{TRC})^s E_{TRC}^{\sum_{i=1}^{n} c_i} \parallel s_1P + c_1y_1 \parallel \cdots \parallel s_nP + c_ny_n \parallel$$

After that, the receiving vehicle updates its own public key set by randomly choosing public keys from S.

4.2.4 OBU fast tracing

A membership tracing operation is performed when solving a dispute, where the real ID of the signature generator is desired. The TRC first checks the validity of the signature and then uses its private key x_{TRC} and determines if

$$E_{TRC} \stackrel{?}{=} \hat{e}(y_i, R)^{x_{TRC}}$$

for some i, $1 \le i \le n$.

If the equation holds at, say when $i = \pi$, then the TRC looks up the record (y_π, RID_π) to find the corresponding identity RID_π meaning that vehicle with identity RID_π is the actual message generator. The TRC then broadcasts the (y_π, RID_π) to all OBUs and each OBU adds the y_π into his local revocation list (RL).

4.2.5 Message verification

Once a message is received, the receiving vehicle V_j, one of the group G_{GNO}, uses his group's shared secret key κ_{GNO} to do the following with ciphertext (C_1, C_2):

1. Recover the session key $k_s \leftarrow b_1/(b_0)^{\kappa_{GNO}}$.
2. Decrypt $D_{k_s}(C_2) = M\|\sigma\|GNO$ with the session key k_s, where $D_{k_s}(\cdot)$ denotes a symmetric decryption with key k_s and $\sigma = (c, s_1, s_2, s_3, s_4, T_1, T_2, T_3)$.
3. Check whether $c \in \{0,1\}^k$, and $s_1 \in_R \pm\{0,1\}^{\epsilon(\gamma_2+k)+1}$, $s_2 \in_R \pm\{0,1\}^{\epsilon(\lambda_2+k)+1}$, $s_3 \in_R \pm\{0,1\}^{\epsilon(\lambda_1+2l_p+k+1)+1}$, and $s_4 \in_R \pm\{0,1\}^{\epsilon(2l_p+k)+1}$ and $T_1, T_2, T_3 \in \mathbb{Z}_n$.
4. Accept the signature if and only if $c = \mathcal{H}(g\|h\|y\|a_0\|a\|T_1\|T_2\|T_3\|d_1'\|d_2'\|d_3'\|d_4'\|M\|C_1)$ where d_1', d_2', d_3', d_4' are computed by the following equations: $d_1' = a_0^c T_1^{s_1-c2^{\gamma_1}}/(a^{s_2-c2^{\lambda_1}} y^{s_3}) \mod n$, $d_2' = T_2^{s_1-c2^{\gamma_1}}/g^{s_3} \mod n$, $d_3' = T_2^c g^{s_4} \mod n$, $d_4' = T_3^c g^{s_1-c2^{\gamma_1}} h^{s_4} \mod n$.

4.2.6 OBU fast tracing

A membership tracing operation is performed when solving a dispute, where the real ID_i of the signature generator is desired. The MM first decrypts (T_1, T_2) in a decrypted C_2 message to find the membership certificate A_i as follows:

1. Recover $A_i = T_1/T_2^x$.
2. Prove that $log_g y = log_{T_2}(T_1/A_i \mod n)$.

Then the MM looks up the record (A_i, ID_i) to find the corresponding identity ID_i meaning that vehicle with identity ID_i is the actual message generator. The MM then broadcasts the (A_i, ID_i) to all OBUs and each OBU adds the ID_i into his local revocation list (RL).

5. Using the taxonomies

In designing the above taxonomies, we selected those components and approach of existing mechanisms that, in our opinion, offer critical information regarding design philosophy and security properties. How can these taxonomies be used?

- *A map of anonymous authentication protocols for VANETs.* For novice researchers, these taxonomies offer a comprehensive overview for a quick introduction to this field. Experienced researchers can use and extend these taxonomies to structure and organize their knowledge in the field.
- *Exploring new strategies.* Besides the existing mechanisms, the taxonomy explored a few strategies seen rarely in the wild and some novel methods.
- *Understanding solution constrains.* The taxonomy highlights common constraints and weaknesses for each class of mechanisms. Understanding these problems will focus research efforts on solving them.
- *Identifying unexplored research areas.* Examining the effectiveness of different mechanism classes achieving different security properties will highlight unexplored venues for research.

6. Conclusion

The anonymous authentication protocols for VANETs can be constructed based on a multitude of cryptographic primitives, which obscures a global view of this field. This chapter is an attempt to cut through the obscurity and structure the knowledge in this field. The proposed taxonomies are intended to help the community think about the constrains of existing works and the possible countermeasures.

7. Acknowledgements

This work is partially supported by National Natural Science Foundation of China under Grant No. 61003230, China Postdoctoral Science Foundation under Grant No. 20100480130, Chongqing Key Lab of Computer Network and Communication Technology under Grant No. CY-CNCL-2010-01 and National Research Foundation for the Doctoral Program of Higher Education of China under Grant No. 200806140010.

8. Nomenclature

Notations	Descriptions
TA:	**T**rusted **A**uthority
OBU:	**O**n**B**oard **U**nit
RSU:	**R**oad**S**ide **U**nit
VANETs:	**V**ehicular **A**d Hoc **Net**works
DSRC:	**D**edicated **S**hort **R**ange **C**ommunications
V2V:	**V**ehicle-to-**V**ehicle
IVC:	**I**nter-**V**ehicle **C**ommunication
FCC:	**F**ederal **C**ommunications **C**ommission
ETSI:	**E**uropean **T**elecommunications **S**tandards **I**nstitute
VSC:	**V**ehicle **S**afety **C**ommunications
DoS:	**D**enial **o**f **s**ervice
TESLA:	**T**imed **E**fficient **S**tream **L**oss-tolerant **A**uthentication
MAC:	**M**essage **A**uthentication **C**ode
CRL:	**C**ertificate **R**evocation **L**ist
TSVC:	**T**ime-efficient and **S**ecure **V**ehicular **C**ommunication

Table 3. Notations

9. References

M. Abe, M. Ohkubo, K. Suzuki. (2002). 1-out-of-n signatures from a variety of keys, In *Proc. ASIACRYPT 2002*, New Zealand, Lecture Notes in Computer Science, 2501, Springer-Verlag, pp.415 432.

G. Ateniese, S. Hohenberger. (2005). Proxy Re-Signatures: New Definitions, Algorithms, and Applications, In: *ACM Conference on Computer and Communications Security (CCS 2005)*, pp. 310-319.

R. Bishop. (2000). A survey of intelligent vehicle applications worldwide, in *Proceedings of the IEEE Intelligent Vehicles Symposium 2000*, Dearborn, MI, USA, Oct. pp. 25-30.

M. Blaze, G. Bleumer, M.Strauss. (1998). Divertible Protocols and Atomic Proxy Cryptography, In: *Nyberg, K. (ed.) EUROCRYPT 1998*, LNCS 1403, pp. 127-144. Springer.

D. Boneh and M. K. Franklin. (2001). Identity-Based Encryption from the Weil Pairing, in: *CRYPTO 2001*, LNCS 2139, pp. 213-229. Springer. SIAM Journal of Computing, Vol. 32, No. 3, pp. 586-615, 2003.

D. Boneh, X. Boyen, H. Shacham. (2004). Short group signatures, In: Franklin, M.K. (ed.) CRYPTO 2004. vol 3152 of LNCS, pp. 227-242, Springer, Heidelberg.

D. Boneh and H. Shacham. (2004). Group signatures with verifier-local revocation, in *Proc. ACM CCS' 04*, pp. 168-177.

E. Bresson, J. Stern, M. Szydlo. (2002). Threshold ring signatures and applications to ad-hoc groups, In *Proc. CRYPTO 2002*, USA, Lecture Notes in Computer Science, 2442, Springer-Verlag, pp.465 480.

G. Calandriello, P. Papadimitratos, J.-P. Hubaux, A. Lioy. (2007). Efficient and robust pseudonymous authentication in VANET, *Vehicular Ad Hoc Networks* pp. 19-28.

D. Chaum, E. van Hevst. (1991). Group Signature, In *EUROCRYPT 1991*,volume 547 of LNCS, pp. 257-265.

L. Chen and S. Ng. (2010). Comments on "Proving Reliability of Anonymous Information in VANETs" by Kounga *et al.*, IEEE Transactions on Vehicular Technology, Vol. 59, No. 3, pp. 1503-1505.

L. Chen, S.-L. Ng and G. Wang. (2011). Threshold anonymous announcement in VANETs. IEEE Journal on Selected Areas in Communications, Vol. 29, No. 3, pp. 605-615.

V. Daza, J. Domingo-Ferrer, F. Sebé, and A. Viejo. (2009). Trustworthy Privacy-Preserving Car-Generated Announcements in Vehicular Ad Hoc Networks", *IEEE Transactions on Vehicular Technology*, vol. 58, no. 4, pp. 1876-1886.

Y. Dodis, A. Kiayias, A. Nicolosi, V. Shoup. (2004). Anonymous identification in ad doc groups, In *Proc. EUROCRYPT 2004*, Switzerland, LNCS 3027, Springer-Verlag, pp.609 626, Full version: http://www.cs.nyu.edu/ nico-lo-si/pa-pers/

U.S. Department of Transportation. (2006). National Highway Traffic Safety Administration, *Vehicle Safety Communications Project*, Final Report. Appendix H: WAVE/DSRC Security.

Dedicated Short Range Communications (5.9 GHz DSRC), Available: http://www.leearmstrong.com/DSRC/DSRCHomeset.htm

J.P. Hubaux, S. Capkun, L. Jun. (2004). The Security and Privacy of Smart Vehicles, *IEEE Security & Privacy Magazine*, Vol. 2, No. 3, pp. 49-55.

Saving Lives Through Advanced Vehicle Safety Technology: Intelligent Vehicle Initiative Final Report. [Online]. Available: http://www.itsdocs.fhwa.dot.gov/JPODOCS/REPTS_PR/14153_files/ivi.pdf

P. Kamat, A. Baliga, W. Trappe. (2006). An Identity-Based Security Framework For VANETs, *VANETqf06*, pp. 94-95.

G. Kounga, T. Walter, and S. Lachmund. (2009). Proving Reliability of Anonymous Information in VANETs, *IEEE Transactions on Vehicular Technology*, vol. 58, no. 6, pp. 2977-2989.

C.-T. Li, M.-S. Hwang, Y.-P. Chu. (2008). A secure and efficient communication scheme with authenticated key establishment and privacy preserving for vehicular ad hoc networks, *Computer Communications*, Vol. 31, pp. 2803-2814.

B. Libert, D. Vergnaud. (2008). Multi-Use Unidirectional Proxy Re-Signatures, *ACM Conference on Computer and Communications Security (CCS 2008)*, Alexandria, Virginia, USA.

D. Y. W. Liu, J. K. Liu, Y. Mu, W. Susilo, D.S. Wong. (2007). Revocable Ring Signature, *J. Comput. Sci. Technol.* 22(6): pp. 785-794.

X. Lin. (2008). Secure and Privacy-Preserving Vehicular Communications, PhD thesis, University of Waterloo, Waterloo, Ontario, Canada.

X. Lin, X. Sun, P.-H. Ho and X. Shen. (2007). GSIS: A Secure and Privacy-Preserving Protocol for Vehicular Communications, *IEEE Transactions on Vehicular Technology*, vol. 56(6), pp. 3442-3456, 2007.

X. Lin, R. Lu, C. Zhang, H. Zhu, P.-H. Ho and X. Shen. (2008a). Security in Vehicular Ad Hoc Networks, *IEEE Communications Magazine*, vol. 46, no. 4, pp. 88-95, 2008.

X. Lin, X. Sun, X. Wang, C. Zhang, P.-H. Ho and X. Shen. (2008b). TSVC: Timed Efficient and Secure Vehicular Communications with Privacy Preserving, *IEEE Transactions on Wireless Communications*, vol. 7, no. 12, pp. 4987-4998.

R. Lu, X. Lin, H. Zhu, P.-H. Ho and X. Shen. (2008). ECPP: Efficient Conditional Privacy Preservation Protocol for Secure Vehicular Communications, *The 27th IEEE International Conference on Computer Communications (INFOCOM 2008)*, Phoenix, Arizona, USA.

R. Lu, X. Lin, H. Zhu, and X. Shen. (2009). SPARK: A New VANET-based Smart Parking Scheme for Large Parking Lots, *The 28th IEEE International Conference on Computer Communications (INFOCOM 2009)*, Rio de Janeiro, Brazil.

R. Lu, X. Lin, and X. Shen. (2010). SPRING: A Social-based Privacy-preserving Packet Forwarding Protocol for Vehicular Delay Tolerant Networks, *The 29th IEEE International Conference on Computer Communications (INFOCOM 2010)*, San Diego, California, USA.

T. K. Mak, K. P. Laberteaux and R. Sengupta. (2005). A Multi-Channel VANET Providing Concurrent Safety and Commercial Services, in *Proceedings of 2nd ACM International Workshop on Vehicular Ad Hoc Networks*, Cologne, Germany, Sep. pp. 1-9.

J. A. Misener. (2005). Vehicle-infrastructure integration (VII) and safety, *Intellimotion*, Vol. 11, No. 2, pp. 1-3.

T. Nakanishi, T. Fujiwara, and H. Watanabe. (1999). A linkable group signature and its application to secret voting, Transactions of Information Processing Society of Japan, vol. 40, no. 7, pp. 3085-3096.

T. Nakanishi and N. Funabiki. (2005). Verifer-local revocation group signature schemes with backward unlinkability from bilinear maps, in *Proc. ASIACRYPT' 05*, LNCS, vol. 3788, pp. 533-548.

L. Nguyen, R. Safavi-Naini. (2005). Dynamic *k*-times anonymous authentication, in *ACNS 2005*, LNCS 3531, pp. 318-333.

A. Perrig, R. Canetti, J. D. Tygar, D. Song. (2002). The TESLA Broadcast Authentication Protocol, RSA CryptoBytes, vol. 5, no. 2, pp. 2-13.

A. Perrig, R. Szewczyk, V. Wen, D. Culler, and J. D. Tygar. (2002). Spins: security protocols for sensor networks, Wireless Networks, vol. 8, no. 11, pp. 521-534.

K. Plößl, H. Federrath. (2008). A privacy aware and efficient security infrastructure for vehicular ad hoc networks, *Computer Standards & Interfaces*, Vol. 30, pp. 390-397.

M. Raya, J. P. Hubaux, (2005). The security of vehicular ad hoc networks, *3rd ACM workshop on Security of ad hoc and sensor networks*, pp. 11-21.

M. Raya and J. P. Hubaux. (2007). Securing Vehicular Ad Hoc Networks, *Journal of Computer Security*, Special Issue on Security of Ad Hoc and Sensor Networks, Vol. 15, Nr. 1, pp. 39-68.

R. L. Rivest, A. Shamir, Y. Tauman. (2001). How to Leak a Secret, In *AsiaCrypt 2001*, volume 2248 of LNCS, pp. 552-565.

X. Sun, X. Lin, P. Ho. (2007). Secure Vehicular Communications Based on Group Signature and ID-Based Signature Scheme, *International Communications Conference (ICC 2007)*, Glasgow, Scotland, June 24-28.

X. Sun. (2007). Anonymous, secure and efficient vehicular communications, Master thesis, University of Waterloo, Waterloo, Ontario, Canada.

J. Sun, Y. Fang. (2009). Defense against misbehavior in anonymous vehicular ad hoc networks, Ad Hoc Networks (Special Issue on Privacy and Security in Wireless Sensor and Ad Hoc Networks), Vol. 7, No. 8, pp. 1515-1525.

Y. Sun, R. Lu, X. Lin, X. Shen, and J. Su. (2010). A Secure and Efficient Revocation Scheme for Anonymous Vehicular Communications, *International Communications Conference (ICC 2010)*, Cape Town, South Africa.

Y. Sun, R. Lu, X. Lin, X. Shen, and J. Su. (2010). An Efficient Pseudonymous Authentication Scheme With Strong Privacy Preservation for Vehicular Communications, *IEEE Transactions on Vehicular Technology*, Vol. 59, No. 7, pp. 3589-3603.

J. Sun, C. Zhang, Y. Zhang, Y. Fang. (2010). An Identity-Based Security System for User Privacy in Vehicular Ad Hoc Networks, IEEE Transactions on Parallel and Distributed Systems, Vol. 21, No. 9, pp. 1227-1239.

I. Teranisi, J. Furukawa, and K. Sako. (2004). *k*-Times Anonymous Authentication, in *ASIACRYPT 2004*, Springer-Verlag, LNCS 3329, pp. 308-322.

Vehicle infrastructure integration. U.S. Department of Transportation, [Online]. Available: http://www.its.dot.gov/index.htm

A. Wasef, Y. Jiang, and X. Shen. (2010). DCS: An efficient distributed certificate service scheme for vehicular networks, IEEE Transactions on Vehicular Technology, vol. 59, no. 2, pp. 533-549.

G. Wang. (2004). Security Analysis of Several Group Signature Schemes. [Online]. Available: http://eprint.iacr.org/2003/194

N. W. Wang, Y. M. Huang, and W. M. Chen. (2008). A novel secure communication scheme in vehicular ad hoc networks, *Computer Communications*, Vol. 31, pp. 2827-2837.

D. S. Wong, K. Fung, J. Liu, V. Wei. (2003). On the RS-code construction of ring signature schemes and a threshold setting of RST, In *Proc. 5th Int. Conference on Infoation and Communication Security (ICICS 2003)*, China, Lecture Notes in Computer Science, 2836, Springer-Verlag, pp.34 46.

Q. Wu, J. Domingo-Ferrer, and Úrsula González-Nicolás. (2010). Balanced Trustworthiness, Safety, and Privacy in Vehicle-to-Vehicle Communications, *IEEE Transactions on Vehicular Technology*, vol. 59, no. 2, pp. 559-573.

Q. Xu, T. Mak, J. Ko and R. Sengupta. (2007). Medium Access Control Protocol Design for Vehicle-Vehicle Safety Messages, *IEEE Transactions on Vehicular Technology*, Vol. 56, No. 2, pp. 499-518.

Y. Xi, K. Sha, W. Shi, L. Scnwiebert, and T. Zhang. (2007). Enforcing Privacy Using Symmetric Random Key-Set in Vehicular Networks, *Eighth International Symposium on Autonomous Decentralized Systems (ISADS'07)*, pp. 344-351.

Y. Xi, W. Shi, L. Schwiebert. (2008). Mobile anonymity of dynamic groups in vehicular networks, *Security and Communication Networks*, Vol. 1, No.3, pp. 219-231.

H. Xiong, Z. Qin, F. Li. (2011). Identity-based Ring Signature Scheme based on quadratic residues, High Technology Letters, Vol. 15, No.1, pp. 94-100.

H. Xiong, K. Beznosov, Z. Qin, M. Ripeanu. (2010). Efficient and Spontaneous Privacy-Preserving Protocol for Secure Vehicular Communication, *International Communications Conference (ICC 2010)*, Cape Town, South Africa.

H. Xiong, Z. Qin, F. Li. (2010). Secure Vehicle-to-roadside communication protocol using certificate-based cryptosystem, IETE Technical Review, Vol 27, No 3, pp. 214-219.

H. Xiong, Z. Qin, F. Li. (2011). A Certificateless Proxy Ring Signature Scheme with Provable Security, International Journal of Network Security, Vol.12, No.2, pp.113-127.

C. Zhang, X. Lin, R. Lu and P.-H. Ho. (2008). RAISE: An Efficient RSU-aided Message Authentication Scheme in Vehicular Communication Networks. IEEE International Conference on Communications (ICC'08), Beijing, China.

C. Zhang, X. Lin, R. Lu, P.-H. Ho and X. Shen. (2008). An Efficient Message Authentication Scheme for Vehicular Communications, *IEEE Transactions on Vehicular Technology*, vol. 57, no. 6, pp. 3357-3368.

3

Security Approaches for Information-Centric Networking

Walter Wong and Maurício Ferreira Magalhães
University of Campinas
Brazil

1. Introduction

The increasing demand for highly scalable infrastructure for efficient content distribution has stimulated the research on new architectures and communication paradigms, where the focus is on the efficient content delivery without explicit indication of the resource location. One of these paradigms is known as information-centric networking (ICN) and its main focus is on data retrieval regardless of the source at the network level. This scenario usually happens when content providers (e.g. Warner Bros, BBC News) produce information (movies, audios, news in a Web page, etc.) and hire delivery systems such as Akamai[1] to deliver their content to the customers. In this model, there is a decoupling between content generation from the server storing the content itself (the actual machine serving the content for clients). Originally, servers used to generate and deliver data to the clients, however, nowadays data may be generated in specialized locations and placed in strategic servers in the network to speed up the content delivery to content consumers.

From the security perspective, the decoupling of data production and hosting opens new challenges for content authentication. The first issue regards the trust establishment for content authentication and a second one is the time decoupling between data consumption and production. Previously, data was generated in servers and the authentication of the hosting server resulted into an *implicit* data authentication because the content producer is the same as the content server. Nowadays, a common scenario is the separation between content generation and delivery, breaking the previous trust relationship established between the serving host and the content. Servers are deployed by content delivery companies to deliver data according to a contract, thus, there might not be a correlation between serving host and the data itself. The second issue regards the time decoupling between data consumption and production, which is a direct consequence of content production and hosting separation. Content providers produce content (e.g. news feeds) that may not be synchronously consumed, i.e., BBC News web-site produces news every 5 minutes, but clients access the data after some period of time. As a consequence, content providers and consumers are *decoupled in time* and *synchronization*, and there might not be any interaction between clients and servers to ensure the content authenticity[2]. Some threats such as fake and unauthorized content publication or content data blocks corruption may appear, requiring a new security model focused on the content itself rather than securing the connection.

---

[1] http://www.akamai.com

[2] Sometimes the original content provider is not online to provide authentication data.

In this paper, we present two hash tree techniques to provide content authentication based on the content rather than the communication channel to provide content authentication in information-centric networks. The authentication model uses *skewed hash trees* (SHT) and *composite hash trees* (CHT) to provide amortized content authentication and integrity for a set of data blocks with one single digital signature. Moreover, the security model is independent of the underlying transport protocol, allowing it to verify the content with the original content owner, regardless of the storage or mirror where it was retrieved. The SHT mechanism allows for secure content caching in the network, enabling data verification by intermediate devices at low processing costs. The CHT mechanism allows for parallel authentication over HTTP, enabling parallel content download in the Internet. As a proof-of-concept, we implemented a prototype with the SHT and CHT libraries and evaluated in these two scenarios, outlining the main experimental results.

The organization of this paper is as follows. Section 2 presents the background information about Merkle Trees. Section 3 presents the SHT and CHT techniques for content authentication in information-centric networks. Section 4 describes the SHT and CHT implementations in the secure caching and parallel authentication scenarios. Finally, Section 5 summarizes the paper.

2. Background

The Merkle Tree (MT) (Merkle, 1989) is a *balanced binary tree* structure containing summary information of a large piece of data or a message set. The data structure was originally proposed in the late 70's as an alternative to provide compact representation of public keys and the main idea is to apply a cryptographic hash over a set of messages and use these hash values as input for a balanced tree. Each parent node contains the hash of the concatenation of the hash values stored in the children's nodes and it goes recursively until reaching the top of the tree. This value is known as *root hash* and it represents the *fingerprint* over a set of messages. Each data block has a list of hash values called *authentication path* (AP) that allows users to verify the integrity by computing the path from the leaves towards the *root hash*, and comparing it with the securely retrieved *root hash* value.

Some applications use MTs to provide efficient content authentication in different scenarios, such as HTTP (Bayardo & Sorensen, 2005) and P2P networks (Tamassia & Triandopoulos, 2007). These applications create a MT over a set of data blocks and append an AP on each block to allow data verification in the receiver side. However, the construction of a MT requires a balanced binary tree, demanding a number of data blocks that are multiple of power of two, otherwise the original MT algorithms will not work due to the unbalance in the tree. There are two simple solutions to tackle this issue: (1) fit the number of blocks to be a power of two; (2) pad with zeros. The first one is restrictive because it intervenes with the application's requirements, e.g., maximum transmission unit, and the second one results in additional computation overhead.

Fig. 1 illustrates the problem with the naive zero padding. The worst case happens when a user has a number of blocks that fits in a balanced tree plus one, requiring a binary tree that is the double of the size. As the height of a MT grows, the number of required zero leaves increases proportionally, resulting in $2^{(H-1)} - 1$ zero leaves, when the number of blocks is equal to $N/2 + 1$, and it requires a tree with height $H + 1$ to hold the hash information of all data blocks. Hence, the number of hash function calls in the zero padding scheme is the same as in the balanced tree since the zero leaves are computed as a regular leaf. Thus, the total number of hash function calls is the sum of all hash functions calls over the N data blocks,

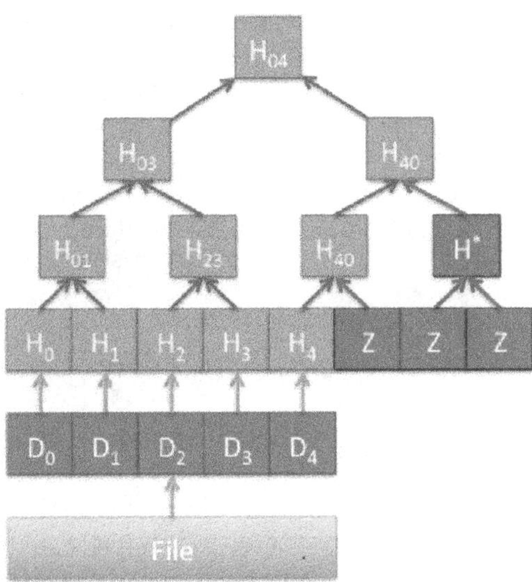

Fig. 1. Naive zero-padding in the Merkle Tree.

plus in the intermediate and top nodes. Consequently, we have:

$$\sum_{i=0}^{H} 2^i = 2^{H+1} - 1 = 2N - 1 \tag{1}$$

Therefore, a MT with N leaves (where $N = 2^H$) requires $2N - 1$ hash function calls to generate the *root hash*, regardless of the number of empty leaves in the tree. In order to tackle this limitation, we propose two mechanisms based on hash trees for information-centric data authentication, called *skewed hash tree* and *composite hash tree* that will be presented in the next section.

3. Security design

In this section we present two hash tree techniques, the skewed hash tree and the composite hash tree, that provide content authentication based solely on the content. These two techniques transfer the trust placed on the root hash to the data blocks through strong cryptographic hash functions, allowing for efficient and trusted content authentication. We start describing the skewed hash tree and then we describe the composite hash tree.

3.1 Definitions

In order to better describe the hash tree data structure and the verification procedures associated to it, we start with some definitions used through the text to ease the comprehension of the proposed mechanism.

- **Block.** A block or data block is a fragment of a larger file and is considered as the *smallest* unity of data used as input of the skewed hash tree algorithms.

- **Leaf.** A leaf is the bottom node of a binary tree. It contains the cryptographic hash value of a data block.
- **Balanced leaf.** A balanced leaf is a leaf of a balanced binary tree. Even though they are leaves, they may have some skewed leaves appended, but they are called balanced leaves to identify the lowest level of a balanced tree. These leaves can be handled using regular Merkle tree algorithms.
- **Skewed leaf.** A skewed leaf is the leaf that is appended under a balanced leaf. It needs special handling in order to generate a coherent root hash value that can be used in the verification process.
- **Height.** The height h is the total height of the entire skewed hash tree, which is the height of a balanced tree if there is no skewed leaf, or the balanced tree plus one if there are skewed leaves.
- **Hash Tree (HT).** A binary hash tree is a complete binary tree with height h and 2^h leaves. Each leaf stores a cryptographic hash value of over a data block and each internal node stores the hash of the concatenation of its children's node;
- **Root Hash (RH).** The *Root Hash* is the hash value in the top of an intermediate hash tree, representing the signature over a set of data blocks. The RH algorithmically binds together all data blocks, and any change in any data block will result in a different signature;
- **Composite Root Hash (CH).** The *Composite Root Hash* is the hash value in the top of a composite hash tree used to authenticate the incoming *Authentication Data Blocks*. The CH can be digitally signed to provide both content authentication and integrity regardless of the number of data blocks;
- **Authentication Data Block (AD).** The *Authentication Data Block* contains intermediate RH values of the hash trees used in the composition. It is used to authenticate the smaller trees and data blocks as they arrive in the receiver side;
- **Authentication Path (AP).** The *Authentication Path* is the list of hash values needed to authenticate a specific data block. The AP hash value in a given height h is the sibling hash in the hash tree towards the root hash. The main difference between AP and AD is that the first one is used to authenticate one data block and the second one is used to authenticate the RH of intermediate hash trees.

3.2 Skewed hash tree

In this section, we present the *skewed hash tree* (SHT), a variant of the original Merkle Tree that supports random size file verification with the minimum overhead associated with each data block. The SHT introduces an easy yet powerful algorithms to leverage the file partitioning procedure, allowing applications to freely divide the data blocks according to their requirements. The proposed mechanism is useful for applications that require: (i) low verification overhead; (ii) content-based or connection-less verification; (iii) random order verification; (iv) random size file authentication.

The SHT extends the original Merkle Tree algorithms to allow data authentication in cases where the number of chunks (data fragments) is not multiple of power of two. In order to achieve this requirement, we separate the hash tree into two parts: one balanced tree and a second one with the *skewed leaves*. A skewed leaf is a leaf that is going to be appended under a balanced leaf and it has a special handling in the algorithm. The balanced tree is created over a partitioned content and later the skewed leaves are added under the balanced tree, creating

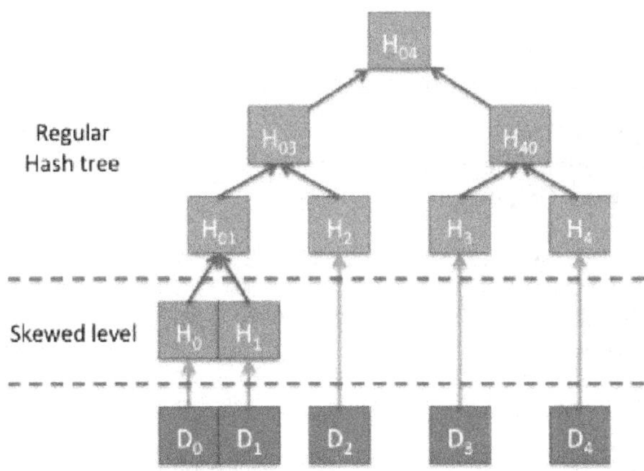

Fig. 2. Skewed Hash Tree proposal.

one extra height in the skewed hash tree. The advantage of splitting the tree in balanced tree and skewed leaves is to maintain the compatibility with the original Merkle tree algorithms for the balanced tree while handling correctly the skewed leaves.

Fig. 2 illustrates an example of skewed hash tree, where the balanced tree comprehends the leaves with hash values H_{01}, H_2, H_3 and H_4 and the skewed leaves contain the hash values H_0 and H_1. The SHT construction starts with the computation of the smallest tree height that can hold all data blocks minus one[3], which in this case is $h = 2$ and results in four balanced leaves. Next, the mechanism computes the number of balanced leaves that will receive the skewed leaves in order to hold all data blocks. Finally, it computes the root hash over the data set.

In order to differentiate the skewed leaves from the balanced ones, the skewed leaves are inserted at the height $h = -1$, indicating that they are appended leaves and they should be handled as a special case when using regular Merkle tree algorithms.

The algorithm to calculate the root hash starts in the first leaf of the balanced tree, in this case, H_{01}. The first step of the algorithm is to check whether it has skewed leaves appended in that leaf or not. In the example, the leaf H_{01} has appended the skewed leaves H_0 and H_1, thus the algorithm must compute first these two leaves and later the algorithm returns again to the balanced tree. The balanced tree algorithm now goes to the second leaf H_2. It checks whether there are appended leaves or not and treats the skewed leaves. From leaf H_2 onward, there is no more skewed leaves, thus, the balanced Merkle tree algorithms can work normally.

3.2.1 SHT construction

The skewed hash tree computation is divided into three phases: *root hash generation, AP generation* and *data blocks verification*. The first phase generates the public signature of a target file, the second phase generates the AP for each data block and the third phase authenticates each data block. In the following algorithms, we use the *stack* data structure to ease the algorithm description and understanding. The decision to use a stack is because it can hold

[3] The motivation to reduce the tree height in one is to avoid empty leaves, for example, if we choose a tree of height $h = 3$ for this example, we would have 5 data blocks and three empty blocks.

the last two values in the top of the stack, easing the comparison process of the last two values. Also, we consider that the stack has the *pop* and *push(element)* primitives, where pop removes the top element of the stack and push adds an element in the top of the stack.

The number of skewed leaves in a skewed hash tree with height h is the number of current leaves in the hash tree minus the number of data blocks of a balanced hash tree with height $h-1$, multiplied by two[4]. Therefore:

$$num\_skewed\_leaves = 2 * (N - 2^{balanced\_tree\_height}) \tag{2}$$

where the *balanced_tree_height* is height of the balanced tree. The number of balanced leaves with appended skewed leaves is:

$$num\_balanced\_leaves = N - 2^{balanced\_tree\_height} \tag{3}$$

Fig. 3 presents a comparison between the number of hash function calls in the MT and SHT.

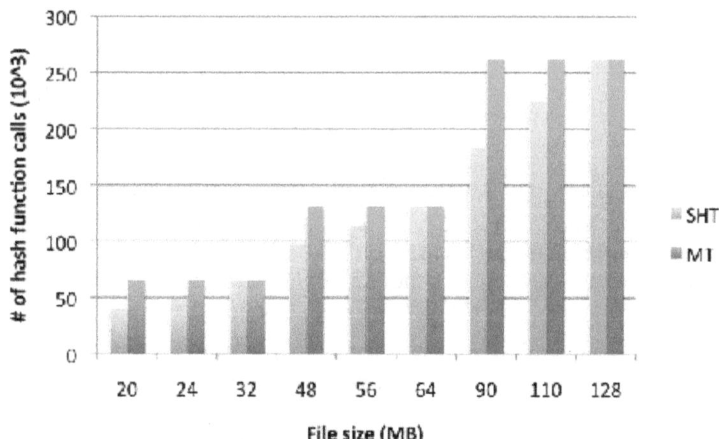

Fig. 3. Comparison between the number of hash function calls in Merkle trees and Skewed hash trees.

Note that MT has a constant overhead per tree height while SHT adapts to the current number of data blocks. The main reason why MT has a constant processing overhead is due to the computation of the empty leaves in order to reach to the *root hash*. On the other hand, SHT just computes the leaves with data blocks, skipping the empty ones. Thus, the worst case for SHT is to have the same computational overhead as regular MT.

3.2.2 SHT algorithms

There are three algorithms associated to SHT: *skewed_treehash*, *skewed_ap* and *skewed_verify*. The skewed_treehash computes the root hash of a skewed hash tree; the skewed_ap computes the authentication path for each data block; and skewed_verify checks whether a data block is consistent with a given root hash or not. We are going to describe each one in detail.

[4] The next height of a binary tree has two times the number of leaves of the previous height.

Algorithm 1 SHT treehash algorithm

```
Input: File, max_height, num_skewed_leaves
Output: Root hash
skewed_count = 0; height = 0;
while height <= max_height do
   if top 2 values have equal height then
      h_R ← pop()
      h_L ← pop()
      height = h_L.height
      h_x ← hash(h_L || h_R)
      stack.push(h_x, height + 1)
   else
      if read_data NOT EOF then
         data = read_data(file)
         if skewed_count < num_skewed_leaves then
            stack.push(hash(data), height=-1)
            skewed_count = skewed_count + 1
         else
            stack.push(hash(data), height=0)
         end if
      end if
   end if
   height ← stack[0].height
end while
Return stack[0]
```

Alg. 1 describes the root hash generation procedure in a skewed hash tree, which is based on the original *treehash* Merkle tree algorithm.

The algorithm receives as input a file, the block size, the maximum height of the tree (which is calculated dividing the file size by data block size and verifying the smallest height of a balanced tree that can hold that number of leaves) and the number of skewed leaves computed with Eq. 2.

The second phase corresponds to the AP generation for each data block and is divided into two steps: (1) initial stack filling and (2) AP generation. The first step uses the skewed treehash algorithm to store all hash values of the leftmost and rightmost leaves ($h_L \leftarrow pop()$ and $h_R \leftarrow pop()$ in Alg. 1) in the S_h and AP_h stacks respectively. The S_h stack contains the hash value to be used in the next AP generation and the AP_h stack contains the AP value at the height h and it contains the authentication path of the first block. These stacks are used as temporary variables to store the previous hash computed hash values to be used in the next AP computation.

The second step uses the pre-filled S_h and AP_h stacks to output each AP in sequence with one tree traversal. Alg. 2 describes the skewed hash tree traversal algorithm. The algorithm receives as input the file, the number of balanced leaves with appended skewed leaves and the height of the balanced tree and outputs the AP for each data block in sequence.

The third phase comprehends the data block verification procedure, described in Alg. 3, where the receiver gets the data block with its corresponding AP and the block index. We assume

Algorithm 2 SHT authentication path generation

```
Input: File, num_balanced_leaves, H
Output: Data blocks with Authentication Paths
leaf = 0, skewed_count = 0
if leaf < 2^H − 1 then
   if skewed_count < num_balanced_leaves then
      data_0 = read_block(); data_1 = read_block()
      Output data_0, hash(data_1), AP; Output data_1, hash(data_0), AP
      skewed_count = skewed_count + 1
   else
      data = read_block()
      Output data, AP
   end if
   for h = 0 to H do
      if (leaf + 1) mod 2^h == 0 then
         AP_h = Stack_h
         startnode = (leaf + 1 + 2^h) XOR 2^h
         Stack_h = skewed_tree_hash(startnode, h)
      end if
   end for
   leaf = leaf + 1
end if
```

Algorithm 3 SHT verification

```
Input: Root Hash, block index, data block, AP
Output: True or False
pos = index
digest = hash(data_block)
for each AP_i value in AP do
   if (pos % 2 == 0) then
      digest = hash(digest || AP_i)
   else
      digest = hash(AP_i || digest)
      pos = ⌊pos/2⌋
   end if
end for
if (digest == Root Hash) then
   Return True
else
   Return False
end if
```

the root hash was previously transferred to the receiver in a secure way, for example, using the security plane model. The algorithm starts reading the data block's AP and appends each hash value in the correct side to reach the root hash.

3.3 Composite hash tree

The Composite Hash Tree (CHT)(Wong et al., 2010a;b) is a data structure created over a set of data blocks belonging to a complete file. The main idea is to create a set of small binary hash trees of fixed height over a set of data blocks and recursively construct other binary hash tree over the previous hash trees in the first level, until reaching one single hash tree in the top level. The motivation for this approach is the high overhead present in the Merkle tree and also skewed hash tree, because the latter one is mainly based on the original Merkle tree algorithms. In these approaches, each data block has a list of cryptographic hash values (authentication path) that is the same length of the hash tree. Therefore, each authentication path has $log_2 N$ values and the sum of all authentication overhead grows $N * log_2 N$, where N is the number of blocks. Thus, for large files, this overhead might be considerable, especially in scenarios using low processing devices such as mobile phones.

In order to attack the authentication overhead problem, we propose CHT as an alternative to both Merkle and skewed hash trees for authentication purposes with low overhead. The proposed mechanism also provides signature amortization, allowing one piece of content to be authenticated with one digital signature regardless of the number of data blocks, requiring on average $O(N)$ fingerprints to authenticate N data blocks that are components of the original content for small composing Merkle tree with height h. A CHT(α, h) is a composite hash tree using smaller Merkle trees of height h (MT(h)) whose root hash values are aggregated in blocks of α elements. Fig. 4 illustrates an example of CHT(1,2) using internal hash tree value $h = 1$ and intermediate RH aggregation of two blocks ($\alpha = 2$). In this example, a file is divided in eight data blocks (D_0 to D_7) and an intermediate hash tree of height $h = 1$ is constructed using the cryptographic hash of the data blocks as input (H_0 and H_1), resulting in an intermediate *Root Hash* (H_{01}). This intermediate RH is used as the verification information for the data blocks D_0 and D_1, which later on will be aggregated in *Authentication Data Blocks*.

The CHT has two configuration parameters: aggregation index (α) and internal hash tree height (h). The α parameter is used to define the aggregation level of the intermediate RH values in the binary hash tree in α values. The internal hash tree height (h) defines the height of the internal hash trees used in the composition. These two parameters allow for the customization of the tree behavior, for instance, the initial verification ordering and the verification overhead, according to the application requirements. Higher h values provide smaller authentication hierarchy, meaning that data and authentication blocks have low interdependency at the cost of higher authentication overhead per data block. On the other hand, small h values results in low authentication overhead, but longer data block authentication hierarchies (thus, higher dependency between data and authentication blocks).

In this example of Fig. 4, intermediate RH values in the first level (H_{01} and H_{23}) are aggregated together in blocks of two ($\alpha = 2$), resulting in the *Authentication Data Blocks* with hash values $H_{01}||H_{23}$ and $H_{45}||H_{67}$, where $||$ represents the concatenation operation. In the second level, the *Authentication Data Blocks* are considered as input data blocks. Hence, the CHT applies the cryptographic hash over the ADs, resulting in the hash values H_{03} and H_{47} and another intermediate hash tree of height $h = 1$ is constructed over these two data blocks, resulting in the *Composite Root Hash* that will be used in the verification procedure. In the case of larger files, this procedure is applied recursively until reaching the *Composite Root Hash*.

In order to provide data verification, each data chunk carries a list of hash values represented by the AP used to verify with the CH. The AP for each data block is the sibling hash value in the hash tree, for instance, in the example described in Fig. 4, the AP for the D_0 is H_1, since

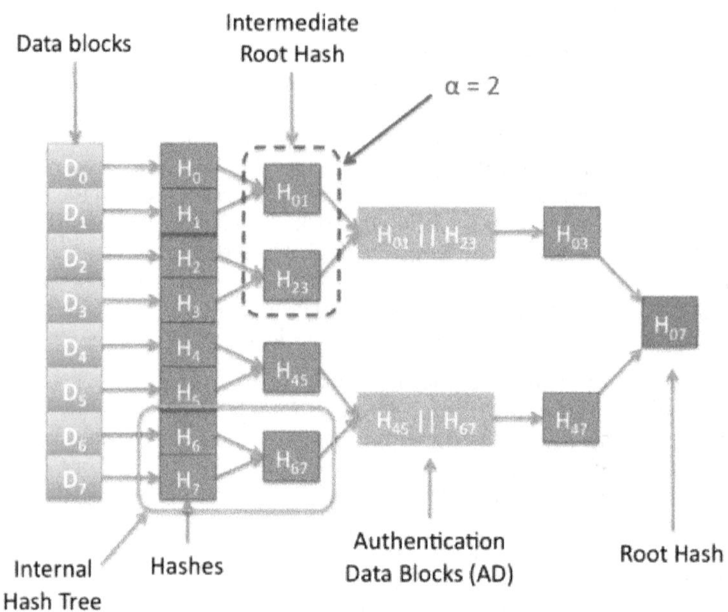

Fig. 4. (a) Composite Hash Tree with internal HT of height $h = 1$ and $\alpha = 2$.

this value is the sibling value of H_0. For larger hash trees, the AP is composed of the sibling hash value at each height towards the RH[5]. Therefore, the overhead per data chunk is defined by the height of the internal hash tree. In this approach, the CHT maintains just one hash value needed to authenticate a target data block, discarding the repeated values of the regular Merkle Tree. On the other hand, this mechanism introduces an authentication hierarchy between data and authentication blocks, requiring that some blocks to be authenticated prior to the data blocks authentication.

The α index reduces the authentication hierarchy needed to authenticate all data blocks in an order of α elements. Thus, the index reduces $\log_{\alpha} N$ authentication levels, where N is the number of partitioned data blocks.

Fig. 5 illustrates an example of authentication hierarchy using a sliding window for a CHT($\alpha = 2, h = 1$). The figure has two columns, the first one indicates the received data blocks in the receiver side and the second column shows the next blocks window to be downloaded. As authentication blocks arrive, the next blocks to be downloaded *slides* to the next set of data blocks that can be downloaded with the arrival of the new set of *Root Hashes*. For example, after the receiver authenticates the AD_0 containing the hash values $H_{01}||$ H_{23}, the user can start downloading data blocks D_0, D_1, D_2 and D_3, in any sequence.

The same procedure is taken when the *AD* with concatenated hash values $H_{45}||H_{67}$ is received in the destination, allowing the download and authentication of data blocks D_4, D_5, D_6, D_7 in any sequence.

[5] Recalling that the AP length is the height of the Merkle Tree, thus, this is the motivation to use really small Merkle trees.

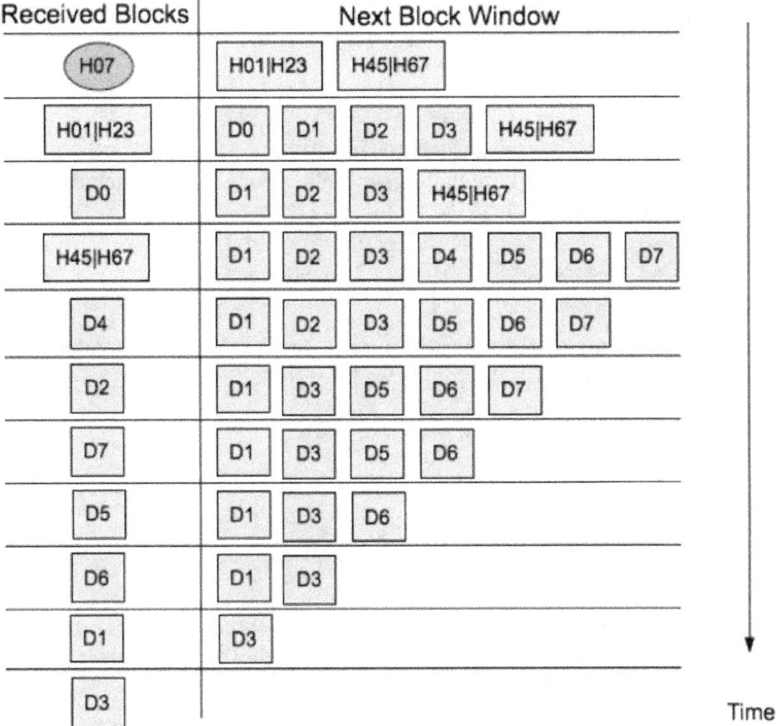

Fig. 5. Authentication Window for CHT.

CHT overhead complexity

The CHT overhead has two components associated, the *Authentication Path* (O_{AP}) overhead of each data and *Authentication Data Block* (O_{AD}) overhead, which are the aggregated *Root Hash* values of the intermediate Merkle Trees. Thus, the total overhead is:

$$O_T = O_{AP} + O_{AD} \tag{4}$$

The O_{AP} is the sum of the product between the number of data blocks on each height by the size of the AP, which is defined by the height of the Merkle Tree used in the CHT. From the CHT construction examples above (Figs. 4), we can notice that the factor $2^h\alpha$ repeats recursively i times to create the CHT over the data blocks. Note that the last MT created over the data blocks does not follow the pattern because they are the data blocks on which the composite hash tree is being created over. These data blocks add 2^h leaves, thus we need to add it separately in the formula to compute the overhead. Therefore, the O_{AP} formula is the product of the i recursions plus 2^h leaves over the data blocks plus the AP length (which is the same as h).

$$O_{AP} = \sum_{i=0}^{H'} (2^h\alpha)^i * 2^h * (AP\ length = h) \tag{5}$$

where H' represents the CHT height minus 1[6]. The H' is the number of data blocks N minus the MT(2^h) over the data blocks that do not repeat. Therefore:

$$H' = \lceil \log_{(2^h\alpha)}(N/2^h) \rceil \tag{6}$$

The O_{AD} is similar to the AP overhead formula and computes the sum of the product of the intermediate *Root Hash* values that are aggregated into α hash values, excluding the MT(2^h) over the data blocks since it starts from the first level. Hence:

$$O_{AD} = \sum_{i=1}^{H'} (2^h\alpha)^i * (AP\ length = h) \tag{7}$$

In order to calculate the overhead complexity with the input, we first calculate the total number of data blocks of a CHT(α, h). From 6, we have that:

$$N = (2^h\alpha)^{H'} * 2^h \tag{8}$$

From 5 and substituting with 8, we have:

$$O_{AP} = \sum_{i=0}^{H'} (2^h\alpha)^i * 2^h * h \approx (2^h\alpha)^{H'} * 2^h * h = N * h \tag{9}$$

Therefore the O_{AP} in the CHT is $N * h$ and grows $O(N)$ when $N >> h$ and h is a constant that does not change with the input size. The maximum value for h in a binary tree is $\log_2 N$, reducing the CHT to a regular Merkle Tree with overhead complexity of $O(N \log_2 N)$.

The *Authentication Data Block* overhead has similar proof to the previous one. Thus, substituting in 7, we have:

$$O_{AD} = \sum_{i=1}^{H'} (2^h\alpha)^i * h \approx (2^h\alpha)^{H'} * h = (N * h)/2^h \tag{10}$$

Therefore, the O_{AD} in the CHT is $N * h/2^h$ and grows $O(N)$ when $N >> h$ and h is a constant parameter that does not change with the input size. The total CHT overhead (O_T) is:

$$O_T = N * h + (N * h)/2^h = O(N) \tag{11}$$

Table 1 compares the overhead of a regular Merkle Tree and a CHT(1,2):

4. Application scenarios

In this section we present two application scenarios for the SHT and CHT. For the first evaluation scenario, we apply the SHT mechanism in the secure content caching mechanism. The SHT allows for content authentication prior to the caching procedure, preventing the unnecessary caching of bogus content. In the second evaluation scenario, we apply the CHT mechanism in the parallel authentication over HTTP scenario.

[6] It is not considered the *Root Hash* in the height computation (thus, $H' = H - 1$).

# of blocks	Merkle Tree	Composite Hash Tree (1,2)	Overhead Reduction(%)
8	24	12	50.00
32	160	48	70.00
128	896	192	78.57
512	4,608	768	83.34
2,048	22,528	3,072	86.36
8,192	106,496	12,288	88.46
32,768	491,520	49,152	90.00
131,072	2,228,224	196,608	91.18
524,288	9,961,472	786,432	92.10

Table 1. Merkle Tree vs. Composite Hash Tree Overhead Comparison

4.1 Secure caching

The fast growth of the user generated content have put pressure on the Internet infrastructure, requiring higher bandwidth capacity and lower latency to connect content providers and users. However, the infrastructure deployment speed has not followed the bandwidth usage mainly due to the lack of incentives to upgrade the infrastructure that interconnects the ISPs, problem known as the *middle mile problem* (Leighton, 2009). In order to reduce the pressure on the infrastructure and also the inter-ISP traffic, ISPs have deployed Web caches (Rodriguez et al., 2001) and content routers (Wong et al., 2011), to reduce the redundant traffic going through their networks. The placement of the caches close to the consumers improves the overall user experience and also temporarily reduces the pressure on the middle mile.

Despite the fact that content caches can be introduced in the network to improve the network efficiency, there is no explicit mechanism to authenticate the cached content, for example, check whether a piece of content is a *malware* or not. As a consequence, caches can be filled with bogus content, reducing the overall cache hit ratio. According to (Reis et al., 2008), 1.3% of the total Web pages downloaded in the Internet are changed during the transfer from the server to the clients, without any explicit knowledge of the receiver. The lack of external security parameters prevents intermediate devices to authenticate content, mainly because current security protocols are end-to-end.

In this section, we present an authentication scheme based on SHT to provide content authentication in network-level caches. The authentication mechanism based on SHT allows for data verification prior to the caching event, preventing the caching of polluted content on *content routers* (CR) (Wong et al., 2011). The CRs are able to route and cache pieces of content in their internal memory for some amount of time. Therefore, these devices have limited storage and they need to optimize the caching capacity and verification mechanisms must be fast enough to be in line speed. The caching mechanism uses high-level content identifiers, resulting in location-independent identifiers to represent content in the Internet and also content self-certification. Some benefits of the secure caching network include improved traffic efficiency by saving the amount of traffic in the network, opportunistic multi-source content retrieval by redirecting requests to nearby caches and security embedded in the content, allowing for authentication directly with the original provider through a security plane.

4.2 Network caching design

This section presents the in-network caching architecture, outlining the main design goals and discussing project decisions regarding content identification, forwarding and authentication.

4.2.1 Design goals

The in-networking caching architecture aims at the following design goals:

- **Protocol independence.** The in-network caching mechanism must be independent of any specific protocol (Arianfar et al., 2010), for instance, peer-to-peer protocols or HTTP.
- **Multi-source content retrieval.** The forwarding mechanism should support multi-source content retrieval from multiple caches on the path towards the original provider.
- **Cache-based forwarding.** The delivery mechanism forwards data requests towards other in-network caches that may have the content, thus, avoiding any lookup process and incurring into a minimum latency towards the original content provider.
- **Content authenticity.** Clients should be able to verify the content integrity despite retrieving data chunks from multiple sources.
- **Provenance.** Data must be always authenticated with the original source or providers, regardless from which mirror (e.g., network cache, peer) that it was retrieved from.

4.2.2 Content router

The *Content Router* (CR) is a network element that acts as a regular router and also provides content routing mechanisms. The main idea is that CRs inspect a CR header in all in-transit data and store some of them with a certain caching probability. Thus, further requests can be served by the cache data in the CR. In addition to the caching feature, CRs also store *pointers* to pieces of data that passed through it, but it decided not to cache it due to space limits. Hence, incoming data requests can be *detoured* to a neighbor CR which may have the requested piece of data, reducing the overall bandwidth consumption and latency in the network that would result by forwarding the request directly to the server.

4.2.3 Content identification

In order to address resources in the Internet and cache them in the CR, we use identifiers that are simultaneously independent from the forwarding, routing, storage location and the underlying transport protocol. Thus, we use content identifiers that are solely based on the content called cryptographic identifiers (cryptoID) (Moskowitz et al., 2008). The benefit of using cryptoIDs are threefold: first, cryptoIDs result from a strong cryptographic hash over a data block, strongly binding the content identifier with the data that it carries; second, the cryptoID namespace is homogeneous since it results from a standard cryptographic hash function and does not need an external authority to manage the namespace; third, cryptoIDs are not bound to any specific protocol, i.e., content identification is not an internal parameter from a protocol but it exists by its own.

The basic unit of communication used in the in-network caching architecture is a data *chunk*. A chunk is a piece of data that is identified by a cryptoID with variable length. Content providers generate data chunks and use a cryptographic hash function to generate the chunks' cryptoIDs. Then, they aggregate the cryptoIDs together into meta information structure called *metadata*. The metadata also contains additional information about the content, for example, version and validity, and the chunk list is ordered to allow the correct reconstruction of the original content. Therefore, clients need to retrieve the content metadata prior to the data chunks download from a trusted place, e.g., a security plane described previously. For legacy applications, we use CR-proxies to perform the name to metadata resolution and the chunk retrieval (described below).

4.2.4 Content security

We use the SHT as the authentication data structure for the secure caching model. Content providers generate SHT over pieces of content and sign the root hash of the SHT of a content. Later, whenever a client request for that content, the provider sends it together with the authentication path, allowing for intermediate CRs to verify the content integrity. CRs also need to have the provider's public key in order to verify the signature on the root hash. Therefore, we assume that CRs are managed by an ISP or a network administrator who has rights to add or remove public keys in the CR. In this scenario, administrators can obtain the public key directly from the content provider and insert into the CRs. Content providers can also publish their public keys into a security plane and administrators can manually verify their digital signature and insert them into the CRs.

4.3 Implementation

In this section we present the implementation of the CR mechanism. The CR is implemented as a background service running in Linux machines, composed of a kernel module and a userspace management unit, shown in Fig. 6.

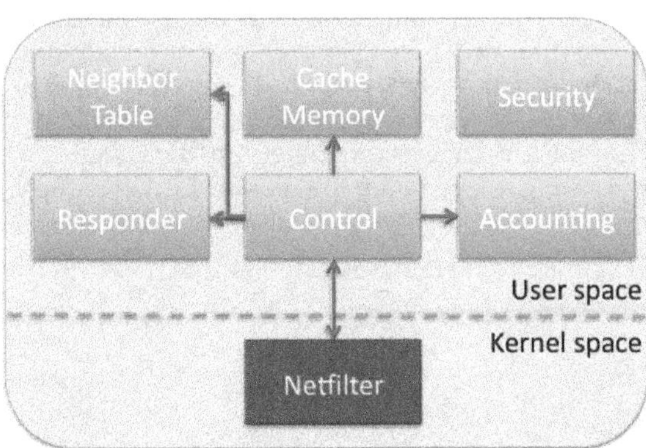

Fig. 6. Internal modules of a content router.

The *Netfilter* module is located in the kernel space and it is responsible for intercepting chunk request and response messages from the network, and delivering them to the *Control* module. This module uses the kernel *netlink* interface to capture packets directly from the kernel space and divert them to the user space in the *Control* module. The *Control* module handles the packet processing and forwarding, receiving data from the kernel space, caching and forwarding based on the *neighborhood table*. The *Security* module is responsible for SHT verification using the appended authentication path. The *Cache Memory* is responsible for storing the data itself and the initial version is implemented as a hash table. The *accounting* module is responsible for collecting the statistics about the data popularity based on the requests and responses passing through the router. These statistics will be used by the *cache memory* to help the cache eviction policies. The *Neighborhood Table* contains forwarding information collected from in-transit data messages in the network together with the last-seen information. Finally, the *Responder* module is responsible for returning cached data to clients on the server's behalf.

The forwarding mechanism based on cryptoIDs between content routers use a special header containing details about the carried data. Fig. 7 illustrates the packet header used for the content discovery and forwarding mechanism based on cryptoIDs.

Type	Crypto ID	Cache Control	Neighbor zones	Visited neighbor	Auth. Path

Fig. 7. Caching control header

The *type* field has a 8-bit field describing the type of the message, for instance, chunk request or response and signaling between CRs. The *cryptoID* is the permanent content identifier and it is generated using a cryptographic hash function, e.g., SHA-1, over the data. The *cache control* field has 8-bit length and provides signaling information for the routers, for example, whether a data chunk has already been previously cached in the network. In this case, the *cached* flag has one bit and it is stored within the *cache control* header. The *neighbor zone* field has 8-bit length and contains the number of neighbors that a message should visit before going directly to the server. The *Auth. Path* field contains the variable length authentication path for data verification.

The current version of the CR is implemented over UDP datagram as the forwarding mechanism, running on ports 22000 and 22001 in Linux OS machines. Clients send data requests to the servers and intermediate CRs cache these information in the popularity table, as they will be used as input parameter for caching policies. Whenever a CR intercepts a passing-by request or response, it may cache it based on the caching policies, e.g., popularity of the requests and responses. Whenever there is a data chunk message, CRs have a probability to cache it in their cache memory to serve for further requests.

4.4 Evaluation

In this section, we evaluate the CR proposal regarding the security mechanism based on the SHT.

4.4.1 Experimental set-up

In order to evaluate the CR authentication mechanism and to compare with per packet signature scheme, we implemented a CR prototype in C language. We used a Mac OSX 10.6, 2.16GHz, 2 GB RAM for the evaluation scenarios. In the first scenario, we evaluated the speed of the RSA public key signature and verification times and the SHA-1 hash function using the OpenSSL cryptographic library. The purpose of the evaluation is to establish the magnitude between a hash verification time and a digital signature and verification times. For the second, third and forth evaluations, we used the topology described in Fig. 8. The topology is composed of a client, a server that sends some data to the client and a CR in the border of the network where the client is located. For each test case, we collected 10 samples and considered the average value to plot the graphics.

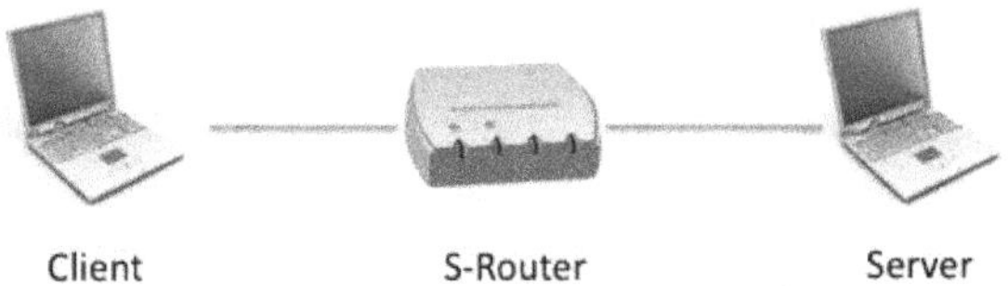

Fig. 8. Evaluation topology with one CR.

4.5 Experimental results & analysis

Tab. 2 shows the experimental evaluation of different cryptographic algorithms for signature and verification. For the SHA-1 verification speed, we considered a packet of 1024 bytes. As the experimental results show, a digital signature costs roughly 388 times slower than a hash verification and 18,51 times slower than a hash verification (SHA-1 vs. RSA 1024). The comparison is to show that if we can reduce the number of digital signatures in a large file transfer, we can considerably reduce the processing overhead resulted from the verification process. In addition, clients generating data wouldn't suffer from the delay due to the signature process.

Type	Signatures/s	Verification/s
SHA-1	-	222,402
SHA-256	-	96,759
RSA 1024 bits	573	12012
RSA 2048 bits	95	3601
ECC 160 bits	4830	1044
ECC 163 bits	1376	563

Table 2. Signature and verification speeds with different cryptographic algorithms

In the second evaluation scenario, we analyzed the root hash generation time using the SHT algorithms with the SHA-256 cryptographic hash function. We selected files ranging from 10 to 50 MB and used block sizes of 1, 2 and 4KB in the algorithm. The results are summarized in Fig. 9(a).

The figure shows that the *Root Hash* computation grows linearly with the file size and the number of data blocks. This result is predicted since the number of hash computations in the hash tree is linear to the number of data blocks. Note that the root hash has an equivalent functionality as the public key in the PKI, since it is used to verify the authenticity of a signature, but with much faster computation time.

In the second evaluation, we compared the SHT authentication path generation time with a 1024-bit RSA signature time, shown in Fig. 9(b). We implemented two applications for this evaluation: the first one reads from an input file in blocks of 1, 2 and 4 Kbytes and apply the skewed hash tree function, and the second one reads from an input file in blocks of 1, 2 and 4 Kbytes and digitally sign each block with a 1024-bit RSA key. Both of them used the SHA-256 cryptographic hash algorithm to produce the digest messages to be signed. We excluded the 1024-bit RSA key generation time from the results, since we generated it once and used the same key in the evaluation.

The results show that SHT mechanism is on average 8 times faster than the per packet signature approach. This result is expected since the digital signature computation uses large prime numbers, requiring high processing in the CPU. One the other hand, hash functions

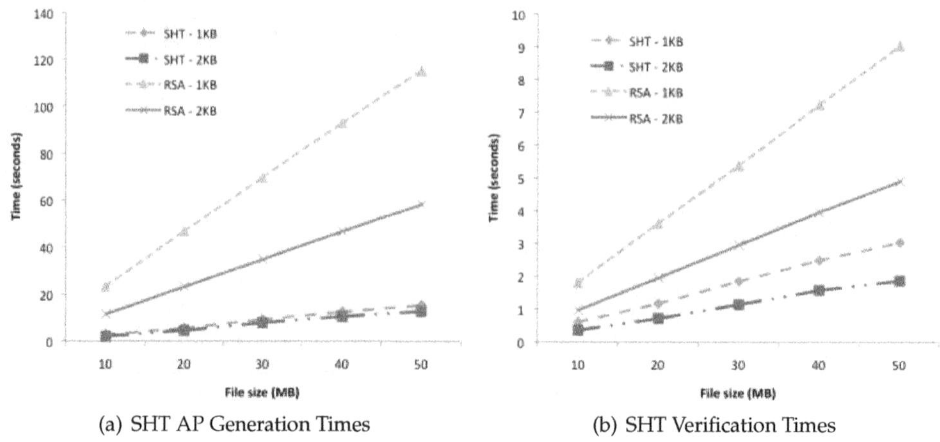

(a) SHT AP Generation Times (b) SHT Verification Times

Fig. 9. (a) SHT Root Hash Generation Times.

rely on bit shifting to generate the digests, resulting in lower power consumption and memory storage.

In the third evaluation, we compared the authentication path verification time in a CR with a 1024-bit RSA verification time considering different file and block sizes. We used the same applications, block size and cryptographic hash function as in the previous scenario. The experimental results from both applications are summarized in Fig. 9. The verification times in the SHT is on average 3 times faster than the per packet signature scheme, which are expected since the hash value computation is much faster than the public key cryptography.

4.6 Parallel authentication over HTTP

Some software companies are already providing Metalink[7] files for users, such as Ubuntu and OpenOffice, so clients have more source options to download the packages. The benefit for the vendors is the reduction on the load on their main servers since users can also use P2P protocols to retrieve data. Apple also started to implement their own protocol for parallel content download, known as *apple streaming* (Pantos, 2010). In this protocol, users receive a *playlist* file containing a list of URLs from where a client can download the data. Each URL points to a segment of the original data, for example, 10 seconds of a music, thus, users can fetch all segments in parallel, reducing the overall download time.

Although the Metalink framework improves the performance of content download, the security mechanisms are not explicitly addressed, and they are basically inherited from the traditional security protocols. Both CDN and Metalink framework use the HTTPS as the default security mechanism to provide content authentication and integrity. For the former case (CDN), it is not actually a problem since the owner of the CDN also owns the infrastructure. Thus, the surrogate servers are considered *secure* servers and the owners are responsible for its maintenance and protection against attacks. But if there is an attack on a

[7] The *metalink* proposal aims to provide Web users with a metadata file containing information about how multiple data chunks can be retrieved from a list of sources, the geographical location of the servers and the preference level on each server.

surrogate server and a target content is tampered, the HTTPS will not accuse any problem, since the end-points are authenticated. Unfortunately, the authenticity of the data is inherited from the authenticity of the host, which is not always true[8]. For the latter case (Metalink), as the content provider may not own the infrastructure that will deliver the content, e.g., a P2P network, the security issues are more critical, as malicious node can tamper the data, preventing users to correctly retrieve the content.

There is no native security mechanism to provide data authentication and integrity efficiently in information-oriented networks, leaving the client unprotected against corrupted data. One naive approach is to establish SSL/TLS tunnels with each server to authenticate the storage place. However, this approach has some drawbacks: first, it is inefficient to open multiple SSL/TLS channels, since it consumes resources on both sides, decreasing the scalability in the server; second, in this specific scenario, we are actually authenticating the storage server and not the data itself. We argue that the trust relationship is misplaced since we are placing the trust in the connection instead of the content itself.

Another approach adopted by content providers is to provide the hash digest (e.g. MD5 or SHA-1) of the entire content to guarantee the content integrity. Although this approach works well for a unicast communication scenario, where there is just one download channel, applications are only able to verify the content integrity after the complete file download, making it hard to spot corrupted data chunks in the middle of the transmission.

In this section, we present an amortized verification mechanism using composite hash trees (Wong et al., 2010b), allowing applications to efficiently verify data chunks as they arrive from multiple sources. The hash tree mechanism allows for fast verification and requires just one hash computation per data segment in the best case. The proposed mechanism can be tweaked to satisfy specific application requirements, e.g., the total overhead and also the dependency between data chunks. The main difference of our approach compared to the traditional SSL/TLS-based authentication is that we enforce the content authentication and integrity based on the information that each data chunk carries instead of binding the authentication procedure to one specific source. The proposed approach has the following benefits: i) data can be more easily shared among users without requiring the verification of the serving host since the authentication information is embedded in the data; ii) fast verification, we just need one hash function per data block to check the integrity in the optimal case; iii) cheap authentication, one digital signature regardless of the number of data chunks; and iv) higher granularity to detect corrupted data chunks, making it possible to re-download it as soon as it is detected.

4.7 Parallel verification proposal

We first start presenting the metrics and design goals for our parallel verification mechanism. Then, we map these requirements on the composite hash tree data structure for authentication and verification procedures. Lastly, we describe an application scenario for the composite

[8] As an illustration of this scenario, consider two friends Alice and Bob. Alice trusts Bob and vice-versa and they know that they will not harm each other. Alice needs to borrow some money from Bob and Bob acknowledges that. Despite the fact that Alice knows Bob (authenticated him), there is no guarantee the bill that Bob will give to her is original or fake one (content authentication). Bob is also honest and does not want to fool Alice, but if he has received a bill that is fake and didn't realize that, he will give to Alice as a original one. Therefore, the authentication of the source does not yield to authentication of the content.

hash tree in the parallel content retrieval context and present an analytical evaluation of the proposed verification mechanism.

4.7.1 Design & rationale

In order to design a parallel verification mechanism, we considered three metrics for our model: *ordering, verification overhead* and *CPU processing cost*.

- *Ordering.* This metric considers the degree of dependency between the data chunks during the verification procedure. For example, hash chains (Yih-Chun Hu, M. Jakobsson and A. Perrig, 2005) require *strict* ordering in the verification procedure, while per packet signature (Catharina Candolin, 2005) or Merkle Trees (Merkle, 1989) can provide independent packet verification (therefore, these mechanisms support *true* parallel verification).
- *Verification information overhead.* The verification information overhead, e.g., the amount of data that a packet should carry in order to provide independent verification, should be as small as possible.
- *CPU processing cost.* The verification should be fast and, preferably, at line speed.

Based on previous requirements, our goal is to have a mechanism that has none (or low) ordering requirements, low verification information overhead and low CPU processing costs. In order to achieve these requirements, we propose an authentication/verification data structure based on *composite hash trees* since it provides an efficient data verification mechanism with *low verification overhead and CPU processing cost* at the cost of *an initial verification ordering* requirement.

4.7.2 Parallel verification procedure

The parallel verification procedure uses the composite hash tree mechanism to provide parallel verification information retrieval together with the data blocks. The goal is to retrieve data chunks from the servers and simultaneously establish a verification relationship between the previously received data authentication blocks with the incoming ones. Fig. 10 shows an example of parallel data chunk retrieval and verification from multiple Web-servers.

In order to enable the parallel verification procedure in the Web, clients must first retrieve the CHT from either a trusted source or embedded in a digital certificate, illustrated in the step 10(a). After the verification procedure of the CHT, the client can initially open two parallel connections to retrieve the two authentication data blocks (AD) that are direct children of the CHT in the tree. After retrieving one AD, the client can verify it and open more connections to retrieve more data chunks in parallel, as shown in step 10(b). The number of connections is limited to two in the beginning of the procedure, increasing by a factor of α connections for every AD retrieved, as illustrated in Fig.10. Finally, in step 10(c), the AD is used to verify the incoming data chunks.

The verification procedure is similar to the one presented in Fig. 5. The figure has two columns, the first one indicates the received data chunks and the second one shows the *next chunk* window which could be downloaded next. As more ADs arrive in the client, there are more options of data chunks to be downloaded since each AD contains a list of RH that can be used to authenticate the data chunks in the hash tree leaves. Therefore, every time that an AD arrives in the left side, it is expanded and the blocks that it can verify are placed in

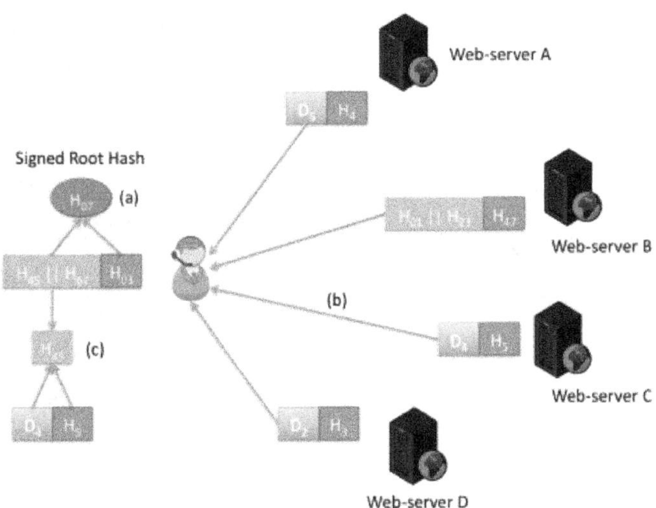

Fig. 10. Parallel data verification scenario. (a) First, the application retrieves the RH and verifies the digital signature. (b) The application retrieves ADs and subsequent data blocks from multiple sources. (c) Data blocks are verified using the previously received ADs.

the right column. For example, after the receiver authenticates the AD_0 containing the hash values $H_{01}||H_{23}$, the user can start downloading data blocks D_0, D_1, D_2 and D_3 in parallel and verify them as they arrive.

After the destination receives the AD with the concatenated hash values $H_{01}||H_{23}$, the receiver can retrieve and authenticate the data blocks D_0, D_1, D_2, D_3 in whichever order. The same procedure is taken when the AD with concatenated hash values $H_{45}||H_{67}$ is received in the destination, allowing the parallel retrieval and authentication of data blocks D_4, D_5, D_6 and D_7.

4.8 Evaluation

In order to compare with other approaches, we perform an analytical evaluation of the CHT overhead using different configurations. As demonstrated in Section 3.3, the composite hash tree has two overhead associated, the *Authentication Path* (O_{AP}) overhead and *Authentication Data Block* (O_{AD}) overhead. The O_{AP} is the sum all AP in each intermediate hash tree, defined by the CHT height h and the O_{AD} computes the sum of the product of the intermediate RH values that are aggregated into α hash values. The total CHT overhead of a CHT (O_T) with height h and aggregation index α is:

$$O_T = N * h + (N * h)/2^h = O(N) \tag{12}$$

The CHT parameters can be tuned to fit the overhead and dependency requirements specific to applications, for instance, in delay sensitive applications, e.g., video streaming, it is interesting that we start downloading the blocks with low latency between them. As applications can open multiple channels, it can check the available bandwidth on each connection and select the one that is providing higher throughput. On the other hand, applications that are not delay sensitive, e.g., file-sharing applications, we can use CHT with higher intermediate hash trees but with lower verification overhead. In that case, smaller data blocks provide faster dissemination, and in our case, it allows us to switch faster between sources after completing a chunk download

In order to analyze the performance of CHT with different parameters, we selected a file of 1 GB which we divided in blocks of 64KB, resulting in 16384 data blocks and we chose an AD with size of 8KB. The decision to choose small data blocks is due to the possibility of switching between sources faster since we can finish one download faster in order to start with another source with higher throughput, similar to the way how P2P systems work. We first start computing the α value:

$$\alpha = \frac{block\ size}{hash\ size} = \frac{8KB}{20B} = 400 \tag{13}$$

Therefore, each AD will hold 400 intermediate *Root Hash*es. The hierarchy dependency will be:

$$H' = \lceil \log_{2^h \alpha}(N/2^h) \rceil = \log_{800} 8192 \approx 1.35 = 2 \tag{14}$$

And the total overhead will be (according to Eq. 12):

$$O_T = N * h + (N * h)/2^h * 20(hash\ size) = 480KB \tag{15}$$

Tab. 3 summarizes the overhead for different h values for a file of 1 GB divided in blocks of 64KB.

CHT configuration	$h = 1$	$h = 2$	$h = 3$	$h = 4$	$h = 5$
Overhead (KB)	480	800	1080	1360	1650

Table 3. CHT overhead vs. authentication hierarchies

Hence, the total overhead for a CHT with $h = 1$ and $\alpha = 400$ is 480KB in a file of 1GB, resulting in less than 0.5% of total overhead at the cost of two verification steps before authenticating the data blocks. Another benefit from the security point of view is the fact that all blocks are algorithmically bound together, making it possible to clients to authenticate the authentication information. Compared to a regular *.torrent* used in BitTorrent, the main benefit is that we provide a mechanism to authenticate the partitioned authentication data, while the transfer of the *.torrent* file would require some other mechanism, e.g., hash chains or a single cryptographic hash over the entire metadata, to authenticate the structure containing all the piece IDs.

Fig. 11 summarizes the CHT overhead using different configurations of h and block sizes. Note that the overhead does not grow linearly, but logarithmically with the height of the internal hash tree (h), and the α parameter does not influence the overhead, but just the hierarchical dependency. Tab. 4 shows a comparison of the overhead with different file sizes and CHT configurations.

Fig. 12 shows the hierarchical dependency needed to authenticate data blocks with different h and α parameters. For this analysis, we considered a file of 1 GB divided in blocks of 64KB, resulting in 16384 data blocks. By using higher values of h, we are able to reduce the number of intermediate AD that we need to authenticate before verifying the data blocks themselves.

The graphic illustrates that for a given α value, the selection of the internal hash tree height h value does not interfere with the number of hierarchy dependencies but changes the overall

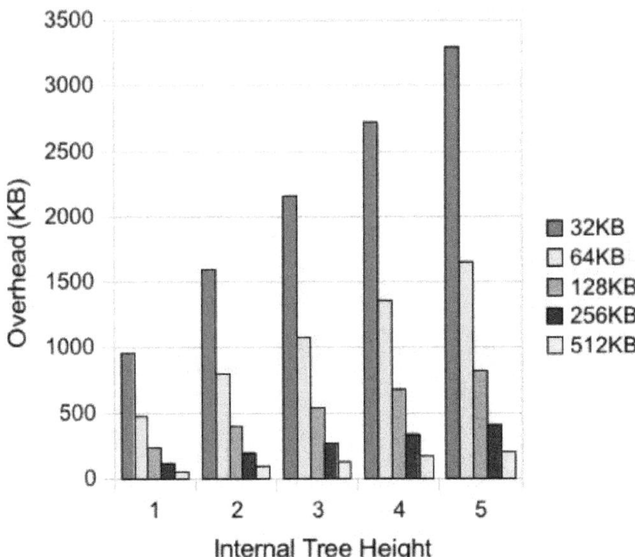

Fig. 11. CHT Overhead comparison using different internal hash trees for a file of 1GB divided in blocks of 32, 64, 128, 256, 512KB.

CHT conf.	1 GB	2 GB	5 GB	10 GB	20 GB	32 GB
CHT(1, 400)	0.47	0.94	2.34	4.68	9.37	15
CHT(2, 400)	0.78	1.56	3.91	7.81	15.62	25
CHT(3, 400)	1.05	2.11	5.27	10.54	21.09	33.75
CHT(4, 400)	1.33	2.65	6.64	13.28	26.56	42.50
CHT(5, 400)	1.61	3.22	8.06	16.11	32.22	51.56
Merkle Tree	4.38	9.38	25.5	54.13	114.51	190

Table 4. CHT overhead (MB) vs. file size using data chunks of 64 KB.

overhead. For instance, if we pick $\alpha = 400$, it is equivalent to select h equal to 1, 2 or 3 since they will result in the same hierarchical dependency between blocks. However, as Fig. 12 shows, higher h values result in higher overhead. Therefore, the best option here is to select the smallest $h = 1$ to minimize the overhead. On the other hand, if we consider $\alpha = 50$, the value of $h = 1$, $h = 2, 3, 4$ and $h = 5$ have different hierarchical values and also overheads, being a choice of the application to select the one that best fits the application's requirements.

4.8.1 Legacy data support

The proposed parallel authentication mechanism also supports legacy data from content providers, meaning that providers do not need to introduce any modifications in the files, for instance, to fragment the files into data chunks beforehand to insert the verification data (AP). As the verification data is unique and it is generated from the data segment, it is possible to detach the verification information from the data. Therefore, applications can retrieve data segments from possible sources and the AP from an authentication server or a security plane.

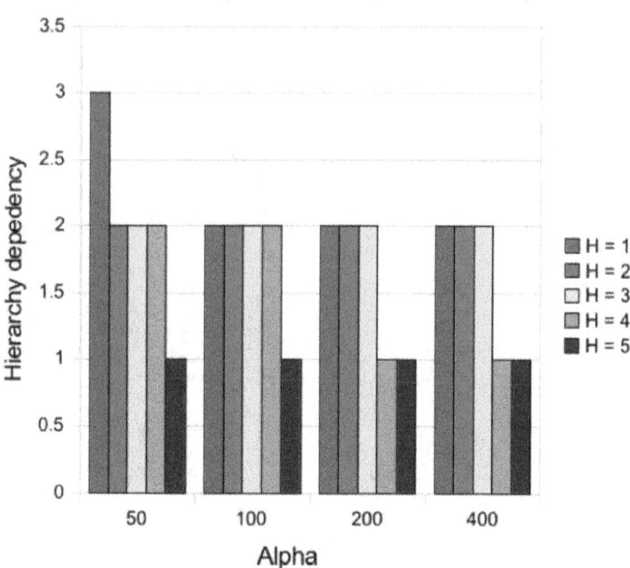

Fig. 12. Hierarchy dependency vs. aggregation index (α) using different internal hash tree heights.

The content retrieval procedure from different sources starts with the metadata file retrieval from a trusted source, e.g. Metalink signed metadata or from a security plane. The metadata contains the segment sizes and the corresponding authentication ID used to authenticate the data block. Then, a client contacts a directory server to retrieve the *authentication data blocks* and the *authentication path* for each segment. Next, the client starts the verification of the AD until reaching the AP of each data block, discarding the intermediate values. In the next step, the client retrieves the metadata containing the segment sizes in order to download the segments from multiple sources using multiple protocols, e.g. HTTP and FTP. In HTTP, it is possible to use the `HTTP Range Request` header to request a specific segment size, and in FTP we can use the `seek` directive to request a data range. After retrieving the data segment, the application applies a cryptographic hash over the data segment and computes the intermediate *root hash* using the previously retrieved AP for the data block.

Another extension supported by the parallel retrieval is the *opportunistic* verification. The idea of the opportunistic authentication is that users start to retrieve both data and authentication data simultaneously from multiple sources instead of downloading the verification information from the authentication server. In this approach, applications do not need to wait for the AD retrieval before the data. The application just places these unverified data blocks in an outstanding table and, as soon as the verification data arrives, it checks the integrity and saves into the destination file.

4.9 Related approaches

SINE (C. Gaspard, S. Goldberg, W. Itani, E. Bertino and C. Nita-Rotaru., 2009) provides Web content integrity using a hash list scheme. The idea is to add the hash of the following block in the previous block and digitally sign the first block sent to the client, which is also known as *chain anchor*. Therefore, modifications in any of the following blocks can be spotted by computing just one hash function over the next block. The main benefits of SINE is that it requires just one digital signature to authenticate an entire piece of data regardless of the number of data blocks and use one hash function to check the integrity, resulting in both low verification header and CPU cost. The main drawback compared to CHT is the strict verification order of the pieces, therefore, not supporting parallel verification of data chunks.

Regular Merkle Trees (Merkle, 1989) create a hash tree over a set of data blocks and each piece of data carries $\log_2 N$ hash values allowing them to authenticate data blocks with the corresponding root hash. The benefits are the independent data block verification and the low CPU processing costs. The main drawback is the verification information that each data block must carry, resulting in a total overhead of $N * \log_2 N$, being a considerable overhead for files with large number of blocks.

Packet Level Authentication (PLA) (Catharina Candolin, 2005) is a security model focused on per packet authentication, providing data authenticity and integrity in the network. Before a data block is sent to the destination, it is digitally signed by its provider, who is also endorsed by a trusted third party. The benefit is the independent block authentication with constant verification information overhead. However, the main drawback is the cost associated to the digital signature and verification, making it unfeasible to use in low processing devices. Tab. 5 summarizes the comparison between these mechanisms with the CHT approach. We took into account the *ordering* requirement, the *verification data overhead* and the *CPU cost associated* with the verification.

Mechanism	Block Association	Verification data	CPU cost
Hash chain	strict ordering	O(N)	low
Merkle Tree	independent	$O(N*\log_2 N)$	low-medium
PLA	independent	O(N)	high
CHT	independent*	O(N)	low

Table 5. Comparison between verification techniques

The CHT mechanism inherits the low verification data overhead and CPU cost from the hash tree mechanism at the cost of an initial dependence between the first data block. After the second one, it works similarly to the regular Merkle Tree, but with linear overhead instead of $O(N*\log_2 N)$.

5. Conclusion

In this paper, we have proposed two hash tree mechanisms, the *skewed hash tree* (SHT) and the *composite hash tree* (CHT) mechanisms to provide efficient content authentication mechanism based on the content rather than the connection. The first technique (SHT) is an extension of the Merkle Tree, which allows for random size authentication. The SHT mechanism can be created over a list of blocks and required one simple digital signature to authenticate all of them. The second mechanism, CHT, allows for efficient content authentication with reduced authentication overhead. CHT uses smaller Merkle Trees to reduce the overall authentication overhead at the cost of some hierarchical authentication dependence.

In order to validate our ideas, we implemented these two techniques and applied into two different scenarios: secure caching and parallel authentication over HTTP. The first evaluation scenario has shown that SHT can provide 8 and 3 times faster signature and verification speeds compared to public key cryptography, and the second evaluation scenario has showed that the CHT authentication overhead for parallel authentication and be less than 1% in some configurations.

6. References

Arianfar, S., Ott, J., Eggert, L., Nikander, P. & Wong, W. (2010). A transport protocol for content-centric networks. extended abstract, *18th International Conference on Network Protocols (ICNP'10), Kyoto, Japan* .

Bayardo, R. J. & Sorensen, J. (2005). Merkle tree authentication of http responses, *Special interest tracks and posters of the 14th international conference on World Wide Web*, WWW '05, ACM, New York, NY, USA, pp. 1182–1183.
URL: *http://doi.acm.org/10.1145/1062745.1062929*

C. Gaspard, S. Goldberg, W. Itani, E. Bertino and C. Nita-Rotaru. (2009). SINE: Cache-Friendly Integrity for the Web, *5th Network Protocol Security Workshop (NPSec'09)* .

Catharina Candolin, Janne Lundberg, H. K. (2005). Packet level authentication in military networks, *Proceedings of the 6th Australian Information Warfare & IT Security Conference.*

Leighton, T. (2009). Improving performance on the internet, *Commun. ACM* 52(2): 44–51.

Merkle, R. C. (1989). A certified digital signature, *Proceedings on Advances in cryptology*, CRYPTO '89, Springer-Verlag New York, Inc., New York, NY, USA, pp. 218–238.
URL: *http://portal.acm.org/citation.cfm?id=118209.118230*

Moskowitz, R., Nikander, P., Jokela, P. & Henderson, T. (2008). RFC 5201: Host Identity Protocol.
URL: *http://www.ietf.org/rfc/rfc5201.txt*

Pantos, R. (2010). HTTP live streaming, Internet Draft draft-pantos-http-live-streaming (Work in Progress).

Reis, C., Gribble, S. D., Kohno, T. & Weaver, N. C. (2008). Detecting in-flight page changes with web tripwires, *NSDI'08: Proceedings of the 5th USENIX Symposium on Networked Systems Design and Implementation*, USENIX Association, Berkeley, CA, USA, pp. 31–44.

Rodriguez, P., Spanner, C. & Biersack, E. W. (2001). Analysis of web caching architectures: Hierarchical and distributed caching, *IEEE/ACM Transactions on Networking* 9: 404–418.

Tamassia, R. & Triandopoulos, N. (2007). Efficient content authentication in peer-to-peer networks, *Proceedings of the 5th international conference on Applied Cryptography and Network Security*, ACNS '07, Springer-Verlag, Berlin, Heidelberg, pp. 354–372.

Wong, W., Giraldi, M., Magalhaes, M. & Kangasharju, J. (2011). Content routers: Fetching data on network path, *IEEE International Conference on Communications (ICC'11), Kyoto, Japan.* pp. 1–6.

Wong, W., Magalhaes, M. F. & Kangasharju, J. (2010a). Piece fingerprinting: Binding content and data blocks together in peer-to-peer networks, *IEEE Global Communications Conference (Globecom'10), Miami, Florida, USA* .

Wong, W., Magalhaes, M. F. & Kangasharju, J. (2010b). Towards verifiable parallel content retrieval, 6th *Workshop on Secure Network Protocols (NPSec'10), Kyoto, Japan* .

Yih-Chun Hu, M. Jakobsson and A. Perrig (2005). Efficient Constructions for One-Way Hash Chains, *Applied Cryptography and Network Security* pp. 423–441.

4

Security from Location

Di Qiu, Dan Boneh, Sherman Lo and Per Enge
Stanford University
United States of America

1. Introduction

The emergence of the Internet and personal computers has led to an age of unprecedented information content and access. The proliferation of Internet connectivity, personal computers, and portable, high density data storage has put volumes of data are at one's fingertips. While the spread of such technology has increased efficiency and knowledge, it has also made information theft easier and more damaging.

The emerging problems have made the field of information security grow significantly in recent years. Geoencryption or location-based encryption is a means to enhance security. Precise location and time information can be used to restrict access of the system or equipment at certain locations and time frames (Qiu et al., 2007). The term "geo-security" or "location-based security" refer to the authentication algorithm that limits the access (decryption) of information content to specified locations and/or times. More generically, the restriction can be based on any set of location-dependent parameters. The algorithm does not replace any of the conventional cryptographic algorithms, but instead adds an additional layer of security.

When a device wishes to determine its position, it does two things (Qiu et al., 2010). First, the hardware uses an antenna and receiver to capture and record a location measurement. Second, the location measurement is converted into a global position in the form of longitude and latitude. Most often these two steps are conflated, and both are seen as necessary to enable location-based applications. In this paper we show that for many security applications only the first step is needed: there is no need to accurately map the location measurement to an accurate global position. Therefore, these location-based security applications can be implemented using a variety of radio frequency (RF) signals, including broadcast communication signals, such as AM/FM, cellular, DTV, Wi-Fi, etc, navigation signals, and an integration of various signals.

While GPS provides accurate position data, other location services are far less accurate. LOng RAnge Navigation (Loran), for example, uses a 3km wavelength, and standalone Loran has an absolute accuracy of several hundred meters (Loran-C, 1994). Loran-C, the most recent version of Loran in use, is a terrestrial navigation system originally designed for naval applications. Its modernized version, enhanced Loran (eLoran), together with differential corrections can achieve an accuracy of 8 to 20 meter. This paper uses standalone Loran-C, which has good repeatable accuracy but low absolute accuracy, as a case study and shows that high absolute accuracy is not a requirement for a number of location-based security applications. As with all radio-based systems, Loran-C radio signals are distorted by buildings and other objects causing measurements to change greatly over short distances. Our main result shows that one can exploit these chaotic changes to obtain a precise and reproducible geotag with an accuracy of about 20 meters. Reproducibility means that measurements at the same location at different times always produce the same tag. While there is no way to map location measurements to an accurate position, there are still many applications, primarily security applications, for which a reproducible and precise tag is sufficient.

We build a reproducible and precise tag using recent results from biometric authentication for location-based security applications. In particular, we rely on fuzzy extractors and secure sketches, originally designed for fingerprint-based authentication. The idea is to store some public information that enables anyone to convert an erroneous measurement into a consistent tag. We develop specific fuzzy extractors designed to handle radio-type errors. The challenge is to correct for signal variations due to day/night, humidity, and seasonal changes.

The rest of the chapter is organized as follows. Section 2 develops a standardized process to quantify the precision, reproducibility and security of a geotag for security applications. Section 3 provides definitions and background information on fuzzy extractors. The design and implementation of fuzzy extractors for location-based security discussed in Section 4 will apply to all radio-based signals. We use Loran-C as a convenient example and evaluate the geotag performance using real data, which will be addressed in Section 5.

2. Geo-security

2.1 System model

The geo-security system works in two steps, calibration and verification, as illustrated in Figure 1. The calibration phase builds the database of geotags for service areas: $\Im = \{T(\ell, t), \forall \ell \epsilon \mathcal{L}\}$, where T is the geotag of the calibration associated with location ℓ, and t represents the time interval when the geotag is generated. The use of time information for geotags is optional. The calibration phase requires one to survey the service areas with a location sensor, such as a Loran receiver that integrates a geotag generation module. Geotags associated with the calibrated areas are computed based on the recorded location information and stored on a database for future use. In the verification phase, a user derives a geotag $T'(\ell', t') \epsilon \Im,\ s.t.\ \ell' \epsilon \mathcal{L}$ using the same geotag generation device and matches it with the pre-computed ones in the database. If the two tags are matched, the user's location is validated and the authorization for an application is granted; otherwise, the authorization is denied.

2.1.1 Geotag generation

In this section we introduce two geotag generation methods: the deterministic approach and the binary approach. The methods differ in geotag representation, efficiency in computation and implementation in practice.

Let $x = f\left(s\left(\ell, t\right)\right)$, be the location-dependent parameters, where $s(\bullet)$ denotes the signals received at location ℓ and time t, and $f(\bullet)$ is the function performed in a receiver. Typical functions in a receiver include signal conditioning, digitizing, and parameter extraction. The extracted x is a vector $x = [x_1, x_2, \ldots, x_n]^T \epsilon \Re^{n \times 1}$, where n is the number of location-dependent parameters.

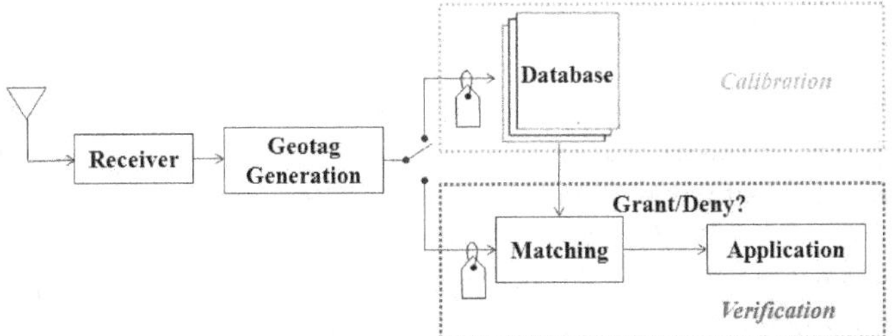

Fig. 1. Geo-security system: Calibration and verification phases

The deterministic approach simply takes the location-dependent parameter vector as a geotag, shown in Equation (1). This technique is similar to the location fingerprinting except that a geotag is computed from various location-dependent parameters rather than the received signal strength (Bahl & Padmanabhan, 2000).

$$T = \epsilon \Re^{n\times 1} \tag{1}$$

The binary geotag generation algorithm consists of three steps: a receiver function $f(\bullet)$ to extract location dependent parameters from the received signals $s(\ell, t)$, a quantizer $\mathcal{E}(\bullet)$ to quantize the parameters with adequate step sizes $\Delta(\ell)$, and a mapping function $\hbar(\bullet)$ to convert the quantized parameters into a binary string T. The binary mapping process can be done using a hash function, which is one-way and collision resistant. A one-way hash function is a fundamental building block in many cryptographic algorithms and protocols (Schneier, 1996), and outputs a fixed-length hash value regardless the length of inputs. One-way-ness means that it is easy to compute but hard or computationally infeasible to invert the function. In addition, since it is collision resistant, it is hard to generate the same hash values from two different inputs. Let q be the quantized parameter vector; its calculation is illustrated in Equation (2). All of these vectors x, q, and Δ have the size n. The quantization steps can be determined based on the standard deviations of the location dependent parameters to allow a certain degree of variations.

$$q_i = \mathcal{E}(x_i) = k; x \epsilon S_i = [k\Delta, (k+1)\Delta), k = 1, ..., N, \tag{2}$$

where S is the partition set and N indicates the number of quantization levels corresponding to a particular Δ. Thus the binary geotag can be calculated as

$$T = \hbar(q) \, \epsilon \, \mathbb{Z}^{m\times 1}. \tag{3}$$

2.1.2 Geotag matching

We next describe different matching algorithms for the two geotag generation functions. Two matching algorithms - the nearest neighbor method (NNM) and the probabilistic approach - can be applied to the deterministic geotag.

Let $\mathcal{M}$ denote the matching function. NNM is a common technique (Roos et al., 2002) used for indoor location estimation and pattern matching. The algorithm measures the distance between the location parameter vector from the verification phase T' and the previously stored vectors in the database, $\Im$. The generalized distance measure D is defined in Equation (4), where w is a weighting factor and p is the norm parameter. For instance, $w = 1$ and $p = 2$ represent the Euclidean distance. Based on the calculated distances between T' and the previously computed $T \epsilon \Im$, the geotag that gives the minimum distance is chosen. It is necessary to set an upper bound d_0 to guarantee that the location is registered at the calibration phase. A modification of NNM that uses the standard deviation σ of the location parameters is called the weighted nearest neighbor method (WNNM). The new distance measure is shown in Equation (5), where C is a covariance matrix, $C = E\{(x - \bar{x})^2\}$ and $\bar{x}$ is the mean value of location-dependent parameters. The matching function for the deterministic geotag is illustrated in Equation (6), where $\tilde{T}$ is the geotag associated with the authorized location.

$$D(x, x') = \frac{1}{n}(\textstyle\sum_{i=1}^{n} \frac{1}{w_i}|x'_i - x_i|^p)^{\frac{1}{p}} \tag{4}$$

$$D(x, x') = \left[(x - x')^T C^{-1}(x - x')\right]^{\frac{1}{2}} \tag{5}$$

$$\mathcal{M}(\tilde{T}, T') = \begin{cases} 1 & \text{if } \underset{T \epsilon \Im}{\arg\min} D(T, T') = \tilde{T},\ D(T, T') \leq d_0; \\ 0 & \text{otherwise.} \end{cases} \tag{6}$$

The probabilistic approach models a geotag with a conditional probability, and uses Bayesian methods to estimate the location (Roos et al., 2002). Both the location-dependent parameters and the standard deviations are estimated at the calibration phase. Assuming that the location-dependent parameters have Gaussian distributions, we use the probability density function shown in Equation (7) to compare the calculated likelihoods. The geotag that gives the maximum probability is chosen. The corresponding matching function is shown as follows:

$$P = \frac{1}{n}\textstyle\sum_{i=1}^{n}[\frac{1}{\sqrt{2\pi}\sigma_i} exp(-\frac{(x'_i - x_i)^2}{2\sigma_i^2})] \tag{7}$$

$$\mathcal{M}(\tilde{T}, T) = \begin{cases} 1 & \text{if } \underset{T \epsilon \Im}{\arg\max} P = \tilde{T}; \\ 0 & \text{otherwise.} \end{cases} \tag{8}$$

The matching process for a binary geotag only involves the correlations between T' and the previously stored ones. The correlation function is shown as follows:

$$\mathcal{M}(\tilde{T}, T') = \begin{cases} 1 & \text{if } \frac{1}{m}\sum_{i=1}^{m} \tilde{T}(i) \oplus T'(i) = 1,\ \forall \tilde{T} \epsilon \Im; \\ 0 & \text{otherwise.} \end{cases} \tag{9}$$

2.2 Loran-C for geo-security

The most important required feature of a signal for geo-security is its ability to generate a strong geotag. The strength of the geotag is determined by the quantity and quality of location-dependent signal parameters. By the quantity, we mean the number of different location-dependent parameters that can be generated. By the quality, we mean the amount of unique location-dependent information provided by each parameter. The information content is related to the spatial decorrelation of the parameter. Greater spatial decorrelation results in more unique information. By having many parameters each providing its unique information content, we can generate a strong geotag.

At the same time, it is desirable to have the parameters be relatively insensitive to temporal changes, which weaken the uniqueness of the information. Temporal variations essentially reduce the uniqueness of the location-dependent information. As a result, repeatability and repeatable accuracy are desirable qualities. They allow a user to have his location-dependent parameters or the derived geotag at one time—and still have those parameters valid at a later time. In other words, the signal characteristics should be consistent enough so that when the user is ready to authenticate, measurements at the same location will yield the same previously generated geotag. These are several features that are highly desirable.

In addition, the signal should have anti-spoofing capabilities. If the signal is vulnerable to spoofing, it may be possible for an attacker to bypass the location check and authenticate correctly. Furthermore, it is desirable that the signal be available indoors. This is because many of the anticipated applications of geo-security will likely occur indoors. This includes applications such as the management and distribution of secure digital data. Often, it is good if this data is only accessible inside certain buildings.

Loran-C is a terrestrial, low frequency, pulsed navigation system that operates in much of the northern hemisphere (Loran-C, 1994). Although the absolute accuracy of standalone Loran-C is not comparable to GPS, it has several advantages over GPS for security applications. First, Loran uses static transmitters and, as a result, its signals provide many parameters that are location-dependent. Each parameter offers different certain amount of information or potential information density. Parameters with higher information density result in stronger security. This is important, as the security strength of the geotag is derived from the information used to generate it. A combination of various parameters and the accuracy of these parameters increase the security strength. Second, Loran has good repeatable position accuracy, which benefits the design and guarantees the reproducibility of the geotag. Furthermore, Loran-C has good regional coverage in Northern Europe and much of East Asia like China, Japan, and Korea. Although the transmission of Loran-C signals in North America has been terminated in Feb. 2010, the decision with eLoran has yet to be made. eLoran will have a data channel (e-Loran, 2007). While some uses of the data have been defined, others have not. Therefore, several message types have been left unassigned to support useful application such as location-based security in the course of eLoran design. Loran antenna size may have been a practical issue in many applications. Recent research (Lee et al., 2009) has shown that a miniature H-field antenna of 2x2 cm can be achieved. With this size, a Loran H-field antenna can be easily fit into a number of portable electronic devices.

2.3 Applications

We discuss a number of potential security applications where the desired properties of geotags - high spatial decorrelation and reproducibility - come into play. Different geotag generation and system implementation methods should be applied to achieve optimized performance for various applications.

2.3.1 Digital manners policies (DMP)

Technologies for digital manners (DMP) (Hruska, 2008) attempt to enforce manners at public locations. A DMP-enabled cell phone can be programmed by the phone provider to turn off the camera while inside a hospital, a locker room, or a classified installation. Or the phone can be programmed to switch to vibrate mode while inside a movie theater. Many other applications have been considered. Although these ideas are highly controversial (Schneier, 2008), we only focus on the technical contents and feasible implementation of the ideas.

To implement DMP one assumes that the device needs to know its precise location. We argue that this is incorrect. Using our radio-based tag, one can build a list of geotags where the camera is to be turned off. The device downloads an updated list periodically. When the device encounters a geotag on this blocklist, it turns the camera off. When the device leaves the blocked location the camera is turned back on. Hence, digital manners are enforced without ever telling the device its precise location.

A DMP system must survive the following attack: the attacker owns the device and tries to make the device think it is somewhere else. Since most places are not blocked, any location confusion will do. To survive this threat any location-based DMP system must make the following two assumptions:

- First the device, including the antenna connection, must be tamper resistant. If the antenna connection is not protected then anyone can tamper with signals from the antenna. The simplest attack is to add a delay loop to the antenna. Since location measurements are time based, the delay loop will fool the device into thinking it is somewhere else.
- Second, it should be difficult to spoof the Loran-C radio signals by transmitting fake signals from a nearby transmitter. The safest defense against spoofing is cryptographic authentication for Loran-C signals. In our previous study we (Qiu et al., 2007) proposed a method for embedding TESLA (Perrig, 2002) authenticators into Loran-C signals to prevent spoofing. We point out that even without cryptography, spoofing Loran-C signals is far harder than spoofing GPS: In fact, GPS spoofers are commercially available and are regularly used by GPS vendors for testing their products.

Both assumptions are necessary to build an effective DMP system regardless of the navigation system used. Our goal is not to promote DMP but rather to show that an accurate DMP system can be built from standalone Loran-C signals.

2.3.2 Location-based access control

While DMP is a blocklisting application, access control is a whitelisting example. Consider a location-aware disk drive. The drive can be programmed to work only while safely in the data center. An attacker who steals the device will not be able to interact with it.

We consider two attack models:

- **Private locations:** suppose the device is located in a guarded data center and the attacker has no access to the insides of the data center. The attacker steals the device (say, while in transit (Sullivan, 2007)) and tries to make the device think it is still in the data center.

- **Public locations:** in this case the attacker has complete access to the data center and the attacker can measure the authorized geotag. After stealing the device the attacker can try to spoof the Loran-C signal to make the device think it is still in the data center. Unlike the DMP application where any location confusion was sufficient for the attacker, here the attacker must cause the device to think it is precisely in the right place in the data center, with 20 meter accuracy. Simply adding delay loops to the antenna will not work.

In both threat models we must assume that the device is tamper-resistant. Otherwise, the attacker can simply modify the device and bypass the location check. In the case of a public location we must also assume cryptographic authentication on Loran-C signals, as discussed in the DMP application.

Interestingly, for the private location settings, the unpredictability of the Loran-C geotag implies that we do not need any signal authentication nor do we need to protect the antenna connection to the device. In Section 5 we show that even if the attacker takes many measurements several hundreds of meters away (say in the parking lot) he still cannot tell for sure what tag to supply.

One option available to the attacker is to build a list of candidate geotags and try them one by one. In Section 5 we show that the list would need to include several dozen candidate tags. But the device can easily shutdown if it ever receives a sequence of incorrect geotags. Consequently, a trial and error attack will not get very far.

We note that location-based access control using encryption was studied by Scott and Denning (Scott & Denning, 2003) under the name Geoencryption, which uses physical locations, such as latitude, longitude and altitude measurements from GPS, for security applications. Our geotag derived from raw location measurements is more unpredictable and provides more information entropy.

3. Background on fuzzy extractors

In the previous section we showed applications for a precise and reproducible geotag. We now show how to build such tags using standalone Loran-C system. To ensure that our tags are reproducible we will make use of fuzzy extractors (Juels & Wattenberg, 1999; Dodis et al., 2004). Fuzzy extractors were originally designed for biometric authentication systems. Since biometric scanners introduce errors, one needs same way to extract a reproducible tag from the scanner's output. While biometric fuzzy extractors are designed with a specific error model in mind, here we need a fuzzy extractor tailored for the Loran error model.

3.1 Fuzzy extractors: Definitions

We follow the definitions in (Dodis et al., 2004). Measurements live in a set M which is equipped with a distance function denoted dis. Roughly speaking, $dis(x, y)$ is small if x is "close" to y.

Fuzzy extractor. A fuzzy extractor works in two steps. During the registration step one runs algorithm Gen on input $x \epsilon M$ to generate a public value P and a tag T. Later, given a noisy version of x, denoted x', one runs algorithm Rep on input x' and P to reproduce the tag T.

The idea is that if x and x' are fingerprint scans of the same finger, then x is "close" to x' and both should produce the same tag T. If T has sufficient entropy then it can used as a login password. Clearly we require that P reveal little or no information about the tag T.

Definition 1. A fuzzy extractor is a tuple (M, t_0, t_1, Gen, Rep), where M is the metric space with a distance function dis, Gen is a generate procedure and Rep is a reproduce procedure, which has the following properties:

If $Gen(x)$ outputs (T, P), then $Rep(x, P) = T$, whenever $dis(x, x') \leq t_0$. If $dis(x, x') \geq t_0$, then there is no guarantee T will be output. In addition, if $dis(x, x') \geq t_1$, $Rep(x', P) = T'$, and $T' \neq T$.

Fig. 2. Fuzzy extractor in action

3.2 Known constructions for fuzzy extractors

Initial constructions were proposed by Juels and Wattenberg (Juels & Wattenberg, 1999). Their scheme uses an error correcting code to handle the hamming metric on binary data. Juels and Sudan (Juels & Sudan, 2002) provide a fuzzy extractor for the set difference metric, which is the first construction for a non-hamming metric. Dodis (Dodis et al., 2004) gives precise definitions for the problem and provide constructions for hamming distance, set distance and edit distance.

All these schemes primarily apply to binary data which does not fit our settings where location measurements are vectors of real numbers. One exception is a construction of Chang and Li (Chang & Li, 2005) that can be adapted to give a fuzzy extractor for the scenario where one of the Loran-C transmitters is offline (e.g. for maintenance).

4. Generating a reproducible and precise geotag from Loran-C

Our goal is to build a reproducible and precise geotag from standalone Loran-C measurements. We first explain what a Loran-C measurement looks like and then discuss the error model for these measurements. Finally, we present a simple fuzzy extractor for this error model.

Loran-C measurements. Radio-based navigation uses signals from multiple transmitters to estimate the receiver's positions. Four transmitters on the west coast of the US, called the west coast Loran chain (GRI9940) are used for navigation in the western US. These four stations are located at Fallon, NV; George, WA; Middletown, CA; and Searchlight, NV. Pulses from this chain are broadcast every 0.0994 seconds (Loran-C, 1994). Fallon is the master station and the remaining three follow in sync. From each station we obtain three values, called location parameters or **features**, per pulse:

- Time-of-arrival (TOA) or time difference (TD): measures the propagation time from the transmitter to the receiver,
- envelope-to-cycle difference (ECD): measures carrier propagation rate, and
- signal-to-noise ratio (SNR).

An example measurement from the Middletown, CA station taken at Stanford is a triple: (496.8 microseconds, -0.145 microseconds, 41dB).

The exact meaning of these numbers is not important for our discussion here. What is important is that each transmitter produces a triple of real numbers (features) per pulse. Collecting the signals from all four stations gives a 12-dimensional real vector from which we wish to derive a geotag.

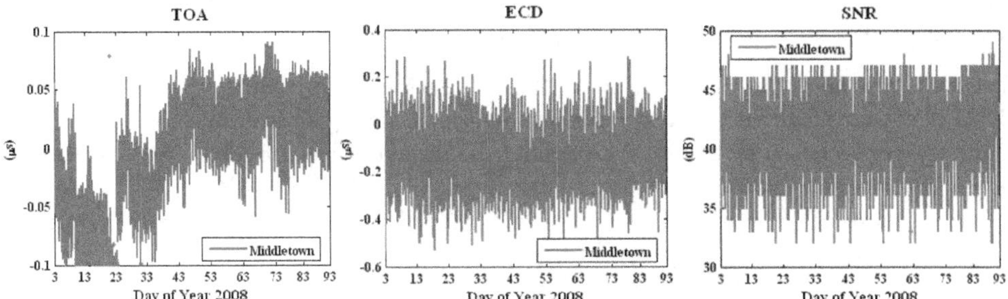

Fig. 3. Stanford seasonal monitor data for 90-day period for Middletown: (a) TOA; (b) ECD; (c) SNR.

Loran-C error patterns. Due to measurement errors and environmental changes, taking multiple measurements at the same location, but at different times, produces different 12 dimensional vectors. Figure 3 shows temporal variations in the triple (TOA, ECD and SNR) as measured from the Middletown station over a 90 day period. These measurements were taken at Stanford, CA. The wild swings in TOA, for example, reflect seasonal variations between winter and spring. We next explain the reason for these variations and how to model them.

- The most common error source is the thermal noise in all electronic devices, considered as white Gaussian noise. This noise cannot be eliminated and is always presenting in all electronic devices and transmission media.
- Many environmental factors cause signal variation, including temperature changes between night and day, changes in soil conductivity over time, humidity, local weather, etc. (Swaszek et al., 2007). In particular, temperature and humidity variations have a considerable effect on propagation speed. The extra delay in propagation time or TOA can introduce a position error of hundreds of meters (Lo et al., 2008). This particular error source in Loran is called additional secondary factor (ASF) and represents one of the largest error sources in Loran.
- Location vectors are continuous and need to be quantized. Quantization error, which is the difference between value of continuous feature and the quantized value, can lead to errors in the derived geotag. The quantization error is usually correlated with the two types of errors discussed above.
- The last type error results from maintenance of any radio-based system. A transmitter can go offline, in which case we lose all measurements associated with that station. Ideally, we would like this to have no effect on the geotag produced by our system.

A fuzzy extractor for Loran signals must take seasonal variations into account and can correct errors differently depending on the time of year.

4.1 Construction 1: Fuzzy extractor for Euclidean distance

We propose a fuzzy extractor when all Loran-C transmitters are present (Qiu et al., 2010). Thus the features are real numbers over R and Euclidean distance is sufficient for the distance metric. Let x be a location feature vector at registration while x' be the feature vector at verification time, Δ is the step size to quantize the feature. The distance $dis(x, x')$ can be bounded by adequate threshold. This threshold, δ, can be a design parameter. We need to develop a fuzzy extractor that can reproduce geotag T when the errors $|x - x'| \leq \delta$. The fuzzy extractor is designed to tolerate the random noise, biases and quantization errors.

Let the metric space $M = [A_i, B_i]^n, n = 12$ if we use the triple from four Loran-C stations. Thus x, x' and Δ are vectors that have n dimensions. The quantization step Δ is a design parameter and chosen by a user. We consider the distance measure for Loran-C features is L_∞ norm to be conservative.

$$dis(x, x') = \left(\max_i \frac{|x_i - x_i'|}{\Delta_i}\right)_{i=1}^{n} \tag{10}$$

The construction of fuzzy extractor for Euclidean distance is as follows: during calibration or registration, feature vector x is quantized to get T and store public value P, whereas, during verification, given a slightly different location feature x' and P, compute T'. P, T and T' are also n-dimensional vectors. P_i represents the ith feature in vector P. The elements in vector T are integers but they are not necessarily positive. For instance, it is possible to result in a negative TD if the distance between the secondary station and a user is shorter than the distance between master station and the user. The basic idea of this fuzzy extractor is to adjust the offsets between the continuous features and the discrete ones due to quantization.

$$Gen(x) = \begin{cases} T = \lfloor \frac{x_i}{\Delta_i} \rfloor_{i=1}^{n} \\ P = \left(x_i - \Delta_i \lfloor \frac{x_i}{\Delta_i} \rfloor\right)_{i=1}^{n} \end{cases} \tag{11}$$

$$Rep(x', P) = \lfloor \frac{x_i' - P_i + \frac{\Delta_i}{2}}{\Delta_i} \rfloor_{i=1}^{n} = T' \tag{12}$$

Claim 1. If $dis(x, x') < \frac{1}{2}$, then a geotag T can be reproduced, that is, $T' = T$. This claim defines the reproducibility of geotags. If x' is measured at the same location of x, we can reproduce T when the distance of x and x' is less than $\frac{\Delta}{2}$.

Claim 2. If $dis(x, x') \geq t_1$, then a geotag $T' \neq T$. This claim defines the precision of geotags. If x' is measured at a different location but close to the location of x, it is not expected that x' achieves the same tag as x.

It is easy to see that our construction is a fuzzy extractor (as in **Definition 1**).

4.2 Construction 2: Secret sharing based fuzzy extractor for hamming distance

The distance metric in this construction is Hamming. The input to the fuzzy extractor is quantized feature vector q_x instead of x, where $q_x = \lfloor \frac{x_i}{\Delta_i} \rfloor_{i=1}^{n}$ is n-dimensional. The scheme is based on the property of secret sharing: a secret can be reconstructed given a subset of shared information. The construction is as follows:

- Create a polynomial $f(x)$, such that $f(i) = q_{x_i}, \forall i = 1, 2, ..., n$.
- Let m be an integer and $m < n$.
- $Gen(x) = \begin{cases} T = \langle f(1), f(2), ..., f(m) \rangle \\ P = \langle f(j), ..., f(j+n-m-1) \rangle \end{cases}, where\ j, ..., j+n-m-1 \notin \{1, ...n\}.$
- $Rep(x', P) = \begin{cases} f'(x) \\ T' = \langle f'(1), f'(2), ..., f'(m) \rangle \end{cases}.$

Claim 3. If $dis(q_x, q_{x'}) \leq n - m$, then a geotag T can be reproduced. When the hamming distance between two vectors is less than $n - m$, the polynomial $f(x)$ can be reconstructed with the assistance of P thus $T' = T$.

Claim 4. If $dis(q_x, q_{x'}) > n - m$, then a geotag $T' \neq T$. The precision of a geotag T relies on the features $x_1, ..., x_m$.

This construction increases reproducibility but reduces entropy because we only use m out of n features to compute a geotag.

5. Experimental results

In this section we use real standalone Loran-C data to evaluate the precision and reproducibility of Loran-C geotag and evaluate the effect of the Euclidean metric fuzzy extractor. We performed two experiments: (1) collected data at various test locations to examine the precision of geotags, and (2) collected data at one location over 90-day period to study the reproducibility of geotags.

5.1 Data at different locations evaluating tag precision

We selected three different environments, where our proposed location-based security applications may occur, to perform the precision test: parking structure, soccer field and office building. At each location we used multiple test points for five minutes at each test point. An H-field antenna and Locus Satmate receiver, shown in Figure 4, were used for the data collection. The receiver averages and outputs Loran location features every minute.

Fig. 4. Loran-C H-field antenna(left) and SatMate receiver (right)

- **Scenario 1.** The first data set was collected at 21 different test points on the top floor of a parking structure at Stanford University. This place has open sky view and no obstruction from the environments but there are some metal structures nearby. The altitude is relatively high compared with the other two scenarios. The dimension of the parking structure is approximately 70 x 50 meters.
- **Scenario 2.** The second data set selected 16 test points in a soccer field. This environment has some obstructions from trees and buildings. The field has a dimension of 176 x 70 meters so the distribution of the test locations are less dense compared to the other two scenarios.
- **Scenario 3.** The third data set, which includes 21 test points, was collected on the top floor both inside and outside a building. The concrete building with metal frames attenuates signal strength more but introduces more uniqueness in the location features, which can be beneficial to the computation of geotags.

We used the triple (TD, ECD, SNR) from four stations in the west coast chain (GRI 9940). Quantization steps are chosen based on the measured SNR. Low SNR signals are often attenuated more and pick up more noise. In general, features from low SNR stations are less consistent; thus larger quantization steps should be applied. We then created two-dimensional cells using Voronoi diagrams and mapped the tags into the cells accordingly. The color map is superimposed on the Google map. A color bar is used to label the hexadecimals of the first 16-bit of tag. This distribution plot can help us visualize how geotag varies in a two-dimensional view. Each black dot together with the numbered label at the center of the cells represents a test location.

The left of Figure 4 is the tag plot on the top floor of the parking structure, the middle plot represents the results of a soccer field, and the right plot shows the top floor/roof of Durand building. Loran signals are very sensitive to the environment, especially to metal structures. The re-radiation of signals from metals can cause more distortion to the RF signals thus higher precision or spatial variation of tags at certain locations. We observe this from the geotag maps of scenario 1 and scenario 3. The locations with very small separations still result in different geotags. It is worth to mention that only two stations, Fallon and Middletown, are used to compute tags for scenario 3 while the other two scenarios use all four stations from GRI 9940. Due to the low signal strength indoors, the SatMate receiver was not able to acquire the other two low SNR stations, George and Searchlight. The averaged precision of three different scenarios is as follows:

- The precision of Loran-C tags in the parking structure ranges from 8 meters to 35 meters. There are four locations that resulted in the same tag shown in dark blue on the left of Figure 5.
- The precision of tags in the soccer field is lower compared with that of the parking structure due to the large separations between the selected test locations or insufficient number of test points used. The averaged size of the colored cells that represents geotag is approximately 30 x 50 meters.
- Although the indoor signals are not good enough to solve a position fix because low-SNR signals are not able to track. The generation of a geotag does not rely on the solved position fix as the geotags are derived from location-dependent features. As a result, it is not required to have more than four transmitters to implement location-based security although more transmitters would provide more information entropy or longer

tag to the system. The smallest colored cell or the highest tag precision in this indoor scenario is approximately 5 meters depicted in purple in the middle of the right plot in Figure 4. An upper bound on actual tag precision at this location is the largest cell, 8 x 20 meters.

Fig. 5. Visualization of Loran geotags: (a) parking structure (left); (b) soccer field (middle); (c) Durand building (right)

5.2 Data at one location evaluating reproducibility

In this section we use the seasonal data shown in Figure 3 to compare the reproducibility of a geotag with and without a fuzzy extractor. Again same triple is used in this experiment. We use TD instead of TOA to minimize the impact of ASF errors: TOA of the master station is used as a reference to mitigate the temporal variations of secondary stations. Our experiments show that the standard deviation of TOA from Middletown is 12.19 meters and the standard deviation of TD from Middletown is reduced to 3.83 meters (Qiu et al., 2008). However, TD provides less information entropy in comparison with TOA as we lose the TOA entropy from master station.

Performance metrics. Before we discuss the experimental results from the seasonal data we introduce the performance metrics that help to quantify and measure the reproducibility of a geotag. The problem of deciding whether the derived geotag is authentic or not, can be seen as a hypothesis testing problem. The task is to decide which of the two hypotheses H_0 (accepting as an authorized user) or H_1 (rejecting as an attacker) is true for the observed location measurements. Location-based system makes two types of errors: 1) mistaking the measurements or derived tag from the same location to be from two different locations and accepting hypothesis H_1 when H_0 is true, called false reject; and 2) mistaking the measurements or derived tags from two different locations to be from the same location and accepting H_0 when H_1 is true, called false accept. Both false reject rate (FRR) and false accept rate (FAR) depend on the accuracy of equipments used, step sizes chosen to quantize location features and environmental conditions. These two types of errors can be traded off against each other by varying the quantization steps. A more secure system aims for low FARs at the expense of high FRRs, while a more convenient system aims for low FRRs at the expense of high FARs. Figure 6 illustrates the two error rates of geotags with the assumption that the probability distributions are Gaussian, which is not necessarily true in practice. The grey tails represent the false reject of an authorized user while the red area is the false accept of an attacker.

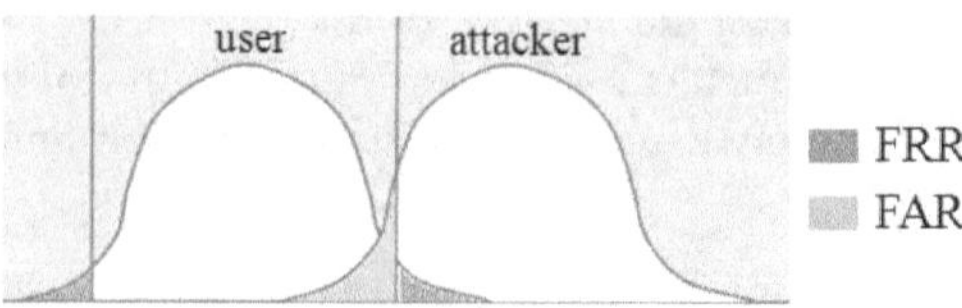

Fig. 6. Performance metrics illustration

Choosing a reliable quantization step for a location feature. Users' false reject rate significantly depends on the standard deviation of the features. Large standard deviation implies high temporal variations; thus the distance between the received features at verification and the ones at registration might be large. Therefore, the quantization step should be chosen to be proportional to the standard deviation σ of features.

In this analysis we show that the quantization step has to be larger than 4σ to achieve reasonably small FRR, less than 0.1. The FRR analysis is illustrated in Figure 7. The quantization step ranges from σ to 6σ. The x-axis is the feature offset between registration and verification. The y-axis is the estimated FRR. The solid lines are analytical results and we assumed the distribution of location feature is near-Gaussian after the ASF mitigation. The dots are derived using the seasonal data. We used ECD from four stations in this experiment. To estimate FRR we take the first day of the 90-day ECD data as registration to compute a geotag and the data from the rest of 89 days for verification. The experimental FRR is the number of days, in which the tags are matched with the registered tag on day one, divided by 89. The experimental results match well with the analytical curves. As expected, FRR increases as offset goes up and quantization step goes down.

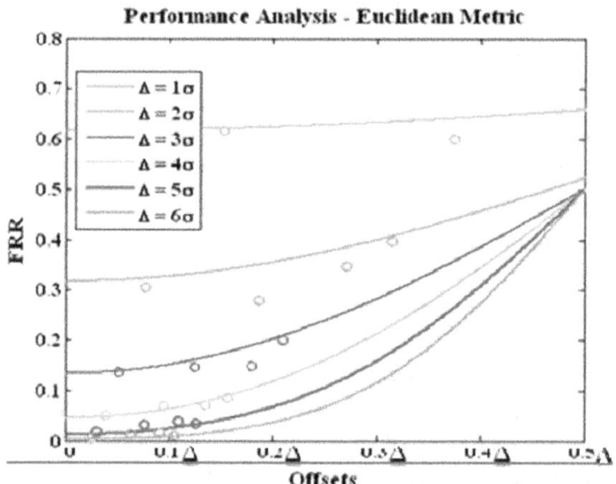

Fig. 7. FRR of a location feature

Using multiple features. The derived FRR in Figure 6 only represents the error rate of one particular location feature. Practically, multiple features are used to achieve more entropy, precision and higher difficulty in predicting the desired tag. However, one drawback using multiple features is that the FRR of the system is increased or reproducibility is reduced.

The system FRR can be estimated as $\Pi_{i=1}^{n} p_i$ if we assume the location features are independent from each other, where p_i is the error rate of one feature. Practically, location features are slightly correlated in some environments. For instance, the signal strength is inversely proportional to the propagation distance, which is determined by TOA. This is true when the antenna is placed in an open sky area and has no obstructions from surroundings. To solve the reliability problem using multiple features, secret sharing based fuzzy extractor can be used together with the Euclidean metric fuzzy extractor. Only a subset of features is used to compute tags thus the total FRR is limited.

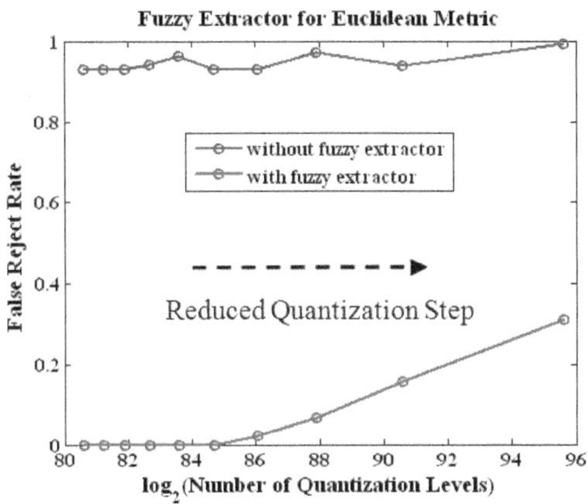

Fig. 8. Performance of Euclidean metric fuzzy extractor

Euclidean metric fuzzy extractor performance of multiple features. Now we use the triple from four stations to evaluate experimentally the performance of Euclidean metric fuzzy extractor. We reduce the quantization steps of the features gradually to observe the change of FRR and the number of quantization levels, which determine the entropy of geotag. The plot is shown in Figure 8. The blue line represents the FRR without the use of the fuzzy extractor while the red line is the results using the fuzzy extractor. As expected, the FRR is dramatically reduced after the use of the fuzzy extractor. The fuzzy extractor guarantees the measurements lying in the center of quantization interval. The graph shows that we can achieve total entropy of 86 bits with FRR is less 0.1 with adequate quantization steps.

5.3 Loran-C geotags are unpredictable

Next we ask whether Loran-C geotags are predictable from a distance. In this chapter unpredictability refers to the difficulty of an individual in predicting the Loran measurements at a given time and place. The temporal variations due to propagation path delay variations and skywave as well as the unexpected distortions in the RF signals due to local features such as buildings and large metallic structures can introduce randomness and entropy in the generation of a geotag, which makes attackers to take more time and effort to break into the system.

We discussed applications for this unpredictability test in Section 2.3. To justify the claim that Loran-C geotags are unpredictable, we perform two experiments.

While we cannot prove the difficulty of prediction mathematically as it is not possible to come up a universal model that suits for all the environments; however, we can show the nonlinear of the Loran-C features experimentally. The predictions can be based on path propagation, reflection, diffraction, diffuse wall scattering and transmission through various materials. The sum of all the components is taken to get TD, ECD and SNR. Moving objects like people can cause not only attenuation but also fluctuation. The irregularities make the prediction even harder.

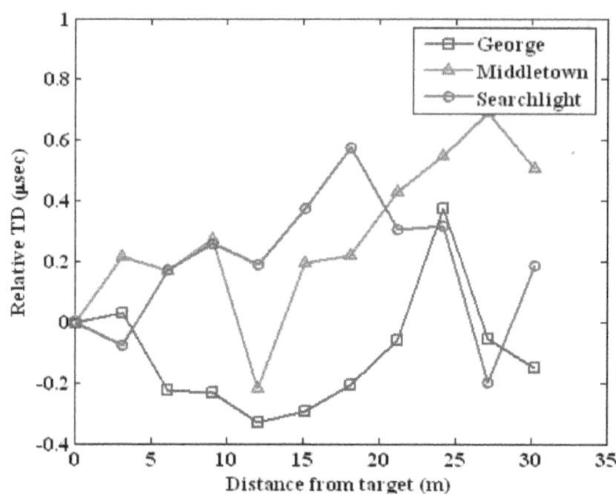

Fig. 9. Spatial variation of TD measurements collected in a parking structure

We perform the following two experiments to test the difficulty to predict a geotag. The first experiment uses the data set collected in a parking structure from 11 test points. The test locations are lined up in one dimension and the separation between adjacent points is approximately three meters. We chose the first point as our target or user location. Figure 8 plots the spatial variations of TD of George, Middletown and Searchlight. The x-axis is the measured distance of test points from the target point. The y-axis is the relative TD in microseconds. We zeroed out the means of the TDs to achieve the same scale for the measurements from three stations. The nonlinearity of the Loran-C measurements is clear from the graph. Low-SNR stations, George and Searchlight, are attenuated more from the obstructions in the environment compared to the strongest station Middletown. This results in more nonlinear variations in the low-SNR stations.

The second experiment uses the same data set collected in Durand building for the precision test discussed in Section 5.1. We chose the center point as our target point and measured Loran-C features with increasing distances from the target point. The point is shown as white dots in the plots of Figure 10. The color contour plot is again superimposed on the Google map. The color bar shown at the bottom represents feature values of various locations. Figure 10 illustrates the spatial variations of TD, ECD and Signal strength measured from Middletown. If feature variations are linearly proportional to distance, the color of the map should change from blue to red gradually with equal diameter. We observe that ECD are more nonlinear in comparison with TD and signal strength because phase is very sensitive to building structures and environments. The non-linearity of location features can significantly benefit the design of location-based security applications as it results in the features are highly unpredictable.

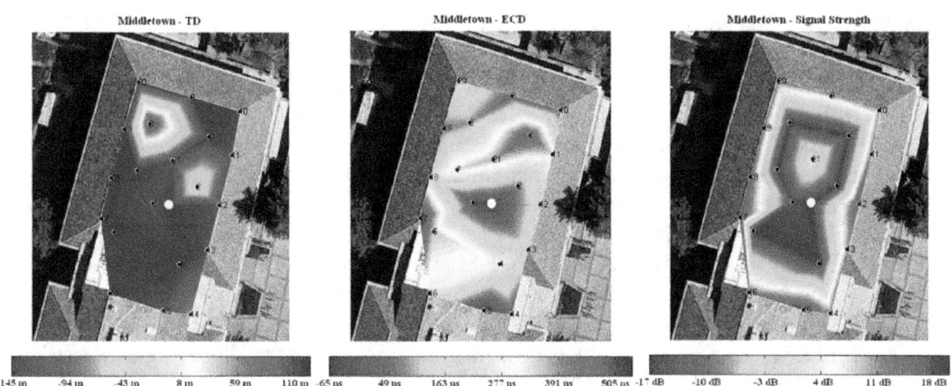

Fig. 10. Spatial variation of location data from Middletown in Durand building: (a) TD; (b) ECD; (c) Signal strength.

6. Conclusion

We showed that a radio navigation system with high absolute accuracy and low repeatable accuracy such as standalone Loran-C can be used to generate a precise and reproducible geotag. A geotag is computed from location-dependent features and can be used for a number of security applications. A geotag is not a replacement but builds on the conventional security schemes. We discussed applications to DMP, inventory control and data access control.

Fuzzy extractors were developed for radio-based signals to achieve high consistency. Euclidean metric fuzzy extractor and Hamming metric fuzzy extractor were designed for different location measurement errors. Adequate quantization step should be chosen as it determines the system performance. FAR and FRR can be traded off by varying the quantization steps of location features. We used Loran-C real data to show that the Euclidean metric fuzzy extractor significantly improves the reproducibility of a generated geotag. In addition we proved that the Loran-C location features can achieve high spatial variation using measurements at three different sites, a parking structure, a soccer field and an office building. In addition, we gave evidence that a geotag is unpredictable from a distance, which is beneficial to location-based security applications.

This paper only focused on the evaluation of geo-security using Loran-C as a case study; however, there are many available radio signals that might be feasible to implement geo-security, such as digital television, cellullar, Wi-Fi, and RFID. The proposed location-based security technique needs to be validated and compared with case studies. Future work shall be directed toward design of experimental setups, evaluating the feasibility and performance of each signal, comparing the different signals in terms of performance, usability and cost, and serivce coverage.

7. References

Enhanced Loran (eLoran) Definitions Document (2007). International Loran Association. URL: *http://www.loran.org/ILAArchive*

Loran-C Signal Specifications (1994). United States Coast Guard (USCG), COMDTINST M15662.4A, May 1994.

Bahl, P. & Padmanabhan V.N. (2000). RADAR: an in-building RF-based user location and tracking system, *Proceedings of IEEE in INFOCOM 2000*, IEEE, Vol. 2 (2000), pp. 775-784.

Boyen, X. (2004). Reusable cryptographic fuzzy extractors, *Proceeding of the 11th ACM Conference on Computer and Communications Security*, ACM Press, pp. 82-91.

Chang, E. & Li, L. (2005). Small secure sketch for point-set difference, *Cryptology ePrint Archive, Report 2005/145.*

Dodis, Y.; Reyzin, L. & Smith, A. (2004). Fuzzy extractors: How to generate strong keys from biometrics and other noisy data, *Eurocrpt'04*, Springer-Verlag, Vol. 3027 of LNCS, pp. 523-540.

Hruska, J. (2008). Microsoft patent brings miss manners into the digital age, *Arstechnica Hardware news*, June 11, 2008.

Juels, A. & Sudan, M. (2002). A fuzzy vault scheme, *Proceeding of IEEE Intl. Symp. on Information Theory*, IEEE Press, pp.408, Lausanne, Switzerland.

Juels, A. & Wattenberg, M. (1999). A fuzzy commitment scheme, *Sixth ACM Conference on Computer and Communications Security*, ACM Press, pp.28-36, 1999.

Lee, D.; Best, S.; Hanna, D. & Rosario, E. (2009). A miniature Loran H-field antenna for low-profile conformal hybrid applications, *Proceeding of ION ITM 2009*, Institute of Navigation, Jan. 2009, Anaheim, California, United States.

Lo, S.; Wenzel, R.; Johnson, G. & Enge, P. (2008). Assessment of the methodology for bounding Loran temporal ASF for aviation, *Proceeding of ION NTM 2008*, Institute of Navigation, Jan. 28-30, 2008, San Diego, California, United States.

Perrig, A.; Canetti, R.; Tygar, J.D. & Song, D. (2002). The TESLA broadcast authentication protocol, *CryptoBytes*, 5:2, Summer/Fall 2002, pp. 2-13.

Qiu, D.; Boneh, D.; Lo, S.; Enge, P. Reliable location-based srvices from radio navigation systems, *Sensors* 2010, *10*, 11369-11389.

Qiu, D.; Lo, S.; Enge, P.; Boneh, D. & Peterson, B. (2007). Geoencryption using Loran, *Proceeding of ION NTM 2007*, Institute of Navigation, Sep. 25-28, 2007, San Diego, California, United States.

Qiu, D.; Lo, S. & Enge, P. (2008). A measure of Loran location information, *Proceeding of IEEE/ION PLANS 2008*, Institute of Navigation, May 6-8, 2008, Monterey, California, United States.

Roos, T.; Myllymaki, P.; Tirri, H.; Misikangas, P. & Sievanen, J. (2002). A probabilistic appraoch to WLAN user location estimation, *International Journal of Wireless Information Networks*, 9(3): 155-164, July 2002.

Schneier, B. (1996). *Applied Cryptography*, John Wiley & Sons, ISBN 0-471-11709-9.

Schneier, B. (2008). Kill switches and remote control, *A blog covering security and security technology*, July 1, 2008.

Scott, L. and Denning, D. (2003). A location based encryption technique and some of its applications, *Proceedings of ION NTM 2003*, Institute of Navigation, Jan. 22-24, 2003, Anaheim, California, United States.

Sullivan, B. (2007). The biggest data disaster ever, *MSNBC news*. Nov. 30th, 2007.

Swaszek, P.; Johnson, G.; Hartnett, R. & Lo, S. (2007). An investigation into the temporal correlation at the ASF monitor sites, *Proceedings of ILA 36th Annual Meeting 2007*, International Loran Association, Oct. 14-17, 2007, Orlando, Florida, United States.

5

Secure Platform Over Wireless Sensor Networks

Marco Pugliese, Luigi Pomante and Fortunato Santucci
Center of Excellence DEWS, University of L'Aquila
Italy

1. Introduction

Homeland security and monitoring of critical infrastructures, such as buildings, bridges, nuclear power plants, aircrafts, etc., represent challenging application domains for modern networking technologies. In this context Wireless Sensor Networks (WSNs) are gaining interest as a fundamental component of an advanced platform that embeds pervasive monitoring, networking and processing. Indeed, recent literature has addressed the perspectives of WSNs for monitoring structural and functional health of industrial plants, e.g. in (Akyildiz, et al., 2002; Bai et al., 2004; Barbaràn et al., 2007; Cho et al., 2008; Flammini et al., 2008; Kim et al., 2007): nevertheless, we can observe that the dominating paradigm is to exploit WSNs features in terms of a "network of small sensors", while almost unexplored is the more advanced paradigm of "networked smart sensors" and the underlying opportunity to actually support autonomous (anomaly) detection processes. A large body of specialized literature deals with this topic and several ad-hoc solutions can be found. On the contrary, we try to develop a different approach in this context: resorting to security mechanisms that are made available in traditional networks can provide a suitable and reliable framework, while smart adaptations are targeted to meet tight resource constraints and possible performance degradation.

Therefore we argue to demonstrate experimentally that, under certain limitations, a WSN can operate as a functionally "autonomous entity" not only for sensing operations. Despite the hard constraints on HW and the computation limitations, a WSN node is not just a sensing device (such as a magnetic contact or an infrared source): it is indeed a smart micro-device equipped with CPU and memory and is able to perform some autonomous data pre-processing, coding and transmission. Moreover the peculiar feature of a WSN with respect to a traditional sensor network is not to rely on fixed devices and cabling: nevertheless this comes at the cost of the availability of the so-called "ad-hoc" network properties (e.g. a sophisticated topology rearrangement mechanism is mandatory to achieve fault tolerance) as well as peer-to-peer frameworks, which imply enhanced protocol complexity and further computational and memory resource.

However, if proper design approaches (Pugliese et al., 2009; Sangiovanni-Vincentelli & Martin, 2001) are adopted, also the provision of fundamental security services (Hu et al., 2004; Law et al., 2005) can be pursued, which is a fundamental step towards the development of WSNs in critical applications; indeed the typical WSN deployment scenarios depicted above are highly exposed to physical capture or signal interception by external attackers much more than traditional sensors, which can be monitored by an extra-surveillance service.

Therefore providing security in a WSN system cannot be restricted to providing a robust cryptographic scheme, also because this kind of schemes are heavy demanding in terms of computational power and memory. Indeed a smart intrusion detection service should be provided also with ciphering and authentication in order to build up a "security service" package that will enhance the typical middleware services provided by an Application Execution Environment (AEE): this service package is the core feature of the proposed "secure platform" that is proposed, analyzed and tested in this chapter.

This chapter is organized as follows: Sec. 2 deals with the security services provided by the "Secure Platform", Sec. 3 and Sec. 4 describe fundamental algorithms and architectures supporting those security services, Sec. 5 reports the design approach of the platform while Sec. 6 is concerned withy a prototype of implementation and related tests. Sec. 7 deals with a viable conformance path to the trusted computing guidelines (TCG, n.d.).

2. Secure platform functions

Fig. 1 shows the main functional blocks of the proposed Secure Platform: apart from the block providing the typical middleware services (MW Services) and shared memory, other specific services (in this case security-oriented) are implemented as customizations of specific SW component and provided to the AEE via different APIs. It is very important to note that the "secure platform approach" offers a promising guideline to design and implement "integrated security" over WSN in a "application-oriented" approach which is aligned to the current SW development paradigms over resource constrained devices (Gay, 2003; Kliazovich, 2009; Sangiovanni-Vincentelli & Martin, 2001).

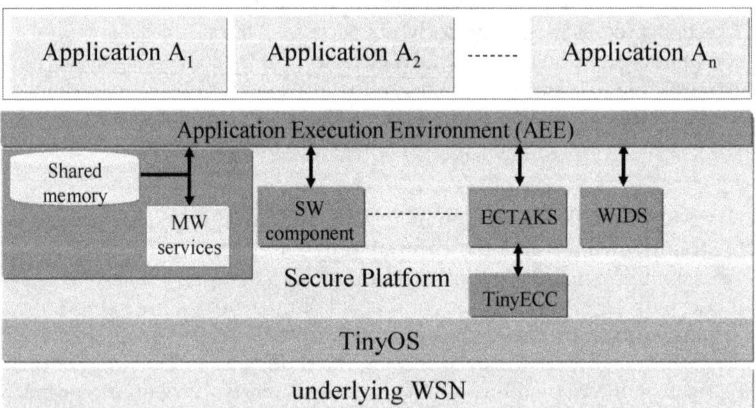

Fig. 1. Secure Platform Architecture

In this case at least two functional blocks are provided: the cryptography module, which implements ECTAKS (Elliptic Curve-based Topology Authenticated Key Scheme), and the intrusion detection module, which implements WIDS (Weak process model-based Intrusion Detection System): the former one represents a novel contribution that enhances the capabilities of the approach in (Pugliese & Santucci, 2008) by exploiting the advanced security features of elliptic curves, while the latter one integrates the developments proposed in (Pugliese et al., 2008, 2009).

TinyECC module (Liu, 2008) represents the ECC security package in WSN as it natively integrated with TinyOS (TinyOS, n.d.), the widely used operating system over WSN: ECTAKS, as we will show in next sections, rely on TinyECC security services to encrypt / decrypt messages.

Next sections, Sec. 3 and Sec. 4, deal with ECTAKS and WIDS modules respectively as well as with security and cost evaluations; however further details, especially about the mathematical proofs of theorems and computation expressions, can be found in (Pugliese et al., 2008, 2009; Pugliese & Santucci, 2008).

3. Elliptic curve-based topology authenticated key scheme (ECTAKS)

3.1 Motivations

In traditional networks such as the Internet, Public Key Cryptography (PKC) has been the enabling technology underlying many security services and protocols (e.g., SSL, IPsec). However, in WSNs PKC has not been widely adopted due to the resource constraints on sensor platforms, in particular the limited battery power and storage capacity. There has been intensive research aimed at developing techniques that can bypass PKC operations in sensor network applications. For example, there has been a substantial amount of research on random key pre-distribution for pair-wise key establishment, e.g. (Eschenauer & Gligor, 2002). However, these alternative approaches do not offer the same degree of security or functionality of PKC. For instance, none of the random key pre-distribution schemes can guarantee key establishment between any two nodes and tolerate arbitrary node compromises at the same time. Pair-wise key establishment can always be achieved, e.g. by resorting to the Diffie-Hellman key exchange protocol (Diffie & Hellman, 1976) without suffering from the node compromise problem and without requiring time synchronization.

Thus, it is desirable to explore the application of PKC on resource constrained sensor platforms (Malan, 2004; Menezes, 1996). Elliptic Curve Cryptography (ECC) has been the top choice among various PKC options due to its fast computation, small key size, and compact signatures: for example, to provide equivalent security to 1024-bit RSA, an ECC scheme only needs 160 bits on various parameters, such as 160-bit finite field operations and 160-bit key size (Gura et al., 2004). TinyECC, targeted at TinyOS, includes almost all known optimizations for ECC operations.

Taking into account the above considerations, we will show how the "hybrid" topology-based authentication logic (Topology Authenticated Key Scheme, TAKS) we proposed in (Pugliese & Santucci, 2008) can be enhanced using an ECC-based vector algebra (and, therefore, we now denote as ECTAKS) and be compatible with TinyECC.

3.2 EC Extensions to vector algebra over GF

Before starting with ECTAKS description, it is necessary to introduce some new algebraic tools and, specifically, the extension to elliptic curves of vector algebra over GF(q). Let $GF(q_E)$ be a finite field and let $x^3 + ax + b$, where $a,b \in GF(q_E)$, be a cubic polynomial with the condition that $4a^3 + 27b^2 \neq 0$ (this ensures that the polynomial has no multiple roots); an elliptic curve E over $GF(q_E)$ is the set of points (x,y) with $x,y \in GF(q_E)$ that satisfies the condition $y^2 = x^3 + ax + b$ and also an element denoted O called the "point at infinity": the point at infinity is the point of intersection where the y-axis and the line at infinity (the collection of points on the projective plane for which z=0) meet. The elements over $E(GF(q_E))$, or the point in E, are denoted #E which results to be a function of q_E. An elliptic curve E can be made into an Abelian group by defining an additive operation on its points (Koblitz, 1987). As the elements of a group can be generated starting from a base element, or generator, by successive multiplications with scalars, we introduce a supplementary field GF(q) with $q \geq \#E$, (therefore q is function of q_E) and, as in TAKS, $q > N$ where N represents the total number of nodes in the network (Pugliese & Santucci, 2008). It is important to note that ECTAK results to be a point on E.

Let V be a vector space over GF(q) with the generic element $\underline{v} \in V$ represented through the 3-pla (v_x, v_y, v_z) with $v_x, v_y, v_z \in$ GF(q), let V_E be a vector space over E with the generic element in $V \in V_E$ represented through the 3-pla (V_1, V_2, V_3) with $V_1, V_2, V_3 \in$ E; let P, Q be points in E. We will denote elements in V as "scalar vectors" because their components are scalars in GF(q), and elements in V_E as "point vectors" because their components are points in E. ECC algebra introduces the "scalar by point product" (the operator symbol is usually omitted) which coincides with the addition of a point by itself many times the value of the scalar.

ECC vector algebra introduces two new operators: the "scalar vector by point product" (denoted by the symbol $\circ$) and the "scalar vector by point vector product" (denoted by the symbol $\otimes$). Identity elements are $0 \in GF(q)$, $\underline{0} = (0,0,0) \in V$ and $\underline{O} = (O,O,O) \in V_E$.

The operator "scalar vector by point product" is a function formally represented as $\circ : V \times E \to V_E$ and defined by

$$\underline{v} \circ P = (v_x, v_y, v_z) \circ P \equiv (v_x P, v_y P, v_z P) \tag{1}$$

It is straightforward to show that

$$\begin{aligned} \underline{0} \circ P &= (0,0,0) \circ P = (0P, 0P, 0P) = (O,O,O) \\ \underline{v} \circ O &= (v_x, v_y, v_z) \circ O = (v_x O, v_y O, v_z O) = (O,O,O) \end{aligned} \tag{2}$$

and the distributive of $\circ$ respect to + and vice-versa:

$$\begin{aligned} &(\underline{a} + \underline{b}) \circ P = \\ &= ((a_x + b_x)P, (a_y + b_y)P, (a_z + b_z)P) \\ &= ((a_x P + b_x P), (a_y P + b_y P), (a_z P + b_z P)) \\ &= \underline{a} \circ P + \underline{b} \circ P \end{aligned} \tag{3}$$

$$\begin{aligned} &\underline{v} \circ (P + Q) = \\ &= (v_x, v_y, v_z) \circ (P + Q) \\ &= (v_x (P + Q), v_y (P + Q), v_z (P + Q)) \\ &= ((v_x P + v_x Q), (v_y P + v_y Q), (v_z P + v_z Q)) \\ &= \underline{v} \circ P + \underline{v} \circ Q \end{aligned} \tag{4}$$

The operator "scalar vector by point vector product" is a function formally represented as $\otimes : V \times V_E \to E$ and defined by

$$\underline{v} \otimes \underline{V} = (v_x, v_y, v_z) \otimes (V_1, V_2, V_3) \equiv v_x V_1 + v_y V_2 + v_z V_3 \tag{5}$$

It is straightforward to show that

$$\begin{aligned} \underline{0} \otimes \underline{V} &= (0,0,0) \otimes (V_1, V_2, V_3) = 0V_1 + 0V_2 + 0V_3 = O \\ \underline{v} \otimes \underline{O} &= (v_x, v_y, v_z) \otimes (O,O,O) = v_x O + v_y O + v_z O = O \end{aligned} \tag{6}$$

and the distributive of $\otimes$ respect to + and vice-versa:

$$\begin{aligned} &(\underline{a} + \underline{b}) \otimes \underline{U} = (\underline{a} + \underline{b}) \otimes (U_1, U_2, U_3) \\ &= (a_x + b_x)U_1 + (a_y + b_y)U_2 + (a_z + b_z)U_3 = \underline{a} \otimes \underline{U} + \underline{b} \otimes \underline{U} \end{aligned} \tag{7}$$

$$\begin{aligned} &\underline{v} \otimes (\underline{V} + \underline{W}) = (v_x, v_y, v_z) \otimes (V_1 + W_1, V_2 + W_2, V_2 + W_2) \\ &= v_x (V_1 + W_1) + v_y (V_2 + W_2) + v_z (V_3 + W_3) = \underline{v} \otimes \underline{V} + \underline{v} \otimes \underline{W} \end{aligned} \tag{8}$$

The following identity $\underline{u} \otimes (\underline{v} \circ P) \equiv (\underline{u} \cdot \underline{v})P$ holds:

$$\begin{aligned} &\underline{u} \otimes (\underline{v} \circ P) = \\ &= \underline{u} \otimes (v_x P, v_y P, v_z P) = (u_x, u_y, u_z) \otimes (v_x P, v_y P, v_z P) \\ &= u_x v_x P + u_y v_y P + u_z v_z P = (\underline{u} \cdot \underline{v})P \end{aligned} \tag{9}$$

where the operator $\cdot$ denotes the usual scalar product between two vectors of scalars.

3.3 The scheme

Along what done for TAKS, ECTAKS is pair-wise, deterministic, shared keys are not pre-distributed but instead generated starting from partial key components. It exploits the impracticability in solving the Elliptic Curve Discrete Logarithm Problem (EDLP), the analogous of the discrete logarithm problem (DLP) applied to integers on GF(q) (Menezes et al., 1996).

Let V be a vector space over GF(q), V_E be a vector space over E, $f()$ be a function defined on GF(q) and $F()$ defined on E satisfying the following requirements:

- R1. Both $f()$ and $F()$ are one-way functions
- R2. $f(\underline{u}) * f(\underline{u}') = f(\underline{u}') * f(\underline{u}) \neq 0$ for $\forall \underline{u}, \underline{u}' \in V$ and for any commutative operator $*$
- R3. $F(\underline{u}, \underline{U}) = F(\underline{U}, \underline{u})$ for $\forall \underline{u} \in V$ and $\forall \underline{U} \in V_E$.

Let $G(.)$ a function defined on E satisfying the following requirements:

- R4. It must be a one-way function
- R5. $G(\underline{u}, \underline{U}) =$ O must hold only for $\underline{u} \in V' \subset V$ and $\underline{U} \in V'_E \subset V_E$, with V' and V'_E predefined sub-spaces of V and V_E respectively.

Definitions stated for TAKS in (Pugliese & Santucci, 2008) still hold true: each node stores the following information:

- Private Key Component (PRKC) which is a vector of scalars over GF(q)
- Public Key Component (PUKC) which is a vector of points over E
- Local Topology Vector (LTV) which is a vector of scalars over GF(q).

Information is classified according to the following definitions:

- *Public*: any information anyone can access (attackers included)
- *Restricted*: any information any node in the network can access
- *Private*: any information only a single node in the network can access
- *Secret*: any information only the planner can access.

According to Kerkhoff's principle, the explicit expressions for both $f()$ and G(.) are public. Fig. 2 reports the conceptual representation of the proposed scheme.

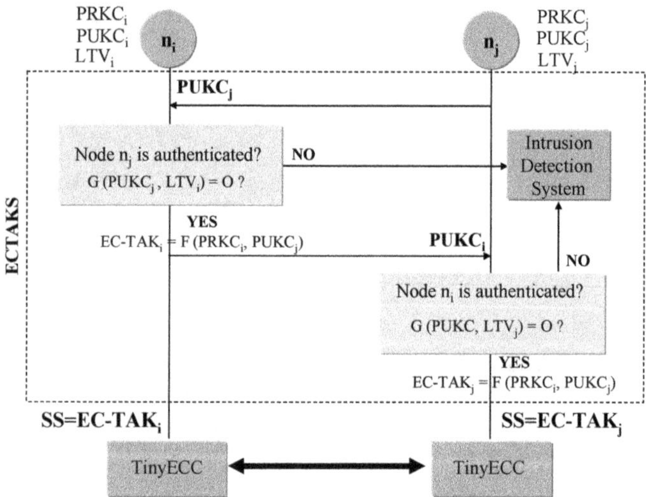

Fig. 2. Conceptual representation of the proposed cryptographic scheme

Node n_j broadcasts $PUKC_j$ and, among the others, node n_i receives it and starts the authentication procedure by executing the verification function $G()$ with inputs LTV_i and $PUKC_j$: if the result is the point at infinity O then node n_j has been successfully authenticated by node n_i and $ECTAK_i$ is generated. The same steps are performed by node n_j and, in case of successful authentication, $ECTAK_j$ is generated. If $f()$ and $F()$ are compliant to requirements R1, R2 and R3, then $ECTAK_i$ and $ECTAK_j$ coincide and ECTAK is a symmetric key shared between nodes n_i and n_j. Therefore ECTAK defines the Shared Secret (SS) which is a mandatory common information shared by parties to encrypt and decrypt messages in standard ECC schemes, such as ECDSA, ECDH, ECIES implemented in TinyECC.

Let n_i and n_j be a nodes pair. The following definitions are assumed:

a. Let $A \subseteq V$, $M \subseteq V$. Elements in A are defined as follows: $\forall \underline{a}_i, \underline{a}_j \in A$ if $\underline{m} \cdot (\underline{a}_i \times \underline{a}_j) \neq 0$ with $\underline{m} \in M$ an arbitrary predefined vector over GF(q): this information is *secret*

b. Let $b \in B \subseteq GF(q)$ be an arbitrary predefined scalar in B but not generator of GF(q): this information is *secret*

c. Let $\underline{c} \in C \subseteq V$ be an arbitrary predefined vector over GF(q): this information is *secret*

d. Let $f() = kb^{\underline{m} \cdot (.)}$ where $\underline{m} \in M$ satisfies (a) and $k \in GF(q)$. This definition for $f()$ is compliant to specified requirements R1, R2 and R3 because for $\forall \underline{v}, \underline{v}' \in V$ and $\forall k \in GF(q)$ is $kb^{\underline{m} \cdot \underline{v}} * kb^{\underline{m} \cdot \underline{v}'} = kb^{\underline{m} \cdot \underline{v}'} * kb^{\underline{m} \cdot \underline{v}} = |k|^2 b^{\underline{m} \cdot (\underline{v} + \underline{v}')} = |k|^2 b^{\underline{m} \cdot (\underline{v}' + \underline{v})}$, where $*$ is the mod q product (commutative) operator. Hereinafter the symbol $*$ will be omitted

e. Let $\underline{k}_{li}$, $\underline{k}_{lj} \in KL \subseteq V$ (this information is *private*)

f. Let $\underline{K}_{ti}$, $\underline{K}_{tj} \in KT \subseteq V_E$ (this information is *public*)

g. Let $LTV_i \in V$. Elements LTV_i are defined to be co-planar to $\underline{m}$ and $\underline{a}_j$ if n_j is an admissible neighbor of node n_i, or is "topology authenticated" (this information is *private*)

h. Let $\alpha, \beta \in GF(q)$ be a random scalars in GF(q) generated by n_i and n_j respectively (this information is *secret*)

i. Let $E: y^2 = x^3 + ax + b$ and $P \in E$ be respectively an elliptic curve E and a point in E both compliant to security requirements in (Certicom Research Standards, n.d.) (this information is *public*).

Setting $k \equiv b^{\underline{m} \cdot \underline{c}}$ in the definition of $f()$:

$$\begin{cases} \underline{k}_{li} \equiv \alpha \underline{a}_i f(\underline{a}_i) = \alpha \underline{a}_i b^{\underline{m} \cdot (\underline{a}_i + \underline{c})} \\ \underline{K}_{ti} \equiv \alpha \underline{k}_{ti} \circ P = \alpha (\underline{s}_i \times \underline{a}_i) \circ P \end{cases} \tag{10}$$

$$\begin{cases} \underline{k}_{l_j} \equiv \beta \underline{a}_j f(\underline{a}_j) = \beta \underline{a}_j b^{\underline{m} \cdot (\underline{a}_j + \underline{c})} \\ \underline{K}_{t_j} \equiv \beta \underline{k}_{t_j} \circ P = \beta (\underline{s}_j \times \underline{a}_j) \circ P \end{cases} \tag{11}$$

where setting now $k \equiv 1$ in the definition of $f()$:

$$\begin{cases} \underline{s}_i = \underline{m} f(\underline{a}_i) = \underline{m} b^{\underline{m} \cdot \underline{a}_i} \\ \underline{s}_j = \underline{m} f(\underline{a}_j) = \underline{m} b^{\underline{m} \cdot \underline{a}_j} \end{cases} \tag{12}$$

According to Kerkhoff's principle, the explicit expressions for $\underline{k}_l$ and $\underline{K}_t$ are *public*.

Given **m**, **c**, b and for $\forall \underline{a}_i, \underline{a}_j \in A$, the following properties hold true:

1. Always $ECTAK \neq O$. This follows from the condition $\underline{m} \cdot (\underline{a}_i \times \underline{a}_j) \neq 0$ assumed in (a) with $\forall P \neq O$
2. Elements in KL are always distinct, i.e. for $\forall \underline{k}_{l_i}, \underline{k}_{l_j} \in KL$ is $\underline{k}_{l_i} \times \underline{k}_{l_j} \neq 0$ which can be derived from $\underline{m} \cdot (\underline{a}_i \times \underline{a}_j) \neq 0$ assumed in (a)
3. Elements in KT are always distinct, i.e. for $\forall \underline{K}_{t_i}, \underline{K}_{t_j} \in KT$ is $\underline{k}_{ti} \times \underline{k}_{tj} \neq 0$ with $\forall P \neq O$ which can be derived from $\underline{k}_{li} \times \underline{k}_{l_j} \neq 0$ and $\underline{k}_{ti} // \underline{m} \times \underline{k}_{li}$ and $\underline{k}_{tj} // \underline{m} \times \underline{k}_{lj}$ (compare (10), (11) and (12))
4. In each node is $\underline{k}_l \otimes \underline{K}_t \equiv O$ that is $\underline{k}_l \cdot \underline{k}_t \equiv 0$ with $\forall P \neq O$ which can de derived from the vector identity $\underline{s} \cdot (\underline{a} \times \underline{a}) \equiv 0$ for $\forall \underline{s}$.

Theorem (ECTAK Generation). In a node pair n_i and n_j, given $\underline{m} \in M$ and $\underline{a}_i, \underline{a}_j \in A$ as defined in (a), $b \in B$ as defined in (b), $\underline{c} \in C$ as defined in (c), $\underline{k}_{l_i}$, $\underline{k}_{l_j}$ as defined in (e), $\underline{K}_{t_i}$ and $\underline{K}_{t_j}$ as defined in (f), α, β as defined in (h), and if $ECTAK_i$ and $ECTAK_j$ are defined as:

$$ECTAK_i \equiv \left| \underline{k}_{l_i} \otimes \underline{K}_{t_j} \right| \tag{13}$$

and

$$ECTAK_j \equiv \left| \underline{k}_{l_j} \otimes \underline{K}_{t_i} \right| \tag{14}$$

then ECTAK is a symmetric key defined as follows:

$$ECTAK = ECTAK_i = ECTAK_j = \alpha\beta b^{\underline{m} \cdot (\underline{a}_i + \underline{a}_j)} k \left| \underline{m} \cdot (\underline{a}_i \times \underline{a}_j) \right| P \tag{15}$$

Proof. The proof is straightforward: putting (10) into (13), exploiting the vector algebra property $\underline{a} \cdot (\underline{s}' \times \underline{a}') \equiv \underline{s}' \cdot (\underline{a}' \times \underline{a})$ and the property (9) then

$$\begin{aligned} ECTAK_i &\equiv \underline{k}_{l_i} \otimes \underline{K}_{t_j} \\ &= \underline{k}_{l_i} \otimes (\underline{k}_{t_j} \circ P) = (\underline{k}_{l_i} \cdot \underline{k}_{t_j}) P \\ &= \alpha \underline{a}_i k b^{\underline{m} \cdot \underline{a}_i} \cdot (\underline{s}_j \times \beta \underline{a}_j)\, P = \alpha\beta b^{\underline{m} \cdot \underline{a}_i} k \underline{s}_j \cdot (\underline{a}_j \times \underline{a}_i)\, P \end{aligned} \tag{16}$$

Putting (11) into (14), exploiting the property $\underline{a}_j \cdot (\underline{s}_i \times \underline{a}_i) \equiv \underline{s}_i \cdot (\underline{a}_i \times \underline{a}_j)$ and the property (9) then

$$\begin{aligned} ECTAK_j &\equiv \underline{k}_{l_j} \otimes \underline{K}_{t_i} \\ &= \underline{k}_{l_j} \otimes (\underline{k}_{t_i} \circ P) = (\underline{k}_{l_j} \cdot \underline{k}_{t_i}) P \\ &= \beta \underline{a}_j k b^{\underline{m} \cdot \underline{a}_j} \cdot (\underline{s}_i \times \alpha \underline{a}_i)\, P = \beta\alpha b^{\underline{m} \cdot \underline{a}_j} k \underline{s}_i \cdot (\underline{a}_i \times \underline{a}_j)\, P \end{aligned} \tag{17}$$

Putting (12) into (16) and (17), the expression (15) is obtained in both cases and the proof is completed. Q.E.D.

Theorem (Node Topology Authentication). In a node pair n_i and n_j, if $LTV_i \otimes \underline{K}_{tj} = O$ then node n_j is an admissible neighbor of node n_i or, node n_j is authenticated by n_i.

Proof. By definition (g) if node n_j is an admissible neighbor of node n_i (or "topology authenticated" by n_i) then LTV_i must be co-planar to $\underline{m}$ and $\underline{a}_j$, hence $LTV_i \cdot (\underline{m} \times \underline{a}_j) \equiv 0$ and therefore $LTV_i \cdot \underline{k}_{tj} = 0$; by multiplying both terms by $P \neq O$, it turns out $LTV_i \otimes \underline{K}_{tj} = O$. It is straightforward to show that function $G(\underline{u},\underline{U}) \equiv \underline{u} \otimes \underline{U}$ is compliant to requirements R4 and R5. QED.

Node authentication by topology information introduces an important security improvement in the family of TinyECC cryptographic schemes because only the integrity check (by means of the Key Derivation Function) of the received crypto-text is actually implemented there.

3.4 Security and cost analysis

We will show how ECTAKS can enhance the security level provided by TAKS: the relevant questions and related answers are as follows:

1. Which is the entropy per binit associated to ECTAK? ECTAK entropy per binit is $\cong 1$ which is the same result for TAKS (Pugliese & Santucci, 2008) as uncertainty about $\underline{K}_t = \underline{k}_t \circ P$ is the same as it is about $\underline{k}_t$ being P a known point.
2. How much complex is the inverse problem to break ECTAKS (security level in a single node)? For the EDLP over E to be intractable, it is important to select an appropriate E (it must be a non-supersingular curve) and q_E such that #E is divisible by a large prime or such that q_E is itself a large prime. Most significantly, no index-calculus-type algorithms are known for EDLP as for the DLP (Menezes et al., 1996). For this reason, the EDLP is believed to be much harder than DLP in that no subexponential-time general-purpose algorithm is known.

The cost is measured in terms of computational time. We assume to employ 128 bit ECTAK keys (i.e. $q = 2^{128}$): it can be shown that (15) can be computed through ~60000 16-bit operations (additions and products). If MicaZ motes are employed (8-bit processor MPR2400 @ 7.4 MHz), and assuming 10 clock cycles / operation, the cost in terms of computation time for the calculation of a 128-bit ECTAK is estimated to be about ~80 ms.

4. Weak process-based intrusion detection system (WIDS)

4.1 Motivations

The further security service component in our Secure Platform is the intrusion detection logic (IDS). Its main function is to identify abnormal network activity that differs from the expected behavior (Kaplantzis, 2004; Karlof & Wagner, 2003; Roosta et al., 2006; Sharma et al., 2010). We will show how a light state-based anomaly-based detection logic can be suited to be implemented over WSN (Ioannis et al., 2007; Jangra et al., 2011; Kalita & Kar, 2009).

Smart nodes are typically provided with mechanisms to identify changes in system parameters or anomalous exchange of information: such data can be used as relevant observations to predict the hidden state of the system and infer whether it is under attack. An Hidden Markov Model (HMM), see e.g. (Ephraim & Merhav, 2002), is a doubly stochastic finite state machine with an underlying stochastic process that represents the real state of the system: the real state of the system is hidden but indirectly observable through another stochastic process that produces a sequence of observable events. The relationships between hidden states and observable data are stochastic as well as the transitions between states. HMMs (Doumit & Agrawal, 2003; Rabiner & Juang, 1986) have been widely used in network-based IDS for wired systems (Al-Subaie & Zulkernine, 2006; Khanna & Liu, 2006; Luk et al., 2007; Sheng & Cybenko, 2005; Yin et al., 2003) as well as for modeling Internet traffic (Dainotti et al., 2008). The Baum-Welch algorithm as likelihood criterion and technique for parameter estimation in HMM is extensively used in (Doumit & Agrawal, 2003) but some training data should be available and still result expensive in terms of computational and memory costs. Some conventional intrusion detection systems perform cross-correlation and aggregation of data, e.g. by analyzing fluctuation in sensor readings (Loo, 2005) or by detecting abnormal traffic patterns (Law, 2005). In general, the application of traditional IDSs to sensor networks is challenging as they require intense computation capability or too limited to a restricted number of threats. The implementation of an effective IDS over a WSN leads to the problem of finding a trade-off between the capability of identifying threats (i.e. with a bounded false alarm rate), the complexity of the algorithms and memory usage (Baker & Prasanna, 2005; Bhatnagar et al., 2010; Jiang, 2005; Kumari et al., 2010).

Our contribution proposes a novel network-layer anomaly detection logic over WSN exploits the Weak Process Models (WPM) and is here simply denoted as WIDS (WPM-based Intrusion Detection System): WPM are a non-parametric version of HMM, wherein state transition probabilities are reduced to rules of reachability in a graph representing the abnormal behaviors (Jiang, 2005). The estimation of a threat in the case of weak processes is greatly simplified and less demanding for resources. The *most probable* state sequence generated by the Viterbi algorithm (Forney, 1973) for HMM becomes the *possible* state sequence generated by simplified estimation algorithms for WPM. The intensity of the attack is evaluated by introducing a threat score, a likelihood criterion based on weighting states and transitions (Pugliese et al., 2008).

4.2 The scheme

As stated before, if WPM are used to model behavior, the algorithm to estimate the possible state sequences (instead of the most probable ones) is much easier than Viterbi estimator (Forney, 1973). But this comes at a cost: due to the cut of lower probabilities (approximated to zero) the expressiveness in WPM could be reduced with respect to HMM and false negatives can increase. However, it has been shown that adding a certain number of further states to WPM, expressiveness could be recovered (Pugliese et al., 2008). Indeed a sort of "state explosion" can require added memory for storage but the binary matrices describing WPM are very low dense (sparse matrix) and some algebraic tricks can be adopted. Given the choice of WPM as behavior model, the question becomes: which behavior should be modeled? Our solution is based on two basic ideas: first, the adoption of an anomaly-based

IDS and, second, a "hierarchical" model for abnormal behaviors. However, even anomaly-based detection algorithms are of lower complexity than misuse-based ones, the problem to model a behaviour still remains (Debar et al., 1999): usually the question is approached by defining different regions in the observation space associated to different system behaviors. Further we apply a "state classification", i.e. we associate each defined region to a specific sub-set (class) of WPM states (not single states) according to WPM topology. State classification can reduce false negatives and false positives in anomaly detection because different state traces (therefore different behavior patterns) contain the same information leading to a useful redundancy. In (Pugliese et al., 2008, 2009) we introduced two classes: LPA (Low Potential Attack) and HPA (High Potential Attack).

Definition 1. Low Potential Attack, LPA. An attack is defined in a "low potentially dangerous" state (or in a LPA state) if the threat is estimated to be in state x_j which is at least 2 hops to the final state.

Definition 2. High Potential Attack, HPA. An attack is defined in a "high potentially dangerous" state (or in a HPA state) if the threat is estimated to be in state x_j which is 1 hop to the final state.

WIDS identifies any observable event correlated to a threat by applying a set of anomaly rules to the incoming traffic. An example of anomaly can be the event of a node receiving multiple "setup" messages in a short time, or two "topologically far" nodes (i.e. nodes whose path length is >>1 hop) to receive similar message sequences. We will show how attacks can be classified into low and high potential attacks according to specific states in the corresponding WPM-based threat model. Alarms are issued as soon as one or more high potential attacks are detected. Considered threats are "hello flooding" and the generalized version of "sinkhole" and "wormhole": we will show that any possible attack against WSN network layer protocols can be derived from these models. The security performance analysis will be carried out by computing the probability of false positives and negatives. However, WPMs technique introduces the following drawback: as very low state transition probabilities are reduced (approximated) to zero, it results an increase of false negatives as some (hazardous) sequences could be classified as not possible when instead in a probabilistic model would be achievable. The number of false negatives decreases if we add states (Pugliese et al., 2008) but the drawback is a larger memory requirement. As it will be shown in the dedicated sections, Boolean matrices that describe the models are sparse and can be compacted for faster computation. The intensity of the attack is evaluated by introducing a threat score, a likelihood criterion based on weighting states and transitions. Intrusions and violations are classified into low potential attacks (LPA) and high potential attacks (HPA) depending on their distance from the state corresponding to a successful attack. When at least one HPA occurs, an alarm is issued. Moreover we introduce a score mechanism to weight state sequences where LPA and HPA contribute differently so that it becomes possible to derive how many LPA and / or HPA states have been experimented.

Definition 3. Threat Score s at Observation Step k [s^k]. It is a weighting mechanism we apply to states and transitions in a given WPM. Weights are represented by a square $n \times n$ matrix (we denote "Score Matrix" S) whose elements are defined as follows (n is the number of states in the WPM): s_{ij} is the score assigned to the transition from x_j to x_i and s_{jj} is the score assigned to the state x_j. In (Pugliese et al., 2008) it has been shown that $s^k = Hn_{hpa}^k + Ln_{lpa}^k$ where n_{hpa}^k and n_{lpa}^k are the number of HPA and LPA states that the system is supposed to have reached up to observation step k, and L, H are values to be assigned depending on LPA and HPA state topology in WPM graph (Pugliese et al., 2008) respectively. Last we introduce the concept of Anomaly Rule, the logic filter applied to incoming signaling messages, which gives two possible results: "no anomalies", resulting in the message being processed further, or "anomaly detected" resulting in a "threat observable".

The main objective of IDS is to detect attacks coming from insider intruders, i.e. only combinations of "hello flooding", "sinkhole" and "wormhole" threats (Debar et al., 1999; Roosta et al., 2006; Singh et al. 2010; Whitman & Mattord, 2011). These attacks are based on well-formed messages generated by authenticated nodes where control information is chosen to generate malicious network topologies. IDS monitoring domain is restricted to observables associated to any combination of these threats (we denote the Aggregated Threat Model).

In summary the process can be stated through the following steps: 1) Analyze the behaviour of the threat; 2) Derive the Anomaly Rules; 3) Derive the WPM-based threat model and 4) Assign weights to WPM states and transitions. WPM-based models for single threats are shown in (Pugliese et al., 2008). Following these steps, we obtain the WPM aggregated model in Fig. 3: ovals represent states, grey border indicate the final states (X_9 and X_10), numbers into brackets the associated threat observables. LPA states are X_1, X_2, X_5 and X_6; HPA states are X_3, X_4, X_7 and X_8. A positive effect of aggregation is to enhance model effectiveness: this is due to the possible sharing of "threat observables" among different threats (as it is for "sinkhole" and "wormhole") and scores can be different. The observable $o^k = o_9$ is produced (defining a RESET state) when no threat observables are produced after K consecutive observation steps, with K a tunable threshold.

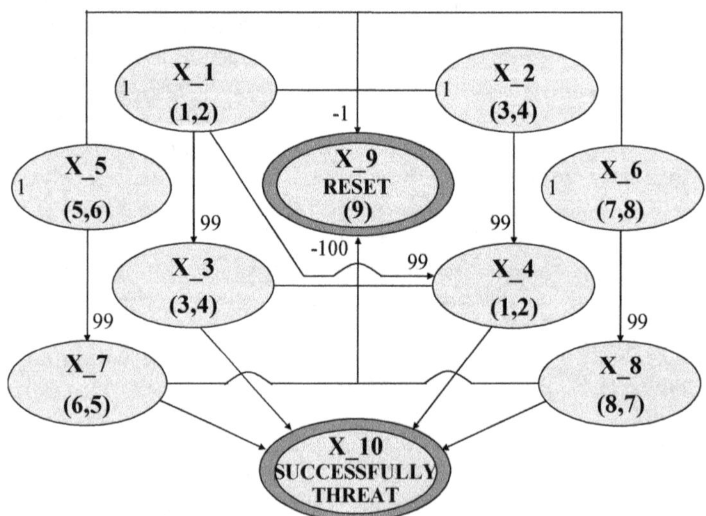

Fig. 3. The Aggregated Threat Model

4.3 Security and cost analysis

The security analysis will verify the effectiveness of the proposed IDS in terms of probabilities of false negatives and false positives. We introduce the false-negative rate (P_{neg}) which represents the rate that the detection algorithm is not able to identify an existing threat (*alarm mis-detections*), and the false-positive rate (P_{pos}) which represents the rate that the detection algorithm identifies undue threats (*false alarm detections*).

Definition 3. WPM Memory Length, WML. It is the length of the state sequence trace considered for alarms detection.

Test for alarm mis-detections (False Negatives). We will compute the false negatives probability P_{neg} by applying "ad-hoc" observables sequences to WPM model in Fig. 3 originated by "hello flooding", "sinkhole" and "wormhole" randomly aggregated. If WPM representation is structurally well-defined we should experiment always $s^k \neq 0$ (and therefore $P_{neg} \to 0$) for increasing observation steps ($k \to \infty$), for any combinations of threat behaviors. Here we report the case study with $k = 32$ observables, $WML = 10$ and $K = 3$: suppose an "hello flooding" attack has been engaged against the WSN: in this case the Anomaly Rules would produce an observable sequence of the type

$$\{5;5;*;8;7;*;*;6;6;8;8;*;*;*;8;*;\ *;5;7;*;*;7;*;6;8;*;*;*;5;5;*;*\} \quad (18)$$

and, in case of an attacking "sinkhole" / "wormhole", observable sequences like:

$$\{2;1;*;*;*;1;*;1;2;2;*;*;*;1;2;*;\ *;1;2;*;*;*;2;2;*;*;1;*;1;*;*;*\} \quad (19)$$

$$\{2;4;*;*;*;3;*;3;4;2;3;*;*;1;3;*;\ *;4;4;*;*;*;2;2;*;*;4;*;3;*;*;*\} \quad (20)$$

The symbol * means "no observable related to this threat". According to the previous considerations, we preliminarily note that:

- There are no observable sharing between "hello flooding" and "sinkhole" or "wormhole";
- Observables for "sinkhole" are also observables for "wormhole" but not vice-versa.

Simulations results are graphically reported in Fig. 4 where dark grey bars refer to scores produced by individual threat models and light grey bars refer to aggregated threat models. As expected the same outputs from both models are obtained only for threats not sharing any observable (Fig. 4 a) while different outputs are obtained for threats, as "sinkhole" and "wormhole", sharing at least one observable (Fig. 4 b).

Test for false alarm detections (False Positives). Not well-defined Anomaly Rules can produce "undecided" threat observables which lead to potential false positives, hence $P_{pos} \neq 0$. False positives are structurally zeroed if no "undecided" threat observables are associated to HPA states. Two approaches can be adopted:

1. Insert further states associated to truly "threat observables into WPM paths where states associated to "undecided" threat observables are leaves: this approach can

decrease the probability for false positives ($P_{pos} \to 0$) because the joint probability to reach the leaf state can be very low in long paths; however a drawback is that long paths could reduce the system reactivity to threats.

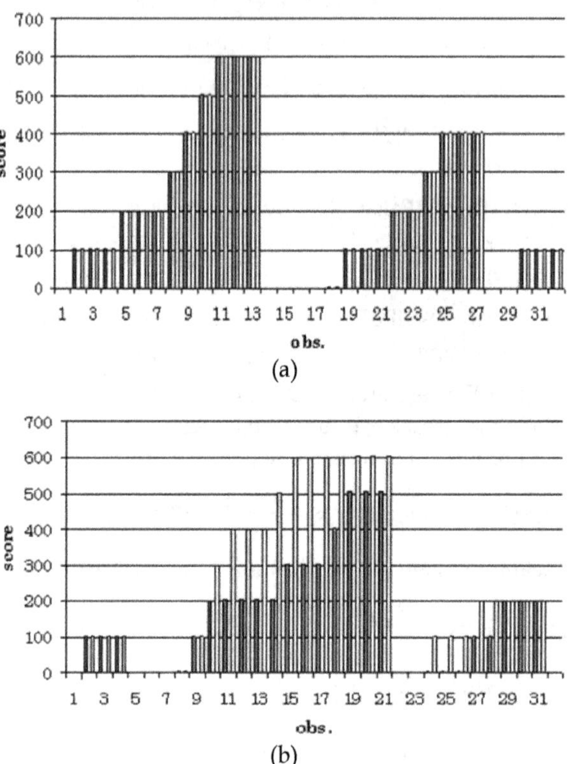

Fig. 4. Scores from single (dark grey) and aggregated model (light grey) when (a) the sequence (18) is applied and (b) the sequences (19), (20) are applied

2. Introduce a further class of states associated to "undecided" threat observables: this approach cannot decrease the probability for false positives, but "ad-hoc" lighter countermeasures can be applied to nodes where alarms from "undecided" observables are generated (e.g. node quarantine rather than link release).

The cost is measured in terms of computational time. If n are the states in the Aggregated Threat Model, we can derive that the upper bound complexity in the computation of scores and alarms is $\approx 6WML \cdot n^2$ if $WML >> n$. If MICA2 motes (CROSSBOW, n.d.) are employed (8-bit processor ATMega128L @ 7.4 MHz), and assuming 20 clock cycles per arithmetic / logic operation, the average computation time per 32-bit operation is ~ 3 μs. If IMOTE motes (MEMSIC, n.d.) are employed (32-bit processor PXA271Xscale@{312, 416} MHz), and assuming 5 clock cycles per arithmetic / logic operation, the average computation time per 32-bit operation is ~ 0.03 μs (assuming 300 MHz for the clock). Suppose the case $n = 10$ and $WML = 100$. For MICA2 the estimated computation time is ≈ 200 ms, for IMOTE ≈ 2 ms.

5. Secure platform design

The adopted architectural design (Roman et al., 2006) will be cross-layered (Kliazovich et al., 2009) and platform-based (Sangiovanni-Vincentelli & Martin, 2001). Cross-layer (CL) results in the interplay between network layer (topology management and routing protocol) and presentation layer (mobile agent based execution environment for distributed monitoring applications): applied to security, an important benefit of CL mechanism is the exploitation of the interplay between different security measures in different layers to provide an enforced security service to applications. Platform-based design (PBD) results in the availability of a software platform where the internal structure is composed by "interconnected" SW components, which represent abstractions of the wired hardware components. Achievements of research goals are sought by taking care of the following major topics: selection of the right layers in the architectural design (a middleware layer is an essential component), application of the platform-oriented concepts for service mappings between layers, enhancement of the middleware layer with security services offered by lower layers entities and, on top, the creation of a flexible AEE by means of agents.

Fig. 5 depicts WIDS functional blocks: the Threat Model (TM) block implements the WPM-based model for abnormal system behavior and the Anomaly Detection Logic (ADL) block implements detection and alarm generation functions. The Intrusion Reaction Logic (IRL) schedules the intervention priority toward the compromised nodes according to specific criteria (defense strategy); IRLA applies the countermeasures against attacks to compromised nodes, including node isolations (quarantine), key revocations, link release or inclusions in black lists / grey lists (Roman et al., 2006).

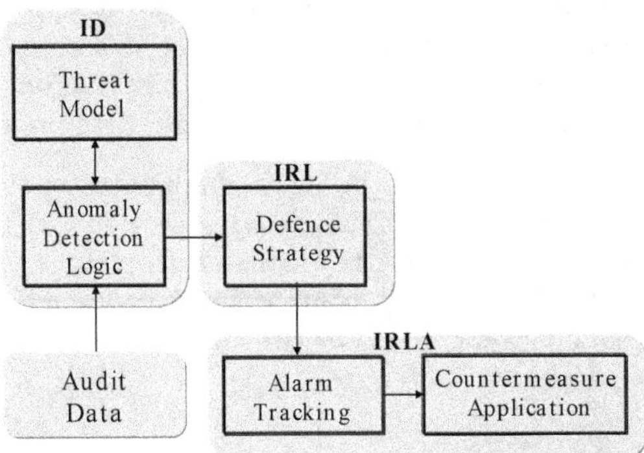

Fig. 5. WIDS functional blocks

6. Mobile agent-based middleware

A key characteristic of mobile agent-based middleware is that any host in the network is allowed a high degree of flexibility to possess any mixture of code, resources, and processors. Its processing capabilities can be combined with local resources. Code (in the form of mobile agents) is not tied to a single host but it is available throughout the network . Moreover, the mobile agent paradigm supports data-centric applications because the implementation code can migrate towards data no matter about node addressing (Hadim & Nader, 2006). Therefore in a mobile-agent application execution environment (Szumel et al.,

2005), each agent implements a sub-set of application components which can be proactively aggregated through agent mobility (code mobility across the network). Among the agent-based middleware solutions available from literature, we will refer to AGILLA (Fok et al., 2006), developed at the Washington University in St. Louis. There are different motivations for this choice. Some of these are listed in the following:

- it is developed using NesC (Gay et al., 2003) which is a component-based programming language (used to develop TinyOS): this occurrence simplifies the integration of further components in AGILLA code
- it is lighter than other mobile agent middleware solutions, e.g. Maté (Levis & Culler, 2002)
- agent mobility is selective, i.e. no code broadcast, e.g. Impala (Liu & Martonosi, 2003)
- agents hosted on adjacent nodes can share memory (through the "Tuple Space")

AGILLA middleware provides two components that facilitate inter-agent coordination: a *Tuple Space* and a *Neighbors List*, both maintained on each node by the middleware services. A Tuple Space is shared by local agents and is remotely accessible and offers a decoupled style of communication where one agent can insert a tuple, another can later read or remove it using pattern matching via a template. The Neighbors List is on every node and contains the location of all one-hop neighbors. Local agents can access it by executing special instructions. The agent architecture is described in (Fok et al., 2006). Code migration is implemented by moving or cloning an agent from one node to another. Migration can be strong or weak dependently if the current execution state is ported on the other node or not. When an agent moves, it carries its code and, if strong move, also state and resumes executing on the new node. When it clones, it copies its code and, if strong clone, state to another node and resumes executing on both the old and new nodes. Multi-hop migration is handled by the middleware and is transparent to the user. It is important to remember that AGILLA can initially deploy a network without any application installed: agents that implement the application can later be injected, actually reprogramming the network.

From the function decomposition shown in Fig. 5, the mapping between WIDS functions and SW components and mobile agents is shown in Fig. 6: ADL and TM blocks are mapped into SW components while IRL and IRLA blocks into a mobile agent, which is denoted by Intrusion Reaction Agent (IRA). SW components are indicated with smoothed squares. This design allows the optimal allocation and code distribution for those functions that should not be implemented anywhere.

6.1 Enhancements to AGILLA middleware

Current version of AGILLA foresees that only the AGILLA Manager can read and write into the Neighbor List and only the AGILLA Manager and Mobile Agents can read and write into Tuple Space.

As stated before, Neighbors List contains the location of all one-hop neighbors but topology authentication provided in ECTAKS should update this list with admissible neighbors only: therefore it would be preferred if ECTAKS could read and write into the Neighbor List as the AGILLA Manager does.

Moreover, WIDS should read and write into Tuple Space in order to manage IRA agents mobility according to the functional mapping shown in Fig. 6.

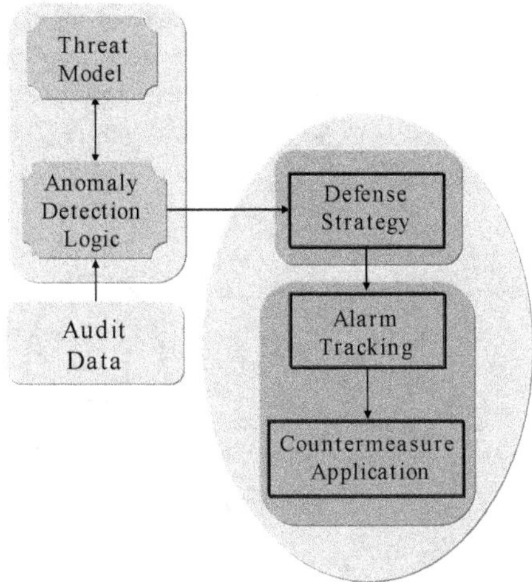

Fig. 6. Mobile Agent-based WIDS architecture

These enhancements have been designed as NesC stubs (Gay et al., 2003) embedded into AGILLA code (Pugliese et al., 2009). Fig. 7 schematically represents this added interfaces as bold arrows.

The first issue that has been actually addressed is related to the interface with the Communication Unit. In particular, the first enhancement made to AGILLA has been to add some basic mechanisms to let the agents able to retrieve some information about the radio traffic from the nodes. More in detail:

- the node-resident part of the middleware has been modified in order to allow the evaluation of some indicators, customizable by the designer, based on the analysis of the radio traffic
- the interface of the middleware towards the agents has been modified to allow an agent to retrieve the value of such indicators by pushing them on its stack.

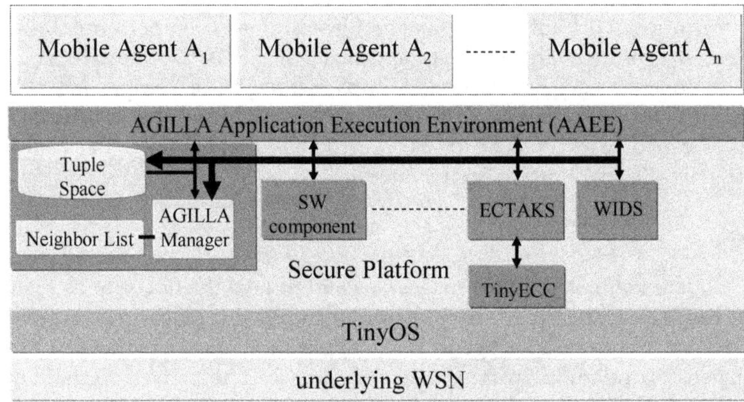

Fig. 7. Enhanced AGILLA Mobile Agent-based Secure Platform Architecture

In this way, the agents are able to check for anomalous values (i.e. alarms), as described in the previous sections. Moreover, this possibility has been added while keeping the existing interaction mechanisms between agents and nodes: the agent sees the added indicators as *virtual sensors* (Fig. 8) accessible as if they were normal sensors (i.e. light, temperature, etc...) by means of the *sense* instruction.

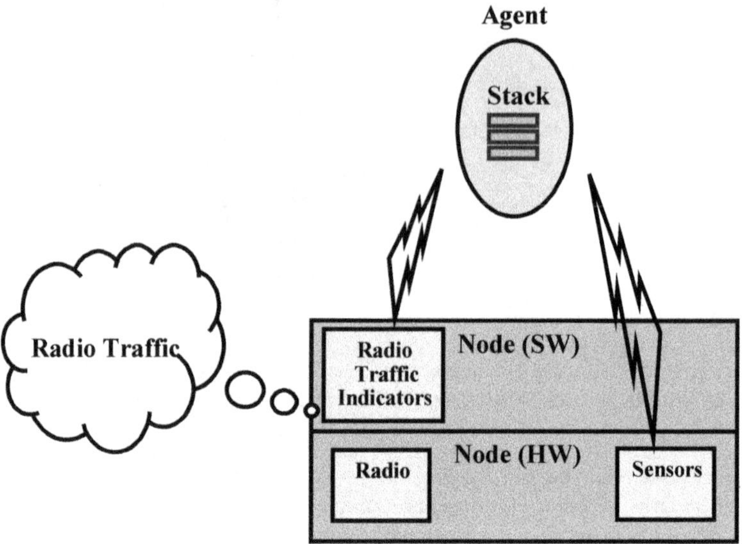

Fig. 8. Virtual Sensor Architecture

As a very simple example, if each node evaluates the number of received packets, an agent could retrieve such an information as shown in Fig. 8. It is worth noting that the approach is exactly the same as the one used to read the temperature sensor. In the sample code the agent turns on the red led when the number of received packets is larger than 10.

In order to make such a first extension to the AGILLA framework, a deep study (that will be very useful for future work) of the original architecture has been performed. First of all, it has been needed to understand the mapping mechanisms between AGILLA instructions and nesC components: each instruction is implemented by a component, stored in the *opcodes* directory, that offers the *BytecodeI* interface that includes the *execute* command. Such a command is called to execute an instruction that is identified by the codes stored in *AgillaOpcodes.h* used as parameters for the interface.

6.2 Validation

In order to validate the first AGILLA extensions and to give the flavor of its exploitation in building up the IDS proposed in the previous sections, the following example has been selected and concerns a sample agent-based application. More in details, as discussed before, by means of the middleware the agents can access to some information about the radio traffic (i.e. in this case just the number of the packets received by a node) as if they were sensor readings and can react if required.

The demo application (Fig. 9) is then based on a sample WSN composed of 4 *MicaZ* nodes and a *MIB510* board (connected to a PC) where 3 Agilla agents are injected for monitoring purposes. Such agents exploit the proposed middleware extensions and the Agilla reaction mechanism while moving on the WSN. The final goal is to detect the nodes that present one or more radio traffic indicators out of standard value (i.e. in this case the agents checks for a number of received packets larger than a defined threshold). The agents developed for such a purpose, called *TupleOut*, *Dynamic* and *Alarm*, are described in the following.

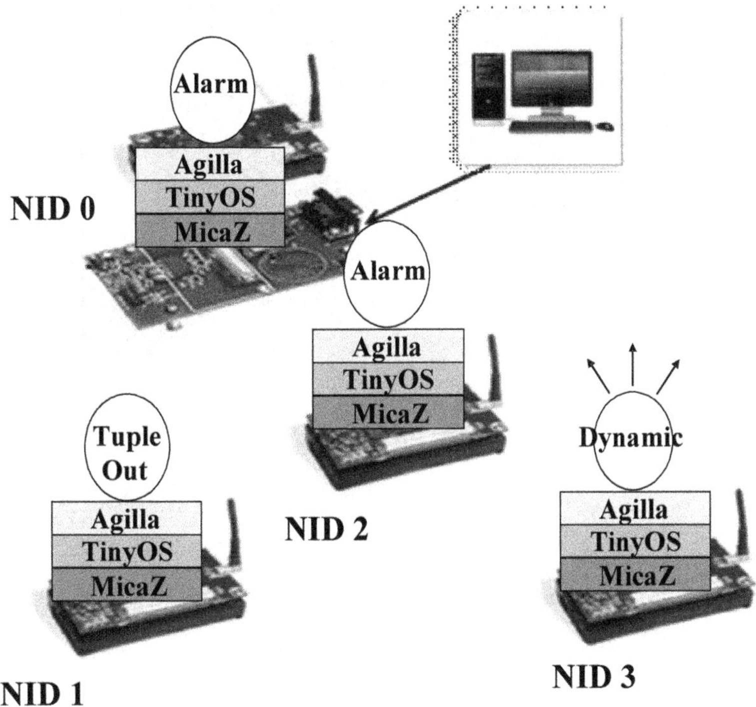

Fig. 9. Demo Application Architecture

TupleOut is a static agent, virtually present on each node to be monitored, that access to the radio traffic indicators evaluated by the node-side middleware, checks for anomalous values and insert a proper tuple on the tuple space of the node to signal an eventual alarm. In the proposed example the agents injected on node #1 checks for a number of received packets larger than 5 and, when the condition met, it inserts the alarm tuple on the Tuple Space of node #1 (Fig. 10). *Dynamic* is a dynamic (strong move in the whole WSN nodes) agent that looks for alarm tuples in the nodes tuple spaces. It exploits a template-based match by type reaction (Fig. 11) to detect an alarm tuple and then to eventually send to the Alarm agent the alarmed node ID. Finally, the *Alarm* agent is a static one that resides in the base station of the WSN (node #0). It receives alarm signals and alarmed node IDs and manages them. In the example, it simply displays by means of the leds the alarmed node ID and sends also such an information to the connected PC.

```
        // INIT
        pushc 0
        setvar 0
        // MANAGEMENT
BEGIN   pushc 25
        putled          // Red led on
        getvar 0
        copy
        inc
        setvar 0
        // CHECK
        pushc num_packets  // ID of the virtual sensor
        sense              // Read the virtual sensor
        pushcl 5           // Threshold
        cgt
        rjumpc OUT         // If > Threshold go to OUT
        pushc BEGIN        // Else go to BEGIN
        jumps
        // ALARM
OUT       pushc num_packets    // ID of the virtual
              sensor
        sense
        pushc 2             // Number of tuple fields
        out                 // Insert the alarm tuple
        rjumpc REDTOGGLE
        // EXIT (ERROR)
        halt
        // EXIT (OK)
REDTGL  pushc 8
        sleep
        pushc 25
        putled
        halt
```

Fig. 10. TupleOut Agent

```
        pusht VALUE              // Type
        pushrt num_packets       // Sensor ID
        pushc 2         // Number of fields
        pushc DO
        regrxn
```

Fig. 11. Agilla reaction

This simple demo application has been very useful to validate the first extension made to the AGILLA middleware and to give the flavor on how AGILLA agents can be used to implement the presented security framework.

7. Compliance to trusted computing paradigm

As a further aspect in performance assessment and evolution perspectives, it is worth noting that the proposed platform can be compliant to the emerging trusted computing guidelines (TCG, n.d.). Nevertheless, some attention should be paid in the mapping process of roles and functions defined in (TCG Best Practice Committee, 2011) to the underlying technology and application scenario of our Secure Platform: as stated in the Introduction, the main service supported and enabled by the Secure Platform consists in monitoring structural and functional health of industrial plants, which indeed can be configured as an "industrial" service. An item-by-item preliminar analysis of compliance to TCG paradigm has lead to the following results.

- **Security**: security modules embedded into the proposed platform can achieve controlled access to some critical secured data (e.g. monitoring measurements). They also provide reliable measurements and reports of the system's security properties through the ciphered mobile code transfer mechanism among sensor nodes. The reporting mechanism can be fully kept under the owner's control through proprietary format messages feedbacks.
- **Privacy**: data mainly refer to physical quantities related to the industrial plant under monitoring in the considered application scenario. Detection data and observable results are transmitted and stored in ciphered mode among Tuple Spaces and the random nature of some one-shot cryptographic parameters (see Sec. 3.3 h) enhance service confidentiality and reliability, so that the system can be reasonably made compliant to all relevant guidelines, laws, and regulations applicable to this case.
- **Interoperability**: the adoption of both a platform-based design and a cross-layered architecture configures primitives, interfaces and protocols as building blocks of the platform model; therefore, the conformance to TCG specifications [TCG WG, 2007] can be achieved when compatible with resource limitations of the underlying WSN.
- **Portability of data**: it does not completely apply in the considered application scenario, as the definition of alarms and observables is based on limited temporal sequences which are gradually overwritten in each Tuple Space.
- **Controllability**: the analysis of this item requests some clarifications about the role of "owner" and "user": in the considered application scenario, for security and safety reasons, the owner of the platform necessarily coincides with the owner of the system under monitoring and the "user" can ultimately be represented by a specialized operator. User-related information is not present in the system and it never affects service operations, the relationship owner - user thus being strictly hierarchical: therefore, some sub-items cannot apply (e.g. the user be able to reliably disable the TCG functionality in a way that does not violate the owner's policy).
- **Ease-of-use**: usually specialized SW applications (installed at user premises) devoted to post-processing and decision support are comprehensible and usable by specialized trained personnel.

8. Conclusions and perspectives

In this chapter we have proposed novel contributions about definition of cryptography and anomaly detection rules in wireless sensor networks and their implementation in a cross-layered framework design that we denote "Secure Platform". Security functions are executed autonomously by nodes in the network without any support from outside (like servers or database). The proposed schemes have been validated using MATLAB simulations and a prototype implementation through mobile agents supported by a MicaZ wireless sensor network. This work is a partial achievement of the internal project WINSOME (**WI**reless sensor **N**etwork-based **S**ecure system f**O**r structural integrity **M**onitoring and Al**E**rting) at DEWS, whose target is to develop a cross-layer secure framework for advanced monitoring and alerting applications.

Current work is concerned with several developments. One objective is to extend WIDS to detect anomalies in data message content and signaling as well: in this frame bayesian analysis and decision techniques (e.g. the Dempster-Shafer theory) have been successfully applied in traditional networks where resource availability is not a problem, but in WSNs it might be a big issue. Current research, jointly done with our research partners, deals with this topic and we are extending the Weak Process Models approach to this case and to derive new "threat observables" in WIDS. Another important issue is to consider monitoring as a component in a control process where correlated actuations on the environment can be performed. This vision implies the integration of Hybrid System Control (Di Benedetto et al., 2009) items into the service platform. Another issue consists in the definition of the defense strategy in IDS: rather than listing the possible countermeasures, the question is about how to schedule the priorities in case of multiple interventions on the network. A multi-constraints (hazardousness and distribution of the estimated threat vs. available resources) optimization problem can be a solution.

Finally, from a signal processing and communication viewpoint, some efforts have been already devoted to optimize the information flow on WSNs: the existing correlation among measurement information taken from "contiguous" sensing units should be exploited to increase coding efficiency without losses (the Slepian-Wolf coding theory).

9. Acknowledgment

We would like to thank Dr. Annarita Giani (UC Berkeley) for the joint work and the long discussions, so stimulating and profitable, on our common research items. Thanks to AGILLA Project group and, in particular, Dr. Chien-Liang Fok (Washington University at St. Louis). We also would like to thank Ms. Francesca Falcone and Ms. Catia Maiorani, two Master students of the University of L'Aquila who have actively collaborated to some of the design and implementation activities reported in this chapter during their thesis work.

Furthermore, the research leading to these results has received funding from the European Union Seventh Framework Programme [FP7/2007-2013] under grant agreement n° 257462 HYCON2 Network of excellence and has been motivated and supported by the ESF-COST Action IntelliCIS (Prof. Fortunato Santucci is participating to this Action).

10. References

Akyildiz, I.F.; Su, W.; Sankarasubramaniam, Y. & Cayirci, E. (2002). A Survey on Sensor Networks, *IEEE Communications Magazine*, August 2002

Al-Subaie, M. & Zulkernine, M. (2006). Efficacy of Hidden Markov Models Over Neural Networks in Anomaly Intrusion Detection, *Proceedings of the 30th Annual International Computer Software and Applications Conference (COMPSAC)*, vol. 1, 2006

Bai, H.; Atiquzzaman, M. & Lilja, D. (2004). Wireless Sensor Network for Aircraft Health Monitoring, *Proceedings of Broadband Networks'04*, 2004

Baker, Z., & Prasanna, V. (2005). Computationally-efficient Engine for flexible Intrusion Detection, *IEEE Transactions on Very Large Scale Integration (VLSI) Systems*, vol. 13, n. 10, 2005

Barbaràn, J.; Diaz, M.; Esteve, I. & Rubio, B. (2007). RadMote: A Mobile Framework for Radiation Monitoring in Nuclear Power Plants," *Proceedings of the 21st International Conference on Computer, Electrical, Systems Science and Engineering (CESSE'07)*, 2007

Bhatnagar, R.; Srivastava, A. K. & Sharma, A. (2010). An Implementation Approach for Intrusion Detection System in Wireless Sensor Network, *International Journal on Computer Science and Engineering*, vol. 2, no. 7, 2010

Certicom Research Standards, http://www.secg.org/

Cho, S.; Yun, C.-B.; Lynch, J. P. ; Zimmerman, A.; Spencer Jr B. & Nagayama, T. (2008). Smart Wireless Sensor Technology for Structural Health Monitoring of Civil Structures, *International Journal of Steel Structures, KSSC*, pp. 267-275, 2008

CROSSBOW Inc., http://www.xbow.com/

Dainotti, A.; Pescapè A.; Rossi, P.; Palmieri, F. & Ventre, G. (2008). Internet Traffic Modeling by means of Hidden Markov Models, Computer Networks, Elsevier, vol. 52, no. 14, 2008

Debar, H.; Dacier, M. & Wespi, A. (1999). Towards a Taxonomy of Intrusion-Detection Systems, *International Journal of Computer and Telecommunications Networking*, pp. 805–822, 1999

Di Benedetto, M. D.; Di Gennaro, S. & D'Innocenzo, A. (2009). Discrete State Observability of Hybrid Systems, *International Journal of Robust and Nonlinear Control*, vol. 19, n. 14 2009

Diffie, W. & Hellman, M.E. (1976). New Directions in Cryptography, *IEEE Transactions on Information Theory, IT-22:644–654*, November 1976

Doumit, S. & Agrawal, D. (2003). Self Organized Critically and Stochastic Learning Based Intrusion Detection System for Wireless Sensor Networks, *Proceedings of the Military Communications Conference (MILCOM)*, 2003

Ephraim, Y. & Merhav, N. (2002). Hidden Markov Processes, *IEEE Trans. Information Theory*, vol. 48, no. 6, 2002

Eschenauer, L. & Gligor, V.D. (2002). A key-management Scheme for Distributed Sensor Networks, *Proceedings of the 9th ACM Conference on Computer and Communications Security*, 2002

Flammini, F.; Gaglione, A.; Mazzocca, N.; Moscato, V. & Pragliola, C. (2008). Wireless Sensor Data Fusion for Critical Infrastructure Security, *Proceedings of International Workshop on Computational Intelligence in Security for Information Systems, CISIS'08*, 2008

Fok, C.-L.; Roman, G.C. & Lu, C. (2006). Agilla: A Mobile Agent Middleware for Sensor Networks, *Technical Report, Washington University in St. Louis,* WUCSE-2006-16, 2006

Forney, G. (1973). The Viterbi Algorithm, *Proceedings IEEE*, vol. 61, pp. 263–278, 1973

Gay, D.; Levis, P.; von Behren, R.; Welsh, M.; Brewer, E. & Culler, D. (2003). The nesC Language: A Holistic Approach to Networked Embedded Systems, *Proceedings of ACM SIGPLAN*, 2003

Gura, N.; Patel, A. & Wander, A. (2004). Comparing Elliptic Curve Cryptography and RSA on 8-bit CPUs, *Proceedings of the 2004 Workshop on Cryptographic Hardware and Embedded Systems (CHES 2004)*, 2004.

Hadim, S. & Nader, M. (2006). Middleware: Middleware Challenges and Approaches for Wireless Sensor Networks, *IEEE Distributed Systems on-line 1541-4922, IEEE Computer Society*, vol. 7, n. 3, 2006

Hu, F.; Ziobro, J.; Tillett, J. & Sharma, N. (2004). Secure Wireless Sensor Networks: Problems and Solutions, *Journal on Systemic, Cybernetics and Informatics*, vol. 1, n. 9, 2004

Ioannis, K.; Dimitriou, T. & Freiling, F. C. (2007). Towards Intrusion Detection in Wireless Sensor Networks, *Proceedings of the 13th European Wireless Conference*, 2007

Jangra, A.; Richa, S. & Verma, R. (2011). Vulnerability and Security Analysis of Wireless Sensor Networks, *International Journal of Applied Engineering Research*, vol. 6, no. 2, 2011

Jiang, G. (2005). Robust Process Detection using Nonparametric Weak Models, *International Journal of Intelligent Control and Systems*, vol. 10, 2005

Kalita, H. K. & Kar, A. (2009). Wireless Sensor Networks Security Analysis, *International Journal of Next-Generation Networks*, vol. 1, n. 1, 2009

Kaplantzis, S. (2004). Classification Techniques for Network Intrusion Detection, *Technical Report*, Monash University, 2004

Karlof, C. & Wagner, D. (2003). Secure Routing in Wireless Sensor Networks: Attacks and Countermeasures, *Proceedings of the 1st IEEE International Workshop on Sensor Network Protocols and Applications*, vol. 10, 2003

Khanna, R. & Liu, H. (2006). System Approach to Intrusion Detection Using Hidden Markov Model, *Proceedings of the International Conference on Wireless Communications and Mobile Computing*, vol. 5, pp. 349 - 354, 2006

Kim, S.; Pakzad, S.; Culler, D.; Demmel, J.; Fenves, G.; Glaser, S. & Turon, M. (2007). Health Monitoring of Civil Infrastructures Using Wireless Sensor Networks, *Proceedings of the 6th International Conference on Information Processing in Sensor Networks IPSN 07*, 2007.

Kliazovich, D.; Devetsikiotis M. & Granelli, F. (2009). Formal Methods in Cross Layer Modeling and Optimization of Wireless Networks, Handbook of Research on Heterogeneous Next Generation Networking, 2009, pp. 1-24.

Koblitz, N. (1987). Elliptic Curve Cryptosystems, *Mathematics of Computation*, vol. 48, pp. 203-229, 1987

Kumari, P.; Kumar, M. & Rishi, R. (2010). Study of Security in Wireless Sensor Networks, *International Journal of Computer Science and Information Technologies*, vol. 1, n. 5, 2010

Law, Y.; Havinga, P. & Johnson, D. (2005). How to Secure a Wireless Sensor Network, *Proceedings of the International Conference on Intelligent Sensors, Sensor Networks and Information Processing*, 2005

Levis, P. & Culler, D. (2002). Matè: a Tiny Virtual Machine for Sensor Networks, *Proceedings of the 10th International Conference on Architectural support for programming languages and operating systems*, ACM Press, 2002

Liu, A.; Kampanakis, P. & Ning, P. (2008). TinyECC: Elliptic Curve Cryptography for Sensor Setworks (v.0.3), http://discovery.csc.ncsu.edu/software/TinyECC/, 2008

Liu, T. & Martonosi M. (2003). Impala: A Middleware System for Managing Autonomic Parallel Sensor Systems, *Proceedings of ACM SIGPLAN Symposium on Principles and Practice of Parallel Programming (PPoPP 2003)*, 2003

Loo, C.; Ng, M.; Leckie, C. & Palaniswami, M. (2005). Intrusion Detection for Routing Attacks in Sensor Networks, *International Journal of Distributed Sensor Networks*, 2005

Luk, M.; Mezzour, G.; Perrig, A. & Gligor. V. (2007). MiniSec: A Secure Sensor Network Communication Architecture, *Proceedings of the 6th International Conference on Information Processing in Sensor Networks (IPSN)*, 2007

Malan, D.; Welsh, M. & Smith, M. (2004). A Public-key Infrastructure for Key Distribution in TinyOS based on Elliptic Curve Cryptography, *Proceedings of IEEE Conference on Sensor and Ad Hoc Communications and Networks (SECON)*, 2004

MEMSIC Inc., http://www.memsic.com

Menezes, A. J.; Van Oorschot, P. & Vanstone, S. A. (1996). Handbook of Applied Cryptography, CRC Press (Ed.), ISBN 0-8493-8523-7, New York, 1996

Pugliese, M. & Santucci, F. (2008). Pair-wise Network Topology Authenticated Hybrid Cryptographic Keys for Wireless Sensor Networks using Vector Algebra, *Proceedings of the 4th IEEE International Workshop on Wireless Sensor Networks Security (WSNS08)*, 2008

Pugliese, M.; Giani, A. & Santucci, F. (2008). A Weak Process Approach to Anomaly Detection in Wireless Sensor Networks, *Proceedings of the 1st International Workshop on Sensor Networks (SN08)*, Virgin Islands, 2008

Pugliese, M.; Giani, A. & Santucci, F. (2009). Weak Process Models for Attack Detection in a Clustered Sensor Network using Mobile Agents, *Proceedings of the 1st International Conference on Sensor Systems and Software (S-CUBE2009)*, Pisa, 2009

Pugliese, M.; Pomante, L. & Santucci, F. (2009). Agent-based Scalable Design of a Cross-Layer Security Framework for Wireless Sensor Networks Monitoring Applications, *Proceedings of the International Workshop on Scalable Ad Hoc and Sensor Networks (SASN2009)*, Saint Petersburg, 2009

Rabiner, L., & Juang, B. (1986). An Introduction to Hidden Markov Models, *IEEE ASSP Magazine*, 1986

Roman, R.; Zhou, J. & Lopez, J. (2006). Applying Intrusion Detection Systems to Wireless Sensor Networks, *Proceedings of the 3rd IEEE Consumer Communications and Networking Conference*, 2006

Roosta, T.; Shieh, S. & Sastry, S. (2006). Taxonomy of Security Attacks in Sensor Networks, *Proceedings of 1st IEEE International Conference on System Integration and Reliability Improvements*, vol. 1, pp. 529-536, 2006

Sangiovanni-Vincentelli, A. & Martin, G. (2001). Platform-based Design and Software Design Methodology for Embedded Systems, *Proceedings of IEEE Computer Design & Test*, vol. 18, n. 6, 2001

Sharma, R.; Chaba, Y. & Singh, Y. (2010). Analysis of Security Protocols in Wireless Sensor Network, *International Journal of Advanced Networking and Applications*, vol. 2, n. 2, 2010

Sheng, Y. & Cybenko, G. (2005). Distance Measures for Nonparametric Weak Process Models, *Proceedings of the IEEE International Conference on Systems, Man and Cybernetics*, vol. 1, 2005

Singh, V. P.; Jain S. & Singhai, J. (2010). Hello Flood Attack and its Countermeasures in Wireless Sensor Networks, *International Journal of Computer Science Issues*, vol. 7, n. 11, 2010

Szumel, L.; LeBrun, J. & Owens, J. D. (2005). Towards a Mobile Agent Framework for Sensor Networks, *2nd IEEE Workshop on Embedded Networked Sensors (EmNetS-TT)*, 2005

TinyOS, http://www.tinyos.net

TCG, http://www.trustedcomputinggroup.org

TCG Best Practise Committee (2011). Design, Implementation, and Usage Principles (v.3.0), February 2011

TCG WG (2007). TCG Specification Architecture Overview Design (rev. 1.4), August 2007

Whitman, M. & Mattord, H. (2011). Principles of Information Security, Thomson (Ed.), Fourth Edition, ISBN-13 978-1-111-13821-9, 2011

Yin, Q., Shen, L., Zhang, R., Li, X., & Wang, H. (2003). Intrusion Detection Based on Hidden Markov Model, *Proceedings of the International Conference on Machine Learning and Cybernetics*, vol. 5, 2003

6

Privacy-Secure Digital Watermarking for Fair Content Trading

Mitsuo Okada
Kyoto University
Japan

1. Introduction

This chapter describes a privacy-secure digital watermarking scheme for fair content trading against cybercrime on digital content piracy and privacy leakage. Conventional digital watermarking schemes are effective only for providers since privacy of a client is not concerned though content is protected. Provider's security as well as client's security need to be considered to enhance security level of privacy management. Blind and Pseudo-blind watermarking schemes utilizing encryption and media processing respectively are the solutions to protect client's security.

In conventional digital watermarking, embedding and extracting are carried out by the same providers. Therefore, a malicious provider could provide fake extracted results to a client. Verification result is considered as trustworthy evidence under the assumption that a provider is trustworthy since most of the providers were owned by enterprises which has relatively high social credibility. However, anyone is able to become a provider these days along with development of technologies. Therefore, improper providers which have insufficient level of knowledge or skill would manage client's privacy information. In other words, a user has to own his/her risk on the privacy information.

Privacy secure watermarking techniques, blind watermarking (Iwamura et al., 1997; Okada et al., 2008) and pseudo-blind watermarking (Okada et al., 2009) are able to protect both content and privacy for the sake of both providers and clients. Blind watermarking based on cryptography and watermarking blinds up content by encryption against a provider to conceal content information. However, the downside is incompatibility of cryptography and watermarking in terms of robustness of watermark and processing cost of cryptography. Pseudo-blind watermarking is another approach that uses media processing to blinds up content instead of using cryptography which enhances compatible with watermarking. The pseudo-blind watermarking provides better performance in robustness and processing cost potentially since media process is compatible to watermarking. The technical detail, features, performance evaluations of both schemes are described in this chapter based on our experimental results.

1.1 History of digital content

Analog content has been alternatively replaced by digital content such as picture, music, movie and book. Analog and digital has completely different features. For example, in analog content such as painting on a canvas, only similar replica or picture which is obviously different from the original piece can be generated instead of making perfect copy. Alteration of content is also easily identified from the original one. On the other hand, digital content can be easily duplicated without any degeneration. Analog content is recorded on physical media while digital content is only data which can be output by a monitor or speaker. Therefore, digital content can be easily distributed to thousands of people at once through the Internet.

The features of digital content, easiness of duplication, alteration and distribution are practical in terms of productivity. For instance, manufacturing and delivering movie through the Internet is much easier and inexpensive than distributing packaged DVD sold in retail stores. Clients also get benefit because they don't have to go to the store, confirm stocks and almost no space is needed to store the purchased content. However, digitalizing content involves many issues regarding to illegal use such as piracy.

In addition to content protection, privacy of a purchaser also needs to be considered. Purchasers (clients) are able to purchase analog content without exposing privacy such as who bought what kinds of content if payment is made by cash. However, purchasing content through the Internet requires user registration containing privacy information which may involve privacy leakage.

1.2 Risk of digital content piracy

Recently, with a rapid development of IT infrastructure, all kinds of digital content can be purchased through the Internet such as music, image, movie, and book as shown in Fig.1. However, an enormous amount of digital content might have been pirated since they can be easily duplicated and distributed through the Internet. In fact, an amount of distributed analog audio content such as CD was peaked out in 1998 toward decreasing as shown in Fig.2 where quantities of distributed content is shown. Note that bars labeled as "CD" in the figure show the amount of CD sold in the store while the other bars show amount of digital music data based on downloaded counting. Decreasing may be because of illegal file sharing using file sharing applications. Napster which had been used to share music content might have been accelerated piracy in 1999. After that, P2P applications such as WinMX Winny and Cabos had been alternatively used for illegal file sharing. Increasing online distribution of music content indicates importance of content protection against piracy of audio data. Because of the property of digital content, much unintentional crime might have been occurring. For example, many people share files illegally using P2P applications without conscious of guilty.

Cryptography or information hiding is digital content protection techniques against piracy. Cryptography encrypts entire content to protect content, but it will be exposed as no protection when decrypted. For example, movie delivered by CATV is encoded by scrambling and then a set top box decodes the encrypted content to play the content. The content is secure as long as encrypted, but once it is decrypted, it would be exposed as no protection (Fig. 3).

Another effective protection technique is digital watermarking that makes some secret data concealed in content. The hidden information, watermark is used for copyright protection, tamper detection, covert communication, source tracking of leakage, and so forth. The ideal form of watermark for copyright claiming is the one in which watermark should not be removed by any manipulations, the watermarked content (endorsed content) should not be

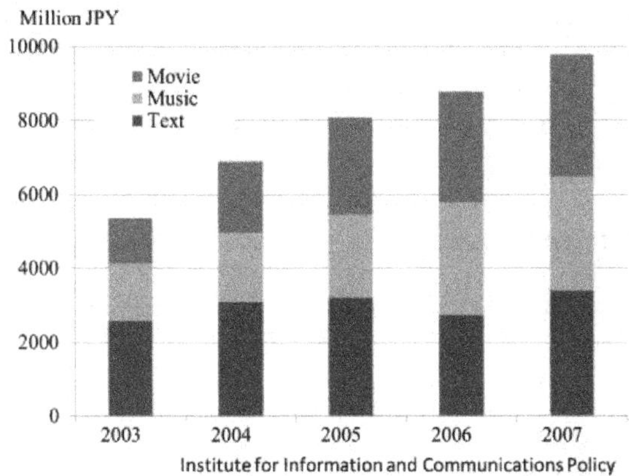

Fig. 1. Distribution Amount of Digital Content

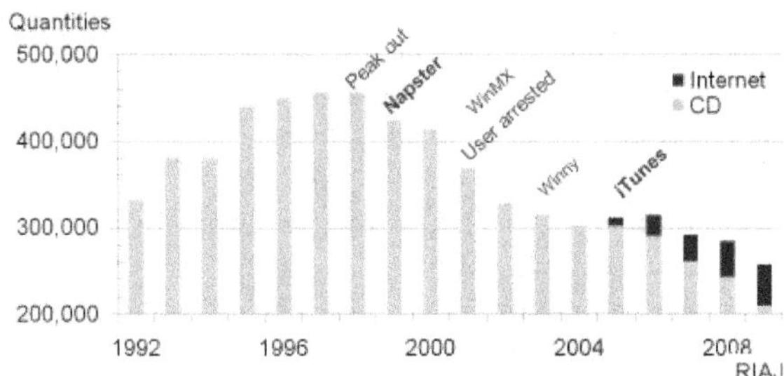

Fig. 2. Distribution Amount on Analog Music Content

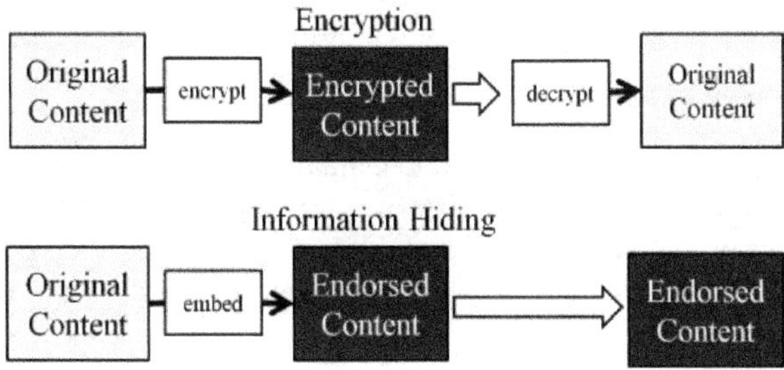

Fig. 3. Protection Techniques

degenerated by embedding watermark and embedded watermark should not perceptually appear.

Two significant issues in the conventional watermarking schemes need to be considered, that is, the provider's security as well as client's security needs to be considered for secure content trading. The issues are fairness and privacy of a client on content trading.

The demand to protect privacy information of client is increasing along with the increment of privacy leakage. Moreover, in a conventional watermarking scheme, a client can be excused from the responsibility of piracy as long as information leakage is technically possible by a provider since the provider also possesses the same delivered watermarked content. In order to resolve the problem, a fair and privacy-secure content trading framework needs to be urgently provided.

2. Content protection techniques

Protection techniques, cryptosystems and information hiding techniques are introduced in this section.

2.1 Cryptosystems

Cryptography protects content entirely by encryption. The content is secure as long as it is encrypted, but once decrypted, the content would be insecure. Cryptography is mainly classified as common key encryption and public key encryption. The former one uses the same key for encryption and decryption in which calculation cost is low, but insecure since the key is exposed when delivering it to a reviver. The latter one uses different keys for encryption and decryption respectively. An encryption key cannot be used for description which enhances security and usability. For example, assume Alice (sender) encrypts data, and Bob (receiver) decrypts it. In the common key encryption, Bob must deliver the encryption key to Alice in a strictly secure method. In other words, a key may be tapped by malicious party during the delivering process. In public key encryption, Bob prepares a pair of public key and secret key which are used for encryption and decryption respectively. Alice uses the public key obtained from Bob to encrypt data and then deliver the encrypted data to Bob. Bob decrypts the encrypted data using the secret key. The public key for encryption cannot be used for decryption and a secret key for decryption is only possessed by Bob. Hence, even though the encryption key is tapped, ciphertext cannot be decrypted.

2.1.1 Public key encryption

A public key cryptography such as RSA and El Gamal is originally proposed in 1976 by Diffie and Hellman. It has advantage in usability, but processing cost is heavy compare to the common key encryption. El Gamal (El Gamal, 1985) and Paillier encryption (Paillier, 1999) which can be adapted to the watermarking schemes are described.

2.1.1.1 El Gamal encryption

El Gamal is proposed in 1982 by El Gamal in which the security relays on the difficulty of the discrete logarithms problem. The asymmetric watermarking (Okada et al., 2008), related work of blind watermarking (Iwamura et al., 1997) uses the modified El Gamal which is customized version of El Gamal. The detail is described below.

STEP 1:(Preliminary) Bob generates a large prime number p and then finds generator g. Multiplicative group of order q on Z_p^* is also figured out. Next, determine $x \in Z_p$ and then calculates $y = g^x \bmod p$ where

$$\begin{cases} x & \text{secret key,} \\ y, g, p & \text{public key.} \end{cases}$$

The public key needs to be shared in prior to trading.

STEP 2:(Encryption) Alice generates ciphertext $E(m) = (c, d)$ by generating a random number $r \in_u Z_q$ and then encrypts the message m using the public key as

$$\begin{cases} c = g^m y^r \bmod p, \\ d = g^r, \end{cases}$$

and then sends the ciphertext to Bob.

STEP 3:(Decryption) Bob decrypts ciphertext (c, d) received by Alice using the secret key x as

$$g^m = D(c, d) = c/d^x \bmod p$$

to obtain m.

2.1.1.2 Paillier encryption

Paillier encryption (Paillier, 1999) is another homomorphic encryption which can be used with watermarking. In a key generation phase, two large prime numbers p, q are generated. $g \in Z_{N^2}$ is selected such that $\gcd(L(g^\lambda \bmod N^2), N) = 1$ where $N = pq$, $\lambda = \text{lcm}(p-1, q-1)$. Note that a public key is g, N and a private key is p, q. For the encryption phase, let m be plaintext to be encrypted, r be a random number chosen from Z_N, and $E(\cdot)$ be an encryption function defined by

$$e = E(m) = g^m r^N \bmod N^2. \tag{1}$$

For decryption phase, the decrypted ciphertext m' is obtained by

$$m' = D(e) = \frac{L(e^\lambda \bmod N^2)}{L(g^\lambda \bmod N^2)} \bmod N \tag{2}$$

where $L(t) = (t-1)/N$ and $D(\cdot)$ is decryption function.

The modified El Gamal and Paillier cryptography satisfy both an additive homomorphism and an indistinguishability denoted by IND [1] which are requirement to be utilized with watermarking. IND is necessary since the only three kinds of plaintexts $(-1, 0, 1)$ would be encrypted in an asymmetric watermarking protocol. Otherwise, the plaintexts can be identified from the ciphertext. The relationship between public-key algorithms and their properties are shown in Table 1.

2.2 Information hiding

Information hiding, in particular watermark has been used for verification in which banknotes are embedded such as the one in paper currency. Watermark can be extracted by anyone,

[1] A cryptosystem is secure in terms of indistinguishability if a ciphertext of given randomly chosen message m_0 or m_1 cannot be identified by any adversary.

Cryptography	Homomorphism	IND	Computation Cost
Modified El Gamal	additive, (multiplicative)	YES	low
Paillier (Paillier, 1999)	additive	YES	high
Okamoto- Uchiyama (Okamoto et al., 1998)	additive	YES	high
RSA	multiplicative	NO	low

Table 1. List of Public-key Algorithms

but difficult to regenerate it. Information hiding had been used for covert communication techniques such as military, diplomacy, spy and so forth that enable to conceal the existence of confidential communication. For example, a sender uses special ink to embed invisible secret message in blank space in the letter which disappears after a certain amount of time to ensure security. The secret message can be extracted only by an authorized receiver who has special liquid. This conceals existence of communication to the others.

Information hiding in digital format embeds secret message in digital content such as images, music, movies, text and so forth. The message is embedded by adding noise-like signals in content. Since the signals are so weak, only a watermark extraction program can recognize it. Basic watermarking models and features are summarized in Fig. 4.

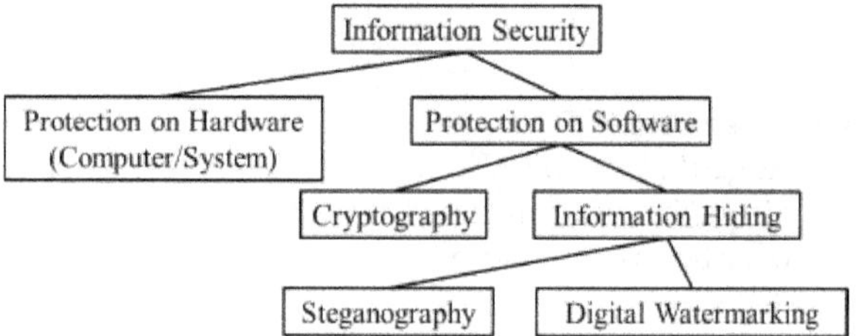

Fig. 4. Classification of Security Techniques

2.2.1 Digital image

Before we get into the watermarking technique, we overview a digital image which is composed of a huge number of small dots called "pixels" standing for a picture cell. These dots represent brightness to form an image. The brightness of Red, Green and Blue known as the three primal colors represents colors of an image. For example, *Lenna* shown in Fig. 25 is composed of 512×512 dots in column and row respectively and 8-bit, 256 levels of brightness.

An index color image such as TIFF or GIF uses less color valuation for smaller data size than full color images. Therefore, they are mostly used for website where quick response is required. Gray-scale images composed of single color valuation, black-white is smaller in file size which are used for surveillance cameras where color information is not needed. Binary images represented in either black or white are used for copy machines and FAX because they were not capable of processing color information when they were invented.

2.2.2 Frequency domain

In this section, we describe frequency which is indispensable on compression for multimedia data. Frequency is very familiar term for audio data. Image can be also represented in frequency component. For example, hair parts in *Lenna* which are considered as complicated area contains high frequency component while flat area such as skin area contains low frequency components.

Multimedia data is often compressed by using frequency component since complicated area where information omitting is hardly recognized can be effectively selected. For example, little noise in hard and noisy parts in music is hardly recognized. Compression formats in images are JPEG, GIF and TIFF. In audio, MP3 and WAV and in movie, MPEG2, MPEG4 and MKV are the major ones.

Frequency domain is more effective for watermark to be embedded because the one embedded in spatial domain somewhat damaged when compressed. However, watermark is hardly influenced if embedded in frequency domain.

An example of watermark embedding process is briefly described below as shown in Fig.5. Following descriptions show rough embedding techniques in spatial domain using x, y coordinates. Watermark is embedded by modifying brightness in either odd or even number. For example, if $\omega = 0$, the value would be changed to odd number. Otherwise, it would be changed to even numbers. Small change in brightness is perceptually unnoticeable. This method is fragile against manipulations, but embedding in frequency domain provides more robust watermark.

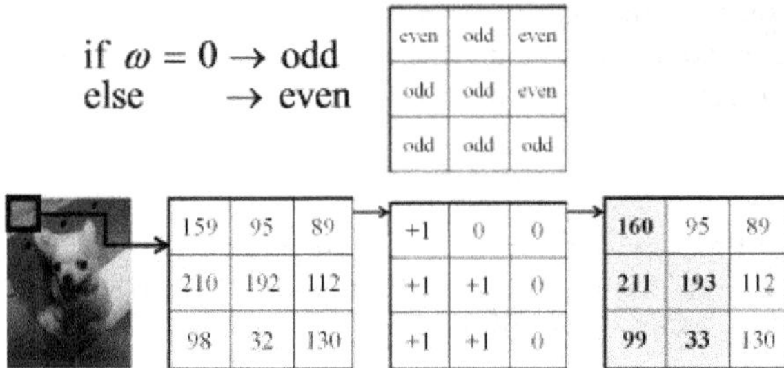

Fig. 5. An Example of Watermark Embedding Procedure

2.2.3 Digital watermark scheme

Digital watermark protects digital content by embedding imperceptive message such as serial numbers, a client ID and copyright notice into the content. The watermark is hardly removed from the watermarked content. If the pirated content had been found, the provider would extract the message to claim the copyright. Watermark is required to be imperceptive and robust against manipulation attacks which is in trade off because embedding robust watermark causes more degradation. If imperceptiveness is increased, watermark becomes fragile.

2.2.4 Potential attacks

Watermark could be removed by manipulations such as compression, re-sizing, rotation and so forth. Stirmark Benchmark Tool is a common benchmark tool for robustness of watermark. Stirmark applies various manipulations to a watermarked image based on media processing and then output attacked images. Robustness is verified by extracting watermark from those attacked images. Alternatively, this tool is called "Dewatermarker" indicating watermark remover. Stirmark covers all major attacks as shown in Table 2.

Methods	Detail
EmbedTime	Overwrite watermark
AddNoise	Noise addition
JPEG	JPEG compression
MedianCut	Smoothing without change of size and channel
ConvFilter	Modification of low-pass, sharpness, histogram
RemoveLines	Remove lines in vertical and horizontal
Cropping	Crop a part of an image
Rescale	Re-scaling
Rotation	Rotating
Affine	Twisting an image horizontally and vertically

Table 2. Attacks in StirMark Benchmark Tools

2.2.5 Tamper detection using fragile digital watermark

Fragile watermark is used for integrity check. If watermark had been damaged, it would indicate that noise or alteration had been added to the watermarked content. Cropping detection techniques based on fragile watermark (Lin et al., 2000) has been proposed in which alternated area can be detected if watermark extracting is failed from the area.

2.2.6 Steganography

Steganography is used for covert communication by hiding message in the dummy content as watermark. For example, assume Alice wants to send strictly confidential message to Bob. Alice embeds very fragile watermark to dummy content. If the content had been attempted to extract watermark while sending, the watermark must be disappear to protect message. In this method, increasing message (watermark) length without degeneration is required.

2.2.7 Digital fingerprinting

In a fingerprinting technique, a provider embeds a unique client ID for every client. If pirated content had been found, a provider would extract watermark from the content to track the source. This deters illegal re-distribution or unintentional leakage. In this technique, only few message for a user ID needs to be embedded robustly against manipulations.

2.3 Extended version of watermarking

2.3.1 Statistical watermarking

Patchwork watermarking (Bender et al., 1995), one of the statistical watermarking, embeds message in statistical value of contents. In this method, an embedding key is a seed of pseudo-random process which chooses a large number of pairs of pixels. Brightness values in the pairs are made slightly brighter and darker for all pairs. Conceptually, the contrast between pixels of the pairs encodes some secret information.

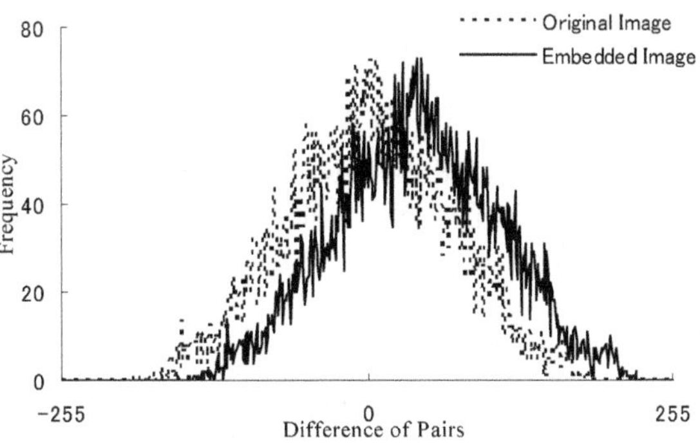

Fig. 6. Distributions of Differences $(a_i - b_i)$ and $(a_i' - b_i')$

The extraction is carried out by finding the same pairs of the pixels chosen in the embedding process and analyzing the difference of their brightness values for all pairs. This provides invisible watermark that has a higher degree of robustness against attacks and image manipulations.

A single-bit embedding process of patchwork watermark is described below. First, choose a large number of pairs from an original image I and then obtain difference in each pair. Let a, b be the first and second pixel of a pair, and S_n be the sum of $(a_i - b_i)$ for n pairs, i.e.,

$$S_n = \sum_{i=1}^{n}(a_i - b_i).$$

Let $\bar{S_n}$ be an expected value defined by $\bar{S_n} = S_n/n$. Note that $\bar{S_n}$ approaches 0 as n increases,

$$\lim_{n\to\infty} \bar{S_n} \to 0. \tag{3}$$

A distribution of differences in *Lenna* (256 × 256 pixels, 256 gray scale levels) with $n = 10000$ is shown in Fig. 6 ("Original Image"). At this experiment, a statistical value of an original image would be $\bar{S_n} = 0.0121$, that satisfies the condition (3).

An embedding process, hiding a secret message ω into I is described. First, choose a seed of pseudo-random sequence to assign two pixels (a_i, b_i) for n pairs. Next, to generate an embedded image I', we modify the assigned pixels as, $a_i' = a_i + \delta$, and $b_i' = b_i - \delta$, for $i = 1, \ldots, n$, where δ is a constant that governs robustness of the watermark. Note that the expected value $\bar{S_n}'$, an average of sum of the difference of the embedded image I', approaches 2δ as

$$\bar{S_n}' = \frac{1}{n}\sum_{i=1}^{n}(a_i + \delta) - (b_i - \delta) = \frac{1}{n}\sum_{i=1}^{n}(a_i - b_i) + 2\delta = 2\delta. \tag{4}$$

with the parameter of $\delta = 20$, the distribution of $(a_i' - b_i')$ is shifted 40 to right as illustrated in Fig. 6. Hence, as δ goes larger, accuracy of detection increases, and as δ goes smaller, the risk of a false detection increases. To extract the hidden message ω, choose a_i', and b_i' according to the random numbers, and then determine,

$$\omega = \begin{cases} 0 & \bar{S_n}' < \tau, \\ 1 & \bar{S_n}' \geq \tau, \end{cases} \tag{5}$$

where τ is a threshold. The optimal threshold is given as $\tau = \delta$ to equalize the false positive and false negative. In the sample image *Lenna*, statistical value is $\bar{S_n}' = 40.0158$, which satisfies the condition of $\bar{S_n} \geq \tau = \delta = 20$.

3. Secure watermarking technique

Consideration of purchaser's privacy is another important issue for fair and secure content trading. Blind and Pseudo blind schemes are solutions to enhance the privacy protection. The big picture of the secure content trading based on three-way communication by interposing TTP (trusted third party) are introduced below (Fig. 7) which are non-blind, blind, pseudo-blind watermarking techniques (Table 3).

The information to be protected is privacy of a client such as who purchased what kind of content. Even though, TTP is trustworthy, there is demand that a client doesn't want to expose privacy information.

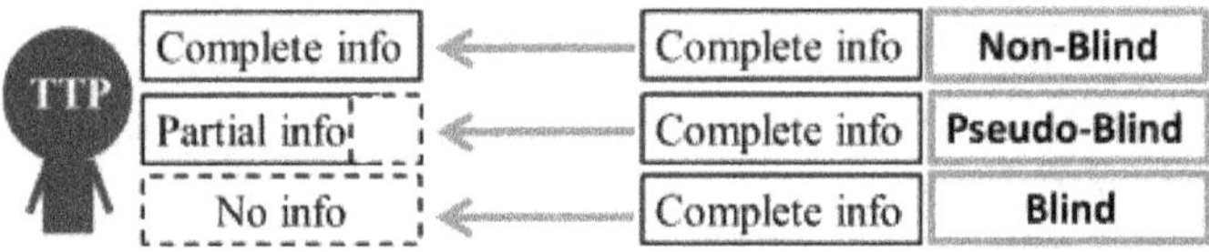

Fig. 7. Big Picture of Secure Content Protection Techniques

3.1 Non-blind watermarking

TTP is interposed for watermark embedding and pseudonymous user verification which is the simplest way to protect privacy against a provider (Fig. 8). However, this scheme doesn't fulfill the needs since content is exposed to TTP. A client doesn't want to expose unnecessary information to TTP even though TTP is trustworthy.

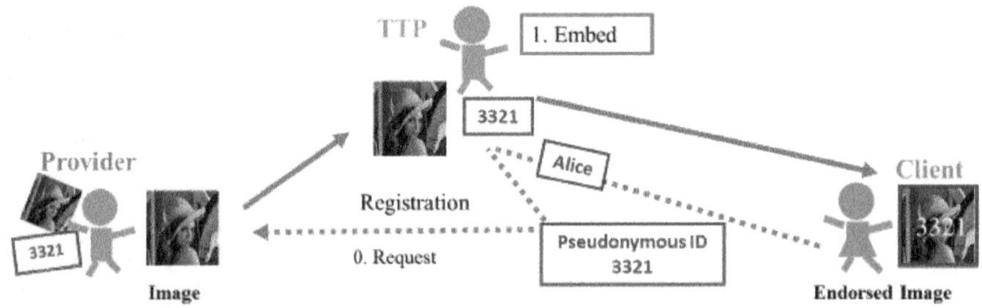

Fig. 8. Non-blind Watermarking

3.2 Blind watermarking, combination of homomorphic encryption and watermark

Blind watermarking blinds up content by encryption against TTP. In this scheme, watermark is able to be embedded even though the content is encrypted. Therefore, TTP cannot obtain information of content. However, it is inefficient in terms of watermark strength and processing cost.

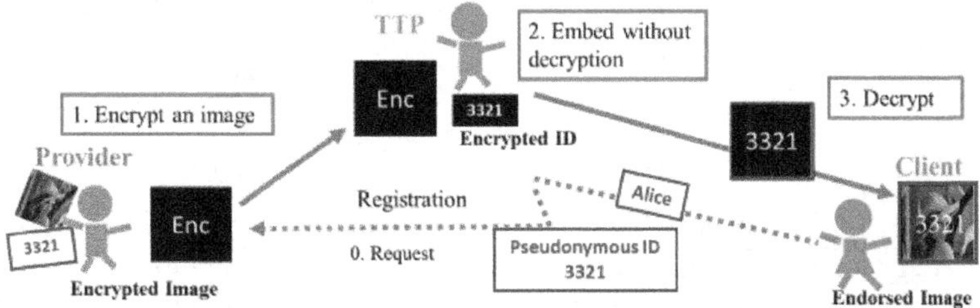

Fig. 9. Blind Watermarking

3.3 Pseudo-blind watermarking, combination of media processing and watermark

Pseudo-blind watermarking (Okada et al., 2009) is an alternative method of blind watermarking which is as secure as blind watermarking and as practical as a non-blind watermarking. The pseudo-blind watermarking partially scrambles the content so that content is blinded against TTP. At the same time, watermark is well embedded since scrambling is designed to preserve feature of the content such as edge of recoded subject where watermark is embedded. Hence the embedded watermark has sufficient level of robustness. A prototype of a content trading system based on the pseudo-blind method has been designed and implemented, and the performance of the pseudo-blind watermarking is evaluated on the system.

The scheme is briefly described below (Fig.10). In prior to trading, a client obtains a pseudonymous ID from TTP. The client requests content by using the ID. If verified, the provider decomposes requested content into two pieces. One of which is blinded by media processing which contains sufficient amount of image feature. Another one is the counterpart. The former one is sent to TTP for watermark embedding and latter one is delivered to the client. At this point, the provider has no information to profile a client because of pseudonymity. Next, TTP embeds watermark into blinded piece (endorse piece) and then delivered to the client. At this point, TTP has no clue as to what kind of content has been traded due to blindness. Finally, the client integrates those decomposed pieces to obtain complete endorsed image. Hence, the client can obtain a complete endorsed image without exposing the privacy information.

4. Verification and performance evaluation

4.1 Performance summary of blind method

Asymmetric watermarking (Pfitzmann et al., 1996) is one of the related works of blind watermarking. Fundamental problems of the blind schemes are specified with our

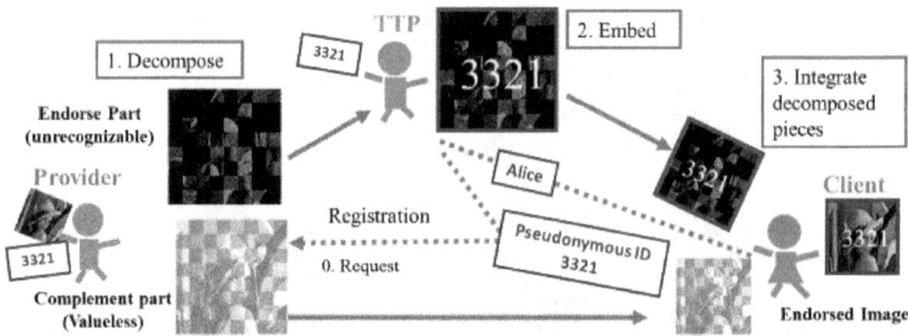

Fig. 10. Pseudo-blind Watermarking

	Non-blind	Blind	Pseudo-blind
Compatibility of watermark and blinding method	applicable to any watermark algorithms	applicable to certain watermark algorithms	applicable to any watermark algorithms
Privacy against TTP	No protection	Blinded by encryption	Blinded by Media processing (scrambling)
Watermark strength	Robust	Fragile	Robust

Table 3. Comparison of Three-way Communication Content Trading

implemented results (Okada et al., 2008) that uses El Gamal encryption and patchwork watermarking.

Suppose that, a provider embeds watermark into content, a client verifies watermark, and TTP generates a secret key *sk* and public key *pk* for the modified El Gamal encryption. Not only does interposal of TTP enhances the reliability of verification, but also prevents a provider from cheating a client. Note that TTP needn't to be fully trustworthy since it does not obtain the embedding key, which is the index of modified pixels determined by a client throughout the embedding process.

Let $I = (x_1, \ldots, x_\ell)$ be an original image, $I' = (z_1, \ldots, z_\ell)$ be an embedded image, and ℓ be the number of pixels in I and I'. An asymmetric watermarking scheme is illustrated in Fig. 11.

4.1.1 The asymmetric protocol

TTP generates the modified El Gamal public key, $y = g^x \bmod p$, where a secret key is x. Let *EXT* be conversion function in the second step, and *IDENTIFY* be a function to obtain ω at the final step, respectively.

STEP1:(Embedding) A client generates random numbers by giving a seed to pseudo-random generator, and obtains subsets A and B of set of indexes $\{1, 2, \ldots, \ell\}$ such that $A \cap B = \phi$ and $|A| = |B| = n$. The client chooses δ and modifies pixels according to (A, B) in the image I to generate I' as

$$z_i = \begin{cases} x_i + \delta & \text{if } i \in A, \\ x_i - \delta & \text{if } i \in B, \\ x_i & \text{otherwise,} \end{cases} \tag{6}$$

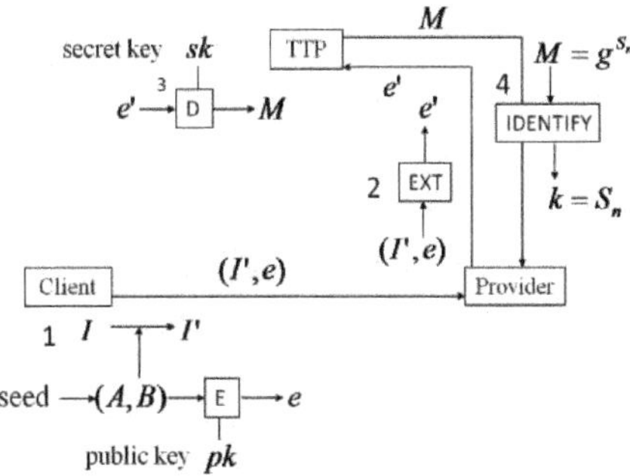

Fig. 11. The Model of the Asymmetric Digital Watermarking

for $i = 1, ..., \ell$. A client computes e, a ciphertext of (A, B) as $e = (c_1, \ldots, c_\ell,\ d_1, \ldots, d_\ell)$, where $c_i = g^{m_i} y^{r_i}$, $d_i = g^{r_i} \bmod p$,

$$m_i = \begin{cases} 1 & \text{if } i \in A, \\ -1 & \text{if } i \in B, \\ 0 & \text{otherwise,} \end{cases} \tag{7}$$

and r_i is random numbers of Z_q, for $i = 1, \ldots, \ell$. Finally, a client sends $I' = (z_1, \ldots, z_\ell)$ to the provider in conjunction with encrypted indexes $e = (c_1, \ldots, c_\ell, d_1, \ldots, d_\ell)$.

STEP2:(Extracting) The provider computes ciphertext $e' = EXT(I', e) = (C, D)$ as follow;

$$C = c_1^{z_1} c_2^{z_2} \cdots c_\ell^{z_\ell} = \prod_{i=1}^{\ell} g^{m_i z_i} y^{r_i z_i} = g^{\sum^\ell m_i z_i} y^{\sum^\ell r_i z_i} = g^{S_n} y^R, \tag{8}$$

$$D = d_1^{z_1} d_2^{z_2} \cdots d_\ell^{z_\ell} = \prod_{i=1}^{\ell} g^{r_i z_i} = g^R,$$

where $R = \sum_{i=1}^{\ell} r_i z_i \bmod q$, and S_n is the sum of difference in patchwork watermark scheme, i.e., $S_n = 2n\delta$ and then sends e' to TTP.

STEP3:(Decrypting) TTP uses its private key x to decrypt $e' = (C, D)$ as $M = D(e') = C/D^x = g^{S_n}$ and then sends back the decrypted text M to the provider.

STEP4:(Identifying) The provider identifies exponent h of M as $IDENTIFY(M)$ such that $M = g^h$ by testing all possible $h = 1, 2, \ldots, n\tau$. Statistically h is distributed around $2n\delta$, which is much smaller than q, and thus able to be identified. The hidden message ω is obtained according to

$$\omega = \begin{cases} 0 & \text{if } h < n\tau, \\ 1 & \text{if } h \geq n\tau, \end{cases} \tag{9}$$

where τ is the threshold. Determine $\omega = 1$, if there is no value matching within the range, $h < n\tau$. Sum of difference, h to form Eq. (9) instead of the average $\bar{S_n}$ in Eq. (5) is used. Note that Eq. (9) is equivalent to Eq. (5).

In other words, $\omega = 0$ does not mean that watermark is not embedded. Difference whether $\omega = 0$ or none can be examined by adopting some optional techniques. One example is that, we assign $\zeta = -1(\omega = 0); 1(\omega = 1)$ as

$$z_i = \begin{cases} x_i + \delta\zeta & \text{if } i \in A, \\ x_i - \delta\zeta & \text{if } i \in B, \\ x_i & \text{otherwise,} \end{cases}$$

which is based on Eq. (6). The above modification provides three conditions such as $\omega = 0$, $\omega = 1$, or none (message is not embedded).

4.1.2 Security

In this section, the security of patchwork watermark is described. First, the embedding key A and B, the indexes of the modified pixels are uniformly distributed over $\{1, \ldots, \ell\}$. The distribution of (A, B) is illustrated in Fig. 12, where white dots represent (A, B). Hence, it is almost impossible to attack to determine (A, B) in I' without the knowledge of the embedding key. Second, the property that the original image is not required in an extraction process improves security against watermark removal due to a leakage of the original image. Third, since the brightness of some of the pixels has slightly changed, the difference is hardly perceptible.

Fig. 12. 1-bit Embedded Images and Distribution of A, B

Fig. 12 illustrates an example of a single-bit information being embedded into *Lenna* (256×256 pixels, 256 gray scale levels) with the parameters of $n = 2053$, and $\delta = 3$. The SNR for Fig. 12 is 50.6[dB] which is considered to be acceptable.

4.1.3 Optimal parameter

In this section, an optimal parameter δ is described in the sense that the least number of δ with an accuracy of 95% succeeds in detection.

Let σ' be standard deviation of n samples of $(a_i - b_i)$, and σ be standard deviation of the average value $\bar{S}_i$. Noting the well-known relation of variances, $\sigma = \sigma' / \sqrt{n}$, we can predict true σ from the sampled σ'. Hence, variance of average S_n decreases as n increases. In other words, an accuracy of S_n increases along with the increment of n. In order to achieve 95% confidence for detection, under an assumption of normal distribution, the embedded image should be shifted by at least 2σ which is identical to δ.

The parameters, average of S_n, μ, standard deviation σ, and optimal δ with respects to n are demonstrated on Table 4, and the optimal δ given n is obtained from Fig. 13. Note that the false positive of 5% with the following δ is not sufficient to practical use. In order to make an image more robust, δ could be increased taking consideration of subjective evaluation. For

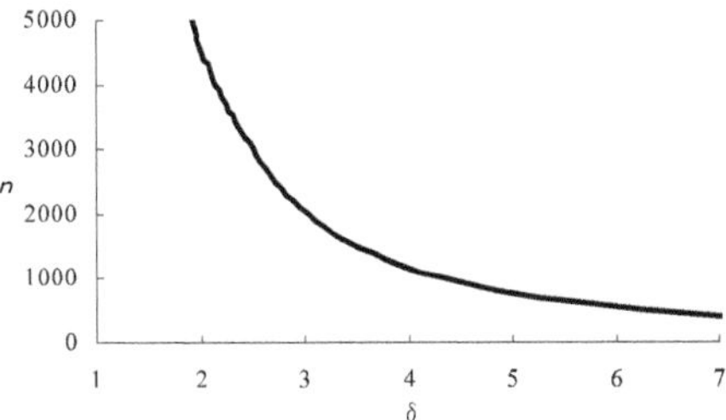

Fig. 13. Optimal δ Distribution

n	μ	σ'	σ	δ
4613	0.8847	67.4449	0.4769	2
2053	1.9206	67.9670	1.5000	3
1165	-0.4335	68.2865	2.0007	4
757	-1.3805	68.8136	2.5011	5
539	-2.0260	69.7601	3.0048	6

Table 4. Parameters for δ Determination

the sake of determination of δ, we study the relation between the number of modified pairs of pixels n and quality of an image, which is estimated by means of Signal to Noise Ratio defined by,

$$\mathrm{SNR} = 10 \cdot \log_{10} \frac{255^2}{\mathrm{MSE}^2} = 10 \cdot \log_{10} \frac{255 \cdot 255}{1/\ell \sum (x_i - z_i)^2}, \tag{10}$$

where MSE is the mean-square error between I and I'. An image *Lenna* of 256×256 pixels is used for this test with the parameters shown in Table 4. Fig. 15 indicates no significant difference between $n = 2053$ and $n = 4613$. This implies the parameter of $n > 2053$, which is $\delta = 3$, is the optimal choice to prevent the embedded image from being spoiled, under the condition that SNR is almost the same. Fig. 14 illustrates how SNR of the image varies for the image size ℓ, where single-bit is embedded and $n = 2053$ pixels are manipulated.

4.1.4 Implementation system

In order to estimate a total performance of asymmetric schemes is described below. Watermark embedding and extracting process for gray scale images are implemented in C, and cryptographic computations are implemented in Java. Environment specifications are described in Table 5. An image *Lenna I* (256 × 256 pixels) with a parameter of $n = 2053$ is used as a host image.

Based on our implementation, we have estimated embedding time and extracting time. Description and decryption time of a single bit embedding based on the 1024-bit modified El Gamal are 0.104 [s], and 0.077 [s], respectively. Those of Paillier encryption are 3.303[s] and 2.127[s].

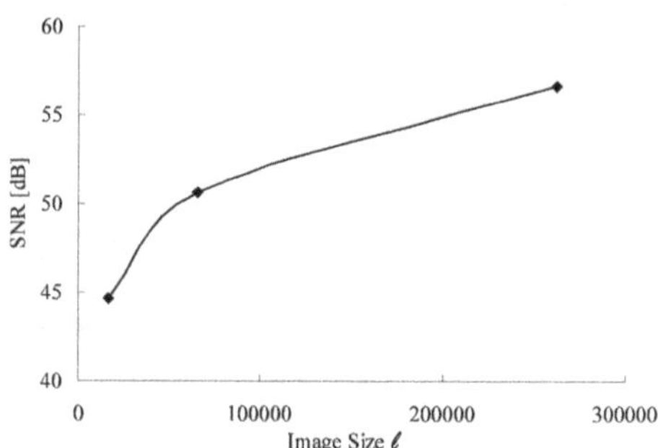

Fig. 14. SNR for Different Image Size ℓ

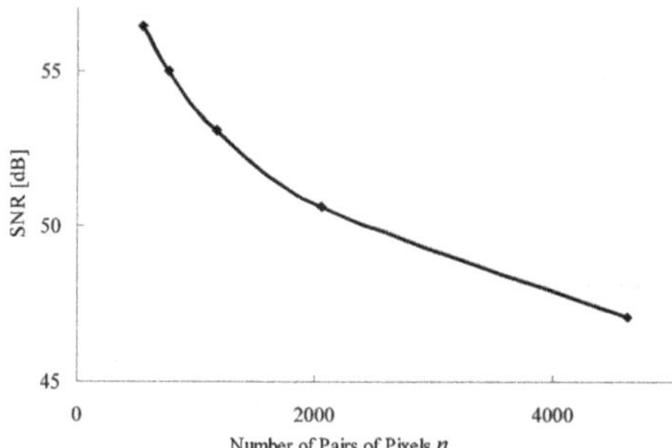

Fig. 15. The Relation between the Number of Modified Pairs of Pixels n and SNR

Detail	Specification
CPU	Xeon 2.3GHz
OS	Redhat 9.0, Linux 2.4.20
Memory	1GB
Encryption Algorithms	1024-bit the modified El Gamal, 1024-bit Paillier
Programming Languages	J2SDK 1.4.2, gcc 3.3.3

Table 5. Implementation Environment

4.2 Robustness against noise addition and JPEG compression attacks

The robustness of patchwork watermarking against attacks of "Add Noise" and "JPEG Compression" using StirMark (Petitcolas, 2000) are evaluated. I' originated from *Lenna* (256×256 pixels, 256 gray scale levels), with the parameters of $n = 2053$, $\delta = 3$, and $\bar{S'_n}$=6.9547. With this sample image, the parameter of τ=3 for all attacked images I' is applied on extraction process.

In JPEG compression attack, watermark has been successfully extracted up to 80% of JPEG quality level as shown in Fig. 16. Evaluation result in Add Noise attack is shown in Fig. 16.

The noise level represents that of normalized from 0 to 100 such that 0 gives no noise while 100 gives a complete random image.

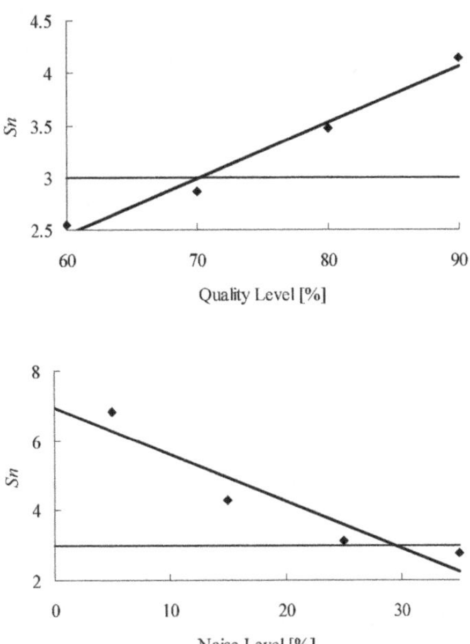

Fig. 16. Robustness on JPEG Compression and Add Noise Attacks

4.2.1 Comparison between Furukawa's method and the proposed scheme

Essential difference between Furukawa's scheme (Furukawa, 2004) and the proposal scheme comes from the cryptographical primitives, that is, the modified El Gamal and Paillier encryption. Fig. 17 shows the processing time of an extracting phase in the modified El Gamal and Paillier encryptions. Processing time for all cases is evaluated. Each of cases is provided average of ten samples of different seeds. The values used to plot in Fig. 17 are shown in Table 6.

For the modified El Gamal encryption, the processing time includes decrypting and identifying process, whereas Paillier encryption includes only decrypting process. The processing time of the modified El Gamal increases proportionally to n while processing time of Paillier encryption remains the same since only single decryption process is needed to extract watermark.

Supposing the processing time follows linearly to n as illustrated in Fig. 17, Paillier processing time would crosses over that of the modified El Gamal at $n^* = 7403$. This result shows that the scheme (Okada et al., 2008) is superior to Furukawa's method (Furukawa, 2004) with the condition when n is less than or equal to n^*.

For the modified El Gamal encryption, it is necessary to examine all possible numbers, which feasibility is stated in section 4.2.1. Whereas, brute force analysis is not necessary in Paillier encryption since exponent can be figured out. Thus, processing cost is the same as encoding value of base ϕ in Paillier encryption.

We recall that as n increase, the detection accuracy improves, but the quality of the image becomes low. According to the section 4.1.3 where we studied the optimal n and δ in terms of SNR, efficient embedding n is estimated between the number of approximately, 2000 to 5000, which is less than threshold $n^* = 7403$.

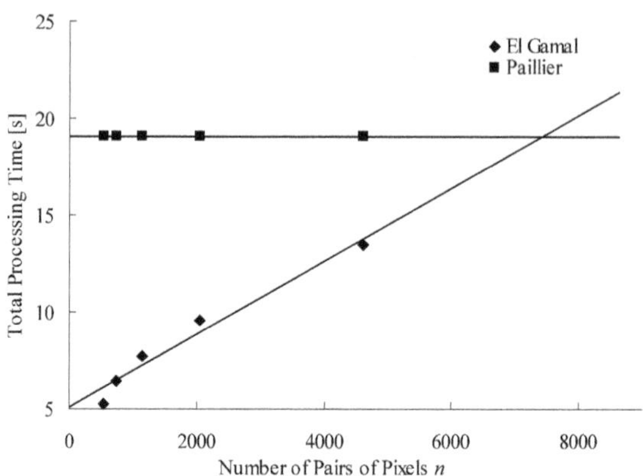

Fig. 17. Processing Time of Proposed Scheme and that of (Furukawa, 2004)

n	539	757	1165	2053	4613
Proposed scheme (the modified El Gamal)	5.279	6.475	7.697	9.590	13.47
Furukawa's scheme (Paillier)	19.11	19.11	19.11	19.11	19.11

Table 6. Processing Time in Watermark Detecting

4.3 Performance summary of pseudo-blind method

In this section, a basic model of practical privacy-secure image trading system based on pseudo-blind watermark is presented. Abstract of implemented system is described with an illustration in Fig.19. Image decomposition and watermark algorithms can be substituted according to the requirement of content trading. The details of image decomposition, embedding process, and integration process are described in Step 1 through 3 respectively in Fig. 19. For the implementation, an image of 512×512 pixels and 256 gray levels, 11-bit of *ID*, and 15-bit ω which includes codeword for ECC are used.

4.3.1 Procedures in the prototype

The procedure of the prototype which mainly contains 3 steps is described below.

4.3.1.1 Verification procedure

A client obtains a pseudonymous ID *ID* through registration page provided by TTP and then get verified by a provider. The provider verifies *ID* in cooperation with TTP by sending *ID* to TTP. If verified, TTP returns the verification result to the provider.

At this point, TTP possesses the client name and the anonymous ID while the provider only possesses the anonymous ID and purchasing history. Therefore, TTP has difficulty to profile what kind of image has been purchased while the provider has no clue as to who the client is.

4.3.1.2 Purchasing procedure

The purchasing procedures is described below (Fig. 18). Assume that the client had been successfully verified anonymously. A client selects an image. Trading procedure which contains image decomposition and watermark embedding process are executed and then two decomposed images are generated. The client receives these two images, an endorse piece and complement piece from TTP and the provider respectively. The images are integrated to be a complete endorsed image as described later on.

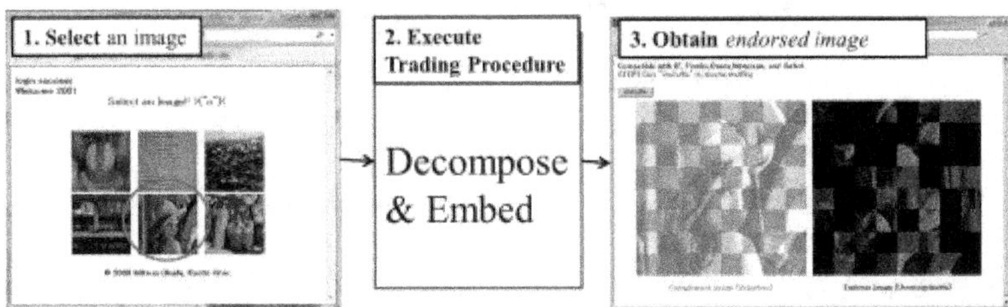

Fig. 18. Purchasing Procedure

4.3.1.3 Trading procedure

The trading procedure is briefly described below. The following instructions can be referred to Fig. 19. We assume that the client has selected an image.

1. A provider receives HTTP post from a client which contains *ID* and information of selected image such as image ID.
2. When the provider receives the data, the selected image is decomposed into a complement piece (I_c) and an endorse piece I_e as $(I_c, I_e) = DCMP(I)$. I_c is allowed to be accessed by the client, whereas I_e is allowed to be accessed by TTP. I_e is number of small $bc \times bc$ pixels of blocked images, $(I_{e_1}, \ldots, I_{e_{bn}}, bn = (Col/bc \times Raw/bc))$ as shown in the figure. In this implementation, $bn = 64 = (512/64 \times 512/64)$ of small blocked images are generated from a 512×512 pixels image.
3. The provider returns HTML content as the response to the client. The HTML content contains links to I_c and I_e. Former one is a single link to I_c while the latter one contains multiple links to small blocked images $(I_{e_1}, \ldots, I_{e_{64}})$. The provider generates a shuffle key *psk* in order to send the small blocks to TTP at random order. I_c and *psk* is sent directly to the client. I_e is sent to TTP at random order.
4. When TTP receives the blocked images, $(I_{e_1}, \ldots, I_{e_{64}})$ from the provider, TTP embeds watermark ω into the blocked images and then the images are forwarded to the client.
5. The client obtains randomly shuffled I_e from TTP and I_c and *psk* from the provider by accessing the links in the HTML content. Finally, the client integrates two images together.

The final step is generating a complete endorsed image by the client as $I' = INTG(I_c, I'_e)$ where $INTG(\cdot)$ is an image integration function.

4.3.2 Technical detail of the prototype

This scheme is mainly composed of verification, trading, and image integration procedures. In the verification procedure, a client obtains pseudonymous ID (ID) from TTP. The client begins trading using ID. A provider verifies ID in cooperation with TTP. If verified, the provider decompose I into an endorsed part I_e and a complement part I_c and then sends HTML content to the client (Step 1 in Fig.19). A client accesses the links to obtains I_c and shuffle key psk from a provider, and then sends request for I_e. I_e is composed of number of divided $zCol \times zRow$ images. As soon as TTP receives the request, TTP obtains divided I_e in which ω will be embedded (Step 2 in Fig.19). The client receives endorsed parts I_e' from TTP.

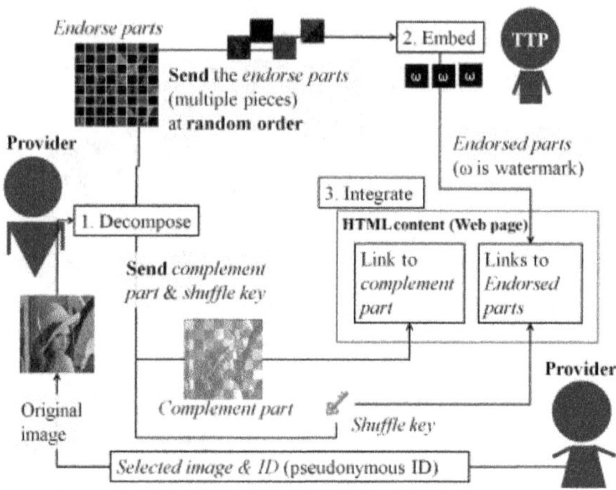

Fig. 19. Trading Procedure

4.3.3 Image decomposition

Image decomposition procedure (step 2 in Fig.19) is described below (Fig.22).

Step 1

FreQuency Decomposition extracts complicated area in an image where watermark is effectively embedded such as edge of recorded subject using high-pass filtering function $FQD(\cdot)$. $FQD(\cdot)$ should be applied to an original image in order to extract correct high-pass component. In other words, if other decomposition elements had been applied before $FQD(\cdot)$, noise or block border would affect high-pass component extraction. A high-pass filtered image is generated as $I_H = FQD(I)$. Next, the counterpart is generated as $I_L = SUB(I, FQD(I))$. $SUB(\cdot)$ is subtraction operation of pixel by pixel of two input images. For example, it subtracts pixels of $FQD(I)$ from those of I. Watermark is effectively embedded in the complicated area of an image since small manipulation is hardly noticed by human eyes. For example, brightness modification of single dot in hair area is almost impossible to recognize the difference, but the modification in skin area is easily recognized. Even though I_H is hardly recognized, detail of an entire figure in the image is somewhat visible. Furthermore, main component of an image remains in the counterpart I_L which may causes re-distribution of it.

Step 2

Block Division ($BRD(\cdot)$), breaks up entire image detail since original condition in I_H may be easily profiled from a high-pass filtered image. $BRD(\cdot)$ is a function which divides an image into $zCol \times zRow$ pixels and outputs two patterns of block-check images as $(I_{Ha}, I_{Hb}) = BRD(I_H)$. The divided blocks are composed of image elements and blank elements sorted alternatively as shown in Fig. 20. In this implementation, the image is divided into square blocks $Z_1, \ldots, Z_\eta$ which is effective universally. η is the total number of blocks in which 64 ($64 = \eta = 512/64 \times 512/64$) blocks such that $Z_1, \ldots, Z_{64}$ is generated where $zCol = zRow = 64$.

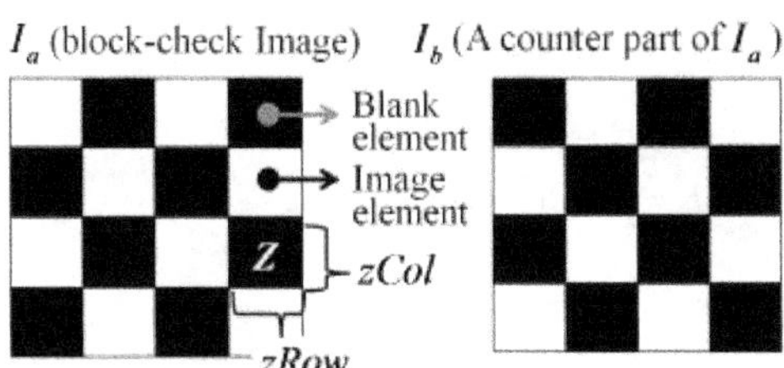

Fig. 20. Block-check Image Generation

Step 3

In order to make a valueless image, Invisible Masking function $IVM(\cdot)$ is used to add noise as $I_{Ln} = IVM(I_L)$ so that the client has no incentive to redistribute I_c without receiving I_e. $IVM(\cdot)$ adds up brightness values as noise in $nCol \times nRow$ pixels for all area $N_j, (1 \leq j \leq (Col/nCol \times Row/nRow))$. Pseudo-random value rnd_j used for noise (block noise) is generated based on minimum brightness of N_j because an input image I_L should be generated by simply summing up the brightness values of block noise image I_{Ln} and the counterpart $SUB(I_L, I_{Ln})$ (Fig. 21). For example, assume the brightness in N_j in I_L is 120,96,209,58, rnd_j in I_{Ln} is 200, the brightness to be assigned to counterpart $SUB(I_L, I_{Ln})$ would be (120-200),(96-200),(209-200),(58-200). Note that since negative integer is invalid for brightness, the pseudo-random value needs to be generated within the range of $1, \ldots, 58$ in order to avoid underflow and overflow when summing up two values together. In this implementation $nCol = nRow = 4$ is used. Block noise should be effective for this case since block noise is able to well conceal recorded subjects compare to every pixel wise noise. If the pixel is large, the subject is concealed well, but it affects watermark embedding due to reduction of feature in the image.

Step 4

Generate the other parts of block-check images as $(I_{Lna}, I_{Lnb}) = BRD(I_{Ln})$. The image element of which will be replaced with the blank parts in I_{Ha}. I_{Lnb} will be used.

Step 5

Block Integration ($BI(\cdot)$) integrates image elements in I_{Lnb} and I_{Ha} as $I_{LnbHa} = BI(I_{Lnb}, I_{Ha})$ which contains frequency components and noise components.

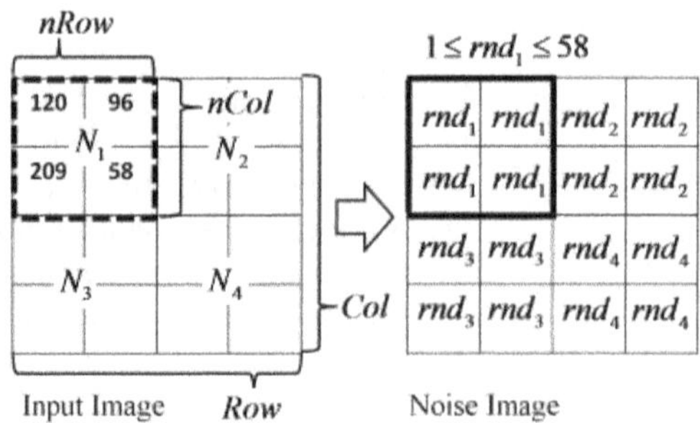

Fig. 21. Noise Generation

Step 6

Generate a complement part $I_c = SUB(I, (I_{LnbHa}))$.

Step 7

Shuffle blocks in I_{LnbHa} by using block shuffling function $RS(\cdot)$ to generate an endorse part I_e and a key psk for reversing shuffle as $(I_e, psk) = RS(I_{LnbHa})$.

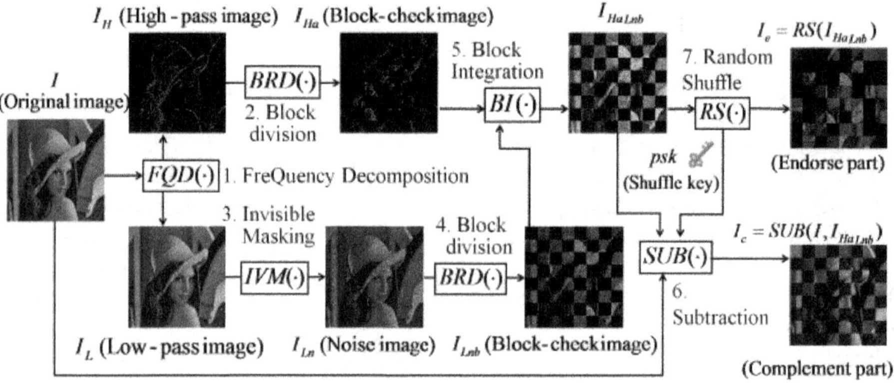

Fig. 22. Image Decomposition Procedure

4.3.4 Watermark embedding

In this section, embedding process is described (Step 2 in Fig. 19). As soon as TTP receives a request from a client, TTP obtains blocked images $I_e = Z_1, \ldots, Z_\eta$ at random to embed ω.

In this prototype, we apply a watermark algorithm that embeds watermark in frequency domain. I_e contains two types of blocks, a high-pass filtered block Z_h and a noise block Z_n. This embedding, effective for high-pass filtered blocks, is applied to Z_h.

Parameters for embedding are summarized below. Let robustness of watermark is δ, pairs of coefficients used for embedding are a_i, b_i, bit string of ω is ω_i, the index of a_i, b_i and ω_i is

$i = 1, \ldots, q$, bit length of ω is q, redundancy (number of Y to be modified) of ω is γ. In this implementation, $q = 15$, $\gamma = 30$, $\delta = 20$, $bCol = bRow = 8$ (ths size of Y_ℓ) is used.

First, finds out small blocks Y_ℓ in a blocked image that contains complicated area where watermark is effectively embedded. In this implementation, standard deviation is used to estimate complexity because standard deviation σ of brightness tends to be large in the complicated area in general. Ordinary images shown in the section 4.4 are used in this implementation. Hence, the block Y_ℓ which contain large σ provides better detection accuracy of watermark. First, divide Z into area Y_ℓ which is $bCol \times bRow$ pixels. Find σ from every Y_ℓ. Next, find Y_ℓ that satisfies $\sigma > \tau$. τ, threshold for complexity, is the average value of σ in all Y_ℓ in this implementation.

Embedding procedure is described below (Fig. 23). Select q pairs of DCT coefficient $a_1, \ldots, a_q, b_1, \ldots, b_q$ from the selected area Y_ℓ to embed watermark $\omega_1, \ldots, \omega_q$.

a_i is selected from low to middle frequency domain, b_i is selected from middle to high frequency domain. For embedding $\omega_i = 0$, the coefficients are modified as $a_i < b_i$, and for $\omega_i = 1$, these are modified as $a_i \geq b_i$. If $\omega_i = 0$ and the selected coefficients are $a_i < b_i$, then the coefficients are modified to satisfy as $a'_i = a_i - \delta, b'_i = b_i + \delta$. Otherwise ($a_i \geq b_i$), the coefficients are modified as $a'_i = b_i - \delta, b'_i = a_i + \delta$. If $\omega_i = 1$ and $a_i \geq b_i$, $a'_i = a_i + \delta$, $b'_i = b_i - \delta$. Otherwise ($a_i \leq b_i$), they are modified as $a'_i = b_i + \delta, b'_i = a_i - \delta$. Apply the above modification to all $i = 1, \ldots, q$.

If δ is large, watermark would be robust, but the image would be degenerated. If δ is small, an image get less degenerated, but watermark would be fragile.

Adding δ causes overflow when integrating two images. However, if the pixels would be larger than 255, we make the brightness in 255.

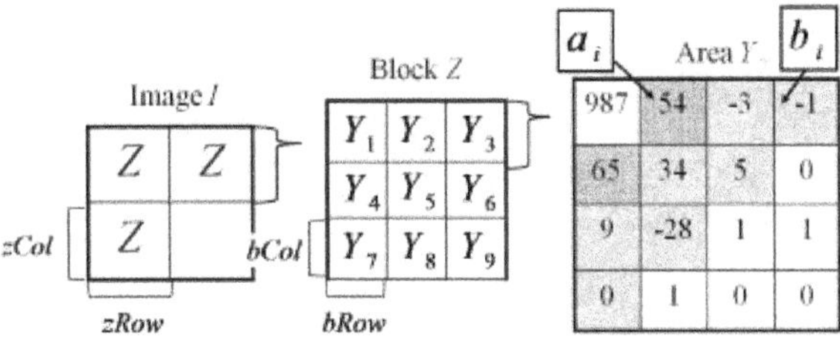

Fig. 23. Coefficients Selection in a block Y

Iterate the above process to all $Y_1, \ldots, Y_\gamma$ which satisfy $\sigma > \tau$. Note that, if γ is large, watermark can be robust, but the image would be degenerated.

Apply the above procedure for all high-pass blocks Z to generate endorsed blocks $Z'_1, \ldots, Z'_{\eta/2}$. Note that total number of Z' is $\eta/2$ since high-pass blocks Z and noise blocks Z exist the equal amount in I' in this implementation.

An extraction method is described below. Extraction requires the information on modified coefficients. Deploy the endorsed image I' into frequency domain as embedding procedure. First, divides the image into Z and then extract $\omega = \omega_1, \ldots, \omega_q$ by examining the condition of DCT coefficients $(a'_1, b'_1), (a'_2, b'_2), \ldots, (a'_q, b'_q)$ in $Y'_1, \ldots, Y'_\gamma$ in every Z' respectively. Next, extracts ω from $Y'_1, \ldots, Y'_\gamma$ and then apply this process for all $Z'_1, \ldots, Z'_{\eta/2}$ to take an average of extracted bit stream.

4.3.5 Obtaining endorsed image

In the final step (Step 3 in Fig. 19), a complete endorsed image I' is generated by integrating I_c and I'_e which can be obtained by tracing links in the HTML content. The client obtains I_c and psk from a provider, and $I'_e = RS(I'_{LnbHa})$ from TTP.

I' is generated by following process. Reverse shuffle by $I'_{LnbHa} = RS^{-1}_{psk}(I'_e)$ and then combine with I_c as $I' = SUM(I_c, I'_{LnbHa})$ where $SUM(\cdot)$ is function that sum up brightness values of two input images. Note that a provider cannot obtain I' illegally because verification is required to obtain I'_e.

4.4 Evaluation

Perceptual and robustness evaluations are shown in this section. The former one shows perceptual condition of decomposed images and a watermarked image. In the latter one, robustness of watermark is shown. The environment used in this implementation is summarized in Table 7.

Detail	Specification
CPU	Intel Xeon E5345 2.33GHz
Memory	4GB RAM
OS	Fedora 10
DCMP, *EMB*	Matlab2009a
Web interface *INTG*	HTML, PHP

Table 7. Environment

Attacks	Description	Total Attacks	Levels	Succeed
AFFINE	Affine transform	8	$1, 2, \ldots, 8$	None
CONV	Gaussian filtering	2	$1, 2$	All
CROP [%]	Cropping	3	$25, 50, 75$	None
JPEG[%]	JPEG compression	7	$20, 30, \ldots, 80$	$30, \ldots, 80$
MEDIAN	Median cut	4	$3, 5, 7, 9$	3
NOISE[%]	Add noise	8	$10, 20, \ldots, 80$	None
RESC [%]	Rescale	6	$50, 75, 90, 125, 150, 200$	All
RML [lines]	Remove lines	9	$10, 20, \ldots, 100$	All

Table 8. Parameters of StirMark and Evaluated Results

4.4.1 Perceptual evaluation

Perceptual evaluation for decomposition using various types of images is shown in Fig. 24 (From top to bottom; *Baboon*, *Book*, *Granada*, *Kyufun*, and *Peppers*). Note that *Baboon* and *Peppers* are provided by USC SIPI database. The other images are prepared by the authors.

An watermarked image I' is shown in Fig. 25 in which high strength-level of watermark has been applied to show distinct embedding effects. Therefore, I' is heavily degenerated.

Original Image I Complement piece I_c Endorse piece I_e

Fig. 24. Various Types of Output Images

4.4.2 Robustness evaluation of watermark using StirMark benchmark

Parameters on StirMark used in this implementation is listed in Table 8. For example of AFFINE, 8 levels of affine transformed images are generated. Robustness is examined by extracting ω from transformed images.

Evaluation results are shown below. Watermark is detected from 24 images out of 47 attacked images as shown in Table 8, labeled as "Succeed." We also show how a watermarked image is affected by decomposition. We have compared robustness of two watermarked images in which combination of embedding and decomposition and the one without decomposition have been applied. The latter one, the one without decomposition shows 31/47 cases are successfully extracted. The comparison of the two methods is shown in Fig. 26. Black lines show robustness of a watermarked image embedded with decomposition, and gray lines show the one without decomposition. The experimental results provide effective evidence showing that robustness of a watermarked image is little affected by decomposition.

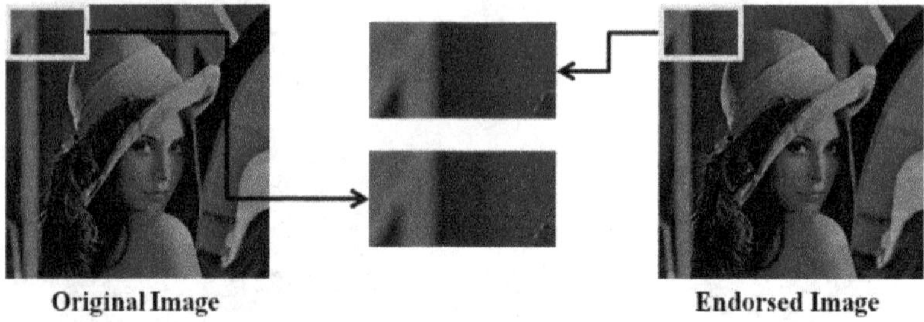

Fig. 25. Original Image I and Endorsed Image I'

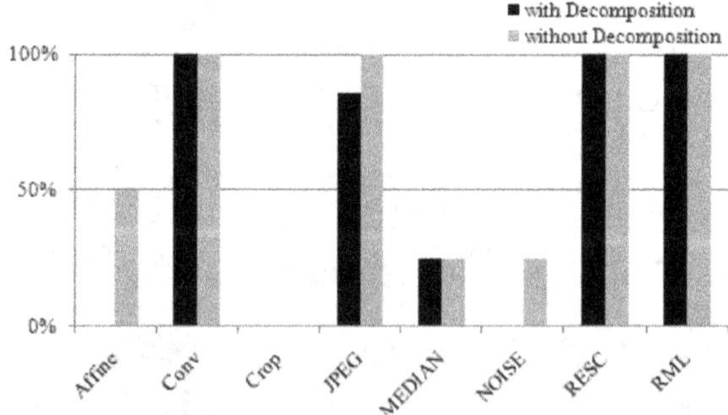

Fig. 26. Robustness of Watermark

5. Conclusion

Our primal consideration is that most of the security applications or tools are difficult to use in which special skill, knowledge and tools are needed. However, majority of the people is not capable of understanding programming or special mean of computer term. Although, the Internet becomes popular commodity, security tool is way behind to be commodity. Practical and secure watermarking is urgently needed. A fair and secure digital content trading scheme that protects both provider's and client's security is introduced in this chapter.

Blind watermarking based on cryptography and watermarking is one of the effective techniques in which performance evaluation is introduced based on our implementation. This satisfies higher level of security at heavy processing cost because cryptography is not compatible with watermarking. Performance evaluation which shows feasibility of blind watermarking is introduced.

Pseudo-blind watermarking (Okada et al., 2009) which uses media processing instead of cryptography is an alternative method of the blind watermarking. This scheme enhances security and compatibility of watermarking. Performance evaluation is also introduced. This scheme is able to resolve the problems of blind watermarking which are robustness and processing cost.

Even though security tools have been developed, most of them are still difficult to use for ordinary people. However, our concern is that providing user-friendly security tools enables to enhance entire security level because if more people use security tools, entire security level would be increased rather than providing absolute security level to only certain people who has high literacy to use security tools. One of our future work (Okada et al., 2011), intuitive watermark extraction is designed for people who have no knowledge nor skill is proposed toward user-friendly digital watermarking.

6. References

Ackerman, M.S. (1999). Privacy in E-Commerce: Examining User Scenarios and Privacy Preferences, *ACM Press*, pp.1-8

Acquisti, A.(2004). Privacy in Electronic Commerce and the Economics of Immediate Gratification, *ACM Electronic Commerce Conference (EC'04), ACM Press*

Bender, W.; Gruhl, D.; Morimoto, N.(1995). Techniques for Data Hiding, *SPIE*, Vol.2020, pp.2420-2440

El Gamal, T.(1985). A Public Key Cryptosystem and a Signature Scheme Based on Discrete Logarithms, *IEEE Trans. on Information Theory*, Vol.IT-31, No.4, pp.469-472

Furukawa, J.(2004). Secure Detection of Watermarks, *IEICE Trans.*, Vol.E87-A, No.1, pp.212-220

Iwamura, K.; Sakurai, K; Imai, H. (1997). Blind Fingerprinting. *Technical report of IEICE. ISEC*, Vol.97, pp. 63-74

Lin, E.; Podilchuk, C. ; Delp, E.(2000). Detection of Image Alterations Using Semi-fragile Watermarks, *SPIE-3971*

Okada, M.; Kikuchi, H.; Okabe, Y. (2008). Multi-Bit Embedding in Asymmetric Digital Watermarking without Exposing Secret Information. *IEICE (The Institute of Electronics, Information and Communication Engineers)*, Vol.E91-D, No.5, pp.1348-1358

Okada, M.; Okabe, Y.; Uehara, T.(2009). A Privacy-Secure Content Trading System for Small Content Providers Using Semi-Blind Digital Watermarking. *The 2009 International Workshop on Forensics for Future Generation Communication environments (F2GC) in conjunction with CSA2009*, Vol.CFP0917F-PRT Vol.2, pp.561-568

Okada, M.; Okabe, Y. ; Uehara, T. (2010). A Web-based Privacy-Secure Content Trading System for Small Content Providers Using Semi-Blind Digital Watermarking, *Annual IEEE Consumer Communications and Networking Conference (IEEE-CCNC2010)*

Okada, M.; Matsuyama, S. ; Hara, Y.(2011). User-friendly Digital Watermark Extraction Using Semi-transparent Image, *8th Annual IEEE Consumer Communications and Networking Conference (IEEE-CCNC2011)*

Okamoto, T. ; Uchiyama, S.(1998). A New Public-key Cryptosystem as Secure as Factoring, *EUROCRYPT'98*, pp.308-318

Paillier, P. (1999). Public-key Cryptosystems based on Composite Degree Residuosity Classes, *EUROCRYPT'99*, pp.223-238

Petitcolas, F.A.P. (2000). Watermarking Schemes Evaluation, *IEEE Signal Processing*, Vol.17, No.5, pp.58-64

Pfitzmann, B. ;Schunter, M. (1996). Asymmetric Fingerprinting, *EUROCRYPT'96 LNCS*, Vol.1070, pp.84-95

7

Key Establishment Protocol for Wireless Sensor Networks

Ali Fanian and Mehdi Berenjkoub
Department of Electrical and Computer Engineering, Isfahan University of Technology (IUT), Isfahan, Iran

1. Introduction

Wireless sensor networks usually comprise a number of sensors with limited resources. Each sensor includes sensing equipment, a data processing unit, a short range radio device and a battery [Pottie & Kaiser, 2000; Kahn et al.,1999; Akyildiz, 2002]. These networks have been considered for various purposes including border security, military target tracking and scientific research in dangerous environments [Perrig et. al., 2002; Kung & Vlah, 2003; Brooks, 2003]. Since the sensors may reside in an unattended and/or hostile environment, security is a critical issue. An adversary could easily access the wireless channel and intercept the transmitted information, or distribute false information in the network. Under such circumstances, authentication and confidentiality should be used to achieve network security. Since authentication and confidentiality protocols require a shared key between entities, key management is one of the most challenging issues in wireless sensor networks (WSNs) [Perrig et. al., 2002].

In the literature, key management protocols are based on either symmetric or asymmetric cryptographic functions [Perrig et. al., 2002]. Due to resource limitations in the sensors, key management protocols based on public keys are not suitable [Perrig et. al., 2002], [Chan et. al., 2003]. Hence, key management protocols based on symmetric cryptographic functions have been extensively investigated [Chan et. al., 2003-Fanian et.al, May 2010]. There are two types of symmetric key management schemes based on an on-demand trust center or key pre-distribution. With an on-demand trust center, the center must generate common keys for every pair of nodes that wish to establish a secure connection. Due to the lack of an infrastructure in WSNs, this scheme is not suitable. With key pre-distribution, key material is distributed among all nodes prior to deployment. In this scheme, each node carries a set of keys to establish a secure connection with other nodes.

A number of key pre-distribution schemes have been developed. A very simple approach is to have a unique pre-loaded key that is shared among the nodes. Then all sensors can encrypt or decrypt data between themselves using this key. Due to its simplicity, this method is very efficient in regards to memory usage and processing overhead, but it suffers from a very serious security problem. If even one of the sensors is captured by an adversary, the security of the entire network will be compromised. Another simple approach, called the basic scheme, is to generate a distinct key between every pair of sensors and store these in the sensors. In this case, if N sensors are deployed in the network, each must store N-1 keys. Despite ideal resilience, this scheme is not scalable, and is not memory efficient, particularly in large networks. In addition, after node deployment, if a new node wants to join the network, none of the previously deployed sensors will have a common key with the new node. Recently, many key establishment protocols have been proposed to address this problem [Chan et. al., 2003- Fanian et. al., 2010], but as we will show most have security or performance issues. These schemes are based on random key pre-distribution, symmetric polynomials and/or the Blom scheme. As shown in the analysis section, with the protocols based on random key pre-distribution, an adversary can obtain the common key between non-compromised sensors by compromising some sensors. Thus, these schemes have a serious security problem. In the symmetric polynomial and/or Blom scheme, however, perfect security can be achieved but resource consumption is an issue. In this chapter, a key establishment protocol employing four key pre-distribution models for sensor networks with different requirements.

In this chpate, we propose a new key establishment protocol called HKey. In this protocol, both efficient resource consumption and perfect security are the goals this protocol. The approach is similar to that of the basic scheme where every pair of sensors has a unique common key. In the proposed protocol, each sensor has a secret key and a unique identity. The common key between two sensors is generated using the secret key of one node and the identity of the other. This key is stored only in the latter node. For example, suppose sensors A and B want to generate a common key. Before deployment, the key distribution center (KDC) generates a key, for example, using the secret key of A and the identity of B, and stores this key only in B. When these sensors want to establish a common key, sensor A can generate the key with its own secret key and the identity of B. Sensor B just retrieves this key from its memory. Hence the memory usage in the proposed scheme is half that of the basic scheme.

In HKey, we propose several different models based on the WSN requirements. In some of these models, the aim is low memory consumption in the sensors. In others, network connectivity and memory usage are equally important. In the last model, the goal is high connectivity. The models are deterministic, so every sensor knows whether or not it can establish a direct common key with another sensor. Since, every pairwise key between two sensors is unique, the security of the protocols is perfect. Also, it this protocol, only one node needs to store a common key, the common key can be generated between a new node and an old one based on the proposed protocol and the key stored in the new node. Therefore, this protocol is scalable. As we will show, this protocol is efficient in comparison other proposed protocols.

The rest of the chapter is organized as follows. Section 2 reviews some required primitives including related work. Details of our key establishment protocol are discussed in Section 3. Performance evaluation and security analysis of the proposed protocol are presented in Section 4. Finally, some conclusions are given in Section 5.

2. Background

Most of the proposed key establishment protocols in WSNs are based on random key pre-distribution, symmetric polynomials and/or the Blom scheme. In this section, we review some well known protocols based on these techniques.

2.1 Key establishment protocols based on random key pre-distribution

Eschenauer et al. [Eschenauer & Gligor, 2002] proposed a random key pre-distribution scheme for WSNs. In this approach, before deployment some keys from a large key pool are selected randomly and stored in the sensors. After deployment in the network, a pair of nodes may have a shared common key to establish a secure connection. If there is no common key between two sensors, they have to establish a key through an intermediate sensor node which has common keys with both sensors. In this method, there is a tradeoff between connectivity and security. Network connectivity is determined from the probability of direct key generation between two adjacent sensors. As the size of the key pool increases, connectivity decreases, but protocol security increases. Due to the distribution of random keys, it may not be possible to establish a common key between every pair of sensors.

Du et al. [Du, 2004] proposed a deployment knowledge key management protocol (denoted Du-1), based on the approach in [Eschenauer & Gligor, 2002]. In this case, deployment knowledge is modeled using a Gaussian probability distribution function (pdf). Methods which do not use deployment knowledge such as in [Eschenauer & Gligor, 2002], assume a uniform pdf for the node distribution in the network. In this case, sensors can reside anywhere in the network with equal probability. In [Du, 2004], the network area is divided into square cells and each cell corresponds to one group of sensors. The key pool is divided into sub key pools of size S, one for each cell, such that each sub key pool has some correlated keys with its neighboring sub key pools. Each sub key pool has αSc common keys with the horizontal and vertical neighboring sub key pools, and βSc common keys with the diagonal neighboring sub key pools, such that $4\alpha + 4\beta = 1$, with $\alpha > \beta$. Each sensor in a cell randomly selects m_R keys from its associated sub key pool.

2.2 Key establishment protocols based on symmetric polynomials

A symmetric polynomial [Borwein & Erde´lyi, 1995; Zhou & Fang, Apr. 2006; Zhou & Fang, Oct. 2006] is a t-degree $(K+1)$-variate polynomial defined as follows

$$f(x_1, x_2, \ldots, x_{K+1}) = \sum_{i_1=0}^{t} \sum_{i_2=0}^{t} \cdots \sum_{i_{k+1}=0}^{t} a_{i_1, i_2, \ldots, i_k, i_{k+1}} x_1^{i_1} x_2^{i_2} \ldots x_K^{i_K} x_{K+1}^{i_{K+1}} \quad (1)$$

All coefficients of the polynomial are chosen from a finite field F_q, where q is a prime integer. The polynomial f is a symmetric polynomial so that [Zhou & Fang, Apr. 2006]

$$f(x_1, x_2, \ldots, x_{K+1}) = f(x_{\partial(1)}, x_{\partial(2)}, \ldots, x_{\partial(K+1)}) \quad (2)$$

where ∂ denotes a permutation. Every node using the symmetric polynomial based protocol takes K credentials $(I_1, I_2, \ldots, I_K)$ from the key management center, and these are stored in memory. The key management center must also compute the polynomial shares using the node credentials and the symmetric polynomial. The coefficients b_i stored in node memory as the polynomial share are computed as follows

$$f_u(x_{K+1}) = f(I_1, I_2, \ldots, I_K, x_{K+1}) = \sum_{i=0}^{t} b_i x_{K+1}^{i} \quad (3)$$

Every pair of nodes with only one mismatch in their identities can establish a shared key. Suppose the identities of nodes u and v have one mismatch in their identities $(c_1,c_2,\ldots,c_{i-1},u_i,c_{i+1},\ldots,c_K)$ and $(c_1,c_2,\ldots,c_{i-1},v_i,c_{i+1},\ldots,c_K)$, respectively. In order to compute a shared key, node u takes v_i as the input and computes $f_u(v_i)$, and node v takes u_i as the input and computes $f_v(u_i)$. Due to the polynomial symmetry, both nodes compute the same shared key. In [Zhou & Fang, Apr. 2006] it was shown that in order to maintain perfect security in the WSN, the polynomial degree must satisfy

$$\begin{cases} 0 \le N_i - 2 \le t \\ N_i K + 1\sqrt{\dfrac{K(K+1)!}{2}} \le t \end{cases} \qquad i = 1,2,\ldots,K \tag{4}$$

where N_i is the number of nodes in group i.

Zhou et al. [Zhou & Fang, Apr. 2007] proposed another key management protocol named LAKE which is based on symmetric polynomials and deployment knowledge. In this scheme, the network is also divided into square cells and each cell is allocated to one group of sensors. A t-degree tri-variate symmetric polynomial is employed. Each sensor in this protocol has credentials (n_1, n_2), where n_1 and n_2 represent the cell identity and the sensor identity, respectively. According to Section 2-1, the sensor polynomial share is calculated and stored in the sensor. After deployment, sensors that have one mismatch in their credentials can directly compute a shared key.

Lin et al. [Liu & Ning, 2003] proposed another key management protocol called LPBK in which the network area is divided into square cells. Each cell has a specific symmetric polynomial which is used to compute the polynomial share for the sensors in the corresponding cell and four adjacent vertical and horizontal cells. Therefore, each sensor must store five polynomial shares in its memory. Then each sensor can directly compute a common key with the sensors in these five cells.

We proposed a key establishment protocol for large scale sensor networks based on both symmetric polynomials and random key pre-distribution called HKEP [Fanian et. al., Apr 2010]. In HKEP, both symmetric polynomials and random key pre-distribution are used to improve efficiency. In this scheme, key information is distributed to the sensors during the pre-deployment stage. Once the sensors have been deployed, they can produce a common key either directly or indirectly. Due to the use of two methods in HKEP, two types of information must be stored in the sensors. One is the sensor polynomial shares generated using the symmetric polynomials and finite projective plan, while the other is a set of random keys. Finite projective plane is a subset of symmetric BIBDs. There are two types of key generation in HKEP. In the first type, a common key between near sensors is generated via their polynomial shares. The polynomial shares for each sensor are distributed by a finite projective plan which is a symmetric design discus in combinatorial design theory. In the second type, a common key between far sensors is generated using the pre-distributed random keys. Since in this case a key may be selected by several sensors, the common key between two far sensors may also be used by other pairs of sensors. Conversely, the common key between near sensors is unique. As we will show, the proposed end to end key establishment protocol between every pair of sensors can be supported without significant overhead.

Another proposed key establishment protocol, called SKEP, is based on symmetric polynomial [Fanian et. al., 2011]. In SKEP, the network area is divided into non-overlapping hexagonal cells, and the sensors are allocated in groups to these cells. The center of a cell is defined as the deployment point of the sensors allocated to that cell. In SKEP, each cell has a distinct t-degree bi-variate symmetric polynomial given by

$$f(x_1, x_2) = \sum_{i_1=0}^{t} \sum_{i_2=0}^{t} a_{i_1,i_2} x_1^{i_1} x_2^{i2}$$

Each sensor has a triplet of credentials, *(i,j,k)*. The first two credentials specify the deployment point of the sensor, while the last uniquely identifies each sensor in the cell. The polynomial share of a sensor, $f_k(x)$, can be computed from the symmetric polynomial assigned to cell *C(i,j)* and the sensor credential *k* as follows

$$f_i(x_2) = f_i(A, x_2) = \sum_{i_1=0}^{t} \sum_{i_2=0}^{t} a_{i_1,i_2} A^{i_1} x_2^{i2} = \sum_{i_2=0}^{t} b_{i_2,A} x_2^{i2}$$

$$, b_{i_2,A} = \sum_{i_1=0}^{t} a_{i_1,i_2} A^{i_1}$$

If the polynomial share of two sensors is generated from the same symmetric polynomial, these sensors can create a common key by exchanging their credentials. Before distributing sensors in the network, the secret information is placed in the sensors. Given the sensor distribution in the network, some sensors in neighboring cells or even non-neighboring cells can be adjacent to each other. In order to connect to the network, these sensors must be able to generate a common key. Therefore, some correlated secret information should be given to these sensors in order to generate this key. However, this should not consume a significant amount of sensor memory. To meet this requirement, SKEP generates a polynomial share from the symmetric polynomial allocated to each cell for a portion of the sensors in neighboring cells. The sensors containing this additional polynomial share can operate as agent nodes to indirectly generate common keys between sensors in neighboring cells. In order to generate this additional polynomial share, we divide each hexagonal cell into six virtual regions. The division of cell *(i,j)* into virtual regions is shown in figure 1.

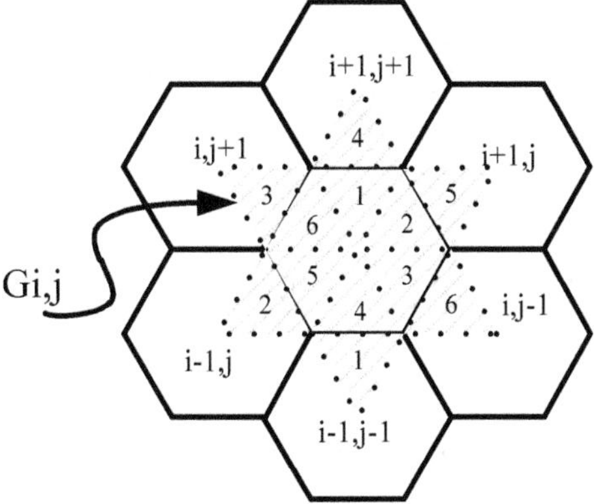

Fig. 1. Dividing each cell into six virtual regions.

Each sensor will belong to one of these virtual regions according to its credential. After deployment, a sensor may not reside in the virtual region it is allocated to. However, each sensor can infer adjacent sensors which have a suitable polynomial share, and can also find suitable agents to generate an indirect common key with the other sensors. As mentioned previously, each sensor has three credential (i,j,k), so two sensors can easily verify whether they are in a common group via their credentials.

2.3 Key establishment protocols based on blom's scheme

Blom proposed a key establishment protocol that allows each pair of nodes to establish a common key [Blom, 1985]. In this method, if no more than t nodes are compromised, the link between non-compromised nodes will remain secure. We refer to this as a *t-secure* method. To guarantee perfect security in a network with N nodes, an (N-2)-secure Blom scheme should be used. In the initialization phase, the key management center constructs a $(t+1)\times N$ matrix G over a finite field F_q, where N is the size of the network and q is a large prime. The matrix G is known by all nodes. Then the center constructs a random $(t+1)\times(t+1)$ symmetric matrix D over $GF(q)$, and an $N\times(t+1)$ matrix $P=(D\cdot G)^T$, where T denotes transpose. The matrix D is kept secret in the center and is not revealed to any user. If D is symmetric, then $K=P\cdot G$ is also symmetric since

$$K=P\cdot G=(D\cdot G)^T\cdot G=G^T\cdot D^T\cdot G=G^T\cdot D\cdot G=G^T\cdot P^T=(P\cdot G)^T \tag{5}$$

Therefore, K_{ij} is equal to K_{ji}, where K_{ij} is the element in the ith row and j^{th} column of K. In the Blom scheme, K_{ij} is used as a secret key between the ith and jth sensors. To generate this common key, the key management center assigns the ith row of P and ith column of G to user i, $i=1, 2, \dots, N$. When nodes i and j want to establish a common key, they first exchange their columns of G. Then they can compute K_{ij} and K_{ji}, respectively, using their private row of P according to

$$K_{ij}=\begin{bmatrix}P_{i,1} & P_{i,2} & \dots & P_{i,t+1}\end{bmatrix}\cdot\begin{bmatrix}G_{1,j}\\ G_{2,j}\\ \cdot\\ \cdot\\ \cdot\\ G_{t+1,j}\end{bmatrix} \tag{6}$$

As mentioned previously, G is public information, so the nodes can freely transmit their columns of G. It has been shown that if any t+1 columns of G are linearly independent then the Blom scheme is t-secure [Blom, 1985]. In this scheme, each sensor must store a row of P and a column of G. Therefore, the memory required is 2t+2. However, the structure of G can be exploited to reduce this memory requirement [Zhou et. al., 2005].

Du [Du et. al., 2006] proposed another key management protocol (denoted Du-2) using the Blom scheme. In this case, many pairs of matrices G and D, called the key spaces, are produced, and some key spaces are assigned to each cell. Adjacent cells have some common key space as in [Du, 2004], where adjacent cells have correlation between their sub key pools. Each sensor selects τ key spaces randomly, and according to the Blom scheme, the required information is stored in the sensors. As a result, sensors with a common key space can produce a common key. As in [Du, 2004], two vertical or horizontal neighboring cells have αSc common key spaces, and two diagonal neighboring cells have βSc common key spaces, where Sc is the number of key spaces assigned to a cell.

Yu and Guan [Yu & Guan, 2008] also proposed a key management protocol based on the Blom scheme. In this protocol, the network area is divided into hexagonal cells and information on the associated matrices is stored in the sensors based on deployment knowledge. The matrices are assigned to the cells such that a confidential exclusive matrix, denoted A_i (equivalent to matrix D in the Blom method), is allocated to cell i. The sensors in a cell, according to their identities, take a row from the corresponding matrix so they can produce a common key directly. To generate a common key between sensors belonging to different cells, another confidential matrix B is employed. The B matrices are allocated to the cells based on two parameters b and w, where b is the number of matrices allocated to a group, and w is the number of rows selected by each sensor from these matrices. The analysis in [Yu & Guan, 2008] shows that the best results are obtained with w=2 and b=2. In this approach, the cells are divided into two categories, base cells and normal cells. Base cells are not neighbors, but normal cells are neighbors with two base cells. To produce a common key between sensors in neighboring cells, a confidential matrix B is allocated to each base cell together with its six neighbors. Using the Blom scheme with this matrix, the necessary information is stored in the sensors. Then the sensors in the seven neighboring cells can produce a common key directly. Since each normal cell is a neighbor with two base cells, normal cell sensors receive information from two B matrices. Although the connectivity of this scheme is close to one, the memory consumption is extremely high.

We proposed another key establishment protocol for low resource wireless sensor networks based on the Blom scheme and random key pre-distribution called KELR [Fanian et. al., May 2010]. In this protocol, the Blom scheme is used to establish common keys between sensors in a cell. Therefore, the key distribution center constructs distinct matrices $G_{i,j}$ and $D_{i,j}$ for each cell $C(i,j)$. Each sensor has a triplet of credentials (i,j,k). The first two credentials specify the deployment point of the sensor and the last is the unique ID of the sensor in the cell. The center uses this unique identifier to construct $G_{i,j}$. Since the sensors belonging to a cell use the same matrix $D_{i,j}$, they can directly generate a common key.

Given the sensor distribution in the network, some sensors belonging to neighboring cells or even non-neighboring cells can be deployed adjacent to each other. In order to connect the network, these sensors should be able to generate a common key, so secret information must be allocated to enable this. However, this should not consume a lot of memory. To meet this requirement, KELR employs random key pre-distribution. We could also use the Blom scheme to establish common keys among sensors in neighboring cells, but this would result in high memory consumption.

3. The new key establishment protocol

Nodes are typically mobile in ad-hoc networks while in sensor networks they are assumed to be static after deployment. Therefore, deployment knowledge can be quite useful in producing common keys among sensors. In addition, in most WSN applications, a secure peer-to-peer connection between remote sensors is unnecessary [Chan et. al., 2003-Fanian et.al, May 2010]. Therefore, the main goal is establishing secure connections between adjacent sensors, so knowledge of probable neighbors can be beneficial in key pre-distribution. In fact, if one can predict the adjacency of sensors in the network, a key management protocol can be developed with high efficiency and low cost. However, due to the inherent randomness of sensor distribution, it is impossible to specify the exact location of each sensor; knowing the probable neighbors is much more realistic. Deployment knowledge is exploited to generate key material in the pre-deployment phase. We first present our key pre-distribution protocol and then consider its use with different models.

3.1 The new key pre-distribution protocol

As mentioned in Section 2, most key establishment protocols are based on symmetric polynomials, the Blom scheme and/or random key pre-distribution [Chan et. al., 2003-Fanian et.al, May 2010]. In this section, a High performance Key establishment protocol, HKey, is proposed which is not based on these techniques. The goal of this new protocol is efficient resource consumptions and perfect security. The approach is similar to that of the basic scheme where every pair of sensors has a unique common key. As mentioned in Section 1, in this case a distinct key must be generated and stored for every pair of sensors, so memory consumption will be excessive in a large scale WSN. Thus while this scheme is quite simple, it has poor scalability. The goal with HKey is to retain the simplicity of the basic scheme while providing scalability and memory efficiency. In the proposed protocol, each sensor has a secret key and a unique identity. The common key between two sensors is generated using the secret key of one node and the identity of the other. This key is stored only in the latter node. For example, suppose sensors A and B want to generate a common key. Before deployment, the key distribution center (KDC) generates a key, for example, using the secret key of A and the identity of B, and stores this key only in B. When these sensors want to establish a common key, sensor A can generate the key with its own secret key and the identity of B. Sensor B just retrieves this key from its memory. Hence the memory usage in the proposed scheme is half that of the basic scheme.

In a group of Ng sensors, each sensor must store $Ng/2$ keys to establish a secure connection with all sensors in the group. To generate common keys, the KDC establishes a key map matrix. This map is an $Ng \times Ng$ matrix which determines whether the secret key or the identity of the corresponding sensor is used to generate the common key. The KDC may generate the key map randomly such that the memory usage for each sensor is not more than $\left\lceil \frac{Ng-1}{2} \right\rceil$. In Table 1 the key map for a group of 8 sensors is shown. We assume the sensor identities are 1 to 8. In Table 1, '√' in location (i,j) indicates that the common key between sensors i and j is generated by the secret key of the jth sensor and the identity of the ith sensor, so the key must be stored in the ith sensor. Conversely, '–' indicates that the common key between sensors i and j is generated from the secret key of the ith sensor and the identity of the jth sensor, so the key must be stored in the jth sensor. Each sensor stores a maximum of only 4 keys.

Sensor Identity	1	2	3	4	5	6	7	8
1	×	-	√	-	√	-	√	-
2	√	×	-	√	-	√	-	√
3	-	√	×	-	√	-	√	-
4	√	-	√	×	-	√	-	√
5	-	√	-	√	×	-	√	-
6	√	-	√	-	√	×	-	√
7	-	√	-	√	-	√	×	-
8	√	-	√	-	√	-	√	×

Table 1. Key Map for a Group with 8 Sensors

The common keys are generated based on the key map generated in the pre-deployment phase. As mentioned previously, each sensor has a unique identity which is a number between 1 and Ng. To generate the common key K_{ij}, the KDC uses a one-way hash function with the secret S_i and identity N_j as follows

$$K_{ij} = H(S_i \,||\, N_j)$$

Unlike the basic scheme, the proposed protocol is scalable. In the basic scheme, since deployed nodes do not have a common key with a new node, they cannot establish a secure connection. In the proposed protocol, since only one node needs to store a common key, it can be generated between a new node and an old one based on the proposed protocol and the key stored in the new node. Therefore, all nodes can establish a secure connection.

3.2 Network and deployment model

In HKey, the network area is divided into non-overlapping hexagonal cells, and the sensors are allocated in groups to these cells. The center of a cell is defined as the deployment point of the sensors allocated to that cell. Figure 2 shows the division of the network into hexagonal cells. Each cell in HKey has a pair of credentials (i,j) which is the cell position. Using two-dimensional Cartesian coordinates and assuming that the deployment point of cell $C(i,j)$ is (x_i, y_i), the pdf of the sensor resident points is

$$f_k^{ij}(x,y|k \in C(i,j)) = f(x-x_i, y-y_j) = \frac{1}{2\pi\sigma^2} e^{-\left[(x-x_i)^2+(y-y_j)^2\right]/2\sigma^2}$$
$$\text{where } f(x,y) = \frac{1}{2\pi\sigma^2} e^{-\left[x^2+y^2\right]/2\sigma^2} \qquad (7)$$

And δ is the standard deviation. Assuming identical pdfs for all group of sensors, we can use $f_k(x,y\,|\,k \in C(i,j))$ instead of $f_k^{ij}(x,y|k \in C(i,j))$. As in [Liu & Ning, 2003-Du, 2006], in HKey it is assumed that the routing protocol delivers transmitted data to the correct destinations. A typical distribution for the sensors belonging to cell $C(1,2)$ is shown in figure 2.

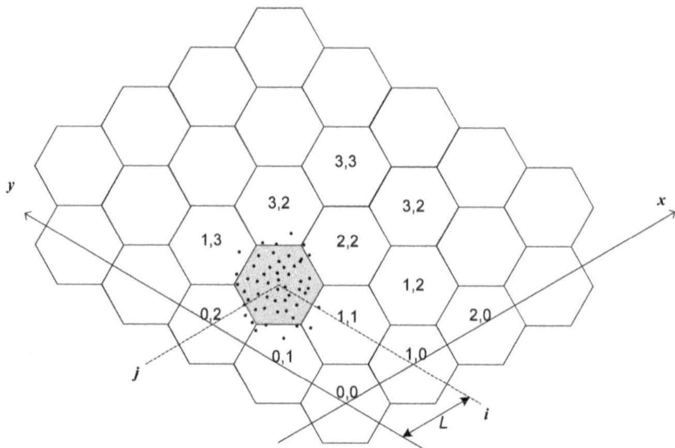

Fig. 2. A sensor network with distance L between adjacent deployment points. The center of each cell is defined as the deployment point.

3.3 Pre-distribution of secret information

The secret information for generating a common key should be produced before deployment. As mentioned in Section 3-1, in the proposed protocol, each sensor has a secret key, a unique identity, and some common keys with other sensors stored in its memory. In HKey, each sensor is able to establish a common key with any sensor in the same cell. If only common keys between sensors in a cell are generated, adjacent sensors belonging to different cells will not be able to establish a secure connection. Since sensor deployment follows a Gaussian distribution, it may be that two sensors from neighboring cells are adjacent to each other. Thus some sensors must be able to establish a common key with sensors in neighboring cells. For this purpose, in HKey the pre-distributed common keys are generated in two phases. In the first phase, the KDC generates the common keys for sensors belonging to a cell based on the proposed protocol in Section 3-1. In the second phase, common keys are distributed so that some sensors belonging to neighboring cells can establish a direct common key.

The percentage of sensors that have second phase keys has a great influence on network connectivity and memory consumption. Thus in HKey, we propose several different models based on the WSN requirements. In some of these models, the aim is low memory consumption in the sensors. In others, network connectivity and memory usage are equally important. In the last model, the goal is high connectivity. The models are deterministic, so every sensor knows whether or not it can establish a direct common key with another sensor. In figure 3, the four models are depicted.

First, a Low Resource consumption (HKey-LR) model is proposed for very low resource sensors. In HKey-LR, each cell is divided into two virtual regions. Virtual regions are also used in some of the other proposed models. In this case, cells are divided into regions, and in the pre-deployment stage each sensor in a cell is assigned to one of these regions. For example, if a cell with Nc sensors is divided into two virtual regions, as shown in figure 3(a), sensors with identities from 1 to $Nc/2$ are assigned to the first virtual region, and the remainder to the second region. After deployment, a sensor may not reside in their virtual region. However, during the key generation process, each sensor will know which adjacent sensors they can establish a common key with. In HKey-LR, a group consists of virtual regions from three neighboring cells. In figure 3(a), the network is divided into triangular areas. In Phase 2, the common keys are generated based on the proposed scheme with a small change. Since common keys among sensors belonging to a cell are generated in Phase 1, we should not produce any more of these keys in Phase 2. Therefore, in the second phase, the KDC only generates common keys among sensors in a group which belong to different cells. For instance, suppose each cell has 6 sensors, so a group has 9 sensors from three neighboring cells. Assume these sensors are A_1, A_2, A_3 in cell A, B_1, B_2, B_3 in cell B, and C_1, C_2, C_3 in cell C. The common keys among sensors in this group are shown in Table 2. In this Table, K_{ij} is the common key between sensors i and j generated using the secret key of sensor i and the identity of sensor j.

A_1	A_2	A_3	B_1	B_2	B_3	C_1	C_2	C_3
$K_{B1\text{-}A1}$	$K_{B1\text{-}A2}$	$K_{B1\text{-}A3}$	$K_{C1\text{-}B1}$	$K_{C1\text{-}B2}$	$K_{C1\text{-}B3}$	$K_{A1\text{-}C1}$	$K_{A1\text{-}C2}$	$K_{A1\text{-}C3}$
$K_{B2\text{-}A1}$	$K_{B2\text{-}A2}$	$K_{B2\text{-}A3}$	$K_{C2\text{-}B1}$	$K_{C2\text{-}B2}$	$K_{C2\text{-}B3}$	$K_{A2\text{-}C1}$	$K_{A2\text{-}C2}$	$K_{A2\text{-}C3}$
$K_{B3\text{-}A1}$	$K_{B3\text{-}A2}$	$K_{B3\text{-}A3}$	$K_{C3\text{-}B1}$	$K_{C3\text{-}B2}$	$K_{C3\text{-}B3}$	$K_{A3\text{-}C1}$	$K_{A3\text{-}C2}$	$K_{A3\text{-}C3}$

Table 2. Common Keys Generated in Phase 2

Second, a Medium Resource consumption (HKey-MR) model is proposed for low resource sensors. Cells in HKey-MR are divided into two types called base cells and normal cells. As shown in figure 3(b), cells $C(i,j)$ and $C(i+1,j+2)$ are base cells. Note that base cells are not neighbors of each other. Each normal cell is the neighbor of two base cells, and is divided into two virtual regions. A group consists of a base cell and virtual regions in the six neighboring cells. Each virtual region belongs to one group. The common keys among sensors belonging to different cells in a group are generated in Phase 2.

Third, an Advanced Medium Resource consumption (HKey-AMR) model is proposed. In HKey-AMR, as shown in figure 3(c), the network cells are divided into even and odd rows. Each cell located in an odd row is divided into two virtual regions. In this model each cell along with its six neighboring cells establishes a group. Each cell along with its neighboring cell that is in the same row establishes one group. In other words, the sensors in cell $C(i,j)$ belong to a distinct group with the sensors in cell $C(i-1,j)$ and also to a group with the sensors in cell $C(i+1,j)$, for j even or odd. If a cell is located in an even row, it will establish four distinct groups with neighboring cells located in odd rows. In figure 3(c), $C(i,j)$ is in an even row, so its sensors along with the sensors belonging to a virtual region of cells $C(i,j+1)$, $C(i+1,j+1)$, $C(i-1,j-1)$ and $C(i,j-1)$ establish four distinct groups. Common keys among sensors belonging to different cells in the groups are generated according to Phase 2 of the proposed protocol.

Finally, a High Performance (HKey-HP) model is proposed. In HKey-HP, similar to HKey-MR, the cells are divided into normal cells and base cells. Each group consists of one base cell and two neighboring normal cells, as shown in figure 3(d) for cell $C(i,j)$. In this case, each cell is a member of three groups. The common keys among sensors within groups are generated in Phase 2.

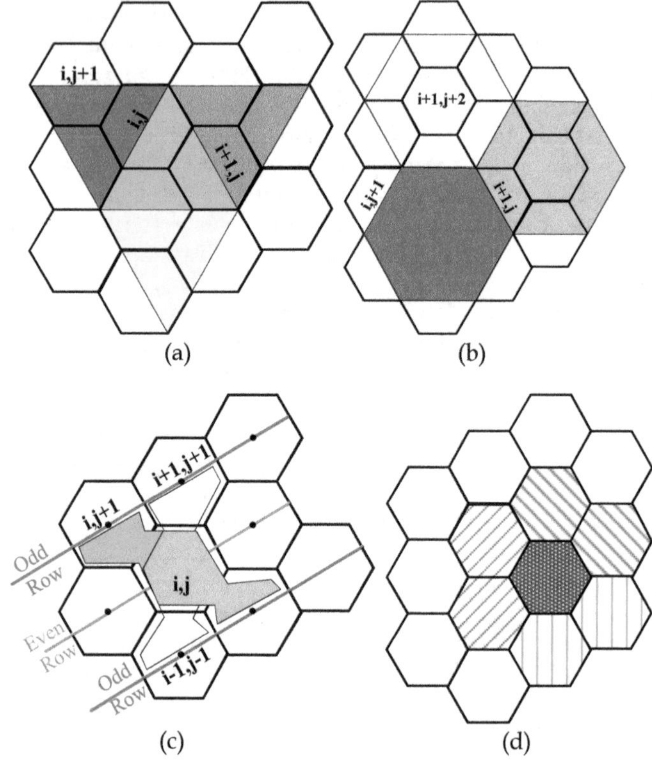

Fig. 3. The proposed key distribution models. a) Low Resource consumption (HKey-LR) b) Medium Resource consumption (HKey-MR) c) Advanced Medium Resource consumption (HKey-AMR) d) High Performance (HKey-HP). In a), b) and c), half of cell $(i,j+1)$ is a virtual region. In b) cells (i,j) and $(i+1,j+2)$ are base cells and their neighbors are normal cells. The shading denotes a group.

3.4 Direct key calculation

In the four proposed models, two sensors belonging to a cell can establish a shared key directly. If they do not belong to the same cell, they may be located in a common group. Based on the model employed, the sensors can easily determine if they are in the same group or not. Sensors in a group can also establish a common key directly.

3.5 Indirect key calculation

Considering the Gaussian distribution for sensor deployment, sensors in two distinct groups may be adjacent to each other. In this case, they cannot generate a common key directly and suitable agents must be found. A proper agent node is one that can generate common keys directly with both sensors. Since a number of sensors in two neighboring cells can directly generate common keys with sensors in both cells, at most two agent nodes suffice to generate a common key between any two adjacent sensors that cannot establish a common key directly. If the distance between sensor deployment points is large, establishing a common key between them may require several agents. Note that if the resident point distance between agents is less than the wireless transmission range, they can communicate with each other directly; otherwise, a routing protocol is needed to connect them such as in [Du, 2004 - Yu & Guan, 2008]. The performance and security of indirect common key generation is greatly affected by the number of agent nodes. In HKey, the number of usable agents is typically high to ensure efficient key generation.

4. Security analysis and performance evaluation

In this section the security analysis and performance evaluation of the proposed protocol are presented and compared with similar protocols including Du-1 [Du, 2004], LAKE [Zhou & Fang, Apr. 2007], LPBK [Liu & Ning, 2003], Du-2 [Du et. al., 2006] and Yu and Guan [Yu & Guan, 2008]. Using the threat model in [Su et. al, 2010], we assume that an adversary can obtain all secret information from compromised sensors, and their goal is to obtain the common keys between non-compromised sensors. An adversary may be an insider or outsider. An outsider does not have any prior information about the network or the relationship between sensors. In contrast, an insider can have significant information about the network such as the deployment model, sensor groups, etc., and thus may know which sensors can establish a common key with a given sensor directly. This information is very useful for some attacks such as network discovery, false route injection, common key compromising, etc [Su et. al, 2010]. Nevertheless, when the common key between every pair of sensors is distinct and independent from any other keys such as in the basic scheme and the proposed protocol, a brute-force attack is the only option for an adversary (insider/outsider) to compromise common keys. In other words, additional information about the sensors and the network does not help in finding a common key between two non-compromised sensors. Unlike the basic scheme and our proposed protocol, with the other protocols based on random key pre-distribution, the Blom scheme and/or symmetric polynomials, insider information can be exploited to compromise the common key between non-compromised sensors. The adversary is assumed to be an outsider who compromises sensor nodes randomly.

4.1 Network configuration

We consider a WSN with the following parameters similar to those in [Du et. al., 2006]:

- The number of sensors in the network is 10,000.
- The network area is $1000m \times 1000m$.
- Sensors have a two dimensional Gaussian distribution with standard deviation $\sigma = 50\ m$.
- The number of sensors in each cell is 100.
- The wireless transmission range is 40 m.

4.2 Local connectivity

Local connectivity is defined as the probability of direct key generation between two adjacent sensors. Each sensor can establish a common key with some adjacent sensors directly, and with other adjacent sensors indirectly. Three parameters are most relevant to the local connectivity. The first is the sensor distribution, which can be uniform or non-uniform. With a uniform distribution, each sensor may reside anywhere in the network. Since the available memory for each sensor is restricted, each sensor can establish a common key with a limited number of sensors. Therefore in this situation the local connectivity is often low [Eschenauer & Gligor, 2002]. With a non-uniform distribution (typically Gaussian), there is a greater chance that two adjacent sensors are members of the same cell or group. Thus in this case the local connectivity can be much higher. The second parameter is the shape and size of the groups. This influences how the correlated key information is distributed among sensors in neighboring cells. The last parameter is the average number of accessible sensors for each sensor. This is related to the sensor wireless transmission range and the density of the sensor distribution.

In this section, we use deployment knowledge to distribute secret information to the sensors. We compare our proposed models with those given above using the specified network parameters. In the scheme in [Du, 2004], each cell has a sub key pool with S keys, and there are some common keys between neighboring cell sub key pools. As mentioned in Section 2-3, the two horizontal or vertical neighboring cell sub key pools have αS common keys, and the two diagonal neighboring cells have βS common keys. The probability of common key establishment between two sensors in a cell with this technique is

$$P_C = 1 - \frac{\binom{S-m}{m}}{\binom{S}{m}} \tag{8}$$

where m is the number of keys in each sensor. The sub key pools of two neighboring cells have ωS shared keys where ω is equal to α for horizontal or vertical neighboring cells and β for the other neighboring cells. Two sensors belonging to neighboring cells can establish a common key if they select at least one common key from the shared keys in their sub key pools. The probability of having i common keys for these sensors is

$$\frac{\binom{\omega S}{i}^2 \binom{S-\omega S}{m-i}^2}{\binom{S}{m}^2}$$

The probability of common key establishment between two sensors belonging to neighboring cells is then

$$P_C = \sum_{i=1}^{\min(\omega.S,m)} \frac{\binom{\omega S}{i}^2 \binom{S-\omega S}{m-i}^2}{\binom{S}{m}^2} \tag{9}$$

With the approach in [Du et. al., 2006], *Sc* key spaces are assigned to a cell, where each key space is a Blom matrix. Similar to [Du, 2004], two neighboring cell key spaces have some common matrices. In this scheme each sensor selects τ matrices from the corresponding key spaces. Thus the probability of establishing a common key between two adjacent sensors can be computed similar to (8) and (9).

In LAKE, a tri-variate *t*-degree symmetric polynomial is used to generate a polynomial share for each sensor. With this scheme, every pair of sensors belonging to a cell can establish a common key, but only one sensor belonging to each cell can establish a direct key with a given sensor in another cell. In LPBK and the approach of Yu and Guan [Yu & Guan, 2008], two adjacent sensors belonging to a cell or neighboring cells can establish a direct common key.

In the proposed models, every pair of sensors belonging to a cell can establish a direct common key. However, only some sensors belonging to neighboring cells can establish a direct common key. In HKey-LR the probability of establishing a common key for these sensors is 1/6. In HKey-MR, if one sensor is in a base cell and another is in a neighboring normal cell, the probability is 0.5. If the sensors are in different normal cells around a base cell, the probability of a common key existing is 0.25. In HKey-AMR, every pair of sensors belonging to neighboring cells in the same row can establish a common key directly. However, the probability for nodes belonging to other neighboring cells is 0.5. In HKey-HP, every pair of sensors belonging to neighboring cells can establish a direct common key.

We simulated the local connectivity of the techniques considered, and the results are given in figure 5. Our simulation program was developed using the C++ language in the Visual Studio .Net environment. This table shows that HKey-LR has lower local connectivity compared to the other proposed models. However, as we will discuss in the next section, the memory usage with this model is lower than with the others. The local connectivity with LAKE is less than the other schemes. Moreover, the local connectivity for HKey-HP, the approach by Yu and Guan [Yu & Guan, 2008], and LPKB are approximately equal to one. However as we will show, the memory usage in our proposed model is lower compared to these schemes. In the simulations, we assumed $\alpha = 15\%$ and $\beta = 10\%$ for the approaches in [Du, 2004] and [Du et. al., 2006].

4.3 Memory usage

Memory in sensors is often very restricted, so the key establishment protocol should use memory efficiently. In this section, the memory usage is determined for the proposed HKey models and the other schemes considering perfect security. With perfect security, an adversary who wants to compromise the common key between two non-compromised sensors cannot do better than a brute-force attack or capturing at least one of these sensors. To achieve perfect security when symmetric polynomials are used, the polynomial degree, *t*, must satisfy (4). The Blom scheme is a *t*-secure scheme, so that if no more than *t* nodes are compromised, the link between non-compromised nodes will remain secure. In this case, *t* specifies the size of the Blom matrix and memory usage. Since in our protocol the common keys among sensors are generated using their secret keys, it intrinsically has perfect security.

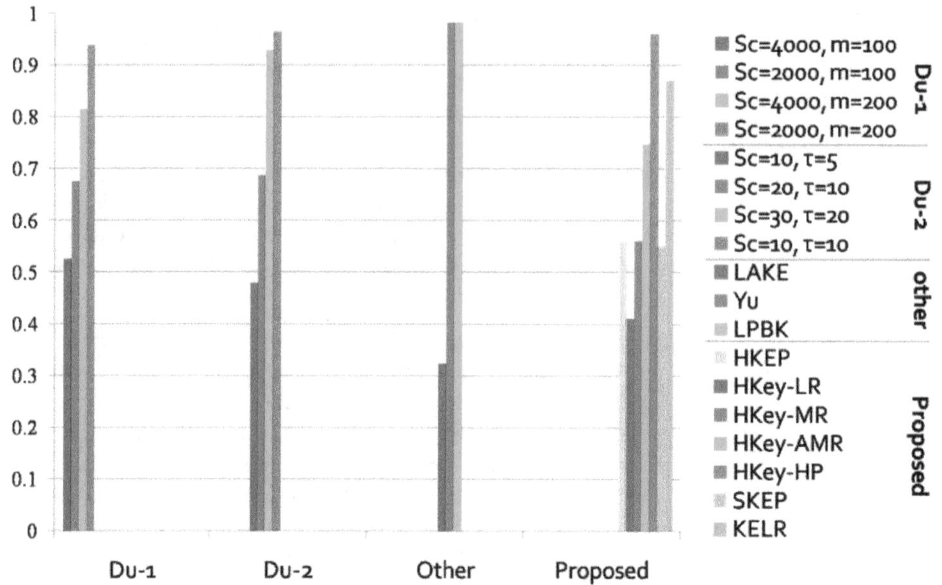

Fig. 4. Comparison of Local Connectivity with Different Techniques

4.3.1 Memory usage for HKey-LR

In HKey-LR, as shown in figure 3(a), each cell is divided into two virtual regions. In this model, a group consists of virtual regions from three neighboring cells. In Phase 2, only the common keys for sensors belonging to different cells are generated. The total memory usage comprises that required for keys generated in Phase 1 ($M_{LR,1}$) and Phase 2 ($M_{LR,2}$). As mentioned previously, in Phase 1 the KDC generates common keys for all sensors in a cell. If the number of sensors in a cell is Nc, the memory usage for each sensor in this phase will be $\left\lceil \frac{N_C}{2} \right\rceil$. In Phase 2, the KDC generates common keys for the groups. Since there are different regions in a group, the KDC generates common keys for the pairs of regions in the group. As shown in figure 3(a), there are three virtual regions in a group each from a neighboring cell. Let the virtual regions in a group be v_1, v_2, and v_3. In Phase 2, the KDC generates common keys among sensors in pairs (v_1, v_2), (v_1, v_3), and (v_2, v_3) independently such that the memory usage for all sensors is similar. If the number of sensors in v_1, v_2, and v_3 is n_1, n_2, and n_3, respectively, the number of common keys among sensors in (v_i, v_j) is $n_i \times n_j$. These keys must be distributed among n_i+n_j sensors. In HKey-LR, since each virtual region has $Nc/2$ sensors, the number of common keys for every pair of virtual regions is $Nc^2/4$. Since the number of sensors in each region is identical and the group structure is the same, the number of common keys distributed to the sensors in every pair of regions is the same. Therefore each sensor in the pair (v_i, v_j) must store $Nc/4$ keys out of $Nc^2/4$ keys. As a result, the memory usage for this model is

$$M_{LR,1} = \left\lceil \frac{N_C}{2} \right\rceil$$
$$M_{LR,2} = 2 \times \left\lceil \frac{N_C}{4} \right\rceil \tag{10}$$
$$M_{LR} = M_{LR,1} + M_{LR,2} \approx N_C$$

4.3.2 Memory usage for HKey-MR

In HKey-MR, as shown in figure 3(b), cells are divided into base cells and normal cells, and each normal cell is divided into two virtual regions. Each group consists of a base cell (v_1) and six virtual regions from neighboring cells (v_2 to v_7). Unlike HKey-LR, in HKey-MR the size of the regions is not equal. Although the number of sensors in six regions of a group is identical, the number of sensors in one region of that group is different. The KDC should generate and distribute common keys such that the memory usage for all sensors is close to identical. In this model, the number of sensors in v_1 is Nc and in the other regions is $Nc/2$. Thus, the number of common keys between v_1 and v_i (i = 2, 3, ..., 7) is $Nc^2/2$ and the number of common keys between v_i and v_j (i,j : 2, 3, ..., 7) is $Nc^2/4$. To balance the memory usage, we assume fractions α and β of the common keys are stored in v_1 and v_i , i = 2, 3, ..., 7, respectively. Since the sensors in v_1 have common keys with all sensors in $v_2, v_3, \ldots, v_7$, the memory usage for each sensor in v_1 is $3\alpha Nc$ in Phase 2. On the other hand, the common keys for the other regions can be equally distributed among them. Therefore, each sensor in v_i (i = 2, 3, ..., 7) has βNc common keys with v_1 and $Nc/4$ common keys with v_j (j=2, 3, ..., 7, $i \neq j$), so that in total there are $\beta Nc + 5Nc/4$ keys in Phase 2. To ensure the same memory usage for all sensors, α and β must satisfy

$$\begin{cases} 3\alpha Nc = \beta Nc + 5Nc/4 \\ \alpha + \beta = 1 \end{cases}$$
$$\text{giving } \alpha = \frac{9}{16} \text{ and } \beta = \frac{7}{16} \tag{11}$$

Therefore, the memory usage for HKey-MR is

$$M_{MR,1} = \left\lceil \frac{N_C}{2} \right\rceil$$
$$M_{MR,2} = \left\lceil \frac{27N_C}{16} \right\rceil \tag{12}$$
$$\text{giving } M_{MR} = \left\lceil \frac{35N_C}{16} \right\rceil \approx 2.2Nc$$

4.3.3 Memory usage for HKey-AMR

In HKey-AMR, as shown in figure 3(c), each cell and its neighboring cells establish six distinct groups. As described in Section 3-3, each cell constructs a group with each of its neighboring cells in the same row. Since the groups are similar, the common keys are distributed equally among the sensors in the group. Therefore, the number of common keys which should be stored in each sensor is $Nc/2$. In addition, each cell located in an even row constructs four separate groups with the virtual regions located in neighboring cells in odd rows. In this case, the two regions have different sizes, and the number of common keys generated for each group is $Nc^2/2$. In order to use the same memory in all sensors, similar to HKey-MR, we assume fractions α and β of the keys are stored in the sensors of even row cells (full-cells) and virtual regions (half-cells). Therefore the number of common keys stored in each sensor belonging to full and half cells is $\alpha Nc/2$ and βNc, respectively. Each virtual region located in an odd row belongs to two groups with neighboring cells in an even row. Since each full cell constructs four distinct groups with four half cells, the Phase 2 memory usage for a sensor belonging to an even row cell is $Nc + 2\alpha NC$, and for a sensor belonging to an odd row cell is $Nc + 2\beta NC$. Thus $\alpha = \beta = 1/2$ provides the required balanced memory usage in all sensors. The required memory for this model is then

$$\begin{aligned} &M_{\text{AMR},1} = \left\lceil \frac{N_C}{2} \right\rceil \\ &M_{\text{AMR},2} = \left\lceil \frac{N_C}{2} \right\rceil + \left\lceil \frac{N_C}{2} \right\rceil + 4 \times \left\lceil \frac{N_C}{4} \right\rceil \\ &\text{giving } M_{\text{AMR}} \approx 2.5 N_C \end{aligned} \tag{13}$$

4.3.4 Memory usage for HKey-HP

In HKey-HP, as shown in figure 3(d), each group consists of regions of three neighboring cells, and each cell is in three groups. The common keys among sensors in different cells are generated in Phase 2. Since groups in this model have the same structure and population, the common keys are equally distributed among the sensors. If the number of sensors belonging to the neighboring cells is n_1, n_2 and n_3, then the number of common keys generated in Phase 2 is $n_1 \times n_2 + n_1 \times n_3 + n_2 \times n_3$. These keys must be equally distributed among $n_1 + n_2 + n_3$ sensors. Since the number of sensors in each cell is N_c, the memory usage for this model is

$$\begin{aligned} &M_{\text{HP},1} = \left\lceil \frac{N_C}{2} \right\rceil \\ &M_{\text{HP},2} = 3N_C \\ &\text{giving } M_{\text{HP}} \approx 3.5 N_C \end{aligned} \tag{14}$$

4.3.5 Memory usage for other schemes

The memory usage for the other schemes is computed based on the perfect security condition. In LPBK, as mentioned previously, the key establishment protocol is based on symmetric polynomials. As shown in (4), in order to maintain perfect security the polynomial degree must be $N_i - 2 \le t$, where N_i is the number of polynomial shares generated from a symmetric polynomial. Therefore, N_i is equal to $5Nc$. To satisfy (4), the degree, t, of each symmetric polynomial must be at least $5Nc - 2$. From Section 2-2, each sensor receives five polynomial shares from five distinct symmetric polynomials. Since each sensor polynomial share has t coefficients and each sensor has five polynomial shares, the memory usage for LPBK with perfect security is $5(5Nc-2)$.

In LAKE, a tri-variate t-degree symmetric polynomial is used. In this scheme, each sensor can establish a direct common key with $2Nc$ nodes. According to (4), to achieve perfect security the polynomial degree and thus memory usage must be at least $2Nc-2$.

The key establishment protocols Du-2 [Du et. al., 2006] and Yu and Guan [Yu & Guan, 2008] are based on the Blom scheme. In this case, the KDC creates an $N_i \times (t+1)$ symmetric matrix. Each sensor stores a row of this matrix. As discussed in Section 2-3, the Blom scheme is t-secure if any subset with a maximum of t colluding sensors cannot compromise the common key between two other sensors. Therefore to achieve perfect security, the number of sensors which receive a row from the matrix must be less than t. With the approach in [Yu & Guan, 2008], in the best case, each base cell has six neighboring normal cells and each normal cell is the neighbor of two base cells. Then sensors in a base cell and the six neighboring normal cells have different rows from a Blom matrix, so t must be at least $7Nc$. Each sensor in a normal cell receives two rows from two matrices corresponding to its two neighboring base cells, so the required memory with the approach in [Yu & Guan, 2008] is at least $14Nc$. With the approach in [Du et. al., 2006], as stated in Section 2-3, each key space may exist in a maximum of two neighboring cells. Therefore, $2Nc$ sensors may select from the shared key space, so t must be at least $2Nc$, and each sensor selects τ key spaces from Sc spaces. The minimum value for τ is one. As τ increases, the memory usage and local connectivity (as shown in figure 4), also increases.

With the approach in [Du, 2004], which is also based on random key pre-distribution, each sensor selects m keys from a sub key pool. In this scheme, perfect security is not possible. Based on the memory analysis above, Table 3 summarizes the required memory for each scheme. This table shows that the memory usage with HKey-LR and HKey-MR is less than with the other schemes. LAKE also has low memory consumption. Although the memory usage with LAKE is almost equal to that with HKey-MR, the corresponding local connectivity is only 0.3228 compared 0.5601. Among the schemes with local connectivity close to one, the memory required with HKey-HP is lowest.

Scheme	Memory cost	Memory required to ensure secrecy of a direct key between sensors
LAKE	$t+1$	$2Nc-1$
LPBK	$5(t+1)$	$5(5Nc-2)$
Yu and Guan	$2(t+1)$	$14N_c+1$
Du-2	$O(\tau(t+1))$	$O(\tau(t+1))$
SKEP	$2(t+1)$	$4Nc$-1
KELR	$t+1$	Nc-1
HKey-LR	-	N_C
HKey-MR	-	$2.2Nc$
HKey- AMR	-	$2.5N_C$
HKey- HP	-	$3.5N_C$

Table 3. Memory Required with Different Schemes

4.4 Resilience against key exposure

Since sensors are deployed in hostile environments and the sensor hardware may not be tamper proof, an adversary may be able to capture key information from one or more sensors. In some key management schemes, it is possible to obtain common keys between uncompromised sensors by compromising some sensors. In methods based on symmetric polynomials or the Blom scheme, as mentioned in Section 2, when an adversary compromises more than t sensors, access can be obtained to the common key of uncompromised sensors. Therefore, by proper selection of t, the probability of keys belonging to uncompromised sensors being compromised can be reduced to an acceptable level, or even 0. However, increasing t directly affects the sensor processing and memory overhead (as shown in Table 4), thus selecting a large value of t may not be practical. Hence, t should be chosen based on the tradeoff between memory/processing cost and the security level. Here, we assume that an adversary can uniformly capture sensors in the network. Let N_i be the number of sensors in each group. If an adversary can compromise the common key between two uncompromised sensors if at least t sensors from the group are compromised, then the probability of a direct common key between two sensors in the same group being compromised is

$$P_{Com} = \sum_{i=t+1}^{N_i} \frac{\binom{N_i}{i}\binom{N-N_i}{X-i}}{\binom{N}{X}} \tag{15}$$

where X is the number of compromised sensors in the entire network and N is the number of sensors in the network.

In [Du, 2004], each sensor selects m_R keys from a sub key pool. An adversary can get more information about the sub key pool by compromising more sensors. In this scheme, each cell has a sub key pool with S keys, and each key exists in two neighboring sub key pools. Thus, the probability of compromising the key between two sensors that have a common key is

$$1-\left(1-\frac{m_R}{S}\right)^{X_i} \tag{16}$$

where X_i is the number of compromised sensors in a group. Since there are two cells in a group, the probability of compromising X_G sensors in a group when X sensors are compromised in the entire network is

$$P(X_G = i) = \binom{X}{i}\left(\frac{2}{n}\right)^i\left(1-\frac{2}{n}\right)^{X-i} \tag{17}$$

where n is the number of cells in the network. Therefore the probability of compromising a common key based on the pre-distributed random key approach in [Du, 2004] is

$$P_{Com} = \sum_{i=1}^{2Nc}\left(1-\left(1-\frac{m_R}{S}\right)^i\right)\binom{X}{i}\left(\frac{2}{n}\right)^i\left(1-\frac{2}{n}\right)^{X-i} \tag{18}$$

In [Du et. al., 2006], each sensor selects τ key spaces from Sc available key spaces, and each key space is a Blom matrix. The value of τ is $m/t+1$, where m is the size of the available memory and t is the size of Blom matrix. Similar to [Du, 2004], each key space is shared between two neighboring cells and may be selected by $2Nc$ sensors. When t sensors having distinct rows of the same key space are compromised, the other common keys in the key space are also compromised. Therefore, assuming X_i sensors in a group are compromised, the probability of compromising a common key between uncompromised sensors is

$$\sum_{i=t+1}^{X_i} \binom{X_i}{i} \left(\frac{\tau}{Sc}\right)^i \left(1-\frac{\tau}{Sc}\right)^{X_i-i} \tag{19}$$

Then the probability of compromising the common key between two uncompromised sensors when X sensors are compromised in the entire network is

$$P_{Com} = \sum_{X_i=1}^{X} \sum_{i=t+1}^{X_i} \binom{X}{X_i} \left(\frac{2}{n}\right)^{X_i} \left(1-\frac{2}{n}\right)^{X-X_i} \binom{X_i}{i} \left(\frac{\tau}{Sc}\right)^i \left(1-\frac{\tau}{Sc}\right)^{X_i-i} \tag{20}$$

Since, our proposed key establishment protocol is not based on symmetric polynomials or the Blom scheme, capturing some sensors has no impact on compromising the common keys between uncompromised sensors. Hence, in the proposed protocol, the probability of compromising a common key between two uncompromised sensors is zero. On the other hand, if the available sensor memory is less than that required to store the Phase 1 and 2 common keys, fewer keys can be stored without any impact on security. However, the local connectivity will be reduced. Thus HKey can be employed when there are memory restrictions. In contrast, with the schemes based on symmetric polynomials or the Blom scheme, each sensor in a group can generate a common key with all other sensors in that group, so there is no flexibility to accommodate memory restrictions.

Using the above analysis, the probability of compromising a common key for all techniques except the proposed one was calculated and the results are shown in figure 5. Note that this probability is zero for all HKey models, so the security of our proposed models is not depicted. With Du-1 [Du, 2004], if the available memory increases, the number of selected random keys can be increased, but the security of this scheme based on (16) will be decreased. Conversely, techniques based on the Blom scheme or symmetric polynomials will have increased security according to (15).

4.5 Computational overhead

Key generation in HKey is based on symmetric cryptography. As mentioned in Section 3-1, a one way hash function is used to generate a common key. For a given pair of sensors, one has the common key in memory, while the other can generate the common key using the hash function. Thus in HKey, key generation is done in only one node, and the other does not require any processing. To estimate the required processing in a sensor, we assume that the key length is 128 bits and the Advanced Encryption Standard (AES) algorithm is used.

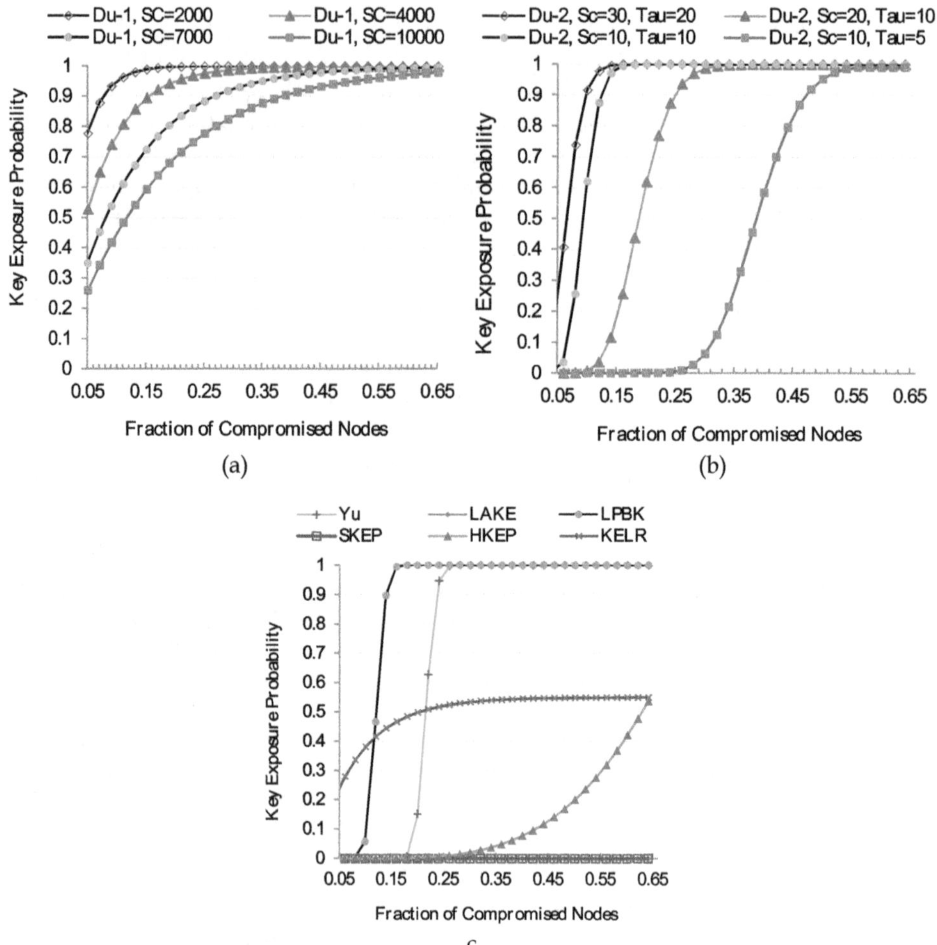

Fig. 5. Key resilience with different protocols for available memory 200 keys for each sensor.

In sensors, a low power microcontroller is typically used as the processing unit, so we assume that an 8-bit microcontroller from the 8051 family [www.atmel.com] is employed. As shown in [Nechavatal, 2000], AES has been implemented on this microcontroller using 3168 instruction cycles. Since key generation between two sensors is done in only one node, the required processing in both sensors to establish a common key is approximately 1600 instruction cycles on average, independent of network parameters. To compare with the other schemes, we have evaluated them assuming sufficient memory is available. LPBK and LAKE are based on symmetric polynomials, and if the polynomial has degree t, $2t$ modular multiplications and t summations are required. Since HKey uses a 128 bit key length, we assume these schemes use 128 bit modular arithmetic. To compute the modular multiplication of two 128 bit numbers, we use the interleaved modulo multiplication algorithm [Bunimov & Schimmler, 2004] which is implemented as follows

$$
\begin{aligned}
&\text{Inputs}: X, Y, M \text{ with } 0 \le X, Y < M \\
&\text{Output}: P = X \times Y \bmod M \\
&n: \text{number of bits in } X; \\
&x_i: i\text{th bit of } X; \\
&P := 0; \\
&\text{for}(i = n-1; i \ge 0; i--)\{ \\
&\quad P := 2 \times P; \\
&\quad I := x_i \times Y; \\
&\quad P := P + I; \\
&\quad \text{if}(P \ge M) \text{ then } P := P - M; \\
&\quad \text{if}(P \ge M) \text{ then } P := P - M; \\
&\}
\end{aligned}
$$

Our evaluation shows that the modular multiplication of two 128 bit numbers requires approximately 4096 instruction cycles. Hence, the number of instruction cycles is approximately $8300\times t$ for LPBK and LAKE. The value of t in these schemes is not identical and is dependent on the group size. With the approach in [Yu & Guan, 2008], which uses the Blom scheme, multiplication of two matrices with dimensions $(1,t+1)$ and $(t+1,1)$ is required. For this operation, $t+1$ modular multiplications and $t+1$ summations are needed. Therefore, this scheme requires approximately $4096\times t$ instruction cycles. The above results are summarized in Table 4 under the condition of perfect security.

Scheme	Required Threshold Value	Average Number of Instruction Cycles per Sensor
HKey (All models) with AES	-	1600
HKey (All models) with MD5	-	638
SKEP	$2Nc$-2	1.66×10^6
KELR	Nc-2	0.86×10^6
LAKE	$2Nc$-2	1.66×10^6
LPBK	$25Nc$-10	2.075×10^7
Yu and Guan	$14Nc$-2	5.734×10^6

Table 4. Computational Overhead for Different Schemes

As mentioned above, generating a common key among sensors with HKey requires a hash function. Although functions such as MD5 or SHA1 are commonly used for this purpose, we use the AES encryption algorithm. Our reason for using this algorithm is that an algorithm must be implemented in the sensors to encrypt transferred data. Due to the restricted sensor code space, it is better to avoid implementing a hash function for key generation. However, as shown in [Venugopalan et. al., 2003], the number of instruction cycles for MD5 is less than for AES. If sufficient memory space is available in the sensors, the MD5 algorithm can easily be used in our protocol. In order to compare results, we extend our analysis to the MD5 hash function as shown in Table 4.

Since in our protocol, key establishment between two sensors is not based on symmetric polynomials or the Blom scheme as in LAKE, LPBK, and the approach in [Yu & Guan, 2008], the computational overhead does not depend on the network or cell size. Thus, the proposed scheme is clearly the best in terms of processing cost.

4.6 Scalability

Wireless sensor networks typically consist of thousands of limited resource nodes which are deployed simultaneously in a network area. Since each sensor has only a small battery, it will be unusable after some period of time. One solution is to add new sensors to replace the dead ones. These new sensors must be able to establish secure connections with each other and with previously deployed sensors. Therefore an important issue for a key establishment protocol is extensibility so new sensors can establish a secure connection with other sensors while maintaining security.

All of the key establishment protocols examined in this chapter are scalable, i.e., new sensors can be added to the network such that they can communicate securely with existing nodes. For example, with the approach in [Du, 2004], if new sensors select their random keys from the current sub key pools, they should be able to establish a common key with the existing sensors. LAKE [Zhou & Fang, Apr. 2007], LPBK [Liu & Ning, 2003], and the approaches by Du [Du et. al., 2006] and Yu and Guan [Yu & Guan, 2008], are based on symmetric polynomials or the Blom scheme. If the secret information for new sensors is computed with the same symmetric polynomial or Blom matrix, these sensors can establish common keys with the old sensors. However, adding new sensors creates security concerns. As mentioned in Section 4-5, if an adversary captures a sufficient number of sensors, they can compromise common keys between uncompromised sensors. Further, once the number of captured sensors (old or new) reaches a threshold, an adversary can easily compromise the entire network. However, if the memory is allocated considering the addition of new sensors, the network will remain secure, but the sensor hardware must be able to support the needed memory.

In our proposed protocol, new sensors can join the network without affecting security. The KDC can generate common keys for the new sensors considering the deployed sensors as well as those which will be distributed in the future. In the initialization phase, the KDC generates common keys for the first group of sensors to be deployed and also the group of sensors to next be deployed. For subsequent distributions, the KDC generates three types of common keys. The first are common keys for sensors to be distributed in the current period. The second are common keys with previously deployed sensors, and the last are common keys with sensors to be distributed next. Consequently, the proposed protocol is simply extensible without any security limitations. This solution can also be used for other schemes. For example, in LPBK, LAKE, and the approach by Yu and Guan, the KDC can generate new secret information for each time interval. In this case, the KDC must generate two shares for each sensor, the first using the new secret and the second using the previous secret. This solution at most doubles the required memory.

4.7 Remarks

As discussed in the previous sections, there are several important parameters in WSN key establishment protocols such as local connectivity, memory usage, key resilience, and computational overhead. Tradeoffs exist between these parameters. For example, to achieve better resilience as shown in figure 5, the memory usage and the computational overhead (as shown in Table 4) must be increased. In this chapter, we proposed an intrinsically secure key establishment protocol for WSNs. In this protocol, the common key between two sensors is generated based on the secret key of one sensor and the identity of the other. It differs from other schemes such as LAKE, LPBK, Du-2, and Yu and Guan in that key resilience does not depend on any other parameters. In addition, the computational overhead in the proposed scheme is independent of other parameters. In other words, in the other schemes based on symmetric polynomials or the Blom scheme, to achieve high key resilience the security threshold must be increased. However, as discussed in Section 4-5, the processing overhead is also increased. The only dependent parameters in our scheme are local connectivity and memory usage. To achieve high local connectivity, the memory usage must be increased. As shown in figure 4, the local connectivity with HKey-HP is close to one, but the memory usage is higher than with the other protocols and the proposed models. Several models were proposed for different applications. For example, when the available memory is very limited, HKey-LR is most suitable. Thus, the proposed protocol provides a number of tradeoffs between local connectivity and memory usage. Since it is sensitive to fewer parameters than the other schemes, the design and analysis of our protocol is more flexible.

5. Conclusions

In this chapter, a new key establishment protocol in which a common key between two nodes is computed using the secret key of one node and the identity of the other has been proposed. Thus, the key is stored in only one sensor and is computed by the other sensor when necessary. Due to the unavoidable need for an offline KDC in wireless sensor networks, this simple idea yields an efficient solution to the challenging key management problem. Four different models were introduced to implement the proposed protocol. The first model, HKey-LR, is memory efficient, but has a local connectivity which is less than with the other models. Conversely, the fourth model, HKey-HP, has high local connectivity, but the memory usage is more than with the others. In all cases, the local connectivity of the proposed models is comparable to that with other well known schemes, and our models are more memory efficient under the perfect security condition. Since the proposed protocol only uses a hash function to compute the common key for one of the two nodes, it has low computational overhead compared with the other schemes. The security analysis shows that the proposed protocol is more robust in low resource situations. In summary, the proposed protocol is a practical, secure, efficient, and scalable key management protocol for wireless sensor networks. As shown in Table 4, the computational overhead for the proposed protocol is considerably less than with the other protocols, which indicates that the energy consumption should be lower.

6. References

Pottie, G.J. & Kaiser, W.J. (2000). Wireless integrated network sensors, *Communication ACM*, vol. 43, no. 5, (May 2000), pp. (51-58)

Kahn, J.M., Katz, R.H. & Pister, K.S.J. (1999). Next century challenges: Mobile networking for smart dust, *Proceeding of ACM Internation Conference on Mobile Computing and Networking (MobiCom)*, (1999), pp. (217-278)

Akyildiz, I.F., Su, W., Sankarasubramaniam, Y., & Cayirci, E. (2002). A survey on sensor networks, *IEEE Communication Magazin.*, vol. 40, no. 8, (2002), pp. (102-114)

Perrig, A., Szewczyk, R., Wen, V., Culler, D.E., & Tygar, J.D. (2002). SPINS: Security protocols for sensor networks, *Wireless Networks*, vol. 8, no. 5, pp. (521-534)

Kung, H.T., & Vlah, D. (2003). "Efficient location tracking using sensor networks," *Proceeding of IEEE Wireless Communication and Networking Conference (WCNC)*, (Mar. 2003), pp. (1954-1961)

Brooks, R., Ramanathan, P., & Sayeed, A. (2003). Distributed target classification and tracking in sensor networks, *Proceeding on IEEE*, vol. 91, no. 8, (Aug. 2003), pp. (1163-1171)

Karlof, C., & Wagner, D. (2003). Secure routing in wireless sensor networks: Attacks and countermeasures, *Proceeding of IEEE Workshop on Sensor Network Protocols and Applications* (*SNPA*), (May 2003), pp. (113-127)

Chan, H., Perrig, A., & Song, D. (2003). Random key predistribution schemes for sensor networks, *Proceeding of IEEE Symposium on Security and Privacy*, (May 2003), pp. (197-213)

Eschenauer, L., & Gligor, V. D. (2002). A key-management scheme for distributed sensor networks, *Proceeding of ACM Conference on Computer and Communication Security*, (Nov. 2002), pp. (41–47)

Du, W., Deng, J., Han, Y.S., Chen, S., & Varshney, P.K. (2004). A key management scheme for wireless sensor networks using deployment knowledge, *Proceeding of IEEE Conference on Computer Communication (INFOCOM)*, (Mar. 2004), pp. (586-597)

Borwein, P. & Erde´lyi, T. (1995). Polynomials and Polynomial Inequalities, New York: Springer-Verlag.

Zhou, Y., & Fang, Y. (2006). Scalable link-layer key agreement in sensor networks, *Proceeding of IEEE Military Communication Conference* (*MILCOM*), (Oct. 2006), pp. (1-6)

Zhou, Y. & Fang, Y. (2006). A scalable key agreement scheme for large scale networks, *Proceeding of IEEE International Conference on Networking, Sensing and Control* (*ICNSC*), (Apr. 2006), pp. (631-636)

Zhou, Y., & Fang, Y. (2007). A two-layer key establishment scheme for wireless sensor networks, *IEEE Transaction on Mobile Computing*, vol. 6, no. 9, (Sept. 2007), pp. (1009-1020)

Liu, D. & Ning, P. (2003), Location-based pairwise key establishments for relatively static sensor networks, *Proceeding of ACM Workshop on Security of Ad Hoc and Sensor Networks* (*SASN*), (Oct. 2003), pp. (72-82)

Blom, R. (1985). An optimal class of symmetric key generation systems, in *Advances in Cryptology: Proc. EUROCRYPT '84*, Springer Lecture Notes in Computer Science, vol. 209, pp. (335-338).

Zhou, Y., Zhang, Y., & Fang, Y. (2005). Key establishment in sensor networks based on triangle grid deployment model, *Proceeding of IEEE Military Communication Conference* (*MILCOM*), (Oct. 2005), pp. (1450-1455)

Du, W., Deng, J., Han, Y.S., Chen, S., & Varshney, P. (2006). A key predistribution scheme for sensor networks using deployment knowledge, *IEEE Trans. Dependable and Secure Computing*, vol. 3, no. 1, (Mar. 2006), pp. (62-77)

Yu, Z., & Guan, Y. (2008). A key management scheme using deployment knowledge for wireless sensor networks, *IEEE Trans. Parallel and Distributed Systems*, vol. 19, no. 10, (Oct. 2008), pp. (1411-1425)

Wei, R. & Wu, J. (2004). Product construction of key distribution schemes for sensor networks, *Proceeding of International Workshop on Selected Areas in Cryptography (SAC)*, Springer Lecture Notes in Computer Science, vol. 3357, (Aug. 2004), pp. (280-293)

Hwang, J., & Kim, Y. (2004). Revisiting random key predistribution schemes for wireless sensor networks, *Proceeding of ACM Workshop on Security of Ad Hoc and Sensor Networks (SASN)*, (Oct. 2004), pp. (43-52)

Ramkumar, M., & Memon, N. (2004). An efficient random key predistribution scheme, *Proceeding of IEEE Global Telecommunication Conference (GLOBECOM)*, (Dec. 2004), pp. (2218-2223)

Liu, D., Ning, P., & Li, R. (2005). Establishing pairwise keys in distributed sensor networks, *ACM Trans. Information and System Security*, vol. 8, no. 1, (Feb. 2005), pp. (41-77)

Chan, H. & Perrig, A. (2005). Pike: Peer intermediaries for key establishment in sensor networks, *Proceeding of IEEE Conference on Computer Communication (INFOCOM)*, (Mar. 2005), pp. (524-535)

Zhou, Y., Zhang, Y., & Fang, Y. (2005). Key establishment in sensor networks based on triangle grid deployment model, *Proceeding of IEEE Military Communication Conference (MILCOM)*, (Oct. 2005), pp. (1450-1455)

Huang, D., Mehta, M., Medhi, D., & Harn, L. (2004). Location-aware key management scheme for wireless sensor networks, *Proceeding of ACM Workshop on Security of Ad Hoc and Sensor Networks (SASN)*, (Oct. 2004), pp. (29-42)

Zhou, Y., Zhang, Y., & Fang, Y. (2005). LLK: A link-layer key establishment scheme in wireless sensor networks, *Proceeding of IEEE Wireless Communication and Networking Conference (WCNC)*, (Mar. 2005), pp. (1921-1926)

Fanian, A., Berenjkoub, M., Saidi, H., & Gulliver, T.A. (2010). A hybrid key establishment protocol for large scale wireless sensor networks, *Proceeding of IEEE Wireless Communication and Networking Conf. (WCNC)*, (Apr. 2010), pp. (1-6)

Fanian, A., Berenjkoub, M., Saidi, H., & Gulliver, T.A. (2010). A new key establishment protocol for limited resource wireless sensor networks, *Proceeding of Conference on Communication Networks and Services Research (CNSR)*, (May 2010), pp. (138-145)

Su, Z., Jiang, Y., Ren, F., Lin, C., & Chu, X.-W. (2010). Distributed KDC-based random pair-wise key establishment in wireless sensor networks, *EURASIP J. Wireless Communication and Networking*, (July 2010), pp. (1-27)

Nechavatal, J. (2000). Report on the Development of Advanced Encryption Standard (AES), *NIST*

Bunimov, V., & Schimmler, M. (2004). Area-time optimal modular multiplication, *in Embedded Cryptographic Hardware: Methodologies and Architectures*

http://www.atmel.com/dyn/products/tools_card.asp?tool_id=3422.

Venugopalan, R., Ganesan, P., Peddabachagari, P., Dean, A., Mueller, F., & Sichitiu, M. (2003). Encryption overhead in embedded systems and sensor network nodes: Modeling and analysis, *Proceeding of ACM International Conference on Compilers, Architecture and Synthesis for Embedded Systems* (*CASES*), (Nov. 2003), pp. (188-197)

Fanian, A., Berenjkoub, M., Saidi, H., & Gulliver, T.A. (2010). "An Efficient Symmetric Polynomial-based Key Establishment Protocol for Wireless Sensor Networks", *The ISC International Journal of Information Security*, pp. (89-105)

8

NLM-MAC: Lightweight Secure Data Communication Framework Using Authenticated Encryption in Wireless Sensor Networks

Pardeep Kumar and Hoon-Jae Lee
Dongseo University
Republic of Korea

1. Introduction

Wireless sensor networks (WSNs) are widely used intelligent technology in the century that provides user-oriented better solutions for real-time environment. WSNs have wide range of applications, such as, habitat monitoring, surveillance, location tracking, agriculture monitoring, structural monitoring, wild-life monitoring and water monitoring, are few examples (Akyildiz et al., 2002). Furthermore, numerous other applications require the fine-grain monitoring of physical environments which are subjected to critical conditions, such as, fires, toxic gas leaks and explosions. Sensors' sense the environmental data and transmit to the sink node using wireless communication, as shown in figure 1. Thus the novelty of WSNs is providing inexpensive yet effective solutions for monitoring unattended physical environments. In addition, the ubiquitous nature of WSNs makes environmental data access possible anytime, anywhere in an ad-hoc manner.

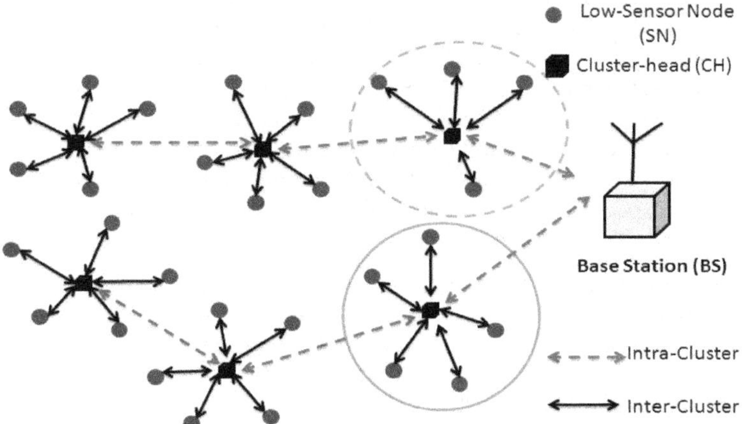

Fig. 1. Wireless sensor networks

A single node consists of on-board sensors, low computation processor, less memory, and limited wireless bandwidth. For example, a typical resource constraint node has 8 MHz microcontroller with 128 KB of read-only memory and 10 KB of program memory (Hill et al., 2000). Furthermore, a node is battery-powered (e.g., AAA batteries), thus it can operate autonomously, if needed. Therefore, a node able to collect the environmental information, processes the raw data, and communicates wirelessly with the sink. Most of WSNs are self-organized that can make self-governing decisions (i.e., turn on/off actuators) and become a part of better distributed management and control system.

The new wireless sensor technology has offered economically viable monitoring solution to many challenging applications (e.g., earthquake monitoring, military, healthcare monitoring, nuclear reactor monitoring, etc). However, deploying new technology without considering security in mind has often susceptible to attacks. As WSNs deals with real-time sensitive data that can be manipulated by any adversary for individual profit. Moreover, wireless nature of sensor node makes network more prone to the attacks. Thus security has always a big concern for wireless communication based applications. In addition, providing security to these resource constraints networks are very tedious task as compared to the resource rich networks, such as, local area networks (LANs) and wide area networks (WANs). While the WSNs security requirements are the same as conventional networks, such as confidentiality, authentication, availability, freshness and integrity. Thus security has emerged as one of the important issues in wireless sensor networks.

Significant cryptographic protocols have been introduced in order to secure the link-layer of wireless sensor networks. These cryptographic schemes are either based on block cipher (i.e., SPINS (Perrig et al., 2001), TinySec (Karlof et al., 2004), MiniSec (Luk et al., 2007)) or on public key cryptosystem (TinyPK (Watro et al., 2004)) and elliptic curve cryptography (TinyECC(Liu & Ning, 2007) and WMECC(Wang et al., 2006)). But due to the fact of limited memory and low computation of sensor nodes these protocol are still expensive in term of memory and computation. Furthermore, block cipher are always centred in cryptology, for instance, data encryption standard (DES) was considered as standard block cipher from 1974-to-2000 (Ahmad et al., 2009). Thereafter, in 2001 Advanced encryption standard (AES) was selected as standard block cipher. In fact the security of AES has been implemented in hardware for sensor nodes (e.g., telosb (Polastre et al., 2005)), and successfully implemented in software as well (Roman et al., 2007). Furthermore, in (Law et al., 2006)) and (Roman et al., 2007), some block ciphers are benchmarked on MSP430 platform and deduced the best block cipher to use in the context of WSNs. In (Roman et al., 2007) authors have surveyed public key cryptography and elliptic curve cryptography primitives for wireless sensor networks. While, the public key cryptosystem and elliptic curve cryptography are computationally expensive and time consuming for sensor networks because they need to generates and verify the digital certificates.

On other hand, stream ciphers have the simple structures, fast computations (i.e., encryption and decryption), but these ciphers are not popular in WSN security. In (Fournel et al., 2007) authors claim that the stream ciphers provide high level security services at low computation time, memory efficient, and easy to implement in software (i.e., few lines of code is required). Moreover, in 2004, the European Union started a project "named eSTREAM" ciphers aim to select a standard stream cipher that has comparable hardware and software security with efficiency (Henricksen, 2008), as AES. In (Fournel et al., 2007) authors have presented a survey and benchmark on stream cipher for dedicated platform and deduce the well-suited stream cipher for constraints devices. Authors argue that the stream ciphers could be a better solution, and could achieves fast encryption in resource constraint network applications.

In Lim et al., 2007 and Kumar & Lee, 2009, proposed authenticated encryption which is known as Dragon-MAC[1] for wireless sensor networks. In Ahmad et al., 2009, have addressed authenticated encryption schemes, namely, HC128 -MAC, SOSEMANUK-MAC using eSTREAM ciphers for wireless sensor networks. In (Kausar & Naureen, 2009), authors have implemented and analyzed the HC-128 and Rabbit encryption schemes for pervasive computing in wireless sensor network environments. They have simulated lightweight stream ciphers (i.e., only encryption) for WSNs.

Consequently, the stream ciphers are not adequately addressed and implemented in wireless sensor networks applications. As the security services such as data authentication, confidentiality, integrity, and freshness are become critical issues in wireless sensor networks and many exiting WSN applications are lacking of the link layer security. As result, there is still research potential at link layer security that would ensure and provide security services at low cost.

In this regard, this chapter proposes a lightweight secure data framework using authenticated encryption. An NLM-128 stream cipher is used for data or packet confidentiality (Lee et al., 2009). In order to achieve the authentication and integrity services, a message authentication code (MAC) "named NLM-MAC" is incorporated into the sensor packets. The NLM-MAC ensures the message integrity and freshness of the authenticated packets. The proposed framework achieves security services at low computation cost (i.e. memory and time efficient). In order to minimize the computation cost of NLM-MAC algorithm, it is using some of the data already computed on NLM-128 stream cipher. In addition, the chapter discusses the following: (1) importance of security at the WSN link layer; (2) an adversary threat model that can be expected in WSNs; and (3) basic security requirements for wireless sensor networks. We have implemented the proposed framework on real-time test bed and our result confirms its feasibility for real-time wireless sensor applications too. In addition, we compared the proposed framework results with the existing stream ciphers that have been implemented in the resource constraints sensor networks.

The rest of chapter is structured as follows: Section 2 discusses (i) importance of security at the link layer; and (ii) an adversary threat model that can be expected in WSNs. Section 3 discusses the basic security requirements for wireless sensor networks, and Section 4 presents the related works with their weaknesses, if any. Section 5 proposed lightweight authenticated encryption framework for wireless sensor networks, and Section 6 evaluation of proposed framework in term of memory and computation time. In Section 7, conclusions are drawn for proposed authenticated encryption (NLM-MAC) and future directions are given.

2. Important of security at the link layer and adversary network model

This section discusses the importance of security at the link layer and adversary network model for wireless sensor networks.

---

[1]MAC is representing as message authentication code, otherwise explain.

2.1 Importance of security at the link layer

End-to-end security mechanisms are not possible in sensor network as compared to traditional computer network (e.g., SSH (Ylonen, 1996), IPSec and SSL protocols). These protocols are based on route-centric. In traditional networks, the intermediate router only need to view the packet header and it is not necessary for them to have access to packet bodies. They are considered inappropriate since they are not allowed in-network processing and data aggregation which plays an important role in energy efficient data retrieval (Karlof et al., 2004).

In contrast, for sensor networks it is important to allow intermediate nodes to check message integrity and authenticity because they have many-to-one multi-hop communication nature. The intermediate nodes carry out some of data processing operation (e.g., data compression, eliminate redundancy and so on) on incoming data packets to be routed towards to the base station. Thus, in-network processing requires intermediate nodes to access, modify, and suppress the contents of messages, if needed. Moreover, it is very unlikely that end-to-end security schemes are used between sensor nodes and base-station to guarantee the message integrity, authenticity and message confidentiality (Karlof et al., 2004). More importantly, the link-layer security architectures can easily detects unauthorized packets when they are first injected into the network, whereas in end-to-end security mechanisms, the network may route packets injected by an adversary many hops before they are detected. These kinds of attacks waste the energy and bandwidth. Hence, security is an imperative requirement at the link layer.

2.2 Adversary network model

WSNs are vulnerable to attacks due to their wireless in nature. In addition the sensor nodes are deployed in hostile or unattended environment, and are not physically protected or guarded. An adversary can directly disturb the functioning of real-time wireless sensor network applications. By applying the adversary model, he/she can handle the application accordingly for their personal benefits. For simplicity, we have divided the adversary model as follows.

- **Data monitoring and eavesdropping:** Since the sensor devices are wireless in nature, and wireless range are not confined. It may happen that an attacker easily snoops data from the wireless channels and have control on network contents, accordingly. Further, he/she may eavesdrop the network contents, such as sensor id, location and others network related information.
- **Malicious node:** An attacker can quietly place his/her malicious node into the network. By deploying malicious node into the network an attacker may control the entire wireless network or may change the route of network.
- **Data corruption:** Any message alteration from the networks, or bogus message injection into the networks could harm to the entire networks. He/she can potentially destroy the whole network and hence, network integrity compromised. Further, an adversary can replay the corrupted messages again and again, by doing so he/she can harm to the critical applications, e.g., healthcare monitoring, military and etc.

3. Security requirements for wireless sensor network at link layer

This section sketches out the important security requirements for WSNs, which are based on the above threat model and link layer requirements, as follows.

- **Confidentiality:** confidentiality, in which message is used by only authorized users. In sensor networks, message should not be leaked to neighboring node because sensor deals with very sensitive data. In order to provide the security, the sensor data should be encrypted with secret key. Moreover, the secret key is intended to recipient only, hence achieved confidentiality.
- **Authentication:** Authentication is associated to identification. Entity authentication function is important for many applications and for administrative task. Entity authentication allows verifying the data whether the data is really sent by legitimate node or not. In node-to-node communication entity authentication can be achieved through symmetric mechanism: a message authentication code (MAC) can be computed on secret shared key for all communicated data.
- **Integrity:** Message integrity, which addresses the illegal alteration of messages. To conformation of message integrity, one must have the ability to identify data manipulation by illegal parties.
- **Freshness:** In wireless sensor networks, data confidentiality and integrity are not enough if data freshness is not considered. Data freshness implies that the sensors reading are fresh or resent and thus an adversary has not replayed the old messages.

4. Related work

This section presents the related work for security protocols that have been proposed for wireless sensor networks.

Perrig et al., 2001, proposed a security protocol SPINS for wireless sensor networks. It consists of two secure building blocks: (1) Secure network encryption protocol (SNEP), provides two party data authentication (point-to-point) communication. (2) micro-Timed efficient streaming loss-tolerant authentication protocol (μ-TESLA), provides efficient authenticated broadcast communication. In their scheme, all cryptographic primitives are constructed based on a single block cipher scheme. Author selected RC5 block cipher because of its small code size and high efficiency. RC5 is also suitable for ATmega platform because of memory constraints. A hash function is used with block cipher.

Karlof et al., 2004, proposed another most popular wireless security architecture known as "TinySec: a link layer security architecture for wireless sensor networks". TinySec achieves low energy consumption and memory usage, and provides access control, message integrity and confidentiality. TinySec consists of two building blocks: (1) *authenticated encryption mode* denoted as TinySec-AE. In this mode, the data packet payload is encrypted and the whole packet is secured by a message authentication code (MAC). (2) *Authentication only* denoted as TinySec-Auth. In this mode, the entire packet is authenticated with a MAC, but the whole data packet is not encrypted. Author has tested two 64-bit block ciphers, i.e. Skipjack and RC5 for *authenticated encryption* mode and *authentication only* mode. Authors claims RC5 is more difficult to implement than Skipjack, so authors' selected Skipjack as the default secure block crypto algorithm. In sensor networks, data travels on carrier sense in which node check, if another node is also currently broadcasting, than node will be vulnerable to denial of service (DoS) attack. TinySec security architecture gives protection from DoS attack, and is able to detect the illegal packets when they are injected into the network. One of the major drawbacks of TinySec, it does not attempt to protect from replay protection (Luk et al., 2007). The replay protection is intentionally omitted from TinySec (Luk et al., 2007).

MiniSec (Luk et al., 2007) is the first fully-carried out general function security protocol, and implanted on the Telos sensor motes. MiniSec provides two controlling modes, i.e., unicast and broadcast, and recognized as MiniSec-U, MiniSec-B, respectively. Both methods use the OCB-encryption system that allows data confidentiality and authentication. By using counter as a nonce MiniSec provides the replay protection to the sensor nodes. For more details reader may refer to the (Luk et al., 2007).

A TinyPK (Watro et al., 2004) protocol has proposed for WSN. It specifically designed for authentication and key agreement. In order to deliver secret key to the protocol, authors implemented the Diffie-Hellman key exchange algorithm. TinyPK is based on public key cryptography, which is memory consuming and time consuming for sensor networks.

Lim et al., 2007 and Kumar & Lee, 2009, proposed Dragon-MAC for wireless sensor networks. In their schemes, *encrypt-then-MAC* is used, i.e., the sensor data first encrypted and then MAC is computed over the encrypted data. Two keys are used for encryption and authentication, respectively. Authors tested their schemes for Telos B family. The main weakness of Dragon, it is not suitable for some real-time applications, such as healthcare monitoring, military, etc. Because it has 1088 bits of internal states, which are not easy to maintain for the resource hungry sensor nodes.

Zhang et al., 2008 proposed a security protocol for wireless sensor networks that exploits the RC4 based encryption cryptosystem and RC4-based hash function "called HMAC (hashed-message authentication code)" is generated for message authentication.

Ahmad et al., 2009 addressed SOSEMANUK-MAC and HC128-MAC authenticated encryption schemes using eSTREAM cipher for sensor networks. They did not provides any analytical or simulation analysis for their proposed work.

In Kausar & Naureen, 2009, authors have implemented and analyzed the HC-128 and Rabbit encryption schemes for wireless sensor networks environment. They have simulated lightweight stream ciphers (i.e., only encryption) for WSNs, but their cost of encryption schemes are very high (Kausar & Naureen, 2009). More importantly, they implemented only encryption, which is not sufficient for real-time WSN applications.

As we have seen the above, only few security schemes are well implemented and provide better security services to the WSNs. Further, many of stream ciphers are not implemented properly and provide less security services at high computation costs. So, next section present a lightweight secure framework for sensor networks that exploits the stream cipher and provides sufficient security services for WSN applications.

5. Proposed authenticated encryption framework

This section is divided into twofold: (1) introduction of NLM-128 keystream generator cryptographic protocol (Lee et al., 2009); and (2) proposed authenticated framework "named NLM-MAC" for wireless sensor networks which is based on a massage authentication code. The proposed scheme exploits the NLM-128 stream cipher based-security and facilitates the confidentiality, authenticity, integrity and freshness to the air messages.

5.1 NLM-128

A NLM-128 keystream generator proposed by Lee et al. in 2009, which is based on LM-type summation generator, and is designed with both security and efficiency in mind. It is a combination of a linear feedback shift register (LFSR) and a nonlinear feedback shift register (NLFSR), which are easy to implement in software as well as in hardware. The length of LFSR and NLRSR is 127 bits and 129 bits, respectively. Both, LFSR and NLFSR give 258 bits of internal states to the NLM-128. Further, it takes 128 bits key-length and 128 bits initialization vector (*IV*) to fill the internal states. The simple structure of NLM-128 is shown in 2.

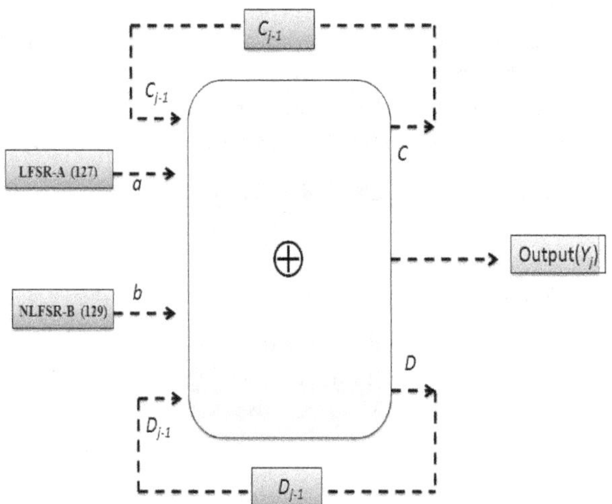

Fig. 2. NLM-128 keystream generator

5.1.1 Keystream generator

The NLM-128 generator generates the output keystream using LFSR and NLFSR sequences, a carry bit (*C*), and a memory bit (*D*). It has two polynomials: a primitive polynomial $P_a(x)$ and irreducible polynomial $P_b(x)$, as following:

$$P_a(x) = x^{127} \oplus x^{109} \oplus x^{91} \oplus x^{84} \oplus x^{73} \oplus x^{67} \oplus x^{66} \oplus x^{63} \oplus x^{56} \oplus x^{55} \oplus x^{48} \oplus x^{45} \oplus x^{42} \oplus x^{41} \oplus x^{37} \oplus x^{34} \oplus x^{30} \oplus x^{27} \oplus x^{23} \oplus x^{21} \oplus x^{20} \oplus x^{19} \oplus x^{16} \oplus x^{13} \oplus x^{12} \oplus x^{7} \oplus x^{6} \oplus x^{2} \oplus x^{1} \oplus 1 \quad (1)$$

$$P_b(x) = x^{129} \oplus x^{125} \oplus x^{121} \oplus x^{117} \oplus x^{113} \oplus x^{109} \oplus x^{105} \oplus x^{101} \oplus x^{97} \oplus x^{93} \oplus x^{89} \oplus x^{85} \oplus x^{81} \oplus x^{77} \oplus x^{73} \oplus x^{69} \oplus x^{65} \oplus x^{61} \oplus x^{57} \oplus x^{53} \oplus x^{49} \oplus x^{45} \oplus x^{41} \oplus x^{37} \oplus x^{33} \oplus x^{29} \oplus x^{25} \oplus x^{21} \oplus x^{17} \oplus x^{13} \oplus x^{9} \oplus x^{5} \oplus \left(\prod_{i=1}^{129} xi\right) \quad (2)$$

The output of keystream Y_j, C_j and D_j are defined as following:

$$Y_j = (a_j \oplus b_j \oplus c_{j-1}) \oplus d_{j-1} \quad (3)$$

$$C_j = a_j b_j \oplus (a_j \oplus b_j) c_{j-1} \quad (4)$$

$$D_j = b_j \oplus (a_j \oplus b_j) d_{j-1} \quad (5)$$

5.1.2 Key loading and re-keying

Initially, 128-bits key (*key*) and 128- bits initialization vector (*IV*) together feed to 257 internal states of NLM-128. To generate the initial state for keystream generator, it uses generator itself twice, as follows.

- The initial state of LFSR-A is simply obtained by *XORing* of two 128-bits binary strings of the key (*key*) and *IV*, i.e., $LFSR\text{-}A = (Key \oplus IV) \bmod 2^{127}$.
- The initial state of 129 bits for NLFSR-B is simply obtained by assuming the 128-bits key are embedded into 129-bits word and shifted one bit left. Then *XORing* with the *IV* embedded into 129 word with a leading zero, i.e., $NLFSR\text{-}B = (key \ll 1) \oplus (0 \mid IV)$.
- Now cipher is runs second time to produce an output string of length 257-bits.

For more detailed specifications and NLM-128 security analysis, reader may refer to the (Lee et al., 2009).

5.2 Proposed authenticated encryption

A secure communication setup is needed in wireless sensor networks between two ends parties (i.e., sensor node and base station). In this regards, this subsection proposed an authentication encryption "named NLM-MAC" that setup secure communication between two ends parties and provides authentication, integrity and confidentiality, to their air messages. The proposed framework effectively utilise: (i) less space for key, and for message encryption, so that application's other functions can have enough room; and (ii) less computation, which helps to increases the network lifetime. The idea of NLM-MAC is very simple: a message authentication code (MAC) is computes over the already encrypted data (i.e., NLM-128), and hence achieve security services, as follows.

5.2.1 Data confidentiality

To achieve the confidentiality, first, NLM-128 keystream generator initialize with 128 bits key length and 128 bits of initialization vector (IV). Later, the keys and IV feed into NLM-128 internal states, which generates 128 bits output keystream, as discussed above (recall section 5.1). Thereafter, the output of NLM-128 keystream generator is *ex-or* with the plaintext that provide data confidentiality. The simplicity and small size of NLM-128 makes it well suitable to the wireless sensor network environments. For NLM-128 security analysis reader may refer to (Lee et al., 2009).

5.2.2 NLM-MAC (authentication and integrity)

A message authentication code (*MAC*) is short piece of information that used to authenticate the two end parties and verify their integrity. For instance, if a sender attached a *MAC* to the message then it must be verified at receiver end in order to manage the access control. The proposed NLM-MAC that is based on Lim et al (2007) and Kumar & Lee (2009) schemes, and offers general security services to the wireless sensor network, as discussed in the section 3. To compute MAC, considers a scenario where a sender (Alice) wants to set up a secure communication with a receiver (Bob), as follows:

- Initially Alice runs NLM-128 and encrypts the plaintext with encryption key (i.e., Key) and initialization vector (*IV*).
- Then Alice computes a *MAC* over the cipher text using MAC-Key (*i.e.*, K_{mac}), the procedure is shown in figure 3.

Pt = plaintext
Ct= Ciphertext
Key= Encryption key
K_{mac}= MAC encryption key
Ct[i]= i^th^ Ciphertext

1. $Ct = E_{key}(Pt)$
2. $\{l, m, n, p\} = K_{mac}$ *(128-bit)*
   IV=
   *[destpan||addr||type||group||count]*2*
3. $\{l, m, n, p\} = Ct[i] \oplus l, m, n, p$
4. *NLM-MAC*= $l \oplus m \oplus n \oplus p$
5. *Output MAC(32-bits)*

Fig. 3. NLM-MAC algorithm

- Thereafter, Alice sends *MAC*, cipher text (*Ct*) and current time (*Ta*) stamp to the receiver end (i.e. Bob).
- Upon receiving Bob the message (i.e., *MAC*, cipher text and time stamp)
- Bob first check time stamp and compare *MAC*, if both checks pass then Alice is authentic and decrypt the cipher text with *Key* and obtained the plain text.

5.2.3 NLM-MAC design

The encrypted cipher text (*Ct*) is splitting into 32-bit blocks, and then padding the last word with zeroes, if required. Meanwhile, the *MAC* encryption key (K_{mac}) is fed through variables *l, m, n, p* and then K_{mac} is *XORing* 32-bit Ct with 32-bit of *l*, and hence obtained 32-bit *MAC*.

To integrate our authenticated encryption procedure into the sensor node, we add 2 bytes counter (*ctr*) and 4-bytes *MAC* into default radio stack (TelosB), as shown in figure 4. The 2 bytes *ctr* used to achieve the semantic security and 4 byte *MAC* ensure the authentication and integrity.

Len	Fcfhi	Fcflo	Dsn	DestPAN	Add	Type	Grp	D_len	Data	CTR	MAC
1	1	1	1	2	2	1	1	1	28	2	4

Fig. 4. Modified Telos B node packet format

5.2.4 NLM-MAC analysis

Generally, the initialization vector (i.e., *IV*) must unique for encrypted packets, the unique *IV* does not give additional rooms to an attacker (Karlof, 2004). Therefore, in the proposed framework, an *IV* is taken from the packet header that is modified radio (refer figure 4) and sends to the recipient end. As shown in the figure 4, a two bytes counter (*ctr*) gives 2^{16} variations to the initialization vector (*IV*). By doing so, it guarantees that message encrypted with same key should give different cipher text every time. The four bytes *MAC* length indirectly implies the computation cost which would be needed to forge the *MAC* in chosen cipher text attack. In, (Chang et al, 2007) , (Zoltak et al., 2004) and (Karlof et al., 2004) suggested 4 bytes *MAC* gives well sufficient security, and easy to implement. Further, (Lim et al., 2007) and (Ahmad et al., 2009) suggested that the strongest definition of security for authenticated encryption can be achieved via *Encrypt-then-MAC* approach only. *Encrypt-then-MAC*: $(E_{key}, K_{mac}(Msg) = E_{key}(Msg) \,||\, K_{mac}(E_{key}(Msg))$ always gives privacy and authenticity to the air messages.

5.2.5 Operation of NLM-MAC

The operation of NLM-MAC is very simple, as follows: suppose, Alice simply computes a *MAC* on the encrypted packet with MAC key (k_{mac}) and sends *MAC* packet and cipher text to the Bob. When Bob received the *MAC* packet (i.e., authenticated packet) and cipher text, then Bob verify the *MAC* packet which is sent by Alice. If *MAC* verified then Alice is authentic and no information has been altered in transit. NLM-MAC is an *Encrypt-then-MAC* stream cipher mode (Lim et al., 2007), as shown in figure 5.

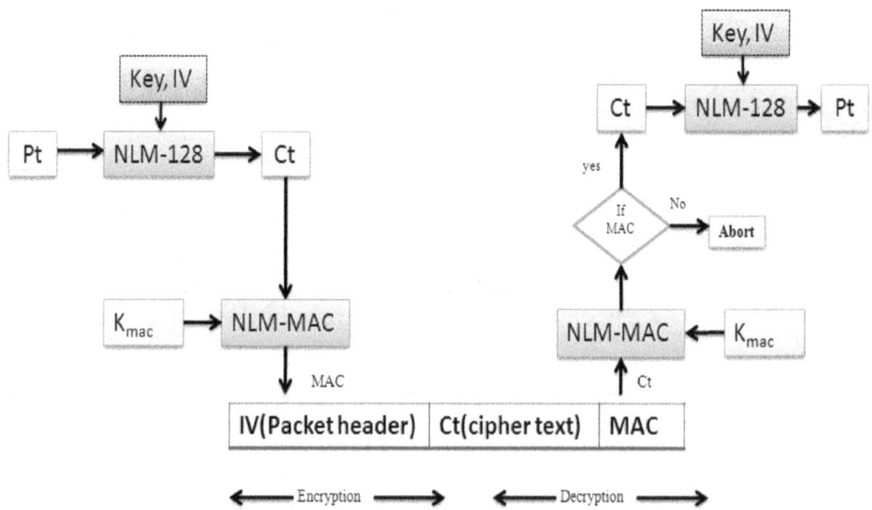

Fig. 5. Flow of NLM-MAC

6. Implementation, evaluation, and security analysis

This section discusses the implementation and evaluation of proposed framework. Further we compare and prove that the proposed scheme is efficient in term of resources consumption (i.e., memory and time efficiency) with existing schemes.

6.1 Experimental set up and implementation

In order to check the feasibility of NLM-MAC, we embedded the proposed scheme on real-time test bed, which ran on two Telos B motes and one personal computer (Intel 3.166GHz) as base station. We have implemented NLM-MAC using TinyOS, an event-driven open source operating system, which is specially designed for wireless sensor networks. The application called "secure chitchat application", and is written in NesC language. The secure chitchat application tested on Telos B sensor node that has a 16-bit, 8MHz MSP430 processor having 48 KB of programme space and 10 KB of flash memory. Further, the specifications of Telos B motes are shown in the table 1.

TelosB specification	
ITEMs	**DESCRIPTION**
Processor	16-bit RICS
Internal Memory	10-kb RAM
Flash Memory	48-kb ROM
Multi-Channel Radio	2.4-GHz(CC2420)
Interface	USB (UART)
Sensors	Temperature, Humidity, Light, etc.

Table 1. Telos B node specification

The experimental set up is depicted in figure 6, where sensor node 'A' acts as sender and the sensor node 'B' as receiver and vice versa. Personal computer (PC) is playing an important role as base station.

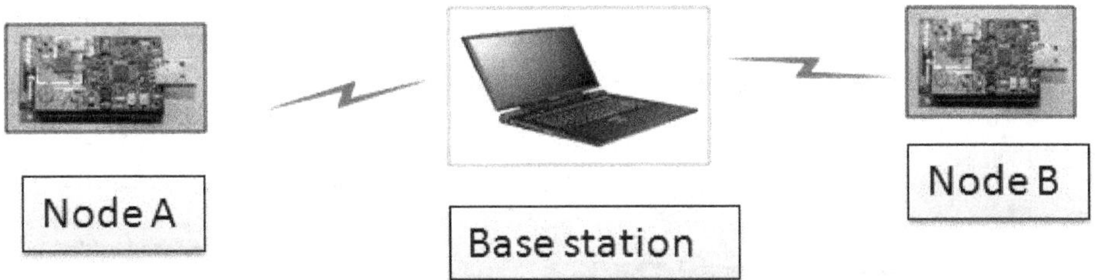

Fig. 6. Experimental set up

6.2 Evaluation

This subsection evaluates the secure chitchat application that integrated with NLM-MAC based security services. For evaluation we have considered mainly, memory and CPU execution time. As shown in table 2, our entire code uses: (i) without security 11 KB of ROM and 450 Bytes of RAM; (ii) with encryption 12.4 KB ROM (i.e., 12.4-11= 1.3KB) and 559 Bytes

RAM (i.e., 559-450 = 109 bytes); and (iii) with NLM-MAC 13.74 KB ROM (i.e., 13.74-12.4 = 1.4KB extra from encryption) and 632 Bytes RAM (i.e., 73 bytes extra from encryption). Further, the proposed scheme takes 13.35 ms time for encryption and 16.74ms for NLM-MAC operation. It is easy to see from the table 2 that the proposed scheme leaves ample space for other application's functions.

Description	ROM (BYTES)	RAM (Bytes)	Execution Time (ms)
Without security scheme	11,412	453	-
NLM-128 (Only Encryption)	12, 442	559	13. 53
NLM-MAC	13,749	632	16.74

Table 2. Occupied memory and execution time of NLM-MAC

In addition, to evaluate the simple performance of symmetric encryption and authentication (i.e. NLM-MAC) on data packets, we conducted some performance evaluation tests. As shown in the experimental set (fig 6), we simply sent 1000 data packets from sensor node A to sensor node B without any packet loss and vice versa. In order to measure the throughput of the proposed scheme, the packet size ranges from 20 bytes to 100 bytes, with an incremental of 20 bytes, as depicted in the figure 7. In only encryption case, the throughput is 23Kbps (i.e., for 20 bytes) to 25.9Kbps (for 100 bytes); and in NLM-MAC operation, it is 13.6Kbps (i.e., for 20 bytes) to 18.5Kbps (for 100bytes), which is reasonable for secure wireless sensor networks.

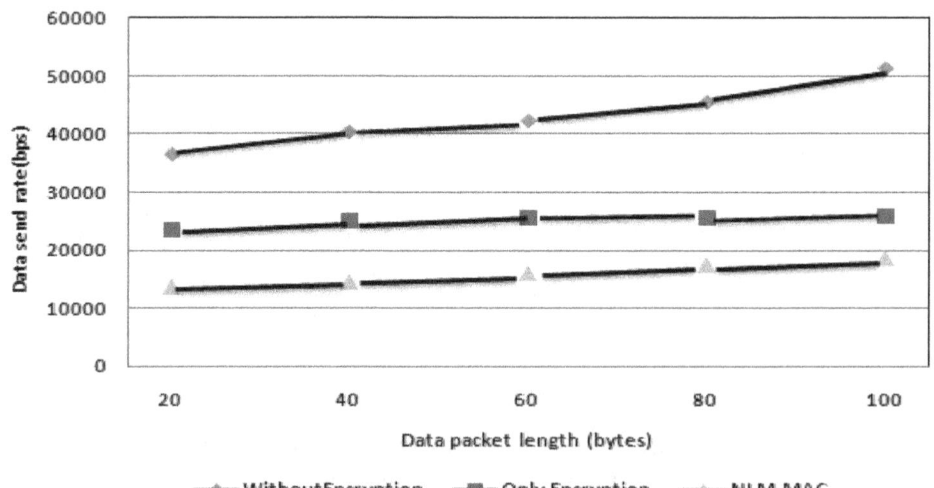

Fig. 7. Data throughput for without Encryption, only encryption, and NLM-MAC.

6.2.1 Memory and execution time comparisons with other exiting stream ciphers

This subsection compares NLM-128 with some existing stream ciphers that have been implemented or simulated in wireless sensor networks, recently. We compared the memory efficiency of proposed scheme with Lim et al.(2007), Kumar & lee (2009) and Kausar & Naureen (2009). Lim et al.(2007) and Kumar & lee (2009) have implemented Dragon stream cipher that support to the link layer security on TelosB sensor platform. Kausar & Naureen (2009) have simulated HC-128 and Rabbit stream cipher on TinyOS and TOSSIM environment for sensor networks. As shown in table 3, the encryption operation of HC-128 simulation is very expensive and it required much memory (i.e., 32.5KB of ROM and 10KB of RAM) and relatively low computation time (.049 ms). Whereas, the proposed scheme required only 12.44KB of ROM and 559bytes of RAM for message encryption, and 13.53 ms of computation time, which is practical on real-time test bed.

		Dragon encryption (Lim et al.,2007)	Dragon encryption (Kumar& Lee, 2009)	Rabbit encryption (Kausar & Naureen, 2009)	HC-128 encryption (Kausar & Naureen,2009)	**Proposed NLM-128 encryption**
MEMORY	Random-access memory (RAM)	18 KB	17.5 KB	14 KB	32.5KB	**12.44KB**
	Read-only memory (ROM)	964 Bytes	915 Bytes	1KB	10KB	**559 Bytes**
Execution time(ms)		17.88	16.25	.039	.049	**13. 53**

Table 3. Memory and execution time comparisons for encryption operation with other stream ciphers.

The table 4 shows the memory comparison for MAC operation. As shown in the table 4, the NLM-MAC needs only 13.7KB of ROM and 632Bytes of RAM; whereas, in (Lim et al., 2007) Dragon-MAC needs 18.9KB of ROM and 982Bytes of RAM; and in (Kumar & Lee, 2009) Dragon-MAC needs 18.13KB of ROM and 948Bytes of RAM. Moreover, NLM-MAC requires 16.74ms computation time for MAC operation, which is significantly low as compared to Lim et al., 2007 and Kumar & Lee, 2009. Whereas, in Kausar & Naureen, 2009, authors did not implemented or analyzed MAC operation, which is paramount operation in WSN security.

Consequently, it is very clear from table 3 and table 4 that the NLM-128 and NLM-MAC operations are memory efficient as compare to existing schemes.

Furthermore, we have calculated the expected latency overhead incurred, if the packet length is increased then transmit time is also increased, as shown in Table 5. Analytically, standard Telos radio stack packet transmission time is 2.016 ms and NLM-MAC radio stack packet transmission time is 2.208 at 250 kbps bandwidth.

		Dragon-MAC (Lim et al.,2007)	Dragon–MAC (Kumar& Lee, 2009)	**Proposed NLM-MAC**
MEM-ORY	RAM	18.9KB	18KB	**13.7KB**
	ROM	982 bytes	948 bytes	**632** bytes
Execution time(ms)		21.40	20.35	**16.74**

Table 4. Memory and execution time comparisons for MAC operation with other stream ciphers.

Description	**Pay-load (Bytes)**	**Packet Over-head (Bytes)**	**Total Size (Bytes)**	**Trans-mission time (ms)**	**Over-head inc. %**
TinySec-AE	24	42	68	28.3	7.9
TinyOS stack	24	39	63	26.2	–
Telos radio stack	24	39	63	2.016	–
MiniSec	24	25	49	1.568	–
NLM-MAC	24	45	69	2.208	9.5

Table 5. Latency analysis

6.3 Security analysis

Based on the above experimental set up, we believe that the proposed NLM-MAC uses NLM-128 in a secure way and uses its strength and makes achieve more secure features, i.e., authentication and integrity. NLM-MAC has achieved basic requirement as discussed in section 3 and protect the air messages from an attacker, as follows.

- Data confidentiality: The proposed framework achieves NLM-128 based data confidentiality through encrypting air messages.
- Data authentication: The proposed framework facilitate data authentication through the *MAC* verification.
- Data integrity: The proposed NLM-MAC also guarantees the data integrity through data authentication verification.

Furthermore, all the operations in proposed schemes are simply uses *XOR* operations, which is cost effective.

7. Conclusions

This chapter tested the feasibility of stream cipher in sensor network where energy and computation time are important factors. We have designed NLM-MAC scheme for resource constrained devices. The proposed scheme employs on some of already computed data underlying NLM-128 cipher. The salient features of NLM-128 keystream generator are its fast key generation and fast software implementation, good primitives for security such as encryption, authentication, decryption and data integrity. The entity verification and message authentication have been tested through the performance of authenticated encryption schemes using Telos B sensor nodes for wireless sensor networks. The implementation of its features can revolutionize the security primitives in wireless sensor networks. As conclusion, this chapter found that the lightweight stream ciphers also can be a substitute of the block ciphers. Furthermore, the remaining feature of NLM-128 can be enhanced and implemented in wireless sensor networks as per the applications scenarios.

8. References

Ahmad, S. ; Wahla, A. & Kausar, F. (2009). Authenticated Encryption in WSN using eSTREAM Ciphers, Proceeding of ISA 2009, LNCS 5576, pp. 741-749.

Akyildiz, I. F. ; Su, W. ; Sankarasubramaniam, Y. & Cayirci, E. (2002). A Survey on Sensor Networks, *IEEE Communications Magazine*, 40(8), pp. 102-114.

Henricksen, M. (2008). Tiny Dragon : An Encryption Algorithm for Wireless Sensor Networks, Proceeding of 10th IEEE International Conference on High Performance Computing and Communications (HPCC'10), Dalian, China, pp. 795-800.

Hill, J. ; Szewczyk, R. ; Woo, A. ; Hollar, S. ; Culler, D. & Pister K.(2000). System Architecture directions for networked sensors, Proceedings of ACM ASPLOS IX, pp. 93-104.

Fournel, N. ; Minier, M. & Ubeda, S. (2007). Survey and Benchmark of Stream Ciphers for Wireless sensor networks, WISTP, 2007, LNCS 4462, pp. 202-214.

KarlOff, C. ; Sastry, N. & Wagner, D.(2004). TinySec : A Link Layer Security Architecture for Wireless Sensor Networks. Proceedings of 2nd ACM Conference on Embedded Networked Sensor Systems(SenSys 2004). Baltimore, MD.

Kausar, F. & Naureen, A. (2009). A Comparative Analysis of HC-128 and Rabbit encryption schemes for pervasive computing in WSN environment, Proceeding of ISA 2009, LNCS 5576, pp. 682-691.

Kumar, P. & Lee, H. J. (2009). A secure data mechanism for ubiquitous sensor networks with Dragon cipher, Proceeding of IEEE 5th International Joint conference INC, IMS and IDC, Seoul, South Korea.

Law, Y. W. ; Doumen, J. & Hartel, P. (2006). Survey and Benchmark of Block Ciphers for Wireless Sensor Networks, ACM Transactions on Sensor Network(TOSN), pp. 65-93.

Lee, H. J. ; Sung S. M. & Kim, H. R. (2009). NLM-128, an Improved LM-Type Summation Generator with 2-Bit memories, in the Proceeding of Computer Sciences and Convergence Information Technology (ICCIT'09), Seoul, South Korea, pp. 577-582

Lim, S. Y. ; Pu, C. C. ; Lim, H. T. & Lee, H. J. (2007). Dragon-MAC : Securing Wireless Sensor Networks with Authenticated Encryption, [http://eprint.iacr.org/2007/204.pdf].

Liu, A. & Ning, P. (2007). TinyECC : A Configurable Library for Elliptic Curve Cryptography in wireless Sensor Networks. North Carolina State University, Department of Computer Science, Tech. Rep. TR-2007-36.

Luk, M. ; Mezzour, G. ; Perrig, A. & Gligor, V. (2007). MiniSec : A Secure Sensor Network Communication Architecture. Proceeding of IPSN'07, Cambridge, USA.

OpenSSL. http://www.openssl.org (Accessed on 12th september 2011).

Perrig, A. ; Szewczyk, R. ; Wen, V. ; Culler, D. & Tygar, J. D. (2001). SPINS : Security protocol for sensor networks. Proceeding of 7th international conference on Mobile Computing and Networks (MOBICOM 2001), Rome, Italy.

Polastre, J. ; Szewczyk, R. & Culler, D. (2005). Telos : Enabling ultra-low power wireless research, Proceeding of Sensor Network (IPSN'2005), pp. 364- 369.

Roman, R. ; Alcaraz, C. & Lopez, J. (2007). A Survey of Cryptographic Primitives and Implementations for Hardware-Constrained Sensor Network Nodes, Mobile Netw Appl (2007), DOI 10.1007/s11036-007-0024-2.

Security Architecture for the Internet Protocol. RFC2401, 1998. (Accessed on 10th september 2011).

Wang, H. ; Sheng, B. ; Tan, C. C. & Li, Q. (2007). WM-ECC : an Elliptic Curve Cryptography Suite on Sensor Motes. College of William and Mary, Department of Computer Science, Tech Rep. WM-CS-2007-11.

Watro, R. ; Kong, D. ; Cuti, S-F. ; Gardiner, C. ; Lynn, C. ; & Kruus, P. (2004). TinyPK : Securing Sensor Networks with Public Key Technology. Proceeding of Security of Ad-hoc and Sensor Networks, Washington DC, USA.

Ylonen, T. (1996). SSH-Secure Login connections over the internet, Proceeding of 6th USENIX Security Symposium, San Jose, California, 1996.

Zoltak, B. (2004). An Efficient Message Authentication Scheme for Stream Cipher, Cryptology ePrint Archieve 2004. (Accessed on 19th september 2011).

Part 2

Quantum Cryptography

9

Quantum Cryptography

W. Chen[1], H.-W. Li[1, 2], S. Wang[1], Z.-Q. Yin[1],
Z. Zhou[1], Y.-H. Li[3], Z.-F. Han[1] and G.C. Guo[1]

[1]Key Lab of Quantum Information, CAS, University of Science and Technology of China,
[2]Zhengzhou Information Science and Technology Institute,
[3]Depart. of Elect. Eng. and Info. Sci., University of Science and Technology of China
China

1. Introduction

Information protection has been an important part of human life from ancient time. In computer society, information security becomes more and more important for humanity and new technologies are emerging in an endless stream. Cryptography or cryptology is a technology to convert the information from readable state into nonsense, or do the contrary transformation. Information transmission and storage can be effectively protected by cryptography. Modern cryptography has been rapidly developed since World War II, along with the fast progress of electronics and computer science. Symmetric-key cryptography and public-key cryptography are two major fields of modern cryptography, depending on if encryption and decryption keys are same or not. One of the symmetric encryption algorithms named one-time pad (OTP) has been proven to be impossible to crack no matter how powerful the computing power is (Shannon, 1949), however, to generate and distribute the true random key steam the same size as the plaintext is a rigorous requirement. Quantum cryptography can provide a secure approach to exchange keys between legitimate users and can be used with OTP to fulfill secure communication sessions. The concept of quantum cryptography was originally proposed by Wiesner in 1960s (Wiesner, 1983), though its real development should be recorded from the first quantum key distribution (QKD) protocol presented by Bennett and Brassard in 1984 (Bennett, & Brassard, 1984). The research fields of quantum cryptography are wider than QKD, including quantum secret sharing , quantum authentication, quantum signature and so on. QKD is a major aspect of quantum cryptography and will be the only topic discussed in this chapter. Unlike public-key cryptography, the security of QKD is guaranteed by quantum mechanics rather than computational complexity. The most important property of QKD is to detect the presence of the behavior to intercept the key information illegally. The single photon used in QKD cannot be divided into smaller parts, which means the eavesdropper cannot hold a part of the particle then measure it. The eavesdropper cannot precisely duplicate a particle with the same quantum state as the original one unknown to her due to the quantum no-cloning theorem. To measure an unknown quantum system will cause it to "collapse" from a range of possibilities into one of its eigenstates. This character, together with the uncertainty principle, ensure the eavesdropper cannot get total information without disturbing the original quantum system.

In this chapter, a short summary of research status of quantum cryptography and the workflow of BB84 protocol is introduced. Then, the security of QKD is discussed and some aspects of practical QKD system are focused on. In section 3, the implementation technolgies of a secure and stable point-to-point QKD system and QKD network are presented. Some field QKD network experiments and their results will be shown in this section. Another section will discuss some technical and non-technical aspects of the applications of QKD. Finally, a short conclusion aiming at the future trends of QKD is proposed.

1.1 The research status of quantum cryptography

The first QKD experiment was implemented by Bennett and Smolin in 1989 (Bennett, et al., 1992) which opened the gate to real-life QKD. According to the implementation scheme of QKD protocol, there are discrete variable, continuous variable and distributed phase reference coding. According to the physical carrier of quantum information, there are polarization encoding, phase encoding, frequency encoding , amplitude encoding and so on. Free-space QKD and fiber QKD can be used as the quantum channel for photon-based QKD. Implementation scheme should be selected according to the channel character, the performance requirements, the operating condition and so on.

Fiber is the most widely used quantum channel, in which the polariztion and the phase encoding QKD schemes can be applied. Polarization encoding QKD schemes use the polarization states of photons to carry key information. Due to the intrinsic birefringence effect in fiber, the polarization states of photons are vulnerable to be interfered, which affects the polarization encoding rather than the phase encoding QKD system in common situation. Although there are some valuable polarization encoding QKD schemes (Ma, et al., 2008; Liu, et al., 2010), phase encoding QKD is still the major scheme used in fiber quantum channel. The encoder and decoder of phase encoding QKD system generally implemented with interferometer, which need to be precisely modulated and adjusted to meet the interference conditions. Some mature phase encoding systems based on different interferomter structures (Ribordy, et al., 1998; Gobby, et al., 2004; Mo, et al., 2005) have been proposed. At present, several experiments in fiber over 100Km (Gobby, et al., 2004; Mo, et al., 2005; Takesue, et al., 2007; Rosenberg et al., 2009; Stucki, 2009; Liu, et. al., 2010) and pulse repetition rate of 10 GHz have been reported (Takesue, et al., 2007). Although fiber is a good media to transmit photons and convenient to be integrated with existing optical communication network, the attenuation of the channel and the performance of practical device still limit the secure key distribution distance. Free space QKD, especially satellite to ground QKD is an available method to build a global secure communication network (Hughes, et al., 2002; Rarity, et al., 2002). Nowadays, a 144 Km free space QKD link has been implemented (Schmitt-Manderbach, et al., 2007) and more experiments aiming to satellite QKD are still in progress (Hughes & Nordholt, 2011).

A lot of countries, including the United State, European Union, Japanese, and China, have spent a lot to develop QKD technology, and some world famous project DARPA and SECOQC were executed. The 973 Program and 863 program of China have funded to support the QKD research from the 1990s. Some companies of quantum technology, such as ID Quantique in Swiss, MaigQ in US and Qasky in China, have been set up, and QKD systems for both education evaluation and telecom communication have been marketed.

1.2 BB84 protocol

QKD protocol is the agreement of particle preparation, information modulation, signal detection and detection results processing, which should be obeyed by communication parties in the key distribution sessions. QKD protocols can be divided into two major categories - preparation and measurement protocols and entanglement based protocols. The first and the most practical implemented QKD protocol, well known as BB84, was originally presented with photon polarization. In fact, any two pairs of conjugate states can be used to implement the protocol, such as the phase of a photon. The flow of BB84 can be described using photon polarization as following, where transmitter named Alice and receiver named Bob:

1. Information Agreement - Alice and Bob make agreements on the correspondence between quantum states and classical bits. For example, 0° and 45°polarization represents the binary bit 0, 90°, 135° corresponds to bit 1.
2. Quantum state preparation and transmission - Alice prepares single photon pulses and modulates their states of polarization to one of the four states according to the random bits stream she generated, then the pulses are sent to the quantum channel.
3. Detection - Bob measures the polarization of photons with random selected bases.
4. Sifting - Bob discloses the bases he used, then Alice tells Bob the bit slots in which she used the same modulation bases. They convert these detection results into binary bits according to the information agreement rules, thus the sifted key stream is generated.

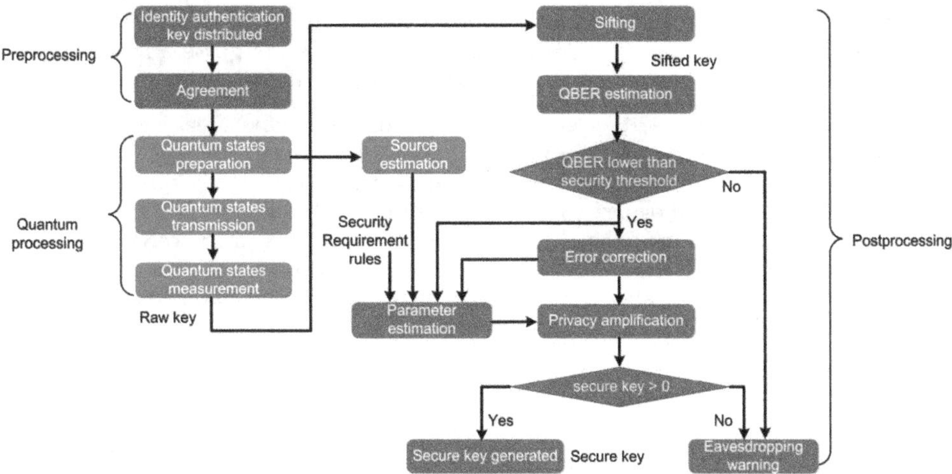

Fig. 1. Integrated QKD procedure

To generate a practice usable key stream in which Alice and Bob share uniform random bits while Eve has no secret key information, there are still some classical post processing works must be fulfilled, such as error correction and privacy amplification. The complete QKD session is shown in Fig. 1. From the diagram, we can see the security of QKD is not only depend on quantum processes, but also classical processes such as error correction, identification and authentication. The QKD without secure preprocessing and post-processing is not really secure. The first key stream used for authentication leads to a chicken-and-egg problem, which means QKD is essentially a kind of key expansion technology.

2. Security of quantum key distribution

The QKD protocol contains the quantum part and the classical part. In the quantum part, quantum states are prepared, transmitted and detected. Assuming that the noisy quantum channel can be controlled by the eavesdropper, the security of quantum channel can be proved by using the basic quantum mechanics property. A classical channel is necessary to apply the sifting, parameter estimation, error correction and privacy amplification to generate the final secure key stream. The classical channel should be authenticated with the unconditional secure authentication protocol based on 2-universal hash functions. The unconditional security analysis of protocols and systems has attracted a lot of attentions since the concept of QKD was proposed.

2.1 Security definition of QKD

Theoretical physicists have analyzed unconditional security of QKD in many respects. Initially, Lo and Chau (Lo, & Chau, 1999) proposed the security analysis with the help of quantum computer. Then, Shor and Preskill (Shor,& Preskill, 2000) proved that the security of prepare-and-measure protocol is equivalent to entanglement-based protocol, thus unconditional security of QKD has been proved combining with the CSS code and entanglement distillation and purification (EDP) technology. Without applying the EDP technology, the security of QKD with information theory method has been analyzed (Renner, 2008). More recently, the security of QKD based on private-entanglement states has been analyzed (Horodecki, 2008). Inspired by Horodecki's mind, Renes and Smith (Renes, & Smith, 2007) have analyzed noisy processing which allows some phase errors to be left uncorrected without compromising unconditional security of the key.

Security proof of perfect QKD protocol can be divided into three levels: physical explanation, physical proof and quantum information theory proof. Physical explanation is based on the no-cloning theorem and the uncertainty principle. Since the quantum state is encoded with two non-orthogonal bases, the eavesdropper Eve can not get the full secret information without disturbing the quantum state. More precisely, the uncertainty relation gives upper bounds on the accuracy by which the outcomes of two incompatible measurements can be predicated, the generalized uncertainty principle (Berta, et al., 2010; Tomamichel, & Renner, 2011) can be given as

$$H_{\min}^{\varepsilon}(X|B)+H_{\max}^{\varepsilon}(Z|E)\geq q \tag{1}$$

where X and Z are measurement outcomes with Pauli matrix $X=\begin{bmatrix}0 & 1\\ 1 & 0\end{bmatrix}$ and $Z=\begin{bmatrix}1 & 0\\ 0 & -1\end{bmatrix}$, the min-entropy $H_{\min}^{\varepsilon}(X|B)$ illustrates Bob's uncertainty about the measurement outcomes X, q quantifies the incompatibility of the two measurements in Bob's side and Eve's side respectively. The max-entropy $H_{\max}^{\varepsilon}(Z|E)$ illustrates Eve's uncertainty about the measurement outcomes Z. From this equation, we find that the upper bound of Eve's information can be estimated by considering Bob's measurement outcomes. In case of BB84 protocol, we can apply the uncertain principle and estimate upper bound of Eve's information as the following

$$H_{\max}^{\varepsilon}(Z|C)\geq 1-H_{\min}^{\varepsilon}(X|B)=1-h(\delta) \tag{2}$$

where h is the binary entropy function, δ is the quantum bit error rate. Physical proof is based on the entanglement based QKD protocol. Since the entanglement quantum state has the monogamy principle, Eve can not get the secret key in case of that Alice and Bob can establish the maximal entangled quantum state $|\varphi\rangle = \frac{1}{\sqrt{2}}(|00\rangle + |11\rangle)$. The monogamy correlation (Scarani, & Gisin, 2001; Pawlowski, & Brukner, 2009) can be given by

$$G_{CHSH}^2(A,B) + G_{CHSH}^2(A,E) \leq 8 \tag{3}$$

where $G_{CHSH}^2(A,B)$ ($G_{CHSH}^2(A,E)$) is the Clauser-Horne-Shimony-Holt (Clauser, et al., 1969)(CHSH) inequality between Alice and Bob (Eve). Information theory proof (Renner, et al., 2005) is the most universal security proof, which illustrates the trace distance between the practical quantum state and the uniformly distributed perfect quantum state

$$\frac{1}{2}\left\| \rho_{practical} - \rho_{perfect} \right\| \leq \varepsilon \tag{4}$$

where $\|M\| \equiv Tr\left\{\sqrt{M^+M}\right\}$ is the trace normal of an Hermitian operator M, the perfect quantum state shared between Alice, Bob and Eve can be given by

$$\rho_{perfect} = \sum_{s \in S} |s\rangle\langle s|_{Alice} \otimes |s\rangle\langle s|_{Bob} \otimes \rho_{Eve} \tag{5}$$

s is the secret key shared between Alice and Bob, ρ_{Eve} is Eve's quantum state. Since Eve's quantum state has no correlation with Alice and Bob's quantum state, Eve can get no secret key. In case of the trace distance between the practical quantum state and the perfect quantum state is lower than ε, the practical quantum state has the same property comparing with the perfect quantum state with probability at least $1 - \varepsilon$.

2.2 Security of perfect quantum key distribution protocol

Suppose that Alice and Bob choose the polarization encoding QKD system in our security analysis, the standard prepare-and-measure QKD protocol will be introduced in the following section (Li, et al., 2011). In Alice's side, the classical bit 0 is randomly encoded by quantum states $|0^o\rangle$ or $|45^o\rangle$, the classical bit 1 is randomly encoded by quantum states $|90^o\rangle$ or $|135^o\rangle$. In Bob's side, he randomly choose rectilinear basis $\{|0^o\rangle, |90^o\rangle\}$ or diagonal basis $\{|45^o\rangle, -|135^o\rangle\}$ to measure the quantum state transmitted through the quantum channel. After Bob's perfect measurement and some classical steps of QKD (sifting, parameter estimation, error correction and privacy amplification), secret key bits can be shared between Alice and Bob. Following the technique obtained by Shor and Preskill, the security of prepare-and-measure QKD protocol is equal to the security of entanglement-based QKD protocol, which can be constructed by considering the corresponding prepare-and-measure encoding scheme as shown in Fig. 2.

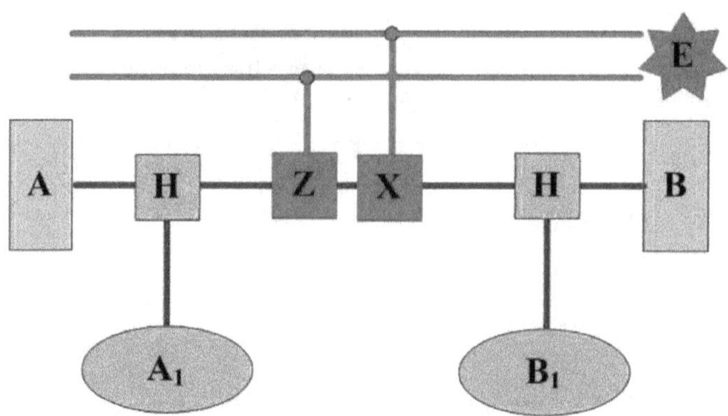

Fig. 2. Entanglement-based protocol with Pauli channel and eavesdropper Eve

Alice prepares maximally entangled pairs $|\phi\rangle = \frac{1}{\sqrt{2}}\left(|00\rangle_{AB} + |11\rangle_{AB}\right)$. After applying the Hadamard operation randomly to the second part of the pair, she sends Bob half of the pair. Bob acknowledges the reception of his state and applies the Hadamard operation randomly. In the security analysis, the most generally noisy channels we need to consider are Pauli channels. By considering Eve's eavesdropping in the Pauli channel, the quantum state about Alice, Bob and Eve is given by

$$\sum_{u,v,i,j} \sqrt{P_{uv} Q_{ij}} \left(I_A \otimes H^i_{B_1} X^u_{E_1} Z^v_{E_2} H^j_{A_1} |\phi\rangle |u\rangle_{E_1} |v\rangle_{E_2} |i\rangle_{B_1} |j\rangle_{B_1} \right) \tag{6}$$

where $H = \frac{1}{\sqrt{2}}\begin{pmatrix} 1 & 1 \\ 1 & -1 \end{pmatrix}$ is the perfect Hadamard operator, which means the transformation between different bases. Note that the Pauli quantum channel can only introduce bit error (X), phase error (Z) and bit phase error (Y) respectively. P_{uv} $u,v \in \{0,1\}$ means the probability of the operator $X^u_{E_1} Z^v_{E_2}$ introduced by Eve, which should be normalized by $\sum_{u,v,i,j} P_{uv} = 1$. Q_{ij} $i,j \in \{0,1\}$ means the probability of $H^i_{B_1} H^j_{A_1}$ matrix introduced by Alice and Bob respectively, which satisfies $Q_{ij} = \frac{1}{4}$ for Alice and Bob's random choice. After the sifting step, the case of $i = j$ will be discarded. We trace out A_1, B_1 and Eve's systems to get the following equation

$$\rho_{AB} = \sum_{u,v} P_{uv} \begin{pmatrix} \frac{1}{2} I_A \otimes X^u_{E_1} Z^v_{E_2} |\phi\rangle\langle\phi| Z^v_{E_2} X^u_{E_1} \otimes I_A + \\ +\frac{1}{2} I_A \otimes H_{B_1} X^u_{E_1} Z^v_{E_2} H_{A_1} |\phi\rangle\langle\phi| H_{A_1} Z^v_{E_2} X^u_{E_1} H_{B_1} \otimes I_A \end{pmatrix} \tag{7}$$

After transmitting through the quantum channel, the initially shared maximally entangled state can be transformed into Bell states using equation (8).

$$\begin{aligned}
|\phi\rangle &= \frac{1}{\sqrt{2}}\left(|00\rangle_{AB} + |11\rangle_{AB}\right) \\
|\phi\rangle_{bit} &= \frac{1}{\sqrt{2}}\left(|01\rangle_{AB} + |10\rangle_{AB}\right) \\
|\phi\rangle_{phase} &= \frac{1}{\sqrt{2}}\left(|00\rangle_{AB} - |11\rangle_{AB}\right) \\
|\phi\rangle_{bitphase} &= \frac{1}{\sqrt{2}}\left(|01\rangle_{AB} - |10\rangle_{AB}\right)
\end{aligned} \tag{8}$$

If the maximally entangled pairs $|\phi\rangle$ is transformed into Bell state $|\phi\rangle$, no error will be introduced in the quantum channel. However, if the maximally entangled pairs $|\phi\rangle$ is transformed into Bell states $|\phi\rangle_{bit}$, $|\phi\rangle_{phase}$ and $|\phi\rangle_{bitphase}$ respectively, the bit error, phase error and bitphase error will be introduced by Eve correspondingly. Thus, the bit error rate and phase error rate can be given by

$$\begin{aligned}
e_{bit} &= {}_{bit}\langle\phi|\rho_{AB}|\phi\rangle_{bit} + {}_{bitphase}\langle\phi|\rho_{AB}|\phi\rangle_{bitphase} \\
e_{phase} &= {}_{phase}\langle\phi|\rho_{AB}|\phi\rangle_{phase} + {}_{bitphase}\langle\phi|\rho_{AB}|\phi\rangle_{bitphase}
\end{aligned} \tag{9}$$

Comparing with the previous two equations, we can get the difference between bit error rate and phase error rate is $e_{bit} - e_{phase} = 0$. Thus, the phase error can be accurately estimated by the bit error rate in the perfect device case. Thus, the final secret key rate can be given by

$$R = 1 - h(e_{bit}) - \mathrm{h}(e_{phase}) = 1 - 2h(e_{bit}) \tag{10}$$

2.3 Security of practical quantum key distribution system

Whereas, security analysis model based on the perfect QKD protocol can not be directly applied to the practical QKD system. Gottesman, Lo, Lukenhaus and Preskill (Gottesman, et al., 2004) analyzed unconditional security of the practical QKD system and gave the famous secret key rate formula GLLP, combining their security analysis result with decoy state method (Hwang, 2003; Lo, et al., 2005, Wang, 2005) , which makes practical QKD system can be realized with weak coherent light source. But their security analysis can not be applied to the practical QKD system with arbitrary imperfections, which will introduce side channel attacks. Xu et al (Xu, et al., 2010) have experimentally demonstrated the imperfect phase modulator will introduce phase-remapping attack. Lydersen et al (Lydersen, et al., 2010) have proposed detector blinding attack with imperfect single photon detector (SPD), they demonstrated that imperfect SPD can be fully remote-controlled by utilizing specially tailored bright illumination. More recently, Weier et al. (Weier, et al., 2011) have proposed dead time attack with imperfect SPD, in which the eavesdropper can exploit the dead time effect of the imperfect SPD to gain almost full secret information without being detected. Thus, practical QKD device imperfections can lead to various types of attacks, which can't be covered by the unconditional security analysis based on the perfect QKD protocol. Major imperfections and attacking methods are summarized in Fig. 3.

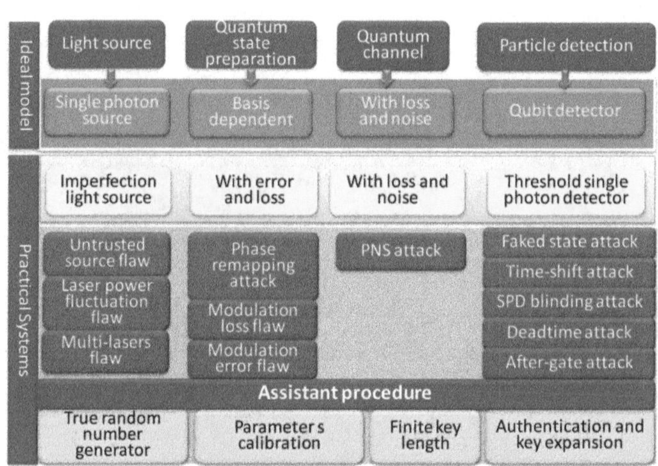

Fig. 3. The imperfections of practical QKD system and quantum hacking methods

Obviously, if the imperfection is basis-dependent, we can consider a slightly changed protocol, where the state preparation and measurement are perfect, while there is a virtual unitary transformation controlled by Eve introduces the basis-dependent imperfection in the quantum channel. Since security of the original protocol is no less than the slightly changed protocol, the final secret key rate can be estimated utilizing the GLLP formula. However, most of the imperfection in states preparation and measurement are state-dependent, which cannot be controlled by Eve in the security analysis. For instance, the wave plate may be inaccurate in polarization based QKD system, while the phase modulator may be modulated by inaccurate voltage in phase-coding QKD system. If the imperfection cannot be illustrated as an unitary transformation, it can't be considered as part of the quantum channel controlled by Eve.

2.3.1 Modulation loss of phase encoding QKD system

Most of real-life QKD implementations are based on phase-coding BB84 protocol, where Unbalanced Mach-Zehnder Interferometer (UMZI) (Gobby, et al., 2004) method is commonly used. However, the Phase Modulator (PM) in the interferometer is always imperfect, where the arm has the imperfect PM will introduce much more loss than the arm has no PM. In this case, photon state emitted by Alice's side is imperfect BB84 states, which we call it unbalanced states in the following.

$$
\begin{aligned}
&\frac{1}{\sqrt{\mu+\nu}}\left(\sqrt{\mu}|1\rangle_s + \sqrt{\nu}|1\rangle_l\right) \\
&\frac{1}{\sqrt{\mu+\nu}}\left(\sqrt{\mu}|1\rangle_s + i\sqrt{\nu}|1\rangle_l\right) \\
&\frac{1}{\sqrt{\mu+\nu}}\left(\sqrt{\mu}|1\rangle_s - \sqrt{\nu}|1\rangle_l\right) \\
&\frac{1}{\sqrt{\mu+\nu}}\left(\sqrt{\mu}|1\rangle_s - i\sqrt{\nu}|1\rangle_l\right)
\end{aligned}
\tag{11}
$$

where, $|1\rangle_s$ is the quantum state in the short arm, $|1\rangle_l$ is the quantum in the long arm after the PM. In this equation, the mean photon number of the short arm μ is larger than the mean photon number in the long arm ν by considering the practical imperfect phase modulator. Correspondingly, secret key rate of QKD based on this states can not be estimated with GLLP formula directly. To give an optimal security key rate of QKD with unbalanced BB84 states, we propose that the real-life source can be replaced by a virtual source without lowering security (Li, et al., 2010).

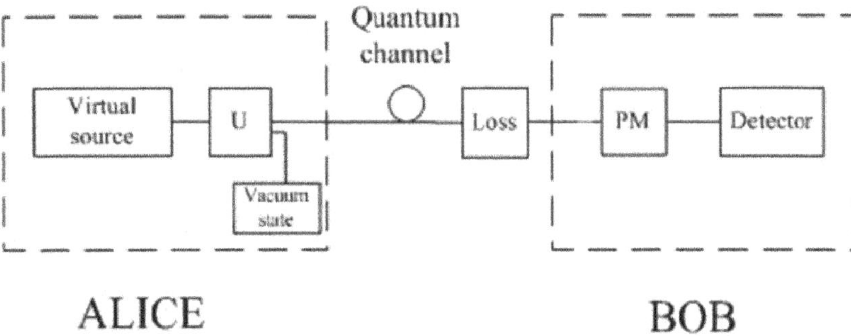

Fig. 4. UMZI method QKD with an imaginary unitary transformation and virtual source.

The unitary transformation does not need to be implemented in practical QKD experimental realizations, the detailed illustration of the unitary transformation is given as the following.

$$\begin{aligned}
&U|0\rangle_l|0\rangle_s|0\rangle_A = |0\rangle_l|0\rangle_s|0\rangle_A \\
&U|0\rangle_l|1\rangle_s|0\rangle_A = |0\rangle_l|1\rangle_s|0\rangle_A \\
&U|1\rangle_l|0\rangle_s|0\rangle_A = \frac{\sqrt{\nu}}{\sqrt{\mu}}|1\rangle_l|0\rangle_s|0\rangle_A + \frac{\sqrt{\mu-\nu}}{\sqrt{\mu}}|0\rangle_l|0\rangle_s|1\rangle_A \\
&U|n\rangle_l|m\rangle_s|0\rangle_A = |n\rangle_l|m\rangle_s|0\rangle_A \qquad n+m \ge 2
\end{aligned} \tag{12}$$

where, $|0\rangle_A$ and $|1\rangle_A$ are mutually orthogonal states. We can simply test and verify that the real-life setup of Alice can be replaced by the virtual source combining with the basis-independent unitary transformation. Obviously, we can even assume the unitary transformation is controlled by Eve, then the security of practical QKD setup is no less than the security of QKD with the virtual source.

2.3.2 Imperfect state preparation and measurement

We apply the entanglement distillation and purification (EDP) technology by considering the most general imperfect state modulation, and a much better secret key rate under constant imperfect parameters has been analyzed in comparation with previous works (Li, et al., 2011). The states prepared by Alice and measured by Bob both have individual imperfections as in Fig. 5, and the whole security analysis can be divided into two steps based on an virtual protocol as in Fig. 6.

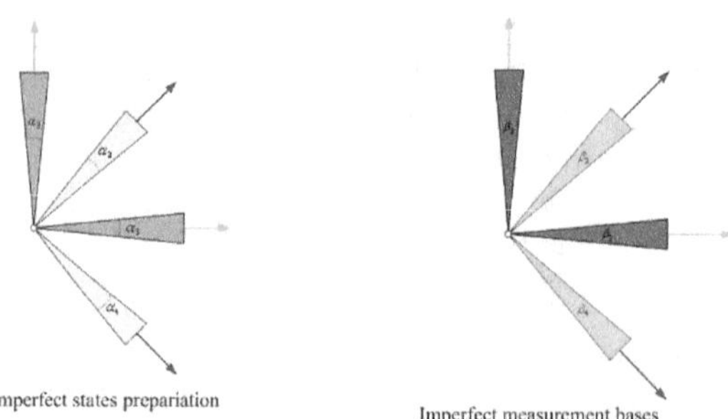

Fig. 5. The most general imperfect states preparation and measurement in practical QKD experimental realization.

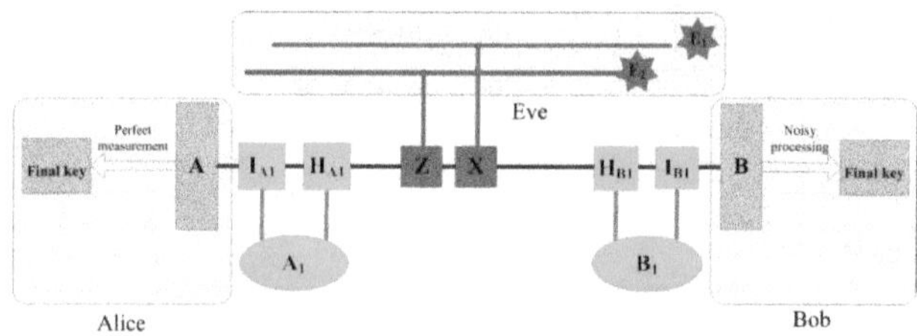

Fig. 6. Entanglement-based quantum key distribution protocol with imperfect devices.

Firstly, we consider that Alice prepares perfect entangled quantum state pairs, then she keeps half of the perfect entangled quantum state and sends half of the imperfect modulated quantum state to Bob, which illustrates the imperfect states preparation. Meanwhile, Bob applies perfect Hadamard transformation in the receiver's side, thus Alice and Bob can share the maximally entangled quantum state utilizing the EDP technology. Secondly, Alice applies perfect measurement with her maximally entangled quantum states, and Bob applies imperfect measurement with his entangled quantum states correspondingly, finally they can establish the raw key. Since the phase error introduced by Bob's imperfect measurement should not be controlled by Eve, we can get a much higher secret key rate correspondingly. The similar result has also been proved that adding noise in the classical post processing can improve the secret key rate by considering that the phase errors introduced in the post processing can not be controlled by Eve (Renner, et al., 2005). Comparing with the above security analysis result, the noise introduced by the imperfect device is precisely known by Eve, while the imperfection can not be corrected or controlled by Eve due to the random encoding choice. Thus, the exactly known but can't be controlled imperfection is similar to adding noise model (Kraus et al., 2005).

3. Realization of quantum key distribution – From point-to-point to network

The QKD system based on weak coherent pulses (WCP) is the most mature QKD technology up to date. The coherent laser pulse is attenuated to the single photon level, where photons are not equally distributed over the pulse train. The average photon number of 0.1 is an accepted secure threshold before decoy state is prompted. The most advantage of WCP QKD system is that the conventional diode lasers and standard single-mode optical fibers of 1550nm can be used, so that the transmission length can get maximum and the system can be realized and integrated into the current fiber network at reasonable price. Here we focus on phase encoding WCP QKD system and fiber QKD network. Security, stability, integration and cost are major aspects of a practical QKD system. We should setup QKD systems with available light sources, encoder, decoder and detector. The flaw between theoretical model and practical devices must be filled by technical skills at acceptable cost .

3.1 Faraday-Michelson QKD system

A typical fiber QKD scheme is based on fiber Mach–Zehnder (M-Z) interferometers, which are unstable due to the polarization fluctuation caused by environment associated fiber birefringence (Han, et al., 2004). The polarization controllers and polarization recovery sessions are necessary in M-Z system to keep the system continuously operating. We presented a Faraday-Michelson (F-M) QKD system which is intrinsic-stable in fiber channel (Mo, et al., 2005). The Faraday rotate mirror can change any imcoming polarization state into its orthogonal state. The system uses this effect to automatically compensate the polarization fluctuation of the fiber channel and the system optical units. The BB84 F-M QKD system with decoy states is implemented, as show in Fig. 7. The quantum and the sync light pulses are generated using different lasers. The energy of the quantum light pulses are attenuated to the single-photon level, then be randomly modulated by the intensity modulator to generate the decoy-state pulses. Alice applies driving signals to her phase modulator to randomly encode binary information onto the photons, with phases of 0, $\pi/2$, π and $3\pi/2$. The receiver Bob also randomly modulates the four phases of his phase modulator, then the interference results are delivered into an InGaAs/InP avalanche single photon detector (SPD). According to the BB84 protocol, the bases are divided into two sets consisting of $\{0, \pi\}$ and $\{\pi/2, 3\pi/2\}$, in which phases 0 and $\pi/2$ denote bit 0, while π and $3\pi/2$ denote bit 1. The users declare the basis sets they selected in every time bin in which the receiver detected photons, and the sifted keys with the same basis sets are kept.

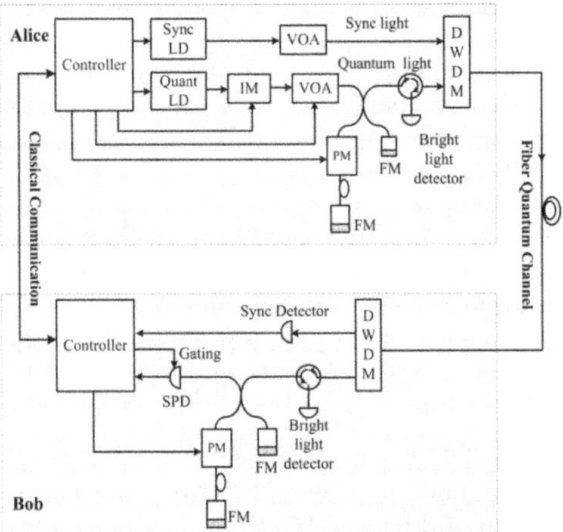

Fig. 7. The schematic diagram of Faraday-Michelson QKD system. Sync LD: Synchronization laser diode; Quant LD: Quantum laser diode; IM: intensity modulator; VOA: Variable optical attenuator; PM: Phase modulator; FM: Faraday rotator mirror; DWDM: Dense wavelength division multiplexer; SPD: Single photon detector.

3.1.1 Implementation essentials of secure QKD system

3.1.1.1 The decoy states

The quantum light source used in the system is the weak coherent pulse laser which follows Poisson distribution and has a chance to prepare multi-photo pulses. The multi-photon part of the quantum signal is vulnerable to photon-number splitting (PNS) attack. Decoy state is proposed to resist the PNS attack by randomly modulating the average photon number of quantum signal. The kernel of decoy method is to estimate the lower bound of the secret key generated by the single photon state. More precisely, applying the formula of key generation rate (GLLP) with practical source as the following

$$r \geq \frac{1}{2}\left[Y_1 P_1 \left(1-h(e_1)\right) - Q_\mu h\left(E_\mu\right)\right] \tag{13}$$

where, r is the final secret key rate, $1/2$ is the sifting efficiency, Y_1 is the yield of the single photon state, P_1 is the proportion of the single photon state, e_1 is the quantum bit error rate (QBER) of the single photon state, Q_μ is the gain of the signal photon states, E_μ is the QBER of the signal photon states, h is the binary Shannon information function. From the secret key rate formula, the upper bound of e_1 and the lower bound of Y_1 can be estimated. In practical side, suppose Alice and Bob choose decoy states with expected photon number ν, then Y_1 and e_1 can be given by

$$\begin{aligned} Y_1 &\geq \frac{\mu^2 e^{-\mu}}{\mu\nu - \nu^2}\left(Q_\nu e^{\nu} - Q_\mu e^{\mu}\frac{\nu^2}{\mu^2} - Q_\mu E_\mu e^{\mu}\frac{\mu^2-\nu^2}{\frac{1}{2}\mu^2}\right) \\ e_1 &\leq \frac{Q_\mu E_\mu}{Y_1 \mu e^{-\mu}} \end{aligned} \tag{14}$$

Combining this inequations with GLLP formula, the final secret key rate can be analyzed with the decoy state method. Note that the security of decoy state QKD protocol is based on that eavesdropper can not distinguish the signal state and decoy state with the same photon number.

The modulation speed of IM is same as the quantum signal generation rate, and the average photon number is randomly modulated to 0.6 and 0.2, which is used for signal and decoy states respectively. To generate the vacuum state, the quant laser will not be triggered. The ratio of the signal pulse, decoy pulse and vacuum pulse is 6:3:1 in the system.

3.1.1.2 The single SPD scheme

In regular BB84 system, two single photon detectors are necessary, which correspond to bit 0 and bit 1 individually, and Bob only perform two-basis modulation. Due to the quantum efficiency mismatch of the multi-SPDs, these schemes are vulnerable to practical attack like fake-state attack and time-shift attack. In our system, the standard BB84 modulation pattern is modified. We use only a single SPD with the four-state modulation in Bob's side. This scheme has advantages to resist these kinds of attacks, but loses half of the detection events.

3.1.1.3 For trojan attack

There are two optical circulators in the system. The optical circulators are used to make the system to immunize from Trojan attack, in which Eve would inject a bright light to the system and get information from reflected light. The optical circulator can restrain the light path as follows: the light incomes from port 1 will exits from port2, and the light from port2 will emit to port 3, as shown in Fig. 8. The bright light detectors of Alice and Bob are used to detect Trojan attack.

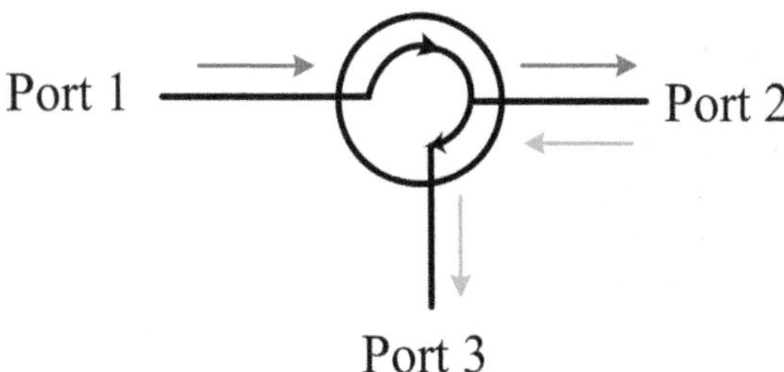

Fig. 8. The light path of optical circulator

3.1.1.4 For bright illumination attack

The bright light detector in Bob's side is not only for detecting Trojan attack, but also for detecting bright illumination attack. The bright light emits into detection system will be reflected by the Faraday rotator mirror and split by a fiber optical coupler, the reflection light will be guided by optical circulator and reaches the bright light detector. The total loss of the bright illumination light is about 3.5~4.5 dB. Since the light power used to effectively blind the SPD is regularly in the level of μW~mW, it can be detected by conventional bright light detectors.

3.1.2 The measures to keep system stable

3.1.2.1 Self-compensation of birefringence

Since the perfect interference requires exactly the same photon polarization, the birefringence also has influence to the phase encoding system. The unbalanced Michelson interferometer combined with Faraday rotator mirror can effectively compensate the birefringence of the fiber devices and channel. The Faraday rotator mirror is designed to rotate a signal's state of polarization (SOP) by 90°. Once 45° when the light enters, and again when the light is reflected back. Since the Faraday effect is non-reciprocal, the resultant SOP is rotated by 90° with respect to the original signal. The birefringence of the fiber channel can be self-compensated thanks to this character of Faraday rotator mirror (Mo, et al., 2005).

3.1.2.2 Synchronization

The SPD used in the system is based on InGaAs/InP avalanche photodiode (APD), which can respond to a single photon. This kind of APD needs to operate in Geiger mode to achieve single photon sensitivity with a low dark count rate. The gating signals of narrow pulses should be added to the bias when the photons arrive, so that sync signals for gating are necessary. Typically, there are two means to transfer synchronization light pulse - to use a standalone fiber or combine the sync single into the quantum channel. Although the crosstalk from sync light is minimum in the former scheme, the time base drift caused by the environment and the length difference between two fibers must be well compensated. The timing drift of the latter scheme is much smaller, but the crosstalk should be effectively reduced. Here we chose the one-fiber scheme not only for gating time stabilization but also to save the fiber sources. In order to suppress the interference from sync light, conventional avalanche photodiodes with typical sensitivites of -35dbm are used as sync detectors, which denotes the power of the sync light can be attenuated much.

3.1.2.3 Phase drift compensation

The phase drift is a common problem in phase encoding QKD system, and must be solved for long time operating QKD sessions, as shown in Fig. 9 (Chen, et al., 2008). Generally, there are three methods to solve the problem: Modify the structure of interferometers such as "plug-and-play" configuration to auto-compensate the phase shift. Use passive compensation to reduce the negative effect of environment fluctuations by strict thermal and mechanical isolation. Acquire drift parameters by active phase tracking then perform compensation. Here, we proposed a four-phase scanning software compensation method without adding additional reference light or hardware feedback unit (Zhang, et al., 2010). The software method is more suitable for high speed QKD system, because the reference light for compensation maybe cause severe crosstalk to quantum signal in this senerio. The four-phase scanning method bases on the interference fringe and the coding matrix. The interference fringe is the curve of the relationship between the SPD counts and the phase difference between Alice's and Bob's phase modulator. Either site, for example Alice, fixes its phase modulation voltage as V_{ref} which denotes the corresponding phase shift as φ_{ref}. The opposite site, i.e. Bob scans its phase modulation voltage from 0 to the full scale range of the DAC (its output voltage controls the phase shift) in a number of steps. In our setup, the phase modulation voltage ranging from -6V to 6V corresponds the phase shift ranging from 0 rad to more than 2π rad. Therefore, scanning the control voltage will traverse 0 to 2π phase differences, as shown in Fig. 10.

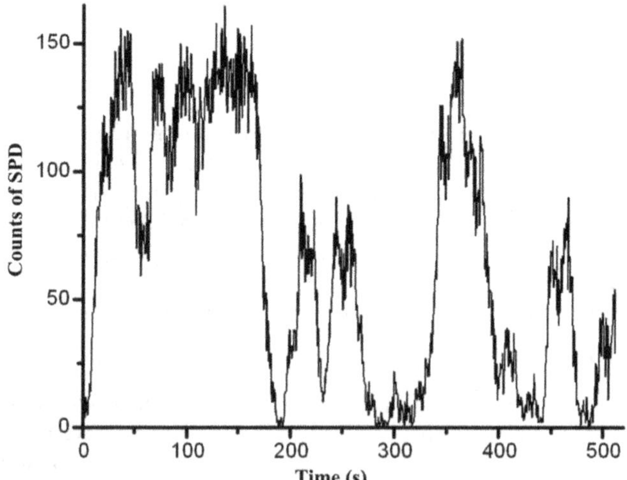

Fig. 9. Phase drift in a QKD experiment

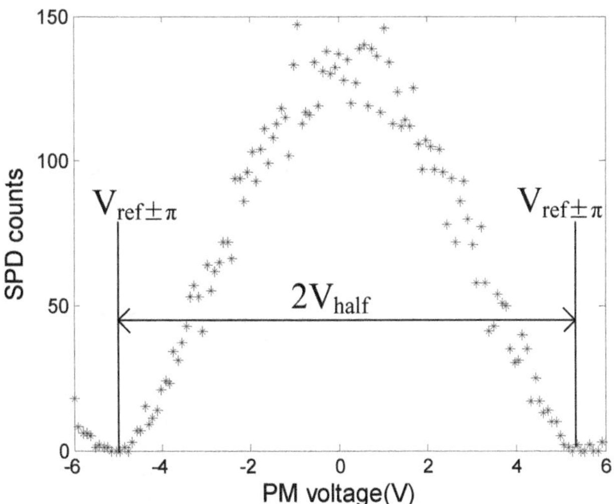

Fig. 10. Interference fringe

At each scanning step, Alice transmits a certain number of photons, meanwhile Bob records the number of photons detected by SPD, so we can get the curve of counting intensity versus the phase difference. The process fixing A-side at $V_{a,\ ref}$ and traversing B-side is called scanning B (relative to $V_{a,\ ref}$). Through the interference fringe from the scanning B, we could get two important parameters on B-side modulator. One is the half-wave voltage (denoted by $V_{b,\ half}$), which is the voltage difference of the half cycle of the interference fringe. The second parameter is the destructive interference voltage, which is the voltage at the valley of the interference fringe, and is denoted as $V_{b,\ ref\pm\pi}$. The phase difference between voltages $V_{a,\ ref}$ and $V_{b,\ ref\pm\pi}$ is π. By the process scanning A, we can get these two parameters for A-side modulator, they are $V_{a,\ half}$ and $V_{a,\ ref\pm\pi}$. The flow of algorithm is described below:

Step 1. Alice gets the half-wave voltage ($V_{a,half}$) by scanning her interference fringe. Assuming its zero phase modulation voltage is $V_{a,0}$, Alice can estimate her voltages for the four phase shifts ($V_{a,0}$, $V_{a,\pi/2}$, $V_{a,\pi}$, $V_{a,3\pi/2}$) as ($V_{a,0}$, $V_{a,0}+1/2V_{a,half}$, $V_{a,0}+V_{a,half}$, $V_{a,0}+3/2V_{a,half}$), respectively.

Step 2. Setting Alice's phase modulation voltage $V_{Alice,ref}$ as 0, $\pi/2$, π, $3\pi/2$ in turn, Bob scans his interference fringes. From these four interference fringes, Bob obtains his destructive interference voltages as ($V_{b,0\pm\pi}$, $V_{b,\pi/2\pm\pi}$, $V_{b,\pi\pm\pi}$, $V_{b,3\pi/2\pm\pi}$). These are exactly equal to Bob's four phase modulating voltages ($V_{b,\pi}$, $V_{b,3\pi/2}$, $V_{b,0}$, $V_{b,\pi/2}$).

Step 3. By checking the difference between the ideal coding matrix and the calculated coding matrix, Alice's four phase modulation voltages ($V_{a,0}$, $V_{a,\pi/2}$, $V_{a,\pi}$, $V_{a,3\pi/2}$) are tuned and step2 and step3 are repeated until the difference is sufficiently small. Then the current voltages ($V_{a,0}$, $V_{a,\pi/2}$, $V_{a,\pi}$, $V_{a,3\pi/2}$) and their scanning results ($V_{b,\pi}$, $V_{b,3\pi/2}$, $V_{b,0}$, $V_{b,\pi/2}$) will be used in the normal transmission process. The diagram of the algorithm flow and the results of the experiment is shown in Fig. 11.

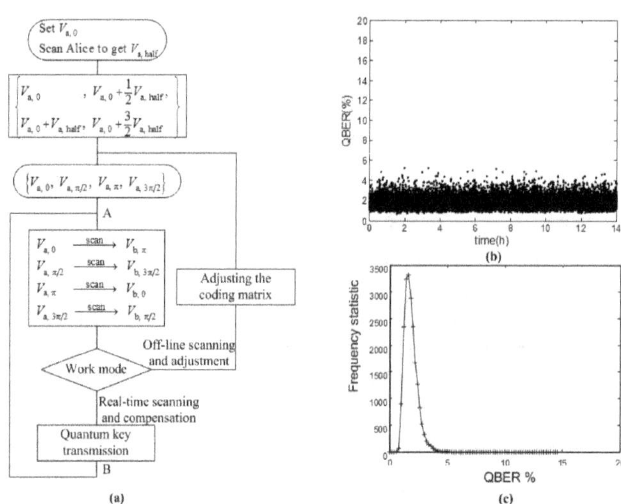

Fig. 11. Flow diagram of the four-phase scanning method and the experiment result. (a) Flow diagram, (b) QBER record of QKD experiment over 1 hours, (c) QBER statistic result.

The Faraday-Michelson (F-M) QKD system has been tested in 125Km dark fiber from Beijing to Tianjin in China in 2004. The QBER was less than 6%, which was mainly limited by the dark count of SPD. This scheme is used as the physical layer apparatus in our next QKD network experiments.

3.2 QKD network

A point-to-point system is not enough to satisfy network communication requirements in real life, so building a quantum key distribution network is not only necessary but also crucial to practical quantum cryptography. Unfortunately, the quantum mechanics make usual network routing methods invalid while keeping the QKD system secure. There are several difficulties to build QKD network.

1. The power of signal is limited at the single-photon level and can't be amplified, which indicates that it is possible but infeasible to get enough signal to noise ratio (SNR) by increasing the light power.
2. The signal can't be relayed in a classical measure and resend manner. Furthermore, it is hard to encode the light signal due to the fiber loss. It indicates the packet switching used in internet is no longer applicable.

The switch units in QKD network can be divided into three categories: optical unit, trusted relay, and quantum repeater. Among them, quantum repeater is still in the lab research stage and far away from real-life applications. Trusted relay requires the quantum signals to be converted into classical binary key bits, so that the quantum features of the keys are eliminated. The security controls of the sites where trusted relay located will become a serious problem while the network scale expands. For now, in existing QKD network, trusted relay is the most available approach to prolong the key distribution distance. Optical components can keep the quantum features of the particles, however the secure key distribution distance can't be extended. So far several optical QKD network schemes have been presented. In the 1990s, A looped and branched network was firstly proposed (Townsend, et al., 1994), then QKD sessions between one controller and several terminals in a branched network were demonstrated, in which the kernel part is a beam splitter (Towsend, 1997). After that, several QKD local network topologies have been proposed with optical methods (Nishioka, et al., 2002; Kumavor , et al., 2006; Fernandez, et al., 2007; Ma, et al., 2007; Zhang, et al., 2008). In this chapter, we will focus on the metropolitan fiber QKD networks set up by optical components.

3.2.1 A QKD network scheme

Here we propose a star topology QKD network based on wavelength-division multiplexing (WDM) in which all users can exchange keys directly and simultaneously, which we call real-time full connectivity (RTFC) network. The center of the network is a "QKD router" (QR). For an N-user network, the QR has N ports and each user connects to one port of the QR via a fiber. A user transfers photons of different wavelengths to the QR and these photons are delivered to a certain user according to their wavelengths. For any two users who want to communicate with each other, a unique wavelength is assigned to them and this is regarded as an address code for the destination of the photons. This scheme provides unique optical links between each two pairs of transmitters and receivers, and arbitrary point-to-point fiber QKD systems can be used as physical equipments into the network. The only change for point-to-point system is that two multiplexers are added into the communication link. However, the maximum secure transmission distance will be reduced a little due to the additional insertion loss.

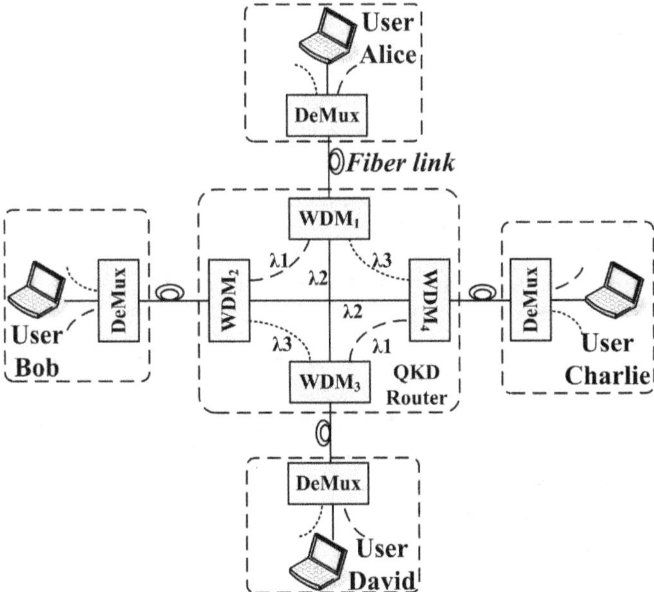

Fig. 12. Structure of four-user QKD router and the star network topology. DeMux: demultiplexer.

As an example, a four-user QKD network is used to describe the topology, as shown in Fig. 12. The router is composed of three-wavelength WDMs. When Alice wants to send quantum signal to Bob, she selects wavelength λ_1 corresponding to the specific connection inside the router, as shown in Fig. 12. These photons will be demultiplexed by WDM_1 and transmitted to WDM_2 through the link λ_1 between WDM_1 and WDM_2, then forwarded to Bob. Alice can transmit photons of λ_1, λ_2 and λ_3 at the same time in principle, then she can exchange keys with Bob, David and Charlie simultaneously, although the cost will increase. The operations of all other users are the same as for Alice. The network can be extended to N users, concurring with the edge coloring theorem in graph theory. Each WDM, link, and wavelength corresponds to a vertex, edge and color in the graph, respectively. From the edge coloring theorem, N-1 colors are required to render a complete graph with N vertices when N is even, and N colors when N is odd. This means that for an N-port router, each WDM should be an N-1 (when N is even) or N (when N is odd) wavelength multiplexer. As the network expanding, crosstalk will become the main constraint.

The crosstalk of the QKD network can be termed as interband (intraband) crosstalk, the wavelength of which falls outside (inside) the same wavelength band as the signal. The interband crosstalk can be removed by narrow-band filter (NBF) in principle. Using thin filmfilter 100GHz dense wavelength division multiplexing (DWDM) filter, less than -32dB (-48dB) adjacent (non-adjacent) channel crosstalk can be obtained experimentally. The maximum QBER caused by 40 interband crosstalk will be $0.5\times10^{-3.2}\times2+0.5\times10^{-4.8}\times38\approx0.10\%$, which validates that the interband crosstalk can be neglected in such a small size QKD network. The intraband crosstalk, which can be categorized into coherent and incoherent crosstalk, can't be eliminated by NBF and will cause non-ignorable QBER. Assuming the counting probabilities of signal and crosstalk photons are a_s and a_c. The total photon counting probability of the coherent crosstalk should be $|a_s+a_c|=|a_s|^2+|a_c|^2+2Re[a_s a_c^*]$, while in the incoherent crosstalk, the third component is 0 in long time statistic. The intraband crosstalk in the network is mainly caused by the multi-path reflection of the quantum signal itself and the same wavelength photons from other users' lasers. The photons from different lasers are generally considered to be incoherent. Since the fiber length in the router is generally much longer than the coherence length of the laser, the mulit-path crosstalk from the same laser is also incoherent. Furthermore, the multi-path crosstalk here can be neglected while taking the return loss of WDM into account.

In QKD network, the average photon number of each user's quantum signal should be fixed and equal when they access into the fiber link, therefore the power penalty model is not suitable for evaluating QKD network. The crosstalk photons generate photon counting only when they fall into the "Geiger" mode SPD triggering gate, and there will be no bit error when the signal and crosstalk photons arrive simultaneously. Thus the maximum QBER is occurred when the crosstalk photons entirely unoverlap with the signal photons, and can be depicted as

$$QBER = \frac{1-V}{2} + \frac{p_{dark} + n_c q\mu\delta 10^{-0.1(\gamma+\alpha+\beta L_c)}\eta}{2(q\mu\delta 10^{-0.1(\gamma+\beta L_s)}\eta + p_{dark} + n_c q\mu\delta 10^{-0.1(\gamma+\alpha+\beta L_c)}\eta)} \quad (15)$$

where V is the fringe visibility of the optical system, which is around 98% in our system. p_{dark} is the dark count rate of SPD, q is the protocol efficiency which is 0.5 with BB84. μ is the average photon number of the signal and crosstalk accessing into the quantum channel. δ is the system-related loss, which is 1/2 in F-M system. γ is the insertion loss of the router (typically 2.5dB). $\beta\approx0.2$dB/km is fiber loss factor. η is the detector's quantum efficient, which is about 10% typically. L_c and L_s is the fiber length of crosstalk and signal link respectively. n_c is the number of the crosstalk and a=32dB is the isolation of the router.

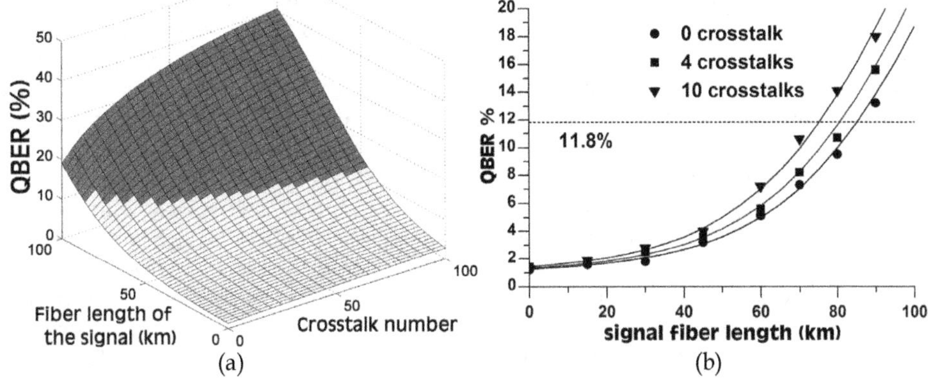

Fig. 13. (a) Simulation result of maximum QBER as a function of intraband crosstalk number and fiber distance, the QBER of the black filled area is more than secure threshold of 11.8%; (b) Experimental results of the maximum QBER of 0, 4 and 10 intraband crosstalk sources in the network, lines are the theoretical value and points are the experimental.

Since simplex transmission is enough to fulfill QKD, only (N-1)/2 or N/2 homodyne links will exist in an odd or even user number QKD network, respectively. Using the parameters in the field experiment and assuming L_c=0, in which the most critical situation is, the maximum QBER of the network is simulated and experimentally evaluated in lab, as shown in Fig. 13. The result indicates that it is possible to build a 200-user QKD network covering a 50km diameter metropolis with the basic QBER requirement. The QBER lower than 5% is generally required to effectively generate secure key if we take practical post processing of decoy into account, so that the valid user number will be a little reduced to 80-100.

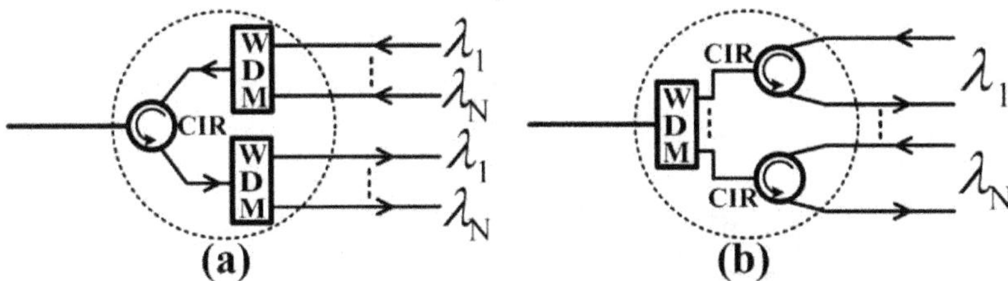

Fig. 14. Two structures of the basic unit. $\lambda_1 \ldots \lambda_N$ are N wavelengths band of WDM, and arrows mark directions.

Wavelength is a strained communication resource. We proposed a wavelength-saving RTFC QKD network scheme utilizing the simplex character of QKD (Wang, et al., 2010). The QKD network with the new topology can support 2N + 1 nodes only with N wavelengths, which saves about 50% of the wavelengths compared with the previous topology. The wavelength-saving topology employs the basic unit consisting of one three-port circulator (CIR) and two N-wavelength WDMs as show in Fig. 14 (a)Fig. 13, or one N-wavelength WDM and N three-port CIRs Fig. 14 (b). This basic unit can be regarded as a multiplexer joining N input signals together and a demultiplexer splitting N output signals apart, denoted as M&D.

As an example, Fig. 15 shows the topology of a five-node RTFC QKD network with two wavelengths. Every node connects to the QKD router, which is composed of five 1 × 4 M&Ds. When node A wants to share secret keys with B, its QKD transmitter A2B sends photons of wavelength λ_1 to its M&D, which multiplexes these photons to the optical fiber channel; while arriving at the router, these photons will propagate from port 1 to 2, then forward to B and be demultiplexed by the M&D, and finally received by the corresponding B QKD receiver A2B. At the same time, node A wants to share other keys with D, which would be required to send photons of wavelength λ_2 to A. Therefore, A can transmit photons of wavelength λ_1 and λ_2 to B and C, and receive photons of wavelength λ_2 and λ_1 from D and E, respectively, simultaneously. Every node in this architecture is on the same term, so every two nodes can share secure keys directly at the same time only with two wavelengths. Because photons in the network propagate is unidirectional (only from one node to the other), any one-way P2P QKD system can be applied on this QKD network independently. According to the Hamiltonian circuits theorem in odd complete graph theory (Deo, 1974).

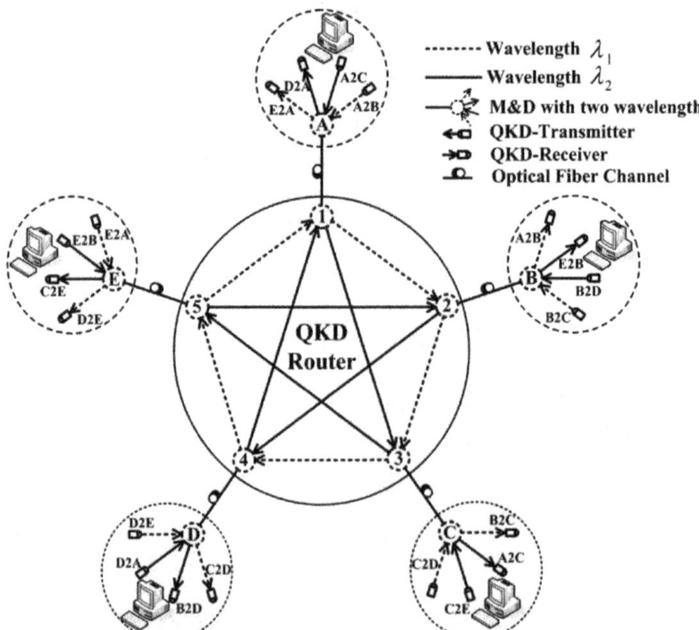

Fig. 15. Schematic diagram of the five-node QKD network topology with two wavelengths. A, B, C, D, and E are the five nodes, and 1, 2, 3, 4, and 5 are the five ports of the QKD router. Arrows indicate the propagation direction of the photons.

3.2.2 The QKD network in field

Some field QKD networks ,such as the DARPA (Elliott, et al., 2006), the SECOQC (Peev, et al., 2009) and the Tokyo QKD network (Sasaki et al, 2011) have been reported in the world. In China, the first field metropolitan QKD network with four users was implemented in the commercial backbone fiber network of China Netcom Company Ltd (CNC) in Beijing, 2007 (Chen, et al., 2009). The longest distance between two users is 42 Km and the shortest is 32 Km. The decoy state F-M QKD system was implemented in the network.

In 2009, A more complex QKD network was implemented in Wuhu, the five users nodes in which located in government bureaus (Xu, et al., 2009). The structure of the network is shown in Fig. 16(a). In this network, we constructed different priorities by considering the requirement of the bureaus. For four important nodes, a high-level full mesh backbone network was built among them and each of them can also operate as a trust relay to expand the net. Two of the others belonged to a subnet, linked with an optical switch matrix to one trust relay node shown as Node "D" in the diagram of the backbone network. In addition, we used one single telecom fiber to add the seventh node into the network, for both the classic network connection and QKD distribution, to infer the potential of our QKD network even if the fiber channel is limited. The whole quantum cryptographic network was built on the inner-city telecom fiber cables with the distribution in the satellite map of Fig. 16 (b). The network was totally implemented with decoy state QKD systems and the wave-length saving scheme was adopted.

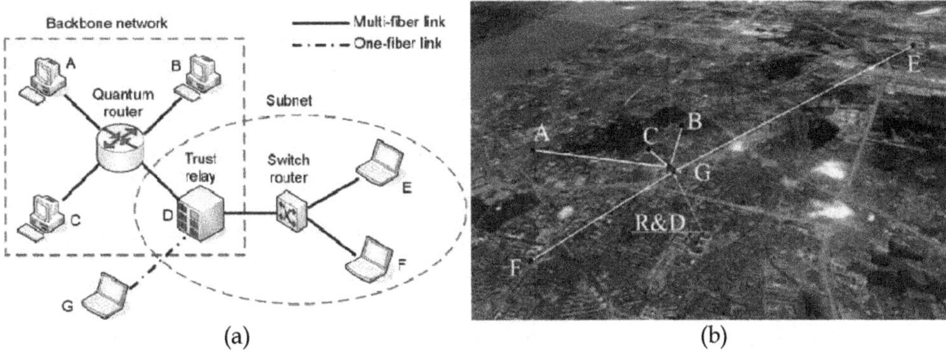

(a) (b)

Fig. 16. (a) Structure of the hierarchical quantum cryptographic network, which contains techniques of QKD router, trust relay and switch router. A to G stand for seven different terminal nodes, which linked to the backbone in the red dash square and the subnet in the blue dash circle individually. (b) Distribution map of the nodes in the network. Node A located in the Bureau of Science and Technology. B stands for the building of Economic Committee. C was in the office of General Labour Union. R stands for the QKD router, which located in the same telecom station with Node D. The backbone network was composed of these four nodes. E and F belonged to the subnet, and was settled in the Bureau of Quality and Technical Supervision and the Civic Commerce Stimulus Bureau respectively. G was in the telecom station as well.

	A2R2B	A2R2C	C2R2E	C2R2F
Wavelength (nm)	1530	1550	1530	1550
Attenuation (dB)	7.24	8.78	14.77	10.79
Sifted key (kbps)	31.00	17.64	3.83	8.16
QBER (%)	2.92	2.84	3.76	2.78
Secure key (kbps)	4.91	2.02	0.41	1.82

Table 1. Field test results for QKD network

The clock of the system was 20MHz, and the test results are shown in Table 1. Using the secure key bits generated by QKD sessions, encrypted tele-meetings between the Bureaus in the network were demonstrated. With the quantum systems used in the network, the key generation rate was insufficient for one-time-pad encryption of high bit rate multimedia data stream, and so therefore, the advanced encryption standard (AES) algorithm with the 128-bit key stream updated every one minute was implemented. The low bit rate speech data in the link A2R2B, text messages and confidential files in all links were transmitted using a one-time-pad encryption.

4. Application of quantum cryptography

Here we would like to survey the quantum cryptography from the user's point of view. Maybe some of the viewpoints expressed here are not original nor objective. These perspectives only represent our understandings of quantum cryptography.

4.1 The application motivation

Undoubtedly, security is the top power to drive scientists, engineers to research quantum cryptography and the customers to keep a watchful eye on this technology. The problems asked by customers may be like if this quantum "unconditional security" can be really realized? and what benefits can this unconditional security bring? How much will it cost? and so on. The customers can be divided into three categories, the representative of which are academy, government, and business users. The academical customers is similar to the researchers, scientific research is their major motivation to adopt quantum cryptography, so that they are regarded as researchers rather than customers. This part of market is limited and no rapid growth can be anticipated. The requirements of the government are a little complex. The perfect secure communication is attractive for the government. On the other hand, they need to keep ability to monitor the communication in necessary occasions in order to keep national security. The contradiction is their original driving force to support quantum cryptography development. This kind of users are strictly care the real-life security rather than cost. The business customers such as group corporations also have remote secure data transfer requirements. There are some motivations to make customers update their technologies when the existing solutions have been adopted:

necessary upgrading functions, much cheaper payments, much more effective or convenient way. In the view of these users, the benefits and the cost must be seriously evaluated.

After more than 20 years of development, quantum cryptography has been understood by a lot of people. The gap between the theoretical description and the real-life realization of quantum cryptography is also well known. Especially, the quantum hacking experiments published in 2010 even lead to a crisis of confidence of quantum cryptography. Since it is well known that unconditional security equals to unconditional investment, making people aware of the weakness of quantum cryptography is not an aggravating situation, but the necessary step to make quantum cryptography technology mature. After that, the proper usage manners and conditions of quantum cryptography can be declared correctly.

From the vendors' and researchers' point of view, the investment of information safety is still not enough and the road of the commercial QKD is full of obstacles. Even if the acceptable security of quantum cryptography is guaranteed, its function is still limited. The information security generally includes storage security, transmission security, authentication security, perimeter security and management security. Quantum cryptography can't solve all these problems. Besides, conventional cryptographers are also developing new crypto technologies to resist future attacking, such as quantum computation, in a much cheaper price than QKD, so that the cost performance will be a critical factor for business users.

4.2 Technology maturity

The secure key generation rate, the maximum key distribution distance, the quantum channel requirements are main technical roadblocks in real-life QKD. At present, the light pulse repetition rate has reached 10GHz and the distance over 200Km, the secure key rate in 50Km fiber can be over 1Mbps, which can support OTP video encryption. The commercial communication for a single mode optical fiber bandwidth has reached 40Gbps and the systems aim at 400Gbps to 1Tbps are in developing. The key generation performance of QKD is far from that record, so that its applications are limited in low speed communication occasions when adopting OTP. Besides that, QKD is mainly restrained in metropolitan area due to its maximum transmission distance. The research achievements of quantum repeater and satellite QKD would help to overcome the defect, however, the trusted relay is still the only choice for now.

The requirement of quantum channel either in fiber or in free space is a serious problem, which is in contradiction with the tendency of network evolution. A single fiber core is necessary to be a quantum channel, due to the SNR requirement. The nonlinear effects of fiber, for example Raman scatting, will lead to a disastrous SNR when the bright light for communication and the quantum signal are transmitted in a single fiber. In short distance, continuous variable QKD scheme may be a usable countermeasure to resist noise interference. However, the real effective scheme to work properly under practical SNR has not emerged yet. The free space channel needs directly visible light path, the good atmospheric condition, and the acceptable SNR, which denotes the valid work time is severely limited.

4.3 Policies, legal and other non-technical obstacles

Cryptography is a strictly controlled technology in all countries. The evaluation and certification must be executed by a special government department following a standardization procedure. The certification is also necessary for business customers to make use of quantum cryptography. A lot of theoretical and experimental works must be achieved to establish the standard for production, security estimation and application of quantum cryptography. Besides, to find the balance between security protection and security control is not only the technical problem for academia, but also for policy makers of the government.

It is difficult for conventional crypto venders to confirm quantum cryptography. Most of the classical cryptographers do not really understand quantum mechanics and have no confidence in quantum cryptography (Lo, 1999). Moreover, some of them are hostile to quantum computation and quantum cryptography, since many classical productions will be no longer in force if these technology become veritable. The benefit alteration will cause a lot of resistance. The new growth points should be vigorously exploited rather than make division from the existing market.

5. Conclusion and future trends

In this chapter we surveyed the concept, security and realization of quantum cryptography, which has huge potentials to achieve physical security. Quantum cryptography is a revolutionary cryptographic technology, which has attracted the attention of various counties over either industrial or academic community. Although great achievements have been achieved in the past 20 years, there are still a lot of real-life difficulties must be overcome. At the end of the chapter, we would like to shortly infer some future evolutionary trends of quantum cryptography.

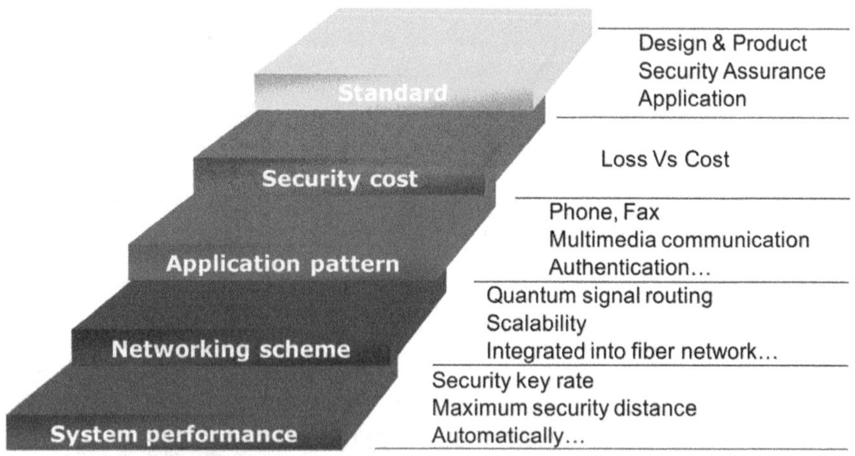

Fig. 17. The road to real-life QKD

Several stages on the road to real-life QKD are shown in Fig. 17. As the prime value, the security loopholes of real-life quantum cryptography system won't be too careful to be assessed. The key generation rate will be nonsense if the security of the procedure can not be guaranteed. This project requires the joint efforts of many people from different areas such as scientists, engineers and users. Especially, quantum hackers are necessary to make quantum cryptography more reliable, while the persuasion to develop QKD rather than destroy it should be kept in mind. The root of the quantum hacking is that we use the untrusted classical devices to perform the practical QKD system, thus how to establish the standard of various devices is very important in future research of the security of practical QKD systems.

To improve the key distribution rate is still an important aspect of futer research, even if the QKD system which can generate Mbps secury key stream over 50 Km fiber channel has been demonstrated (Dixon, et al., 2008). The development step maybe retarded due to the performance limitation of SPD, modulation, post procession, and so on. The next hot research area will be in engineering field rather than physical area, aiming at making the effective and economic QKD equipment to be integrated into existing security infrastructure.

Networking is a nature evolution way of QKD. The infrastructure of large scale QKD networks is still immature. The quantum repeater to extend the secure transmission distance, the technolgy to integrate QKD network into exsisting optical communication network will be the hot research field. The real quantum cryptography network, in which the end users can use it in their real-life information transfer applications will be the next milestone.

At last, as the core of industry, standards for security evaluation, the production, and the application of QKD are already in development (ETSI, 2011) and will continuously attract the attention of researchers.

6. References

Bennett C. H, & Brassard, G. (1984). Quantum cryptography: Public-key distribution and coin tossing, *Proceedings of IEEE International Conference on Computers, Systems and Signal Processing*, pp. 175 - 179.Bangalore, India, December 1984

Bennett C. H.; Bessette F.; Brassard G.; Salvail L. & Smolin J. (1992), Experimental quantum cryptography, *Jour. of Cryptology*, 5(1):3-28.1992.

Berta,M.; Colbeck, M. R.; Renes, J. M.; & Renner, R. (2010) The uncertainty principle in the presence of quantum memory, *Nature Physics*, Vol. 6. Issue 9, 659, 2010

Clauser, J. F.; Horne, Ma.; Shimony, A., Holt, R. A. (1969). Proposed Experiment to Test Local Hidden-Variable Theories, *Phys. Rev. Lett.*, 23, 880-884, 1969

Chen, W.; Han, Z.-F.; Yin, Z.-Q.; Wu, Q.-L.; Wei, G. & Guo, G.-C. (2007). Decoy state quantum key distribution in telecom dark fiber, *Proceedings of the SPIE*, Vol. 6827, 682709-1-6, 2007

Chen, W.; Han. Z.-F.; Xu, F.-X.; Mo, X.-F.; Wei, G. & Guo, G.C. (2008). Active phase compensation of quantum key distribution system, *Chinese Science Bulletin*. Vol. 53, 1310-1314, 2008

Chen, W.; et al., (2009). Field experiment on a "star type" metropolitan quantum key distribution network, *IEEE Photonics Technology Letters*, Vol. 21, 575-577, 2009.

Chen, T.-Y.; et al., (2010) Metropolitan all-pass and inter-city quantum communication network, *Optics Express*. Vol. 18, Issue 26, pp. 27217-27225, 2010

Choi,I.; Young, R.J. & Townsend, P.D. (2010). Quantum key distribution on a 10Gb/s WDM PON, *Optics Express,* Vol. 18, No. 9, 2010

Deo, N. (1974). Graph Theory with Applications to Engineering and Computer Science (Prentice-Hall, 1974), pp. 33–34. theorems 2–8

Diffie W. & Hellman M. E. (1976). New Directions in Cryptography, *IEEE Transactions on Information Theory,* Vol. IT-22, pp. 644–654, 1976

Dixon, A.-R.; Yuan, Z.-L.; Dynes, J.-F.; Sharpe, A. W. & Shields, A. J. (2008). Gigahertz decoy quantum key distribution with 1 Mbit/s secure key rate, *Optics Express,* Vol. 16, Issue 23, pp. 18790-18979, 2008

Elliott, C.; Colvin, A.; Pearson, D.; Pikalo, O.; Schlafer, J.& Yeh, H. (2006). Current status of the DARPA quantum network,*Proc. of the SPIE,* Vol. 6372, pp. U270-U275, 2006

ETSI (2011). http://www.etsi.org/WebSite/Technologies/QKD.aspx

Fernandez, V.; Collins, R.J.; Gordon, K.J.; Townsend, P.D. & Buller, G.S. (2007). Passive optical network approach to gigahertz-clocked multiuser quantum key distribution, *IEEE J. Quantum Electron.* Vol. 43, No. 2, pp. 130-138, 2007

Gobby, C.; Yuan, Z. L. & Shields, A. J. (2004). Quantum key distribution over 122 km of standard telecom fiber, *Appl. Phys. Letts.* Vol. 84, Issue 19, 2004

Gottesman, D.; Lo, H.-K.; Lukenhaus, N. & Preskill, J.(2004). Security of quantum key distribution with imperfect devices, *Quantum Information and Computation,* Vol. 4, 325, 2004

Han, Z.-F.; Mo, X.-F., Gui, Y.-Z. & Guo, G.C., (2005). Stability of phase-modulated quantum key distribution systems, *Applied. Physics. Letters,* 86, 221103, 2005

Horodecki, K.; Pankowski, L.; Horodecki, M. & Horodecki, P. (2008). Low-dimensional bound entanglement with one-way distillable cryptographic key, *IEEE Trans. on Infor. Theory,* Vol. 54, Issue 6, p 2604-2620, 2008.

Hughes, R. & Nordholt, J. (2011). Refining Quantum Cryptography, *Science,* Vol. 333, 1584-1586, 2011.

Hwang, W.-Y. (2003). Quantum key distribution with high loss: Toward global secure communication, *Phys. Rev. Lett.* 91, 057901, 2003.

Kraus, B.; Gisin, N. & Renner, R. (2005). Lower and Upper Bounds on the Secret-Key Rate for Quantum Key Distribution Protocols Using One-Way Classical Communication, *Phys. Rev. Lett.* 95, 080501, 2005

Kumavor, P. D.; Beal, A. C.; Donkor, E. & Wang, B. C. (2006). Experimental multiuser quantum key distribution network using a wavelength-addressed bus architecture, *IEEE J. Light Tech.* Vol. 24, pp. 3103-3106, 2006

Li, H-W. Yin, Z.-Q.; Han, Z.-F.; Bao, W.-S. & Guo, G. C. (2010). Security of practical phase-coding quantum key distribution, *Quantum Information and Computation,* Vol. 10, No. 9 & 10 0771–0779, 2010

Li, H.-W.; Yin, Z.-Q.; Han, Z.-F.; Bao, W.-S. & Guo, G. C. (2011). Security of quantum key distribution with state-dependent imperfections, *Quantum Information and Computation,* Vol. 11, No. 11 & 12 0937–0947, 2011

Liu Y.; Chen, T.-Y.; Wang, J.; et al. (2010). Decoy-state quantum key distribution with polarized photons over 200 km, *Opt. Express.* 18(8):8587-94, 2010.

Lo, H.-K. (1999). Will Quantum Cryptography ever become a successful technology in the marketplace?, arXiv:quant-ph/9912011v1, 1999

Lo, H.-K.; & Chau, H. F. (1999). Unconditional security of quantum key distribution over arbitrarily long distances, *Science* 283, 5410, 1999.

Lo, H.-K.; Ma, X.-F., & Chen, K. (2005). Decoy state quantum key distribution, *Phys. Rev. Lett.* 94, 230504, 2005.

Lydersen, L.; Wiechers, C.; Wittmann, C.; Elser, D.; Skaar, J.& Makarov, V. (2010). Hacking commercial quantum cryptography systems by tailored bright illumination, *Nature Photonics* 4 686-689., 2010

Ma, L.-J.; Mink, A.; Xu, H.; Slattery, O. & Tang, X. (2007). Experimental demonstration of an active quantum key distribution network with over gbps clock synchronization, *IEEE Communications Letters*, Vol. 11, No. 12, 1019 -1021, 2007

Ma, L.-J.; et al., (2008). Experimental demonstration of a detection-time-bin-shift polarization encoding quantum key distribution system, *IEEE Comm. Lett.*, Vol. 12, No. 6, 2008.

Mo, X.-F.; Zhu, B.; Han, Z.-F.; Gui, Y.-Z. & Guo, G. C. (2005). Faraday–Michelson system for quantum cryptography, *Optics Letters*, Vol. 30, No. 19, pp.2632-2634, 2005.

Nishioka, T.; Ishizuka, H.; Hasegawa, T.& Abe, J. (2002). "Circular type" quantum key distribution, *IEEE Photonics Technology Letters*, Vol. 14, No. 4 , pp. 576-578, 2002

Pawlowski, M.; & Brukner, C. (2009). Monogamy of Bell's inequality violations in nonsignaling theories, *Phys. Rev. Lett.*, 102, 030403, 2009

Peev, M.; Pacher, C.; Alleaume, R.; et al. (2009). The SECOQC quantum key distribution network in Vienna, *New Jour. Of Phys.*, Vol. 11, 075001, 2009

Rarity, J. G.; Tapster, P. R.; Gorman, O.M. & Knight P. (2002). Ground to satellite secure key exchange using quantum cryptography. *New Journal of Physics*, 4. 82.1–82.21, 2002.

Renes, J. M. & Smith, G. (2007). Noisy processing and distillation of private quantum states, *Phys. Rev. Lett.* 98, 020502, 2007

Renner, R.; Gisin, N. & Kraus, B. (2005), Information-theoretic security proof for quantum-key-distribution protocols, *Phys. Rev. A.* 72,012332, 2005

Renner, R. (2005), PhD thesis, ETH No 16242, 2005 *http://quant-ph/0512258, 2005.*

Ribordy, G.; Gautier, J.-D.; Gisin, N.; Guinnard, O. & Zibinden, H. (1998). Automated "Plug &Play" quantum key distribution, *Electronics. Letters.* 34, (22), pp. 2116 - 2117, 1998

Rosenberg, D.; Peterson, C.G.; Harrington, J. W.; Rice, P. R., Dallmann, N., Tyagi, K. T., McCabe, K. P.; Nam S.; Baek, B.; Hadfield, R. H.; Hughes, R. J. & Nordholt J. E. (2009). Practical long-distance quantum key distribution system using decoy levels, *New Jour. of Phys.* 11, 045009, 2009.

Sasaki, M; et al., (2011). Field test of quantum key distribution in the Tokyo QKD Network, *Optics Express,* Vol. 9, Issue 11, pp. 10387-10409, 2011.

Scarani, V. & Gisin,N. Quantum communication between N partners and Bell's inequalities, *Phys. Rev. Lett*, Vol. 87, No.11, 117901,2001

Schmitt-Manderbach, T.; Weier, H.; Fürst, M.; Ursin, R.; Tiefenbacher, F.; Scheidl, T.; Perdigues, J.; Sodnik., Z.; Kurtsiefer, C.; Rarity, J.G.; Zeilinger, A & Weinfurter, H. (2007). Experimental Demonstration of Free-Space Decoy-State Quantum Key Distribution over 144 km, *Phys. Rev. Lett.* 98, 010504 (2007)

Shannon, C. (1949). *Bell System Technical Journal* 28 (4): 656–715, 1949.

Shor, W.; Preskill, J. (2000). Simple proof of security of the BB84 quantum key distribution protocol , *Phys. Rev. Lett.*, 85, pp.441-444, 2000.

Stucki D.; Walenta, N.; Vannel, F.; Thew, R. T.; Gisin, N.; Zbinden, H.; Gray. S.; Towery, C. R &Ten, S. (2009). High rate, long-distance quantum key distribution over 250 km of ultra low loss fibres, *New Jour. of Phys.* 11, 075003, 2009.

Takesue, H.; Nam, S. W.; Zhang, Q., Hadfield, R. H.; Honjo, T.; Tamaki, K. & Yamamoto, Y. (2007). Quantum key distribution over a 40-dB channel loss using superconducting single-photon detectors, *Nature Photonics,* 1, 343 - 348, 2007

Tomamichel, M.; Renner, R. (2011). Uncertainty relation for smooth entropies, *Phys. Rev. Lett.,* 106, 110506, 2011.

Townsend, P.D.; Phoenix, S.; Blow, K.J. & Barnett, S. (1994). Design of quantum cryptography systems for passive optical networks, *Electronic Letters.* 30 , 1875, 1994

Townsend, P.D. (1997). Quantum cryptography on multiuser optical fibre networks, *Nature,* 385, 47, 1997

Wang, X.-B. (2005). Beating the photon-number-splitting attack in practical quantum cryptography, *Phys. Rev. Lett.* 94, 230503, 2005

Wang, S.; et al., (2010). Field test of wavelength-saving quantum key distribution network , *Optics Letters,* Vol. 35 Issue 14, pp.2454-2456, 2010

Weier, H.; Krauss, H.; Rau, M.; Furst, M.; Nauerth, S.& Weinfurter, H. (2011). Quantum eavesdropping without interception: an attack exploiting the dead time of single-photon detectors, *New Jour. of Phys.* 13, 073024, 2011

Wiesner, S, (1083), Congjugate coding, *SIGACT news,* 15(1):78-88, 1983

Xu, F.-X.; et al., (2009). Field experiment on a robust hierarchical metropolitan quantum cryptography network, *Chinese Science Bulletin,* Vol. 54, 2991-2997, 2009.

Xu, F.-H.; Qi, B. & Lo, H.-K. (2010). Experimental demonstration of phase-remapping attack in a practical quantum key distribution system, *New Jour. of Phys,* 12, 113026, 2010

Zhang, L.-J.; Wang, Y.-G.; Yin, Z.-Q.; Chen, W.; Yang, Y.; Zhang, T.; Huang, D.-J.; Wang, S.; Li, F.-Y. & Han, Z.-F. (2011) Real-time compensation of phase drift for phase-encoded quantum key distribution systems, *Chin. Sci. Bull.,* Vol 56, 2305-2311, 2011

Zhang, Tao.; Mo, X.-F.; Han, Z.-F. & Guo, G.-C. (2008). Extensible router for a quantum key distribution network et al., *Phys Lett. A.,* Vol.372, 3957-3962, 2008

10

Securing a Telecom Services Using Quantum Cryptographic Mechanisms

Abdallah Handoura
Ecole Nationale Supérieure des Télécommunications de Bretagne
France

1. Introduction

The architectural model of Internet telephony is rather different than that of the traditional telephone network. The base assumption is that all signaling and media flow over an IP-based network, either the public Internet or various intranets. IP-based networks, present the appearance at the network level that any machine can communicate directly with any other, unless the network specifically restricts them from doing so, through such means as firewalls. This architectural change necessitates a dramatic transformation in the architectural assumptions of traditional telephone networks. In particular, whereas in a traditional network a large amount of administrative control, such as call-volume limitation, implicitly resides at every switch, and thus additional controls can easily be added there without much architectural change, in an Internet environment an administrative point of control must be explicitly engineered into a network, as in a firewall; otherwise end systems can simply bypass any device which attempts to restrict their behavior. In addition, the Internet model transforms the locations at which many services are performed. In general, end systems are assumed to be much more intelligent than in the traditional telephone model; thus, many services which traditionally had to reside within the network can be moved out to the edges, without requiring any explicit support for them within the networks. Other services can be performed by widely separated specialized servers which result in call setup information traversing paths which might be extremely indirect when compared with the physical network's actual topology.

Most of the services and service features of ITU-T Q.1211 can be provided by the IETF's draft signaling standards for Internet Telephony, SIP (the Session Initiation Protocol) (Schulzrinne, 2001) and, for some more specialized features, its Call Control extensions (Johnston, 2002).

However, The growing globalization and the liberalization of the market telecommunications, necessitates a more global infrastructure of IN that satisfies the needs of different subscribed legal implied, especially for multinational services subscribed. A lot of these services are offered on a current system, but are often realized with specialists of the system. The concepts of IN for giving such service is a coherent and stable basis (Schulzrinne, 2001). Some security functions have been introduced already in current systems, but they define constraints to user groups with the private line means, the proprietor equipment and proprietor algorithms or secrets.

There is a major difference between the realization of today service (limited) and the goals of the introduction of IN, however, the IN offer its services to a public world, open, and especially to offer the services that allow user groups to communicate by the public transmission and to change the equipment without unloading their intimacy and affluence of employment. Therefore, the services of security provides for the current network will not be sufficient for IN, the goal is more long. The defying of the aspect of the new security functions has to make then be publicly usable, economically feasible and insured all its at the same time.

2. Interconnecting SIP and telecom service application

The IN (Intelligent Network) functional architecture identifies several entities such as the service switching function (SSF), the service control functions (SCF), and the call control function (CCF) that model the behavior of the IN network. The CCF represents the normal activities of call and the connection processing in traditional switch, for two clients. The SSF model's additional functionality required for interacting with a service logic program executed by the SCF. The CCF and the SSF are generally co-located in specific switching centers, known as SSP, while the SCFs are hosted on dedicated computers known as SCP. The communication between the different nodes uses the INAP protocol.

Accessing IN services from the IMS network requires that one or more entities in these networks can play the role of an SSP and communicate with existing SCPs via the INAP protocol.

To realize services with SIP it is important that the SIP entity be able to provide features normally provided by the traditional switch, including operating as a SSP for IN features. The SIP entity should also maintain call state and trigger queries to IN-based services, just as traditional switches do.

The most expeditious manner for providing existing IN services in the IP domain is to use the deployed IN infrastructure as much as possible.

The creation of a service by SIP is possible by the three methods INVITE, Bye and options and fields of header SIP Contact, Also, Call-Disposition Replace and Requested-by that are extensions of SIP specified by IETF (Fing, 2001). Some services are already specified by IETF (Gisin, Ribordy, 2001) by using methods and fields of already quoted header: Call, Hold, Transfer of call, Return of call, Third party control.

The key to programming telecom services with SIP is to add logic that guides behavior at each of the elements in the system (Johnston, 2002). In a SIP proxy server, this logic would dictate where the requests are proxies to, how the results are processed, and how the packet should be formatted.

The basic model for providing logic for SIP services is shown in Figure 1. The figure shows a SIP server that has been augmented with service logic, which is a program that is responsible for creating the services. When requests and responses arrive, the server passes information up to the service logic. The service logic makes some decisions based on this information, and other information it gathers from different resources, and passes instructions back to the server. The server then executes these instructions (Johnston, 2002).

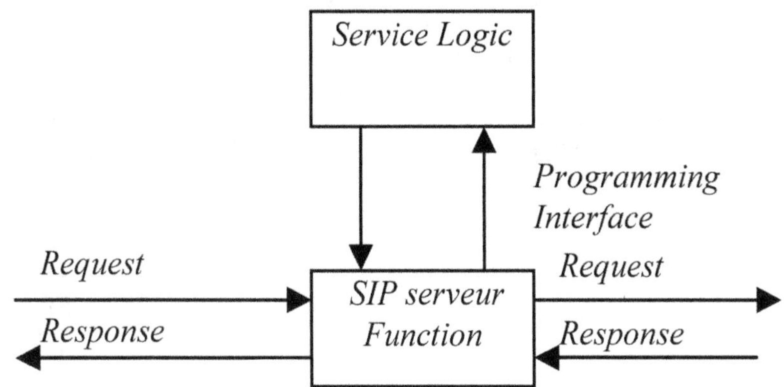

Fig. 1. Model for Programming SIP Services

The separation of the service logic from the server is certainly not new. This idea is inspired by the Intelligent Network (IN) concept (Chapron, 2001). This separation enables rapid development of new services; the idea also exists on the web.

The mechanisms used in these environments can provide valuable insight on how a solution for SIP, IN integration. SIP does not operate the model of call IN directly to access to services IN, the trick is then to bypass the machine of states of the entity SIP with the layer IN such that the acceptance of the call and the routing is executed by the native states and service machine are accessed to layers IN with the model of call IN (El Ouahidi, 2000). The model of service programming with SIP consists therefore in add on SIP server an IN layer, that manages the interconnection with the IN called SIN (SIP Intelligent Network) (Gurbani, 2002). This operation necessitates the definition of a correspondence between the model of call IN and the model of call SIP, it is to tell a correspondence between the state machine of the SIP protocol (SIP defines the header Record_Route that allows to order SIP server to function in mode with the states until the liberation of the call) and the state machine of IN. A call will be processed by the two machines, the state machine SIP processes the initiation of a call and the final reply deliverance, and the IN layer communicate with the intelligent point SCP to provide services during processing of the call (Gurbani, 2002). The figure 2 illustrates the integration SIP-IN.

Similarly to the machine of states IN, one defines the quoted calling and called the entity (O-SIP) and (T-SIP) which are entities corresponding, respectively, to the O-BCSM and T-BCSM of the model IN.

In the basic system of SIP, the SIP proxy with this control of call " intelligent " is defined to interconnect with intelligent network, this intelligence is realized by the use of control calls, that can synchronize with the model of call IN (BCSM). According to RFC 2543 (SIP) one can define calls of the state machine of the SIP client and SIP server [7,8]. The 11 PICs of O_BCSM come into play when a call request (SIP INVITE message) arrives from an upstream SIP client to an originating SIN-enabled SIP entity running the IN call model. This entity will create an O_BCSM object and initialize it in the O_NULL PIC. The next seven IN PICs -- O_NULL, AUTH_ORIG_ATT, COLLECT_INFO, ANALYZE_INFO, SELECT_ROUTE, AUTH_ CALL_SETUP, CALL_SENT, O_Alerting and O_Active, can all be mapped to the SIP "Calling" state. Figure 3 below provides a visual mapping from the SIP protocol state machine to the originating half of the IN call model. Note that control of the call shuttles between the SIP protocol machine and the IN O_BCSM call model while it is being serviced.

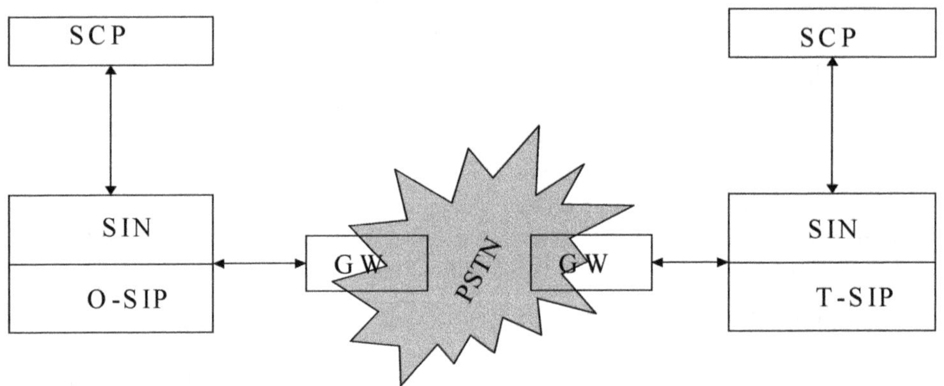

Fig. 2. Interconnection SIP-IN

The SIP "Calling" protocol state has enough functionality to absorb the seven PICs. From server of SIP proxy point of view, its initial state could be corresponded to the O_NULL PIC of the O_BCSM. Its processing state could be corresponded to the Auth_Ori_att, Collect_Info, Analyse_info, Select_ Route, Auth_Call_Setup, Senf_Call and O_Alerting PICs. Its success, confirmed and complete states could be corresponded to the O_Active PIC. Figure 4 below provides a visual mapping from the SIP protocol state machine to the terminating half of the IN Call model.

When the SIP server of termination receives the message INVITE, it creates the T_ BCSM object and initials it to the PIC T_Null, this operation is realized by the state " Proceeding " that orders the five PICs : T_Null, Auth_Ter_Att, Select_Facility, PICs of the T_BCSM. Its calling state could be corresponded to the prrsent_Call PIC. Its call processing state could be corresponded to the T_Alerting. Its complete state could be corresponded to the T_Active PIC.

The service-level call flows for Voice over IP communication where interconnecting between the PSTN and IP-based networks are necessary to complete a call.

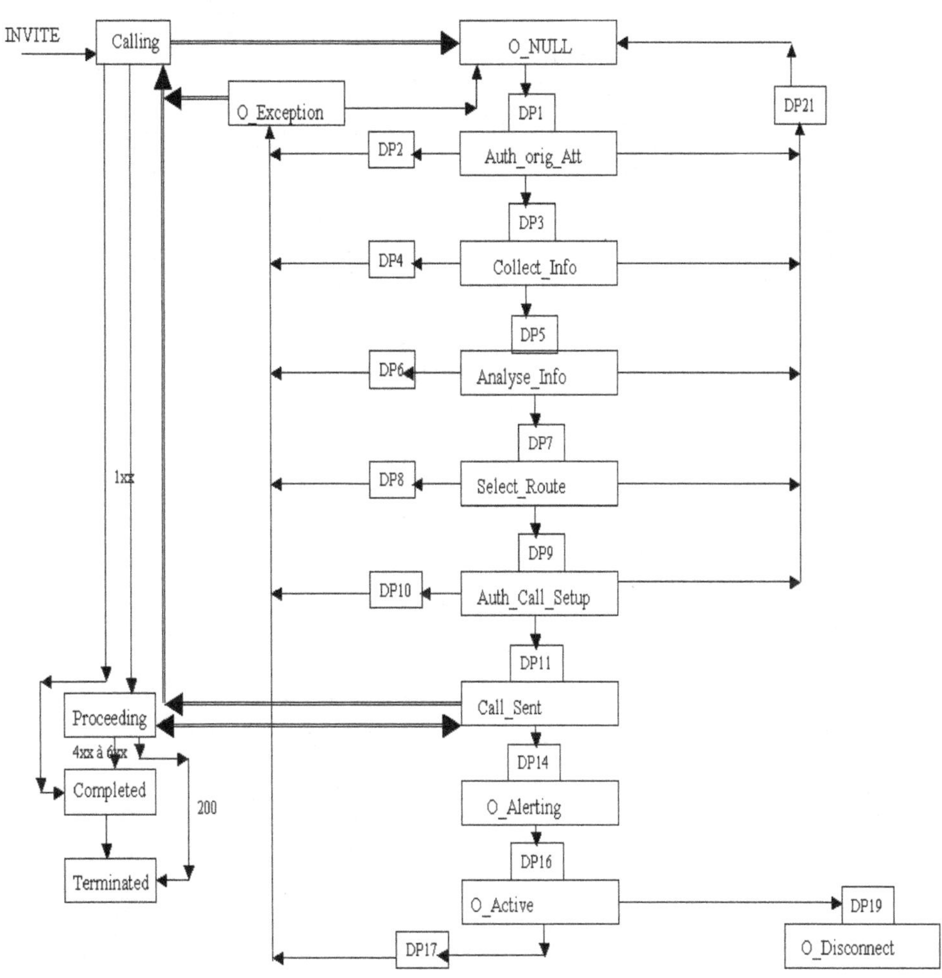

Fig. 3. Mapping from SIP to O_BCSM

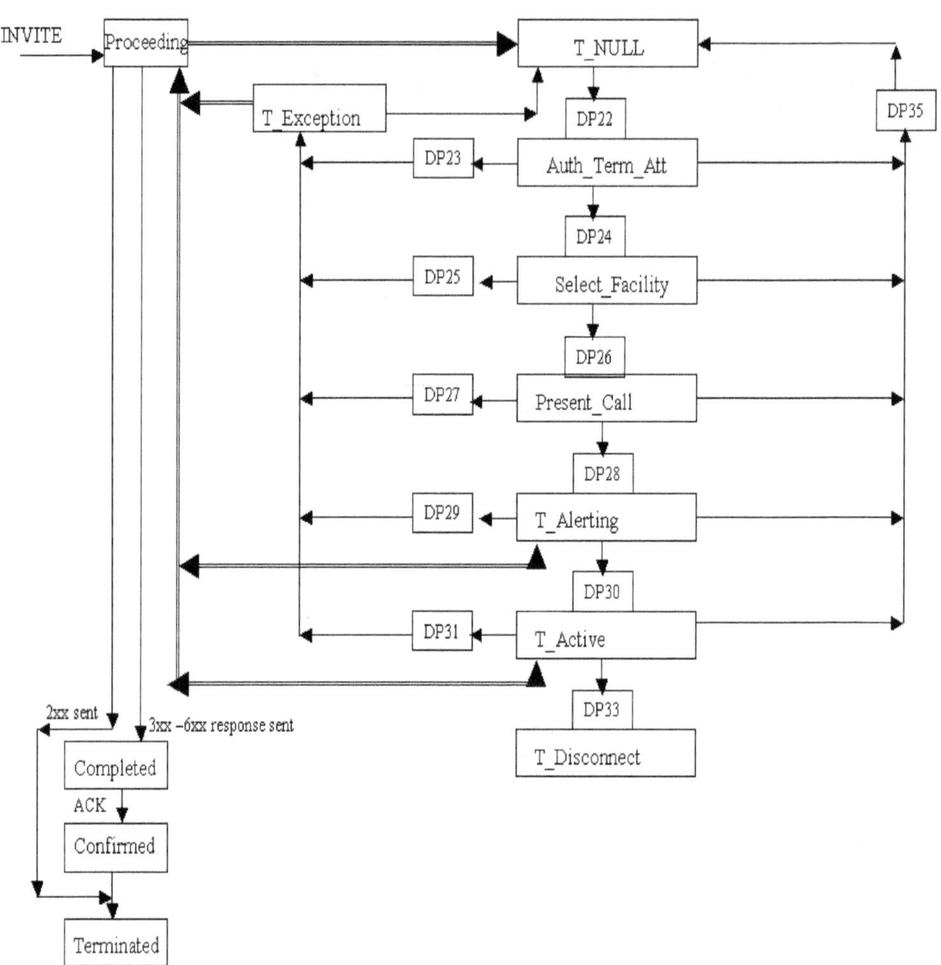

Fig. 4. Mapping from SIP to T_BCSM.

3. Threats in the intelligent network (telecom service)

As all elements of a network can be distributed geographically and that element of system IP is totally opened, several threats of security can rise and attack these different elements. The interconnection IN, is the process to execute a demand of service IN on the part of the user of service through at least two different autonomous areas. Typically, each area represents a system IN separated with different legal entities and entities of resource IN. The limp of the IN service is only to be executed, if the two different areas cooperates by exchanging management, control, and services of data on the basis of a legal contract (co-contract of operation). In this competition, each area applies these clean mechanisms to provide the integrity, the availability, and the intimacy of service users. If the two operators that distribute cooperate, they have to apply the same totality of mechanisms to exchange data between their SCPs and SDPs.

The main problems of security that pose in the multimedia communication area and the telephony over IP as well in a system IN under IP are following:

- Imitation of attack: users not authorized can try to access to services of IN. For example, in the case of service IMR a user not recorded can try to see video services.
- Simulating attack: A recorded user can try to avoid the policy of security and obtains illegitimately access to sensitive services. For example, a user with common access privileges can try to act as an administrator of service IN.
- Denial of Service attack: an adversary can try to block users to access to the services of IN. For example to send a great number of requests to the system simultaneously
- Communication to spy and alter: an adversary can try to spy and/or to modify the communication between a legitimate user and elements of service IN.
- Lack of responsibility: if IN is not capable to verify the communication between users and its elements of service, then it will not be possible to make these users responsible for their actions.

The list is not complete. In practice, nevertheless, one can be found confronted with others problems of security, considered as not belonging of the area of application (for example, problems linked, the policy of security, the security of the management system, to security of the implementation, the operational security or to the processing of security incidents). As well as the technological evolution on the soft, does not cease to increase in a manner not estimable, similarly, the technological connection tools to the system and the attack passive and active become impressive things?

If the system and its components are not sufficiently secured, a lot threats can occur. However, it is necessary always to consider:

- What is the probability of a threat (occurrence; likelihood)?
- What are the potential damages (impact)?
- What are the costs to prevent a threat?

Depending on these suppositions, the cost and the efficiency of security mechanisms has to be implemented. The potential of the threat depends on the implementation of IN, the specific service IN. They depend also on the implementation of security mechanisms (ex. PIN, strong authentication, placement of authentication, management of key, etc.).

Manufacturers as well as the groups of standardization make the work of the analysis of risks in the order to improve the security of systems IN. Although a many improvements have already been realized, concerning the security of access to SCP and SMP. New services and new architectural concepts necessitate supplementary improvements. The next figure, figure 5, presents places of the different threats.

Intelligent networks are distributed by nature. This distribution is realized not only to the superior level where the services are described as a collection of service feature (SF), but to too low levels, where the functional entities (FE) can be propagated on different physical entities (PE). Like the communications of various elements of the network are realized on the open and uncertain environment, the security mechanisms have to be applied.

A responsible of the system can prevent these threats of security by using the various mechanisms. The authentication has to be applied in the order to prevent users not authorized to earn the access to the distribution of services.

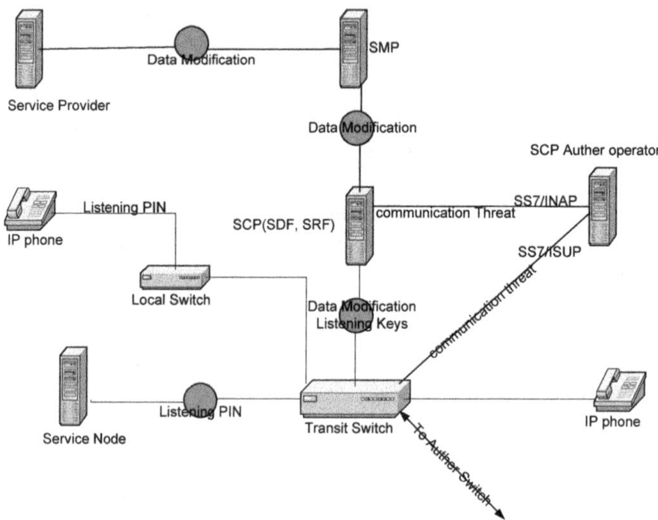

Fig. 5. Places of the different threats.

4. Secure the telecom service with SIP

SIP Communication is susceptible to confront several types of attack. The simplest attacks in the SIP permit to a hacker of earning the information on users' identities, services, media and topology of the distribution. This information can be employed to excute others types of attacks. The modification of attack occurs when an assailant intercept the effort and covers the signal and modify the SIP message in the order to change a certain characteristic of a service. For example, this sort of attack can be employed for diverting the flow of signaling by forcing a particular itinerary or for changing a recording of the user or modifying a profile of service (Profos, 2002). The sort of attack depends on the type of security (or insecurity) employed (the type of authentication, etc.). These attacks can also be employed for the denial of service.

The main two mechanisms of security employed with SIP: authentication and the encryption data. The authentication of data is employed to authenticate the sender message and insure that certain sensitive information of the message was not modified in the transit. It has to prevent an assailant to modify and/or listen in SIP requests and reply. SIP employs Proxy -Authentication, Proxy -Authorization, authorization, and WWW - Authentication of areas of the letterhead, similar to these of HTTP, for the authentication of the terminal system by the means of a numerical signature. Rather, proxy-by-proxy authentication can be executed by using the authentication protocols over Internet such that, the transport layer TLS or SSL and the network layer IPSEC.

The cryptography of data is employed to, ensure the confidentiality in SIP communication, allowing only the legal receiver client to decrypt and read data. It is usual of using algorithms of cryptography such that the DES (DES: Data Encryption Standard) and Advanced AES (AES: Advanced Encryption Standard). SIP endorses two forms of cryptography: end-to-end and hop-by-hop. The end-to-end encryption provides confidentiality for all information (some letterhead and the body of SIP message) that needs to be read by intermediate servers or proxy. The end-to-end encryption is executed by the mechanism S/MIME. On the contrary, the hop-by-hop encryption of whole SIP message can be employed in the order to protect the information that would have to be accessed by intermediate entities, such that letterhead *From, To* and *Via*. The security of such information prevents malevolent users to determine that calls, or to access to the information of the itinerary. The hop-by-hop encryption can be executed by external security mechanisms to SIP (IPSEC or TLS).

Before closing this poll of security mechanisms in SIP, it is necessary to consider the efforts of standardization processing to improve the security mechanisms for SIP. The most important matter here is the problem of the agreement on the chosen security mechanism between two SIP entities (user agents and/or proxy) that want to communicate by applying a level of «sufficient» security. For this reason, it is very important to define how a SIP entity can select an appropriate mechanism for communicating with a next proxy entity. One of the proposals for an agreement security mechanism that allows two agents of exchanging their clean security aptitudes of preferences in the order to select and apply a common mechanism is, when a client initiated the procedure, the SIP agent include in the first request sent to the neighbor proxy entity the list of its mechanisms of security sustained. The other element replies with a list of its clean security mechanisms and its parameters. The client selects then the common security mechanism preferred and use this chosen mechanism (ex, TLS), and contact the proxy by using the new mechanism of security (Jennings, 2002).

With this technique, another problem should be handled. It is the problem with the assertion and the validation of the identity of the user by SIP server. The SIP protocol allows a user to assert its identity by several manners (ex, in the letterhead); but the information of identity requested by the user is not verified in the fundamental SIP operation. On the other hand, an IP client of telephony could have required and insure the identity of a user in order to provide a specific service and/or to condition the type of service to the identity of the user himself. The model of SIP authentication could be a way of obtaining such identity; however, the user agents have not always the necessary information on key to authenticate with all the other agents. A model is proposed in (Profods, 2002) for «confirmed identity» which is based on the concept of a «confirmed area». The idea is, that when a user authenticates its clean identity with a proxy, the proxy can share this authenticated identity (the confirmed identity) with all the other proxies in the «confirmed area». A confirmed area is a totality of proxies that have a mutual configuration of a security association. Such association of security represents a confidence between proxies. When a proxy in a «confirmed area» authenticates the identity of the author of a message, it adds a new letterhead to the message containing the confirmed identity of the user. Such identity can be employed by all other proxies belonging to the «confirmed area».

Using this mechanism the client UAC, is capable to identify himself to a proxy UAS, to an intermediate proxy or to a registration proxy. Therefore, the SIP authentication is applied only to the communications end-to-end or end-to-proxy; the authentication proxy-by-proxy would have to count on others mechanisms as IPsec or TLS.

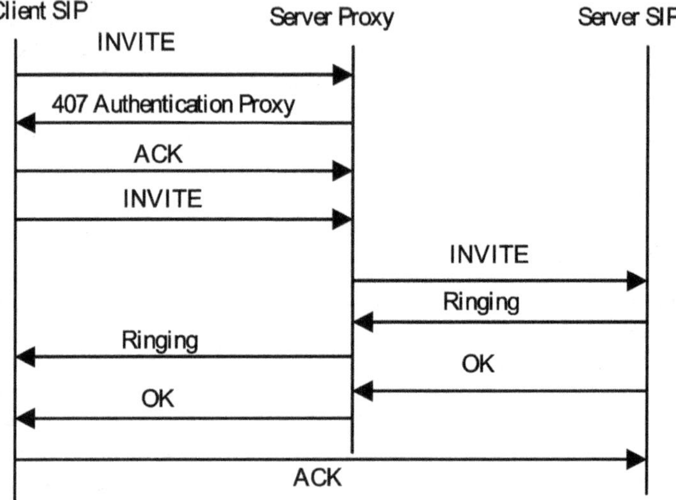

Fig. 6. Authentication SIP

The procedure of authentication is executed when the UAS, the proxy intermediate, or the necessary recording proxy for the call of the UAC has to be authenticated before accepting the call, or the recording. In the beginning the UAS sends a request of SIP message «text» (ex, INVITE). In the reception of this message, the UAS, proxy, or recording proxy decides that the authentication is necessary and sent to the client a specific SIP error message of the request of authentication. This error message represents a challenge. In the particular case, where the message of error is 401 (Unauthorized) is sent by UAS and recording, while when the message of error is 407 (Proxy Authentication Required) is sent by proxy server. The UAC receives the message of error, calculates the reply, and includes it in a new message of the SIP request. The next figure 6 shows the sequence of message for the case of request of authentication by the proxy server.

The UAC sends a message ACK immediately after that the message of error is received. This message closes the first transaction; then the second message INVITE opens a new transaction.

```
INVITE sip:xy@domain SIP/2.0
Via: SIP/2.0/UDP
To: xy <sip:xy@domain>
From: yx <sip:yx@domain>
Call-ID:
CSeq: 1 INVITE
Contact: <sip:yx@domain>
Content-Type: multipart/signed;boundary=...;
micalg=sha1;protocol=application/pkcs7-signature
Content-Length:
Content-Type: application/pkcs7-mime;
smime-type=envelopeddata; name=smime.p7m
Content-Disposition: attachment;handling=required;filename=smime.p7m
Content-Transfer-Encoding: binary
<envelopedData object encapsulating encrypted SDP attachment not shown>
Content-Type: application/pkcs7-signature;name=smime.p7s
Content-Disposition: attachment;handling=required;filename=smime.p7s
Content-Transfer-Encoding: binary
<signedData object containing signature not shown>
```

Fig. 7. S/MIME encryption in SDP

But this technique is a classic and it's based on a standard and classical mechanism. It will thus be preferable to propose a new technique based on sure cryptographic algorithms such as the quantum cryptography.

5. Elements necessitates security in telecom service

Manufacturers as well as the groups of standardization make the work of the analysis of risks in the order to improve the security of systems IN. Although a lot of improvements have already been realized, concerning the security of access to SCP and SMP. New services and new architectural concepts necessitate supplementary improvements. The next figure, figure 7, presents places of the different threats.

Intelligent networks are distributed by nature. This distribution is realized not only to the superior level where the services are described as a collection of service feature (SF), but to too low levels, where the functional entities (FE) can be propagated on different physical entities (PE). Like the communications of various elements of the network are realized on the open and uncertain environment, the security mechanisms have to be applied.

A responsible of the system can prevent these threats of security by using the various mechanisms. The authentication has to be applied in the order to prevent users not authorized to earn the access to the distribution of services.

The cryptography technique that allows detecting a spy and realized the security is the technique of quantum cryptography

6. Quantum cryptography

Quantum cryptography does not base security on unproven mathematical problems. Instead, the foundation of security lies in the properties of quantum mechanics (Gisin, Ribordy, 2001). Three such properties essential for quantum cryptography are:

1. We cannot make a measurement on an unknown quantum system without perturbing unless the measurement is an eigen operator to the quantum state being measured. This implies that an eavesdropper (conventionally called Eve) cannot make a measurement of an unknown quantum state in order to obtain some information about the key without introducing disturbances that can in turn be discovered by Alice and Bob.
2. We cannot make a copy of an unknown quantum state. This property is usually referred to as the no cloning theorem. It prevents an eavesdropper from simply intercepting the transmission and making copies of the transmitted quantum states in order to keep copies to make measurements on, while passing on an unperturbed quantum state to Bob.
3. We cannot measure the simultaneous values of non commuting observables on a single copy of a quantum state.

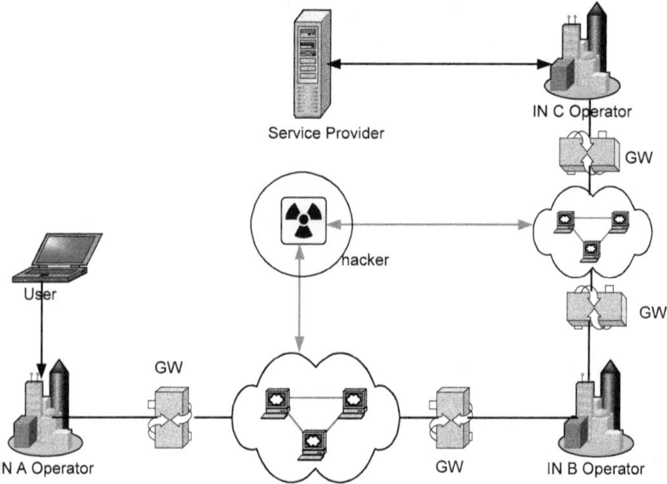

Fig. 8. Place of the hacker.

It ensures that the eavesdropper cannot construct a measurement that is an eigen operator to all quantum states used for the key distribution, i.e., it guarantees that it is impossible for the eavesdropper to only perform measurements that leave the quantum states unperturbed (Hoi, 2008).

Quantum cryptography cannot securely transmit predetermined information; it can only securely generate a random key. Once generated, this random key can be subsequently used in a symmetric cipher, such as the one-time pad or one of the modern symmetric ciphers, to securely transmit data over a classical communication channel. A running quantum cryptography channel will steadily generate new secret key material. Thus, quantum cryptography is solving the most difficult problem in modern cryptography, that of key distribution.

There are mainly two types of quantum key distribution (QKD) schemes. One is the prepare-andmea sure scheme, such as BB84, in which Alice sends each qubit in one of four states of two complementary bases; B92, in which Alice sends each qubit in one of two non-orthogonal states; six-state, in which Alice sends each qubit in one of six states of three complementary bases. The other is the entanglement based QKD, such as E91, in which entangled pairs of qubits are distributed to Alice and Bob, who then extract key bits by measuring their qubits; BBM92, where each party measures half of the EPR pair in one of two complementary bases.

6.1 BB84 algorithm

BB84 is a quantum key distribution scheme developed by C. Bennett and G. Brassard in 1984. It is the first quantum cryptography protocol. The protocol is provably secure, relying on the quantum property that information gain is only possible at the expense of disturbing the signal if the two states we are trying to distinguish are not orthogonal. It is usually explained as a method of securely communicating a private key from one party to another for use in one-time pad encryption. It has the following the phases.

Step 1. Alice sends a random stream of bits consisting of 1's and 0's using a random selection of rectilinear and diagonal scheme over the quantum channel. On the other side Bob has to measure these photons. He randomly uses one of the two schemes (+ or X) to read the qubits. If he has used the right scheme he notes down the correct bits or he ends up noting down the wrong bits. This is because one cannot measure the polarization of a photon in 2 different 'basis' (rectilinear and diagonal in our case) simultaneously. For example, suppose Alice sends | using '+' scheme to represent 1 and Bob uses '+' scheme and notes down the bit as 1. For the second bit Alice sends \ using the 'X' scheme to represent 1 but Bob uses an incorrect scheme + and miss interprets it as either | or - noting it down correctly as 1 or 0 incorrectly.

Step 2. Alice talks to Bob over a regular phone line and tells the polarization schemes (and not the actual polarization) she had used for each qubit. Bob then tells Alice which of the schemes he had guessed it right. This gives the correct bits noted down by Bob. Based on this they discard all the bits Bob had noted down guessing the wrong scheme.

Step 3. The only way for Alice and Bob to check errors would be to read out the whole sequence of bits on an ordinary telephone line. This wouldn't be a wise idea. So Alice randomly picks some (say 100) binary digits out of the total number of bits that were measured using the correct scheme and checks just these. The probability of Eve being online and not affecting Bob's measurements of 100 bits is infinitesimally small. So if they find any discrepancy among the 100 digits they will detect Eve's presence and will discard the whole sequence and start over again. If not then they will just discard only those 100 digits discussed over phone and use the remaining 1000 digits to be used as one time pad (Johnston, 2002)

One advantage of quantum cryptography is the ability to detect an eavesdropper since Eve can never read the values with out altering them. For example, if Eve reads \ polarization using + scheme then he will be altering the polarization of the photon to either - or ↕, resulting in binary values 0 or 1 respectively. Eve might be able to get the actual (binary) value of 1 but ends up altering the polarization for Bob. If Bob uses X scheme to measure the values he might get either \, which is what Alice sent or /, which is an incorrect measurement.

Bit Number	1	2	3	4	5	6	7	8
Alice : Bits	1	1	0	1	0	0	1	1
Alice : Scheme	+	+	+	+	X	X	X	+
Alice : Qubit	↕	↕	↔	↕	/	/	\	↕
Eve: Scheme	X	+	X	+	+	X	+	X
Eve: Qubit	/	↕	↕	↕	↔	/	↕	/
Bob: Scheme	+	X	X	+	+	X	X	+
Bob: Qubit	↕	\	\	↕	↔	/	/	↔
Bob: Bits	1	1	1	1	0	0	0	0
Selection	√			√		√	√	√

Fig. 8. Key Selection and detecting Eve's presence

Here the bits 1, 4, 6, 7, 8 are selected by Alice and Bob since both of them use the same detection scheme. But when they randomly check bits 1, 7 and 8 they find that the values are different. Through this they can detect the presence of the eavesdropper.

6.2 BB92 algorithm

In 1992, Charles Bennett proposed what is essentially a simplified version of BB84 in his paper, "Quantum cryptography using any two non-orthogonal states". The key difference in B92 is that only two states are necessary rather than the possible 4 polarization states in BB84. As 0 can be encoded as 0 degrees in the rectilinear basis and 1 can be encoded by 45 degrees in the diagonal basis. Like the BB84, Alice transmits to Bob a string of photons encoded with randomly chosen bits but this time the bits Alice chooses dictates which bases she must use. Bob still randomly chooses a basis by which to measure but if he chooses the wrong basis, he will not measure anything; a condition in quantum mechanics which is known as an erasure. Bob can simply tell Alice after each bit she sends whether or not he measured it correctly.

This security feature results from the use of a single or two photons. We know from quantum properties of photons that the measurement of spin of one gives the spin of the other. So if a given pulse sent from Alice is formed by entangled photons then Eve can split these photons using a beam splitter in such a way that he can direct one photon to his polarization detector and another to Bob's. But if only single photons are generated then in presence of a beam splitter the photons have to choose between Eve's and Bob's polarization detectors. This increases the error rate which the BB84 protocol will detect.

Thus, it is the singleness of the photon that guarantees security (Mohamed, 2007). The figure 9 represents a probability to spy detected vs photon number:

Pdet(n) = Pr{MBB84 |= Φdet} with Φdet = a PCTL equation, is True if spy is detected.

PCTL : probabilistic temporal logic (Xu, 2009)

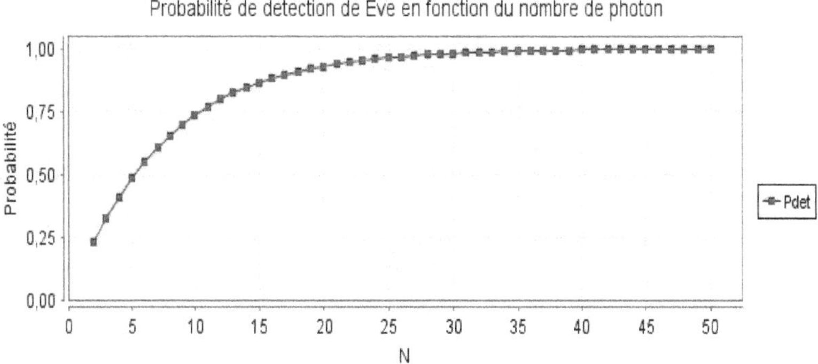

Fig. 9. Probability to spy detected

6.3 Quantum key distribution QKD

The BB84 protocol and its variants are the only known provably secure QKD protocols. Other QKD protocols (BB92), although promising, have yet to be proven secure. The benefits of QKD are that it can generate and distribute provably secure keys over unsecured channels and that potential eavesdropping can be detected (Mohamed, 2007). QKD can defeat the current computationally complex key exchange methods. Because QKD generates random strings for shared secrets, attaining a QKD system and reverse engineering its theory of operation would yield no mechanism to defeat QKD.

7. Implementation a quantum cryptography in SIP protocol over IMS network

The IMS has been *originally* conceived for mobile systems, but with the addition of *TISPAN* works in the *7* version 7, *the PSTN* are equally supported.

The IMS is a structured *of the architecture of Next* Generation *Network* (NGN) that allows the progressive introduction of *voice* application and multimedia in mobile and permanent *network*. The IMS *is used* with all types of systems (permanent, mo*bile* or wireless), including *a switching functions,* as GPRS, UMTS, CDMA 2000, WLAN, WiMAX, *DSL. An open interface between control and service layers allows mixing* calls/*session in a* different *access networks*. The IMS use*d a* cellular technolog*y* to provide an access in every *position,* and *Internet* technology to provide services.

The principle of the IMS consists on the one hand in *clearly* separate the transport layer of the *service* layer and on the other hand to use the transport layer for control and *signaling* functions so as to insure the quality of service wished for the *desired* application. IMS aims, to make the *network* a sort of middleware *layer* between applications and the access. Applications are been SIP, *or* not SIP, they pass by a *Gateway* before the connection to the controller of sessions.

Despite considerable advantages of the IMS, several limit render the IMS all alone is incapable to be beneficial for the creation and the exploitation of services by operators to the near users, it is in order that, one uses IN service into SIP protocol.

In my Application, I'm proposing a several IMS networks nodes for mobile application (figure10). The signaling into the different elements is assured with SIP over MAP (Mobile Application Protocol).

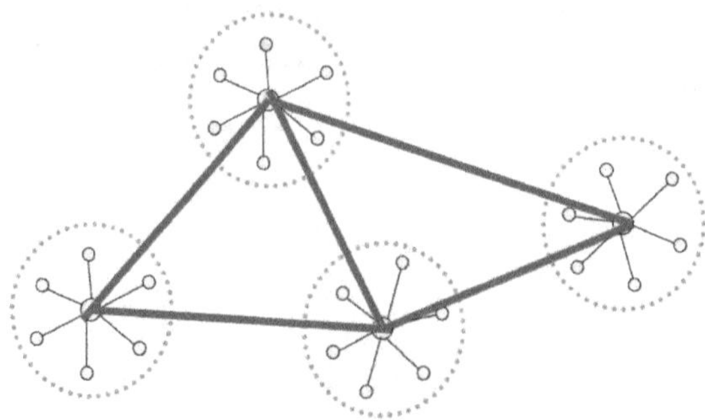

Fig. 10. IMS Network node

After this I'm developing a quantum cryptographic key distribution in SIP Body based on the BB84 algorithm (Bernhard, 2003), named qc:

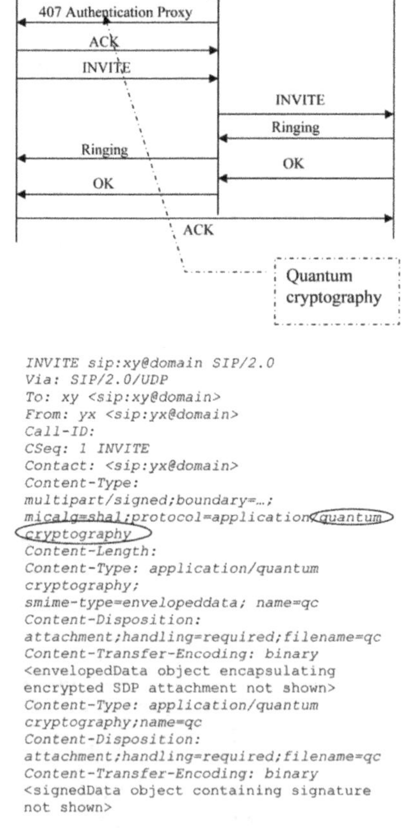


```
INVITE sip:xy@domain SIP/2.0
Via: SIP/2.0/UDP
To: xy <sip:xy@domain>
From: yx <sip:yx@domain>
Call-ID:
CSeq: 1 INVITE
Contact: <sip:yx@domain>
Content-Type:
multipart/signed;boundary=…;
micalg=sha1;protocol=application/quantum
cryptography
Content-Length:
Content-Type: application/quantum
cryptography;
smime-type=envelopeddata; name=qc
Content-Disposition:
attachment;handling=required;filename=qc
Content-Transfer-Encoding: binary
<envelopedData object encapsulating
encrypted SDP attachment not shown>
Content-Type: application/quantum
cryptography;name=qc
Content-Disposition:
attachment;handling=required;filename=qc
Content-Transfer-Encoding: binary
<signedData object containing signature
not shown>
```

Fig. 11. QC into SIP request

The different ID of IMS clients is registered in a database developed with sql in QC server. I am proposing one QC server for one IMS server (see figure) and the transaction into these IMS servers is authenticate with BB84 protocol like a Kerberos protocol (Butler, 2006), figure 12.

After this, I am implementing my application over an IMS core (http://www.openimscore.org) open source IMS network and IMS client is UCT client IMS (http://uctimsclient.berlios.de). The figure 13 show a SIP client Request and figure 14 show an IMS network with QKD server.

8. Conclusion

Mobile networks has adopted the IN technology to provide to users of the new services that can be only obtained in the permanent system and improved management of mobility. With the SIP protocol under IP an attempt of the Mobile connection has IP and IN to define the new services as well as to exploit advanced techniques in the security developed for IP network becomes possible especially for IMS network. The SIP authentication is the alone technique proposed by SIP for the security for the terminal and subscribed. With quantum cryptography mechanism into SIP Authentication, the security between IMS client and P-CSCF or I-CSCF is assured and sure.

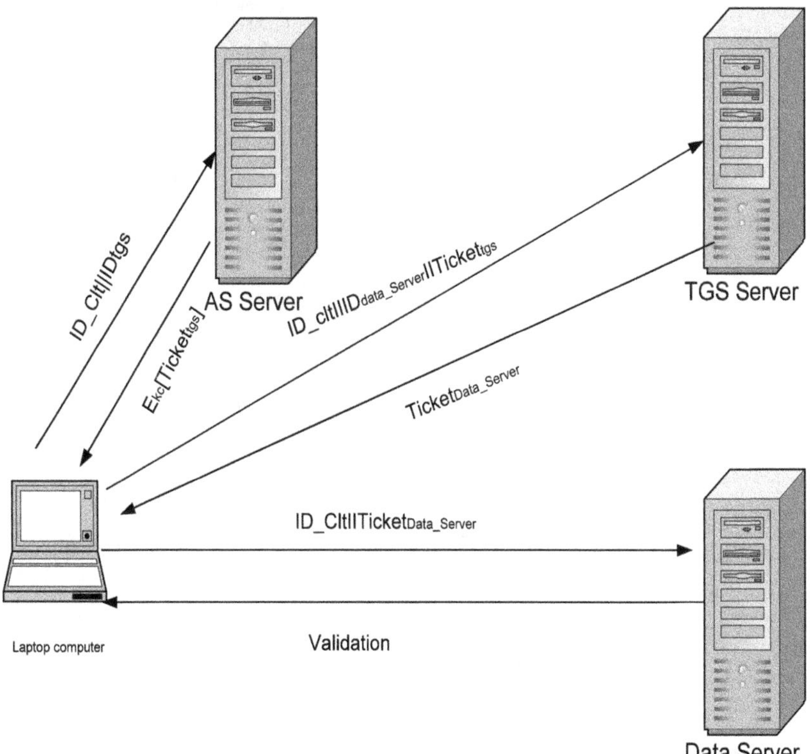

Fig. 12. Kerberos mechanism

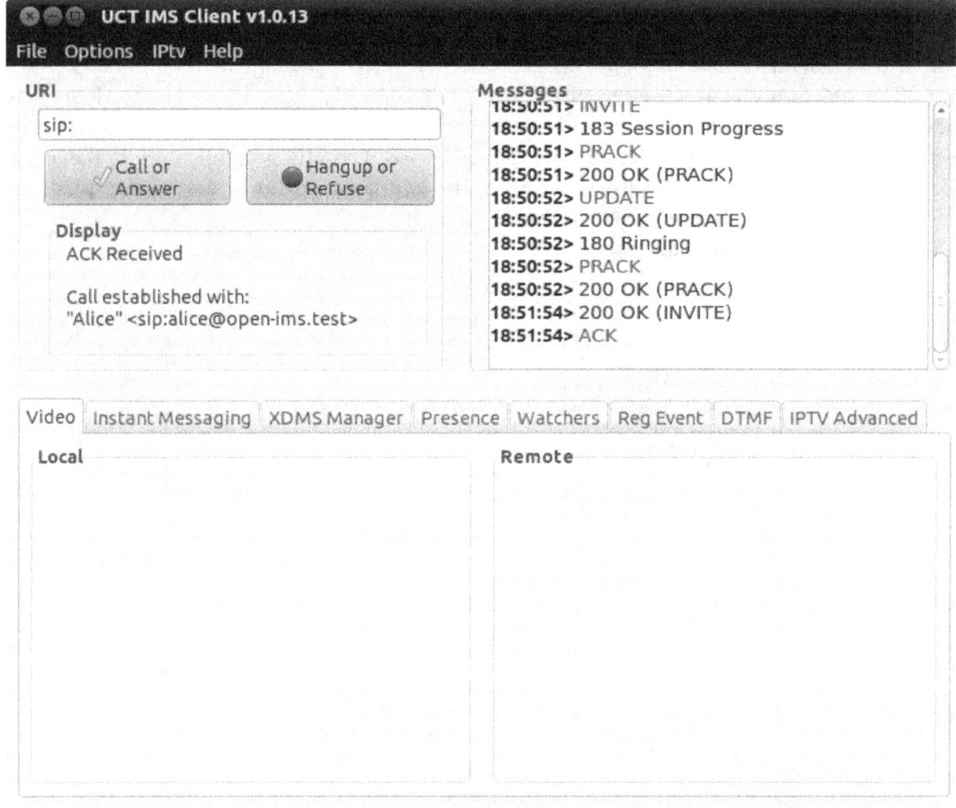

Fig. 13. SIP client request

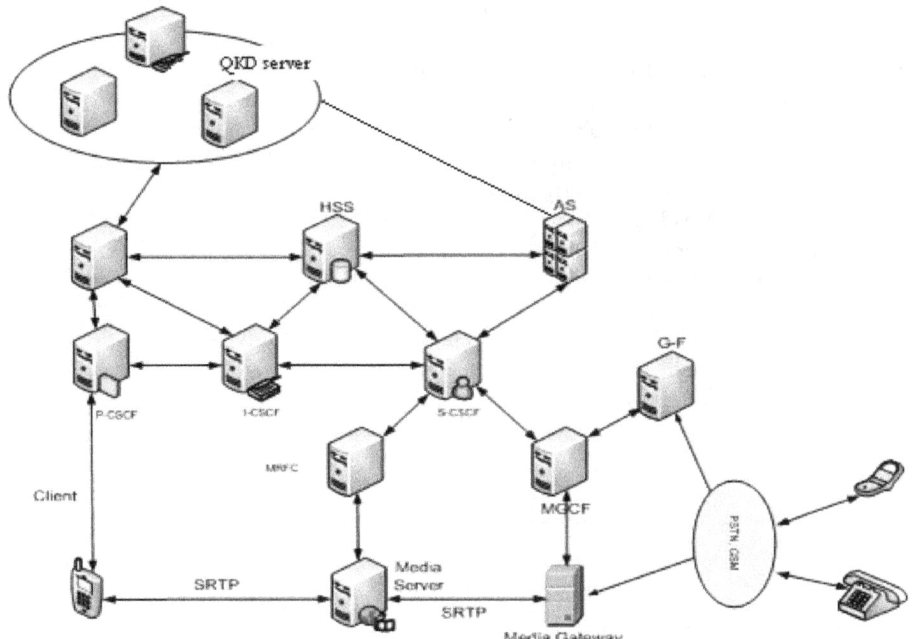

Fig. 14. IMS network with QKD server

9. References

Bulter, F. I, Cervesato, A. D. Jaggard, A. Scedrov,C. Walstad, Formal analysis for Kerberos 5, Theoretical Computer Science 367 (2006) 57 - 87.

Schulzrinne, H. The Session Initiation Protocol (SIP); hgs/SIP Tutorial may 2001.

Johnston, A & al, SIP service examples; draft-ietf-sip-service-examples-03.txt, June 2002.

Chapron, J. B, Chatras, An analysis of the IN call model suitability in the context of VoIP; Compter Networks 35 (2001) 521-535.

Hoi-Kwong Lo and Yi Zhao, Quantum cryptography. arXiv:0803.2507v4,1 Apr 2008.

El ouahidi, B & al, Internet/Telecommunication integration : Towards IN-capable SIP network; Revue internationale: Calculateurs parallèles réseaux et systèmes repartis, Hermès-Editions, Edition spéciale ingénierie des services de télécoms, 12(2) :259-280, December 2000.

Internet Draft , VK. Gurbani, Interworking SIP and Intelligent Network (IN) Applications; draft-gurbani-sin-02.txt, June 2002

EEEurescom Project P916 Supporting of H323 by IN, Providing IN functionality for H323 telephony calls, October 2000.

Gisin, N. G.Ribordy, W.Tittel and H.Zbinden, Quantum cryptography. arXiv:quant-ph/0101098v2 18 Sep 2001.

Fing, Principes et conditions de mise en oeuvre du standard ENUM en France; http://www.art-telecom.fr/publications/index-cp-enum.htm. 18 juin 2001.

Bernhard Omer, Classical Concepts in Quantum Programming. arXiv:quant-ph/0211100v2 29 Apr 2003.

Mohamed Saleh Mourad Debbabi, Verifying Security Properties of Cryptoprotocols: A Novel Approach. Fifth IEEE International Conference on Software Engineering and Formal Methods, IEEE 2007.

Xu Wei, Ma Yan, Liu Nan, Wu Dong-ying, A Formal Method for Analyzing Fair Exchange Protocols. 2009 WASE International Conference on Information Engineering.

Schweizer.L, Scripts et APIs pour la gestion de serveurs SIP ; www.tcom.ch; 23/12/2001.

http://www.openimscore.org.

Profos.D "Security requirements and concepts for Intelligents networks" , *Ascom Tech AG Bielstrasse 122, 4502 Solthurn.*

Jennings, C. Peterson, J and M. Watson,"Private Extensions to the Session Initiation Protocol (SIP) for Asserted Identity within Trusted Networks", *<draft-ietf-sip-asserted-identity-01>, June 2002.*

11

Quantum Key Management

Peter Schartner[1], Stefan Rass[1] and Martin Schaffer[2]
[1]*Alpen-Adria Universität Klagenfurt*
[2]*NXP Semiconductors Austria GmbH Styria*
Austria

1. Introduction

Quantum key distribution (QKD), invented by Bennett & Brassard (1984) based on previous work of Wiesner (1983), has been recognized as a key-technology of the upcoming decades. With various (experimental) quantum networks existing (cf. the reports of Poppe et al. (2008) and Elliott (2004)), questions regarding the efficient construction and management of such networks arise. While much has been achieved in proving security of QKD under various assumptions (trusted devices as proposed by Salvail et al. (2009) vs. non-trustworthy devices as discussed by Elliott (2008b)), and many cryptographic primitives have been transferred to the quantum setting by Buchmann et al. (2004) and Damgård et al. (2004), some questions are still waiting to be answered. With the invention of public-key cryptography, key management has become an issue of major importance. Authentication is equally crucial for QKD-enhanced links, but authenticating keys here is inherently different to the public key setting. Nevertheless, why should quantum cryptography not benefit from the lessons learnt in classic, particularly public-key, cryptography (one of which is the strict principle not to use one key in two different applications)? Elegant ideas for key management and authentication have arisen in public-key cryptography (such as identity-based cryptography invented by Shamir (1985) or certificateless cryptography discussed in Al-Riyami & Paterson (2003)). Are similarly elegant solutions imaginable for the problem of entity authentication in the quantum setting? More importantly, with the one-time pad (OTP) as the encryption of choice, the key demand equals the data transmission demand in terms of size, so an effective management of keys is crucial for a reasonable quality of service of quantum networks. The whole security can be at stake if (quantum-)key generators cannot cope with the flood of information and run empty, thus logically (in terms of secrecy) cutting the link.

Summarizing some lessons learnt from public-key cryptography, the management of keys includes their creation, activation, assignment, binding (to identities), escrow, recovery, as well as revocation and destruction. Particularly the last point is sometimes neglected, but is of no less importance than any of its predecessors.

What has all this to do with quantum cryptography? At first glance, secret-key cryptography does not suffer from such complicated issues as public-key cryptography does. Once a key has securely been created (or exchanged), why bother with key-management? In fact, public-key cryptography has evolved early enough to have become a fundament to almost all nowadays existing networks. While symmetric encryption is (often, perhaps not always) used for data transfer based on session keys that have been exchanged by virtue of public-key means (hybrid cryptosystem), its (session) keys do require some management too. Indeed, side-channel attacks and remote timing attacks have demonstrated the need to change symmetric session keys periodically and frequently, in order to avoid the adversary collect sufficiently many transcripts (involving the same key) to potentially breach the system's secrecy. Besides this, data recovery fields that allow for emergency reconstruction in case of lost keys are just one simple example, but many more scenarios exist where authorities may have legitimate interest in "opening" a channel, protected by symmetric cryptography. Guarding against terrorism is only one critical example, which back in the days gave rise to the well-known Escrowed Encryption Standard (1994).

Quantum key management

The core of this chapter is about management of keys created by QKD devices. Several proposals tackling various aspects of this problem are around, such as the quantum network manager proposed by Mink et al. (2008). Commercial solutions, such as the "Scalar Key Manager Appliance" due to Quantum (2009), originally dedicated to the management of keys for tape storages, could be used as a starting point for effective quantum key management. In particular, once the keys are created, the quantum-related part is mostly over, and when it comes to storing the goods in secure places, this expertise becomes valuable.

From the experimental point of view, SwissQuantum (2011) reports on a running quantum network, with a dedicated key management layer. Speaking of the latter, a patent has been submitted by Berzanskis & Gelfond (2009), employing a centralized quantum key certificate authority. Of course, it would be desirable to have a fully decentralized management of such a network, for not only resilience against attacks, but also for relieving trust requirements in each node.

The randomness of QKD keys is vital to the security of subsequent applications based on these keys. Several proposals exist; see the work of Tanaka et al. (2008) as one example. Finally, one should consider the possibility to strengthen existing standards by virtue of QKD. Some steps towards this have been taken, as indicated by Mink et al. (2009).

Chapter organization

Section 2 presents some arguments to substantiate the need for research towards quantum key distribution. Although nowadays cryptography appears to be capable of sufficient protection, it nevertheless pays to look at its (theoretical) limits to motivate why practical quantum key distribution devices are needed at the earliest possible stage. In Section 3, we discuss various ways to attack and defend a quantum network on a higher level than where the QKD protocols run. Since QKD has been extensively studied by researchers with ingenious proofs of security, an attacker will most likely focus his efforts on attacking elsewhere than on the quantum link. Guarding against such incidents, which include denial-of-service attacks or attacks on the perhaps not-so-well protected devices, are subject of this section. Section 4 addresses the benefit that a quantum infrastructure provides from the viewpoint of a decision-maker. After all, the decision maker will be concerned mostly with two questions: how much does it cost and what is the benefit? QKD as such is only capable of point-to-point security, but getting end-to-end security is a completely different problem. The main goal in Section 4 is to analyze the power of quantum networks in terms of end-to-end security. The ability to talk privately is worthless if we cannot assure who we are talking to, hence authentication is crucial to avoid person-in-the-middle attacks. Section 5 briefly discusses continuous authentication in the context of QKD and contains further details about authentication *without* end-to-end shared secrets. Applications of QKD in a wireless area are a live area of research, and Section 6 is a compilation of selected results on wireless QKD performance and some thoughts towards extending the application scenarios to an indoor and ad hoc domain. Final conclusions are drawn in Section 7.

2. Why quantum cryptography matters

Several arguments seemingly limiting the value of quantum key distribution exist. First, it does not come with a natural defense against impersonation attacks, and authentic channels are an inevitable ingredient for secure QKD. As already outlined by Paterson, K.G. and Piper, F. and Schack, R. (2004), this is an occasionally overlooked fact, leading to wrong expectations and perhaps flawed security arguments. Moreover, Shor (1997) has presented algorithms to solve the factorization and discrete logarithm problem, which are a severe threat to many public-key environments once quantum computers come to operation. Fortunately, up to now there is no significant evidence of symmetric algorithms like AES being in danger too. So even if hybrid cryptography fails by Shor's algorithms becoming standard, there are still other public key schemes available residing on problems that are not easily solved on a quantum computer too. Furthermore, post-quantum cryptographic primitives such as signatures (discussed by Buchmann et al. (2004)) or zero-knowledge proofs (discussed by Damgård et al. (2004)) are being developed. It follows that we could just "evade" the technological progress by enlarging the parameter spaces faster than the bit-lengths increase that quantum computers could handle. This is just what is happening nowadays, but transferred to a world full of quantum computers.

Anyone who feels uneasy about computational intractability assumptions (for their validity is hard to assure reliably) will agree that provable security is the more desirable good, compared to keeping the actual scenario alive.

Moreover, much of the field of multi-party computation (cf. the work of Hirt (2001)) relies on secure channels between any two participants. QKD is a natural tool for achieving this. Though this assumption is not obligatory (with corresponding results comprehensively discussed by Goldreich (2008) for instance), perfect end-to-end security between any two players in a multi-party protocol is often implicitly assumed, but rarely explicitly ensured in the literature. As we cannot expect a fully meshed network between players of a multi-party computation, end-to-end security is a vital point of these applications.

3. Trusted nodes, denial-of-service, maintenance and recovery

Since QKD networks use one-time pad encryption to protect the secrecy of the transmitted messages, the attacker basically has two options:

1. attacking the nodes and extracting the key material, or
2. forcing the QKD nodes into the usage of classical encryption by means of a denial-of-service attack on the (optical) QKD links.

In the remainder of this section, we will describe two methods which will help to mitigate the threats described above. The first method proposed by Schartner & Rass (2009) results in so called strengthened QKD nodes. These nodes are in fact not invulnerable to physical attacks, but these strengthened nodes will stay secure for some period of time even in the case of a physical attack. This time span may be used to securely transmit an alarm message to the network management center. The second approach proposed by Schartner & Rass (2010) resurrects the idea of keeping public parameters secret, like proposed by Kaabneh &

Al-Bdour (2005). Here the idea is to use the remaining key material in the most efficient way and maintain a high level of secrecy during the DOS attack on the QKD link(s).

3.1 Strengthening QKD nodes

As it is with other cryptographic protocols, the security of QKD protocols massively depends on the security of the keys (one-time pads). In contrast to classical cryptographic protocols the space needed to store these keys is quite large (more precisely: as large as the messages). Unfortunately secure storage, can only partially be settled on cryptographic grounds, as leaking key material is in any sense not acceptable. Although the problem of physically stealing a keystore from a QKD-repeating node can be made less emergent using the technique proposed in Schartner & Rass (2009), it cannot be fully overcome. A full solution for that case is presented in Rass (2009), but at the cost of increased communication overhead and a threshold assumption on the number of so compromised nodes. The construction in Rass (2009) is simple, yet too lengthy to be repeated here, but the basic idea of Schartner & Rass (2009) can be sketched as follows: once a node shares (via a QKD channel, denoted as ←----→) a key k_A with one neighbor (predecessor A), and another key k_B with another neighbor (successor B), then, instead of storing the pair (k_A, k_B), why not store $k_{AB} := k_A \oplus k_B$, where $\oplus$ denotes the bitwise exclusive-or. Passing a one-time pad encrypted message $c_A := m \oplus k_A$ onwards to the successor is trivial by sending $c_B = c_A \oplus k_{AB} = m \oplus k_B$ straight away. The process is sketched in Figure 1, where Node R forwards an encrypted message from Node A to Node B.

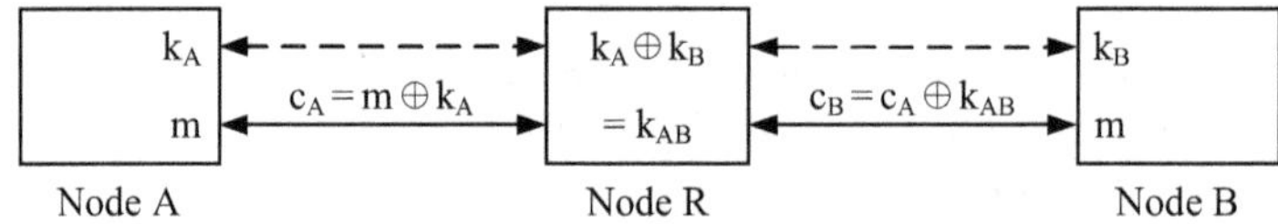

Fig. 1. Protected forwarding of messages

Notice that this re-encryption never reveals the plain text m, and no decryption of c can be performed using only k. This way, the adversary has to wait until all key material is used up, and fresh key material is created, which can then be prevented from being discarded after XORing it pairwise.

This scheme renders information streams between different ports independent from each other, as each pairwise connection enjoys its own key-store. Contrary to the classical design (see Figure 2 (left)), information being passed from port A to port B does not draw from the same key-store as the flow from A to C would do. This naturally facilitates efficient load balancing. Comparing the two designs (the new one shown in Figure 2 (right)) in terms of buffers and keys, reveals that the new design cuts down the number of keys by a factor of two, thus doubling the efficiency. Giving some numbers, a trusted relay with 5 links requires 5 buffers storing 4 keys per buffer (making a total of 20 keys), whereas the design of Schartner & Rass (2009) does this with 10 buffers filled with only 1 key (ending up with only 10 keys). Even this higher number of buffers is no real restriction, as these are located within the same physical memory anyway.

A yet open issue is how the network management traffic can be exploited for mounting attacks or deriving information about the information flow. As key-management is a core task that cannot autonomously be done by a single node, can the "background traffic" be manipulated to mount attacks? This question cannot be answered on general grounds, as it depends on

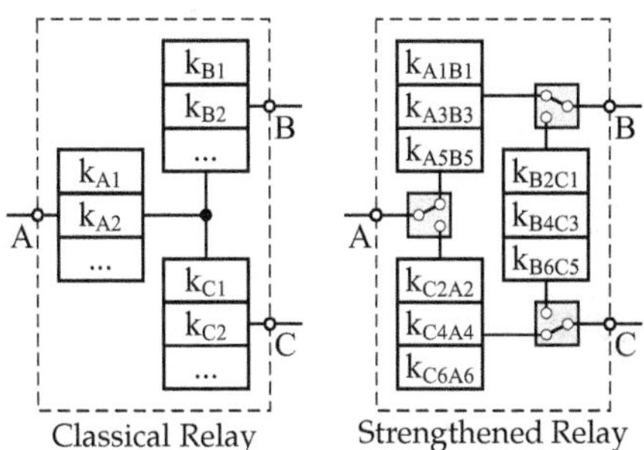

Fig. 2. Two relay methods

the particular implementation of the quantum network (we refer the reader to the report of Los Alamos National Security (2009) for an overview). However, the possibility should be considered when designing such network managers. A problem that has not received much attention yet, as it seems.

A different possibility is offered by secret-sharing. If the secret key is shared among many parties, can this somehow prevent access if only one party is compromised? The question might be trivial and with a negative answer if we really ask for one-time pad keys, but the management of shares in a multi-party computation environment may offer interesting ideas applicable to securing QKD keys as well, if we are willing to use keys shorter than the messages to encrypt. Although this is no secrecy in the sense Shannon envisioned, but still unconditionally provable and could be good enough for practical use. Apart from this, it seems that the keystore has to be secured by non-cryptographic means in order to protect keys from unauthorized access.

3.2 Counteracting DoS-attacks

In case of a denial of service attack on the QKD links, the first option ist to suspend the transmission of messages when the nodes run short of key material. Unfortunately, there may be scenarios where no communication is no option. So we can continue to use the remaining key material in the most secure way: as one-time pads. Unfortunately, in this case each encrypted and transmitted bit "costs" one bit of key material. If we have to transit more message bits, than key bits remaining, we could switch to some emergency communication mode, which uses the key material already stored in the connected nodes in the most efficient way and continues to send (encrypted) messages on an alternate path. Figure 3 shows such a QKD network, which securely connects a sending node A and a receiving node B. There are several paths between A and B, like $A \leftrightarrow B$, $A \leftrightarrow 1 \leftrightarrow B$, $A \leftrightarrow 1 \leftrightarrow 2 \leftrightarrow B$ or $A \leftrightarrow 4 \leftrightarrow 2 \leftrightarrow B$, but obviously all these paths start at A and end in B. So a good place to mount a DoS attack is somewhere nearby the sending node A or receiving node B. Even worse, if the links directly connected to A or B are bundled, because now the attacker can affect all of them with a single strike. As shown in Figure 3, the attacker has brought down all links directly connected to B. Hence, secure key exchange over the QKD network and subsequently secure communication between A and B becomes impossible.

In order to keep secure communication alive, A and B use an alternate communication path somewhere outside the QKD network. The only question remaining is how to secure this link, if there is no way to generate new key material. The straight forward solution is to use the

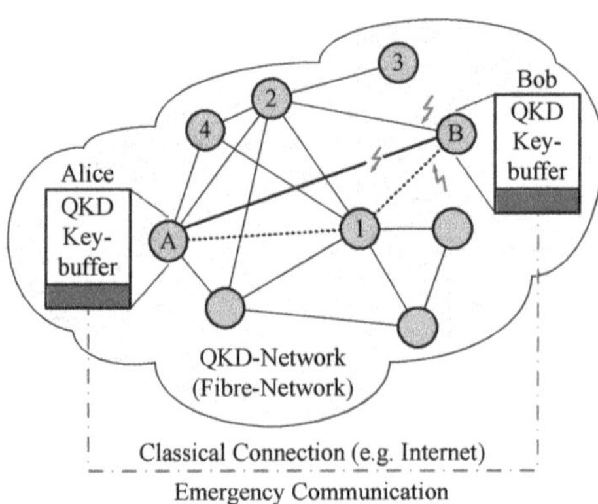

Fig. 3. Usage of the proposed scheme

remaining key material as keys for classical symmetric encryption (e.g. AES). Note that this is exactly the way, some commercial products like Cerberis (ID Quantique ID Quantique (2011)) use to exchange keys for classical symmetric encryption by means of OTP-protected links.

When using such a hybrid scheme of QKD and symmetric encryption, we should keep in mind that the strongest assumption on the attacker is, that he knows the protocol, the cipher, the block length and the key length. Hence, if the attacker gets hold of transmitted ciphertexts, he can (at least) start a brute force attack to find the key. If the attacker can insert some plaintext into the encryption system, he can start a known plaintext attack as well. After retrieving the key, all messages encrypted with this key can be decrypted. Hence, the key has to be changed quite often if we want to keep the damage low in case of a successful attack on the key.

If we want the attacker to face a harder problem, the idea is to hide essential parameters from the attacker (but assume that the employed protocols and algorithms are still known). In case of symmetric encryption (like AES) there is nothing to hide except the key length (128, 192, or 256 bit). All other parameters (like block length) are fixed. In order to overcome this drawback, the scheme proposed by Schartner & Rass (2010) uses a hybrid encryption system which consists of three layers (also see Figure 4):

1. QKD is used to establich OTP in connected nodes. These OTPs are used to encrypt parameters of a public key encryption scheme (message c_1).
2. The public key encryption scheme is used to transmit the keys for the classical symmetric encryption (message c_2).
3. Finally the (fast) symmetric encryption scheme secures the transmitted messages m_1 to m_n (ciphertexts c_{31} to c_{3n}).

The best attacking method on RSA, known by now, is factorizing the modulus and deriving the private key from the public key. If the attacker never sees the modulus (as it is encrypted by use of an OTP), he has no chance to factorize it. And if the attacker retrieves the primes of the modulus by other means, he is still missing the public key (which is also transmitted encrypted by use of an OTP). For assessing how hard these problems really are, and an alternative that replaces RSA and AES by ECC, we refer the reader to Schartner & Rass (2010).

It is clear, that the key for the symmetric encryption has to be changed quite frequently (as mentioned above). But now, this does not cost valuable QKD key material.

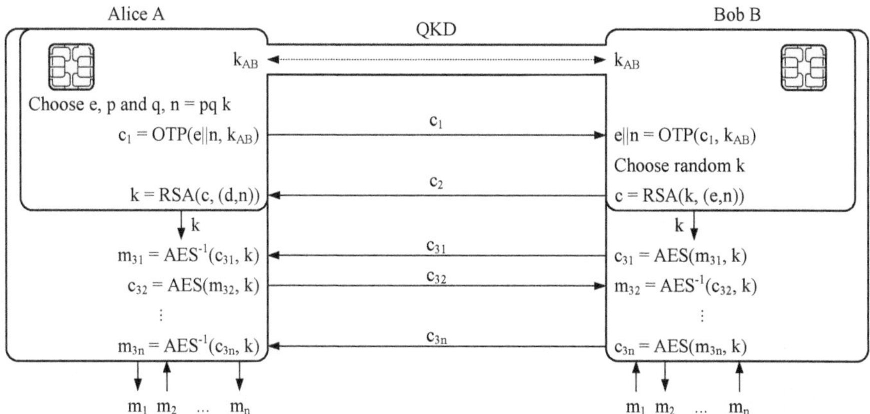

Fig. 4. A three step hybrid system: QKD+RSA+AES

Note that this special mode of operation of the QKD nodes may be used during the maintenance of QKD links as well.

4. Risk management in a quantum network

It is well-known that quantum key distribution is limited in terms of distance and that it can create cryptographically strong keys between directly connected peers. Also, most plain QKD protocols are intended for two-party key-exchange. The problem of *quantum conference keying* has been studied and some interesting solutions were proposed by Jin et al. (2006) and Hwang et al. (2007). However, we will confine ourselves to the simpler two-party point-to-point key-exchange here. The problem of achieving end-to-end security from this kind of point-to-point security is nontrivial, and several solution proposals to overcome the distance limitation exist. Among the most important are the following:

- Quantum repeater
- Trusted relay
- Multipath transmission

The well-known no-cloning theorem due to Wootters & Zurek (1982) rules out the possibility of copying photons in a similar manner as electrical signals can be reproduced for amplification. Hence, a quantum repeater appears impossible at first glance. Fortunately, however, entanglement of photons can be exploited to achieve almost the same effect as a (classical electrical) repeater would have. This concept is known as *quantum repeater*. The theory behind this is much beyond the scope of this chapter and the interested reader is referred to the work of Dür et al. (1999) and Yuan et al. (2008) for a theoretical as well as practical introduction. Here, we will confine ourselves to conveying the underlying ideas. Unfortunately, however, quantum repeaters have not yet reached a level of maturity beyond experimental implementations in the laboratory.

Roughly speaking, the idea behind a quantum repeater is to create a chain of entangled photons. That is, one starts with a single pair of entangled photons ϕ_1, ϕ_2, and creates another pair of photons ϕ_3, ϕ_4 such that ϕ_2 is in addition entangled to ϕ_3. Hence, the states

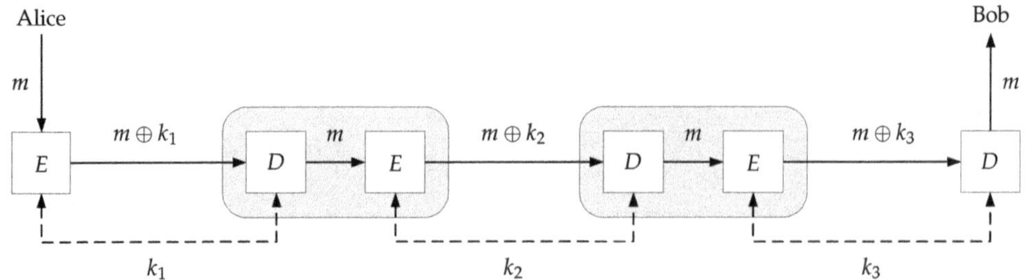

Fig. 5. One-time pad based single path transmission with two intermediate nodes

of ϕ_1 and ϕ_4 are entangled, meaning that information can be transported from ϕ_1 to ϕ_4. This idea can be repeated (endlessly) to bridge arbitrary distances. It goes without saying that practical implementations are far more complex than this simple sketch. For instance, entanglement purification (a highly nontrivial process on its own) are crucial ingredients to avoid the entanglement becoming "messed up" with noise. Nevertheless, various approaches and implementations exist in the lab, and future networks might employ such technology soon.

Trusted relay is the simple concept of having each intermediate node along a lengthy chain re-encrypt its incoming payload before forwarding it to the next hop. This comes at the price of each intermediate node getting to see the message. Figure 5 illustrates the problem. Still, this transmission paradigm finds itself implemented in various quantum demonstration networks, such as the SECOQC network (cf. Peev et al. (2009)) or the DARPA network (cf. Elliott (2007)). From a risk manager's perspective, such trust assumptions are rather undesirable, since it is difficult to quantify the risk and hence to meaningfully relate it to business assets (confidential information) that are communicated over the quantum network. *Multipath transmission* is a straightforward remedy to relieve the stringent assumptions that trusted relay requires, and to avoid complex technologies like the quantum repeater. Hence, we describe this third paradigm in more detail now. As usual in quantum cryptography, we consider a computationally unbounded adversary. The only constraint that we require is his incapability of compromising more than a fixed portion of the network. That is, we cannot allow the adversary to conquer arbitrary large parts in the network, for otherwise we would have a classical person-in-the-middle situation. In the absence of end-to-end shared secrets, confidential communication is impossible in this situation (for obvious reasons).

Consider the well-known polynomial (k, n)-secret-sharing due to Shamir (1979) as a motivating example, and let the adversary's threshold be t, i.e. no more than t nodes in the network can be compromised. Furthermore, assume that the network topology (graph) G connecting Alice and Bob admits r node-disjoint paths between them. Obviously, if $r > t$, then we transmit a secret message in a perfectly secure manner as follows:

1. Choose a set of at least k out of $r > t$ node-disjoint paths for transmission (a simple choice is $k = n$ so that the adversary is forced to intercept all n paths, which is impossible if $t < n$. However, more careful choices of $k \leq n$ can yield to protocols with less overhead but no loss of security).
2. Decompose the secret message into k shares traveling over the k paths from Alice to Bob.

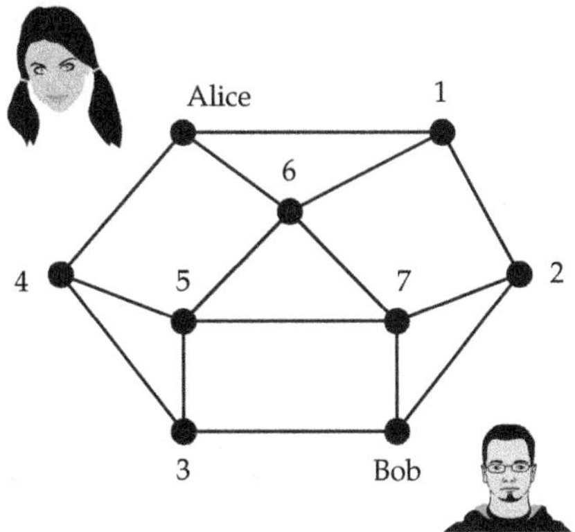

Fig. 6. Example network topology

3. Let the receiver reconstruct the secret from the received shares, possibly invoking an error correction algorithm (perhaps the one devised by Berlekamp & Welch (1986)) to recover from corrupted shares.

This is the rough skeleton that many protocols for multipath transmission embody. Moreover, it constitutes a necessity for perfectly secure communication, as has rigorously been proven by Wang & Desmedt (2008), Fitzi et al. (2007) and Ashwin Kumar et al. (2002). The remaining problem with these results still is their limited applicability in real-life networks, as many known criteria for perfectly secure communication impose strong requirements on the graph's (vertex) connectivity. We shall not go into details about this, and confine ourselves to the following simple observation:

Provided that $r > t$, it is easy to see that even if $k \leq t$, we still have some chance to have chosen paths that the adversary has not yet intercepted. In other words, as long as he cannot have all paths under his control, we have some chance of at least partially circumventing the adversary. Now, the problem has changed into finding a clever way of choosing these paths. It is trivial to enumerate all possible choices, along with all possibly compromised sets of nodes. Having these lists, we can set up a matrix whose entries contain either zero if the transmission failed, or 1 if the transmission was successful. At this point, we can invoke *game-theory* to provide us with the best way of choosing among our options (paths). A full discussion of this idea is given by Rass & Schartner (2010b), and we will use a simple example to illustrate the idea here.

Suppose Alice and Bob being interconnected through the simple network depicted in Figure 6. Implementing the above skeleton, they use multipath transmission based on a $(2,2)$-sum-sharing of the form $m = s_1 \oplus s_2$, where m is the secret message and $\oplus$ is the bitwise exclusive-or. This scheme directly resembles a one-time pad encryption and is therefore information-theoretically secure, as Shannon (1949) has proved. For illustration, let the adversary have the assumed threshold $t = 2$. Call PS_1 the list of all selections of two disjoint paths, and write PS_2 to denote the list of all nodes that are possibly compromised (two-element subsets of $V = \{1,2,\ldots,7\}$). Let S_1 and S_2 be the set of *probability distributions* over PS_1, PS_2, respectively. For each scenario $(s_1, s_2) \in PS_1 \times PS_2$, we decide about success for Alice and Bob (outcome 1) or failure (outcome 0). Collect all these in a matrix $A \in \{0,1\}^{n \times m}$. Let $\theta_1 \in S_1$ be the probability distribution from which Alice and Bob draw their paths

PS_1 (Alice and Bob)	PS_2 (adversary)
s_1^{AB}: $\{A—4—3—B, A—1—2—B\}$	s_1^{adv}: $\{1,4\}$
s_2^{AB}: $\{A—4—5—7—B, A—1—2—B\}$	s_2^{adv}: $\{1,6\}$
s_3^{AB}: $\{A—6—5—3—B, A—1—2—B\}$	s_3^{adv}: $\{4,6\}$
s_4^{AB}: $\{A—6—7—B, A—1—2—B\}$	s_4^{adv}: $\{1,7\}$
s_5^{AB}: $\{A—6—7—B, A—4—3—B\}$	s_5^{adv}: $\{1,3\}$
	s_6^{adv}: $\{1,5\}$

(a) Strategies

A	s_1^{adv}	s_2^{adv}	s_3^{adv}	s_4^{adv}	s_5^{adv}	s_6^{adv}
s_1^{AB}	0	1	1	1	0	1
s_2^{AB}	0	1	1	0	1	0
s_3^{AB}	1	0	1	1	0	0
s_4^{AB}	1	0	1	0	1	1
s_5^{AB}	1	1	0	1	1	1

(b) Utility matrix

Fig. 7. Security Game

(randomized routing), and let θ_2 describe the probabilities for certain subsets of nodes to be compromised. Then, the bilinear form ${\theta_1}^T A\theta_2$ is the long-run average success-rate, or in other words the probability for Alice and Bob being successful. Presuming the adversary having precisely opposite intentions than Alice and Bob have, we can set up a zero-sum competition giving the best strategy of path selection and the strongest strategy for attacking. Formally, this is the *Nash-equilibrium* of the game induced by A. Its average outcome is the value $v(A)$ of the game, and defined as

$$v(A) = \max_{\theta_1 \in S_1} \min_{\theta_2 \in S_2} {\theta_1}^T A\theta_2$$

because Alice and Bob try to maximize their success-rate, while the adversary tries to minimize it (thus maximizing his chances of eavesdropping).

Observe that ${\theta_1}^T A\theta_2$ is just the expected value of the random variable selecting an entry from the matrix A, if the rows and columns are chosen according to the distributions θ_1 and θ_2. Because A is set up over the set $\{0,1\}$, this is essentially the expectation of an indicator variable, and therefore nothing else than a probability. By construction, we therefore have

$$\mathsf{P}(\text{successful transmission}) = v(A), \tag{1}$$

assuming a zero-sum competition. In case that the adversary does not play a zero-sum regime, the equality changes into a lower-bound to the probability (this can be proven by twice-exploitation of the saddle-point property of the Nash-equilibrium; cf. Rass & Schartner (2010b)).

Carrying out the above sketched method for all path selections and possibly compromised nodes, we end up with a 34×21-matrix. In doing so, we notice that some rows are element-wise greater or equal than others, so we can delete the respective "smaller" rows, because these are obviously suboptimal strategies (as the alternative will give better revenue in every case). Such a uniformly better strategy is said to *dominate* the other one. Analogously, from the adversary's point of view, we can delete all columns for which another column gives less utility in every row, because the latter strategy is obviously a better way of attacking. Repeating this reduction, we end up with a 5×6-matrix and corresponding strategies as shown in Figure 7. The core concept introduced by Rass & Schartner (2010b) is the *vulnerability*, defined as the difference between the maximum possible outcome and the average outcome. Formally, the vulnerability $\rho(A) := 1 - v(A)$ for a (zeros-sum) game-matrix $A \in \{0,1\}^{n \times m}$. Based on this quantity, the following result has been obtained. Notice that Theorem 4.1 *does not* assume a zero-sum competition, i.e. the adversary is not bound to behave according to a Nash-equilibrium.

Theorem 4.1 (Rass & Schartner (2010b)). *Let Alice and Bob set up their matrix (game) with binary entries $a_{ij} \in \{0,1\}$, where $a_{ij} = 1$ if and only if a message can securely be delivered by choosing the i-th (set of) paths, and the adversary uses his j-th strategy of attacking. Then $\rho(A) \in [0,1]$, and*

1. *if $\rho(A) < 1$, then a protocol exists upon which Alice and Bob can secretly communicate with an eavesdropping probability of at most ε for any $\varepsilon > 0$ (arbitrarily small).*
2. *if $\rho(A) = 1$, then the probability of the message becoming extracted by the adversary is 1.*

Summarizing this result, we can say that perfectly secure transmission is possible if and only if $v(A) > 0$ for a game-matrix A modeling the underlying multipath transmission scenario. Notice that this generalizes previous results due to Ashwin Kumar et al. (2002) and Wang & Desmedt (2008) along these lines.

Generalized risk management

If we work through the above arguments carefully, we observe that neither the theory nor its results hinge on the binary scale for setting up the game-matrices. It turns out that we can fill in any meaningful number in the slots of the game-matrix. Hence, we can use discrete scales modeling nominal valuation of messages, say a classification in terms of "public" (i.e. no particular protection required), "confidential" (protection is required) or "top secret" (eavesdropping would have devastating consequences). Also, one can use a continuous scale $[a,b]$ with $a,b > 0$ to directly associate the monetary loss suffered from a message that falls into the adversary's hands. In other words, we can equally well set up the game with a utility functional that gives the monetary value of a secretly delivered message, or 0 otherwise (in case of eavesdropping). The *vulnerability* in this case is the monetary loss suffered when communicating valuable data over the network. Rephrasing this differently, the vulnerability directly equals the decision-theoretic risk.

A valuable application of such quantitative risk assessment is the design of quantum networks. As the technology has reached a state of maturity that permits thinking about globally spanning networks, a considerable number of research articles (Alleaume et al. (2009); Dianati et al. (2008); Elliott et al. (2005); Fernandez et al. (2007); Kumavor et al. (2006); Le et al. (2008); Rass & Schartner (2009); Tang et al. (2006) and many more), as well as several patents (by Elliott (2008a) and Elliott (2008b) among others) have arisen. An economic implementation of such networks can be tackled from various directions. One approach is presented by Alleaume et al. (2009), where the network topology is optimized to provide best performance, assuming that security is retained by secure point-to-point connections. In particular, this article employs the trusted node relay and optimizes the costs for building a secure network on this paradigm. In contrast to this, the approach presented by Rass & Schartner (2009) aims at squeezing out a maximal level of secrecy, assuming that point-to-point connections are perfectly secure. This approach is more focused on maximizing security with given environmental constraints. We believe that a successful roll-out of such networks amounts to a highly constrained optimization problem that has to account for both, topological aspects (to be tackled with stochastic geometry, such as done by Alleaume et al. (2009)), as well as taking security not for granted by QKD itself, such as posed by Rass & Schartner (2009).

5. Authentication with and without pre-shared keys

It is easy to see that a quantum channel is only as secure as it is authentic. For otherwise, an adversary may easily become the person-in-the-middle acting as a proxy and reading all the traffic through his node in plain text. Quantum cryptography is therefore often misunderstood as a method of creating a key "from nothing", while it is actually a method of "expanding" an already existing shared key. This pre-shared secret is required for authentication purposes, and the most common way of authenticating the channel is authenticating each message flowing over it. This approach is known as *continuous authentication*. Key-management for this form of authentication is involved, as the amount of produced key-material has to exceed the respective expenditure for authentication. Hence, the actual amount of key-material that is consumed for creating authentication tags crucially depends on the specific QKD protocol in charge. Gilbert & Hamrick (2000) provide a full-detailed discussion of the key-consumption for the BB84 and related protocols. The calculations are a matter of simple yet messy algebra. We leave this to the interested reader consulting the work of Gilbert & Hamrick (2000) for details. In the following, we shall sketch an alternative way of authentication that is compatible with the game-theoretic risk-management approach sketched in Section 4.

The idea of PGP's web-of-trust can be rephrased into setting up a threshold authentication scheme based on shared secrets between adjacent nodes and not requiring any end-to-end shared secrets (cf. Rass & Schartner (2010a)). If Alice wishes to authenticate a message for Bob, without having a secret in common with him, she may use her current or past direct neighbors to prove her reputation. Notice that this scheme is easily transferred to a *wireless* setting too: suppose that Alice's neighborhood looks as sketched in Figure 8. Because she does not have any secret with Bob in common, her only way of proving her reputation to Bob is by having her neighbors confirm her identity to Bob. Let a general message authentication code be given by a mapping $MAC : \{0,1\}^* \times \{0,1\}^{l_1} \to \{0,1\}^{l_2}$ that takes a message m of arbitrary length and a key of length l_1, returning a MAC of length l_2. We denote the MAC for m with key s by $MAC(m,s)$. Furthermore, let $H : \{0,1\}^* \to \{0,1\}^{l_3}$ be any collision-resistant cryptographic hash function (e.g. SHA-256).

To let Alice's neighbors confirm her identity without telling them the message m that is intended for Bob, Alice authenticates the hash-value $H(m)$ instead of m, so that Bob can present $H(m)$ to the neighbors to let them check the MACs that he received from Alice. The verification is done over disjoint paths, and he accepts if and only if all verifications come back positive.

Security

We assume the hash-function H collision-resistant, as well as the MAC to be secure in the sense of permitting a negligible chance of forgery, if we choose a universal hash-family for both purposes. Appropriate constructions are given by Krawczyk (1994), Shoup (1996) and Bierbrauer (1998) for instance. We therefore focus on the threshold property, taking the threshold t of the adversary into account. Let Alice have attached k MACs for her message. It is easy to see that if $t \geq k$, then the adversary can conquer and control all of Alice's neighbors thus successfully fooling Bob into thinking a forged message is authentic. On the other hand, if $t < k$, then at least one verification will reveal the impersonation, and Bob will reject the message as not coming from Alice.

Similarly as for a multipath transmission scenario, we require node-disjoint paths here too. Alas, graphs with sufficiently strong connectivity are rarely found in real-life infrastructures. At this point, we can re-use the ideas described in Section 4: just as for multipath transmission, it is equally trivial to set up a similar matrix over $\{0,1\}$, storing a "1" for a successful

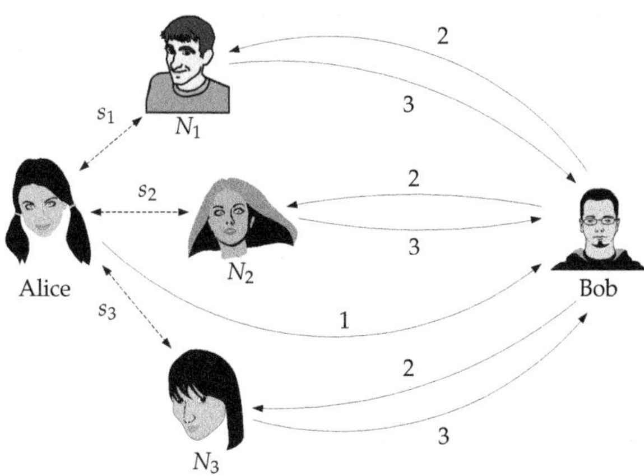

Initialization:
Alice shares secrets $s_1, \ldots, s_k$ with her neighboring nodes $N_1, \ldots, N_k$.
Protocol:

1. Alice $\rightarrow$ Bob $(m, MAC(H(m), s_1), MAC(H(m), s_2) \ldots, MAC(H(m), s_k))$
2. Bob $\rightarrow N_1$ $(H(m), MAC(H(m), s_1))$
   Bob $\rightarrow N_2$ $(H(m), MAC(H(m), s_2))$
   $\vdots$
   Bob $\rightarrow N_k$ $(H(m), MAC(H(m), s_k))$
3. $N_1, \ldots, N_k \rightarrow$ Bob each neighbor responds with either "OK" or failure ("NOK")

Bob accepts if all verifications come back OK

Fig. 8. Threshold authentication protocol and example

authentication and "0" for a successful impersonation attack. An analogue result as Theorem 4.1 can be stated for this kind of authentication too:

Theorem 5.1 (Rass & Schartner (2010a)). *Let A denote the matrix, modeling the authentication game as described above, and let Alice share secrets of length l with $n > 1$ neighbors of hers, but no secret with Bob is shared. If $\rho(A) < 1$, then Alice can transmit a message to Bob in an authentic manner, where the probability of forgery is less than 2^{-l}. If $\rho(A) = 1$, then the adversary can forge messages with probability 1.*

We draw almost an analogous conclusion as before: perfectly secure authentication is possible, if and only if $v(A) > 0$ for the game-matrix A modeling the authentication in the way as described above.

6. Outlook: Towards mobile and Ad-hoc QKD networks

The question, regarding the possibility of mobile or ad-hoc quantum networking, is perhaps the most promising one, which if it can be answered positively, would drastically increase the call for QKD in daily work environments. Sheikh et al. (2006) discuss various QKD-algorithms in terms of their applicability in a wireless setting. In particular, they consider attenuation and losses in the atmosphere, and report on various environmental influences that free-space QKD may suffer from. Interestingly, the first demonstration of QKD has been using a wireless channel with about 30 cm distance between the sender and the receiver. Using strongly

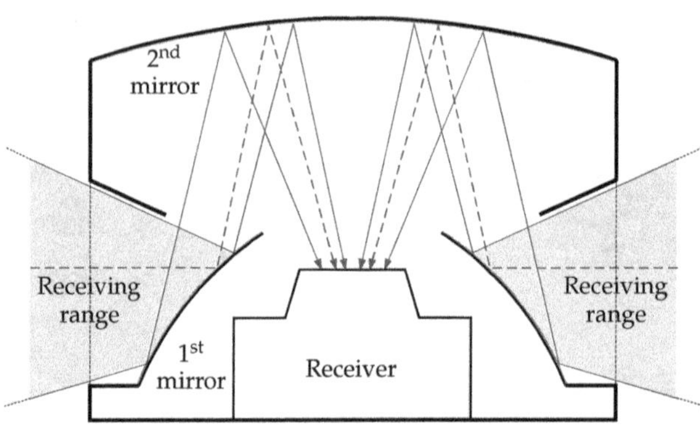

Fig. 9. Table-mounted omnidirectional Receiver

attenuated laser pulses, distances of 500 m have been bridged, as reported by Weier et al. (2006). Hughes et al. (2002) described experiments over a distance of 10 km at daylight and at night, and Kurtsiefer et al. (2002) demonstrated the possibility of globally spanning networks. Studies regarding QKD between a terrestrial station and an orbit satellite have been conducted by Rarity et al. (2002) and Pfennigbauer & Leeb (2003). Experimental implementations covering a distance of about 144 km have been reported by Schmitt-Manderbach et al. (2007).

Free-Space QKD in the standard form requires a straight line of sight connection. It is thus fair to assume that the connection may be temporarily unavailable and in possible misalignment for short periods of time, particularly in a mobile ad-hoc environment. We could therefore focus on wireless networks with (almost) static participants. Such peers naturally arise in any environment where environmental conditions disallow using cables of any kind. Newly created networks within buildings, within or between cities or spanning mountainous terrain are only some examples, not to mention communication among geostationary satellites. Transferring the techniques to a mobile environment, however, is indeed possible, as the key-establishment can run entirely decoupled from the encryption process. A simple approach is loading a mobile device with key material for subsequent encryption, and then cut the quantum channel. Kollmitzer & Pivk (2010) further elaborate on this. A much simpler application of QKD in an in-door environment, the receiver that might be placed in the middle of a conference table (Figure 9) could be built similar to an omnidirectional (surveillance) camera. This could make QKD feasible even in a wireless setting within buildings.

7. Conclusion

Quantum key distribution has reached a level of maturity that renders a vast range of applications in sight. However, while the basic technology has been studied extensively, most solutions remain focused on perfect point-to-point security. Careful management of keys created by QKD is vital to any application, building upon a quantum network infrastructure, because end-to-end security, authenticity and availability cannot be assured by QKD alone. Here, we surveyed a selection of ideas related to the management of quantum networks, covering various topics such as failure and recovery management, general end-to-end security and risk-management, as well as authentication and possible applications in the wireless setting. Quantum key distribution is for sure a promising direction of research, in fact a key technology of upcoming decades. Nevertheless, it is only another brick in the wall which cannot by itself do all the protection. It is the combination of mechanisms (and QKD is only one of them), that makes the defense against an adversary strong. Key-management is another often neglected but nevertheless important building block for a successful defense. In the public-key domain, its importance has been widely recognized. In the quantum domain, the issue remains equally important, but seemingly has not yet received the full amount of attention that it deserves.

8. References

Al-Riyami, S. S. & Paterson, K. G. (2003). Certificateless public key cryptography, *ASIACRYPT*, pp. 452–473.

Alleaume, R., Roueff, F., Diamanti, E. & Lütkenhaus, N. (2009). Topological optimization of quantum key distribution networks, *New Journal of Physics* 11: 075002.

Ashwin Kumar, M., Goundan, P. R., Srinathan, K. & Pandu Rangan, C. (2002). On perfectly secure communication over arbitrary networks, *PODC '02: Proceedings of the twenty-first annual symposium on Principles of distributed computing*, ACM, New York, NY, USA, pp. 193–202.

Bennett, C. & Brassard, G. (1984). Public key distribution and coin tossing, *IEEE International Conference on Computers, Systems, and Signal Processing*, IEEE Press, Los Alamitos, pp. 175–179.

Berlekamp, E. & Welch, L. (1986). Error correction of algebraic block codes, US Patent Nr. 4,633,470.

Berzanskis, A. & Gelfond, R. (2009). Key management and user authentication for quantum cryptography networks. IPC8 Class: AH04L906FI, USPC Class: 380277.

Bierbrauer, J. (1998). Authentication via algebraic-geometric codes, *Rend. Circ. Mat. Palermo (2) Suppl.* 51: 139–152.

Buchmann, J., Coronado, C., Döring, M., Engelbert, D., Ludwig, C., Overbeck, R., Schmidt, A., Vollmer, U. & Weinmann, R.-P. (2004). Post-quantum signatures, Cryptology ePrint Archive, Report 2004/297.

Damgård, I. B., Fehr, S. & Salvail, L. (2004). Zero-knowledge proofs and string commitments withstanding quantum attacks, *in* M. Franklin (ed.), *Advances in Cryptology (CRYPTO)*, LNCS 3152, pp. 254–272.

Dianati, M., Alleaume, R., Gagnaire, M. & Shen, X. (2008). Architecture and protocols of the future european quantum key distribution network, *Security And Communication Networks* 1: 57–74.

Dür, W., Briegel, H.-J., Cirac, J. I. & Zoller, P. (1999). Quantum repeaters based on entanglement purification, *Phys. Rev. A* 59(1): 169–181.

Elliott, B. B. (2008a). Key distribution center for quantum cryptographic key distribution networks.
URL: *http://www.freepatentsonline.com/7457416.html*

Elliott, B. B. (2008b). Quantum cryptographic key distribution networks with untrusted switches.

Elliott, C. (2004). The DARPA Quantum Network, *ArXiv Quantum Physics e-prints* .
URL: *http://adsabs.harvard.edu/abs/2004quant.ph.12029E*

Elliott, C. (2007). The DARPA quantum network. arXiv:quant-ph/0412029v1.

Elliott, C., Colvin, A., Pearson, D., Pikalo, O., Schlafer, J. & Yeh, H. (2005). Current status of the DARPA quantum network, arXiv:quant-ph/0503058v2.

Escrowed Encryption Standard (1994). Federal Information Processing Standards (Publication 185).

Fernandez, V., Collins, R. J., Gordon, K. J., Townsend, P. D. & Buller, G. S. (2007). Passive optical network approach to gigahertz-clocked multiuser quantum key distribution, *IEEE Journal Of Quantum Electronics* 43(2): 130–138.

Fitzi, M., Franklin, M. K., Garay, J. & Vardhan, S. H. (2007). Towards optimal and efficient perfectly secure message transmission, *in* S. Vadhan (ed.), *4th Theory of Cryptography Conference (TCC)*, Lecture Notes in Computer Science LNCS 4392, Springer, pp. 311–322.

Gilbert, G. & Hamrick, M. (2000). Practical quantum cryptography: A comprehensive analysis (part one).
URL: *http://www.citebase.org/abstract?id=oai:arXiv.org:quant-ph/0009027*

Goldreich, O. (2008). *Computational Complexity*, Cambridge University Press.

Hirt, M. (2001). *Multi-Party Computation: Efficient Protocols, General Adversaries, and Voting*, PhD thesis, ETH Zürich.

Hughes, R. J., Nordholt, J. E., Derkacs, D. & Peterson, C. G. (2002). Practical free-space quantum key distribution over 10 km in daylight and at night, *New Journal of Physics* 4: 43.1–43.14.

Hwang, T., Lee, K.-C. & Li, C.-M. (2007). Provably secure three-party authenticated quantum key distribution protocols, *IEEE Transactions On Dependable And Secure Computing* 4(1): 71–80.

ID Quantique (2011). Website of "CERBERIS – A fast and secure solution: high speed encryption combined with quantum key distribution". http://www.idquantique.com/network-encryption/cerberis-layer2 -encryption-and-qkd.html (last access: September 27th, 2011).

Jin, X.-R., Ji, X., Zhang, Y.-Q., Zhang, S., Hong, S.-K., Yeon, K.-H. & Um, C.-I. (2006). Three-party quantum secure direct communication based on GHZ states, *Physics Letters A* 354(1-2): 67–70.

Kaabneh, K. & Al-Bdour, H. (2005). Key Exchange Protocol in Elliptic Curve Cryptography with No Public Point, *American Journal of Applied Sciences* 2(8): 1232–1235.

Kollmitzer, C. & Pivk, M. (eds) (2010). *Applied Quantum Cryptography*, Lecture Notes in Physics 797, Springer.

Krawczyk, H. (1994). LFSR-based hashing and authentication, *CRYPTO '94: Proceedings of the 14th Annual International Cryptology Conference on Advances in Cryptology*, Springer, London, UK, pp. 129–139.

Kumavor, P. D., Beal, A. C., Donkor, E. & Wang, B. C. (2006). Experimental multiuser quantum key distribution network using a wavelength-addressed bus architecture, *Journal Of Lightwave Technology* 24(8): 3103–3106.

Kurtsiefer, C., Zarda, P., Halder, M., Weinfurter, H., Gorman, P. M., Tapster, P. R. & Rarity, J. G. (2002). A step towards global key distribution, *Nature* 419(2): 450.

Le, Q.-C., Bellot, P. & Demaille, A. (2008). *Information Security Practice and Experience*, Springer, chapter Towards the World-Wide Quantum Network, pp. 218–232.

Los Alamos National Security (2009). Quantum cryptography roadmap, *Technical report*, Los Alamos National Security. http://qist.lanl.gov/qcrypt_map.shtml (last accessed: September 27th, 2011).

Mink, A., Frankel, S. & Perlner, R. (2009). Quantum key distribution (qkd) and commodity security protocols: Introduction and integration, *International Journal of Network Security & Its Applications (IJNSA)* 1(2): 101–112.

Mink, A., Ma, L., Nakassis, T., Xu, H., Slattery, O., Hershman, B. & Tang, X. (2008). A quantum network manager that supports a one-time pad stream, *Proceedings of the second*

International Conference on Quantum, Nano and Micro Technologies, IEEE Computer Society Press, pp. 16–21.

Paterson, K.G. and Piper, F. and Schack, R. (2004). Why Quantum Cryptography?, http://eprint.iacr.org/2004/156.pdf.

Peev, M., Pacher, C., Alleaume, R., Barreiro, C., Bouda, J., Boxleitner, W., Debuisschert, T., Diamanti, E., Dianati, M., Dynes, J. F., Fasel, S., Fossier, S., Furst, M., Gautier, J. D., Gay, O., Gisin, N., Grangier, P., Happe, A., Hasani, Y., Hentschel, M., Hubel, H., Humer, G., Länger, T., Legre, M., Lieger, R., Lodewyck, J., Lorünser, T., Lütkenhaus, N., Marhold, A., Matyus, T., Maurhart, O., Monat, L., Nauerth, S., Page, J. B., Poppe, A., Querasser, E., Ribordy, G., Robyr, S., Salvail, L., Sharpe, A. W., Shields, A. J., Stucki, D., Suda, M., Tamas, C., Themel, T., Thew, R. T., Thoma, Y., Treiber, A., Trinkler, P., Tualle-Brouri, R., Vannel, F., Walenta, N., Weier, H., Weinfurter, H., Wimberger, I., Yuan, Z. L., Zbinden, H. & Zeilinger, A. (2009). The SECOQC quantum key distribution network in vienna, *New Journal of Physics* 11(7): 075001. URL: *http://dx.doi.org/10.1088/1367-2630/11/7/075001*

Pfennigbauer, M. & Leeb, W. R. (2003). Free-space optical quantum key distribution using intersatellite links, *Proceedings of the CNES Intersatellite Link Workshop*.

Poppe, A., Peev, M. & Maurhart, O. (2008). Outline of the SECOQC Quantum-Key-Distribution network in vienna, *International Journal of Quantum Information* 6(2): 209–218.

Quantum (2009). Scalar key manager. http://quantum.com/products/tapelibraries/scalarkeymanager/index.aspx, (last access: September 27th, 2011).

Rarity, J., Tapster, P., Gorman, P. & Knight, P. (2002). Ground to satellite secure key exchange using quantum cryptography, *New Journal of Physics* 4: 82.1–82.21.

Rass, S. (2009). *On Information-Theoretic Security: Contemporary Problems and Solutions*, PhD thesis, Klagenfurt University, Institute of Applied Informatics.

Rass, S. & Schartner, P. (2009). Security in quantum networks as an optimization problem, *Proceedings of the International Conference on Availability, Reliability and Security*, pp. 493–498.

Rass, S. & Schartner, P. (2010a). Multipath authentication without shared secrets and with applications in quantum networks, *Proceedings of the International Conference on Security and Management (SAM)*, Vol. 1, CSREA Press, pp. 111–115.

Rass, S. & Schartner, P. (2010b). A unified framework for the analysis of availability, reliability and security, with applications to quantum networks, *IEEE Transactions on Systems, Man, and Cybernetics – Part C: Applications and Reviews* 40(5): 107–119.

Salvail, L., Peev, M., Diamanti, E., Alleaume, R., Lütkenhaus, N. & Länger, T. (2009). Security of trusted repeater quantum key distribution networks, `arXiv:0904.4072v1 [quant-ph]`.

Schartner, P. & Rass, S. (2009). How to overcome the trusted node model in quantum cryptography, *Proceedings of the 12th IEEE International Conference on Computational Science and Engineering*, Los Alamitos, California, pp. 259–262.

Schartner, P. & Rass, S. (2010). Quantum key distribution and denial-of-service: Using strengthened classical cryptography as a fallback option, *Proceedings of ICS 2010 Workshop of Information Security*, IEEE, pp. 131–136.

Schmitt-Manderbach, T., Weier, H., Fürst, M., Ursin, R., Tiefenbacher, F., Scheidl, T., Perdigues, J., Sodnik, Z., Kurtsiefer, C., Rarity, J. G., Zeilinger, A. & Weinfurter, H. (2007). Experimental demonstration of free-space decoy-state quantum key distribution

over 144 km, *Physical Review Letters* 98(1): 010504.
URL: *http://link.aps.org/abstract/PRL/v98/e010504*

Shamir, A. (1979). How to share a secret, *Commun. ACM* 22(11): 612–613.

Shamir, A. (1985). Identity-based cryptosystems and signature schemes, *Proceedings of CRYPTO 84 on Advances in cryptology*, Springer-Verlag New York, Inc., New York, NY, USA, pp. 47–53.

Shannon, C. (1949). Communication theory of secrecy systems, *Bell System Technical Journal* 28: 656–715.

Sheikh, K. H., Hyder, S. S. & Khan, M. M. (2006). An overview of quantum cryptography for wireless networking infrastructure, *CTS '06: Proceedings of the International Symposium on Collaborative Technologies and Systems*, IEEE Computer Society, Washington, DC, USA, pp. 379–385.

Shor, P. (1997). Polynomial-time algorithms for prime factorization and discrete logarithms on a quantum computer, *SIAM Journal on Computing* 26: 1484–1509.

Shoup, V. (1996). On fast and provably secure message authentication based on universal hashing, *CRYPTO '96: Proceedings of the 16th Annual International Cryptology Conference on Advances in Cryptology*, Springer-Verlag, London, UK, pp. 313–328.

SwissQuantum (2011). Key management layer. http://www.swissquantum.com/?-Key-Management-Layer (last access: September 27th, 2011).

Tanaka, A. andMaeda, W., Takahashi, S., Tajima, A. & Tomita, A. (2008). Randomize technique for quantum key and key management system for use in qkd networks, *SECOQC Demonstration Conference*.

Tang, X., Ma, L., Mink, A., Nakassis, A., Xu, H., Hershman, B., Bienfang, J., Su, D., Boisvert, R. F., Clark, C. & Williams, C. (2006). Demonstration of an active quantum key distribution network, *Technical report*, National Institute of Standards and Technology.

Wang, Y. & Desmedt, Y. (2008). Perfectly secure message transmission revisited, *IEEE Transactions on Information Theory* 54(6): 2582–2595.

Weier, H., Schmitt-Manderbach, T., Regner, N., Kurtsiefer, C. & Weinfurter, H. (2006). Free space quantum key distribution: Towards a real life application, *Fortschritte der Physik* 54(8-10): 840–845.

Wiesner, S. (1983). Conjugate coding, *Sigact News* 15(1): 78–88. original manuscript written circa 1970.

Wootters, W. K. & Zurek, W. H. (1982). A single quantum cannot be cloned, *Nature* 299(802): 802–803.

Yuan, Z.-S., Chen, Y.-A., Zhao, B., Chen, S., Schmiedmayer, J. & Pan, J.-W. (2008). Experimental demonstration of a BDCZ quantum repeater node, *Nature* 454: 1098–1101.

Part 3

Evolutionary Concepts and Techniques in Security

12

Chaotic Electronic Circuits in Cryptography

Matej Šalamon
University of Maribor, Faculty of Electrical Engineering and Computer Science
Slovenia

1. Introduction

Chaotic electronic circuits represent deterministic systems which can be used as random number generators in cryptography. Truly chaotic signals can only be generated by analog chaotic circuits. In a cryptosystem a synchronization of the encryption and decryption sides has to be secured, which can be very problematic due to the high sensitivity of the chaotic circuits (Koh & Ushio, 1997; Ogorzalek, 1993). Total inversion of the encryption and decryption sides can only be achieved by using digital chaotic circuits, which act only as pseudo random number generators (Kocarev & Lian, 2011).

In a digital chaotic cryptosystem the chaotic analog circuit is replaced by a suitable mathematic model. The latter is usually represented by equations which are solved with corresponding numerical algorithms, using computers. The digital model of the chaotic circuit therefore represents a mere approximation of its analog variant, and only acts as a pseudo random number generator (PRNG) and not as a truly random number generator (TRNG). Namely, the number of various values is always final in a computer, whereas the values themselves are represented by a limited number of bits.

This article deals with a model of a well-known analog chaotic circuit - the Chua's Circuit, which was used in the cryptosystem as a pseudo random sequence generator. With the mathematical tool Matlab we created a prototype of the cryptosystem and carried out its cryptanalysis. The purpose of the article, however, is not only the presentation of a new chaotic cryptosystem. It tends to point out a few potential problems which can be expected in cryptosystems of this kind.

This article is organised as follows. In the chapter two is presented a phenomenon of chaotic electronic circuits. In the subsequent sub-chapters detailed analysis of chaos in the Chua's circuit is given. The circuit's behaviour is analysed through the three-dimensional state space and the bifurcation diagrams. From the bifurcation diagrams we can read out the parameters at which the circuit's behaviour is chaotic and thus appropriate for random sequences generation. In a cryptographic system, random sequences should be uniformly distributed. Since the basic variant of the Chua's circuit is not able to generate uniformly distributed values, in the continuation the modified Chua's circuit with a more complex chaotic behaviour was introduced. Chaotic state variables in cases of 3-, 4- and 5-scroll chaotic attractors were analysed. All discussed variants of the Chua's circuit were analysed also with the Lyapunov exponents. Based on theirs maximum values, sensitivities to initial conditions were estimated. The most sensitive variant of the Chua's circuit was chosen for the random sequences generator.

The third chapter deals with a usage of chaotic circuits in cryptography. The subsequent sub-chapters describe three basic analog encryption techniques and the structures of a chaos based digital cryptographic system.

The fourth chapter describes the example of digital chaotic cryptosystem with the previously chosen variant of the Chua's circuit. In the sub-chapters are described details of used encryption function and the structure of the entire cryptographic system, adapted for a digital images encryption. In the continuation the cryptanalysis of the described cryptographic system is also presented. Analysis of ciphertexts histograms points out the problem of not uniformly distributed pseudo-chaotic sequences. We have presented also the solution that assures a uniform distribution of pseudo-chaotic sequences. Further we have analysed the statistical and correlation properties of ciphertexts, obtained with different secret keys. Therefore, we performed the auto-covariance and cross-covariance analysis. The problem of a slow initial divergence of pseudo-chaotic sequences is also emphasised. This problem is very evident by an encryption with very similar secret keys.

The last fifth chapter is assigned to the summary of findings and possibilities to solve some problems of the so called chaotic cryptography.

2. Chaotic behaviour of electronic circuits

Electronic circuits can generally be linear or non-linear. As no complete linearity exists in the real world, all circuits are actually non-linear. Their analysis is usually mathematically difficult as it is linked to solving non-linear differential equations.

The multitude of non-linear circuits comprises a huge number of circuits with various behaviour. Concentrating only on autonomous non-linear circuits, we can classify them according to the solutions of equations, describing their behaviour (Ogorzalek, 1997). The solutions can:

- converge to a unique equilibrium point - operating point (RLC-filters, amplifiers etc.);
- converge to one of several possible equilibrium points (bistable circuits, memory cells, sample-and-hold circuits, Schmitt trigger circuits etc.);
- be periodic or quasi-periodic (oscillators, periodic signal generators etc.).

The types of solutions stated above describe the so called »normal« circuit behaviour (Ogorzalek, 1997). However, circuits with a much more exotic - chaotic behaviour have joined the circuits with »normal« behaviour during the last forty years. They are non-linear circuits whose behaviour cannot be determined precisely despite a precise analytic description, as they are high sensitive to initial conditions and some parameters.

Different chaotic circuits have been mentioned in numerous scientific articles like e.g. (Kennedy, 1993a, 1993b, 1994; Sharkovsky & Chua, 1993; Suykens & Vandewalle, 1993; Kolumban & Vizvari, 1994; Šalamon & Dogša, 1995; Hongtao & Zhenya, 1996; Ogorzalek, 1997; Hilborn, 2000). These are simple RLC-circuits, various oscillators, capacitive-trigger circuits, digital filters, flip-flops, adaptive filters, power supplies and converters, power circuits. Figure 1 presents three examples of simple chaotic circuits.

Among the chaotic circuits the most established one - being an object of numerous scientific activities (Chua et al, 1993), is the Chua's oscillator. Kennedy asserts (Kennedy, 1993a,

1993b) that the Chua's oscillator is the only physical system for which the presence of chaos has been established experimentally, confirmed numerically (with computer simulations) and proven mathematically (Chua et al, 1986).

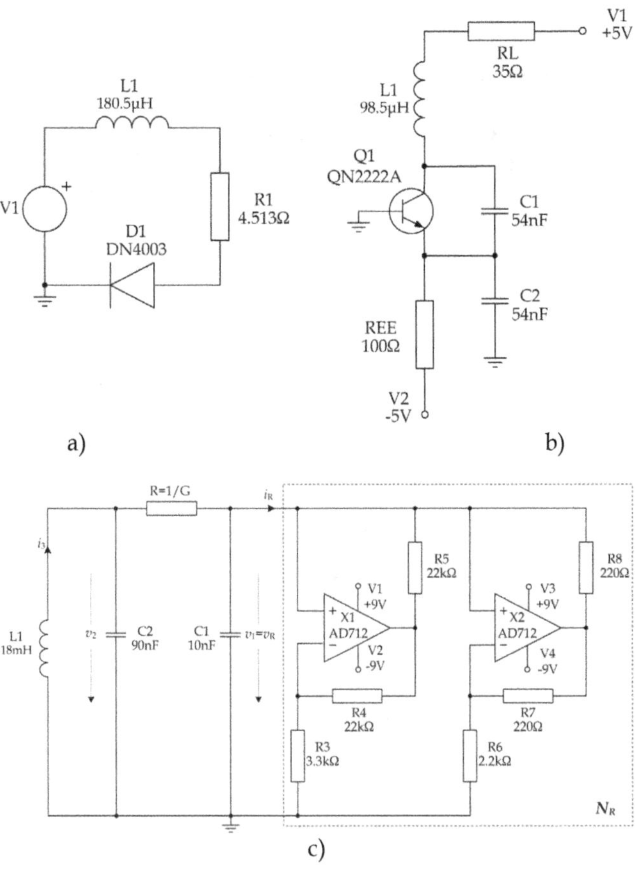

Fig. 1. Examples of simple chaotic circuits: a) diode resonator; b) Colpitts oscillator; c) Chua's oscillator.

Chaotic signals cannot be classified among any of the sorts of solutions of non-linear differential equations stated above. Although their time waveforms are similar to random signals time waveforms, there are substantial differences between them as they are predictable, but only within a short time interval.

The behaviour of chaotic circuits is orderly disordered. Experiments show that in specific conditions (chosen parameters, initial conditions, input signals ...) almost all electric and electronic circuits behave chaotically (Ogorzalek, 1997).

Chaotic circuits and other kinds of chaotic systems have certain common characteristics like: high sensitivity to initial conditions, bifurcations, positive Lyapunov exponents, chaotic attractors, fractals etc. (Hilborn, 2000; Sprott, 2009). When using this kind of systems in cryptography, these characteristics are consequently transferred into cryptosystems. First of all, let us discuss some characteristics of the chaotic Chua's Circuit.

2.1 Chua's circuit

Chua's Circuit, shown in figure 1c, represents an oscillator and a third-order autonomous circuit, respectively (Kennedy, 1993b). It consists of simple electronic components: resistors, inductor, capacitors and operational amplifiers. The *L1* inductor and *C2* capacitor build a resonant circuit, whereas their values determine the basic oscillation frequency. The operational amplifiers *X1* and *X2* as well as the resistors *R3* to *R8* form a voltage-controlled negative resistor (N_R), also called the *Chua's diode* which sustains the oscillation. Basically, the Chua's diode v_R-i_R characteristic has three piecewise-linear segments with two different negative slopes G_a and G_b and two segments with positive slope G_c (figure 2).

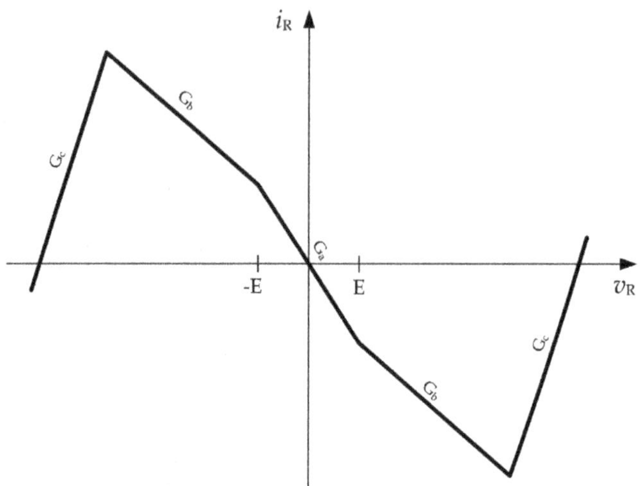

Fig. 2. The Chua's diode v_R-i_R characteristic.

If *R4*=*R5* and *R7*=*R8*, the values of the negative slopes of the v_R-i_R characteristic are determined by the equations:

$$G_a = -\frac{1}{R3} - \frac{1}{R6} \tag{1}$$

$$G_b = \frac{1}{R5} - \frac{1}{R6} \tag{2}$$

C1 can be represented as a parasitic capacitor without which the Chua's circuit cannot behave chaotically. Similarly to the resistor *R*=1/*G*, we can also use the capacitance *C1* as a bifurcation parameter (Kennedy, 1993b). By changing the bifurcation parameter we can influence the behaviour of the Chua's circuit, described by the following differential equations:

$$\frac{dv_1}{dt} = \frac{1}{C1}\left[G(v_2 - v_1) - f(v_1)\right] = \begin{cases} \frac{G}{C1}v_2 - \frac{G_b^{'}}{C1}v_1 - \left(\frac{G_b - G_a}{C1}\right)\cdot E & ; \quad v_1 < -E \\ \frac{G}{C1}v_2 - \frac{G_a^{'}}{C1}v_1 & ; \quad -E \le v_1 \le E \\ \frac{G}{C1}v_2 - \frac{G_b^{'}}{C1}v_1 - \left(\frac{G_a - G_b}{C1}\right)\cdot E & ; \quad v_1 > E \end{cases}$$

$$\frac{dv_2}{dt} = \frac{1}{C2}\left[G(v_1 - v_2) + i_3\right] \qquad (3)$$

$$\frac{di_3}{dt} = -\frac{1}{L1}v_2$$

Here v_1, v_2 and i_3 are state variables. The rest of the parameters are: $G=1/R2$, $G'_a=G+G_a$ and $G'_b=G+G_b$.

A detailed analysis of the Chua's circuit follows, enabling a better understanding of its features and showing possibilities of its use in cryptography.

2.2 The model and the analysis of the Chua's circuit

The analog electronic circuits are usually analysed with analog electronic circuit simulators. SPICE simulators are the best known ones. Up to a certain degree also the chaotic behaviour of circuits can be analysed by them. They can predominantly be used for the time analysis of the voltage and currents in circuits, and also of the so called bifurcation diagrams, given an additional spice macro model (Šalamon & Dogša, 2009).

The use of mathematical tools is necessary for a more detailed analysis of chaotic circuits. The circuit must be described by a suitable mathematical model - by corresponding differential equations. The solution of the equations is carried out by a mathematical tool which - beside the basic time analysis of the state variables - also enables the determination of the bifurcation diagrams, Lyapunov exponents, Poincare's sections of attractors etc.

A more detailed analysis of Chua's Circuit cannot be carried out with an electronic circuit simulator. Therefore we used the mathematical tool Matlab where we initially described the Chua's Circuit by a corresponding model. We used the so called normalized dimensionless form of the Chua's equations (Fortuna et al, 2009). These are acquired by introducing new variables: $x=v_1/E$, $y=v_2/E$, $z=i_3/(E\cdot G)$, $\tau=t\cdot G/C2$, $a=G_a/G$, $b=G_b/G$, $\alpha=C2/C1$, $\beta=C2/(L1\cdot G^2)$ into the equations (3):

$$\begin{aligned} \dot{x} &= \alpha\left[y - x - g(x)\right] \\ \dot{y} &= x - y + z \\ \dot{z} &= -\beta y \end{aligned} \qquad (4)$$

Here the following function is marked as g(x):

$$g(x) = \begin{cases} bx + b - a, & x \le -1 \\ ax, & |x| < 1 \\ bx + a - b, & x \ge 1 \end{cases} \qquad (5)$$

Let us also define the following function:

$$h(x) = x + g(x) = m_1 x + \frac{1}{2}(m_0 - m_1)(|x+1| - |x-1|) \tag{6}$$

which represents the piecewise-linear characteristic (figure 3) with two negative slopes: $m_0=a+1$ in $m_1=b+1$.

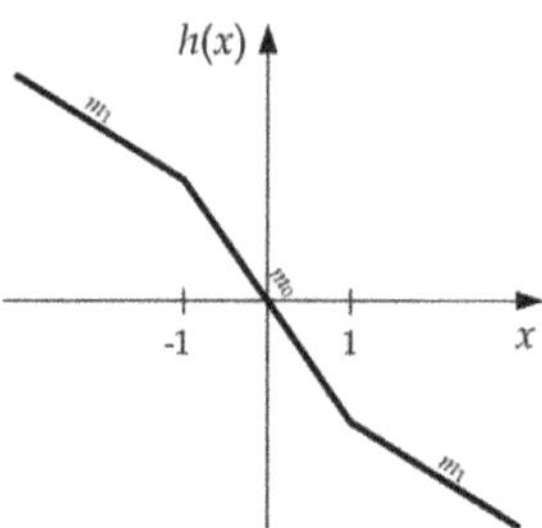

Fig. 3. Piecewise-linear characteristic *h(x)*.

Considering the function *h(x)* in the equations (4) we can describe the Chua's Circuit by an equivalent form of Chua's equations:

$$\begin{aligned} \dot{x} &= \alpha\left[y - h(x)\right] \\ \dot{y} &= x - y + z \\ \dot{z} &= -\beta y \end{aligned} \tag{7}$$

We have analysed the Chua's Circuit behaviour with solutions of the differential equations shown above. The solutions of the equations are represented by the state variables time waveforms: *x(t)*, *y(t)* and *z(t)*. These are equivalent to the voltage time waveforms $v_1(t)$, $v_2(t)$ and the current time waveform $i_3(t)$ in the circuit as shown in figure 1c.

The analysis was carried out at different parameters a and β which in a real circuit depend on the values of the circuit components *R*, *C1*, *C2* and *L1*. We chose the following constant values of the elements: *C1*=10nF, *C2*=90nF, *L1*=18mH and the parameters of the Chua's diode: m_0=-1/7, m_1=2/7. The resistance *R* is variable and represents a bifurcation parameter to which the circuit is very sensitive. By changing it we achieve an alteration of the circuit's global behaviour. According to the selected values of elements parameters: a=9 and $\beta=5 \cdot 10^{-6} \cdot R^2$ can be calculated.

The solutions of Chua's equations can be presented by trajectories in the three-dimensional state space. Some of them are shown in figure 4. The Chua's Circuit at the value of β>15.4 behaves as a common harmonic oscillator. In this case the trajectory represents a limit cycle, shown in figure 4a. At the value of β=16.4 a doubling of the period occurs and the presence of bifurcations, respectively, where the state variables have two different amplitudes. Within the state space, the trajectory only ends after two turns (figure 4b). The reduction of parameter β causes a further orbit splitting, thus causing the formation of period 4, period 8, period 16 etc. Figure 4c presents the period 4, where individual state variables have four different maximum values. By reducing parameter β the orbit splitting becomes more and more frequent, up to the formation of the orbit with an infinite period, which represents the chaotic regime of the circuit operation. This is achieved at the parameter value of β=15.4. In this case an unusual spiral

Chua's attractor appears in the state space, its form being shown in the figure 4d. The trajectory which in such cases never closes, encircles one of the three virtual equilibrium circuit states (Kennedy, 1993b). A further reduction of the parameter β causes the transition of the spiral Chua's attractor into a double-scroll Chua's attractor (figure 4f). Here the trajectory randomly traverses and circles around two different virtual states.

The chaotic regime of the circuit operation is interrupted by several narrow so called »periodic windows« within the Chua's Circuit periodically oscillates again. Figure 4e presents an example of a periodic window, described by a closed trajectory within the state space. Given a small change of the bifurcation parameter, the periodic window disappears and the circuit begins to oscillate chaotically again.

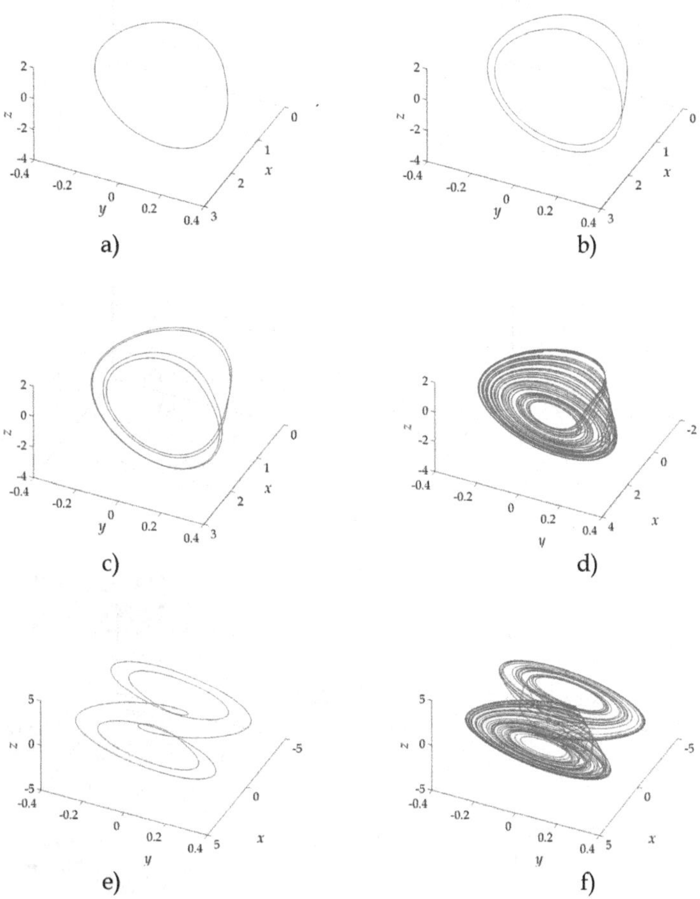

Fig. 4. The behaviour of the Chua's Circuit at different values of the bifurcation parameter β: a) limit cycle (β =17); b) period 2 (β =16.2); c) period 4 (β =15.7); d) spiral Chua's attractor (β =14.9); e) periodic window (β =14.31); f) double-scroll Chua's attractor (β =14.2).

The circuit behaviour described above can be more explicitly presented through the bifurcation diagrams. Bifurcation diagrams of state variables x, y and z are shown in the figure 5. The number of maximum extreme values depends on the bifurcation parameter β. The dark spaces in the bifurcation diagrams represent the chaotic regime of the circuit operation. This regime is interrupted by periodic windows, showing as light spots among dark chaotic areas.

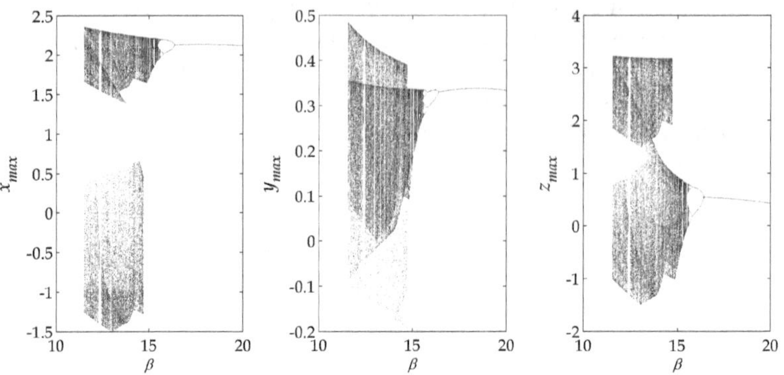

Fig. 5. The Chua's circuit bifurcation diagrams of the state variables x, y and z.

From the cryptographic point of view only the chaotic behaviour of the Chua's Circuit is interesting, being that random signals can only be generated in this mode of operation. It is the characteristics of chaotic signals that although they are non-periodic, certain patterns can be traced in them which do not appear in truly random signals.

Figure 6a shows an example of the state variables time waveforms $x(t)$, $y(t)$ and $z(t)$ in the chaotic regime of the Chua's Circuit operation, described by the double-scroll Chua's attractor; figure 6b shows the corresponding histograms - statistical distribution of the chaotic state variables. We can see that they are not uniformly distributed, showing that some time signal values are more probable than others.

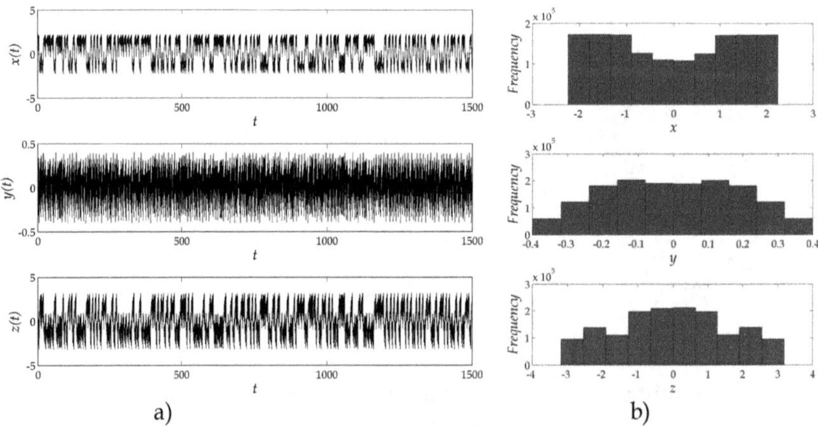

Fig. 6. a) The state variables waveforms by the double-scroll Chua's attractor (β=14.2); b) Histograms of the state variables.

On the basis of the analysis results so far obtained we can conclude that it is possible to generate random signals with the Chua's Circuit, but their individual time values will not be uniformly distributed. As this is one of the characteristics required in the random number generators in cryptosystems, which we wanted to come as close to as possible with the Chua's Circuit, we subsequently modified the basic Chua's Circuit (figure 1c). We wanted to achieve more complex circuit dynamics and a uniform distribution of time values.

2.3 The model of the Chua's circuit with a more complex chaotic behaviour

A more complex chaotic behaviour of the Chua's Circuit can be obtained by modifying the Chua's diode characteristic or by a modification of the function $h(x)$, defined by the equation (6). Suykens and Vanewalle ascertained in their article (Suykens & Vandewalle, 1993) that with the Chua's Circuit even more complex signals or more complex attractors can be generated. This can be achieved with several additional segments of the Chua's diode characteristic which is in such cases described by the following function:

$$h(x) = m_{2q-1}x + \frac{1}{2}\sum_{i=1}^{2q-1}(m_{i-1} - m_i)(|x + c_i| - |x - c_i|) \tag{8}$$

Here q is a natural number, c_i is the breakpoint of i-th segment and m_i is the slope of i-th segment of the piecewise-linear characteristic $h(x)$. Thus n-scroll or multi-scroll chaotic attractors with n=1, 2, 3… scrolls can be achieved with the Chua's Circuit.

More complex attractors also represent more complex time waveforms of voltages and currents in the Chua's Circuit. Different attractors can be obtained by choosing appropriate breakpoints and slopes of the characteristics $h(x)$ and with suitable parameters α and β. In our case we have limited ourselves to discussing the variants of the circuit with a 3-, 4- and 5-scroll chaotic attractor at the following parameters:

- 3-scroll chaotic attractor: α=9; β=100/7; m_0=0,9/7, m_1=-3/7, m_2=3.5/7, m_3=-2.4/7, c_1=1, c_2=2.15, c_3=4;
- 4-scroll chaotic attractor: α=9; β=100/7; m_0=-1/7, m_1=2/7, m_2=-4/7, m_3=2/7, c_1=1, c_2=2.15, c_3=3.6;
- 5-scroll chaotic attractor: α=9; β=100/7; m_0=0.9/7, m_1=-3/7, m_2 =3.5/7, m_3=-2/7, m_4=4/7, m_5=-2.4/7, c_1=1, c_2=2.15, c_3=3.6, c_4=6.2, c_5=9.

Figures 7a-c show obtained 3-, 4- and 5-scroll chaotic attractors.

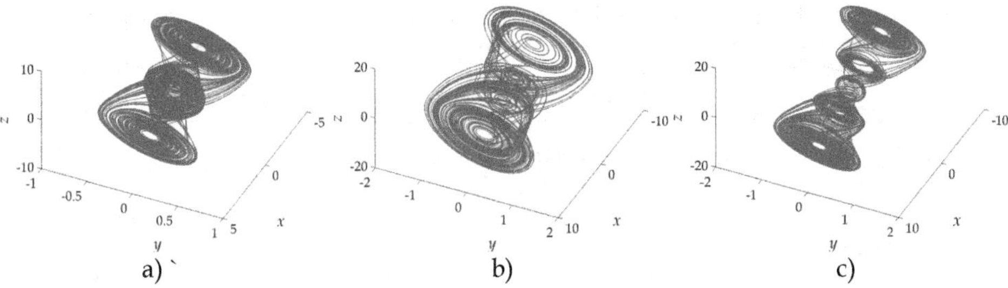

Fig. 7. a) 3-scroll chaotic attractor, b) 4-scroll chaotic attractor and c) 5-scroll chaotic attractor.

Figure 8a shows the time waveforms of the state variables $x(t)$, $y(t)$ and $z(t)$ in the case of the 5-scroll chaotic attractor, and figure 8b shows statistical distributions of their time values.

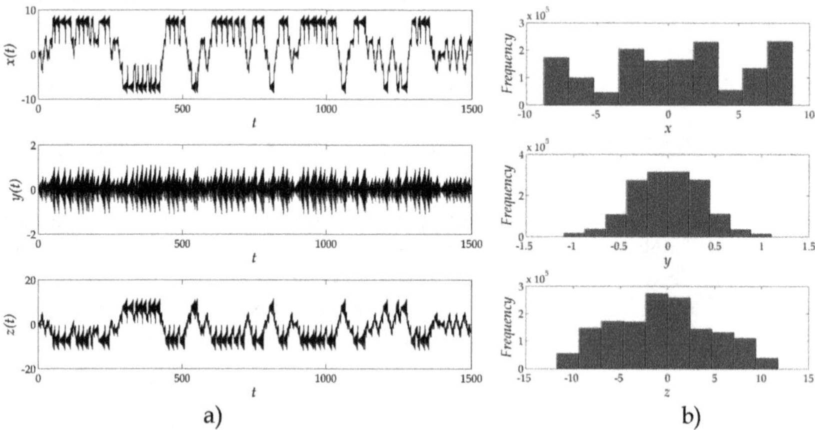

Fig. 8. a) Time waveforms of the state variables in the 5-scroll chaotic attractor (β=14.2); b) Histograms of the state variables.

The results show that despite the more complex chaotic behaviour of the Chua's Circuit the time values of the state variables are not more uniformly distributed than in the case of the two-scroll attractor. Despite this fact we used the variant of the Chua's Circuit with a 5-scroll chaotic attractor in planning the encryption system, described later in the article. This circuit variant enabled us the fastest divergence of two trajectories; the evaluation was carried out with the Lyapunov exponent analysis.

2.4 Lyapunov exponents analysis of the Chua's circuit

The basic feature of all chaotic systems is high sensitivity dependence to initial conditions and some system parameters. This feature prevents a long-term prediction of their behaviour. The chaotic trajectories, starting in the state space from close initial conditions, begin to diverge very quickly from each other as time progresses. The speed of their divergence which occurs due to infinitesimal deviation in the initial conditions is evaluated with the Lyapunov exponent (Hilborn, 2000; Sprott, 2009).

The positive Lyapunov exponent is characteristic of all chaotic systems. A higher value of the Lyapunov exponent represents a higher divergence speed of two adjacent trajectories in the state space or more sensitive and faster changing of the chaotic variables. The negative value of the Lyapunov exponent represents a periodic behaviour of the system, whereas the value zero represents the presence of bifurcations which do not represent chaotic behaviour either.

The calculation of the Lyapunov exponent calls for the use of an appropriate mathematical tool and procedure. In our case the Lyapunov exponents were calculated with a procedure suggested by Sprott (Sprott, 2009). Using the Matlab tool, we calculated the average values of the Lyapunov exponents for all four previously discussed variants of the Chua's Circuit at a constant parameter a=9 and at a variable bifurcation parameter β. Figure 9 shows the obtained average values of the Lyapunov exponents λ in the case of the Chua's Circuit with 2-, 3-, 4- and 5-scroll chaotic attractor at various parameter β values.

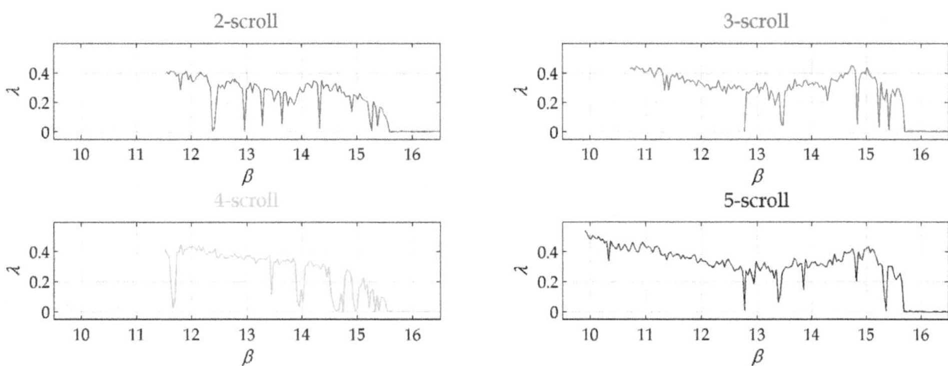

Fig. 9. Average values of the Lyapunov exponent λ vs. β calculated for the Chua's Circuit with 2-, 3-, 4- and 5-scroll chaotic attractor.

The results show that the values of the Lyapunov exponent slightly rise with the complexity of the attractors. Maximum values of the Lyapunov exponents are written in table 1.

	2-sroll	3-scroll	4-scroll	5-scroll
λ_{max}	0.4125	0.4461	0.4467	0.5412
ß	11.6280	14.7620	11.8080	9.9000

Table 1. Maximum values of the Lyapunov exponent, achieved by the 2-, 3-, 4- and 5-scroll chaotic attractor of the Chua's Circuit.

According to the presented dependency of the Lyapunov exponents and their maximum values we can conclude as follows:

- the value of the maximum Lyapunov exponent of the Chua's Circuit with a 5-scroll chaotic attractor is by 31% higher than with a 2-scroll attractor. By a more complex behaviour of the Chua's Circuit faster divergence of the state variables can be achieved;
- individual positive values of the Lyapunov exponent are comparatively small - in the case of a truly random sequence the values of the Lyapunov exponents would be infinitely large;
- Lyapunov exponent values depend largely on the parameter β. In an encryption system it can be a part of the secret key, which in our case cannot be an arbitrary value. Namely, there is a large number of very small and even negative values of the Lyapunov exponent where the Chua's Circuit would surely not behave chaotically;
- if the bifurcation parameter represents a part of the secret key, in the case of the Chua's Circuit there is a strong probability of selecting the so called weak keys which prevent safe ciphering. Namely, the chaotic regime of the circuit operation is limited to several relatively narrow areas, interrupted by periodic windows. They can only be avoided by precise knowledge of the Chua's Circuit behaviour.

The presented results of the analysis of Chua's Circuit indicate problems which can be expected when using it in cryptography. The same problems are also to be expected in the case of other chaotic circuits.

3. The principles of chaotic encryption

When the phenomenon of chaos was discovered in the electronic circuits, questions about the possibility of their use in practice appeared. The similarity among chaotic signals, generated by deterministic systems and random signals which cannot be generated by deterministic systems, led many researchers to the idea of the applicability of chaotic circuits in cryptography. In the beginning, mostly analog cryptosystems were used. Three basic encryption techniques appeared where a complete synchronization of chaotic circuits of the encryption and decryption sides is needed. Due to high sensitivity to initial conditions, external impacts (temperature, noise, ageing of components) and the tolerances of the components, analog chaotic circuits cannot be completely synchronized. Despite this fact analog chaotic encryption proved to be useful predominantly in ciphering undemanding audio signals.

Besides the analog chaotic encryption systems there are also the digital ones. Here instead of truly chaotic analog circuits their discrete models are used. In such cases we are dealing with a digital chaos-based cryptosystems (Kocarev & Lian, 2011).

3.1 Analog encryption techniques

Through the years the following techniques of the analog chaotic encryption were predominantly carried into effect (Dedieu et al. 1993; Ogorzalek, 1993; Koh & Ushio, 1997):

- chaotic masking where the continuous chaotic signal is added to the input analog signal,
- chaotic modulation where the input analog signal is modulated by the chaotic carrier,
- chaotic switching - also known as CSK (Chaotic Shift Keying) where the input digital signal is ciphered by switching between two different attractors. Also the chaotic phase-shift keying - CPSK, and the modulation on the basis of M-synchronized chaotic systems - M-CPSK, are based on the principle of chaotic shifting.

Chaotic masking and chaotic modulation are used at ciphering analog signals while the technique of chaotic switching is used in the case of ciphering digital signals.

3.1.1 Chaotic masking

This is the simplest encryption method where the analog input signal *i(t)* is masked with a chaotic signal *k(t)*. The transmitter contains a chaotic circuit - a generator of a chaotic signal which generates the signal *k(t)*. The latter is added to the signal *i(t)* and then sent to the receiver (figure 10).

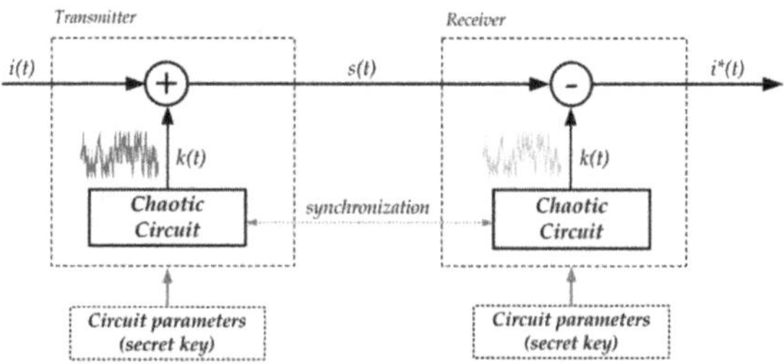

Fig. 10. The principle of chaotic masking.

The masked or ciphered signal *s(t)* is deciphered on the receiver side in the way that the chaotic signal *k(t)*, which has to be the same as the one on the receiver side, is subtracted from it. The signal *i*(t)* shall only be equal to the signal *i(t)* when the transmitter and the receiver have equal and time synchronized chaotic signal generators at their disposal. Further information on the synchronization of chaotic circuits and various methods of synchronization can be found in the literature (Cuomo et al., 1993; Ogorzalek, 1993).

3.1.2 Chaotic modulation

The essence of the chaotic modulation is the modulation of the input signal *i(t)* by a chaotic signal *k(t)* generated by the chaotic signal generator. The signal *i(t)* is modulated by the signal *k(t)* in the chaotic modulator where their multiplication occurs. The modulated signal *s(t)* is transmitted over the communication channel to the receiver where in the chaotic demodulator the demodulation or division of the modulated signal *s(t)* with the chaotic signal *k(t)* is carried out. The equality of the receiver's and the transmitter's parameters and their synchronization is a condition for successful demodulation (Dedieu et al. 1993; Ogorzalek, 1993).

3.1.3 Chaotic switching

The method of chaotic switching represents the simplest form of modulation with chaotic attractors. It is suitable for deciphering digital signals. Let's observe a case of ciphering a binary input signal *i(t)*, shown in the figure 11.

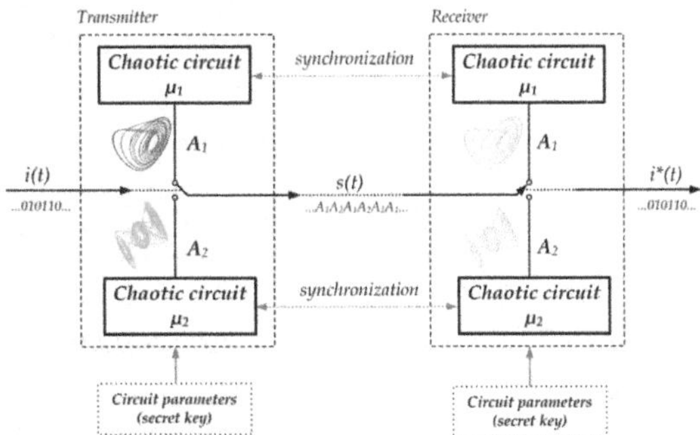

Fig. 11. The principle of the chaotic switching.

The signal *i(t)* controls the switch which toggles between the chaotic systems with different parameters μ_1 and μ_2.

The transmitter consists of two chaotic subsystems:

- the subsystem with the parameters μ_1 - active when $i(t) = 0$,
- the subsystem with the parameters μ_2 - active when $i(t) = 1$.

Transmission of the chaotic attractor A_1, generated by the first chaotic circuit (with the parameters μ_1), corresponds to the logical zero, transmission of the attractor A_2, generated by the second chaotic circuit (with the parameters μ_2), corresponds to the logical one. The entire system acts as a switch which switches between the attractors A_1 and A_2.

The receiver also consists of two chaotic subsystems which have to be identical to and synchronized with the ones on the transmitter side. The first one is designed for demodulating the zeros, the second one for the ones. The demodulation is carried out on the basis of decisions within an individual time interval. A successful demodulation of a logical zero or one is only possible when the chaotic systems on the transmitter and the receiver sides are precisely synchronized (Cuomo et al., 1993; Ogorzalek, 1993; Corron & Hahs, 1997; Yang & Chua, 1996).

3.2 Digital chaotic cryptosystems

Nowadays digital cryptosystems are predominantly used. In general they are divided into symmetric and asymmetric ones (Schneier, 1996; Stallings, 1999). The symmetric ones which only use one secret key, are divided into stream and block systems. The asymmetric ones use two secret keys, the public and the private key.

Chaotic circuits and their digital models, respectively, can be included in any sort of cryptosystems. Here a "naturally" digital chaotic circuit can be used (Šalamon & Dogša, 2000), (e.g. a digital filter), or an analog chaotic circuit can be digitalized.

The digital cryptosystem has several advantages over the analog one:

- it enables complete inversion between the encryption and decryption sides;
- the encryption and decryption algorithms can easily be changed and updated as it is usually implemented with a programme code;
- there is no need for the problematic synchronization of the analog chaotic circuits;
- the digital structure is insensitive to numerous disturbances like the ageing of elements, temperature, noise . . .

The basic structure of the digital chaotic cryptosystem is evident from the figure 12.

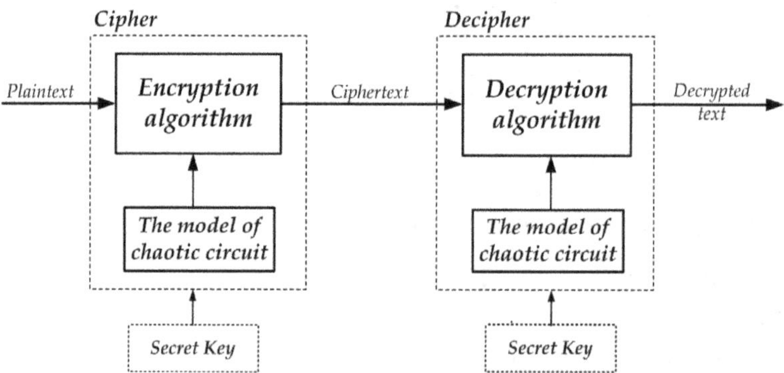

Fig. 12. The basic structure of a simple symmetric chaotic cryptosystem.

Like in the analog cryptosystem, also in the digital cryptosystem the chaotic circuit or its model is the basic component, performing the function of the random number generator. In analog cryptosystem these generators are analog circuits and they generate truly chaotic signals. In digital cryptosystem the generators are discrete systems which generate digital, pseudo chaotic signals.

According to the sort of the encryption algorithm the chaotic cryptosystem can be symmetric, stream or block and asymmetric. The secret key consists of the values of the parameters of the encryption function and/or the parameters of the pseudo random number generator.

Among the first patented symmetric chaotic cryptosystem were block as well as stream cryptosystem (Bianco & Reed, 1991; Gao, 1997). In stream ciphers, the encryption function is a simple logical operation XOR. A plaintext is ciphered by carrying out a logical XOR operation between the bits of the plaintext and the bits of the pseudo random sequence. The latter is generated on the basis of various algorithms (logistic equation, Lorenz's chaotic equations etc.) The ciphertext is deciphered with a XOR function of the ciphertext bits and the pseudo random sequence which equals the one used at ciphering (Fridrich, 1998).

In more recent chaotic cryptosystems the chaotic systems are incorporated into the encryption function in various ways. These systems are much more complex and also offer higher security. Their characteristics are perfectly comparable with the characteristics of the classical cryptosystems (Kocarev, 2001, Kocarev, & Lian, 2011).

4. The cryptosystem with the model of Chua's circuit

In this chapter a simple example of a chaotic cryptosystem, realized in the Matlab environment, is described. The model of the Chua's Circuit with a 5-scroll chaotic attractor discussed previously was used for generating pseudo random sequences; as the encryption algorithm a special multi-shift encryption function was used which is described in detail below.

4.1 The encryption function

The N-shift or the multi-shift encryption function can be described with the iterative algorithm described by the following equation (Yang et al. 1997, Šalamon & Dogša, 2002):

$$s(n) = \underbrace{f_1(\ldots f_1(f_1(}_{N} i(n), \underbrace{k(n)), k(n)), \ldots, k(n))}_{N} \, . \tag{9}$$

where N is the number of iterations, $i(n)$ the value of n-th sample of the plaintext, $k(n)$ is the n-th value of the chaotic variable, and f_1 is a non-linear function, described by the equation:

$$f_1(x,k) = \begin{cases} (x+k) + 2 \cdot h & -2 \cdot h \le (x+k) \le -h \\ (x+k) & -h < (x+k) < h \\ (x+k) - 2 \cdot h & h \le (x+k) \le 2 \cdot h \end{cases} \, . \tag{10}$$

Its graphic presentation is given in figure 13.

The encryption function will be bijective if the value of the variable h is chosen in the way that x and k will always be within the interval ($-h$, h):

$$-h < x < h \tag{11}$$

$$-h < k < h \tag{12}$$

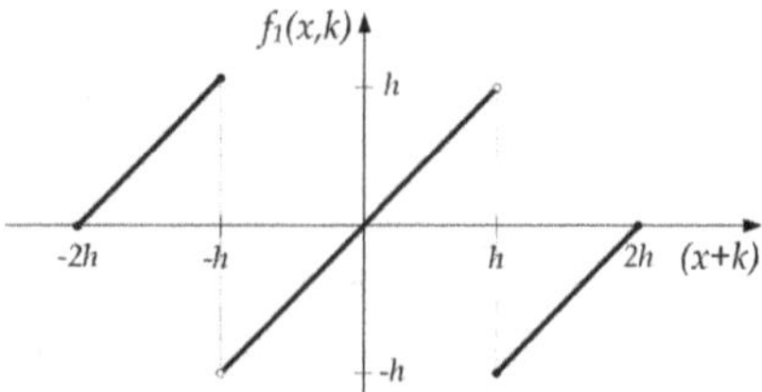

Fig. 13. The graph of non-linear function f_1.

In this case there is also the inverse - decryption algorithm described by the equation:

$$i(n) = \underbrace{f_1(\ldots f_1(f_1}_{N}(s(n), \underbrace{-k(n)), -k(n)), \ldots, -k(n))}_{N} \qquad (13)$$

where: $s(n)$ is n-th sample of the ciphertext and $i(n)$ is n-th sample of the decrypted text. f_1 is a non-linear function described by an equation (10). As the encryption and the decryption functions are recursive, a certain time is necessary to calculate the individual values of the ciphertext or the sample of the deciphered text. The time depends on the selected number of iterations N.

4.2 Details of the chaotic cryptosystem

Our cryptosystem belongs to the symmetric cryptosystems and can be used to cipher various kinds of plaintexts (text files, pictures, sound …) It is designed in the mathematical environment Matlab which enables flexible designing of prototypes and performing the cryptanalysis.

In this article a variant of a chaotic cryptosystem is described which has been adapted to ciphering and deciphering digital images. Its principal structure is shown in figure 14. The unit to be encrypted is represented by the pixel $i(n)$ on the image. The pixel is represented by three component intensities of primary colours: red $i_{red}(n)$, green $i_{green}(n)$ and blue $i_{blue}(n)$. Each component is represented by an 8-bit number.

Within a single encryption cycle all three components of an individual pixel are ciphered with three equal encryption functions. At the selected number of iterations of the encryption function N the cryptosystem ciphers the pixel $i(n)$ into pixel $s(n)$.

The pseudo random values are formed by three chaotic sate variables of the model of Chua's Circuit $x(n)$, $y(n)$ and $z(n)$. According to the necessary condition of inversion of the encryption and decryption algorithms, described by the equation (12), the state variables x, y and z are properly normalized.

The samples of the plaintext, ciphertext and the secret keys are values, represented by a number of bits in the digital cryptosystems. In the prototype realization of our cryptosystem, individual samples of the plaintext and random values $x(n)$, $y(n)$ and $z(n)$ were treated as double precision numbers, limited to the interval $(-h, h)$.

The secret key is composed of the values of the Chua's Circuit parameters: α, β, m_1-m_5, c_1-c_5, the initial values of the state variables $x(0)$, $y(0)$, $z(0)$ and the number of iterations N of the non-linear function f_1.

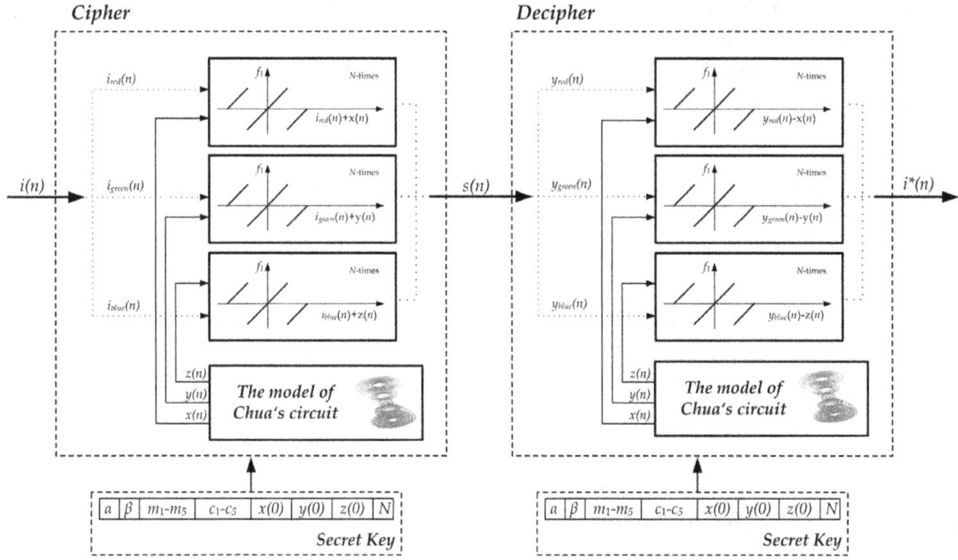

Fig. 14. The structure of the chaotic cryptosystem.

The encryption procedure is as follows: the random value $(x(n), y(n), z(n))$ is added to the n-sample of a plaintext $(i_{red}(n), i_{green}(n), i_{blue}(n))$. After N iterations have been carried out, the n-sample of the ciphertext $s(n)$ is generated by the function f_1. It is then transformed into the decrypted sample $i^*(n)$, being only equal to the original sample $i(n)$ if the key used at decryption equals the secret key used by encryption.

In cryptosystems the secret key is an optional value, represented by a definite number of bits. This is not valid for our cryptosystem as we have not ensured safe encryption with arbitrary values of its parameters. Safe encryption could only be ensured by providing automatic elimination or disabling of those circuit parameters where the circuit would not behave chaotically. In this article we did not deal with the automatic generation of suitable secret keys. The secret keys were adequate and carefully chosen values.

4.3 Cryptanalysis

We do not only wish to present the cryptographic features of our cryptosystem by cryptanalysis. Above all, we wish to present the problems which can be expected in systems of this kind.

In the cryptanalysis we have mostly kept to discussing some statistical characteristics. We have carried out the statistical analysis of ciphertexts, and on the basis of the statistical distribution of the ciphertext we made inferences as to their being random. We carried out an even more detailed analysis of the ciphertext with auto-covariance and cross-covariance, thus searching for possible correlation between ciphertexts and plaintexts as well as the correlation among various ciphertexts.

4.3.1 Statistical analysis of ciphertexts

In the statistical analysis of ciphertexts we mainly focused on the statistical distributions of their samples. The ciphertext samples must be uniformly distributed in order to be equally probable. In such case they will enable no conclusions about any kind of corresponding plaintext information.

In the following part of the article the cryptanalysis is presented where a digital image with dimensions 640x320, format JPG, shown in figure 15a, was used as the plaintext. As the random number generator we used the Chua's Circuit with the parameters: $a=9$, $\beta=9.9$, $m_0=0.9/7$, $m_1=-3/7$, $m_2=3.5/7$, $m_3=-2/7$, $m_4=4/7$, $m_5=-2.4/7$, $c_1=1$, $c_2=2.15$, $c_3=3.6$, $c_4=6.2$, $c_5=9$ and the initial conditions: $x(0)=0.5$, $y(0)=0$, $z(0)=0$.

The figures 15b-d show encrypted images with corresponding histograms at different numbers of iteration of the encryption function $N=1$, $N=10$ and $N=1000$. It is evident from the figure 15b that uniformly distributed values of the ciphertext cannot be obtained at $N=1$. Encryption with $N=1$ is not secure enough. Obtained results are comparable to the results achieved by the analog chaotic masking technique.

As the number N increases, the distribution of the ciphertext approaches to the uniform distribution, thus showing the need for the highest possible number of iterations of the encryption function. A higher number of iterations mean a longer lasting encryption procedure, but it also ensures decreased statistic dependence between plaintext and ciphertexts.

The analysis of the ciphertext histograms does not enable a more detailed insight into the characteristics of the ciphertext patterns and their correlations with patterns of the corresponding plaintext. This is the reason why we proceeded with the cryptanalysis with correlational and covariance analysis, respectively.

4.3.2 Auto-covariance and cross-covariance analysis

For better understanding let us first observe some basic features of the auto-correlation and cross-correlation. The cross-correlation of M samples of the random sequence $x(n)$ and $y(n)$ is defined by the equation:

$$\varphi_{xy}(m)=\begin{cases}\sum_{n=0}^{M-m-1} x(n)\cdot y(n+m), & m\geq 0\\ \varphi_{yx}(-m), & m<0\end{cases}, \tag{14}$$

where n and m are arguments limited within intervals: $0\leq n\leq M-1$ and $-(M-1)\leq m\leq (M-1)$. Auto-correlation is a special case of the cross-correlation, therefore it can be written on the basis of the equation (14):

$$\varphi_{xx}(m)=\begin{cases}\sum_{n=0}^{M-m-1} x(n)\cdot x(n+m), & m\geq 0\\ \varphi_{xx}(-m), & m<0\end{cases}. \tag{15}$$

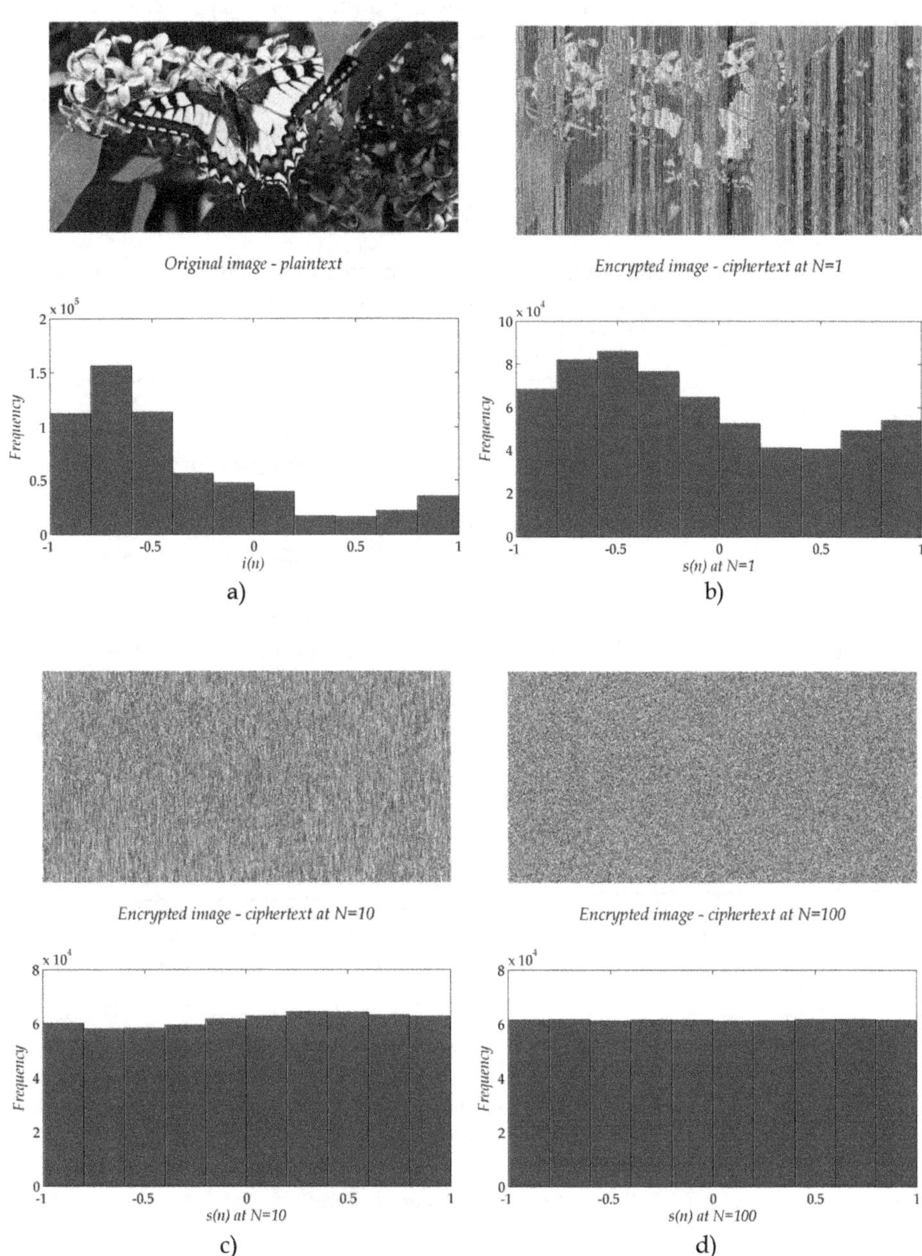

Fig. 15. a) Original image (plaintext) and its histogram. Encrypted images with the corresponding histograms at: b) N=1, c) N=10, d) N=100.

In the theory of probability and statistics covariance is also frequently used beside the correlation. The cross-covariance of the sequences $x(n)$ and $y(n)$ equals their cross-correlation if their mean value is eliminated from the sequences $x(n)$ and $y(n)$. It is described by the following equation:

$$c_{xy}(m) = \begin{cases} \sum_{n=0}^{M-m-1} \left(x(n) - \frac{1}{M} \sum_{i=0}^{M-1} x_i \right) \cdot \left(y(n+m) - \frac{1}{M} \sum_{i=0}^{M-1} y_i \right), & m \geq 0 \\ c_{yx}(-m), & m < 0 \end{cases} . \tag{16}$$

In the case of statistically completely independent sequences $x(n)$ and $y(n)$ the values of the cross-covariance for each argument m are equal zero. The more the sequences are correlated, the higher are the values of their cross-covariance.

The auto-covariance $c_{xx}(m)$ of the sequence $x(n)$ is only a special case of the cross-covariance. Its features are as follows:

- if the sequence $x(n)$ is periodical, its auto-covariance is also a periodical function $c_{xx}(m)$, retaining the period of the sequence $x(n)$;
- if the sequence $x(n)$ is random, its auto-covariance is an even function $c_{xx}(m)=c_{xx}(-m)$ and has the following characteristics: at the argument $m=0$ it has its maximum, at an infinite argument it equals zero $c_{xx}(\pm\infty) = 0$, which means that »the beginning« and »the end« of the random function $x(n)$ are statistically independent or non-correlated. There is no causal relationship between them or, »the end« of the sequence does not remember its »beginning«.

In cryptography the characteristics of the auto-covariance and cross-covariance can be used for a more detailed analysis of the ciphertext and their dependence of plaintext. In this way we can also make conclusions about the security which can be provided by an encryption system.

In the figure 16 the results of the covariance analysis with three different numbers of iterations of the encryption function N=1, N=10 and N=100 are shown. The blue graphs represent the auto-covariance of the ciphertexts, shown in figures 15b-d, the red graphs represent the cross-covariance of the same ciphertexts with the plaintext shown in figure 15a.

The auto-covariance of the ciphertexts obtained by encryption of the same plaintext at different numbers of iterations of the encryption function show that the ciphertexts are the more statistically independent the higher is the number of iterations. On the other hand, the cross-covariance of the ciphertext and the corresponding plaintext show that at N=1 we are dealing with a slightly emphasized statistical dependence of the original and encrypted image which decreases with the increasing number of iterations. At N=10 and N=100 the cross-covariance is very close to the zero value.

In the following part of the cryptanalysis we analysed the dependence of the statistical characteristics of ciphertexts on the secret key. Namely, the encryption system must ensure independence and insensitivity of the ciphertext to the selected secret key.

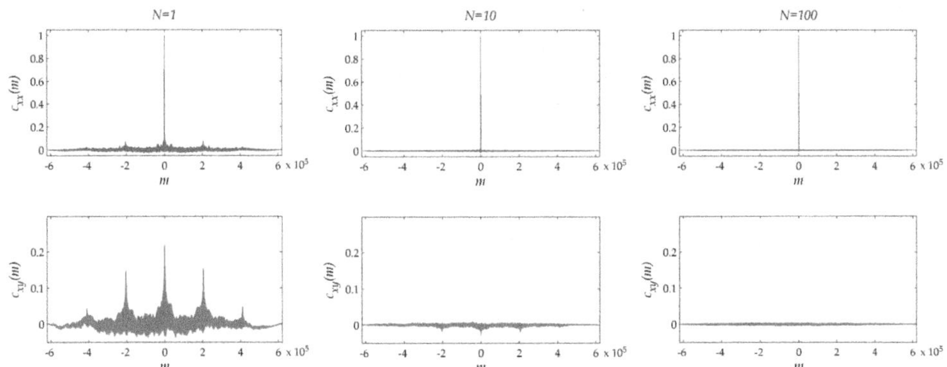

Fig. 16. Normalized auto-covariance $c_{xx}(m)$ of the ciphertexts, shown in figures 15b-d and their cross-covariance $c_{xy}(m)$ with the plaintext shown in figure 15a, at different numbers of iterations of the encryption function N=1, N=10 and N=100.

Example 1

We have analysed the differences between two ciphertexts A and B, obtained at the encryption of the same plaintext (figure 15a) with two very similar secret keys. They only differed from each other in the initial state of the chaotic state variable y. The initial state in the case of the ciphertext A was: $x(0)=0.5$, $y(0)=0$, $z(0)=0$, in the case of the ciphertext B it was: $x(0)=0.5$, $y(0)=10^{-12}$, $z(0)=0$. The rest of the secret key parameters were the same in both cases: $a=9$, $\beta=9.9$, $m_0=0.9/7$, $m_1=-3/7$, $m_2=3.5/7$, $m_3=-2/7$, $m_4=4/7$, $m_5=-2.4/7$, $c_1=1$, $c_2=2.15$, $c_3=3.6$, $c_4=6.2$, $c_5=9$, $N=100$.

Figure 17 illustrates the results of the encryption: ciphertext A (figure 17a), ciphertext B (figure 17b) and the difference between them (figure 17c).

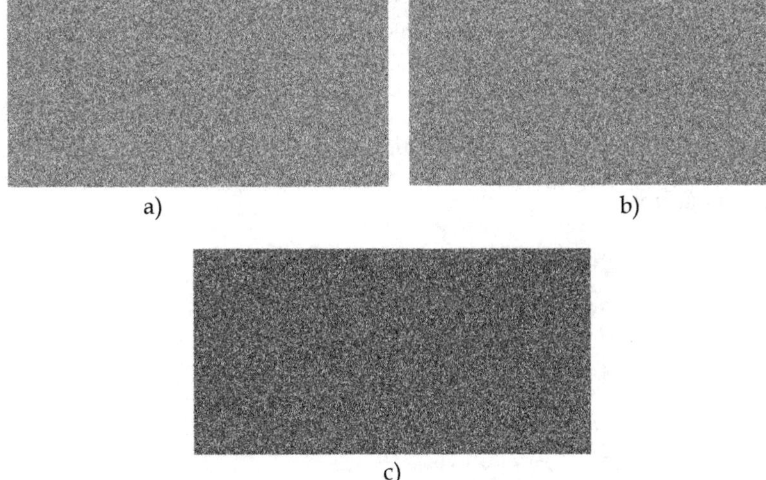

Fig. 17. a) Ciphertext A at $y(0)=0$; b) Ciphertext B at $y(0)=10^{-12}$; c) The difference between the ciphertexts A and B.

The difference between ciphertext A and B is practically imperceptible. In spite of this, the figure 17c showing the difference between both images, enables us to see an exposed area. The reason for this area is a very small initial difference between the pseudo-random sequences which do not start to diverge more quickly till after a certain time and several generated values, respectively.

Although the behaviour of the Chua's Circuit is very sensitive to the change of the initial conditions, the chaotic sequences begin to diverge noticeably only after several thousand samples which is clearly shown in figure 18.

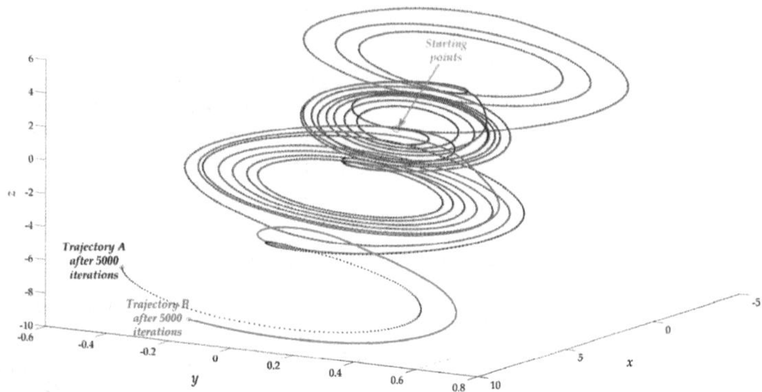

Fig. 18. Sensitivity to the initial conditions in the case of the trajectories A and B.

The figure shows the trajectories A and B in the state space, which start very close together and diverge from each other considerably after a certain time. This is the reason why the initial several thousand samples of the ciphertext A and B are very similar (black dots in image 17c). As the divergence of the trajectories depends on the size of the Lyapunov exponent value, we wish it to be as large as possible.

Example 2

In this case the encryption was carried out in the same way as in the example 1, but we left out the initial 20000 samples of the chaotic state variables. Thus we ensured a large divergence of the trajectories A and B at the very beginning of the encryption. The results are shown in figure 19.

Fig. 19. The difference between the ciphertexts A and B. The initial 20000 samples of random sequences, generated with a model of the Chua's Circuit, were left out.

The difference between the ciphertexts A and B (figure 19) shows that the similarity area of the ciphertexts, which was evident before, has disappeared. This can be more accurately evaluated with a cross-covariance of both ciphertexts. For the purpose of comparison figure 20 shows the cross-covariance of the ciphertexts A and B for both examples described above.

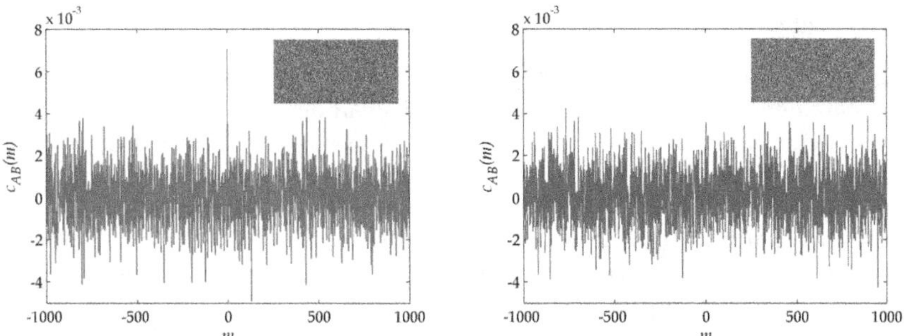

Fig. 20. Cross-covariance of the ciphertexts from examples 1 and 2, respectively.

In the first example (red graph) the aberrated cross-covariance value at the argument m=0 is noticeable, proving the initial correlativity of the compared ciphertexts. This is the consequence of the fact that the initial divergence of the pseudo-random sequences used was too slow. In the second example (blue graph) we do not notice any evident correlativity of the ciphertexts A and B, as the initial 20000 very similar or even equal samples of pseudo-random sequences were left out before the beginning of the encryption.

5. Conclusion

Chaotic electronic circuits generate chaotic, non-periodic signals. With an appropriate correction they can be modified into truly random signals, useful in cryptography. In the article we present the alternative for the random number generation with the chaotic Chua's circuit. We found out, that the basic variant of the Chua's circuit is not able to generate uniformly distributed random signals. Equally applies also for the modified Chua's circuit with 3-, 4-, 5-scroll chaotic attractors. Lyapunov exponent analysis points out that a sensitivity of the Chua's circuit to initial conditions increases with the complexity of chaotic attractors.

If the initial conditions of chaotic state variables represent the parts of secret key, in a cryptographic sense, a sensitivity to initial conditions should be as large as possible. Therefore, we have chosen for the random number generator, the variant of Chua's circuit with 5-scroll chaotic attractors. With the digital model of this circuit and the appropriate recursive function we have designed the cryptographic system adapted for a digital images encryption. For an individual image pixel encryption we have used three available chaotic state variables. Theirs uniform distribution was assured with the additional recursive function used for an encryption. The secret key could not be an arbitrary value but an adequate and a carefully chosen value consisting of the Chua's circuit parameters, initial conditions and a number of encryption function iterations. Namely, the bifurcation diagrams and Lyapunov exponents show that the Chua's circuit only behaves chaotically at certain values of components and parameters.

From a cryptographic point of view uniformly distributed ciphertexts are always required. In our crypto system, we could satisfy this requirement only by using an additional recursive function with a large enough number of its iterations. In such cases, the auto-covariance of ciphertexts was always very close or equal to the zero value. Similar conclusions were reached also in the ciphertexts cross-covariance analysis with the corresponding plaintexts. Statistical independence of ciphertext and plaintext samples was assured only with a large enough number of encryption iterations.

One of the essential properties of all chaotic systems is a high sensitivity to initial conditions and some parameters. Despite of the infinitesimal small deviation of two initial conditions, the Chua's circuit generates signals with several thousand very similar initial time-values. This is obviously undesirable, since each of so small secret key changes, should be reflected with a very large ciphertext change. Thus, the problem of ciphertexts initial similarity appears by encryption with the very similar secret keys. In our case, we have analysed this problem with a cross-covariance of ciphertexts. By elimination of the initial 20000 chaotic values the problem was completely resolved.

In the paper, we have pointed out the problems that may occur when the chaotic circuits are using in the cryptographic systems. Described problems can be avoided by appropriate automatic secret keys generation, which requires precise knowledge of the chaotic circuit behaviour and the properties of encryption function.

Automatic secret keys generation for a chaotic cryptographic system can be a challenge for a further research work that links two interesting areas: deterministic chaos and cryptography.

6. References

Bianco, M. E. & Reed, D. A. (1991). *Encryption system based on chaos theory*. US Patent No. 5048086, (September 1991), USA

Chua, L. O.; Komuro, M. & Matsumoto, T. (1986). The double scroll family. *IEEE Transactions on Circuits and Systems*, Vol.33, No.11, (November 1986), pp. 1072-1118, ISSN 0098-4094

Chua, L. O.; Wu, C. W.; Huang, A. & Zhong (1993). A universal circuit for studying and generating chaos. I. Routes to chaos. *IEEE Transactions on Circuits and Systems I: Fundamental Theory and Applications*, Vol.40, No.10, (October 1993), pp. 732-744, ISSN 1057-7122

Corron, N. J. & Hahs D. W. (1997). A new approach to communications using chaotic signals. *IEEE Transactions on Circuits and Systems I: Fundamental Theory and Applications*, Vol.44, No.5, (May 1997), pp. 373-382, ISSN 1057-7122

Cuomo, K. M.; Oppenheim, A. V. & Strogatz, S. H. (1993). Synchronization of Lorenz-based chaotic circuits with applications to communications. *IEEE Transactions on Circuits and Systems-II: Analog and Digital Signal Processing*, Vol.40, No.10, (October 1993), pp. 626-633, ISSN 1057-7130

Dedieu, H.; Kennedy, M. & Hasler, M. (1993). Chaos shift keying: modulation and demodulation of a chaotic carrier using self-synchronizing Chua's circuits. *IEEE Transactions on Circuits and Systems-II: Analog and Digital Signal Processing*, Vol.40, No.10, (October 1993), pp. 634-642, ISSN 1057-7130

Fortuna, L.; Frasca, M. & Xibilia, M. G. (2009). *Chua's Circuit Implementations – Yesterday, Today and Tomorrow*. World Scientific Publishing Co. Pte. Ltd., ISBN-13 978-981-283-924-4, Danvers, USA

Fridrich, J. (1998). Symmetric Ciphers Based on Two-Dimensional Chaotic Maps. *International Journal of Bifurcation and Chaos*, Vol.8, No.6, (June 1998), pp. 1259-1284, ISSN 0218-1274

Gao, Z. (1997). *Method and apparatus for encrypting and decrypting information using a digital chaos signal*. US Patent No. 5696826, (December 1997), USA

Hilborn, R. C. (2000). *Chaos and Nonlinear Dynamics, An Introduction for Scientists and Engineers, Second Edition*, Oxford University Press, ISBN 0198507232, New York, USA

Hongtao, L. & Zhenya, H. (1996). Chaotic Behavior in First-Order Autonomous Continuous-Time Systems with Delay. *IEEE Transactions on Circuits and Systems I: Fundamental Theory and Applications*, Vol.43, No.8, (August 1996), pp. 700-702, ISSN 1057-7122

Kennedy, M. P. (1993). Three steps to chaos. I. Evolution. *IEEE Transactions on Circuits and Systems I: Fundamental Theory and Applications*, Vol.40, No.10, (October 1993), pp. 640-656, ISSN 1057-7122

Kennedy, M. P. (1993). Three steps to chaos. II. A Chua's circuit primer. *IEEE Transactions on Circuits and Systems I: Fundamental Theory and Applications*, Vol.40, No.10, (October 1993), pp. 657-674, ISSN 1057-7122

Kennedy, M. P. (1994). Chaos in the Colpitts oscillator. *IEEE Transactions on Circuits and Systems I: Fundamental Theory and Applications*, Vol.41, No.11, (November 1994), pp. 771-774, ISSN 1057-7122

Kocarev, L. (2001). Chaos-based cryptography: a brief overview. *IEEE Circuits and System Magazine*, Vol.1, No.3, (Third Quarter 2001), pp. 6-21, ISSN 1531-636X

Kocarev, L. & Lian, S. (2011). *Chaos-Based Cryptography Theory, Algorithms and Applications*. Springer-Verlag, ISBN 978-3-642-20541-5, Berlin, Germany

Koh, C. L. & Ushio, T. (1997). Digital communication method based on M-synchronized chaotic systems. *IEEE Transactions on Circuits and Systems I: Fundamental Theory and Applications*, Vol.44, No.5, (May 1997), pp. 383-390, ISSN 1057-7122

Kolumban, G. & Vizvari, B. (1994). Nonlinear dynamics and chaotic behavior of the sampling phase-locked loop. *IEEE Transactions on Circuits and Systems I: Fundamental Theory and Applications*, Vol.41, No.4, (April 1994), pp. 333-337, ISSN 1057-7122

Ogorzalek, M. J. (1993). Taming chaos. I. Synchronization. *IEEE Transactions on Circuits and Systems I: Fundamental Theory and Applications*, Vol.40, No.10, (October 1993), pp. 693-699, ISSN 1057-7122

Ogorzalek, M. J. (1997). *Chaos and complexity in nonlinear electronic circuits*. World Scientific Publishing Co. Pte. Ltd., ISBN 981-02-2873-2, Danvers, USA

Schneier, B. (1996). *Applied cryptography: protocols, algorithms, and source code in C*. John Wiley and Sons, ISBN 0471128457, Canada

Sharkovsky, A. N. & Chua, L. O. (1993). Chaos in some 1-D discontinuous maps that appear in the analysis of electrical circuits. *IEEE Transactions on Circuits and Systems I: Fundamental Theory and Applications*, Vol.40, No.10, (October 1993), pp. 722-731, ISSN 1057-7122

Sprott, J. C. (2009). *Chaos and Time-Series Analysis*. Oxford University Press, ISBN 978-0-19-850839-7, New York, USA

Stallings, W. (1999). *Cryptography and Network Security Principles and Practice, Second Edition*. Prentice-Hall, ISBN 0138690170, Upper Saddle River, New Jersey USA

Suykens, J. A. K. & Vandewalle, J. (1993). Generation of n-Double Scrolls (n = 1, 2, 3, 4, ...). *IEEE Transactions on Circuits and Systems I: Fundamental Theory and Applications*, Vol.40, No.11, (November 1993), pp. 861-867, ISSN 1057-7122

Šalamon, M. & Dogša, T. (1995). Analysis of chaos in the Chua's oscillator. *Electrotechnical review: journal of electrical engineering and computer science*, Vol.62, No.1, (October 1995), pp. 50-58, ISSN 0013-5852

Šalamon, M. & Dogša, T. (2000). Danger of Chaos in a second-order Digital Filter. *Informacije MIDEM - Journal of microelectronics, electronic components and materials*, Vol.30, No.1, (March 2000), pp. 37-42, ISSN 0352-9045

Šalamon, M. & Dogša, T. (2002). A comparative analysis of chaotic encryption systems with the XOR encryption function and multishift encryption function. *Electrotechnical review: journal of electrical engineering and computer science*, Vol.69, No.2, (June 2002), pp. 107-112, ISSN 0013-5852

Šalamon, M. & Dogša, T. (2009). The model of chaoticness detector. *Informacije MIDEM - Journal of microelectronics, electronic components and materials*, Vol.39, No.2, (June 2009), pp. 93-99, ISSN 0352-9045

Yang, T. & Chua, L. O. (1996). Secure communication via chaotic parameter modulation. *IEEE Transactions on Circuits and Systems I: Fundamental Theory and Applications*, Vol.43, No.9, (May 1997), pp. 817-819, ISSN 1057-7122

Yang, T.; Chai, W. W. & Chua, L. O. (1997). Cryptography based on chaotic systems. *IEEE Transactions on Circuits and Systems I: Fundamental Theory and Applications*, Vol.44, No.5, (May 1997), pp. 469 - 472, ISSN 1057-7122

13

Notions of Chaotic Cryptography: Sketch of a Chaos Based Cryptosystem

Pellicer-Lostao Carmen and López-Ruiz Ricardo
Department of Computer Science and BIFI, University of Zaragoza, Spain

1. Introduction

Chaotic cryptography describes the use of *chaos theory* (in particular physical dynamical systems working in chaotic regime as part of communication techniques and computation algorithms) to perform different cryptographic tasks in a cryptographic system.

Then, we can start by answering the questions: what exactly is chaos?, how is it used in cryptography?. First of all, let us say that there is not an universally mathematical accepted definition of the term "chaos". In general sense, it refers to some dynamical phenomena considered to be complex (lack of time and spatial order) and unpredictable (erratic). Although it was precluded by Poincaré at the end of the XIX century (Poincaré, 1890), chaos theory begins to take form in the second half of the XX century (Lorenz, 1963; Mandelbrot, 1977) after observations of the evolution of different physical systems. These systems revealed that despite of the knowledge of their evolution rules and initial conditions, their future seemed to be arbitrary and unpredictable. That opened quite a revolution in modern physics, terminating with Laplace's ideas of casual determinism (Laplace, 1825).

Chaos has been observed in nature, in weather and climate (Sneyers, 1997), population growth in ecology (May & McLean, 2007), economy (Kyrtsou & Vorlow, 2005), to mention only a few examples. It also has been observed in the laboratory in a number of systems such as electrical circuits (van der Pol & van der Mark, 1927), lasers (Casperson, 1988), chemical reactions, fluid dynamics, mechanical systems, and magneto-mechanical devices.

In essence, chaos theory studies systems that evolve in time presenting three particular properties of movement: sensitivity to initial conditions (dynamical instability), stretching and folding of the phase space (topological mixing) and aperiodic trajectories arbitrary close to an infinite set of periodic orbits (dense orbits). Chaos theory provides the means to explain chaos phenomena, control and make use of chaotic dynamical systems.

A remarkable characteristic of chaotic systems is their capability of producing quite complex patterns of behavior. This is done from simple real systems or in simulations from low dimensional systems given by a small set of evolution equations. This quality has made them particularly useful for application in a wide variety of disciplines, such as biology, economics, engineering and others (Cambel, 1993; Kocarev et al., 2009). In these applications, chaotic systems are used to produce, simulate, assist or control different processes improving their performance or providing a more suitable output.

The use of chaos in cryptography seems quite natural, as its inherent properties connect it directly with cryptographic characteristics of *confusion* and *diffusion*. This idea is present in Shannon's works (Shannon, 1949), even earlier than the term "chaos" appeared in scientific literature. Additionally, chaotic dynamical systems have the advantage of providing qualitatively simple mechanisms to generate deterministic pseudo randomness. For cryptography, this could be the promise of producing simpler or better randomness in terms of performance (Tenny et al., 2006).

By now, the history of chaos-based cryptography is more than two decades long. First, some works appear in the 80's (Wolfram, 1985; Guan, 1987), but it is in the 90's, when chaotic cryptography really takes off. Two papers mark this beginning (Matews, 1989) and (Pecora, 1989). The first one proposes a digital stream cipher where a signal generated from a chaotic system is used to mask the clear message. The second proposes chaos synchronization to mask the clear message with a chaotic signal at the physical level of the communication channel and to use synchronization techniques at the receiver to filter the chaotic signal. These two papers also open two different views of the application of chaos to cryptography that will be later referred as digital or analog techniques (Alvarez & Li, 2006).

Since then, the number of chaotic cryptosystems that have been proposed is too large to be covered in this chapter. The interested reader can find a complete and updated view of this field in (Kocarev, 2011). In addition, for more recent developments, some time is also needed to assess their security. Nevertheless these works have been published in journals of physics or engineering; they have revealed the potential of this field, but also a series of errors and weak points that need to be overcome. As a consequence, chaotic cryptography has been an active research field but with marginal impact in classical cryptography (Dachselt & Schwarz, 2001; Amigó, 2009).

In the end, the question is, can chaotic systems provide alternative techniques able to enhance cryptographic algorithms?. This chapter can be a worthy material to guide the reader in order to answer himself this question. Thus, the objective of this chapter is to give a general vision of what chaotic cryptography is and a comprehensive example that illustrates the main techniques used in this field. In it, the authors are intended to present a series of selected topics of special interest in this field.

In successive sections of this chapter the reader will be introduced to the following topics: fundamentals of chaos, relation between chaos and cryptography, different kinds of chaotic cryptosystems and their main characteristics, Pseudo-Random Number Generation (PRNG) based on digitized chaos, cipher design based on two dimensional chaotic maps, and the corresponding best practices and guidelines required for designing good cryptographic algorithms.

2. Chaos and cryptography

This section explains the basic concepts of chaos theory. Then, the focus is set on those properties that seem relevant for its application to cryptography. In particular, first it is given a conceptual introduction to chaotic systems, to follow with a practical approach through non-linear dynamical systems. The section concludes considering how chaos theory can be useful for cryptographic applications.

2.1 Basic properties of chaotic systems

Chaos has been observed in numerous natural and laboratory systems (Sneyers, 1997; May, 1976; Casperson, 1988; Kyrtsou & Vorlow, 2005; van der Pol & van der Mark, 1927) covering a substantial number of scientific and engineering areas (physics, biology, meteorology, ecology, electronics, computer science and economy, among others). These phenomena, as mentioned before, show specific properties that make them complex and unpredictable.

Chaos theory deals with systems that evolve in time with a particular kind of dynamical behaviour. As this is a vast mathematical theory, the interested reader is addressed to (Robinson, 1995) for a broader introduction. In general, these systems obey a certain set of laws of evolution, and so, they are deterministic. It has to be said, that chaos occurs only in some deterministic non-linear systems. Explicitly, chaos appears when there is a sustained and disorderly-looking long-term evolution that satisfies certain mathematical criteria.

There is a set of properties that summarize the characteristics observed in chaotic systems. These are considered the mathematical criteria that define chaos. The most relevant are:

- **Dynamic instability:** also referred as butterfly effect, it is the property of sensitivity to initial conditions, where two arbitrarily closed initial conditions evolve with significantly different and divergent trajectories (Boguta, 2011).
- **Topological mixing**: intuitively depicted as mixing coloured dyes, it means that the system will evolve in time so that any given region of states is always transformed or overlaps with any other given region (Mahieu, 2011).
- **Aperiodicity**: the system evolves in an orbit that never repeats on itself, that is, these orbits are never periodic (Zech et al., 2011).
- **Dense periodic orbits**: it means that the system follows a dynamics that can arbitrarily closely approach every possible asymptotic state.
- **Ergodicity:** statistical measurements of the variables give similar results no matter if they are performed over time or space. Put it in another way, the dynamics shows similar statistics when measured over time or space.
- **Self-similarity:** the evolution of the system, in time or space, shows the same appearance at different scales of observation. This characteristic makes the system to appear auto-repetitive at different scales of observation (Fabre, 2011).

The references included above show interactive demonstrations of these properties. The following section introduces some notions of non-linear dynamical systems.

2.2 Non-linear dynamical systems (NLDS)

A dynamical system is a physical phenomenon that evolves in time. In mathematical terms, the states of the system are described by a set of variables and its evolution is given by an equation and the value of the initial state. This is summarized in Eq. (1),

$$\frac{dX_i(t)}{dt} = F_i(X_j(t), \Lambda) \tag{1}$$

where $X_i(t)\in R^N$ is the coordinate i of the state of the system at instant t, that is X is an N-dimensional vector with $i,j=0,1,\ldots N$ with $N\geq 1$, F is a parametric function that describes the evolution of the system and Λ is the vector of parameters that control the evolution of the system.

As chaotic systems only occur in non-linear dynamical systems, F will be considered to be non-linear. For digital cryptographic applications we centre our attention on discrete-time NLDS. Then, a *discrete-time NLDS* is given by the following equation:

$$X_{i+1} = F(X_i, \Lambda) \tag{2}$$

The significance of the mathematical symbols in Eq. (2) is the same as in Eq. (1) but now the time t is discrete. It is observed that this kind of systems is deterministic, thus the time evolution of X can be calculated with F and Λ from a given initial state X_0. They are also *recursive*, as the next state is calculated from the previous state.

There are a series of concepts or terms that are of special interest in the study of NLDS. The first one is the *phase space* that is the subspace of R^N, where all possible states of the system are confined:

$$U \subset R^N \text{ and } F: U \rightarrow U, \tag{3}$$

where N is the dimension of the phase space or *degree of freedom* of the system. The evolution in space of an initial state when time passes is called *orbit*. As we are considering F a discrete-time function, the orbits of these systems will be a collection of real pairs of numbers:

$$(t_0, X_0), (t_1, F(X_0)), \ldots, (t_i, F_i(X_0)), \ldots \tag{4}$$

Then there is the central concept in chaos theory, the *attractor*. The term attractor refers to the long-term behavior of the orbits, and it represents the region of phase space where the orbits of the system converge after the transitory. The attractor A is a compact region where all orbits converge and where the system gets trapped,

$$A \subset U \quad \text{and } A = F(A). \tag{5}$$

Geometrically, an attractor can be a point, a curve, a manifold, or even a complicated set with a fractal structure known as a *strange attractor*. A brief description of them is given:

- **Fixed point,** it corresponds to a stationary state of the system.
- **Limit cycle,** which is associated with a periodic behaviour of the system. Once the system enters this attractor the states of the system repeat periodically.
- **Manifold,** where there are more than one frequency in the periodic trajectories of the system. For example, in the case of two frequencies, the attractor is a 2D-torus.
- **Strange attractor,** it is informally said to have a complex geometric shape with non-integer dimension. Any state in the attractor evolves within it and never converges to a fixed point, limit cycle or manifold. The dynamics on this attractor is normally chaotic, but there exist also strange attractors that are not chaotic (Mahieu, 2011).

After reviewing the main characteristic of NLDS, one could define the term *chaotic system* as a NLDS that have at least a chaotic strange attractor.

NLDS are usually studied only in a qualitative and computational way, as opposed to the study of linear systems, where there is a set of analytical tools (Devaney, 1989). Different models of N-dimensional discrete-time mappings have been studied, and under certain circumstances complex behaviour in time evolution has been shown. The 1-dimensional cases have been deeper analyzed (Collet & Eckmann, 1980), cases of N=2 have also several well explored examples (Mira et al., 1996) and (López-Ruiz & Fournier-Prunaret, 2003), but as N increases, the complexity grows and less literature is found with a well documented analysis of the chaotic properties of the mapping (Fournier-Prunaret et al., 2006).

In chaotic cryptography the behaviour of the dynamical system is fully studied to assess the security of the cryptosystem. Due to the nature of NLDS, chaotic cryptography does not have analytic tools, as those that exist in classical cryptography. Then, qualitative techniques have to be applied in chaotic cryptoanalysis. In particular, the study of the sensitivity to the initial conditions and to the control parameters is considered of importance. Normally these elements are also a key part of the cryptosystem.

a. Assessing the sensitivity to initial conditions

Lyapunov exponents are used as a quantifier of the divergence of the orbits in NLDS. N exponents can be calculated for a N-dimensional system. These exponents allow us to decide if the dynamical system has sensitivity to initial conditions. A system is considered to be chaotic when it has a dense aperiodic orbit, and at least the higher of the Lyapunov exponents is positive.

The study of the value of *Lyapunov exponents* as a function of the control parameters (vector Λ in Eq. (2)) is a matter of interest as it allows to discover windows of non chaotic behaviour of the system, where periodic patterns may appear.

b. Assessing the sensitivity to control parameters

Chaotic systems are also sensitive to the variation of the control parameters (vector Λ in Eq. (2)). This dependence may produce completely different dynamics in the system (chaotic, periodic, divergent, etc...) depending on the values of Λ. A substantial change in the dynamics of the system due to a variation of the values of the control parameters is called a *bifurcation* (Mahieu, 2011).

The *bifurcations diagrams* are used to study the dynamics of the system as a function of the values of Λ. These unfolding diagrams allow knowing the regions of the phase space where the system displays chaotic or regular behaviour, depending on the values of the control parameters.

2.3 Connection between chaos and cryptography

As it has been said previously, the main characteristics of chaotic systems make them intuitively interesting for their application in cryptography. Here, this connection is explored in more detail.

Chaotic systems are implemented with deterministic NLDS, being able to produce the deterministic pseudo-randomness required in cryptography. In addition to that, NLDS are able to produce complex patterns of evolution. This gives to chaotic systems the algorithmic complexity required in cryptographic systems.

Now, let us examine how the inherent properties of chaos connect it directly with cryptographic characteristics of *confusion* and *diffusion* (Shannon, 1949). Referring to the properties discussed of chaotic systems, it is clear that the properties of ergodicity, auto-similarity, topological mixing are directly connected with confusion. The dynamics in the chaotic attractor is given by aperiodic orbits that generate similar statistical patterns. These patterns can be used to mask clear messages by means of substitution-like techniques.

On the other hand, diffusion is closely connected with the sensitivity that chaotic systems present to initial conditions and control parameters. Diffusion produces the avalanche effect, where a minimum difference in the input of the cryptosystem gives a completely different output. A chaotic system produces this behaviour when a small change is applied to its initial conditions or control parameters. The use of these variables as input in the cryptosystem algorithm may produce the same avalanche effect.

Table 1 obtained from (Alvarez & Li, 2006), summarizes the connection between chaos and cryptography.

Chaotic characteristic	**Cryptographic property**	**Description**
Ergodicity Mixing property Auto-similarity	Confusion	The output of the system seems similar for any intput
Sensitivity to initial conditions and control parameters	Difusion	A small diference in the input produces a very different output
Deterministic	Deterministic pseudorandomness	A deterministic procedure that produces pseudo-randomness
Complexity	Algorithmic complexity	A simple algorithm that produces highly complex outputs

Table 1. Comparisons of chaotic and cryptographic properties (from Alvarez & Li, 2006).

To conclude, it would be interesting to describe particular potential advantages that chaotic cryptosystems may provide to cryptography (Tenny et al., 2006). First of all, chaotic systems appear spontaneously in nature and can be directly applied to security processes, as it is the case of physical devices used in communications. Those show naturally non-linear and chaotic behaviours that can be straightforwardly used to secure communications.

Also chaotic NLDS have the advantage of being implemented with simple computable deterministic algorithms. Additionally these algorithms may refer to N-dimensional equations or to several systems combined at a time. They could be subject of implementation with parallel computing and become faster algorithms.

3. Chaotic based cryptosystems

This section presents two specific examples of chaotic based cryptosystems. Full versions of them can be found in (Pellicer-Lostao & López-Ruiz, 2008, 2009). These are specially suited to illustrate in detail some relevant techniques used in chaotic cryptography. In particular, they cover three interesting topics: Pseudo-Random Number Generation (PRNG) based on digitized chaos, cipher design based on two-dimensional chaotic maps and the role of symmetry and geometry of chaotic maps in encryption algorithms.

Along with that, an introduction provides a global (though not extensive) picture of different techniques used in chaotic cryptography.

3.1 Review of chaos based encryption techniques

The number of chaotic cryptosystems proposed in literature is too large and diverse to be covered in this chapter. Valuable overviews with corresponding references can be found in (Li, 2003; Kocarev, 2011). It is important as well, to have in mind that it is an active area of research and recent developments need some time to assess their security.

To keep this review sufficiently small and clear, it will only cover a general view of the main techniques and their basic concepts of operation. See Table 2 for a brief summary of them obtained from (Li, 2003). To conclude and provide a comprehensive background, a detailed description is dedicated to the specific technique used in the examples described later in this section.

CATEGORY	METHOD		DESCRIPTION
Analog cryptosystems	Additive chaos masking		A chaotic signal is added to the message
	Chaotic shift keying		A digital message signal switches among different chaotic systems to be added to the message
	Chaotic modulation		A message signal is used to change the parameters or the phase space of the chaotic transmitter
	Chaotic Control		A message signal is ciphered in a classical way and used to perturbate the chaotic system
Digital cryptosystems	Stream ciphers	Chaotic PRNG	A chaotic signal generates a pseudorandom sequence (keystream) to XORed the message
		Chaotic Inverse System approach	A message signal is added to the output of the chaotic signal, which has been feeded by the ciphered message signal in previous instants
	Block ciphers	Backwards iterative	A block of a clear message is ciphered using of inverse chaotic systems
		Forwards iterative	A block of ciphered message is obtained by pseudoramdom permutations obtained from a chaotic system
		S-Boxes	An S-Box is created from the chaotic system. There can be dynamic or static S-Boxes
	Miscellaneous	Searching based chaotic ciphers	A table of characters is generated from a chaotic system. The table is used to cipher the characters of the message text
		Cell. Automata	The chaotic system is a Cellular Automata

Table 2. Different kinds of chaos based cryptosystems presented in literature (Li, 2003).

As it is seen in Table 2, the application of chaotic systems to cryptography has followed two main approaches. These have been called, analogue and digital techniques (Alvarez & Li, 2006). Let us discuss in further detail their principal concepts and features of operation.

a. Analogue chaos-based cryptosystems

These systems are mostly used to secure communications and have attracted very extensive research activity lately (Larson et al., 2006). In them, the clear message is masked with a chaotic signal at physical level of the communication channel. The natural non-linearity of electric and optical communication devices is controlled to produce a chaotic waveform that modulates the message in a secure way for transmission. At the receiver, chaotic synchronization techniques demodulate the signal and produce the clear message. Though no completely secure their implementation results straightforward.

Main techniques of chaotic modulation (Yang, 2004), described in Table 2, are shown in Fig.1

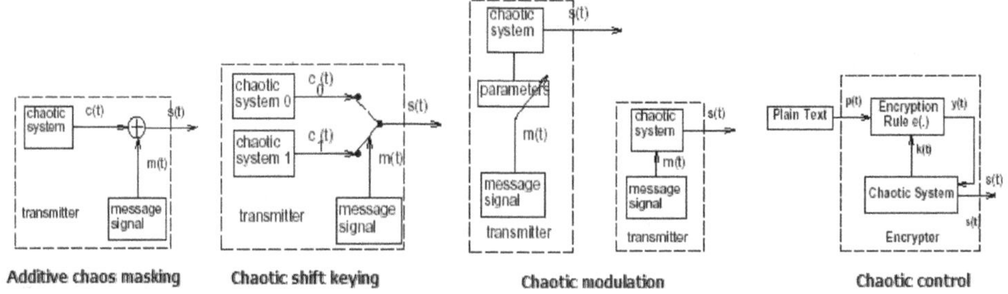

Fig. 1. Modulation techniques used in analogue chaotic cryptosystems (Yang, 2004).

Typically used in optical communications with high rates of transmission, synchronization techniques become critical, also due to the fact that chaotic performance implies highly sensitivity to small deviations. Here, a chaotic control signal is used to provide a synchronous performance of transmitter and receiver. Though not necessary to be equal (Femat et al., 2005), they require careful fabrication and operation within specific conditions.

These systems are not cryptographically secure (Larson et al., 2006), due to intrinsic limitations of their design. As it has been seen in previous section, chaotic signals are deterministic and though they appear to be random, they are intrinsically correlated. This means that patterns can be found in the communication signals that may allow an attacker to decipher the message. Even though, their technical complexity and high transmission rates makes them valuable for communications that only require security for a limited period of time.

b. Digital chaos-based cryptosystems

These cryptosystems are basically algorithms implemented in digital circuits or computers. These algorithms are based in iterative computations of chaotic functions that produce digital signals. Then, basic cryptographic operations (substitution and mixing) are used to mask the clear message with the chaotic signals. These cryptosystems involve one or more chaotic systems in the algorithm and use their initial conditions and/or control parameters as secret keys.

But chaos implemented on computers with finite precision may diverge from real-precision chaos. This is why it is normally called "pseudo chaos". In pseudo chaos, the chaotic properties of the system may suffer dynamical degradation, for pseudo orbits may depart from the real ones in many manners (Guckenheimer & Holmes, 1983; Li, 2003; Li et al, 2005). Even so, it is possible for these pseudo chaotic systems, to minimize their dynamical degradation. In this matter, the idea of using high dimensional chaotic systems may also be helpful. While less known, these systems whirl many variables at any calculation and the periodic patterns produced by the finite precision are diminished (Falcioni et al., 2005). Anyway, only a detailed study of the dynamical system may guarantee their performance.

Main techniques used here are algorithms that implement stream or block ciphers (Li, 2003). Understanding by them, the encryption of individual bits or blocks at a time, respectively. There are also miscellaneous systems that use characteristic techniques or systems and belong to specific families. As for security, cryptographers demand more rigorous studies of security in publications (Alvarez & Li, 2006). Also the novelty of chaotic cryptography shows a lack of tools for cryptanalysis as the ones of classical cryptography (Amigó, 2009).

c. Digital stream ciphers implemented with chaotic PRBG

Pseudo Random Bit Generation (PRBG) is a topic of high interest. As it is shown in Table 2, these are used in stream cipher encryption but they are also a subject of broad application in many scientific and engineering areas. This is why, since 1990 the proposals of chaos based PRBG have demonstrated great development (Kovarev, 2001; Kocarev & Jakimoski, 2003).

To build a chaotic PRBG, we take an N-dimensional deterministic discrete-time dynamical system. As seen in Eq. (2), it is an iterative map $f: R^N \rightarrow R^N$ of the form:

$$X_{k+1} = F(X_k, \Lambda) \tag{6}$$

where $k = 0, 1, \ldots, n$ is the discrete time, Λ vector of parameters, X_0 initial condition and $X_1, \ldots, X_n$ states of the system in the following instants of time. Then it is necessary to construct a numerical algorithm that transforms the states of the system into binary numbers. Additionally not all states of the orbit are used to produce the pseudo-random sequence. Normally the orbit is sampled in order to get rid of the correlation existent between consecutive states. The existing designs of chaotic PRBGs use different techniques to pass from the continuum to the binary world (Li, 2003). The most relevant are:

- **Extracting bits** from each state along the chaotic orbits (Protopopescu, 1995; Bodgan et al., 2007; Fournier-Prunaret &Abdel-Kaddous, 2012).
- **Dividing the phase space into m sub-spaces**, and output a binary number $i = 0, 1, \ldots, m$ if the chaotic orbit visits the i-th subspace (Stojanovski &Kocarev, 2001; Suneel,2009).
- **Combining the outputs of two or more chaotic systems** to generate the pseudo-random numbers (Li et al, 2001; Po et al., 2003).

The binary sequence generated with the chaotic PRBG algorithm is used as a keystream. To mask the clear message, the keystream is added to it through a binary XOR operation. The initial conditions and the vector of parameters are used as the secret key.

3.2 First example: Building a stream cipher based on 2D chaotic maps

This subsection presents an asymmetric or secret key chaotic cryptosystem. It describes a chaotic digital stream cipher. Its nucleus is a Pseudo-Random Bit Generation (PRBG) based on 2D chaotic mappings of logistic type (Pellicer-Lostao & López-Ruiz, 2008). This chaotic PRBG produces pseudorandom binary sequences out of the chaotic dynamics of the considered maps. The sequences produced are used as the keystream in the cipher.

To illustrate its implementation and functionality, the design of the chaotic PRBG algorithm is fully described and different evaluations are presented, such as statistical tests, predictability and speed measurements. Considering the application of this PRBG in cryptography, the size of the available key space is also calculated.

First let us see the chaotic systems that are going to be used in this example. In (López-Ruiz & Pérez-García, 1991) the authors analyze a family of three chaotic systems obtained by coupling two logistic maps. The focus here will be made on models (a) and (b), which will be referred as System A and B:

$$\begin{array}{ll} SISTEM\ A: & SISTEM\ B: \\ T_A:[0\ 1]\mathrm{x}[0\ 1]\to[0\ 1]\mathrm{x}[0\ 1] & T_B:[0\ 1]\mathrm{x}[0\ 1]\to[0\ 1]\mathrm{x}[0\ 1] \\ x_{n+1}=\lambda(3y_n+1)x_n(1-x_n) & x_{n+1}=\lambda(3x_n+1)y_n(1-y_n) \\ y_{n+1}=\lambda(3x_n+1)y_n(1-y_n) & y_{n+1}=\lambda(3y_n+1)x_n(1-x_n) \end{array} \qquad (7)$$

The interest of using these systems is their symmetry properties ($T_A(x,y) = T_B(y,x)$ and $T^2{}_A(x,y) = T^2{}_B(x,y)$) wich will be of used in 3.3 to improve the algorithm. From a geometrical point of view, both present the same chaotic attractor in the interval $\lambda \in [1.032\ \ 1.0843]$. The parameter λ in Eq. (7), could be considered different for the calculus of x and y coordinates. This would give two independent control parameters λ_x and λ_y, which in a similar range *[1.032, 1.0843]* maintain the system in a chaotic regime due to its structural stability. The dynamics in this regime (Pellicer-Lostao & López-Ruiz, 2011a) is particularly interlaced around the saddle point *P4*:

$$P4=\left[P4_x,\ P4_y\right]\ P4_x=P4_y=\frac{1}{3}\left(1+\sqrt{4-\frac{3}{\lambda}}\right) \qquad (8)$$

Despite of the similarities of these systems, their dynamics have some differences. In Fig. 2 one can see one orbit and its spectrum for both systems with equal initial conditions.

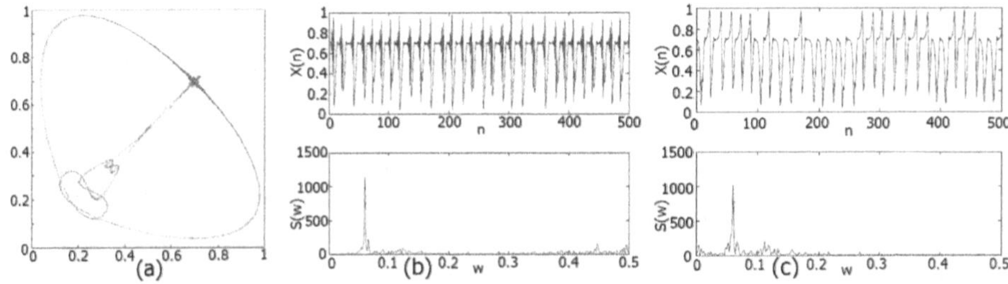

Fig. 2. Chaotic Attractor with λ= 1.07 , X_0=[0.737,0.747] for System A in (a). Orbit $x(n)$ and spectrum $S(w)$ for and Systems A and B in (b) and (c) respectively for the same λ and X_0.

Second, let us present the algorithm used to obtain the Symmetric Coupled Logistic Map PRBG. In (Suneel, 2009) the author presents an algorithm to build a PRBG based on a 2D chaotic system, the Hénon map (Hénon, 1976; Pellicer-Lostao & López-Ruiz, 2011b). This algorithm is based on the technique of subspace division. The pseudorandom sequences generated with this algorithm show good random properties when subjected to different statistical tests. The author indicates that the choice of the Hénon map is rather arbitrary and similar results should also be attainable with other 2D maps. This algorithm is then taken and the chaotic Hénon map is substituted by the Symmetric Coupled Logistic Map.

But, as it normally happens in chaotic cryptosystems, this algorithm is dependent of the chaotic system and the mere substitution of the chaotic systems is not enough to maintain its performance (Li, 2003). In particular, it is found that the sub-space division method has also to be adapted to fit the geometrical characteristics of the new chaotic systems. In (Pellicer-Lostao & López-Ruiz, 2008) the interested reader can find these details. The final algorithm applied to the Symmetric Coupled Logistic Maps is shown in Fig.3 through a functional diagram. In the following paragraphs the details of its implementation are described.

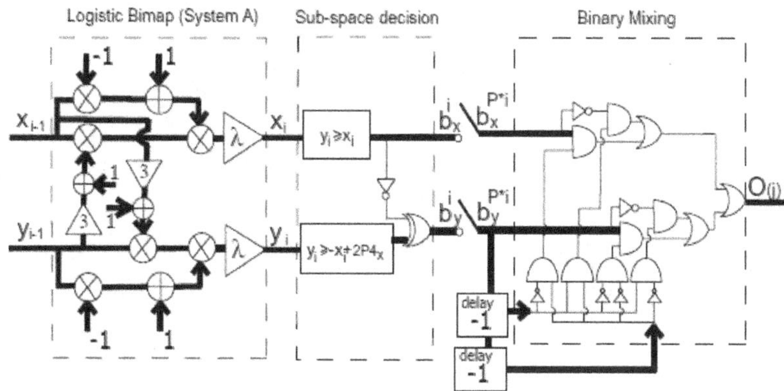

Fig. 3. Functional block structure of the proposed algorithm (example for System A)

The input of the algorithm are a state of initial conditions $X_0 = [x_0, y_0]$ and a value of the parameters (λ_x, λ_y). The functional block named as *Logistic Bimap* produces a series of iterations through Eq.(7). Whenever the initial input values produce chaotic regime this block produces a chaotic sequence of 2D real states $X_i = [x_i, y_i]$. Then, it is used the technique of dividing the phase space in four sub-spaces to transform the 2D states into binary vectors $[b^i_X, b^i_Y]$. This is done in the block named as *sub-space decision*. This produces two binary sequences $S_X = \{b^i_X\}^{\infty}_{i=1}$ and $S_Y = \{b^i_Y\}^{\infty}_{i=1}$.

As it is said before, the division of the phase space in four sub-spaces must be defined, in a way that the Logistic Bimap system visits each subspace as the Hénon map does in (Suneel, 2009). A finite automata that summarizes the pattern of visits is used to obtain that. A finite automata is inferred from the Hénon map in (Suneel, 2009) and a division of sub-paces is chosen in the Logistic Bimaps in order to get the same finite automata. In particular, if we name the sub-spaces corresponding to $[b^i_X , b^i_Y]$ with values *[0, 0]*, *[1, 0]*, *[0, 1]* and *[1, 1]* as *1,2,3* and *4*, we can analyze the detail of this pattern of visits. This is shown in Fig.4.

In (Suneel, 2009) the Hénon map does not visit the four sub-spaces equally. It is observed that there exists a symmetry of movements between sub-spaces *1-3* and *2-4*, which has a characteristic mixing of *50%* and *50%*, as long as a predominant (*80%*) and constant transition between *3* and *2*. This leads to a highly variation of binary values in sequences S_x, S_y. In the end, these conditions give the final result of an output sequence $O(j)$ with a proper balance of zeros and ones, or put it in another way, with pseudo-random properties.

To get this automata for the symmetric coupled logistic maps Systems A and B, one should chose the diagonal axis, which divides phase space in two parts, each of which is equally visited (*50%*). And additional statistical calculus is required to divide these two sub-spaces, in another two with a visiting rate of *40%-10%* each one. When this is done, one can observe that this is got by merely selecting *P4* and the line perpendicular to the axis in *P4* as the other division line.

The final sub-space division for each system is presented in Fig. 4(a) and 4(c), along with the indications of the evolution of the visits to each sub-space. For Systems A and B, this finite automata is depicted in Fig. 4(b) and 4(d).

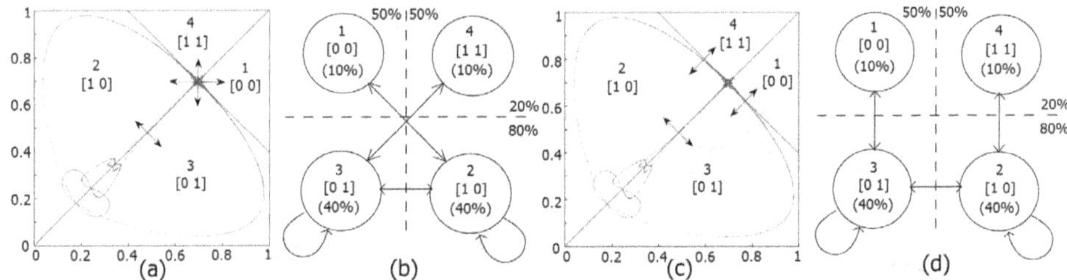

Fig. 4. (a) Final sub-space division and (b) finite automata for System A. (c) Final sub-space division and (d) finite automata for System B. (In both cases, $\lambda = 1.07$).

Finally the operation performed in the sub-space decision block is summarized in Eq (9):

$$b_x = \begin{cases} 0 & \text{if } y<x \\ 1 & \text{if } y\geq x \end{cases} \quad b_y \begin{cases} 0 & \text{if } (y<x \,\&\, y\geq -x+2P4_x) OR (y\geq x \,\&\, y<-x+2p4_x) \\ 1 & \text{if } (y<x \,\&\, y<-x+2P4_x) OR (y\geq x \,\&\, y\geq -x+2P4_x) \end{cases} \tag{9}$$

After obtaining $S_X = \{b^i{}_X\}^{\infty}{}_{i=1}$ and $S_Y = \{b^i{}_Y\}^{\infty}{}_{i=1}$, they are sampled with a frequency of $1/P$ (each P iterations) and $B_X = \{b^{P*i}{}_X\}^{\infty}{}_{i=1}$ and $B_Y = \{b^{P*i}{}_Y\}^{\infty}{}_{i=1}$ are obtained. The effect of skipping P consecutive values of the orbit is necessary to get a random macroscopic behaviour. With this operation, the correlation existing between consecutive values generated by the chaotic system is eliminated.

This is done in a way that over a P_{min}, sequences generated with $P > P_{min}$ will appear macroscopically random. Although P is normally introduced as an additional key parameter in pseudo-random sequences generation (Kocarev, 2001), it strongly determines the speed of the generation algorithm, so it is recommended to be kept as small as possible.

The output binary pseudorandom sequence $O(j)$ is obtained by a mixing operation of the actual and previous values of the sequence $B(j) = [BX(j), BY(j)]$ given by the truth table sketched in Table 3.

	$B_Y(j\text{-}1)$	
$B_Y(j\text{-}2)$	0	1
0	$B_X(j)$	$Not(B_X(j))$
1	$B_Y(j)$	$Not(B_Y(j))$

Table 3. Truth table generating the binary sequence $O(j)$.

As a direct application for cryptography, the above described PRBG could be used in the construction of a stream cipher. Different initial conditions, x_0 and y_0 and parameters λ and P, can be applied to the input of the system and be used as a key to generate the keystream, or output sequence $O(j)$. The keystream $O(j)$ can be XORed directly with a clear text, obtaining that way the ciphertext.

In rest of this example, we evaluate the functionality of the chaotic PRBG with the calculus of the size of the key space, applying statistical and predictability tests to different sequences produced with it and measuring its speed.

a. Calculus of the key space

Let us determine the operative range of initial conditions and parameters values that can be applied to the PRBG in Fig. 3. This range, when the PRBG is used in cryptography applications is known as the key-space. Then, the key space is determined by the interval of the parameter and the initial conditions that keep the dynamical system in the chaotic regime. These are $\lambda \in [1.032, 1.0843]$, $x_0 \in (0, 1)$ and $y_0 \in (0, 1)$. The parameter λ can be considered as two independent parameters λ_x y λ_y, and the dynamic properties of the system still remain chaotic in the same interval. The sampling parameter can also be considered as another parameter of the key space. One must observe that P should be kept in a suitable range, so that the PRBG is fast enough for its desired application. These intervals can be denoted with brackets and calculated as $[\lambda_x]= [\lambda_y]=0.0523$, $[x_0]=1$, $[y_0]=1$ y $[P]=890$, when taking $[P] \in [110,1000]$ as the functional range of the sampling factor.

The size of the key space will be determined by the numeric representation used in the calculus of the algorithm. If floating-point representation under standard IEEE 754 is chosen, the smallest available precision is $\varepsilon_{32} \approx 1.1921 \times 10^{-7}$ for simple precision with 32 bits and $\varepsilon_{64} \approx 2.2204 \times 10^{-16}$for double precision with 64 bits. These quantities give the maximum number of possible values of every parameter in any of the two representations. This is easily computed dividing the intervals by ε, as $K_{\lambda x}=[\lambda_x]/\varepsilon$, $K_{\lambda y}=[\lambda_y]/\varepsilon$, $K_{x0}=[x_0]/\varepsilon$, $K_{y0}=[y_0]/\varepsilon$, and $K_P=[P]$. Notice that the calculus of K_P is different as P can only take integer values.

The total size of possible parameter values is given by K, calculated as $K=K_{\lambda x}\times K_{\lambda y}\times K_{x0}\times K_{y0}\times K_P$. K is the size of the available key-space and its logarithm in base 2 gives us the available length of binary keys or entries to produce pseudo-random sequences in the generator. The values obtained for each number precision, are $K_{32}=1.21\times 10^{28}$, with a key length of *93* bits for single precision and $K_{64}=1.00\times 10^{63}$, with a key length of *209* bits for double precision.

These results are fine for the use of the chaotic PRBG in cryptography, where a length of keys greater than *100* is considered strong enough against brute force attacks, (Alvarez & Li, 2006). Nevertheless, it has to be said for accuracy's sake, that the calculus of the key space is a coarse estimation and a deeper study is required (Alvarez & Li, 2006) for accurate evaluation. The high sensitivity to parameter values and initial conditions of chaotic systems may produce windows on periodicity in the key space. Another possibility is that the dynamics can diverge towards infinity. In the systems presented here an initial calculus of *100* iterations is enough to ensure the boundless or goodness of the initial conditions.

b. Statistical testing

In general, randomness cannot be mathematically proved. Alternatively, different statistical batteries of tests have been proposed over time to assess randomness. Each of these tests evaluates a relevant random property expected in a true random generator. Then, to test a certain randomness property in a PRBG, several output sequences are taken from the generator. As one knows a priori the statistical distribution of possible values that true random sequences would be likely to exhibit for that property, a conclusion can be obtained upon the probability of the tested sequences to be random.

There exist different well-known sources of test suites available in literature, such as those described by Knuth (Knuth, 1997), the Marsaglias Diehard test suite (Marsaglia, 1995) or those of the National Institute of Standards and Technology (NIST) (Rukhin et al., 2010). But there are many more (Rütti et al, 2004; Mascagni, 1999), perhaps not so nicely packaged, but still useful. In these collections of tests, each test tries a different random property and gives a way of interpreting its results. In this example, the Diehard test suite (Marsaglia, 1995) and the NIST Test Suite (Rukhin et al., 2010) are selected, for they are very accessible and widely used. Table 4 lists the tests comprised in these suites.

*N^er^*	***Diehard test suite***	***NIST test suite***
1	Birthday spacings	Frequency (monobit)
2	Overlapping 5-permutation	Frequency test within a block
3	Binary rank test	Cumulative sums
4	Bitstream	Runs
5	OPSO	Longest run of ones in a block
6	OQSO	Binary matrix rank
7	DNA	Discrete fourier transform
8	Count-the-1's test	Non-overlapping template matching
9	A parking lot	Overlapping template matching
10	Minimum distance	Maurer's universal statistical
11	3D-spheres	Approximate entropy
12	Squeeze	Random excursions
13	Overlapping sums	Random excursions variant
14	Runs	Serial
15	Craps	Linear complexity

Table 4. List of tests comprised in the Diehard and NIST test suites.

In each test, a *p-value* is obtained. This value summaries the strength of evidence against the randomness of the tested sequence. In Marsaglia's Diehard test suite, *p-values* should lie within the interval *[0, 1)* to accept the PRBG. In NIST Statistical Test Suite, the acceptance happens when the *p-values* are greater than *a*, the significance level of the test.

To assess the randomness of the PRBG obtained in the previous section with systems A and B, several sequences are obtained and submitted to the Diehard and NIST test suites described in Table 4. The significance level of the tests is set to a value appropriate for cryptographic applications (a= 0.01). Similar results are found for both systems and for simplicity, only those obtained with system A will be presented here after. Ten sequences are generated with six different sets of initial conditions and considering $\lambda = \lambda_x = \lambda_y$. Their characteristics are described in Table 5.

Sequence	*S1*	*S2*	*S3*	*S4*	*S5*	*S6*
x_0	0.9891	0.4913	0.6727	0.7268	0.3956	0.9998
y_0	0.6891	0.6913	0.4977	0.9018	0.4956	0.6498
λ	1.048	1.053	1.069	1.080	1.064	1.074
P_{Dmin}	55	45	35	47	n.a.	n.a.
P_{Nmin}	83	105	83	83	100	85

Table 5. Parameters P_{Dmin} and P_{Nmin} for different sequences Si , $i = 1,...,6$, with different initial conditions (x_0, y_0) and control parameter λ.

Six of them (*S1, S2, S3, S4, S5* and *S6*) are tested with Nist tests suite with *200 Mill.* of bits and four of them (*S1, S2, S3* and *S4*) are tested with Diehard tests suite with *80 Mill.* of bits. Here, the parameters P_{Dmin} and P_{Nmin} are the minimum sampling rate or shift factor, P_{min}, over which, all sequences generated with the same initial conditions and $P > P_{min}$ pass Diehard or Nist tests suites, respectively. It is observed here, that the Nist tests suite requires a higher value of P_{min} and that *S5* and *S6* are not tested with Diehard battery of tests.

In the Diehard tests suite, each of the tests returns one or several p-values which should be uniform in the interval *[0,1)* when the input sequence contains truly independent random bits. The software available in (Marsaglia, 1995) provides a total of *218* p-values for *15* tests, and the uniformity requirement can be assessed graphically, when plotting them in the interval *[0,1)*. For example Fig. 5 shows the *p-values* obtained for three sequences (a),(b) and (c) with the same initial conditions *S1*, and different sampling factor *P*. The first one, Fig. 5(a), demonstrates graphically the failure of the tests, for there is a non-uniform clustering of p-values around the value *1.0*. Fig. 5(b) shows the uniformity obtained with $P_{Dmin}= 55$ over the interval *[0,1)*. A better uniformity can be appreciated when $P > P_{Dmin}$ in Fig. 5(c). Sequences *S1* to *S4* are proved to pass the Diehard battery of tests with significance level $a= 0.01$. Fig. 5(d) presents a graphical representation of the *p-values* obtained for each sequence with sampling factor $P=P_{Dmin}$ of Table 6. It can be observed that some *p-values* are occasionally near *0* or *1*. Although it can not be well appreciated in the figure, it has to be said that those never really reach these values.

In the Nist tests suite, one or more p-values are also returned for each sequence under test. These values should be greater than the significance level a, which was selected as $a=0.01$ (as in the Diehard case). These tests also require a sufficiently high length of sequences and to prove randomness in one test, two conditions should be verified. First, a minimum percentage of sequences should pass the test and second, the p-values of all sequences should also be uniformly distributed in the interval *(0, 1)*. For this case, each of the six sequences with initial conditions *S1* to *S6* are arranged in *200* sub-sequences of *1Mill.* bits each and submitted to the Nist battery of tests. Sequences *Si* prove to pass all tests over a minimum value P_{Nmin}, shown in Table 5.

In Fig.5(e) and 5(f), the results obtained for *S1* and *S4* respectively are graphically presented, as an example of what is obtained for each *Si*. The tests in the suite are numbered according to Table 4. Fig. 5(e) represents the percentage of the *200* sub-sequences of *S1* that pass each of the *15* tests of the suite. These percentages are over the minimum pass rate required of *96.8893%* for a sample size of *200* binary sub-sequences.

Fig. 5(f) describes the uniformity of the distribution of *p-values* obtained for the *15* tests of the suite. Here, uniformity is assessed. The interval *(0, 1)* is divided in ten subintervals (**C1,C2,...,C10**) and the number of *p-values* that lay in each sub-interval, among a total of *200,* are counted and proved to be uniform.

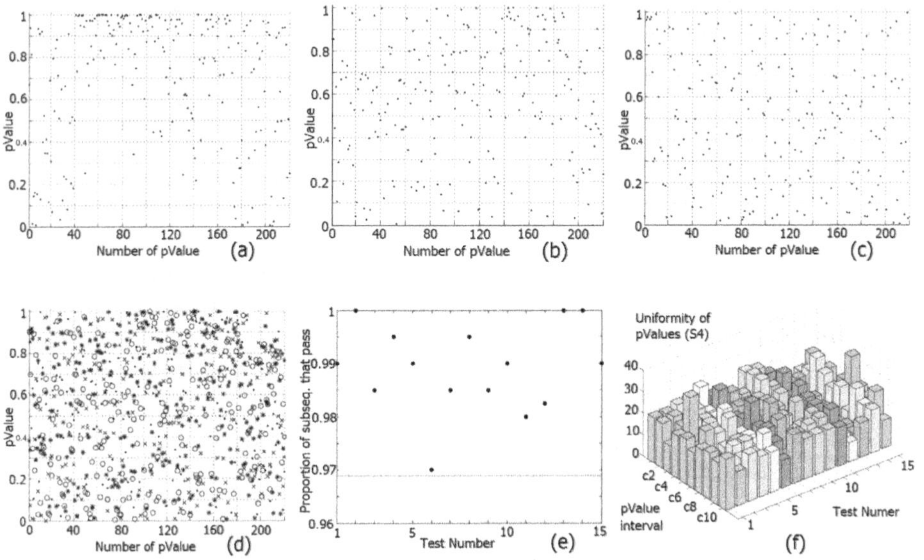

Fig. 5. Diehard test suite *p-values* obtained for initial conditions *S1* with (a) $P = 20$, (b) $P = P_{Dmin} = 55$ and (c) $P = 110$. In (d), *p-values* obtained for initial conditions *S1, S2, S3* and *S4* with $P = P_{Dmin}$ of Table 5. NIST test results, in (e) the proportion of sub-sequences of *S1* that passes each test, in (f) the distribution of *p-values* of *S4* is examined for each test to ensure uniformity.

The results above obtained are finally compared with the ones produced by other standard PRBG. To do that, two generators provided in the software packet of Diehard (Marsaglia, 1995) are submitted to the statistical tests.

The first one is the shift-register, generator number *13* with parameters *L1= 13, R=17* and *L2=5*. The second one is a extended congruential generator; the first one provided in the packet with seeds *78, 29* and *33*. These generators produce two sequences of *11 Mill.* of bytes, more than *80 Mill.* bits. Another two generators given in NIST (Rukhin et al., 2010) are also used to produce another two standard pseudorandom sequences. In particular two sequences of *200 Mill.* bits were produced with the ANSI X9.17(3-DES) and the linear congruential generator.

The results obtained for these standard generators are similar to the ones obtained with the Symmetric Coupled Logistic Map PRBG and they are presented in Fig.6. Only one of the standard generators shows poorer performance than the chaotic PRBG. This is the shift-register generator that fails with *p-value=1* the following tests: binary rank test and count-the-1's test.

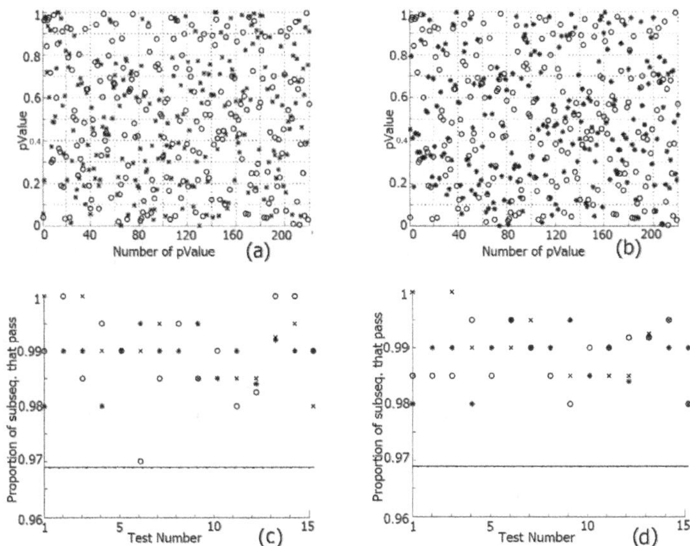

Fig. 6. Diehard test suite *p-values* obtained with a sequence generated with the chaotic PRBG and initial conditions *S1* and *P=110* (circles) and for the sequence generated with the standard generators (stars). (a) The shift register. (b) The extended congruential generator. (c) Proportion of sub-sequences that passes each one of NIST tests with generator ANSI X9.17 (black cross) and linear congruential generator (asterisk) and chaotic PRBG (circles) with initial conditions *S1* and *P=50* (c) or *P=90* (d).

c. Predictability testing

A PRBG is called a cryptographically secure pseudorandom bit generator (CSPRBG) when is not predictable [Menezes et al, 1996]. To assess the unpredictability, it is necessary to pass any of the following tests: the polynomial-time statistical test or the next-bit test. Both tests are equivalent.

A PRBG passes the first one if no polynomial-time algorithm can correctly distinguish between an output sequence of the generator and a truly random sequence of the same length with probability significantly greater than *0.5*. A PRBG passes the next-bit test if there is no polynomial-time algorithm which, on input of the first *L* bits of a generated sequence *s*, can predict the *(L + 1)*st bit of *s* with probability negligible greater than *0.5* (a function is negligible if it is eventually smaller than the inverse of any positive polynomial). As it is not possible to prove the non existence of something, a generator is considered to pass these tests if it is possible to verify the above conditions under some plausible but unproved mathematical assumption.

Conventional cryptography has a framework of concepts and techniques that allows conclude on predictability, based on number and computation theories. In chaotic cryptography one may expect predictability to be a function of the dynamical parameters of the chaotic system. However, here there is a lack of theoretical tools to carry out such kind of analysis. In return, one can perform empirical measurements.

This part presents several measurements to assess the predictability of the PRBG. These will show, that due to the characteristics of the design of the PRBG, the probability of producing a *0* or a *1* at a given instant *t=j* is:

$$P(O(j)=1) = P(O(j)=0) = 0.5+\Delta\varepsilon \tag{10}$$

and the maximum value of $\Delta\varepsilon$ will be measured ($\Delta\varepsilon_{max}$).

To do that, the chaotic PRBG algorithm is revised. The conditions necessary for unpredictability are analyzed. After that, a binary pseudorandom sequence is generated, the probability of obtaining a *0* or a *1* bits is measured on that sequence and the error magnitude $\Delta\varepsilon$ is evaluated. Our discussion is centred in System A, but measurements could also be performed to System B the same way and similar results should be obtained.

The design of the generator is depicted in Fig.3. There it can be seen that the output bit generated at instant *t=j*, *O(j)* is generated by means of Table 3 as a function of the binary vectors *BY(j-1)* , *BY(j-2)* and *B(j) = [BX(j),BY(j)]* where at instant *t=j=P*i*, *BX(j)= bP*iX* and *BY(j)= bP*iY*. As a result the output bit is produced explicitly as it is shown in the following Table 6.

	$[B_X(j),B_Y(j)]$			
$[B_Y(j-2),B_Y(j-1)])$	[0,0]	[0,1]	[1,0]	[1,1]
[0,0]	0	0	1	1
[0,1]	1	1	0	0
[1,0]	0	1	1	0
[1,1]	1	0	0	1

Table 6. Truth table generating the output bit *O(j)*.

From Table 6 one observes that the output *O(j)* will have a *0.5* probability of being a *0* or *1* bit whenever the probabilities of the vectors *BY(j-1)* , *BY(j-2)* and *B(j) = [BX(j), BY(j)]* are also 0.5. And we can say that the distribution of *0*'s and *1*'s the output binary sequence will be uniform as long as the distribution of the sequence of the binary vector *B(j) = [BX(j), BY(j)]* is uniform.

But *B(j)* is obtained in the output of the sub-space division block, as *t=j=P*i*, $B_X(j)= b^{P*i}{}_X$ and $B_Y(j)= b^{P*i}{}_Y$, and as it was seen the pattern of visits of any sub-space is not uniform, it depends of the dynamic of the chaotic attractor. The dynamic of visits of every sub-space is analyzed in Fig. 7.

In Fig.7, it is observed that the sequences of binary vectors $[b^i{}_X , b^i{}_Y]$ in (a) and $[b^{P*i}{}_X , b^{P*i}{}_Y]$ in (b) have a characteristic evolution. In particular, from the Fig.7 (a) is easy to conclude that it is possible to predict next states in the automata given and initial state for *P=1*. For example $P([b^i{}_X , b^i{}_Y] =[0,0])/([b^{i-1}{}_X , b^{i-1}{}_Y] = [1,0])=1$. On the other hand, in Fig.7 (b) this sequence is sampled at *P* rate, when *P* is taken sufficiently high, *P>>1*. Then, the correlation of the states in the chaotic system disappears and any transition is possible.

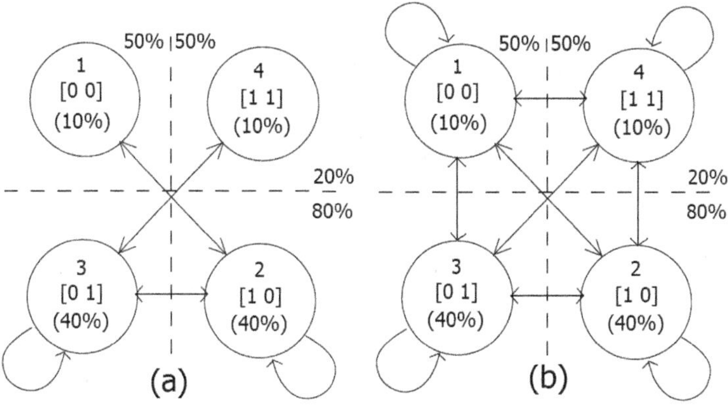

Fig. 7. Finite automata for the evolution dynamics of binary vector $[b^{P*i}_X, b^{P*i}_Y]$ generated in the chaotic PRBG with system A (a) when *P=1* and (b) when *P>>1*.

To measure the predictability, different binary sequences are produced in the chaotic PRBG with initial conditions *S2* of Table 5, a length of *n=2Mill* of bits and different values of sampling factor *P=1, 101* y *151*. With these sequences, it is measured the probability of transition from a state $B(j-1) = [B_X(j-1), B_Y(j-1)]$ at instant $t=j-1$ to the state $B(j) = [B_X(j), B_Y(j)]$ in the next instant. These measurements can be seen in Table 7.

NUMBER OF VISITS OF EVERY SUBSPACE (from B[j-1] to B[j]) (P=1)

2000000	211026	788125	789279	211570	TOTAL
B(j-1) \ B(j)	[0,0]	[1,0]	[0,1]	[1,1]	2000000
[0,0]	0	211025	0	0	211025
[1,0]	211026	104267	472832	0	788125
[0,1]	0	472833	104877	211570	789280
[1,1]	0	0	211570	0	211570

(a)

PROBABILITY OF VISITS OF EVERY SUBSPACE (from B[j-1] to B[j]) (P=1)

TOTAL	0,105513	0,394062	0,394639	0,105785
t=j-1 \ t=j	[0,0]	[1,0]	[0,1]	[1,1]
[0,0]	0	1	0	0
[1,0]	0,267757	0,132298	0,599945	0
[0,1]	0	0,599069	0,132877	0,268054
[1,1]	0	0	1	0

(b)

NUMBER OF VISITS OF EVERY SUBSPACE (from B[j-1] to B[j]) (P=101)

2000000	210811	788153	789383	211653	TOTAL
B(j-1) \ B(j)	[0,0]	[1,0]	[0,1]	[1,1]	2000000
[0,0]	14243	91059	90979	14530	210811
[1,0]	91236	302043	303811	91063	788153
[0,1]	90827	303940	302989	91627	789383
[1,1]	14505	91111	91604	14433	211653

(c)

PROBABILITY OF VISITS OF EVERY SUBSPACE (from B[j-1] to B[j]) (P=101)

TOTAL	0,105406	0,394077	0,394691	0,105827
t=j-1 \ t=j	[0,0]	[1,0]	[0,1]	[1,1]
[0,0]	0,0675629	0,431946	0,431567	0,0689243
[1,0]	0,115759	0,383229	0,385472	0,11554
[0,1]	0,115061	0,385035	0,38383	0,116074
[1,1]	0,068532	0,430473	0,432803	0,0681918

(d)

NUMBER OF VISITS OF EVERY SUBSPACE (from B[j-1] to B[j]) (P=151)

2000000	211841	788804	788004	211351	TOTAL
B(j-1) \ B(j)	[0,0]	[1,0]	[0,1]	[1,1]	2000000
[0,0]	24757	81217	81281	24586	211841
[1,0]	81133	313633	313237	80800	788803
[0,1]	81244	312899	312659	81203	788005
[1,1]	24707	81055	80827	24762	211351

(e)

PROBABILITY OF VISITS OF EVERY SUBSPACE (from B[j-1] to B[j]) (P=151)

TOTAL	0,105921	0,394402	0,394002	0,105676
t=j-1 \ t=j	[0,0]	[1,0]	[0,1]	[1,1]
[0,0]	0,116866	0,383387	0,383689	0,116059
[1,0]	0,102856	0,397606	0,397104	0,102434
[0,1]	0,103101	0,397077	0,396773	0,103049
[1,1]	0,1169	0,383509	0,38243	0,117161

(f)

Table 7. Measurements of the probability of transition from one subspace to another.

Table 7 shows two tables for every value of P used in the measurements. The table on the left counts the visits or transitions from the sub-space where $B(j\text{-}1) = [B_X(j\text{-}1),B_Y(j\text{-}1)]$ was at instant $t=j\text{-}1$ to the sub-space where $[B_X(j),B_Y(j)]$ is at the following instant. The table on the right calculates the probability of transition between the four subspaces calculated from the table on the left. The values in the different tables are obtained in (a), (b) with $P=1$, in (c), (d) $P=101$, and in (e), (f) $P= 151$. As a conclusion of these, it is found that the system at instant $t=j$ has the following probabilities for being in any of the four possible states:

$$P([BX(j),BY(j)]=[0,0])= P(([BX(j),BY(j)=[1,1])= 0.1$$
$$P([BX(j),BY(j)]=[0,1])= P(([BX(j),BY(j)=[1,0])= 0.4 \tag{11}$$

It is observed that the greater the value of P, the closer the probabilities to 0.5. The case where $P=151$ is then considered to proceed with the measurements. Now it is possible to calculate from Table 7 the probability of obtaining $B_X(j) = 0$ or $B_X(j)=1$ from a given predecessor state $B(j\text{-}1) = [B_X(j\text{-}1),B_Y(j\text{-}1)]$. And the same for the probabilities of $B_Y(j) = 0$ or $B_Y(j)=1$ from the state $B(j\text{-}1)$. These calculus can be done by the reader in all cases with the data of Table 7(f), but here the first one is illustrated as an example:

$$P(BX(j) = 0/B(j\text{-}1)=[0,0]) = 0{,}116866^*\ P(B(j\text{-}1)=[0,0])+ 0{,}383689^*\ P(B(j\text{-}1)=[0,0])=$$
$$0{,}500555^*\ P(B(j\text{-}1)=[0,0]) \tag{12}$$

All results are summarized in Table 8, where $\Delta\varepsilon$ is the deviasion from probability 0.5:

P=151

t=j / t=j-1	By=0	By=1	Δε	Δε
[0,0]	0,500253	0,499748	0,000253	0,000252
[1,0]	0,500462	0,499538	0,000462	0,000462
[0,1]	0,500178	0,499822	0,000178	0,000178
[1,1]	0,500409	0,499591	0,000409	0,000409

(a)

P=151

t=j / t=j-1	Bx=0	Bx=1	Δε	Δε
[0,0]	0,500555	0,499446	0,000555	0,000554
[1,0]	0,49996	0,50004	0,000040	0,000040
[0,1]	0,499874	0,500126	0,000126	0,000126
[1,1]	0,49933	0,50067	0,00067	0,00067

(b)

Table 8. Calculus of the probability of obtaining from the estate $B(j\text{-}1) = [B_X(j\text{-}1),B_Y(j\text{-}1)]$ (a) $B_X(j) = 0$ or $B_X(j)=1$ and *(b)* $B_Y(j) = 0$ *or* $B_Y(j)=1$.

From Table 8 it can be seen that:

$$P(BX(j) = 0) \approx P(BX(j) = 1) \approx P(BY(j) = 0) \approx P(BY(j) = 1) = 0.5 \pm\Delta\varepsilon \tag{13}$$

The error $\Delta\varepsilon$ is different in each case of Eq. (13). To get this equation we have taken the approximations of Eq. (14) for all cases:

$$P(BX(j) = 0) \approx 0.5 * (P([BX(j\text{-}1)/BY(j\text{-}1)=[0,0])+ P([BX(j\text{-}1)/BY(j\text{-}1)=[0,1])+$$
$$P([BX(j\text{-}1)/BY(j\text{-}1)=[1,0])+ P([BX(j\text{-}1)/BY(j\text{-}1)=[1,1])) \approx 0.5 \pm\Delta\varepsilon \tag{14}$$

Considering all cases, we obtain that $\Delta\varepsilon<0.0006$. This result can be compared with the acuracy of this measurement $\delta=1/n= 5x10^{-7}$, where n is the length of the sequence. Finally it can be concluded that the distribution of the binary vector $B(j)$ is uniform with an error of $\Delta\varepsilon_{max}<0.0006$. And from Table 8 we conclude that the probability of producing a bit *0* or *1* given a sequence *S2* of $n=2Mill$ bits is almost *0.5* within a maximum error of $\Delta\varepsilon_{max}<0.0006$. This gives a quantitative magnitude of the chaotic PRBG predictability.

d. Performance test

To assess the functionality of the PRBG for its use in cryptography, it is necessary to measure its speed. As it is said, an allegedly "secure" cipher is not acceptable for real applications if it is not efficient.

To establish the complexity, and consequently the performance of the chaotic PRBG, the principle of invariance is observed. This says that the efficiency of one algorithm in different execution environments differs only in a multiplicative constant, when the values of the parameters of cost are sufficiently high. In this case, the asymptotic behavior of the computational cost of the PRBG is governed by the calculus performed in the chaotic block of Fig.3. This block makes P iterations for each output bit, $O(j)$. The capital theta notation (Θ) can be used to describe an asymptotic tight bound for the magnitude of cost of the PRBG. And consequently, the 2D symmetric coupled logistic maps have a computational cost or complexity of order $\Theta(P^*n)$. This result is typical in chaotic based cryptosystems where multiple iterations are required for each encryption step. In this case the number of iterations required for good statistical quality is around *100* iterations and this can be considered small compared with other cryptosystems (Examples: larger than *250* or *65536* in (Kocarev, 2001)). Nevertheless in our case, the calculus is two dimensional and two real variables are computed for each step.

To measure the speed of the chaotic PRBG the following test is performed: the algorithm is implemented in C++ code with the compiler *Bloodshed C++ 4.9.9.2* and run in PC with *Windows 2000 5.00.2195 SP4 - Intel Pentium 4 - CPU 2.80GHz – 515.056 KB RAM*. Generally speaking, on a PC with a f_z Hz CPU, it is acceptable if the encryption speed is f_z/a bps, where $a <=100$ (Alvarez & Li, 2006). In our case the chaotic PRBG gives a speed of $a=2394$ if $P=25$ and $a=4219$ when $P=47$.

The results obtained show no optimal performance, but as it is known (Alvarez & Li, 2006) besides the CPU frequency, the encryption speed of a software implementation is tightly dependent on other issues, such as the CPU structure, the memory size, the underlying OS platform, the developing language, all options of the compiler, and so on. In consequence one could say that this speed needs to be increased with code optimization. In this case, among other things, it could be convenient to use hardware implementations with parallel mechanisms for calculating simultaneously each variable of the 2D chaotic iterations.

3.3 Second example: Improving encryption with symmetry swap of chaotic variables

In this example it is explored how the geometric and symmetric characteristics of the chaotic maps can be used to improve the encryption algorithm. In particular, these characteristics are studied in the chaotic logistic bimap attractors and a mechanism called "*symmetry-swap*" (Pellicer-Lostao & López-Ruiz, 2009) is introduced to enhance the previous PRBG. It is shown that this mechanism can increase the degrees of freedom of the key space, while maintaining the performance of the PRBG algorithm.

Let us observe that the maps under consideration present symmetry with respect to the diagonal axis. Now let us consider a point $[x_0, y_0]$ and its conjugated $[y_0, x_0]$ with respect to the diagonal $[x_0, y_0]$ as two different initial conditions. It can be seen, that starting from any of these points systems A and B produce different but symmetric orbits (conjugated orbits).

Now it becomes clear that an interchange (or swap) of coordinates x and y in an orbit state will to produce a jump to a conjugated orbit, while the attractor and the chaotic regime are not affected. These facts are illustrated in the schematic diagram of Fig. 8 for Systems A and B. When starting with the same initial conditions, one orbit and its conjugated are presented, jumping from one to the other is possible by swapping the coordinates.

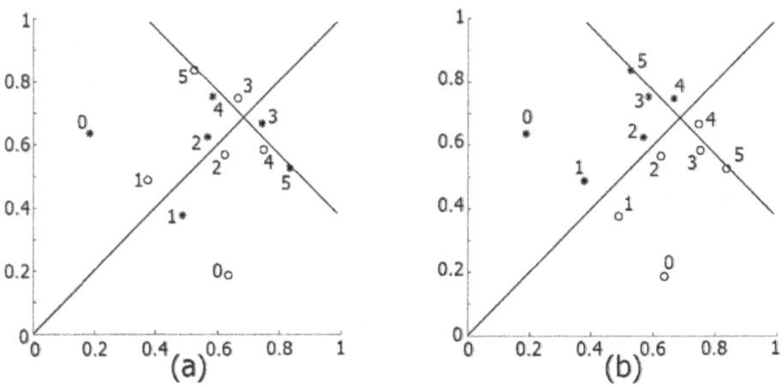

Fig. 8. Five points in the evolution of trajectories for System A (a) or B (b) when starting with $\lambda = 1.07$ and the same initial conditions $[x_0, y_0]$ (point *0* with the star-marker) and its coordinate conjugated $[y_0, x_0]$ (point *0* with the circle-marker).

In these circumstances, a swapping of coordinates could be introduced in the algorithm of Fig. 3, without altering its pseudorandom properties. This mechanism is named by the authors as "*symmetry-swap*". In practice, the s symmetry-swap can be an additional step at the input of the system, which is applied at specific instants $t=i-1$ as desired. When the swapping is applied at a constant rate S, a swap of coordinates is introduced every S iterations and the algorithm has the following performance: the map evolves along one specific orbit during S iterations and after a swap in the coordinates (swapping $x \leftrightarrow y$), the map jumps to a conjugated orbit. Let us call S the rate of swapping or the swapping factor.

a. Calculus of the key space

It is important to observe at this point, that the introduction of a swapping factor S does not penalizes the computational cost of the resulting PRBG. The chaotic block again dominates its asymptotic behavior. As a result, the swapped 2D symmetric coupled logistic maps PRBGs have an asymptotic tight bound of order $\Theta(P^*n)$. Then we must expect a similar performance as for the algorithm in the first example. Another valuable aspect to remark is that the swapping factor S can offer an improvement in the range of input values of the initial PRBG algorithm. In cryptography, this means an enhancement in security and it can be obtained straight from the fact that S, considered as a constant value, may represent a new free parameter in the key-space.

Let us consider that the useful values of S could range in the interval $S = [1,n]$, where n is the number of bits generated. Taking n for a typical value of *1 Mill.* of bits, this would enlarge the key space calculated last example. Following analogous calculations and S taking integer values, then *[S] =1000000* , $K = K=K_{\lambda X}\times K_{\lambda Y}\times K_{x0}\times K_{y0}\times K_P\times K_S$. This increases the key size from *93* to *113* for single precision and from *209* to *229* for double. The enlargement of the key space makes the swapped algorithm stronger against brute force attack than the non swapped one.

b. Statistical testing

The interesting point about the symmetry-swap, is that no matter what number of consecutive iterations and swaps are performed to the system, the chaotic behavior always prevails. Logically, this particular fact will make pseudorandomness to prevail too.

The authors explore the construction of a swapped PRBG. This is, following algorithm in Fig. 3 with system A and adding a constant swapping factor of value *S* in the input. Ten pseudo-random binary sequences are generated with the same characteristics (initial conditions and length) as the ones described in Table 5. A swapping factor of $S = 90$ is applied for sequences to be tested with Diehard test suite. To illustrate a different value, a swapping factor of $S = 50$ is chosen with NIST's suite. The sequences of the swapped PRBGs demonstrate similar random results when submitted to the tests. Very similar P_{min} values to those in Table 5, or even the same, are obtained in all cases. Fig. 9 shows graphically the results obtained and illustrated the success of the tests. Unsurprisingly, this demonstrates that in this case the symmetry-swap maintains pseudo randomness.

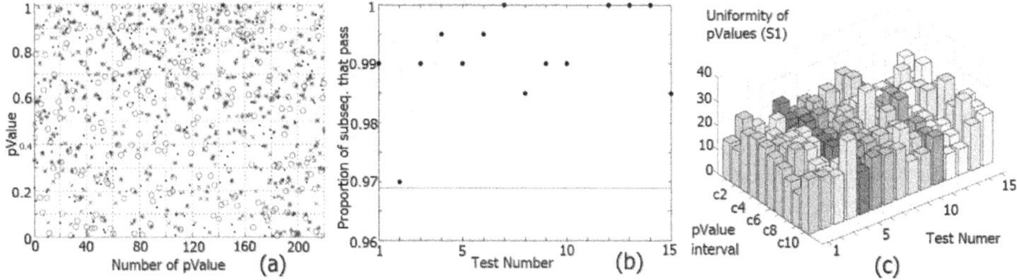

Fig. 9. In (a), *p-values* obtained with all tests of Diehard suite for initial conditions *S1, S2, S3* and S4 with $P = P_{Dmin}$ and $S = 90$. In (b) the proportion of sub-sequences that pass NIST test suite with initial conditions *S1*, $P = P_{Nmin}$ and $S = 50$. In (c) The distribution of p-values for each test with the same conditions of (b) demonstrates the required uniformity.

In addition, one may think that the introduction of a swapping factor *S* can be applied in multiple ways. Consider, for example, different values of *S* used alternatively in the process, this may make the swapping factor many dimensional. Another way could be to consider an *S* value variable in time. The swapping factor can also offer an easy feedback mechanism, when making its value dependable of the output. Therefore the symmetry-swap mechanism is a very flexible tool. In the end, it can be observed that the symmetry-swap offers a remarkable advantage, while maintaining speed and simplicity of the initial PRBG algorithm.

To conclude, the symmetry swap mechanism represents an interesting strategy for finding additional degrees of freedom in the key space with no extra computational costs. This is possible thanks to the symmetric and geometric properties observed in the chaotic attractor. Unlike what happens when introducing the sampling factor *P*, the swapping factor *S* doesn't force the designer to consider a trade-off between its range of values and the speed of the algorithm. Moreover this degree of freedom can be introduced in multiple ways. Therefore the swapping factor S can increase the security of the system with great flexibility.

4. Conclusion and perspectives

Chaotic cryptography has experienced significant development since its birth in the early 90's. Nevertheless, as other interdisciplinary areas of research, it has encountered many difficulties in its way through. Chaotic cryptographers have been censured by conventional cryptographers of a lack of deep knowledge in cryptography.

Chaotic cryptography appears as an applied branch of non-linear dynamical systems. Initial works were discussed in the area of applied cryptology (Dachselt & Schwarz, 2001; Amigó, 2009) but soon demonstrated low security or performance, being discarded before long. Since then, numerous cryptosystems have been proposed, many still lacking of thorough security and efficiency analysis or difficult to implement in practice. This has damaged the image of chaotic cryptography in the cryptographic community.

Nevertheless hard work has been done to this respect (Alvarez & Li, 2006) and relevant aspects have been identified as important in the process of designing good chaotic cryptosystems. As a consequence, there are a series of guidelines to assist designers to fulfil some basic cryptographic requirements (Alvarez & Li, 2006). They address three main issues: implementation, key management and security analysis. Implementation guidelines take into account the necessity of a detailed description of the cryptosystem and measurements of its performance. Regarding to the key, a complete analysis should be done to guaranty the required behaviour of the chaotic algorithm in the key space. This means looking for regions of weak keys or windows of non chaotic behaviour, among others. The definition of the key and the procedure to build it, should be also clearly specified.

As for the security analysis, the novelty of chaotic cryptography makes difficult a rigorous study on the security of these algorithms (Amigó, 2009). As well as it is not yet established a general analytical methodology to study non-linear dynamical systems, there is also a lack of adequate analysis tools to assess the behaviour of these systems as part of the cryptographic algorithm. In this case, conventional cryptography tools cannot be directly applied to chaotic cryptographic algorithms. This is another reason why these totally new schemes seem doubtful to conventional cryptographers.

However, lessons have been learnt and the work done in this area isgiving a series of mathematical tools to assess the security of the algorithms (Arroyo, 2009; Alvarez et al, 2011). Chaotic cryptoanalysis works show examples of the tools used to assess security and the details of their realization. The analysis of the dynamical properties of the systems as the bifurcation diagrams and the Lyapunov's exponents is considered a basic security analysis. These tools allow the designer to discover regions of the parameters of design where the chaotic system shows windows of periodic behaviour. Furthermore a study of the statistical characteristics of the cryptosystem must be recommended. This is done, through the study of the histograms looking for uniformity in the distribution of ciphertexts and calculating for different values of the parameters the entropy of the orbits and the statistical complexity.

Today chaotic cryptography remains a very active field, with many publications in different areas of modern cryptography. This interdisciplinary approach has been quite successful in pseudo random number generation. But it is still in the side of chaotic cryptography to develop the necessary analytical tools and prove the compliance of the required security standards.

The chapter concludes here. It has intended to give a vision of what chaotic cryptography is and a comprehensive example of the techniques used in this field. This example gathers a series of topics considered of interest in the field of chaotic cryptography, such as digital chaotic cryptosystems, chaos based Pseudo-Random Bit Generation (PRBG) and the use of chaotic two-dimensional maps. It also covers a detailed explanation of its implementation and describes the measurements performed to assess its performance characteristics. This provides a display of how digital chaotic cryptosystems are built and the tools used in this area to evaluate their quality. Additionally it is presented a mechanism that illustrates how the geometry characteristics of the chaotic attractors can be used to improve the security of the cryptographic algorithm.

The authors would like to leave a final remark. This is that, though chaotic cryptography may be considered at present peripheral in circles of conventional crypto, chaotic number generation may have attractive applications as simulation engines in computational science (Pellicer-Lostao & Lopez-Ruiz, 2011c, 2011d). Chaos based number generators are easy to use and highly configurable. This makes them a valuable tool for this application.

5. Acknowledgment

The authors thank the BIFI Institute of the Universidad de Zaragoza by financial support.

6. References

Alvarez, G., Li, S. (2006). Some Basic Cryptographic Requirements for Chaos-Based Cryptosystems. *International Journal of Bifurcation and Chaos*, World Scientific, Vol. 16, pp 2129-2151.

Alvarez, G., Amigó, J.M., Arroyo, D., Li, S. (2011). Lessons Learnt from Cryptoanalysis of Chaos-based Ciphers, in *Chaos-Based Cryptography. Theory, Algorithms and Applications*. Studies in Computational Intelligence, Vol. 354, ISBN 978-3-642-20542-2, Berlin, pp. 257-295.

Alligood, K. T., Sauer, T., & Yorke, J.A. (1997). *Chaos: an introduction to dynamical systems*. Springer-Verlag, ISBN 0-387-94677-2, New York.

Amigó, J.M. (2009). Chaos-Based Cryptography. In: *Intelligent Computing Based on Chaos*, Springer, ISBN 978-3-540-95971-7, pp. 291-313, Berlin.

Arroyo Guardeño, David (2009). *Framework for the analysis and design of encryption strategies based on discrete-time chaotic dynamical systems*, Ph.D. thesis, Universidad Politécnica de Madrid, Escuela Técnica Superior de Ingenieros Agrónomos, Madrid, Spain. Available on line: http://oa.upm.es/1808/

Bogdan, C., Chargé, P., Fournier-Purnaret, D. (2007). Behavior of Chaotic Sequences Under a Finite Representation and its Cryptographic Applications, *IEEE Workshop on Nonlinear Maps and Applications (NOMA)*, Toulouse, 2007.

Boguta, K.. (2011). *Sensitivity To Peturbation in Elementary Cellular Automata*, from the Wolfram Demonstrations Project http://demonstrations.wolfram.com/SensitivityToPeturbationInElementaryCellularAutomata/

Cambel, A. B., (1993). *Applied Chaos Theory: A Paradigm for Complexity.* (Ed. 1). Academic Press, ISBN 0-12-155940-8, London.

Casperson, L. W. (1988). Gas laser instabilities and their interpretation. In: *Instabilities and Chaos in Quantum Optics II.* Proceedings of the NATO Advanced Study Institute, Italy, June 1987 pp. 83–98, Springer Verlag.

Collet, P., Eckmann, J. P. (1980). Iterated Maps on the Interval as Dynamical Systems, *Progress in Physics*, Birkhauser, Cambridge.

Dachselt, F., Schwarz, W. (2001). Chaos and Cryptography, IEEE Transactions on Circuits and Systems, Part 1, Special Issue. IEEE Transactions on Circuits and Systems I: Fundamental Theory and Applications, Vol. 48, No. 12, pp. 1498-1509.

Devaney, R. L. (1989). *Introduction to chaotic dynamical systems.* Addison-Wesley Publishing Company, Inc., ISBN 13: 9780201130461, pp. 161-172.

Fabre, C. (2011). *Chaos Game 2D/3D*, from the Wolfram Demonstrations Project http://demonstrations.wolfram.com/ChaosGame2D3D/

Fournier-Prunaret, D., Lopez-Ruiz, R., Taha, A. K. (2006). Route to Chaos in Three-Dimensional Maps of Logistic Type, *Grazer Mathematische Berichte*, Vol. 350, pp. 82-95.

Fournier-Prunaret, D., Abdel-Kaddous T. (2012). Chaotic sequences as pseudo-random sequences obtained from 2-dimensional maps, *International Journal of Applied Mathematics & Statistics*, Special Issue on Statistical Chaos and Complexity, Vol. 26, No. 2, pp. 92-105.

Guan, P. (1987). Cellular automaton publick-key cryptosystem. *Complex Systems*, Vol. 1, pp.51-57.

Guckenheimer, M., Holmes, P. (1983). *Nonlinear Oscillations, Dynamical Systems and Bifurcation of Vector Fields*, Applied Mathematical Sciences Vol. 42, Springer-Verlag, ISBN-13: 978-0387908199

Kocarev, L. (2001). Chaos-based Cryptography: A Brief Overview, *IEEE Circuits and Systems Magazine*, IEEE Publications, Vol. 1, pp. 6-21.

Kocarev, L., Jakimoski, G. (2003). Pseudorandom Bits Generated by Chaotic Maps", IEEE Transactions on Circuits and Systems I: Fundamental Theory and Applications, Vol.50, No. 1, pp 123-126.

Kocarev, L., Galias, Z., & Lian, S. (2009). Intelligent Computing Based on Chaos. Studies in Computational Intelligence, Vol. 184 Springer-Verlag, ISBN 978-3-540-95971-7, Berlin.

Kocarev, L., Lian, S. (2011). *Chaos-Based Cryptography. Theory, Algorithms and Applications.* Studies in Computational Intelligence, Vol. 354, ISBN 978-3-642-20542-2, Berlin.

Falcioni, M., Palatella, L., Pigolotti, S., Vulpiani, A. (2005). Properties Making a Chaotic System a Good Pseudo Random Number Generator, *Physical Review E*, Elsevier, 016220, pp. 1-10.

Femat, R., L. Kocarev, L., van Gerven, L., Monsivais-Pérez, M.E. (2005). Towards generalized synchronization of strictly different chaotic systems, *Physics Letters A*, Vol. 342, pp. 247–255.

Hénon, M. (1976). A Two-dimensional Mapping with a Strange Attractor, *Communications in Mathematical Physics*, Springer, Vol. 50, pp 69-77.

Knuth, D. E. (1997). *The Art of Computer Programming*, Vol. 2, (3rd Ed.): Seminumerical Algorithms, Addison-Wesley Longman Publishing Co., ISBNv13: 978-0-201-89684-8, pp. 38-113.

Kyrtsou, C., & Vorlow, C., (2005). Complex dynamics in macroeconomics: A novel approach. In: *New Trends in Macroeconomics*, Diebolt, C., and Kyrtsou, C., (eds.), pp. 223-245, ISBN-13: 978-3-540-21448-9, Springer Verlag, Berlin.

Laplace, P. S. (1825). *Traité du Mécanique Céleste.* Oeuvres complètes de Laplace (vol. 5), Gauthier-Villars, Paris.

Larson, L. E., Liu, J. M., Tsimring, L. S. (2006). *Digital Communications Using Chaos and Nonlinear Dynamics*, Springer-Verlag, ISBN-13: 978-0387-29787-3, New York.

Li, S., Mou, X., Cai, Y. (2001). Pseudo-random Bit Generator Based on Couple Chaotic Systems and Its Application in Stream- Ciphers Cryptography", INDOCRYPT 2001, LNCS, Springer, Vol. 2247, pp 316-329.

Li, S. (2003). *Analyses and New Designs of Digital Chaotic Ciphers*. Ph.D. thesis, School of Electronic and Information Engineering, Xi'an Jiaotong University, Xi'an, China. Available online at http://www.hooklee.com/pub.html

Li, S., Chen, G., Mou, X. (2005). On the Dynamical Degradation of Digital Piecewise Linear Chaotic Maps, *International Journal of Bifurcation and Chaos*, World Scientific, Vol.15, pp. 3119-3151.

López-Ruiz, R., Fournier-Prunaret, D. (2003). Complex Patterns on the Plane: Different Types of Basin Fractalization in a Two-Dimensional Mapping, *International Journal of Bifurcation and Chaos*, World Scientific, Vol. 13, pp. 287-310.

López-Ruiz, R., Pérez-García, C. (1991). Dynamics of Maps with a Global Multiplicative Coupling, *Chaos, Solitons and Fractals*, Elsevier, Vol.1, pp 511-528,

Lorenz, E. N. (1963). Deterministic non-periodic flow. *Journal of the Atmospheric Sciences*, vol. 20, pp 130–141.

Mahieu, E. (2011). *Ikeda Attractor*, from the Wolfram Demonstrations Project *http://demonstrations.wolfram.com/IkedaAttractor/*

Mandelbrot, B. (1977). *The Fractal Geometry of Nature* (Ed. 1), W.H. Freeman & Company, ISBN-13: 978-0-7167-1186-5, New York.

Mahieu, E. (2011). *Bifurcation Diagram of the Hénon Map* from the Wolfram Demonstrations Project *http://demonstrations.wolfram.com/ BifurcationDiagramOfTheHenonMap/*

Marsaglia, G. (1995) .The Diehard Test Suite. Available in: *http://stat.fsu.edu/geo/diehard.html*

Mascagni, M. (1999). *The Scalable Parallel Random Number Generators Library (SPRNG) for ASCI Monte Carlo Computations.* Available in: http://sprng.cs.fsu.edu/

May, R. M., McLean, A. R. (2007). *Theoretical Ecology: Principles and Applications*, Blackwell, Oxford, ISBN 978-0-19-920998-9

Menezes, A. J., Paul C. van Oorschot, P. C., Vanstone, S. A. (1996). Handbook of applied Cryptography, CRC Press, ISBN: 0-8493-8523-7, Available at: *http://www.cacr.math.uwaterloo.ca/hac/*

Mira, C., Gardini, L., Barugola, A., Cathala, J. C. (1996). *Chaotic Dynamics in Two-Dimensional Noninvertible Maps*, World Scientific Series on Nonlinear Science, WorldScientific. Series A, vol. 20, ISBN: 978-981-02-1647-4.

Pellicer-Lostao, C., Lopez-Ruiz, R. (2008). Pseudo-Random Bit Generation based on 2D chaotic maps of logistic type and its Applications in Chaotic Cryptography. LNCS, Vol. 5073, pp. 784-796, Springer, Heidelberg. (Available pre-print at: arXiv:0801.3982)

Pellicer-Lostao, C., Lopez-Ruiz, R. (2009). Role of Symmetry and Geometry in a Chaotic Pseudorandom Bit Generator, *International Journal of Computer Science and Software Technology*, Vol. 2, No. 1, International Science Press, ISSN: 0974-3898, pp. 43-53. (Available pre-print at: arXiv:0802.4350)

Pellicer-Lostao, C., Lopez-Ruiz, R. (2011a). Orbit Diagram of Two Coupled Logistic Maps, from the Wolfram Demonstrations Project, http://demonstrations.wolfram.com/OrbitDiagramOfTwoCoupledLogisticMaps/

Pellicer-Lostao, C., Lopez-Ruiz, R. (2011b). *Orbit Diagram of the Henon Map*, from the Wolfram Demonstrations Project, http://demonstrations.wolfram.com/OrbitDiagramOfTheHenonMap/

Pellicer-Lostao, C., Lopez-Ruiz, R. (2011c). Transition from Exponential to Power Law Income Distributions in a Chaotic Market, *International Journal of Modern Physics C*, Vol. 22, No. 1 pp. 21–33.

Pellicer-Lostao, C., Lopez-Ruiz, R. (2011d). *Application of Chaotic Number Generators in Econophysics*, to appear in Journal of Engineering Science and Technology Review, Available on line: arXiv:1110.4506v2

Po Han, L., Soo Chang, P., Yih Yuh, C. (2003). Generating Chaotic Stream Ciphers using Chaotic Systems, *Chinese Journal of Physics*, The Physical Society of the Republic of China, Vol. 41, pp 559-581,.

Poincaré, J. H. (1890). Sur le problème des trois corps et les équations de la dynamique. Divergence des séries de M. Lindstedt. *Acta Mathematica*, vol. 13, pp 1–270.

Protopopescu, V. A., Santoro, R. T., Tollover, J. S. (1995). *Fast Secure Encryptiondecryption Method Based on Chaotic Dynamics*, US Patent 5479513.

Robinson, C. (1995). *Dynamical Systems*, (Ed. 2), CRC Press, ISBN 13: 9780849384936, New York.

Rukhin, A., Soto, J., Nechvatal, J., Smid, M., Barker, E., Leigh, S., Levenson, M., Vangel, M., Banks, D., Heckert, A., Dray, J., Vo, S. (2010). Special Publication 800-22 Revision 1 a (http://csrc.nist.gov/publications/nistpubs/800-22-rev1a/SP800-22rev1a.pdf

Rütti, M., Troyer, M., Petersen, W.P. (2004). *A Generic Random Number Generator Test Suite*. Available in: http://arXiv:math/0410385v1

Suneel, M. (2009). Cryptographic Pseudo-Random Sequences from the Chaotic Hénon Map. *Sadhana*, Indian Academy of Sciences, Vol. 34, pp. 689 - 701 Available pre-print in: http://arxiv.org/abs/cs/0604018.

Stojanovski, T., Kocarev, L. (2001). Chaos Based Random Number Generators. Part I: Analysis, *IEEE Transactions on Circuits and Systems I: Fundamental Theory and Applications*, IEEE Publications, Vol. 43, pp 281-288.

Tenny, R., Tsimring, L. S., Abarbanel, H. D. I., and Larson, L. E. (2006). Security of chaos-based communication and encryption. In: *Digital Communications Using Chaos and Nonlinear Dynamics* (Institute for Nonlinear Science). Springer, 2006, pp. 191–229.

van der Pol, B., & van der Mark, J. (1927). Frequency demultiplication, *Nature*, vol. 120, pp. 363–364.

Wolfram, S. (1985). Cryptography with cellular automata. In: *Advances in Cryptology-Crypto'85*, Lectures Notes in Computer Science, Vol. 218, pp.429-432, Springer-Verlag, Berlin.

Zech, A., Donges, J. F., Marwan, N. & Kurths, J. (2011). Frequency Distribution of the Logistic Map, from the Wolfram Demonstrations Project, *http://demonstrations.wolfram.com/FrequencyDistributionOfTheLogisticMap/*

14

Modern Technologies Used for Security of Software Applications

Tatiana Hodorogea[1] and Ionas Szilard Otto[2]
[1]*University of Basel,*
[2]*Bogdan-Voda University, Cluj-Napoca,*
[1]*Switzerland,*
[2]*Romania*

1. Introduction

Nowadays information systems security services involve more complexity because of there heterogeneity involving very big threats and attacks on such kind of networks, which are widely spread, open and interconnected. The security attacks and the technologies to exploit security attacks are growing continuously.

The importance of providing and maintaining the data and information security across networks is a major enterprise business activity, resulting in a big demand and need to ensure and maintain information security.

Cryptographic algorithms for confidentiality and authentication play a major importance role in nowadays information security.

With current network, Internet, and distributed systems, cryptography has become a key technology to ensure the security of today's web-Software Applications. A cryptographic system that an attacker is unable to penetrate even with access to infinite computing power is called *unconditionally secure*. The mathematics of such a system is based on information theory and probability theory. The goal of every cryptographer is to reduce the probability of a successful attack against the security of an encryption system - to zero and the probability theory provides the answer for this goal.

The aim and objective of this chapter is the development of a DNA Cryptographic Keys Based on Evolutionary Models, for the integration in our DNAProvider as Java Cryptographic Extension (JCE) with DNA Encryption (DNAE) system for use in security of our developed Web-based Software Applications.

Java Cryptography Extension (JCE) was developed as an extension package which includes implementation for cryptographic services. JCE offers a provider implementation plus API packages providing support for key agreement, encryption, decryption and secret key generation. JCE offers a provider implementation plus API packages providing support for key agreement, encryption, decryption and secret key generation. The security provider interface the means by which different security implementations may be plugged into the security package as message digests, encryption, digital signatures and keys, through JCE,

JSSE and authentication through JAAS. Thus, JCE support allowed us to provide our independent implementation of DNA Cryptographic Keys Based on Evolutionary Models used for Security of Web-based Business Processes.

As Public-Key algorithms are based on mathematical functions rather than on substitution and permutation involving the use of two separate keys, in contrast to symmetric encryption, which uses only one key we developed, implemented and tested the Security System Software Applications based on the Central Dogma of Molecular Biology (CDMB), where we derived DNA Cryptographic Keys based on evolutionary models. Our cryptographic system has one or more algorithms which implements a computational procedure by taking a variable input and generating a corresponding output.

If an algorithm's behavior is completely determined by the input, it is called *deterministic,* and if its behavior is not determined completely by input and generates different output each time executed with the same input, it is *probabilistic.*

Our work was based on the complexity of developing, as a subset of JCE, an unconditionally secure DNAE System as part of our security provider, named DNAProvider, (Hodorogea, Ionas, 2011).

Our work is based on Deriving DNA Cryptographic Keys Based on Evolutionary Models for Security of Software Applications.

Biotechnological Methods as recombinant DNA have been developed for a wide class of operations on DNA and RNA strands.

When aligning the DNA sequences of the same gene from related species, there will usually be differences between the sequences because of evolution and because of the degeneracy of the genetic code. Based on evolutionary models we extract and align the DNA sequences of the same gene from related chosen species with respect to human DNA Sequences. The alignment in the evolutionary system pipeline is realized with ProbCons tool, which is a pair-hidden Markov model-based on progressive alignment algorithm that primarily differs from most typical approaches in its use of maximum expected accuracy. After aligning our extracted DNA Sequences with ProbCons we derive the private/public pair DNA cryptographic keys based on evolutionary models mathematical functions. The molecular evolution model assigns probabilities to multiple-alignment columns in terms of the the philogenetic tree branches and is time dependent of frequency selections. Based on Kimura-Ohta theory Halpern and Bruno who have shown that mutation limit can be determined by substitution rates in terms of the mutation rates and equilibrium frequencies. Our work described in this chapter was based on the complexity of deriving DNA Cryptographic Keys Based on Evolutionary Models for Security of Software Applications.

2. Data security and cryptography

Networks are based on a number of network level equipments and servers as:

- **Dynamic host configuration protocol (DHCP)**, server dynamically assigns an IP address.
- **Domain name system (DNS)**, server translates a domain name (URL) into an IP address.

- **Network address translation (NAT)**, performs translation between private and public addresses.
- **E-mail server** supports electronic mailing
- Internet/Intranet/Extranet Web servers
- **Access points (AP),** giving wireless equipments access to wired network.
- **Virtual LAN (VLAN)** which virtually separate flows over the same physical network, so that direct communications between equipments from different VLANs could be restricted and required to go through a router for filtering purposes
- **Network access server (NAS) / Broadband access server (BAS),** gateways between the switched phone network and an IP-based network
- **Intrusion detection system (IDS) / Intrusion prevention system (IPS)** used to detect intrusions based on known intrusion scenario signatures.

More than 20 years information security considers confidentiality, integrity and availability, known as CIA as the base of information security. Cryptography gives us all of these services, linked with transmitted or stored data.

Considering GRID computing security where the heterogeneous resources are shared and located in different places belonging to different administrative domains over a heterogeneous network, additional security requirements must be satisfied compare to classical network security.

A GRID is a software toolbox and provides services for managing distributed software resources. Securing information in GRID computing encompasses verifying the integrity of the message against malicious modification, authenticating the source of a message and assuring the confidentiality of the message being sent.

The key points of information security are:

- Confidentiality- keeping the data secret
- Integrity - keeping the data unmodified
- Authentication - certifies the source of the data
- Non-repudiation - the process of the sent data can't be negated

Confidentiality implies the prevention to disclosure information by individuals and unauthorized systems.

In information security integrity implies the impossibility of data modification without the authorization and keeping the data unchanged. Authentication means the knowledge of the source, from where the data was received.

The information needs to be available when necessary. The assurance of availability implies the prevention of denial of service attacks.

Communication between GRID entities must be secure and confidentiality must be ensured for sensitive data, from communication stage, to potential storage stage. Problems of integrity should be detected in order to avoid treatment faults, availability is directly linked to performance and cost in GRID environment.

Cryptographic algorithms for confidentiality and authentication play a major importance role in nowadays information security.

2.1 Security services, threats and attacks

The main threats to WLAN networks are the radio waves since the radio waves broadcast, without respect to neither walls nor other limit. Denial of service (DoS) makes the network ineffective. It is easy to jam a radio network and network becomes unusable. By the use of rush access the network is overloaded with malicious connection request. Tools are able to detect this kind of traffic and help network administrator to identify and locate the origin.

Intrusions threats are most common attacks where the intrusion is done via client station and protection is the same as for wired networks, the use of firewall.

The most critical attack that aims to take the control of network resources of the enterprise is the network intrusion and in this case Wi-Fi dedicated intrusion detection systems (IDS) are efficient against such attacks.

With falsification of access points the hacker fetches the traffic on the network and the security protection from such attacks is by detecting abnormal radio transmission in unexpected areas.

Security protections can be applied to WLAN: network monitoring is a good defense to observe the network to be informed if something strange happens.

The intrusion detection system (IDS) is used against network intrusions. IDS correlates suspect events, tries to determine if they are due to an intrusion.

Traffic monitoring prevents against spoofing due to permanence observing of the Wi-Fi traffic in order to detect any inconsistent situations.

Network engineering is another security mechanism for network protection. It is strongly recommended to deploy WLAN using switches instead hubs and to control the traffic between wired networks. WLAN dedicated switch manages radio, networking and security functions and access points are used only as emitters and receptors providing a better protection against attacks. The firewalls manage protections at addressing level by providing filters and log connections, managing access control list (ACL) which are used for access filtering and monitor the connections. The firewalls must be installed in a DMZ, VPN authentication with encryption mechanisms activated. The use of VLAN must be done in order to split the network for the isolation of strategic data from the radio network. For this VLAN must be deployed on a dedicated virtual LAN structure where network contains several VLANs and each associated to a WLAN subnet with own SSID. All VLANs must be connected on the WLAN switch.

Encryption is the security mechanism at the application level by its use if the information is intercepted is unusable. In this scope standard protocols like transport layer security (TLS) may be used. Authentication is done by a login password sequence and link between client and server is secured by TLS, authentication is done via a local authentication database.

MAC addresses filtering is a non cryptographic security feature uses the unique link layer (MAC) address of the WLAN network card and identifies legitimates users.

One of security feature based on cryptography is wired equivalent privacy (WEP), defined in the initial IEEE 802.11 standard and provides authentication and encryption with 40-128 bit key length. The key should be changed in all nodes and in the access points, frequently and simultaneously.

Because of WEP weakness, the IEEE designed a protocol named 802.11i, known as WPA 2 (Wi-Fi Protected Access 2). Temporal key integrity protocol (TKIP) is used for generating per-packet keys for the RC4 ciphering used. The key is called temporal because is changed frequently and is combined with the sender's MAC address using the exclusive OR-operation. Resulting in the usage of different keys for upstream and downstream transmissions,

Two types of security mechanisms are known: first type is the one which are implemented in a certain protocol layer. Second type of the security mechanisms are not related to protocol layers or any security services.

Cryptography encrypts the data by the mean of using encryption security mechanism.

Encryption security mechanism is an encryption algorithm which encrypts and decrypts the data, transforming it into unreadable format.

The encryption mechanism depends on encryption keys being used (zero or more) and encryption algorithm. After the readable data is cryptographically transformed, digital signature is appended to it as a second security mechanism. *Digital signature security mechanism* proves the integrity of the data, the source of the data and protects the information send against forgery.

The access right to information and resources is realized thought the third security mechanism known as: *access control security mechanism.*

For preventing traffic analysis attempts the bits are inserted into the gaps of the data stream and this constitutes the *traffic padding security mechanism.*

Data security model represents a secure transfer of information across information channel (internet), between two principals: sender and receiver, by the use of communication protocols. Data security model implies the protection of data against confidentiality and authentication threats coming from an opponent. Security related transformation is needed to satisfy these conditions of data protection during transfer through information channel. Encryption transforms the message in an unreadable format, by the opponent. The additional code is added to the secret information based on the content of the message and this way the identity of the sender is verified.

3. DNA cryptography model

With current network, Internet, and distributed systems, cryptography has become a key technology to ensure the security of today's information infrastructure.

Biotechnological Methods as recombinant DNA have been developed for a wide class of operations on DNA and RNA strands. Bio Molecular Computation (BMC) makes use of biotechnological methods for doing computation and splicing operations allow for universal computation.

The first applications of DNA-based cryptography systems using biotechnologies techniques included: methods for 2D data input and output by use of chip-based DNA micro-array technology and transformation between conventional binary storage media via (photo-sensitive and/or photo emitting) DNA chip arrays

Lately DNA Cryptosystem using substitution and biotechnologies have been developed: *Substitution* one-time-pad encryption: is a substitution method using libraries of distinct pads, each of which defines a specific, randomly generated, pair-wise mapping. The decryption is done by similar methods. The *Input is a* plaintext binary message of length n, partitioned into plaintext words of fixed length.

Substitution One-time-pad, a table randomly mapping all possible strings of plaintext words into cipher words of fixed length, such that there is a unique reverse mapping and the *encryption is done by* substituting each i-th block of the plaintext with the cipher word given by the table, and is decrypted by reversing these substitutions. Using long DNA pads containing many segments, each segment contains a cipher word followed by a plaintext word and the cipher word, acts as a hybridization site for binding of a primer. Cipher word is appended with a plaintext word to produce word-pairs. The word-pair DNA strands are used as a lookup table in conversion of plaintext into cipher text.

*One-time-pad DNA Sequence with l*ength n, contains d = n/(L1+ L2+ L3) copies of repeating unit *Repeating unit* made up of:

1. Bi = a cipher word of length L1 = c1log n
2. Ci = a plaintext word length L2= c2log n

Each sequence pair uniquely associates a plaintext word with a cipher word and the Polymerase acts as a "stopper" sequence of length L3 = c3.

To generate a set of oligonucleotides corresponding to the plaintext/cipher and word-pair strands, ~Bi used as polymerase primer and *extended* with polymerase by specific attachment of plaintext word Ci. The *Stopper sequence* prohibits extension of growing

DNA strand beyond boundary of paired plaintext word.

Methods for Construction of DNA one-time pads are based on the biotechnologies rather than bioinformatics and present difficult to achieve both full coverage and yet still avoiding possible conflicts by repetition of plaintext and cipher words.

This methods make use of DNA chip technology for random assembly of one-time pads.

The advantages are that are currently commercially available (Affymetrix) chemical methods for construction of custom variants are well developed.

Other method also based on biotechnologies is so called method *DNA chip Method* for Construction of DNA one-time pads where is used an array of immobilized DNA strands and multiple copies of a single sequence are grouped together in a microscopic pixel which is optically addressable. Using the technology for synthesis of distinct DNA sequences at each (optically addressable) site of the array and combinatorial synthesis conducted in parallel at thousands of locations, prepared of oligonucleotides of length L, the 4L sequences are synthesized in 4n chemical reactions.

As an Example: 65,000 sequences of length 8 use 32 synthesis cycles and 1.67x107 sequences of length 10 use 48 cycles. The construction of DNA One-time pads based on biotechnologies was first developed by the pioneer in this field (Adleman 1997).

XOR One-time-pad (Vernam Cipher) Cryptosystem based on biotechnologies One-time-pad: S is a sequence of independently distributed random bits

M is a plaintext binary message of n bits resulting in the following cipher text ,

Ci = Mi XOR Si for = 1,…,n .

*Decrypted bits, u*se commutative property of XOR Ci XOR resulting in:

Si = (Mi XOR Si) XOR Si= Mi XOR (Si XOR Si)= Mi.

DNA Implementation of XOR One-time-pad Cryptosystem:

The *plaintext messages is* one test tube of short DNA strands

The *encrypted message is* another test tube of different short DNA strands

Encryption by XOR One-time-pad maps these in a random and reversible way such as plaintext is converted to cipher strands and plaintext strands are removed. For the *efficient* DNA encoding Adleman proposed to use *modular base 4 as* DNA has four nucleotides. Encryption constitutes the addition of one-time-pad elements modulo 4 and decryption is the subtract one-time-pad elements modulo.

Details of DNA Implementation of XOR One-time-pad Cryptosystem based on biotechnologies:

Each plaintext message has appended a unique *prefix index tag* of length L indexing it.

Each of one-time-pad DNA sequence has appended unique *prefix index tag* of same length L, forming *complements* of plaintext message tags. Using recombinant DNA bio techniques such as annealing and ligation in order to *concatenate into a single DNA strand* each corresponding pair of a plaintext message and a one-time-pad sequence resulting in *enciphered by bit-wise XOR computation and* fragments of the plaintext are converted to cipher strands using the one-time-pad DNA sequences, and plaintext strands are removed.

The reverse decryption is similar using commutative property of bit-wise XOR operation.

BMC Methods to effect bit-wise XOR on Vectors. This method can adapt BMC methods for binary addition and similar to bit-wise XOR computation can disable carry-sums logic to do XOR

*BMC techniques for Integer Addition were implemented by (*Guarnieri, Fliss, and Bancroft 96), first BMC addition operations (on single bits) by (Rubin el al 98, OGB97, LKSR97, GPZ97) permit chaining on n bits.

Addition by *Self Assembly* of DNA tiles was exploited by (Reif, 97) and (LaBean, 99)

*XOR by Self Assembly of DNA tiles (*LaBean, 99)**:** *XOR by Self Assembly of DNA tiles includes that f*or each bit Mi of the message, construct sequence ai that represents the ith bit.

Scaffold strands for binary inputs to the XOR are the usage of linkers to assemble the message M's n bits into scaffold strand sequence *a1, a 2 … a n.*

The One-time-pad is further portion scaffold strand *a' 1a' 2… a'n* and is created from random inputs add output tiles, the annealing give self assembly of the tiling.

The next step: adding ligase yields to the reporter strand:

R = a 1 a 2 ... a n.a' 1 a' 2... a'n.b 1 b 2 ... b n, where b i = a i XOR a'i, for i = 1,...,n.

In the next step the reporter strand is extracted by biotechnique of melting away the tiles, smaller sequences, and purifying it, contains concatenation of input message, encryption key, ciphertext.

Before the final last step using a marker sequence the ciphertext can be excised and separated based on its length being half that of remaining sequence. In the last step ciphertext is stored in a compact form.

These increasing importances of information security and the protection of human privacy rights as Confidentiality lead me to develop new security solutions based on modern technologies: Bioinformatics and Biotechnology.

In this work we present a technical process for protecting data assets such as personal medical information using Bioinformatics and a DNA cryptography technique based on bioinformatics rather then biotechnologies in this bioinformatics technique a person's own blood mineral levels serve as a seed for selecting, transmitting, and recovering his sensitive personal data.

As we know that the management of security keys remains a challenge, we also developed a bioinformatic mechanism to generate encrypt-decrypt keys by taking into consideration specifics of the cryptography method and the individual's DNA genome analysis.

Our work was based on the complexity of developing, as a subset of JCE, an unconditionally secure DNAE System as part of our security provider, named DNAProvider, (Hodorogea, Ionas 2011).

A cryptographic system that an attacker is unable to penetrate even with access to infinite computing power is called *unconditionally secure*. The mathematics of such a system is based on information theory and probability theory. When an attacker is theoretically able to intrude, but it is computationally infeasible with available resources, the cryptographic system is said to be *conditionally secure*. The mathematics in such systems is based on computational complexity theory. To design a secure cryptographic system is a very challenging. A cryptographic system has one or more algorithms which implement a computational procedure by taking a variable input and generating a corresponding output. If an algorithm's behavior is completely determined by the input, it is called *deterministic*, and if its behavior is not determined completely by input and generates different output each time executed with the same input, it is *probabilistic*. A distributed algorithm in which two or more entities take part is defined as a protocol including a set of communicational and computational steps. Each communicational step requires data to be transferred from one side to the other and each computational step may occur only on one side of the protocol. The goal of every cryptographer is to reduce the probability of a successful attack against the security of an encryption system - to zero. Probability theory provides the answer for this goal. Our work is based on the complexity of developing an unconditionally-secure DNA Encryption System as part of DNA Provider.

Java Cryptographic Extension (JCE) offers support for developing cryptographic package providers, allowing us to extend the JCE by implementing faster or more secure cryptographic algorithms. By the same means we shall provide our independent implementation of a DNA Encryption (DNAE) system, based on the Central Dogma of Molecular Biology (CDMB).

4. Complexity of DNA encryption system as a subset of Java cryptography extension

Java Cryptography Extension (JCE) was developed as an extension package which includes implementation for cryptographic services.

The goal of the security provider interface is to allow a means whereby specific algorithm implementations can be substituted for the default provider, SUN JCE. JCE was developed as an extension package which includes implementation for cryptographic services. JCE offers a provider implementation plus API packages providing support for key agreement, encryption, decryption and secret key generation. Thus, JCE offers support for developing alternative cryptographic package providers, (Fig.1)

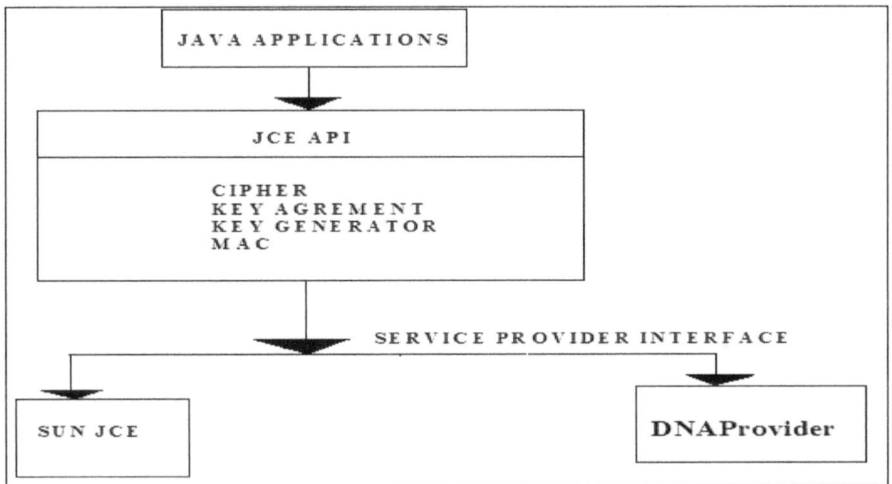

Fig. 1. Java Cryptography Extensions architectural model with unconditional secure DNA Encryption as part of our security provider (DNAProvider)

This support allows us to provide our independent implementation of DNAE System, based on the CDMB (Central Dogma of Molecular Biology).

The application code calls the appropriate JCE API classes. The JCE API classes invoke the classes in a provider that implements the interface classes, JCE SPI. The JCE SPI classes, in turn, invoke the requested functionality of the DNA Provider.

The security provider interface the means by which different security implementations may be plugged into the security package as message digests, encryption, digital signatures and keys, through JCE, JSSE and authentication through JAAS. Thus, JCE support allowed us to provide our independent implementation of DNA Cryptographic Keys Based on Evolutionary Models used for Security of Web-based Business Processes.

The classes necessary to handle secret keys come only with JCE. Keys and certificates are normally associated with some person or organization, and the way in which keys are stored, transmitted, and shared is an important topic in the security package.

When the Java Virtual Machine starts execution, it examines the user's properties to determine which security providers should be used. The user's properties are located in the file *java.security,* in which each provider is also enumerated. If users prefer to use DNAProvider as an additional security provider they can edit this file and add the DNA Provider. When the Security Class is asked to provide a particular engine and algorithm, it searches the listed providers for the first that can supply the desired operation,(Fig.2).

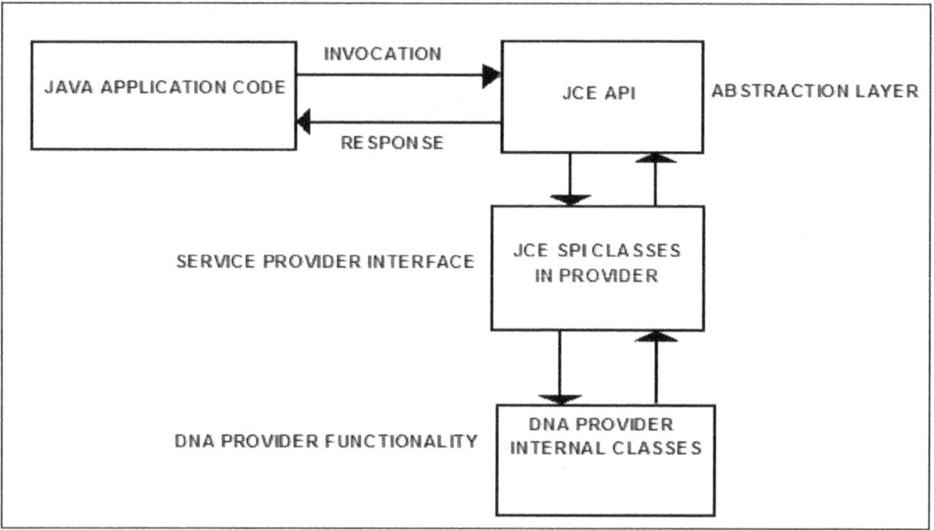

Fig. 2. Invocation of DNAProvider for providing requested functionality

The security provider abstracts two ideas: engines and algorithms. An Engine Class defines an abstract cryptographic service, without its concrete implementation. The goal of the security provider interface is to allow an easy mechanism where the specific algorithms and their implementations can be easily changed or substituted. The architecture including all of this contains:

Engine classes, these classes come with the Java virtual machine as part of the core API.

Algorithm classes, at the basic level, there is a set of classes that implement particular algorithms for particular engines.

A default set of these classes is provided by the supplier of the Java platform. Other third-party organizations or individual can supply additional sets of algorithm classes. These classes may implement one or more algorithms for one or more engines.

Going to provide my own set of classes to perform security operations, I must extend the Provider class and register that class with the security infrastructure

Provider class is abstract, none of its methods are abstract, I need do is subclass the Provider class and provide an appropriate constructor.

The basic implementation of a DNAProvider security provider is:

```
public class DNAProvider extends Provider
{
public DNAProvider( )
{
super("DNAProvider", 1.0, "DNA Security Provider v1.0");
}
}
```

Here we define the skeleton of a DNAProvider that is going to provide certain facilities based on Central Dogma of Molecular Biology(CDMB).

Java Cryptographic Extension (JCE) offers support for developing cryptographic package providers, allowing us to extend the JCE by implementing faster or more secure cryptographic algorithms. By the same means we provide our independent implementation of a DNA Encryption (DNAE) system, based on the Central Dogma of Molecular Biology (CDMB). In this work we present a technical process for protecting data assets such as personal information using a DNA cryptography technique in which a person's own blood mineral levels serve as a seed for selecting, transmitting, and recovering his sensitive personal data.

Adleman began the new field of bio-molecular computing research. His idea was to use DNA biochemistry for solving problems that are impossible to solve by conventional computers, or that require an enormous number of computation steps. The DNAE technique simulates the CDMB steps: transcription, splicing, and translation process. The time complexity of an attack on a message of length n, is $O(2^n)$. DNA computing takes advantages of combinatorial properties of DNA for massively-parallel computation.

Introducing DNA cryptography into the common PKI scenario, it is possible to follow the pattern of PKI, while also exploiting the inherent massively-parallel computing properties of DNA bonding to perform the encryption and decryption of the public and private keys. The resulting encryption algorithm used in the transaction is much more complex than the one used by conventional encryption methods.

To put this into the common description of secure data transmission and reception with respect to DNA cryptography, let us say Stefani is the sender, and Otto, the receiver. Stefani provides Otto her public key which will comprise someone's unique blood analysis. The Public Key (PK) encryption technique splits the key into a public key for encryption and a secret key for decryption. As an example: Otto generates a pair of keys and publishes his public key, while only he knows his secret key. Thus, anyone can use Otto's public key to send him an encrypted message, but only Otto knows the secret key to decrypt it.

A secret DNA data strand contains three parts: a secret DNA data strand in the middle, and unique primer sequences on each side S1. Stefani uses the technique of deriving DNA private key.

Using an information conversion program, Stefani encodes the medical records in a DNA data strand flanked by unique primer sequences S1 and mixes it among other decoy DNA strands.

According to the CDMB, during the process of transcription, Stefani removes the introns from the data-encoded DNA, resulting in encryption key 1, E1 (starting and pattern codes of introns). Thus, E1 => C1 = E1(P), where P is plain-text and C is the cipher-text. Stefani translates the resulting spliced form of the data from which she derives Encryption key 2, E2 (codon-amino acid mapping). E2 => C = E2(C1) obtains the data-encoded protein after the translation process. Stefani sends Otto the keys E1 and E2 through a public channel.

Then she sends Otto the encoded protein form of the data through a public channel. Otto uses the key E2 to recover the mRNA form of the data from the protein form of the data. Decryption key, D1 = E2 => P1=D1(C). Otto recovers the DNA form of the data in the reverse order that Stefani encrypted it. Decryption key, D2 = E1 => P = D2(P1). Otto identifies the secret data-carrying DNA strand using the program that associates the nucleotide sequence based on someone's blood mineral analysis.

He obtains the unique primer sequences S1 that mark the beginning and end of the secret data DNA strand hidden among the decoy strands. In this last step, Otto uses the information conversion program and reads the medical record of the individual.

4.1 The DNA encryption protocol

Resent research considers the use of the Human genome in cryptography and the famous DNA one-time-pad encryption schemes utilizing the indexed of random key string was first developed by Ashish Gehani, Thomas H. LaBean and John H. Reif.

At the lowest level, a genome can be described as a long string of nucleotides. It could be compared to a very long text made of four letters (strings of DNA). All living organisms consist of cells and in each cell there is the same set of chromosomes. Chromosomes are strings of DNA and serve as a model for the whole organism made from genes, which are made from blocks of DNA. Complete set of genetic material (all chromosomes) is called genome. The assumption of evolutionary models is that biological systems have evolved from the same origin, constantly reusing some basic building blocks and through the cycles of mutation and selection that constitute evolution, new functions have been created by reusing pieces of already existing DNA machinery. If we consider this problem in terms of sequences, this means that two sequences responsible for similar functions may be different, depending on how long they have been diverging. Many of the problems in bioinformatics and more specifically in sequence alignment are said to be NP complete as the number of potential solutions rises exponentially with the number of sequences and their length and the solution cannot be found in polynomial time and space. A sequence alignment is the representation of two sequences in a way that reflects their relationship and if the alignment is designed to reflect phylogenetic relationships, the residues will be aligned when they originate from the same residue in the common ancestor. If a given sequence lacks one residue, a gap will be inserted in its place at the corresponding position, in an evolutionary model context, a null sign means that a residue was inserted in one of the sequences or deleted in the other while the sequences were diverging from their common ancestor.

As Public-key algorithms are based on mathematical functions rather than on substitution and permutation and involves the use of two separate keys, in contrast to symmetric encryption, which uses only one key. When aligning the DNA sequences of the same gene from related species, there will usually be differences between the sequences because of evolution.

We developed a Unique Process System Pipeline Evolutionary Models of deriving DNA Cryptographic

Keys Sequences by deriving the DNA private/public keys from human genome analysis by computing the philogenetic tree relating and the branch length during evolution for chosen species. The molecular evolution model assigns probabilities to multiple-alignment columns in terms of the the philogenetic tree branches and is time dependent of frequency selections. Based on Kimura-Ohta theory Halpern and Bruno, have shown that mutation limit can be determined by substitution rates in terms of the mutation rates and equilibrium frequencies.

Models of DNA evolution were first proposed in 1969 by Jukes and Cantor, assuming equal transition rates and equal equilibrium frequencies for all bases.

In 1980 Kimura-Ohta introduced a model of DNA Evolution with two parameters: one for the transition and one for the transversion rate.

To estimate evolutionary distances in terms of the number of nucleotide substitutions and the evolutionary rates when the divergence times are known by comparing a pair of nucleotide sequences. There are two types of differences when homologous sites are occupied by different nucleotide bases and both are purines or both are pyrimidines. The difference is called Transition type when one of the two is a purine and the other is a pyrimidine then the difference is called transversion type.

Let P and Q be the fractions of nucleotide sites, showing between two sequences compared the transition and transversion type differences, then:

The Evolutionary Distance per Site is:

$$K = -(1/2)\ln\{(1-2P-Q)\} \tag{1}$$

The Evolutionary Rate per Year is then given by:

$$k = K/(2T) \tag{2}$$

T is the time since the divergence of the two sequences. If only the third codon positions are compared, then *the Synonymous Component of Evolutionary Base Substitutions per Site* is:

$$K'_S = -(1/2)\ln(1-2P-Q) \tag{3}$$

In biology, a substitution model describes the process from which a sequence of characters changes into another set of traits.

Each position in the sequence corresponds to a property of a species which can either be present or absent.

4.2 The technique of deriving DNA cryptographic keys based on evolutionary models

We developed and implemented a software tool for aligning the DNA Cryptographic Keys Sequences of the same gene from related chosen species with respect to Human DNA Sequences.

The alignment in the evolutionary system pipeline of DNA Cryptographic Keys Sequences was realized with trained ProbCons tool which is a pair-hidden Markov model-based on progressive alignment algorithm, that primarily differs from most typical approaches in its use of maximum expected accuracy.

As Public-key algorithms are based on mathematical functions rather than on substitution and permutation and involves the use of two separate keys, in contrast to symmetric encryption, which uses only one key. When aligning the DNA sequences of the same gene from related species, there will usually be differences between the sequences because of evolution, (Ochman, 2003). Some of these will lead to differences in the amino acids of the encoded protein (non-synonymous changes). Because of the degeneracy of the genetic code leave the protein unchanged (synonymous, or silent changes). If Ka/Ks< 1 *Purifying (negative) selection,* most proteins are well adapted to carry out their function change would not lead to the creation of selective advantage. If *Ka/Ks >1 Diversifying (positive),* selection has acted to change the protein and if *Ka/Ks= 1 Neutral evolution,* (Mustonen, Lässig, 2005). After aligning our extracted DNA Sequences with ProbCons tool, we derive the private/public pair DNA cryptographic keys based on evolutionary models and based on mathematical functions.

ProbCons is a tool for generating multiple alignments of protein sequences. It uses a combination of probabilistic modeling and consistency-based alignment techniques and has achieved the highest accuracies of all alignments methods. The basic for ProbCons algorithm is the computation of pairwise posterior probability matrices, P(xi ~ yi | x, y), which give the probability that one should match letters *xi* and *yi* when aligning two sequences *x* and *y*. ProbCons uses a simple probabilistic model that allows for efficient computation of this probabilities. Given a set of sequences ProbCons computes the posterior probability matrices for each pair of sequences and computes the expected accuracy of each alignment.

As Public-key algorithms are based on mathematical functions rather than on substitution and permutation and involves the use of two separate keys, in contrast to symmetric encryption, which uses only one key. When aligning the DNA sequences of the same gene from related species, there will usually be differences between the sequences because of evolution.

We developed a Unique Process System Pipeline Evolutionary Models of deriving DNA Cryptographic

Keys Sequences by deriving the DNA private/public keys from human genome analysis by computing the philogenetic tree relating and the branch length during evolution for chosen species. The molecular evolution model assigns probabilities to multiple-alignment columns in terms of the the philogenetic tree branches and is time dependent of frequency selections. Based on Kimura-Ohta theory Halpern and Bruno, have shown that mutation limit can be determined by substitution rates in terms of the mutation rates and equilibrium frequencies.

For every alignment column, we calculated the likelihood under two evolutionary models: a "foreground" and a "background" model.

The background model assumes a rate model (Felsenstein 1981), parameterized by the branch lengths of the phylogenetic tree:

w is a vector of nucleotide frequencies, with w_α the frequency of nucleotide α,

$r_{\alpha\beta}$ -the rate of substitution from base β to base α which is proportional to w_α, independent of β.

For every background evolution models we have a corresponding foreground model. The difference between the foreground model and background model is that the background model assumes that all positions undergo substitutions from base β to base α at the same rate $r_{\alpha\beta} \propto w_\alpha$.

The foreground model I assume that, at a given position i, the substitution rates $r^i_{\alpha\beta} \propto w^i_\alpha$ are altered due to specific selection preferences for certain bases at this position, parameterized by nucleotide frequencies w^i_α.

The parameters w^i_α, at each position are unknown, integrated out of the likelihood.

For each alignment column of the reference species, in intergenic regions and in genes, we calculate the ratio R, representing the likelihoods of foreground and background evolutionary models.

Halpern and Bruno in 1998 estimated the evolutionary distances from coding sequences taking into account protein-level selection to avoid relative underestimation of longer evolutionary distances.

The equilibrium frequencies determine the maximum dissimilarity expected for highly diverged but functionally and structurally conserved sequences and crucial for estimating long distances (Molina, Nimwegen 2008).

Halpern and Bruno introduced a codon-level model of coding sequence evolution in which position-specific amino acid equilibrium frequencies were free parameters. They demonstrated the importance and feasibility of modeling such behavior as the model produced linear distance estimated over a wide range of distances. Some alternative models underestimated long distances, relative to short distances.

If r is the rate of substitution from a base a to a base b at position i, μ is the rate of mutation from a to b and w is the equilibrium frequency of nucleotide i, at this position, (Halpern AL, Bruno WJ, 1998).

Following Golding and Felsenstein (1990), Halpern and Bruno (1998) who have shown that mutation limit of the standard Kimura-Ohta theory, one can uniquely determine substitution rates in terms of the mutation rates and the equilibrium frequencies w^i_α if $r^i_{\alpha\beta}$ is the rate of substitution from β to α at position i, $\mu_{\alpha\beta}$ the rate of mutation from β to α, and w_{α}^{i} the equilibrium frequency of α at this position, we have (Halpern and Bruno 1998).

We derive the private/public pair DNA cryptographic keys based on evolutionary models and based on mathematical functions.

We started with extracting from public available database all orthologus DNA coding sequences for all genes, from related species with respect to Human Genome sequences. A genome of a reference species in our case is Human Genom (hg18) and two more additional genomes are: Taurus Genome (bosTau3) and Dog Genome (canFam2). We extracted the DNA sequences for 29.000 genes which equals to 44103 pages in printable format. Using a trained parameter set for ProbCons tool we aligned all orthologus DNA coding sequences of our choosen species for all genes with respect to Human DNA coding sequences.

ProbCons achieved the highest accuracies of all multiple alignments methods as it uses probabilistic modeling and consistency-based alignment techniques.

We computed the philogenitic tree for our chosen species and the branch length during evolution, (Fig. 4) with respect to human genome (hg18).

A Software Application, reeds the tree, computes the pairwise alignment, computes the branches of the tree for our

chosen mammalian species. Public-key algorithms are based on mathematical functions, rather than on substitution and permutation and involve the use of two separate keys in contrast to symmetric encryption, (Fig. 3).

In Table 1, Second Column (C2) model represents the computed DNA Public Keys, with respect to Colum C1 and assumes substitution rate model which is calculated by the branch lengths of the phylogenetic tree and a vector of nucleotide frequencies, (Table 1) and represents the public keys.

Given the transition probabilities and given a phylogenetic tree we calculated the ratio for an alignment column C3/C2, which is the product over transition probabilities for each branch of the tree we summed over all possible nucleotides for internal nodes calculated by recursive algorithm introduced by Felsenstein.

The first column C1 represents all possible three base sequences with respect to human species. Second Colum (C2) model, with respect to C1 assumes substitution rate model which is calculated by the branch lengths of the phylogenetic tree and a vector of nucleotide frequencies, and represents the public key. The third Colum (C3) assumes that at a given position, the substitution rates are altered during due to specific selection preferences for a certain base. The last Colum is the ratio C3/C2 and represents the private key, (Table 1).

Using the same model and desired length of bases from the first column we can derive the public/private keys used in Java KeyStore with respect to human or desired number of species. Resulting in new set of public/private *DNA Cryptographic Keys for our Java DNA KeyStore usage.*

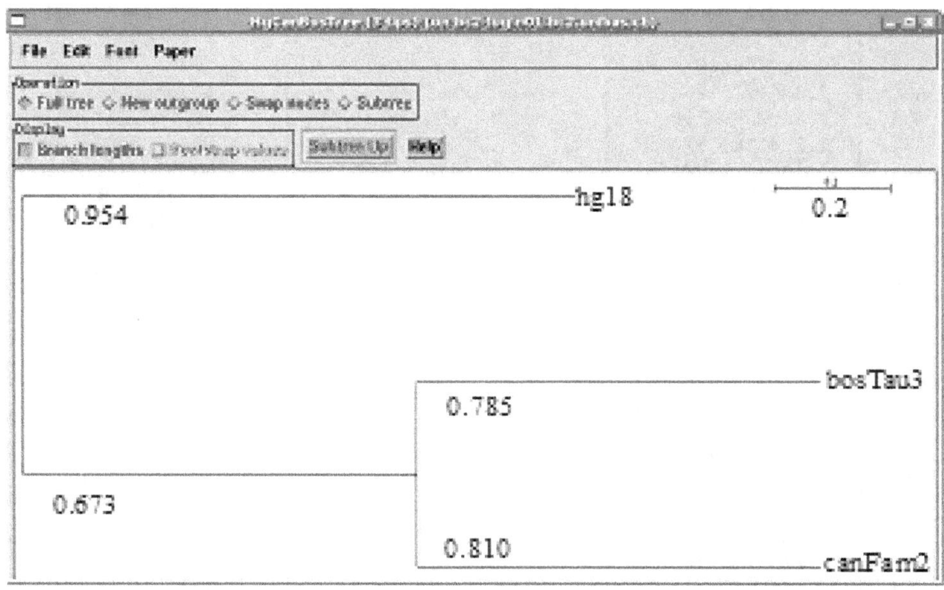

Fig. 3. Computed philogenetic tree and the branch length

C1	C2	C3	C3/C2
Applications Places System			
			chontoro@bc2-
File Edit View Terminal Tabs Help			
AAA	1.6597000119e-01	2.3079619624e-01	1.3905898330e+00
AAC	2.4681019326e-02	1.3278568674e-02	5.3800730425e-01
AAG	1.6454012884e-02	8.8523791160e-03	5.3800730425e-01
AAT	1.6454012884e-02	8.8523791160e-03	5.3800730425e-01
AA-	2.2355904628e-01	2.6177952314e-01	1.1709636782e+00
ACA	1.4264544699e-02	8.0703313604e-03	5.6576158094e-01
ACC	1.2867509971e-02	7.3718139965e-03	5.7290136265e-01
ACG	2.8141770326e-03	4.6902950543e-04	1.6666666667e-01
ACT	2.8141770326e-03	4.6902950543e-04	1.6666666667e-01
AC-	3.2760408735e-02	1.6380204368e-02	5.0000000000e-01
AGA	9.5096964661e-03	5.3802209069e-03	5.6576158094e-01
AGC	2.8141770326e-03	4.6902950543e-04	1.6666666667e-01
AGG	7.6402809700e-03	4.7581994958e-03	6.2277807774e-01
AGT	1.8761180217e-03	3.1268633695e-04	1.6666666667e-01
AG-	2.1840272490e-02	1.0920136245e-02	5.0000000000e-01
ATA	9.5096964661e-03	5.3802209069e-03	5.6576158094e-01
ATC	2.8141770326e-03	4.6902950543e-04	1.6666666667e-01
ATG	1.8761180217e-03	3.1268633695e-04	1.6666666667e-01
ATT	7.6402809700e-03	4.7581994958e-03	6.2277807774e-01
AT-	2.1840272490e-02	1.0920136245e-02	5.0000000000e-01
A-A	1.9925393882e-01	2.4962696941e-01	1.2528082049e+00
A-C	4.3176883363e-02	2.1588441681e-02	5.0000000000e-01
A-G	2.8784588908e-02	1.4392294454e-02	5.0000000000e-01
A-T	2.8784588908e-02	1.4392294454e-02	5.0000000000e-01
A--	3.0000000000e-01	3.0000000000e-01	1.0000000000e+00
CAA	1.2867509971e-02	7.3718139965e-03	5.7290136265e-01
CAC	1.4264544699e-02	8.0703313604e-03	5.6576158094e-01
CAG	2.8141770326e-03	4.6902950543e-04	1.6666666667e-01
CAT	2.8141770326e-03	4.6902950543e-04	1.6666666667e-01
CA-	3.2760408735e-02	1.6380204368e-02	5.0000000000e-01
CCA	2.4681019326e-02	1.3278568674e-02	5.3800730425e-01
CCC	1.6597000119e-01	2.3079619624e-01	1.3905898330e+00
CCG	1.6454012884e-02	8.8523791160e-03	5.3800730425e-01
CCT	1.6454012884e-02	8.8523791160e-03	5.3800730425e-01
CC-	2.2355904628e-01	2.6177952314e-01	1.1709636782e+00
CGA	2.8141770326e-03	4.6902950543e-04	1.6666666667e-01
CGC	9.5096964661e-03	5.3802209069e-03	5.6576158094e-01
CGG	7.6402809700e-03	4.7581994958e-03	6.2277807774e-01
CGT	1.8761180217e-03	3.1268633695e-04	1.6666666667e-01
CG-	2.1840272490e-02	1.0920136245e-02	5.0000000000e-01
CTA	2.8141770326e-03	4.6902950543e-04	1.6666666667e-01
CTC	9.5096964661e-03	5.3802209069e-03	5.6576158094e-01
CTG	1.8761180217e-03	3.1268633695e-04	1.6666666667e-01

Table 1. Public/Private DNA Cryptographic Keys

5. Conclusion

Considering GRID computing security where the heterogeneous resources are shared and located in different places belonging to different administrative domains over a heterogeneous network, additional security requirements must be satisfied compare to classical network security. Communication between GRID entities must be secure and confidentiality must be ensured for sensitive data, from communication stage, to potential storage stage. Cryptographic algorithms for confidentiality play a major importance role in nowadays information security.

Our work described in this chapter was based on the complexity of developing the cryptographic package provider, named DNAProvider as Java Cryptographic Extension (JCE), where we derive the DNA Cryptographic Keys Based on Evolutionary Models for Security of Software Applications, extending the JCE by implementing faster and more secure DNA Encryption (DNAE) system based on the Central Dogma of Molecular Biology (CDMB). Sun Microsystems certified and signed our DNAProvider as Java Cryptographic Extension (JCE) with DNA cryptographic algorithm. We got the Code Signing Certificate from Sun Microsystems for our DNAProvider as Java Cryptographic Extension (JCE) with DNA cryptographic algorithm which is available for 5 years, until with the reference #679, when renewing it in 2013.

In our future research work we intend to integrate our developed system pipeline of deriving DNA Cryptographic Keys Based on Evolutionary Models implemented and tested at University of Basel, Switzerland, in our DNAProvider as Java Cryptographic Extension (JCE) with DNA Encryption (DNAE) system for use in security of our developed Web-based Business Processes Software Applications. We aim to use DNA Provider with unconditional secure DNAE system to ensure security of today's web-based business processes. as e-commerce and Internet banking. (Hodorogea, Ionas, 2011).

6. Acknowledgment

This research work is supported by the Company INNOVA BIOTECH, Cluj-Napoca, Romania.

7. References

Abad, C., Taylor, J., Sengul, C., Yurcik, W., Zhou,Y., & Rowe, K. (2003). Log correlation for intrusion detection: A proof of concept. In *Proceedings of the 19th Annual Computer Security Applications Conference (ACSAC 2003).* Los Alamitos, CA: IEEE Computer Society Press.

Almgren, M., & Jonsson, E. (2004). Using active learning in intrusion detection. In *Proceedings of the 17th IEEE Computer Security Foundations Workshop (CSFW'04).* Los Alamitos, CA: IEEE Computer Society Press.

Anderson, J. P. (1980). *Computer security threat monitoring and surveillance* (Tech.l Rep.). FortWashington, PA: James P. Anderson.

Alberts C., Audrey D., "Managing Information Security Risks: The OCTAVESM Approach ", Addison Wesley Professional, July 09, 2002.

Bace, R., & Mell, P. (2001). *Intrusion detection systems.* NIST special publication in intrusion detection systems. Retrieved from http://csrc.nist gov/publications/nistpubs/800-31/sp800-31.pdf

Beznosov, K. (2004). *On the benefits of decomposing policy engines into components.* Third Workshop on Adaptive and Reflect Middleware, Toronto, Canada.

Blobel, B. (2001). The European TrustHealth project experiences with implementing a security infrastructure. *International Journal of Medical Informatics, 60,* 193-201.

Blobel, B., Hoepner, P., Joop, R., Karnouskos, S., Kleinhuis, G., & Stassinopoulos, G. (2003). Using a privilege management infrastructure for secure Web-based e-health applications. *Computer Communication, 26*(16), 1863-1872.

Blobel, B. (2004). Authorisation and access control for electronic health record system. *InternationalJournal of Medical Informatics, 73,* 251-257.

Hodorogea T., Ionas O., (2011), "Security of Business to Business and Business to Customer Software Applications Based on the Central Dogma of Molecular Biology (CDMB) and Evolutionary Models", IEEE Explore (ITI) 2011, International Conferince on Information Technology Interfaces, June, 2011, Cavtat, Croatia.

Halpern, A.L. and Bruno, W.J. 1998. Evolutionary distances forprotein-coding sequences: Modeling site-specific residue frequencies.Mol. Biol. Evol. 5: 910–917.

Halligan, D.L., Eyre-Walker, A., Andolfatto, P., and Keightley, P.D. 2004, Patterns of evolutionary constraints in intronic and intergenic DNA of *Drosophila. Genome Res.* 14: 273–Rajewsky, N., Socci, N.D., Zapotocky, M., and Siggia, E.D. 2002. The evolution of DNA regulatory regions for proteo-gamma bacteria by interspecies comparisons. *Genome Res.* 12: 298–308

Rogozin, I.B., Makarova, K.S., Natale, D.A., Spiridonov, A.N., Tatusov, R.L., Wolf, Y.I., Yin, J., and Koonin, E.V. 2002. Congruent evolution of different classes of non-coding DNA in prokaryoticgenomes.Nucleic Acids Res. 30: 4264–4271. doi:2001. Codon bias at the 3_-side of the initiation codon is correlated

van Nimwegen, E. 2003. Scaling laws in the functional content of genomes. Trends Genet.

van Nimwegen, E. 2004. Scaling laws in the functional content of genomes: Fundamental constants of evolution In Power laws, scale-free networks and genome biology (eds. E. Koonin et al.), pp.236–253 Landes Bioscience, Austin, TX.

15

Research on DNA Cryptography

Yunpeng Zhang* and Liu He Bochen Fu
College of Software and Microelectronics, Northwestern Polytechnical University, Xi'an, China

1. Introduction

The 21st century is a period of information explosion in which information has become a very important strategic resource, and so the task of information security has become increasing important. Cryptography is the most important component part of the infrastructure of communication security and computer security. However, there are many latent defects in some of the classical cryptography technology of modern cryptography - such as RSA and DES algorithms - which have been broken by some attack programs. Some encryption technology may set a trap door, giving those attackers who understand this trap door the ability to decipher this kind of encryption technology. This information demonstrates that modern cryptography encryption technology based on mathematical problems is not so reliable as before.

The relation between cryptography and molecular biology was originally irrelevant, but with the in-depth study of modern biotechnology and DNA computing, these two disciplines begin to work together more closely. DNA cryptography and information science was born after research in the field of DNA computing field by Adleman; it is a new field and has become the forefront of international research on cryptography. Many scholars from all over the world have done a large number of studies on DNA cryptography. In terms of hiding information, there are such results as "Hiding messages in DNA microdots," "Cryptography with DNA binary strands" and so on. In terms of DNA algorithms, there are such results as "A DNA-based, bimolecular cryptography design," "Public-key system using DNA as a one-way function for key distribution," "DNASC cryptography system" and so on. However, DNA cryptography is an emerging area of cryptography and many studies are still at an early stage.

DNA Cryptography is based on biological problems: in theory, a DNA computer will not only has the same computing power as a modern computer but will also have a potency and function which traditional computers cannot match. First, DNA chains have a very large scale of parallelism, and its computing speed could reach 1 billion times per second; second, the DNA molecule - as a carrier of data - has a large capacity. It seems that one trillion bits of binary data can be stored in one cubic decimetre of a DNA solution; third, a DNA molecular computer has low power consumption, only equal to one-billionth of a traditional computer.

*Corresponding author

2. Technology and software

DNA cryptography is a subject of study about how to use DNA as an information carrier and it uses modern biotechnology as a measure to transfer ciphertext into plaintext. Thus, biotechnology plays an important role in the field of DNA cryptography. In this part we will introduce some of the DNA biotechnology and software of the field of DNA.

2.1 Gel electrophoresis

Electrophoresis is a phenomenon where one charge moves in the opposite direction of its electrode in an electric field. This is an important method for the separation, identification and purification of DNA fragments. At present, there are two kinds of medium: agarose and polyacrylamide. Both of these can be made for a gel with different sizes, shapes and diameter. In causing electrophoresis on different devices, we call it either agarose gel electrophoresis or polyacrylamide gel electrophoresis. When DNA molecules go through the sieves which are formed by the gel, the short DNA molecule moves faster than the longer one and so we can discriminate between them easily.

2.2 The technology of DNA fragment assembly

DNA fragment assembly is a technology which attempts to reconstruct a large number of DNA fragments into the original long chain of DNA. In order to solve the limit of the length of the sequence, the researchers developed this technology. The measures are as follows: First, the researchers amplified the DNA chain and got lots of backup; second, they obtained a large number of short DNA fragments by cutting the DNA long chain at random locations; finally, the researchers recombined the DNA fragments - which have an overlapping part - back into the original DNA chain. This strategy is called "shotgun sequencing."

2.3 DNA chip technology

DNA chip technology is to the manuscript should be presented without any additional comments in the margins.synthesis oligo probe on solid substrates or else directly solidifies a large amount of a DNA probe in an orderly fashion on the surface of substrates using the method of micro-printing. It then hybridises with the labelled sample, through the testing and analysis of the hybridised signal, so as to get the genetic information (the gene order and the information it gives) about the sample. Since silicon computer chips are usually used as solid substrates, it is called a DNA chip.

DNA chip encryption technology has two layers of security: one layer is provided by the limitations of biotechnology and it is also the security that the system primarily based on. The other layer is that of computing security - even if an attacker breaks through the first layer of security - in the case where they do not have the decipher key - they must have strong computing power and data storage capacity in order to decipher the DNA chip. Now, the encryption progress of DNA chip technology will be presented.

2.4 PCR technology

PCR Technology is also called "polymerase chain reaction" and it is a rapid amplification technology of DNA. Because it is very difficult to manipulate small amounts of DNA, PCR

Technology usually used to amplify the DNA which has been determined. In practice, DNA amplification techniques include cloning. The amplification efficiency of PCR is very high, and can amplify a large number of chosen DNA in a short period of time. Moreover, PCR will achieve the amplification by using natural nucleotide molecules. In order to achieve PCR amplification, the experimenter needs to know the sequence of the chosen DNA chain, and use it to design primers for amplification. Actually, the primer is also a DNA sequence which contains a number of nucleotides. It is certain that the primer can be amplified for the chosen DNA. In short, the PCR process can be divided into two stages:

1. The design of two primers, separately loaded onto the target DNA in the beginning and at the end;
2. The finding of the target DNA under the action of the polymerase and its amplification.

2.5 The DNA code

DNA is the genetic material of eukaryotes, with a double-helix molecular structure and two single-strands parallel to each other. DNA is something which is called a polymer, which composed of many small nucleotides. Each nucleotide consists of three parts:

1. The Nitrogenous bases;
2. Deoxyribose;
3. Phosphate.

DNA coding is a new area of cryptography which has appeared in recent years along with DNA computing research. Originally there was no connection between these two disciplines -- cryptography and molecular biology (also known as genetics or genomics). However, with the study of DNA - especially after Adleman put forward DNA computing in 1994 - and with more in-depth study, this research can be used in the field of information security. Ultimately, DNA cryptography appeared only gradually. DNA cryptography is built on DNA - which is an information carrier - and modern biotechnology for its tools, and it achieves the encryption process by the use of the characteristics of DNA of massive parallelism and high storage density. In addition, the reason why we can combine cryptography and molecular biology is the encoded plaintext, which can combine the computer and the use of molecular biological techniques, such as polymerase chain reactions, polymerisation overlapping amplification, affinity chromatography, cloning, mutagenesis, molecular purification, electrophoresis, magnetic bead separation and other techniques of molecular biology, and then obtain the final ciphertext. Most importantly, DNA code abandons that traditional cryptography which uses the intractable mathematical problem of the security guarantee, instead using the limited nature of the learning of biology. In theory, DNA code is mainly based on the biology's limitations for security, and has nothing to do with computing ability; as such, it is immune to the attacks of both modern computers and even the quantum computers of the future. Therefore, many scholars have already started to study the better encryption effect of DNA code.

2.6 The chaos code

Chaos will be included in the example of the chapter, and so we discuss the chaotic system only simply, leading to two tracks from two initial points concerning such systems.

Sometimes these tracks will infinitely close, and sometimes they are away from each other. Both cases will appear numerous times - this indicates that the system's long-term behaviour has no rules. It is a pseudo-random phenomenon which can be used in cryptography.

A chaotic system has three key advantages:

- The sensitive dependence on initial conditions;
- The critical level. This is the point of non-linear events;
- The fractal dimension, which shows the unity of order and disorder.

Usually, it is a self-feedback system and so this leads to the system itself being unable to forecast for the long-term.

At present, many chaotic cryptosystems have been used in the iterative process in order to complete data encryption or decryption. The security of ciphertext mainly benefits from the effect of chaotic dynamics. The more dimensions the equation has, the greater the security that will be obtained. However, the time of encryption or decryption will increase, and the ciphertext will soon become longer. Chaotic encryption mainly uses the random sequence - generated by the chaotic system's iteration - as an impact sequence of the encryption transform. This sequence inherits the pseudo-randomness of the chaotic system. Moreover, it can make and spread confusion and it does not identify characteristics of the obtained ciphertext after the use of this sequence to treat the plaintext. This is a great challenge for cryptanalysts. Therefore, the chaos code has been used in some encryption recently.

2.7 Software

DNA fragment stitching software - the DNA Baser Sequence Assembler. The DNA Baser Sequence Assembler is used for splicing DNA fragments fatly. It should be noted that we must prepare some DNA fragments for splicing before using this software.

3. Biological problems

An unintelligible problem in biology is due to the limits of human cognitive and experimental means as well as the problems which have resulted from other scientific laws and which will not be solved in the visible future.

The known biological problems are, mainly:

1. That we do not know the proper primers at present: it is difficult in that we have to separate the unknown and specific sequences of DNA from the unknown mixed liquids of DNA and then sequence them. In the literature, by using DNA synthesis, PCR amplification and DNA digital coding adequately, and with the combination of traditional cryptography, Guangzhao Cui proposed a DNA-based encryption scheme. Unfortunately, the author did not make an adequate difficulty of this biological problem. Therefore, the lack of difficult problems in the literature does not provide sufficient reliability and theoretical support.
2. We have to perform completely accurate sequencing in order to decipher the unknown hybrid DNA (PNA) probe information where the DNA chip (microarray) is only a different nucleotide arrangement. This is the second biological problem.

Now there are two main types of sequencing method:

1. The Maxam-Gilber method, which has also been known as the "chemical degradation method;"
2. The Sanger method, which is also known as the "enzyme method."

Neither of the two methods are suitable for sequencing a little of the unknown mixed sequence of a DNA chip.

In the literature, the author had a discussion as to this problem. He proposed a non-deterministic symmetric encryption system - DANSC-based on this problem. Generally speaking, the biological problem in the literature depends on the sequencing technology, which is still in the primary stages and has its own weaknesses. This will generate a hidden danger when we build the encryption scheme; what is more, the DANSC will also likely face a fate of being cracked in the future.

Of course, there are other difficult biological problems that can be used in DNA cryptography which will be discovered in the future.

4. Analysis DNA encryption which is based on PCR amplification technology

4.1 DNA encoding scheme

In the field of information science, the most basic encoding method is binary encoding. This is because everything can be encoded by the two states of 0 and 1. However, for DNA there are four basic units:

1. Adenine (A);
2. Thymine (T);
3. Cytosine (C);
4. Guanine (G).

The easiest way to encode is to represent these four units as four figures:

1. A(0) -00;
2. T(1) -01;
3. C(2)-10;
4. G(3)-11.

Obviously, by these encoding rules, there are 4! = 24 possible encoding methods. For DNA encoding, it is necessary to reflect the biological characteristics and pairing principles of the four nucleotides. Based on this principle, we know that:

A(0) - 00 and G(3) - 11 make pairs,
T(1) - 01 and C(2) - 10 make pairs.

In these 24 programs, there are only 8 programs

0123/CTAG,
0123/CATG,
0123/GTAC,
0123/GATC,
0123/TCGA,

0123/TGCA,
0123/ACGT,

0123/AGCT match the DNA pair of a complementary principle. The coding scheme should be consistent with the weight of a molecular chain, so we get that 0123/CTAG is the best encoding scheme.

4.2 Encryption process

If the encrypter wants to encrypt the plaintext, he first needs to transform the plaintext by using the code rules. Next, he obtains the DNA sequence with its base sequence represented a special meaning and he then uses the biotechnology and - according to DNA sequences - artificially synthesises the DNA chain as the target DNA. After this, he can design the appropriate primers as the key. When the sender has the key, he loads them onto the target DNA for its strand and end according to the sequence synthesis primers of the primer. On this basis, we use DNA technology to cut and splice, and implant this DNA to a long DNA chain. Finally, he adds an interfered DNA chain, namely the common DNA chain. The sequence of these chains does not contain any meaningful information.

4.3 Analysis of DNA encryption based on PCR technology

4.3.1 Safety analysis

For this encryption scheme - and because the ciphertext includes the DNA chain for the carrier, its message will be represented by the base sequence of the DNA chain. When the cryptographers intercept the ciphertext, what is obtained is a DNA mixture in which there is a lot of confusion in the DNA chain. As with the technology of PCR itself, this technology has high requirements for the correctness of the primers of the sequence. If starting amplification experiment, then it is impossible to try to find out the target gene without knowing of the primer sequence. Because, in this case, (if) cryptographers designed the primer by themselves, then first, they do not know the molecule length of the correct primer. For any different length that they have, they will get the wrong message. Even if the length is right, and supposing there are 25 base sequences, in theory there will be 4^{25} kinds of primers. If cryptographers experiment on them one by one - and they assume that taking one PCR amplification requires 2 or 3 hours - they would need 10^{27} years to finish it. This is impossible.

However, only using DNA Encryption based on PCR Technology is not always safe, because the plaintext and the converted DNA are in a one-to-one relationship, and the ciphertext contains the plaintext's unique statistical properties. In this case, the cryptanalyst can decipher it though statistical attacks, giving the password a security risk.

4.3.2 Feasibility analysis of the experimental operation

The primers that are designed must comply with the following principles:

1. Specificity.

Primers should be arranged in a specific way - especially with regard to the amplified target sequences between the two primers - and we should make sure of at least a 30% difference and the arrangement of 8 consecutive Bases cannot be the same;

2. Length.

Statistical calculations indicate that the 17 base sequences in the human DNA are likely to occur at one time, and so the primer length general controls more than 17; however, it cannot have unlimited length and at most it cannot longer than 30 Bases sequence. Usually, the best length is 20 to 24 Bases. This length of DNA primer has a strong stability when reacting, and does not produce hybrids;

3. The content of C and G bases.

The content of C + G needs to be controlled at 40% to 60% so as to avoid containing too many bases polymers, and the percentage of the C + G in the two primers should be similar;

4. Random Distribution of bases.

The distribution of bases in the primer should be random so as to avoid more than three consecutive identical bases;

5. The primer Itself.

The complementary sequence should not appear in the primer sequence itself, and if it cannot be avoided we must ensure that there are less than 3 bases in a complementary situation, at the very least;

6. Between the Primers.

Each primer should avoid appearing in the complementary sequence;

7. The End of Primer 3′.

Not using Base A at the 3′ end, because A has a high rate of mismatch, and it cannot make any modification at the 3′ end;

8. The End of Primer 5′.

The 5′ end of the primer limits the length of PCR amplification's product, but it is less demanding and some fluorescent markings can be modified.

Because PCR primer design is a crucial part of the technology, and because the use of PCR technology is at the core of this encryption algorithm - as well as for its safety and security conditions - if we use inappropriate PCR primers, it will lead to experiment failure. Therefore, the design of the primers must comply with the above principles. Here, we can use the biological expertise software to help design the primers. The software called - Primer Premier 5.0.

5. The united chaos encryption algorithm based on the logistic map and the henon map

5.1 Research for the logistic map

The logistic map is the most widely used chaotic map. It is a one-dimensional chaotic map with the advantages of a high efficiency and simplicity. A logistic map is defined as:

$$x_{n+1} = \lambda \times x_n \times (1 - x_n), \quad \lambda \in (0,4), n = 0,1,... \tag{1}$$

We use Parameter λ and the initial value x_0 as a key. Parameter λ can be divided into three parts and start parameter validation. Make x_0 equals to a random value of 0.79284, and then take the above data into formula 1 which is as the defination of a logistic map, and making it iterate 100 times. Next, make a picture to analyse each x. There are three kinds of situations, as follows:

When $\lambda \in (0,1)$ and where we have a random value for λ=0.5789757497. Then we iterate it 100 times and the value is shown in Figure 1. We can see that after 10 times, the values of x have tended to 0. Here, it is already doesn't have any random features which the chaos should have.

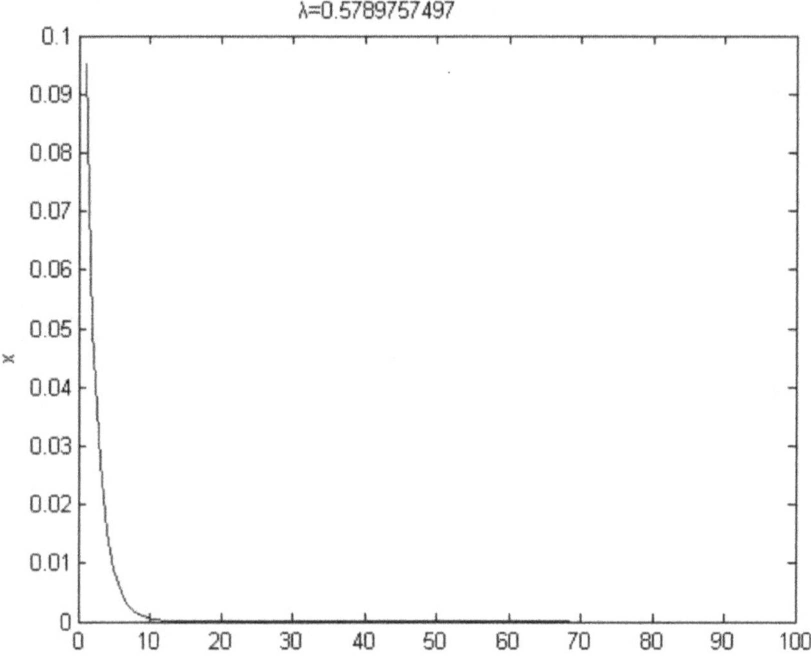

Fig. 1. Logistic experiment 1

When $\lambda \in (1,2)$ and where we have a random value for λ= 1.8438643285. As shown in Figure 2, in the case of 100 iterations, the value of x after 10 times is little changed. However, the data shows that if we take 17 decimal places after the decimal point for x, the top 15 are identical, but only the last two have subtle differences. And the following value of x became periodicity,(And always became periodicity,) these values are 0.45766074838406956, 0.45766074838406962, 0.45766074838406973. It is always these three numbers, and so the overall system does not appear to have the features of chaos.

When $\lambda \in (2,3)$ and where we have a random value for λ= 2.4829473982. As shown in Figure 3, it is a similar situation for $\lambda \in (1,2)$ when, after 10 iterations, the figure tends to be stable. The data shows that there are two numbers in circulation: 0.59725284525763811 and 0.59725284525763822, and the overall system does not appear to have the features of chaos.

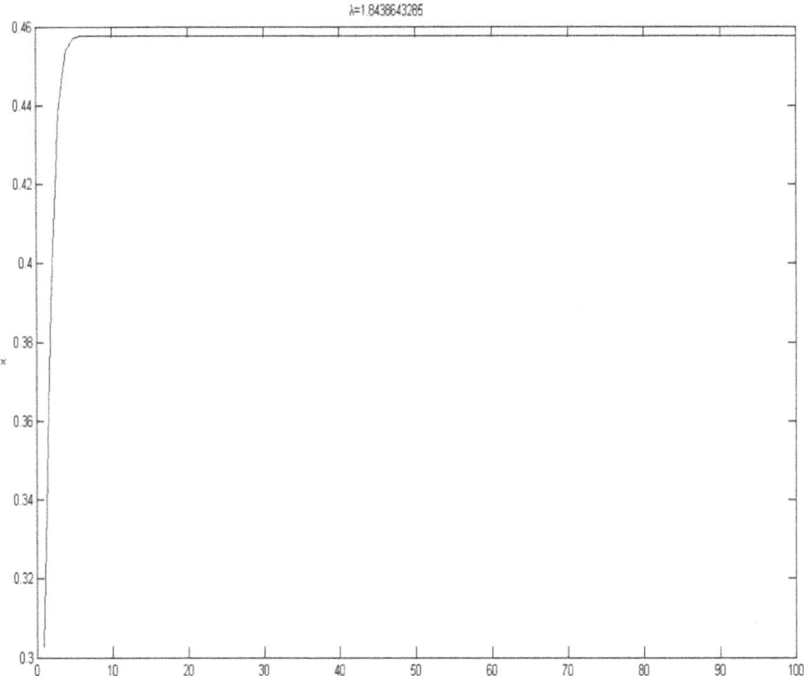

Fig. 2. Logistic experiments 2

When λ ∈(3,3.6) and where we have a random value for λ= 3.3483997432. It is iterated 100 times, as is shown in Figure 4: the value of x has relatively large fluctuations and becomes a discrete state. However, the data shows that although the value of x is volatile, it is still a circulation. Moreover, although this periodicity is not as obviou as the former two have, it still has some implications for encryption security.

When λ ∈(3.6,4) and where we have a random value for λ= 3.8374666542. The value of x after it is iterated 100 times is shown in Figure 5. We can see that the value of x has a more significant fluctuation. After analysis, it was shown that this result is not a circulation. As such, this system will be a chaotic system.

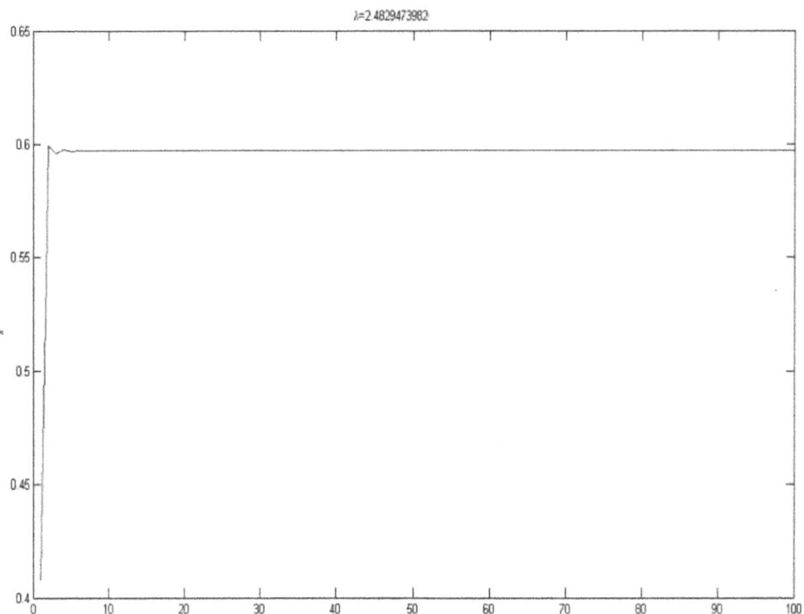

Fig. 3. Logistic experiments 3

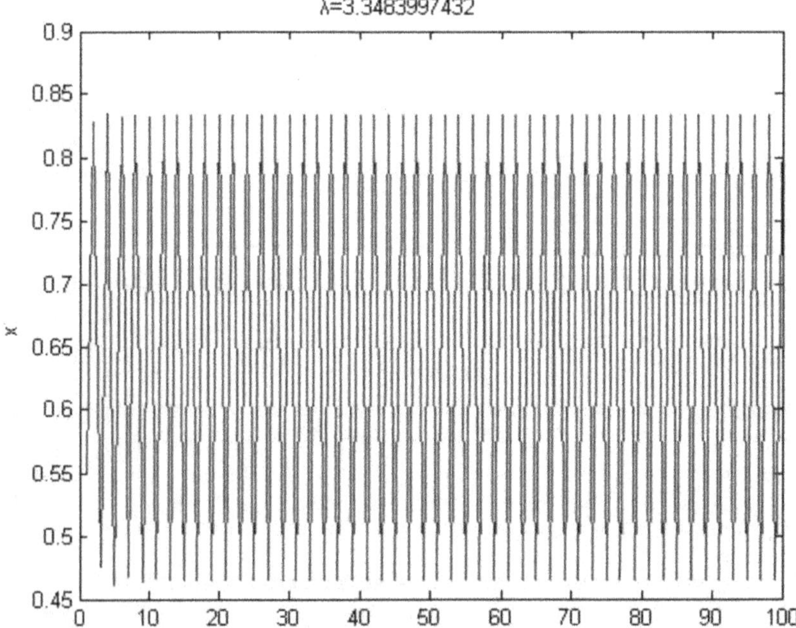

Fig. 4. Logistic experiments 4

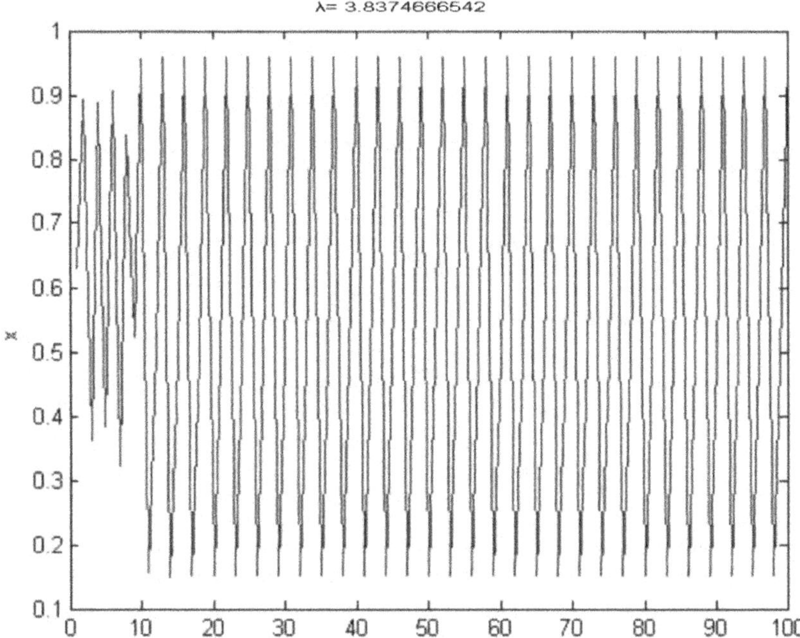

Fig. 5. Logistic experiments 5

5.2 The united chaos encryption algorithm based on logistic map and henon map

We can add a two-dimensional chaotic map in the circumstances that ensures that the efficiency is not too bad. This chaotic map is called a Henon map. We can use it to start encryption united with a Logistic map. Moreover, this can be achieved without losing efficiency while strengthening its security.

A Henon map as a two-dimensional chaotic map, and its equation is:

$$\begin{cases} X_{n+1} = 1 + Y_n - a \times X_n^2 \\ Y_{n+1} = b \times X_n \end{cases} \quad (2)$$

When using this map, we need to set initial values for x_0 and x_1 and the parameters a and b. The algorithm flow is shown in Figure 6.

This chaotic system is used mainly to generate a chaotic sequence of random numbers. It could have chaotic characteristics. The purpose of using this chaotic system is in the pre-treatment of the encrypted plaintext. The whole of the algorithm's flow of chaotic pre-processing is:

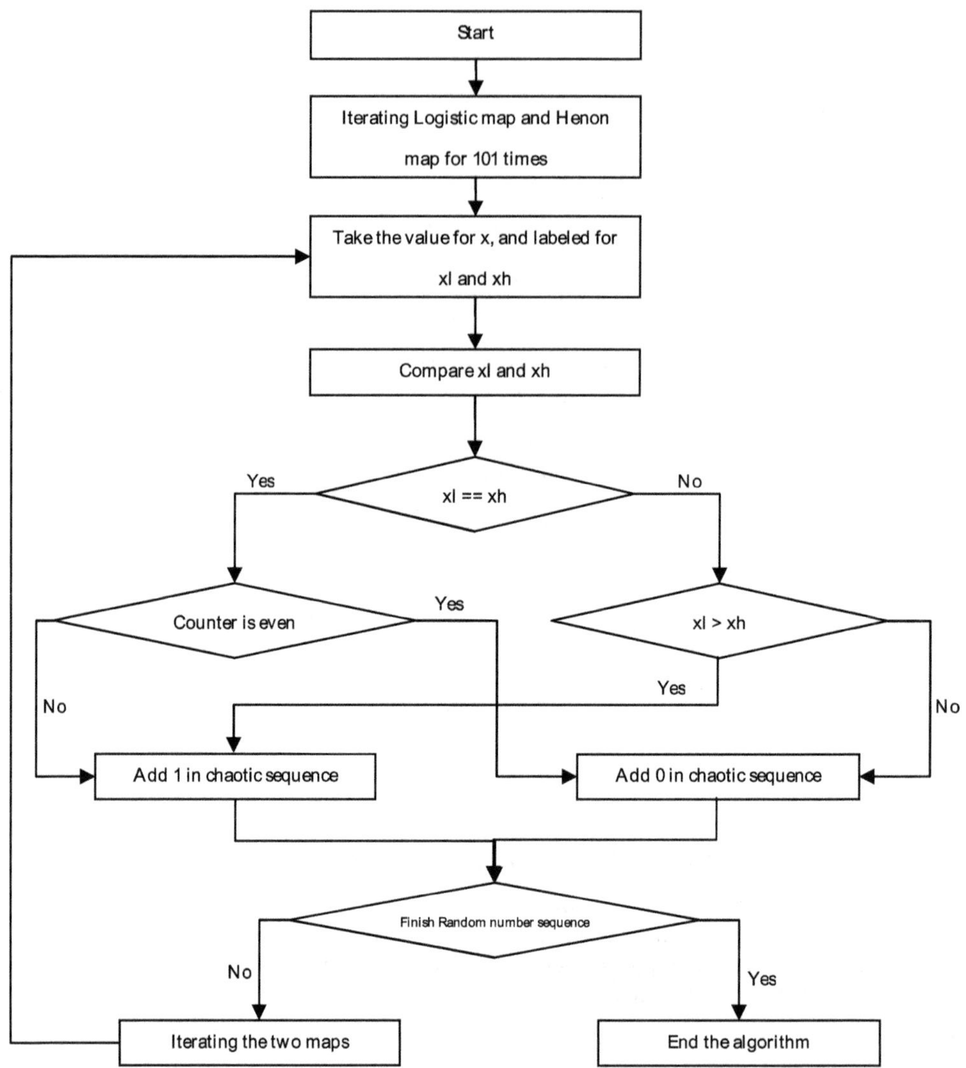

Fig. 6. The algorithm flow

1. Make an encoding conversion for the encrypted plaintext; transfer the ASCII code which corresponds to the plaintext character into n-bit binary code;
2. Use the n-bit pseudo-random number sequence which is produced by the chaotic system to conduct XOR with the plaintext's binary sequences. All of these sequences are 0, 1 sequences. Obtain the binary sequences after treatment;
3. Obtain the DNA chain by using the digital coding rules of DNA to transfer these binary sequences into a DNA base sequence.

The entire process shown in Figure 7:

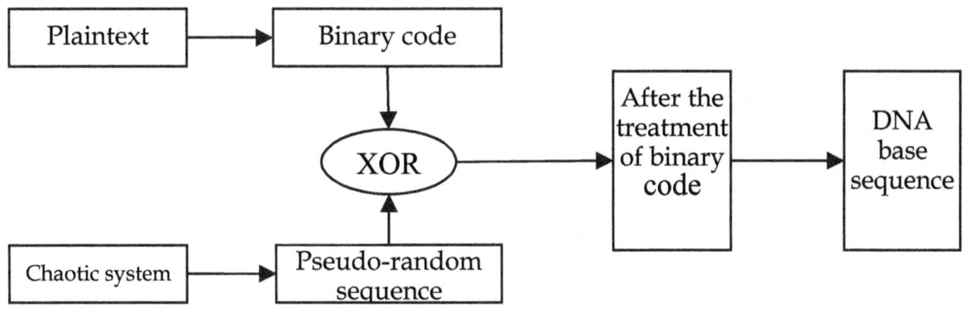

Fig. 7. XOR processing

5.3 Security verification

1. Key Analysis

In this encryption system, as a key, the initial values are xl_0 = 0.3, xh_0 = 0.5, xh_1 = 0.4 and the three parameters of the chaotic maps are λ = 3.8264775543, a = 1.3649226742, b = 0.3. The initial value range of these two parameters is (0, 1) and the value is a real number. The logistic map's parameter has a value in the range of (3.6, 4). In the two parameters of the Henon map, one is the fixed value for b=0.3, the other parameter we assume it to a. Moreover, its value range had better be in (1.07, 1.4), as this range can better reflect the characteristics of chaos. Sensitivity can be reflected in the key, and now we keep all of the parameters of the encryption system at a correct value, only changing λ = 3.8264775543 to λ = 3.8264775544 for the logistic map. We add 10^{-10}, which means that we only change a tenth of a decimal number. Next, we take this kind of key into the chaotic system in order to have it decrypted. The result is shown in Figure 8.

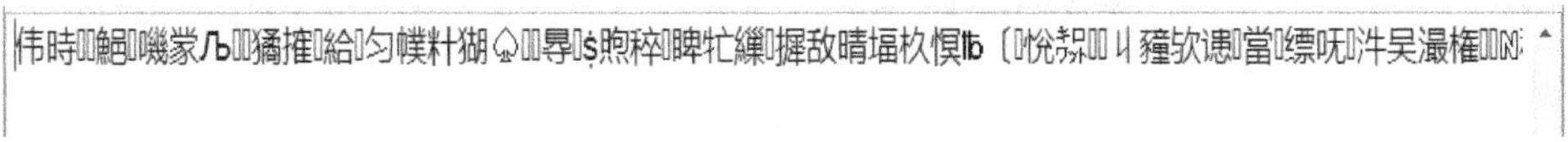

Fig. 8. Decrypt results of the wrong key.

2. Statistical analysis

Generally the message of plaintext is text or other information and they all follow certain statistical laws, such as in English words the letters r, a, e, etc. have a high frequency of use, but letters q, z, u, etc. do not. It is a law of English words, and so it brings some security risk to the password. If the encrypted ciphertext still has the characteristics of these statistics, it is easy for statistical attacks. Next, we use encryption to analyse an English article -- Martin Luther King's speech "I have a dream."

The original is shown in Figure 9.

Everyone has a dream. I often ask myself. When I was a little boy, I wanted to be a soldier with a gun so that I could defend our motherland. Now I am a young boy with a new dream to be a doctor. I want to be a famous doctor, helping the sick and saving their lives.

I also saw some people who were suffering and dying of illnesses. I made up my mind to become a doctor, so that I can help the sick people and cure them of their diseases. China is a developing country. She needs good medicine and good doctors, especially in the countryside and lonely villages.

I want to try my best to help the poor sick people of our country. I want to let them have an opportunity to receive excellent treatments for their illnesses without having to pay much or any money.

I will do every bit to cure the incurable. I hope to see a world where there is no cancer, no Aids, no fatal diseases. I am confident that through the joint efforts of you and me, man will put an end to his bodily sufferings and this dream of mine will one day be brought into reality.

Fig. 9. Plaintext examples

We analyse this article, and add up the letters in terms of the number of their occurrence. As is shown in Figure 10, we found that the frequency of letters that appear in each word is not the same. The letter e occurs the most, the letter o is second, and so on. In this article, we cannot find the letters q and z. So, the statistical law is very clear and the cryptanalyst can make attack according to the number of times the characters appear in the ciphertext.

Fig. 10. Statistical laws of the letters in plaintext.

In this case, we use the chaotic system and its key to encrypt the article. The encrypted file is shown in Figure 11. The figure told us that after encryption the article - which is also called the ciphertext - has a lot of confusing characters. Equally, they do not have any statistical features: all of the characters are randomly distributed and they do not follow any law. So, this kind of encryption has the ability to avoid statistical attacks.

```
◘↑|&,I┬"LO%4Q17B├┬bK>♀?|┴,'←w=┬dJ‼♀"f-('Fk`#wWC;#9→JCFecH[ ♫K}←0?_pxFT$FY<]↕?┼→←=H;J|[9[┐├jV*)yD!◘[N7
[;L☼J↑)┘♀1Q☼ ┼1→4soL ‼          b‼
c?c
@n+┘┬wAZ =~┴B♂?→ <B)8GYgErjAYdRa└8/1.┌^KG^e          ^-
)↕F•6←I┐yZ
w┴¶Cy 3U‼R#┐F((i¶| 7┐"┼1◄*☼Yy          |W◄g┬-5>nyR]‼ q ┘9@O$G%n←a C-15d•♫9-dY\[uK8‼↑vd♀Z3K└y ]f♂
[:cm☼└<↕w◘-psD↕jX|◄<┬R%-k├Y6F0☼)eb-┌ye(x↑[G6A-|\x•
22|V_;◄rw:S'V'\#7+┼O~`┤W`.I<x"8♂9>←/z\QJ(;,.2↕┤9=,.(          ┬=6x♂#B5_          ┼L1z<&5/>S[Y→KKtArZ1hpWw6?
<¶a! 65PP┴9_!2>
@VmL♀Oa♂)FhVom<♫_"┴^•O:└)‼Px↕|d0-/<◄4h5     V\S#w]<◄$s←Wa|dX‼├V &k├,{N[:g#┴x:☼┘A├.i
FA|E)C6(5,♀|m>├&|:b3◄{┌
p`<&=4>┐← \‼♂Q#<-┴N_←K|r┴(L#0nz
rp1]←┬$4a☼┬F☼‼pK?h|♂-sS}◘-RSH,♀oUv‼BRr9?7-◘└IC>‼2Q→O.
ak♫|TbU5Y┬):@◘+@J┬├>>%9MI¶a-Y~'^Y.RD
└#IU&
jv)          .1{→rdg→21uW<M{%↕1
FGXU5Qg|"M☼♫-┤p$3t/←e┐;J*t↕OX2}|O(?xN¶♀‼WJXM+w461O\☼Tk┐8>◘PO3↕i├Qz♫q,FX◄oO-by↕%;;-"J_nOrO)R;m64
Z<‼¶‼j!i◘z|S←aV0Bc"(K1-♂|cwe{@Po$Y→L ┴R└9OPOP.C%♀=}3¶Q M•→=◄
"G[oOv2.t↕↕
dWk7e`◘┴2.,8!]t♀r,}•┼XJ \:‼♀07qZ\Io%;→o,c3Dr9U^-{`zJsvW cH|├i?~e‼t;G['WtxV├☼0/┐.yp↕A2W┤[>G-L┐☼- m*├v├r←N┐D
{¶uH~Gb=Pa>(♀%Jo~|♀┤`t)┘{Z NIQM→E♫[ol#
```


Fig. 11. Example of ciphertext.

6. A new cryptographic algorithms based on PCR and chaos optimisation

6.1 Encryption system design

6.1.1 Key generation

In this encryption system, we use the united keys instead of a single key. The key is divided into two parts: the first part is a PCR technique used in the primers, with the primer sequences as a key - KeyA; The second part concerns the initial conditions and parameters which are used in the chaotic system, and the system is called KeyB.

The password system is the most important which relies on bio-security. As such, the DNA code of the key has the requirement of high quality. However, in the united key, key KeyB is related with the DNA code. For the generation of KeyA, KeyA is a string of bases of the DNA sequence, which is used for the PCR amplification primers. Password security and systems can be realised, which is determined by the success of the primer design system. Accordingly, the design of this key is very important. If the key is designed strictly according to the design principles of the design primer, it will cause limited limitation of primer shortage space. Therefore, the primer design of the encryption system is designed by software Primer Premier 5.0, which is used in biological simulation.

The design shown in Figure 12:

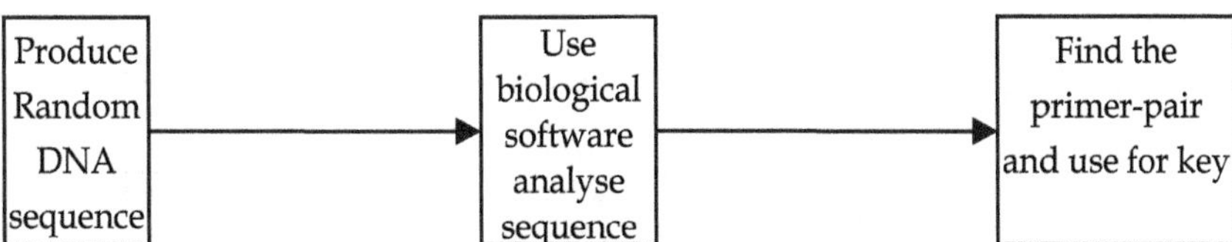

Fig. 12. Key preparation processes

For the production of KeyB, we select the appropriate parameters in the chaotic system as keys. The parameter selection rules have been talked about in the preamble, so it need not be repeated. For the median of the parameters selected, this can be based on the security of encryption strength in order to develop the key's length.

6.1.2 Encryption process

The message sender is also called the encrypter: after completing the key design it begins to encrypt the plaintext and makes a ciphertext.

1. Explicating that which is converted into binary code;
2. Using the DNA encoding rule pre-treatment the binary code for chaos;
3. Bringing KeyB into the chaotic system to produce the chaotic pseudo-random number sequence;
4. Operating the sequence and the plaintext sequence corresponding to the binary by XOR so as obtain the processed binary sequence.

This binary sequence is divided into n sub-sequences and the specific number is decided by the length of the ciphertext. The pair sequence is numbered l_1, $l_2 \ldots l_n$ and is followed by the following operations:

$$l_1 \oplus l_2 = s_2,$$

$$s_2 \oplus l_3 = s_3$$

$$\ldots$$

$$s_{n-1} \oplus l_n = s_n$$

Get s_2, s_3, …, s_n n-1 sequences and then l_1, s_2, s_3, …, s_n, and its subscript number of these sequences. The sequences were added to each sequence at the beginning. Next, the sequence was transformed into a DNA base sequence according to DNA coding. The coding rules are 0123/CTAG (it has been illustrated in the fourth part of this chapter). Afterwards, select the stand-n-primer from that obtained in the previous primer sequence step added to the front of the sequence. The ciphertext sequence propagated successfully. It is shown in Figure 13.

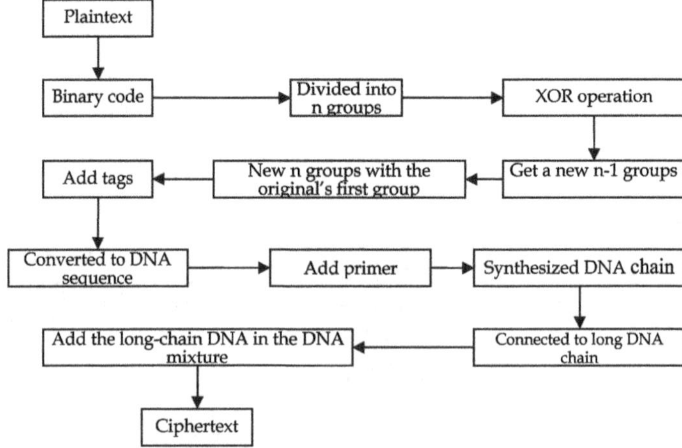

Fig. 13. Encryption Process

The use of biological experimental techniques - using mainly artificial DNA synthesis technology - see the formation of DNA sequences into short-chain DNA synthesis. Next, using cutting and splicing, the DNA technology is used to make short-chain n-DNA, splicing into a long DNA template chain. We complete this long-chain DNA system and add it to the DNA mixture. In the DNA mixture there are many different lengths of DNA, such as interference DNA. The ciphertext is thereby produced.

6.1.3 Decryption process

First, the cracker has to get KeyA using key information that is obtained from safe prior sources and then carry out PCR amplification. For the second step, the DNA to be amplified will be selected by using electrophorus and these DNA have the information we need. For the third step, through the sequencing of the DNA chain, we can draw the corresponding DNA sequence. For the fourth step, the DNA sequence was restored to a binary sequence by the DNA encoding. At this time, the obtained binary sequence is l_1 , s_2 , s_3 , ... , s_n in the encrypted process. After sorting it is then calculated:

$$s_{n-1} \oplus s_n = l_n$$

$$\dots$$

$$s_2 \oplus s_3 = l_3$$

$$l_1 \oplus s_2 = l_2$$

We can get l_1 , $l_2 \dots l_n$. For the fifth step, the binary sequences are spliced together, and we can get a sequence that is a clear binary sequence after the sequence of the pre-treated. For the sixth step - the building of the chaotic system - we bring the parameters of KeyB into the chaotic system. After these operations, we can obtain a binary sequence corresponding to the plaintext. For the seventh step, through transcending and the restoration of the character data, we can get clear.

The entire process is shown in Figure 14.

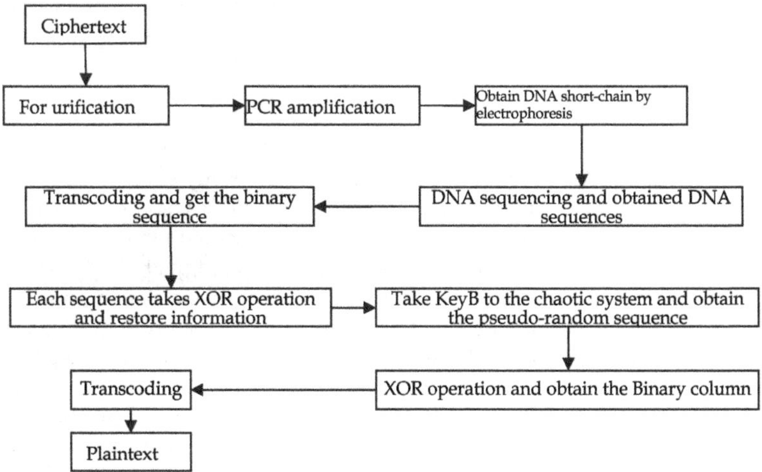

Fig. 14. Decryption Process

Now, the information transmission process is over. When the sender sends a successful message, the receiver will get safe information and they will get plaintext.

7. Analysis of cryptographic algorithms

7.1 Key space

The size of the key space is very important for the security of the encryption system. A good cryptographic algorithm should have enough key space to ensure its safety. The traditional encryption schemes of the PCR amplification technology of encrypted DNA witnesses a problem where it does not have enough key space. As such, we present three ways for improving the security problem of the system.

1. Using a method for combining PCR technology and chaos technology.
2. If we do not know the correct primers, we cannot start PCR amplification and, at the same, we cannot obtain the DNA which has the plaintext information. This is the feature of encryption system we described above and on security issues this method will be more stronger than others.
3. This encryption system is a common encryption system for the combination of DNA code and chaotic encryption. Here, we use a chaotic system to pre-treat the plaintext.

This encryption system has the three above features and it can adjust to the size of the entire key space dynamically, and especially to the key of the adjusted DNA code.

7.2 Features and benefits of the system

In this system, we use chaotic encryption for encryption systems dealing with plaintext. This encrypted system eliminates the statistic rules in plaintext and loads chaotic encryption into DNA code. This means that the DNA code has the same advantages that traditional encryption has. As such, security has been improved. Even if the attacker deciphered the DNA code, he will still face a lot of chaos code that it would be necessary to decrypt. This increases the difficulty of decryption. In order to be a new type of encryption system, DNA code is based on a different security to the traditional code. Accordingly, we can obtain a complementary effect when we combined these two systems.

8. Conclusion

This paper mainly discusses DNA Cryptography and one example algorithm, analysing the encryption algorithm of the PCR-based amplification technology of DNA, improving security and the key space, and it provides an operational test of it. In order to solve the key space-constrained problem that the PCR amplification technology of DNA has, the authors used a method for building a chaotic system. This system includes a logistic chaotic map and a Henon chaotic map. We can generate a chaotic pseudo-random sequence which could handle the plaintext for eliminating the statistical rules in it with the two maps. On the one hand, it makes the encryption algorithm immune of statistical attack. On the other hand, it increases the key space. After using the binary code of the message of plaintext to make an XOR operation, we can obtain a new binary code. We can then ensure an increase in the number of primers, and we add some primers to it; this is one of the primers' features. After all of this, we have increased the security of the entire system.

In addition, during the PCR amplification experiment, if the amplified target DNA is too long, it may lead to a failure of the amplification. In this encryption algorithm, we separate the binary code of the plaintext into many small sequences. In this manner, we guarantee that the amplification could be carried out smoothly during its operation.

This chapter used the encryption instance to describe all of the encryption algorithm. Moreover, we have analysed each encryption effect. Finally, we analysed the security and operability of the entire system, and used biology software to demonstrate the bio-security of the analogue of the amplification primers, using computer to analyse the statistics and demonstrate the effect of the chaotic system.

9. Acknowledgements

This work is supported by the Aero-Science Fund of China (2009ZD53045), Science and Technology Development Project of Shaanxi Province Project (2010K06-22g), Basic research fund of Northwestern Polytechnical University (GAKY100101), and the R Fund of College of Software and Microelectronics of Northwestern Polytechnical University (2010R001), Xi'an science and technology plan (CXY1118).

10. References

Leier A et al. Cryptography with DNA binary strands [J]. Biosystems, 2000, 57(1): 13-22.

Beenish Anam et al. "Review on the Advancements of DNA Cryptography", eprint arXiv:1010.0186, 10/2010

Cui G et al. DNA computing and its application to information security field [C]. IEEE Fifth International Conference on Natural Computation, Tianjian, China, Aug. 2009.

Xiong Fuqin, Cryptography Technology and Application [J]. Science, 2010.

Luque G et al. Metaheuristics for the DNA Fragment Assembly Problem. International Journal of Computational Intelligence Research, 2005, 1(2), 98–108.

Hayashi et al. Anonymity on paillier's trap-door permutation[C]. Springer Verlag, 2007 , 200-214.

Huo J-J et al. Encoding Technique of DNA Cryptography [J]. Information Security and Communications Privacy, 2009, 7: 90-92.

Chen J. A DNA-based, biomolecular cryptography design [J]. ISCAS, 2003, 3:822-825.

Adleman L, Molecular computation of solutions to combinatorial problems [J]. Science, 1994, 266: 1021-1024.

Limin Qin. The Study of DNA - Based Encryption Method [D]. Zheng Zhou: Zheng Zhou University of Light Industry, 2008.)

Borda M. & Tornea O. DNA secret writing techniques [C]. In COMM(2010), Chengdu: IEEE, June 10-12, 2010: 451-456.

C Popovici. Aspects of DNA Cryptography [J]. Annals of the University of Craiova Mathematics and Computer Science Series, 2010, 37(3).

Limin Qin. The Study of DNA - Based Encryption Method [D]. Zheng Zhou: Zheng Zhou University of Light Industry, 2008.

Kazuo T, Akimitsu O, Isao S. Public-key system using DNA as a one-way function for key distribution[J]. Biosystems, 2005, 81: 25-29.

Celland C T et al. Hiding messages in DNA microdots [J]. Nature, 1999, 399: 533-534.

Xing-Yuan Wang et al. A chaotic image encryption algorithm based on perceptronmodel [J]. Nonlinear Dyn, 2010, 62: 615-621.

Luo Ming Xin et al. A Symmetric Encryption Method Based On DNA Technology [J]. Science in China (Series E:Information Sciences),2007,37(2): 175-182.

http://baike.baidu.com/view/107254.htm, 2011.7

http://baike.baidu.com/view/25110.htm, 2011.7

16

An En/Decryption Machine Based on Statistical Physics

Annie Perez, Céline Huynh Van Thieng,
Samuel Charbouillot and Hassen Aziza
*Aix-Marseille Univ., IM2NP ; CNRS, IM2NP (UMR 6242)
IMT, Technopôle de Château-Gombert, Marseille Cedex 20
France*

1. Introduction

Internet-based communications, multimedia systems, telemedicine or military communications, need high-speed data encryption. Thus, in various fields, high-speed cryptosystems are necessary for the large data size transfers and real-time constraints. A secret key stream cipher is suitable for these high-speed encryption systems.

The stream cipher generates long unpredictable key sequences. These pseudo-random key bits, or Cipher Keys, are then bitwise XORed with the data to encrypt/decrypt. Since many processes in the nature include the randomness in themselves, the main idea of this study is to use this natural randomness to generate Cipher Keys.

Physical systems containing randomness appear to follow no definite rules, and to be governed merely by probabilities. Moreover, there are systems that can also generate apparent randomness internally, without an external random input. For instance, a cellular automaton (Bagnoli & Francescato, 1990; Sarkar, 2000; Vichniac, 1984; Wolfram, 1983) evolving from a simple initial state can produce a pattern so complicated that many features of it seem random.

The physical system considered in this chapter is a ferromagnetic material. As the temperature increases, thermal oscillation, or entropy, competes with the ferromagnetic tendency for dipoles to align. At high temperature the magnetization is destroyed and the dipoles are disordered.

In order to simulate this system at high temperature to obtain these predicted disordered dipoles features, we used the well-known two-dimensional Ising model (Ising, 1925; Onsager, 1944) where a spin (encoded on one bit) represents a dipole. Space and time are discrete in this model. The evolution law of the spin lattice (or bit array) is defined by local rules between neighbour spins.

A mapping between the spin lattice and a cellular automaton cell array seems obvious. What are the more suitable local rules for a fast and few resources consuming secret key cryptosystem? We shall try to answer this question. In the framework of secret key cryptography (Chen & Lai, 2007; Sathyanarayana et al., 2011; Seredynski et al., 2004), we shall propose an Ising Spin Machine (ISM) as a feasibility model for data stream encryption.

ISM is synchronous and needs an initialization phase through a parameter set. Then, at each time step, ISM generates a pseudo-random array of bits, shifts the data flow to encrypt from south towards north, and combines (logic XOR operation) the data with the random bits. The decryption process is identical to the encryption one.

ISM can be used to secure communication over an unsecure channel. If Alice wants to send to Bob a secret data flow which may be trapped by an adversary, she can encrypt this data flow using an ISM. Alice initializes her ISM and communicates the initialization parameter set to Bob (through a secure channel). This set of parameters builds the secret key. Then Bob initializes his own ISM and waits. Alice introduces the data flow to encrypt into her ISM which generates the encrypted flow that is sent to Bob. When Bob receives the first encrypted word, he enables his ISM for a real-time data flow decryption process. The estimated throughput of this enc/decryption process is 2 Gbps.

The rest of this chapter is organized as follows: Section 2 presents the Ising model. Then two algorithms to simulate the 2D-Ising model are described in Section 3. Next, section 4 proposes a parallel implementation of the Reservoir algorithm to generate Cipher Keys. Section 5 is dedicated to the architecture and performances of the Ising Spin Machine, and an image encryption/decryption application example is proposed. Finally, section 6 concludes the chapter.

2. A model for nature randomness

An example of randomness in the nature can be found in an iron bar. Consider this iron bar in a strong magnetic field, H, parallel to its axis. In these conditions the bar is almost completely magnetized. Its magnetization is M_1. Now decrease H to zero: the magnetization will decrease but not to zero. Rather, at zero field a spontaneous magnetization M_0 will remain. Now suppose that the temperature T is increased slightly. It is found that M_0 decreases. Finally, if T is increased to a critical value T_C (the Curie point), M_0 vanishes. The spontaneous magnetization curve $M_0(T)$ is given in Figure 1.

Spins models were invented as simple statistical physics models of ferromagnetism. In most cases they exhibit the cooperative behaviour found in phase transitions. The well known Ising model describes the phase transition occurring at the temperature T_C, between a low temperature phase (called ferromagnetic phase) with a spontaneous magnetization M_0 and a high temperature phase (called paramagnetic phase) where the magnetization M_0 vanishes.

The Ising model is the most famous model in Statistical Physics (Onsager, 1944). The aim of statistical physics is to predict the relations between the observable macroscopic properties of the system, given only the knowledge of the microscopic forces between its components. In the Ising model the magnet is made up of molecules that are constrained to lie on the sites of a regular lattice. Suppose that there are N such sites and molecules, labeled i = 1, 2, …, N.

Let us consider a molecule as a microscopic magnet which either points along some preferred axis, or points in exactly the opposite direction. So molecule *i* has two possible states, which can be described by a spin variable S_i with a value "up" when it is parallel to the axis, and "down" when it is anti-parallel to the axis. Thus there are 2^N configurations of the lattice, called "spin configurations" or "micro-states" of the system. The spin-spin interaction is described by the coupling constant J. Figure 1 gives two spin configurations:

one at the transition temperature T_C (a), and the other one above T_C (b). Spins are organized in clusters at T_C and begin to be disordered at 1.28 T_C. More details can be found in (Perez et al, 1995).

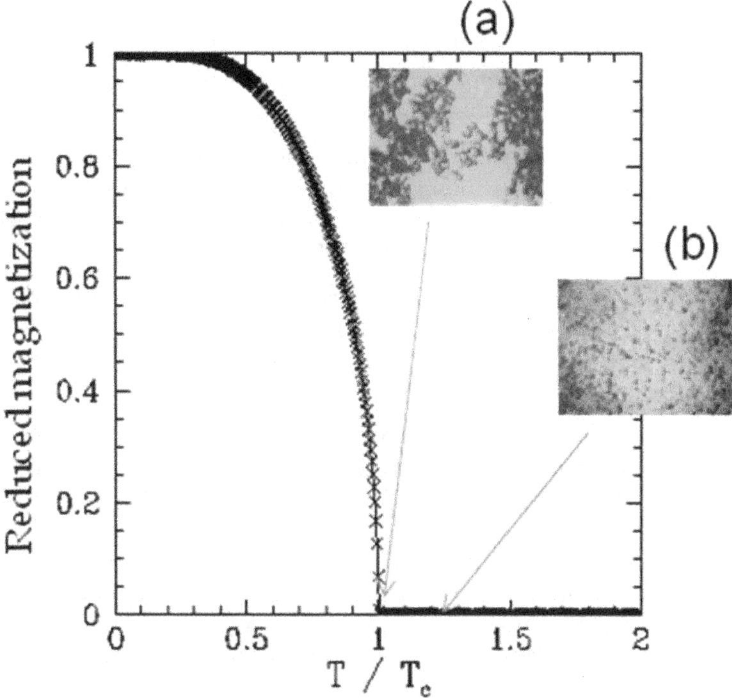

Fig. 1. Reduced magnetization versus temperature. Two spin configurations are shown: (a) clusters of spins at T_C, (b) disordered spins at 1.28 T_C. (Blue pixel = spin down, green pixel = spin up).

Once the spin model is established, it is simulated and the macroscopic properties of the statistic system are extracted from simulation results. For instance, the magnetization is extracted from the simulation results of the Ising model and we can see in Figure 1 that it vanishes when the system temperature reaches T_C. Physicists are interested in calculating the critical exponent of the magnetization at the phase transition.

In this study, we focus on the high temperature phase where the magnetization is equal to zero because fifty percent of the spins are "up". Moreover, the spins are entirely disordered at these temperatures. The time evolution of the disordered spin configurations can generate series of pseudo-random array of bits (since one spin can be coded on one bit). This feature makes this Pseudo-Random Number Generator (PRNG) usable in a symmetric crypto-system.

After adopting the Ising model, we have to choose the corresponding simulation algorithm. In addition, we want an algorithm suitable for an optimized hardware implementation of the PRNG and the associated crypto-system.

3. An algorithm suitable for hardware implementation

3.1 Introduction

Except some spin models solved analytically (Baxter, 1982), statistical models are more generally solved by numerical techniques. The most popular technique is the Monte Carlo computer simulation (Baillie, 1990; Metropolis & Ulam, 1949). The goal of computer simulations is to generate spin configurations typical of statistical equilibrium, in order to obtain the physical observable value of the macroscopic system.

Starting from any spin configuration, the algorithms used to simulate the Ising model aim to generate a series of spin configurations appearing with a probability in accordance with the statistical thermodynamics, i.e. proportional to $e^{-(E/kT)}$ where E is the internal energy of the configuration, T the system temperature and k the Boltzmann constant.

The trajectory through the configuration space is induced by local microscopic rules that can be probabilistic or determinist. In this chapter, we are only interested in the algorithms based on local microscopic rules completely determinist in order to design a machine dedicated to a symmetric crypto-system. In this case, the machines used for encryption and for decryption process must be identical.

First, we describe the standard and most common example of Ising simulation algorithm: the Metropolis algorithm (Metropolis et al., 1953). Then we focus on the "Reservoir algorithm" particularly suitable for the hardware implementation of our enc/decryption machine. We will not describe the huge number of algorithms proposed in the literature for the 2D-Ising model, because most of them are intended to improve the so called "critical slowing down" (Selke, 1993) appearing at the phase transition. Since we want to study the physical system at high temperature, far from the transition, we do not need so sophisticated algorithms.

3.2 Metropolis algorithm

We focus on the 2D-Ising model. Let us consider a square lattice of N sites with one spin S at each site. Each site interacts with its four nearest neighbours. The spins may be "up" or "down". A spin "up" is coded "1". A spin "down" is coded "0". The energy of a link between two neighbour spins pointing towards the same direction (parallel spins) is 0. This link energy is equal to 1 if the two spins are anti-parallel. The total energy of this system is the sum of the energies of the 2N links.

The main idea of the Metropolis algorithm (Metropolis et al.,1953) is to slightly modify a spin configuration and to accept or not this modification versus a probabilistic rule related to the Boltzmann weight. The Metropolis algorithm generates a Markow chain of spin configurations. Starting from any initial spin configuration, the successive configurations lead to the macroscopic equilibrium. The algorithm itself is described thereafter:

Metropolis algorithm

a. Choose an initial spin configuration
b. Select one spin S_i (represented by the red arrow in Figure 2) to be updated and try to flip its spin. Nevertheless flipping a spin has a cost in terms of magnetic energy. Indeed, if the spin S_i of site i flips, the magnetic energy varies as:

$$\Delta M_i = -2\,[\Sigma_j(S_i \text{ xor } S_j) - 2] \qquad (1)$$

where j refers to the four neighbours of the site i.

For instance, if we focus on the first configuration presented in Figure 2, the four neighbours spins are parallel to the central spin, so the magnetic energy (sum of the link energies) is equal to 0. Now, if we flip the central spin, the four links become twisted and the magnetic energy becomes equal to 4. So, flipping the central spin costs $\Delta M_i = 4$. Notice that ΔM_i is always even.

c. Will the central spin flip or not? If ΔM_i lowers the system energy or let it unchanged ($\Delta M_i \leq 0$) then the spin flips. Otherwise the spin flips only with the probability $p = e^{-\Delta Mi/kT}$. Notice that, at constant ΔM_i, this probability increases with T. In practice, a random number r ($0 \leq r \leq 1$) is generated and, if $r \leq e^{-\Delta Mi/kT}$, the spin S_i can flip. Otherwise, it remains unchanged.

d. Return to step (b) until all the spins are updated.

The description of this algorithm leads to two important remarks: during step (c) the Metropolis algorithm needs a real number r randomly chosen (this is not suitable for an optimized hardware implementation of the Metropolis algorithm) and the control parameter is the temperature T.

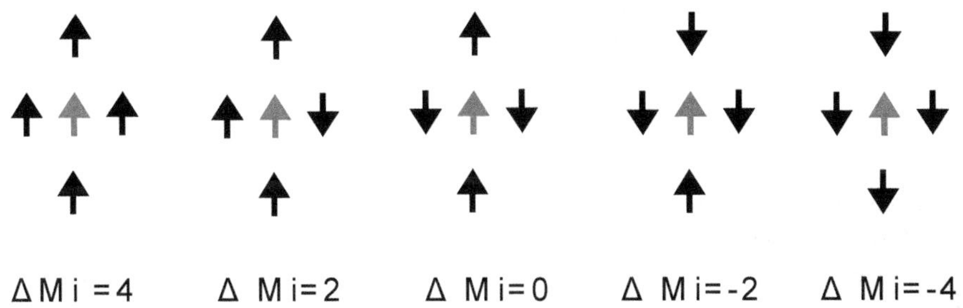

Fig. 2. Magnetic energy cost ΔMi to flip the red spin of the central site i

3.3 Microcanonical Reservoir algorithm

First, notice that the Reservoir algorithm (Ottavi & Parodi, 1989; Perez & all, 1995) and the Creutz microcanonical algorithm (with fixed demons) (Creutz, 1986) are very similar. However the Reservoir algorithm offers solutions for some low temperature simulation problems. These improvements are not considered in the present work since we are only interested in simulating the high temperature phase of the Ising model.

The statistical system to simulate is the same as the previous one except that each site i has one spin S_i and also a reservoir containing an energy E_{ri}. So, two kinds of energies are involved in this model. The first one is the magnetic energy, sum of all the link energies of the system. The second kind of energy is called "reservoir" energy, sum of all the private site reservoir energies E_{ri} of the system.

The algorithm itself is described thereafter:

Reservoir algorithm

a. Choose an initial spin configuration and an initial reservoir energy configuration.
b. Select one spin S_i (represented by the red arrow in Figure 2) to be updated and try to flip its spin. Nevertheless flipping a spin has a cost in terms of magnetic energy. Indeed if the spin S_i of site i flips, the magnetic energy varies as:

$$\Delta M_i = -2 \, [\Sigma_j (S_i \text{ xor } S_j) - 2] \quad (1)$$

   where j refers to the four neighbours of the site i.
c. Will the central spin flip or not? The local rule is: if ΔM_i is smaller than or equal to E_{ri}, the spin S_i flips. Otherwise, S_i does not change. In other words, if the site has enough reservoir energy to pay the flip then the spin can flip effectively.
d. Return to step (b) until all the spins are updated.

Some important comments can be made:

1. The total energy E of the system is the sum of the magnetic energy and of the reservoir energy. E remains constant since the Reservoir algorithm is a microcanonical algorithm. This energy conservation is a very useful tool to test a hardware (or software) implementation of this algorithm.
2. The control parameter is the total energy E and no more the temperature T as is the case in Metropolis algorithm. Nevertheless, we shall see later that we can establish a relation between E and T (Equ. 3).
3. Another important point is that no random number r ($0 \leq r \leq 1$) is needed as input. Moreover, the reservoir energy can be encoded on few bits.

We can conclude that the Reservoir algorithm is more suitable for hardware implementation than the Metropolis algorithm. Next sections will describe the parallelization of the selected algorithm in a Cellular Automata (CA) fashion, and its hardware implementation in a symmetric cryptosystem.

4. Parallel implementation of Reservoir algorithm

4.1 Mapping a cellular automaton?

The qualities of simplicity, parallelism, and locality of the CA are very appreciated for hardware implementations. Moreover, a uniform two-dimensional CA with the von Newman neighbourhood is quite similar to a two-dimensional Ising spin lattice.

We already described (Charbouillot & all, 2008) the software implementation of Reservoir algorithm rules in a multi-purpose hardware cellular automaton named Programmable Hardware Cellular Automata (PHCA). Here, we present a hardware parallel structure dedicated to the Reservoir algorithm. The design of this fine-grained structure was inspired by the mapping between the 2D-Ising model and a 2D-Cellular Automaton.

Cellular Automata are dynamical systems where space, time, and variables are discrete. They are traditionally implemented as an array of cells with a specific rule. The rule can be seen as a function whose arguments are the states at time t of the neighbouring cells (and possibly the state of the considered cell itself) and whose value is the state of the considered cell at time t+1. If all the cells obey to the same rule, the CA is uniform.

Let us focus on two-dimensional CAs. Two kinds of neighbourhoods are usually considered: five cells, consisting of the considered cell and its four nearest neighbours respectively situated at East, South, West and North. This is the von Newman neighbourhood. The second kind of neighbourhood is obtained by also including the cells situated at East-South, South-West, West-North and North-East. This is the Moore neighbourhood implying eight surrounding cells.

To implement the 2D-Ising model, we choose the von Newman neighbourhood, so the next state of cell(*i;j*) is defined by Equ. 2:

$$x_{i,j}(t+1) = f\,[x_{i,j}(t), x_{i-1,j}(t), x_{i+1,j}(t), x_{i,j-1}(t), x_{i,j+1}(t)] \quad (2)$$

Fixed or null boundary conditions can be added at the boundary of the external cells of the array. More often, to avoid finite-size array effects, cyclic boundary conditions are applied. In this last case, the two-dimensional array becomes a torus.

Starting from the 2D-Ising model, replace "lattice" by "array", "sites" by "cells" and "iteration step" by "time step" and you have a cellular automaton. However, a problem appears when we want to simultaneously update all the spins at each time step. The so-called "feedback catastrophe"(Vichniac, 1984) illustrates this problem as follows.

Start the simulation with an aligned configuration (all the spin are parallel) below the Curie temperature (say, 0.8 T_C). During the first time steps, some spins flip and flip back like in a standard Monte Carlo calculation, but as soon as two spins (or cells) with contiguous corners flip during the same time step, a spurious chessboard pattern starts to grow. This can lead to two antiferromagnet spin configurations (one corresponds to the last scheme of Figure 2, and the other one corresponds to the complementary situation). These two configurations alternate because each spin "up", surrounded by four spin "down", will flip in order to align itself with its neighbours, which themselves will also flip, doing "the same reasoning".

This problem can be solved if we distinguish two kinds of sites: the black ones and the white ones, distributed in a chessboard fashion in the 2D-lattice. With this process, all the white sites can be updated simultaneously. Then, at the next time step, all the black sites will be updated simultaneously. So, two time steps are necessary for an entire lattice update and the parallel array of cells is no more exactly a CA. When the state of a white site has to be updated, its four nearest neighbours are black and cannot be updated, and the "feedback catastrophe" is avoided.

In conclusion, the Reservoir algorithm was easily amenable to true parallel processing. The variables assigned to each site are: a reservoir energy coded on few bits (the number of bits depends on the number of sites in the lattice, and on the global reservoir energy), a spin encoded on one bit, and a colour encoded on one bit. However an "iteration step" is equal to two "time steps".

4.2 Initialization phase and result extraction

At the beginning of the simulation, an initial spin configuration must be established and the total reservoir energy must be shared among the lattice sites. Then, we have to choose an initial spin configuration, for instance uniform: all the spins are down. Notice that, in this particular case, the total energy E of the lattice is only constituted by the reservoir energy since the initial magnetic energy is equal to zero.

At the beginning, the system is not in its statistical equilibrium and physical quantities (magnetization, energies) fluctuate considerably. Even though, in this study, we do not want to use these quantities but only the spin configurations of the disordered phase, we need to know the temperature of the system.

Starting from any initial reservoir energy distribution, it is interesting to see that after a transient regime, the reservoir contents obey to the Boltzmann statistical law. At this step, Equ. 3 allows to compute the system temperature T.

$$T = \frac{2.J}{k.Ln[(2j/ < Er >) + 1]} \tag{3}$$

where $< Er >$ is the mean value of the reservoir energy.

Simulating the Ising model using either the Metropolis algorithm or the Reservoir algorithm, leads to the same statistical results. Indeed, the same M(T) curve is obtain by both algorithms and the same precision is reached for its critical exponent. Figure 1 presents the M(T) curve and some corresponding spin configurations. We are interested in the rightmost one, which corresponds to apparent disorder.

At each iteration step, the spin configurations evolved, from a simple initial state and under simple rules without external random input, towards more and more complicated patterns. Once the statistical equilibrium is reached, these patterns appear to be random. These successive bit array configurations could be the long unpredictable key sequences (or Cipher Keys) necessary for en/decrypting a data flow. However, it is necessary to test the quality of the generated randomness.

4.3 Test of randomness

Randomness is one of the crucial points of a key stream for secure stream ciphers. Various types of statistical tests for randomness have been proposed (Kim & Umeno, 2006, Tomassini et al., 2000). We will focus on the Diehard random number generator testing suite proposed in (Marsaglia, 1998). The list of the Diehard tests is given in Table 1. Generators that pass these tests are considered "good".

Most of the Diehard tests need a 12 Mbytes input file, but three of them need a 270 Mbytes input file. Most of these tests return "p-values", which should be uniform on [0,1] if input files contain truly random bits. If the PRNG is bad, most of the p-values will be 0 or 1.

We applied the Diehard tests to successive spin configurations generated by the simulation of the 2D-Ising model at high temperature paramagnetic phase. We have tested the Ising system for different initial reservoir energies.

1. Birthday Spacings
2. GCD
3. Gorilla
4. Overlapping Permutations
5. Ranks of 31x31 and 32x32 Matrices
6. Ranks of 6x8 Matrices
7. Bitstream
8. OPSO Overlapping-Pairs-Sparse-Occupancy
9. OQSO Overlapping-Quadruples Sparse-Occupancy
10. DNA
11. Count the 1's in a Stream of Bytes
12. Count the 1's in Specific Bytes
13. Parking Lot
14. Minimum Distance
15. 3D Spheres
16. Sqeeze Test
17. Overlapping Sums
18. Runs Up and Down
19. Craps

Table 1. List of Diehard tests

The tests were carried on under the following conditions:

- During the initialization phase, all sites have the same reservoir energy except some sites (called "hot points") which have a higher one.
- Then, lattice iterations are performed till the successive patterns of the spin configurations seem disordered as presented in Figure 1 or in Figure 7.

The input file for the Diehard test program is a binary file resulting from the concatenation of the random keys C_i generated by the Ising spin configuration. These keys are built as follows. Let $K_i(t)$ be the concatenation of all the spin values of lattice row i at time t, the first encryption key of the random sequence is:

$$C(t_m) = K_0(0) \text{ xor } K_1(1) \text{ xor} \ldots \text{xor } K_m(t_m) \tag{4}$$

where t is the iteration step (equal to two time steps).

The curve in Figure 3 gives an example of test results. It is obtained by applying the Diehard tests to a sequence of 70M keys $C(t_m)$, $C(t_m +1)$, …, $C(t_m + a)$ extracted from a 128x128 2D-Ising lattice (Figure 7). Figure 3 gives the proportion of pass tests versus R (where $R = E_R/2$). These results come from interpretation of p-values. If all the p-values within a test are greater than 0.01 and less than 0.99, the test is considered as "pass".

These results show that, in this example, R must be chosen between 1000 and 3000 to obtain high-quality randomness. The test fails for low reservoir energies because the system is not in the paramagnetic phase. It also fails for too higher energies because all spins flip simultaneously.

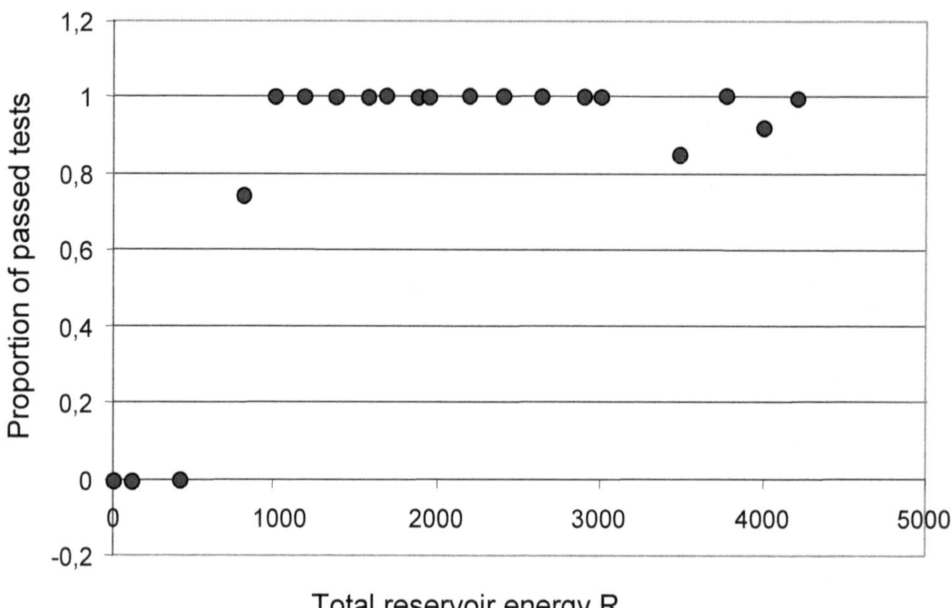

Fig. 3. Example of Diehard test results

5. Ising spin machine

We designed an Ising Spin Machine (ISM) dedicated to simulate the 2D-Ising Model with the Reservoir algorithm and to enc/decrypt a data flow.

5.1 ISM architecture

ISM is a parallel machine, entirely synchronous and autonomous, containing a finite state machine which controls a 2D-array of cells. This array contains n x m identical cells (Figure 4). Each cell is linked to its North, East, West, and South nearest neighbours (NEWS array). We implemented the NEWS array with cyclic boundary conditions: the North border is linked to the South border, and the West border is linked to the East one. All these local links are bidirectional.

The array has n parallel 1-bit data-in inputs, n parallel 1-bit data-out outputs, some control inputs and some state outputs. We add n global connection lines, with South to North direction (represented by grey arrows in Figure 4), to ensure data shifts.

The structure of a cell is detailed in Figure 5. Each cell is designed to manage a site of the Ising lattice under the established rule. So, a cell contains a combinational logic block $\Delta M'$, an adder, registers and multiplexors. $\Delta M'$ computes ($-\Delta Mi/2$) where ΔMi is the cost of the spin flip (Figure 2). ΔMi is divided by 2 since we noticed that this quantity is always even; in return the user has to distribute twice lower initial reservoir energy. The adder computes the reservoir energy which remains if the spin flips. If this energy is positive, this energy and the flip of the spin are registered.

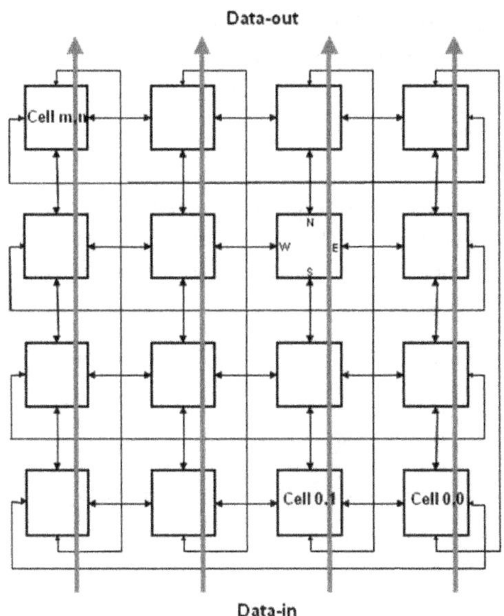

Fig. 4. Cell array architecture

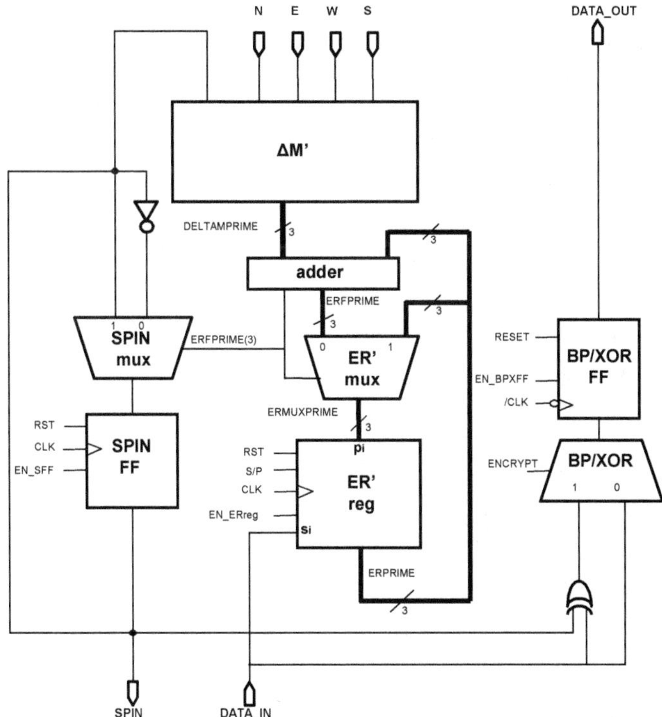

Fig. 5. Cell architecture

The data-in input is used during the initialization phase (encrypt = 0) to introduce the reservoir energy, and during the encryption phase (encrypt = 1) to "XOR" each bit of data with the registered spin bit.

5.2 Data encryption with ISM

At time $t = 0$, at the beginning of the encryption process illustrated in Figure 6, the first row R_0 of clear data is introduced through the south input of the PE array and "XORed" with $K_0(0)$. Then, at time $t = 1$ (time is here the iteration step), the result $D_0(0)$ is shifted to the north and "XORed" with $K_1(1)$ and so on.

At time $t = t_m$, the first encrypted data row $D_0(t_m)$ available at the north of the PE array, is given by :

$$D_0(t_m) = R_0 \text{ xor } C(t_m) \tag{5}$$

where $C(t_m) = K_0(0)$ xor $K_1(1)$ xor ... xor $K_m(t_m)$ is the first encryption key.

The second encrypted data row $D_1(t_m+1)$is

$$D_1(t_m+1) = R_1 \text{ xor } C(t_m+1) \tag{6}$$

where $C(t_m+1) = K_0(1)$ xor $K_1(2)$ xor ... xor $K_m(t_m+1)$ is the second encryption key and so on.

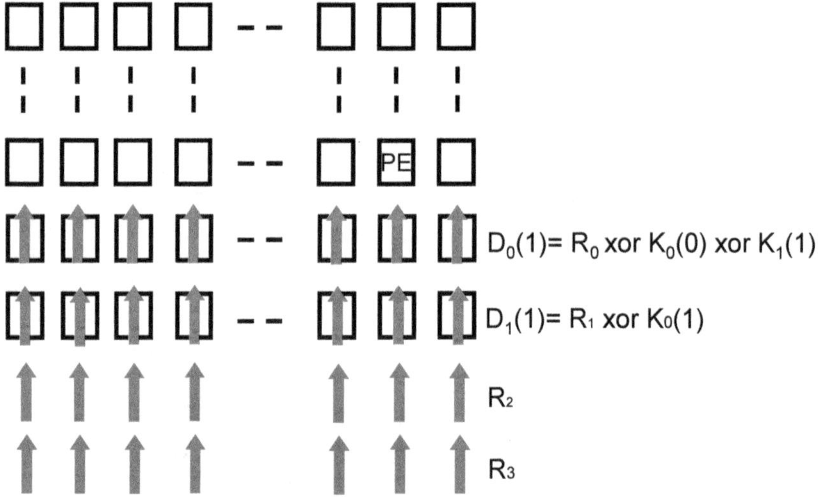

Fig. 6. South-North shift of the data to encrypt

5.3 ISM-based image encryption/decryption system

An application example of a 128x128 cell array ISM, is the colour image enc/decryption system shown in Figure 7. The clear original image given in Figure 8 is a colour image of size 640x853 pixels. Each pixel is coded on 3 bytes (Red, Green, Blue) so each line of this image can be divided into 120 128-bit words to fit in the cell array horizontal size. This resizing operation is not presented in Figure 7.

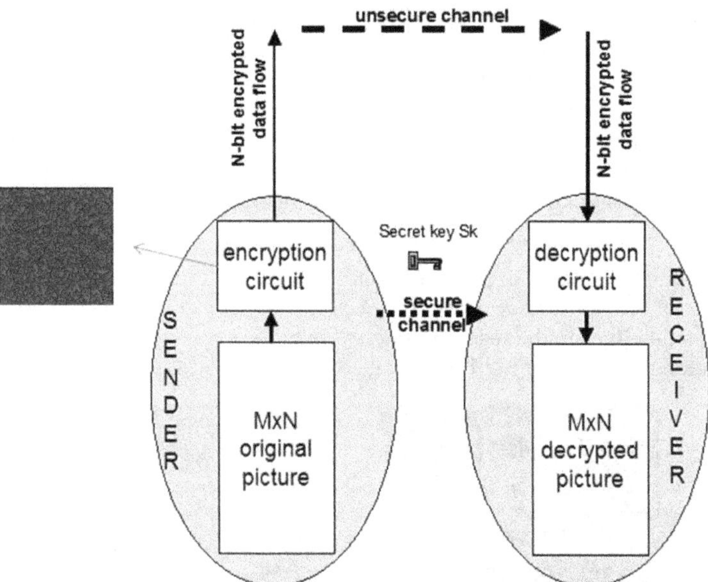

Fig. 7. Image encryption/decryption system. A disordered spin configuration generated by the Ising Spin Machine is shown at the left side.

In order to ensure a secure data exchange, both the Sender and the Receiver need an ISM. The operations to encrypt and decrypt the data are detailed thereafter:

- The Sender imposes the initial spin values S and distributes the total reservoir energy R. Then, the U initial spin lattice configuration updates are performed. The spin configuration shown in Figure 7 was obtained after 2000 iterations, starting with all the spins "down" (S = 0) and with a reservoir energy of 2 for each cell except for 3 cells (called "hot points") which received an energy of 4. Hot points coordinates constitute the information H. The concatenation of S, H and U builds the secret key S_k that must be transmitted to the Receiver through a secure channel, before the encrypted image is sent.
- After a resizing operation, the clear image is introduced through the South data-in of the Sender's ISM, one 128-bit word at a time. These data shift to the North and are encrypted at each iteration step. The resulting encrypted image is shown in Figure 8 (after inverse resizing). One can notice that the initial picture is completely scrambled at this step.
- Before receiving the encrypted image, the receiver gets the secret key S_k through a secure channel. He initializes its ISM with S and H, and controls U spin lattice configuration updates.
- Then, the encrypted image is introduced into the Receiver's ISM for the decryption process. After an inverse resizing operation, the decrypted image is exactly identical to the original clear image.

Two types of keys are involved in this process: the long sequence of the C_k Cipher Keys generated by ISM and the secret key S_k (Seredynski et al., 2004).

In order to test the feasibility of the Ising Spin Machine we have implemented an ISM version with a 32 x 32 cell array into a XC3S5000-5 Xilinx FPGA. As expected, the hardware implementation was easy since the architecture is simple, regular, and involves integer arithmetic and logic operations. This ISM provides good performances since the throughput is 2.02 Gbps (a 32-bit data is encoded every 2 time steps). However, ISM is resource consuming compared to other simple stream ciphers (Chen & Lai, 2007; Machhout et al., 2009). This is due essentially to its fully parallel structure: 5123 Flip-Flops are needed (five per cell, and three for the Finite State Machine).

An important point is related to the microcanonical quality of the Reservoir algorithm. The fact that the total energy is kept constant is a powerful tool to test the Ising Spin Machine. One erroneous bit either in the reservoir energy or in the spin has irreversible consequences when simulations are in progress. The fault is immediately detected.

Fig. 8. Clear image and encrypted image.

6. Conclusion

This work starts with a Physicist point of view on some algorithms invented for Statistical Physics, and moves towards a Cryptosystem Designer point of view. This approach is not new since the Ising model invented for a physical system was very useful in a large spectrum of domains. Our contribution consists in taking a "determinist Monte Carlo" method to simulate the Ising model for finally generating pseudo-random bit streams. This method, called "Reservoir algorithm", involves only integer arithmetic and logic operations and can be easily implemented either in hardware or in software.

We designed the Ising Spin Machine by adding data flow encrypting capabilities to the hardware implementation of the Reservoir algorithm. ISM has a fine-grained parallel structure and is based on Statistical Physics. In the Metropolis algorithm, the Boltzmann law, basis of the Statistical Physics, is introduced through the local rule to flip a spin. In the Reservoir algorithm no such a law is introduced. However, it is very interesting to see that the system itself, more exactly its reservoir energies, finally obey to this law. So, the reservoirs of the Ising Spin Machine intrinsically obey to the Boltzmann law and, under this energy condition, its spin configurations can generate the Cipher Keys to encrypt/decrypt data streams.

A FPGA implementation of a 32x32 cell array version of ISM is used in a symmetric stream cipher crypto-system for an image enc/decryption process. It performs 2 Gbps and could be used for real-time video applications. Moreover, ISM throughput could be improved. We saw that the chessboard trick is a solution to avoid the "feedback catastrophe" that could occur when all the sites are updated concurrently. The consequence of this solution is that two time steps are necessary to update the whole array of cells. Instead of the chessboard trick, a solution could be to endow each cell with four states in order to accommodate for two spins. This last solution could multiply the ISM throughput by a factor 2.

A same approach consisting in modeling the nature with fine-grained fully parallel systems can be adopted in other investigation domains. Adding high degree of redundancy to such systems is our inspiring source to design nanotechnology device architectures.

7. References

Bagnoli, F. & Francescato, A. (1990). Cellular Automata and Modeling of Complex Physical Systems, Boccara; N, Vichniac, G. & Bidaux, R. Springer-Verlag, (Ed.) (1990), pp. 312

Baillie, C. (1990). Lattice spin models and new algorithms : a review of Monte Carlo computer simulations. *International Journal of Modern Physics C,* Vol.1, Issue 01, (1990), pp.91-117

Baxter, R. (1982). *Exactly Solved Models in Statistical Mechanics* (1982), Academic Press Inc. LTD, ISBN 0-12_083180-5, London

Charbouillot, S.; Perez, A. & Fronte, D. (2008). A programmable Hardware Cellular Automaton: Example of Data Flow Transformation. *VLSI Design Journal,* Vol.2008, (2008), pp. 1-7

Chen, R. & Lai, J. (2007). Image security system using recursive cellular automata substitution, *Pattern Recognition,* Vol.40, (2007), pp.1621-1631

Creutz, M. (1986). Deterministic Ising Dynamics. *Annals of Physics,* Vol.167, (1986), pp. 62-72

Ising, E. (1925). Beitrag zur Theorie des Ferromagnetismus. *Zeitschrift fur Physik,* Vol.31 (1925), pp. 253-258

Kim, SJ. & Umeno, K. (2006). Randomness Evaluation and Hardware Implementation of Nonadditive CA-Based Stream Cipher, Available from http://citeseerx.ist.psu.edu/viewdoc/summary?doi=10.1.1.135.3466

Machhout, M.; Guitouni, Z.; Zeghid, M. & Tourki, R. (2009). Design of reconfigurable image encryption processor using 2-D Cellular Automata generator. *International Journal of Computer Science and Applications,* Vol.6 (2009), pp. 43-62

Marsaglia, G. (1998) "Diehard", Available from http://www.cs.hku.hk/cisc/projects/va/diehard.html

Metropolis, N & Ulam, S. (1949). The Monte Carlo method. *Journal of American Statistical Association,* Vol.44 (1949), pp. 335-341

Metropolis, N; Rosenbluth, AW.; Rosenbluth, MN.; Teller, AH. & Teller, E. (1953). Equation of State Calculations by Fast Computing Machines. *The Journal of Chemical Physics,* Vol.21, No.6, (1953), pp. 1087-1092

Onsager, L. (1944). Crystal Statistics. I. A Two-Dimensional Model with a Order-Disorder Transition. *Physical Review,* Vol.65 (1944), pp. 117-149

Ottavi, H. & Parodi, O. (1989). Simulation of the Ising Model by Cellular Automata. *Europhysics Letters,* Vol.8 (1989), pp. 741

Perez, A.; Ottavi, H. & Cotton, M. (1995). The Ising model as a test for a personal parallel computer. *Computational Materials Science,* Vol.4 (1995), pp. 133-142

Sarkar, P. (2000). A Brief History of Cellular Automata. *Journal of ACM Computing Surveys,* Vol.32, No.1, (March 2000), pp.80-107

Sathyanarayana, S.; Aswatha, M. & Hari Bhat, K.. (2011). Symmetric Key Image Encryption Scheme with Key Sequences derived from Random Sequence of cyclic Elliptic Curve points, *International Journal of Network Security,* Vol.12, No.3, (2011), pp.137-150

Selke, W; Talapov, A. & Schur, L. (1993). Cluster-flipping Monte Carlo algorithm and correlations in "good" random number generators. *JETP Letters,* Vol.58, No.8, (1993), pp. 665-668

Seredynski, F.; Bouvry, P. & Zomaya, Y. (2004). Cellular automata computations and secret key cryptography, *Parallel Computing,* Vol.30, (2004), pp.753-766

Tomassini, M; Sipper, M. & Perrenoud, M. (2000). On the Generation of High-Quality Random Numbers by Two-Dimensional Cellular Automata. *IEEE Transactions on Computers,* Vol.49, (2000), pp. 1146-1151

Vichniac, G. (1984). Simulating Physics with Cellular Automata. *Physica 10D* (1984), pp. 96-116

Wolfram, S. (1983). Statistical mechanics of Cellular Automata. *Reviews of Modern Physics,* Vol.55, No.3, (1983), pp. 601-644

Permissions

The contributors of this book come from diverse backgrounds, making this book a truly international effort. This book will bring forth new frontiers with its revolutionizing research information and detailed analysis of the nascent developments around the world.

We would like to thank Jaydip Sen, for lending his expertise to make the book truly unique. He has played a crucial role in the development of this book. Without his invaluable contribution this book wouldn't have been possible. He has made vital efforts to compile up to date information on the varied aspects of this subject to make this book a valuable addition to the collection of many professionals and students.

This book was conceptualized with the vision of imparting up-to-date information and advanced data in this field. To ensure the same, a matchless editorial board was set up. Every individual on the board went through rigorous rounds of assessment to prove their worth. After which they invested a large part of their time researching and compiling the most relevant data for our readers. Conferences and sessions were held from time to time between the editorial board and the contributing authors to present the data in the most comprehensible form. The editorial team has worked tirelessly to provide valuable and valid information to help people across the globe.

Every chapter published in this book has been scrutinized by our experts. Their significance has been extensively debated. The topics covered herein carry significant findings which will fuel the growth of the discipline. They may even be implemented as practical applications or may be referred to as a beginning point for another development.

The editorial board has been involved in producing this book since its inception. They have spent rigorous hours researching and exploring the diverse topics which have resulted in the successful publishing of this book. They have passed on their knowledge of decades through this book. To expedite this challenging task, the publisher supported the team at every step. A small team of assistant editors was also appointed to further simplify the editing procedure and attain best results for the readers.

Our editorial team has been hand-picked from every corner of the world. Their multi-ethnicity adds dynamic inputs to the discussions which result in innovative outcomes. These outcomes are then further discussed with the researchers and contributors who give their valuable feedback and opinion regarding the same. The feedback is then collaborated with the researches and they are edited in a comprehensive manner to aid the understanding of the subject.

Apart from the editorial board, the designing team has also invested a significant amount of their time in understanding the subject and creating the most relevant covers. They scrutinized every image to scout for the most suitable representation of the subject and create an appropriate cover for the book.

The publishing team has been involved in this book since its early stages. They were actively engaged in every process, be it collecting the data, connecting with the contributors or procuring relevant information. The team has been an ardent support to the editorial, designing and production team. Their endless efforts to recruit the best for this project, has resulted in the accomplishment of this book. They are a veteran in the field of academics and their pool of knowledge is as vast as their experience in printing. Their expertise and guidance has proved useful at every step. Their uncompromising quality standards have made this book an exceptional effort. Their encouragement from time to time has been an inspiration for everyone.

The publisher and the editorial board hope that this book will prove to be a valuable piece of knowledge for researchers, students, practitioners and scholars across the globe.

List of Contributors

Jaydip Sen
Innovation Lab, Tata Consultancy Services Ltd., India

Hu Xiong, Zhi Guan, Jianbin Hu and Zhong Chen
Key Laboratory of Network and Software Security Assurance of the Ministry of Education, Institute of Software, School of Electronics Engineering and Computer Science, Peking University, P. R. China

Walter Wong and Maurício Ferreira Magalhães
University of Campinas, Brazil

Di Qiu, Dan Boneh, Sherman Lo and Per Enge
Stanford University, United States of America

Marco Pugliese, Luigi Pomante and Fortunato Santucci
Center of Excellence DEWS, University of L'Aquila, Italy

Mitsuo Okada
Kyoto University, Japan

Ali Fanian and Mehdi Berenjkoub
Department of Electrical and Computer Engineering, Isfahan University of Technology (IUT), Isfahan, Iran

Pardeep Kumar and Hoon-Jae Lee
Dongseo University, Republic of Korea

W. Chen, S. Wang, Z.-Q. Yin, Z. Zhou, Z.-F. Han and G.C. Guo
Key Lab of Quantum Information, CAS, University of Science and Technology of China, China

H.-W. Li
Key Lab of Quantum Information, CAS, University of Science and Technology of China, China Zhengzhou Information Science and Technology Institute, China

Y.-H. Li
Depart. of Elect. Eng. and Info. Sci., University of Science and Technology of China, China

Abdallah Handoura
Ecole Nationale Supérieure des Télécommunications de Bretagne, France

Peter Schartner and Stefan Rass
Alpen-Adria Universität Klagenfurt, Austria

Martin Schaffer
NXP Semiconductors Austria GmbH Styria, Austria

Matej Šalamon
University of Maribor, Faculty of Electrical Engineering and Computer Science, Slovenia

Pellicer-Lostao Carmen and López-Ruiz Ricardo
Department of Computer Science and BIFI, University of Zaragoza, Spain

Tatiana Hodorogea
University of Basel, Switzerland

Ionas Szilard Otto
Bogdan-Voda University, Cluj-Napoca, Romania

Yunpeng Zhang and Liu He Bochen Fu
College of Software and Microelectronics, Northwestern Polytechnical University, Xi'an, China

Annie Perez, Céline Huynh Van Thieng, Samuel Charbouillot and Hassen Aziza
Aix-Marseille Univ., IM2NP; CNRS, IM2NP (UMR 6242), IMT, Technopôle de Château-Gombert, Marseille Cedex 20, France

Printed in the USA
CPSIA information can be obtained
at www.ICGtesting.com
JSHW011505221024
72173JS00005B/1210